Modern American Extremism and Domestic Terrorism

Modern American Extremism and Domestic Terrorism

An Encyclopedia of Extremists and Extremist Groups

BARRY J. BALLECK

An Imprint of ABC-CLIO, LLC

Santa Barbara, California • Denver, Colorado

Library of Congress Cataloging-in-Publication Data

Names: Balleck, Barry J., author.
Title: Modern American extremism and domestic terrorism : an encyclopedia of extremists and extremist groups / Barry J. Balleck.
Description: Santa Barbara, California : ABC-CLIO, [2018] | Includes bibliographical references and index.
Identifiers: LCCN 2018010857 (print) | LCCN 2018013255 (ebook) | ISBN 9781440852756 (ebook) | ISBN 9781440852749 (set : alk. paper)
Subjects: LCSH: Radicalism—United States. | Terrorism—United States.
Classification: LCC HN90.R3 (ebook) | LCC HN90.R3 B333 2018 (print) | DDC 303.48/4—dc23
LC record available at https://lccn.loc.gov/2018010857

ISBN: 978-1-4408-5274-9 (print)
        978-1-4408-5275-6 (ebook)

22 21 20 19 18   1 2 3 4 5

This book is also available as an eBook.

ABC-CLIO
An Imprint of ABC-CLIO, LLC

ABC-CLIO, LLC
130 Cremona Drive, P.O. Box 1911
Santa Barbara, California 93116-1911
www.abc-clio.com

This book is printed on acid-free paper ∞

Manufactured in the United States of America

I would like to dedicate this book to my wife and eternal partner, Deana, who has always been my biggest fan and supporter.

Contents

Alphabetical List of Entries

INTRODUCTION

An extremist is defined as one who holds extreme or fanatical political or religious views, especially one who resorts to or advocates extreme action. Synonyms of extremist include fanatic, radical, zealot, fundamentalist, hard-liner, militant, and activist. The problem with this definition, or its alternate descriptions, is that extremism is always defined in opposition to a normal state or condition. But what is normalcy? Extremists and extremism are determined by the prevailing social agreement of a particular point in historical time. The extremist, or what is considered extreme, may or may not have been considered so in the past, and it may not hold sway in the future. Any consideration of extremism must be viewed within the historical time frame in which it is situated.

Extremism is a hallmark of the American social, cultural, economic, and political experience. American patriots who took up arms against what they considered a tyrannical British government are generally viewed with great admiration and reverence in the United States. The actions of "patriots" at Lexington and Concord ignited the American Revolution, an act that eventually led to the creation of the United States of America. The selfless sacrifices of these patriots are celebrated, and their actions are marked with days of observance, reenactments, and even sporting events, rivaling observances of the most significant events in American history. Yet these American "patriots" were also extremists. At the time of the American Revolution, there was not universal acceptance of the need for a political break from Great Britain. Once the enthusiasm of the initial American victories waned, the colonists discovered how difficult and dangerous military service could be, and many returned home (Ferling 2010). One "extremist" group in contemporary times, known as the Three Percenters (III Percenters), takes its name from the claim that no more than 3 percent of American colonists were actively fighting against the British at any one time (TheThreePercenters.org). In today's parlance, the American colonists fighting against a vastly superior power—the most formidable in the world at the time—were "extremists." They held radical, hard-line, and militant positions. Yet today they are viewed in the context of American history as eponymous of patriot sacrifice.

A line that first appeared in the 1975 novel *Harry's Game* by Gerald Seymour quipped that "one man's terrorist is another man's freedom fighter." This line was later repeated by American president Ronald Reagan, who, in a radio address to the American people on terrorism in May 1986, used the quote to illustrate how difficult it is to distinguish those who fight for justice and freedom in opposition to political and social repression from those who use "terror" to accomplish such ends. Reagan had invoked the phrase in referring to the Nicaraguan Contra rebels who were fighting the communist Sandinista government in that country. The glaring weakness with President Reagan's assessment is that the differences between terrorists and freedom fighters are completely subjective; they are distinguishable only by those who are doing the viewing. "Freedom fighters" may oppose tyranny and fight for freedom and justice, but those dubbed "terrorists" may fight for exactly the same things. "Where you stand depends on where you sit" is a line first used in American politics to describe bureaucratic decision-making processes that involve actors who come to a "game" with "varying preferences, abilities, and positions of power" (Durbin). The assessments and decisions of the actors are colored by the determination of what will best serve the interests of the actor and the organization that he or she represents. In the same manner, designating one as a "terrorist" or a "freedom fighter" is a function of the end result desired by the players of the game—in other words, suppression of undesirable elements (terrorist) or support of desirable elements (freedom fighter).

Interestingly, terrorists rarely, if ever, refer to themselves as such. They use the terms "revolutionaries," "militants," "freedom fighters," or "activists." Thus, both extremists and terrorists, however they are designated, articulate that the cause for which they are fighting is just and honorable, thereby suggesting that the moniker that is applied to them should be more descriptive of their overall purpose—to bring about change: change that will be beneficial to the greatest number of people over the longest period of time.

This text identifies extremists and extremist groups as well as incidents of domestic terrorism in American history. However, as discussed above, these terms are highly charged and subject to debate. There are several individuals and groups within these pages who have been designated as "extremist" because of their attitudes and actions toward issues, groups, and ideologies. Some are even branded with the viscerally charged term "hate." Yet many groups and individuals so designated reject these labels. They argue that they are being characterized as racist, intolerant, misogynistic, or hateful because of their beliefs. In some circumstances, however, these beliefs are informed by religious or personal convictions, so there is the countercharge that those making the characterizations are themselves intolerant. In like manner, the term "domestic terrorism" is difficult to pin down, as the understanding of the phrase may depend greatly upon whether violent actions are considered as pro- or antiestablishment. This is the same conundrum that plagues attempts to define incidents of international terrorism.

Many of the individuals and groups identified in this text have been labeled extremists from a variety of sources. However, the most definitive sources used in this text are the designations provided by the Southern Poverty Law Center (SPLC), the Anti-Defamation League (ADL), and the U.S. Federal Bureau of Investigation (FBI). The SPLC is undoubtedly the preeminent tracker of hate groups in the United States, defining "hate group" as "an organized group or movement that advocates and practices hatred, hostility, or violence towards members of a race, ethnicity, nation, religion, gender, gender identity, sexual orientation or any other designated sector of society" (Phillips 2016). However, there is no universal agreement as to which groups fit this designation, and opponents of such designations make the countercharge that the organizations that define hate, extremism, or racism often do so with their own philosophical, ideological, and political agendas.

Nevertheless, this text examines dozens of individuals and groups variously defined as extremist or terroristic by virtue of one or more of the organizations discussed above. Acts of terror or extremism, as well as movements defined as such, are examined, and readers are left to draw their own conclusions as to whether the terms affixed to subjects of this work are appropriate.

This text examines extremists and extremist groups that have been part of the American scene in the post–World War II era. Some groups that were active before the end of World War II (e.g., the Ku Klux Klan) are covered, but the vast majority of the information presented will focus on the activities of these groups after 1945. Also, there may be a variety of groups or individuals that appeared as extremist on the domestic political scene very briefly, but their impact and influence was marginal, and they are therefore not included in this examination.

As this work progressed, it became apparent that extremist groups cannot be easily placed into one category or another. For instance, contemporary Ku Klux Klan (KKK) groups do not confine themselves to merely a hatred of blacks or protection of Southern culture and values. Rather, KKK groups today may have multiple affiliations and sympathies with neo-Nazis, sovereign citizens, patriot or militia groups, or various other antigovernment adherents. In the same manner, individuals do not fall neatly into a definitive category but may exhibit multiple affinities for different ideologies at a single point in time, or across multiple points in time. The most definitive passages found within are those dealing with particular events that have a discernible beginning and ending (e.g., Ruby Ridge or the Waco standoff). But even in these circumstances, the effects of the event are not confined to the event itself or its immediate aftermath. Rather, the event may ripple through time and be a motivating factor for individuals or groups many years after the event's culmination.

Ruby Ridge and the Waco standoff are perfect illustrations of this point. In and of themselves, Ruby Ridge and Waco had discernible beginnings and endings, even though some might quibble about the contributing factors that led to the initiation of one event or another. In the case of these two incidents, Ruby Ridge began and ended in 1992, and the Waco standoff began and ended in 1993. Yet in 1995, Timothy McVeigh bombed the Alfred P. Murrah Federal Building in Oklahoma City, Oklahoma, killing 168 people, including 20 children. McVeigh's justification for his actions was that the U.S. federal government had become illegitimate as evidenced by the impunity with which it "murdered" (according to McVeigh) American citizens for the simple transgression of possessing illegal weapons. McVeigh's rationale was that the U.S. government was a "bully," and if no one stands up to a bully, he will continue to ride roughshod over his victims.

But Ruby Ridge and the Waco standoff have reverberated through the years beyond Oklahoma City. In their immediate aftermaths, the incidents spawned both the patriot and militia movements. At their inception, these two movements were motivated by antigovernment sentiments and the belief that the United States government had become illegitimate. Fears arose about government attempts to seize weapons—in what these movements believed was an explicit violation of the Second Amendment to the Constitution—but there were also conspiracy fears that the federal government was being manipulated by behind-the-scenes forces or being co-opted by the United Nations, which was seeking to establish a one-world government. Though the patriot and militia movements waned at the turn of the 21st century, they roared back to life with the election of the United States' first black president. Convinced President Barack Obama was ineligible for the presidency due to his alleged country of birth (the so-called Birther argument) and that he was secretly a Muslim who was advancing Islamic causes in the United States, the patriot and militia movements became even more virulent in their antigovernment activities and rhetoric. In their contemporary iterations, these movements now spew anti-Semitic vitriol and are viscerally opposed to immigration and government programs, such as health care.

But even tragedies such as the Columbine shooting have not been contained within their event horizon. Since teenagers Eric Harris and Dylan Klebold killed 12 and injured more than 20 in 1999, more than 50 attacks on schools, or plots to attack schools in a Columbine style, have occurred (Thomas et al. 2014). Among these were the Virginia Tech shooting in 2007, in which student Seung-Hui Cho shot and killed 32 people and injured 17 others, and the Sandy Hook Elementary School shooting, in which 20-year-old Adam Lanza shot and killed 26 people, including 20 six- and seven-year-olds. The Virginia Tech shooting remains the most deadly mass school shooting in U.S. history. However, the most deadly mass shooting of any kind in the United States occurred on October 1, 2017, when gunman Stephen Paddock opened fire on a music festival in Las Vegas, Nevada. The shooting resulted in 59 deaths and more than 850 injuries (Associated Press 2017).

In each of the incidents described in the paragraph above, the discernible event appeared to have been concluded when the killers were either killed or apprehended. Yet in each of these circumstances, the events spawned "copycat killings," though these killings may not have occurred until years after the original event. Another interesting facet of these particular extremist events is that none of the killers had apparent political motivations behind their attacks. In almost every circumstance, the killers had emotional and psychological issues that led them to strike out against the innocent. This begs the question, then, are these individuals considered extremists? Certainly in the context of their actions they were extreme in grappling with their emotional problems through violence. They might even be categorized as terrorists if we define a terrorist simply as one who terrorizes. Certainly, in each of the circumstances described above, the emotional, psychological, and physical trauma experienced by the victims of these incidents has lasted far beyond the culmination of the event. Recalling the definition of extremism offered at the beginning of this introduction, the killers in these events perpetrated their acts for neither political nor religious reasons. Yet their heinous actions certainly are extreme by any reasonable definition as there are millions of Americans with mental health issues who do not attack and kill innocents.

Perhaps a more suitable example for an extremist as presented within the context of this work would be Dylann Roof, the 21-year-old white supremacist who killed nine black parishioners at the Emanuel African Methodist Episcopal Church in downtown Charleston, South Carolina, on June 17, 2015. After attending Bible study with his victims for nearly an hour before the shootings, Roof brutally killed nine individuals, ages 26 to 87 (Coleman). Roof was not a lifelong white supremacist. Yet as a lone shooter, he too was troubled and searching for answers for his anger. Unfortunately, as is far too common in the modern world, Roof found his answers on the Internet. When Roof began questioning the national debate that took place after the death of black teenager Trayvon Martin—who, on the evening of February 26, 2012, was shot to death by neighborhood watch coordinator George Zimmerman—Roof turned to the Internet for answers. Googling "black-on-white crime," Roof was confronted with information from the Web site of the Council of Conservative Citizens (CCC), a white nationalist group that preaches segregation and is the successor to the virulent white citizens' councils that were pervasive in the South during the civil rights era. The CCC presented page after page of incidents and statistics related to black-on-white crime. Roof was enraged. He stated, "I was in disbelief. At this moment I realized that something was very wrong. How could the news be blowing up the Trayvon Martin case while hundreds of these black on White murders got ignored?" (NPR 2017).

Dylann Roof was "radicalized" or, more aptly, became an extremist, after reading information on the Internet and then reinforcing those ideas with comparable messages from other sources that echoed the original message. In this same manner, mass killers Nidal Hasan (Fort Hood shooting), Sayed Farook and Tashfeen Malik (San Bernardino shooting), and Omar Mateen (Orlando nightclub shooting) were also radicalized online and became extremists. In each of these circumstances, either a political or a religious motivation applied to the actions of the killers, and the murders they committed were for a "cause," though it is not always clear even after the fact how or why the pursuit of a particular cause spurred them to action.

Though it is less common, extremism does not always take the form of violent actions against other individuals. There are groups discussed in this text that have taken it upon themselves to be the protectors of animals, the earth, or other causes that are not as spectacular as to make the headlines. Yet groups such as the Animal Liberation Front (ALF), the Earth Liberation Front (ELF), and Greenpeace epitomize extremist activity in their own realms. Both ALF and ELF have perpetrated attacks against business interests that have led to millions of dollars in damages and have forced the closures of some enterprises. Greenpeace, too, has interfered with legitimate business ventures in preventing whaling vessels from seeking their prey. Though the actions of any of these groups may be applauded by a significant proportion of the world's population, these organizations nevertheless are pursuing political ends through extremist means. Talking, cajoling, lobbying, or demonstrating is not enough for these groups. Through "direct action," they attempt to bend the will of actors who they believe are harming the planet—through their exploitation of animals, their exploitation of the earth's resources, or their disregard for the balance of life that these groups contend is essential for a civilized society to exist.

The vast majority of the entries found within this work focus on individuals and groups who are considered extremist or terroristic within the post–World War II time frame. Within this span of time can be found groups and individuals on both the left wing and the right wing of political extremism. Given the nature of this work, there is a far greater focus on extremists on the right wing than on the left. Yet there are entries that pertain to a brief period in American history when left-wing extremism was prominent in the United States. During the mid to late 1960s and early 1970s, several left-wing groups existed in the United States that were intent on radically reorienting American society and culture. Groups such as the Symbionese Liberation Army, the Students for a Democratic Society, and the Weathermen all carried out extremist actions that were politically motivated. At the time, groups on the left wing of the political spectrum were determined to bring down the old political order of the United States and replace it with a new order based on collective principles motivated by communism. These groups were largely anticapitalist and urban, and the number of women in these groups far exceeded any numbers that would be found in right-wing groups. These groups were antigovernment, as many right-wing groups were and later would be. Yet extremists on the left were not beholden to an idealized version of American life. They believed that modern life ("modernity") was "revolutionary" and that to meet the challenges of the future, Americans had to throw off their preconceptions, prejudices, and allegiances in order to pledge fealty to a new order wherein people would be equal. This sentiment directly challenged the long-established American morals and values that characterized the "exceptional" American experience. As might be expected, there was significant opposition to these groups, and by the 1980s they had largely disappeared from the American political scene.

Extremism on the right, however, has endured. Whereas left-wing extremism is "revolutionary" and forward looking, right-wing extremism tends to be much more concerned with returning the social, cultural, and political milieu of the United States to an idealized version of the past. Indeed, there is ample evidence that a large plurality of Americans believe that the current decade in which they live is not the best in the history of the United States. Though Americans today live longer, enjoy higher standards of living, travel more quickly around the world, communicate instantaneously, and have achieved higher levels of freedom and equality than ever before in their history, there is a significant number of Americans today who long for the past (Bailey 2017). Many Americans today long for the 1950s, believing it to be the last "great" American decade (Harper 2013). Many extremists on the right wing of the political spectrum view the 1950s as a time when whites were still indisputably in control of government, the United States was the most economically and militarily powerful country in the world, and society "made sense"—in other words, women knew their place (as did minorities), prayers were said in schools, everyone pledged allegiance to the flag, gays stayed in the closet, and the vast majority of immigrants coming into the United States were from majority-white countries (Balleck 2015). For conservatives on the extreme right, everything started to go to hell when civil rights were enacted, women burned their bras, gays demanded equal rights, and you could no longer hurl racial or ethnic epithets because they were not "politically correct." The longing for a "simpler time"—a less complicated time—has largely driven the growth of extremism on the political right wing in the United States.

Today, there are those who are extremist because they hate the government, believing it to be illegitimate because it has strayed so far from the founding principles that were articulated by the framers of the Constitution. They contend that the government has no powers except those accorded to it by the Constitution, and any additional powers that the government has taken unto itself through precedent, legislation, tradition, fiat, or any other manner is abusive and not what the founders intended. Therefore, as the patriots of the American Revolution took up arms against an abusive and tyrannical government, so too do "patriots" today take up arms and fight against a government that they believe no longer appropriately represents the American people.

Antigovernment sentiments are seen today in the patriot and militia movements, which are organizations that realize that they are outgunned by the federal government but nevertheless intend to arm themselves against the eventuality of government abuses (i.e., gun control measures and the possibility of the usurpation of American sovereignty by the United Nations or some shadowy cabal of Jewish leaders who are intent on controlling international financial institutions in order to bend governments to their will). Though a great deal of hate runs through these groups, they are most interested in being left alone by a government that has overreached its authority and has allowed the devolution of American society to the point that whatever made "America great" is no longer recognizable.

A variation on the patriot and militia disdain for the government is found within the sovereign citizens and common-law court movements. Whereas patriot and militia groups distrust the government and prepare themselves for the eventuality of a government takeover, they still by and large obey government laws. They do not actively seek to usurp government power. Sovereign citizens, on the other hand, interpret the role of the government much differently. Their interpretation of the Constitution is that power was never intended to be concentrated in either the national (federal) or state governments. Rather, local control was always the level at which government governed best (Balleck 2015). Thus, sovereign citizens generally do not recognize either state or federal laws, and they believe that the highest authority to which they must answer is the county sheriff. Many sovereign citizens do not possess driver's licenses, refuse to pay taxes, and do not recognize the state or federal governments' power or authority to own or administer public lands. In 2014 and 2016, sovereign citizen members of the Bundy family confronted government authorities, challenging them on whether the federal government has the power to charge money for grazing cattle on land or whether the federal government has the authority to administer millions of acres of land in the western United States. These actions are typical of sovereign citizens who are determined to take back power that they believe has been unlawfully usurped by the federal government.

Sovereign citizens often make their claims through mechanisms within common-law courts. Again, primarily located within local jurisdictions, common-law courts are held by sovereign citizens to be the only legitimate sources of legal jurisprudence. Many sovereign citizens disdain state and federal courts and prefer to take their cases to common-law courts, where judges are universally accepted by a community and where verdicts almost always favor the litigants when there is a question of rights between a citizen and the federal government. Of course, common-law courts have no legal standing and are not recognized as valid in any part of the American justice system. Nevertheless, common-law courts continue to exist, even issuing arrest warrants for government officials, declaring federal laws null and void, and convening to adjudicate matters of citizen rights (Balleck 2015).

Antigovernment sentiments have elicited some tense confrontations between adherents and government authorities. However, even more virulent forms of right-wing extremism are found in those that express hate for entire races, groups of people (e.g., LGBT people), or ideas. Hate is a powerful motivator, and many individuals and groups today openly express their hatred of one thing or another. The KKK is perhaps the United States' most infamous hate group, having existed for over 150 years. Yet the scope and impact of the KKK pales in comparison to hate groups that have arisen since World War II. Aryan Nations and the National Alliance are two neo-Nazi organizations that preach white supremacism and white nationalism. While maintaining a traditional hatred of blacks and other racial minorities and often carrying out acts of intimidation and violence against these people, Aryan Nations and the National Alliance have perpetrated an unparalleled hatred of Jews in the United States. Much of this hate stemmed from the "religion" of Christian Identity embraced by Aryan Nations as preaching the "true" nature of the Jews. According to Christian Identity theology, the white race, and not Jews, are God's chosen people. Jews, in fact, are inherently evil as they are actually the product of a sexual liaison between the devil—Satan—and Eve. All other people besides whites are "mud people" and are not worthy to be accorded the same rights in society as white people.

The hatred of Jews (anti-Semitism) is a prominent theme in this text and is expressed in the rhetoric and actions of dozens of individuals and groups. Such hatred is not new to the Jewish people, who have been hated and persecuted throughout history. Yet anti-Semitism today is not just about the hatred of Jews; it is also found in the disavowal of their history. For instance, Holocaust denial has become a hallmark of anti-Semitism, and it has gone so far as to be institutionalized in organizations such as the Institute for Historical Review, which is a Holocaust denial outfit that uses pseudoacademic means to perpetuate a revisionist view of the Holocaust. Modern forms of communication have been used to spread the conspiracy theories and tropes that for centuries have been used against the Jews. There are right-wing extremists who are firmly convinced that a secret cabal of Jews control the world. Adherents of this idea contend that a secret meeting of Jewish leaders gathered decades ago to concoct a plot whereby Western civilization would be "mongrelized" through societal and political devolution, thereby allowing these countries to be more easily co-opted into a new world order. The blueprint for this assimilation is purportedly found in a document known as the *Protocols of the Elders of Zion*, a tract first published in Czarist Russia in the early

20th century. As the tract spread from Russia to the rest of the world, anti-Semites, including prominent Americans such as Henry Ford, distributed the *Protocols* and perpetuated the myths of a secret Jewish organization that have no basis in fact (Anti-Defamation League).

The hatred elicited by the *Protocols* has been repeated in other tracts, perhaps none more infamous than William Luther Pierce's dystopian novel, *The Turner Diaries*. Pierce, the founder of the neo-Nazi National Alliance, wrote *The Turner Diaries* as an antigovernment novel that presents a fictional future in which Jews, fully in control of the American government, institute laws that eliminate private gun ownership and empower minority groups against the white majority. *The Turner Diaries* envisions a race war in which Jews and other "race traitors" are eventually destroyed in the United States and throughout the world. Other races, too, are destroyed through the use of nuclear, chemical, and biological weapons, and the white race is left alone to administer the new world. *The Turner Diaries* is considered the "Bible" of the extremist right and has motivated some of the most violent acts of American extremism. For instance, Timothy McVeigh's bombing of the Oklahoma City federal building was inspired by a similar bombing in *The Turner Diaries*. The Order, at one time the most wanted terror group in the United States, also took its name from the book, after a group in *The Turner Diaries* that was largely responsible for eliminating Jews in the country. Today, *The Turner Diaries* still inspires new generations of antigovernment extremists (Jackson 2004).

Post–World War II United States has witnessed many changes, and there have been milestones that have fomented the extremist sentiments present in the country today. Fears of communism, as expressed by the right-wing group the John Birch Society, caused Americans to hate and mistrust every aspect of communism. The revelations that communists had infiltrated the government, though not to the extent claimed by McCarthyism, confirmed Americans' worst nightmares of losing their democratic freedoms and independence. The social and political upheavals of the 1960s and 1970s forever changed the country from its bucolic sentiments—where the simple life was expressed in rural memories—to an urban setting where Americans were suspicious of the growing number of people coming to the country who never seemed to assimilate the culture and values of the United States as their ancestors had done. A growing mistrust of government was perpetuated by revelations that the government had lied about U.S. advances in Vietnam, and the Watergate scandal that precipitated the first resignation of an American president in history. Later, the economic "stagflation" of the late 1970s and 1980s saw hundreds of farmers throughout the country lose their family farms to large investment banks or in favor of large agricultural conglomerates. Average Americans began to believe that the government was hampering their efforts to achieve the American dream as opposed to advancing the conditions that would make the dream more realizable.

The federal government's missteps at Ruby Ridge and Waco created new government distrust and hate, while Bill Clinton's support of increased gun control restrictions convinced many that the conspiracies that had swirled for years about government's intentions of seizing weapons was coming to pass. While the United States enjoyed a brief respite from domestic extremist groups during the administration of George W. Bush—as the country focused its efforts on fighting the global war on terror—the election of the country's first black president fostered a precipitous rise in extremist and hate group activity. Soon after Barack Obama was elected president in 2008, registered users on white supremacist Web sites tripled to more than 300,000 (Lee, Canon, and Patterson 2015). However, it was not only the election of the country's first black president that heightened anxieties among extremists that explains the precipitous rise of extremist activity. In 2008, there was also an economic and financial crisis unlike any experienced in the United States since the Great Depression of the 1930s. Moreover, debates over immigration, social changes, and a growing uneasiness among conservative white Americans that whites would soon be a minority in the country prompted the formation of new groups.

Today, there are still vestiges of old extremist groups that have expressed their hatred or antigovernment sentiments for decades. Now, however, the rise of groups that completely disdain the current government are in the ascendancy. Sovereign citizens, for instance, do not really care about a reformation of government. Rather, they wish government to shrink to the size where all government is local. Though this ideal has never been a reality in the United States, sovereign citizens would be content to never interact with the government and would prefer to be largely self-sufficient with as little government interference in their lives as possible. The most recent alt-right movement is also antigovernment, disdaining traditional party politics and agitating for a complete overhaul of the domestic and foreign policies that have characterized the United States since the end of World War II. Alt-right advocates, for instance, call the government corrupt, assail the Republican establishment, flout almost every rule of political etiquette, and openly advocate for policies that will be advantageous to an increasingly dispossessed and disheartened white majority (Caldwell 2016). Alt-righters claim that unchecked immigration is contributing to "white genocide" as the values and principles that were once the hallmark of American society are now lost in a multicultural society where political correctness and government paralysis reign.

The election of Donald Trump to the U.S. presidency has given hope to many extremists. Though Trump himself has disavowed many of the associations with extremists—and the endorsements that he has received before and after his election—his presence in the White House is nevertheless the most significant sign that extremism has found a new voice in American politics. For months, as Trump ran to secure the Republican nomination for president, his total disregard for the standards of American political campaigns and the undercurrents of hate he professed caused the establishment in Washington, D.C., liberal Americans, and many in the rest of the world to cringe about the possibility that he might actually be elected president. When the fears of many finally came to pass, Trump was hailed by right-wing extremists for his victory. Indeed, Richard Spencer, founder of the alt-right movement, shouted at a gathering of alt-righters soon after Trump's election: "Hail, Trump! Hail, our people! Hail, victory!" As Spencer raised his hands, a scattered half dozen or so men stood in solidarity and raised their arms in Nazi salutes (Caldwell 2016).

Though Trump has been deemed a populist, his message resonates with the right-wing extremists (Taub 2016). Fears of social change, including women's rights, gay rights, and greater equality for minorities; fears of unchecked immigration, particularly from nonwhite, non-Christian countries; fears of threats around the world, from militant Islam, to hyperbolized threats enunciated by foreign governments and the United Nations, to the rise of a nuclearized North Korea; and fears of a collapse of traditional white identity have all contributed to the rise of extremist sentiments in the modern United States. Where once the United States led the world in its vision for the future, extremists and extremist groups have now turned back the clock as millions of Americans wish to recapture a mythical point in time in order to "Make America Great Again." Unfortunately, this time has never existed in American history nor in the history of any civilization. Indeed, civilizations exist on a continuum, and the social, economic, cultural, and political conditions of any point in time on that continuum are the reality with which citizens have to contend. Though there is nostalgia for times in our childhoods when we lived in idyllic circumstances, reality dictates that we live in the present and attempt to make the future as palatable as possible. That future will not be secured by returning to the past but rather by inculcating the lessons of the present into a collective view of the future.

As you read this encyclopedia, remember that extremism has been part of the American experience since its founding. Though it has always been manifested by groups and individuals on the political left and the right, as of this writing it appears that both the left and the right are becoming ever more vocal in pursuit of their goals. In August 2017, events in Charlottesville, Virginia, illustrated extremism across the political spectrum in the United States. Far-right groups, including factions of the KKK as well as white nationalist and white supremacist groups, faced off against far-left groups, such as Black Lives Matter and Antifa, an antifascist organization that reemerged into prominence in the wake of Donald Trump's ascendancy to the U.S. presidency. The confrontation arose as white nationalist and white supremacist groups objected to the removal of symbols deemed relevant to the Old Confederacy that had long been part of public life in Charlottesville. These symbols, now seen by many as oppressive reminders of hate, elicited a clash between those on the right wishing to preserve such symbolism and those on the left wishing to discard such symbols as relics of a past best forgotten. The events in Charlottesville punctuated the deep divide that has always existed in the United States over issues of race, privilege, equity, justice, and freedom. But those who agitate on behalf of these issues are not confined just to the United States. They can be found around the world and are manifested in radical Islamic movements that intend to return traditional Muslim populations to a more strict observance of Islamic law. This trend has been best exemplified by the rise of ISIS, the Islamic State of Iraq and Syria. In short, extremism can be found anywhere in the world at any time. Whether the actions of individuals or groups will be deemed "extreme" will depend entirely on the perspective of those doing the viewing.

Though the present moment makes those on both the left and the right of the political spectrum apprehensive, there is every reason to believe that extremists and extremism will continue to flourish in our foreseeable future.

Further Reading

Anti-Defamation League. "A Hoax of Hate: The Protocols of the Learned Elders of Zion." https://www.adl.org/education/resources/backgrounders/a-hoax-of-hate-the-protocols-of-the-learned-elders-of-zion (Accessed June 10, 2017).

Associated Press. October 2, 2017. "Death Toll Rises to 59; Investigators Find Explosives and 18 Guns at Gunman's Home." *Los Angeles Times.* http://www.latimes.com/nation/la-las-vegas-shooting-live-updates-death-toll-rises-to-59-investigators-1506983486-htmlstory.html (Accessed January 23, 2018).

Bailey, Sarah Pulliam. January 5, 2017. "How Nostalgia for White Christian America Drove So Many Americans to Vote for Trump." *The Washington Post.* https://www.washingtonpost.com/local/social-issues/how-nostalgia-for-white-christian-america-drove-so-many-americans-to-vote-for-trump/2017/01/04/4ef6d686-b033-11e6-be1c-8cec35b1ad25_story.html?utm_term=.8def10f8a872 (Accessed June 10, 2017).

Balleck, Barry J. 2015. *Allegiance to Liberty: The Changing Face of Patriots, Militias, and Political Violence in America.* Praeger.

Caldwell, Christopher. December 2, 2016. "What the Alt-Right Really Means." *The New York Times.* https://www.nytimes.com/2016/12/02/opinion/sunday/what-the-alt-right-really-means.html (Accessed June 10, 2017).

Coleman, Arical. "Remembering the Charleston Nine." *LA Progressive.* https://www.laprogressive.com/charleston-nine/ (Accessed June 10, 2017).

Durbin, Brent. "Bureaucratic Politics Approach." *Encyclopedia Britannica.* https://www.britannica.com/topic/bureaucratic-politics-approach#ref1181380 (Accessed June 9, 2017).

Ferling, John. January 2010. "Myths of the American Revolution." Smithsonian.com. http://www.smithsonianmag.com/history/myths-of-the-american-revolution-10941835/ (Accessed June 9, 2017).

Google. "Extremist." https://www.google.com/search?q=extremist+defintion&ie=utf-8&oe=utf-8#q=extremist+definition (Accessed June 9, 2017).

Harper, Jennifer. August 16, 2013. "What Other Decade Would You Live In? Most Americans Choose the 1950s." *The Washington Times.* http://www.washingtontimes.com/blog/watercooler/2013/aug/16/what-other-decade-would-you-live-most-americans-ch/ (Accessed June 10, 2017).

Jackson, Camille. October 24, 2004. "The Turner Diaries, Other Racist Novels, Inspire Extremist Violence." *Southern Poverty Law Center—Intelligence Report.* https://www.splcenter.org/fighting-hate/intelligence-report/2004/turner-diaries-other-racist-novels-inspire-extremist-violence (Accessed June 10, 2017).

Lee, Jaeah, Gabrielle Canon, and Brandon E. Patterson. June 30, 2015. "The Rise of Violent Right-Wing Extremism, Explained." *Mother Jones.* http://www.motherjones.com/politics/2015/06/right-wing-extremism-explainer-charleston-mass-shooting-terrorism/ (Accessed June 10, 2017).

NPR. January 10, 2017. "What Happened When Dylann Roof Asked Google for Information About Race?" http://www.npr.org/sections/thetwo-way/2017/01/10/508363607/what-happened-when-dylann-roof-asked-google-for-information-about-race (Accessed June 10, 2017).

Phillips, Craig. April 1, 2016. "Who Is Watching the Hate? Tracking Hate Groups Online and Beyond." PBS.org. http://www.pbs.org/independentlens/blog/who-is-watching -the-hate-tracking-hate-groups-online-and-beyond/ (Accessed June 9, 2017).

Reagan, Ronald. May 31, 1986. "Radio Address to the Nation on Terrorism." The American Presidency Project. http://www.presidency.ucsb.edu/ws/?pid=37376 (Accessed June 9, 2017).

Seymour, Gerald. 1975. *Harry's Game*. Random House.

Taub, Amanda. November 9, 2016. "Trump's Victory and the Rise of White Populism." *The New York Times*. https://www.nytimes.com/2016/11/10/world/americas/trump-white -populism-europe-united-states.html (Accessed June 10, 2017).

Thomas, Pierre, Mike Levine, Jack Cloherty, and Jack Date. October 7, 2014. "Columbine Shootings' Grim Legacy: More Than 50 School Attacks, Plots." *ABC News*. http://abcnews.go.com/US/columbine-shootings-grim-legacy-50-school-attacks-plots /story?id=26007119 (Accessed June 10, 2017).

The Three Percenters. "What Is the Three Percenters?" http://www.thethreepercenters.org /about-us (Accessed June 9, 2017).

ALT-RIGHT MOVEMENT

The alternative right (alt-right) movement has been described by the Southern Poverty Law Center (SPLC) as

> a set of far-right ideologies, groups and individuals whose core belief is that "white identity" is under attack by multicultural forces using "political correctness" and "social justice" to undermine white people and "their" civilization. Characterized by heavy use of social media and online memes, Alt-Righters eschew "establishment" conservatism, skew young, and embrace white ethno-nationalism as a fundamental value.

Besides its bent toward white nationalism, racism, and neo-Nazism, the alt-right movement has also been described as embracing anti-Semitism, nativism, Islamophobia, antifeminism, and homophobia (Krieg 2016). Alt-right ideology portends to break with mainstream conservatism and large portions of the Republican Party (GOP), as defined by values espoused by the party upon the nomination of Barry Goldwater for president in 1964. This brand of conservatism, which included an emphasis on liberty, freedom, free markets, and capitalism, is considered by those in the alt-right movement as "anti-ideals" and the reasons why the movement wants to define a new kind of conservatism (Southern Poverty Law Center).

Richard Spencer is credited with coining the term "alt-right" in 2010 when he created the Web site AlternativeRight.com. Spencer describes alt-right adherents as "younger people, often recent college graduates, who recognize the 'uselessness of mainstream conservatism' in what he describes as a 'hyper-racialized' world" (Southern Poverty Law Center). As such, the alt-right has opposed the immigration and resettlement of Syrian refugees in the United States and has been a major proponent of U.S. president Donald Trump's plan to crack down on illegal immigration, particularly from across the United States' southern border with Mexico. The alt-right movement has been associated with American identitarianism, an iteration of a European ideology "that emphasizes cultural and racial homogeneity within different countries" (Southern Poverty Law Center). Like their European counterparts, alt-right members believe that older conservatives within their countries have sold out the younger generations in support of worn-out and dated conservative values (Southern Poverty Law Center).

One critical aspect in the growth of the alt-right movement has been the organization's use of social media. As noted by the SPLC, "Legions of anonymous Twitter users have used the hashtag #AltRight to proliferate their ideas, sometimes successfully pushing them into the political mainstream." One example of this proliferation of ideas is the popularization of the term "cuckservative," a combination of the words "cuckold" and "conservative"; it designates mainstream conservative (mostly Republican) "politicians who are seen as traitors to the American people" inasmuch as they are willing to sell out their traditional beliefs in order to support programs and policies related to globalism and certain liberal ideals (Southern Poverty Law Center). The phrase is racist and sexist in its overtones as the term "cuckold" implies "that establishment conservatives are like white men that allow black men to sleep with their wives" (Southern Poverty Law Center).

Donald Trump's 2016 presidential campaign attracted great attention from the alt-right movement. During the Republican primaries, Trump was the only male Republican candidate to which the term "cuckservative" was not applied. Reportedly, alt-right adherents are drawn to Trump, in part because he eschews political correctness and regularly rails against Muslims, immigrants, Mexicans, Chinese, and others (Southern Poverty Law Center).

The alt-right movement is hardly monolithic and attracts some diverse characters. Milo Yiannopoulos, whose Jewish roots have put him at odds with some in the neo-Nazi and white supremacist movements, has become a noted alt-right apologist. Yiannopoulos was once a senior editor at *Breitbart News* but was fired after he was banned from Twitter in 2016 for "inciting or engaging in the targeted abuse or harassment of others" (Isaac 2016). In an article written for *Breitbart News* in March 2016 before his firing, Yiannopoulos said that the alt-right movement is "fundamentally about youthful provocation and subversion, rather than simply another vehicle for the worst dregs of human society: anti-Semites, white supremacists, and other members of the Stormfront set" (Bokhari and Yiannopoulos 2016). In the final analysis, as pointed out by the SPLC, "coat-and-tie racists like Richard Spencer and Jared Taylor [a neo-Nazi who runs the white supremacist publication *American Renaissance*], and oddball figures like Yiannopoulos have more in common, in terms of sharing a vision of society as fundamentally determined by race, than they disagree about" (Southern Poverty Law Center).

See also: American Renaissance; Bannon, Steve; Neo-Nazis; Spencer, Richard Bertrand; Taylor, Jared; White Nationalism; White Supremacist Movement

Further Reading

Bokhari, Allum and Milo Yiannopoulos. March 29, 2016. "An Establishment Conservative's Guide to the Alt-Right." *Breitbart News*. http://www.breitbart.com/tech/2016/03/29/an-establishment-conservatives-guide-to-the-alt-right/ (Accessed March 15, 2017).

Caldwell, Christopher. December 2, 2016. "What the Alt-Right Really Means." *The New York Times*. https://www.nytimes.com/2016/12/02/opinion/sunday/what-the-alt-right-really-means.html (Accessed March 15, 2017).

Isaac, Mike. July 20, 2016. "Twitter Bans Milo Yiannopoulos in Wake of Leslie Jones' Reports of Abuse." *The New York Times*. https://www.nytimes.com/2016/07/20/technology/twitter-bars-milo-yiannopoulos-in-crackdown-on-abusive-comments.html (Accessed March 15, 2017).

Krieg, Gregory. August 25, 2016. "Clinton Is Attacking the 'Alt-Right'—What Is It?" *CNN*. http://www.cnn.com/2016/08/25/politics/alt-right-explained-hillary-clinton-donald-trump/ (Accessed March 15, 2017).

Southern Poverty Law Center. "Alternative Right." https://www.splcenter.org/fighting-hate/extremist-files/ideology/alternative-right (Accessed March 15, 2017).

Wallace-Wells, Benjamin. May 5, 2016. "Is the Alt-Right for Real?" *The New Yorker*. http://www.newyorker.com/news/benjamin-wallace-wells/is-the-alt-right-for-real (Accessed March 15, 2017).

AMERICAN BORDER PATROL/AMERICAN PATROL

The American Border Patrol (or American Patrol, sometimes called Voice of Citizens Together) is an anti-immigration group largely based in Arizona. Its founder, Glenn Spencer, has called Mexican immigration a "cultural cancer" in the United States, and the group often rails against what it calls the Mexican plan to reconquer the parts of the American Southwest that used to be Mexican territory.

The conspiratorial theories of a Mexican attempt to retake the American Southwest now permeate other groups of the radical right. On the group's website, an article purported that President Obama has concluded a secret deal with the Mexican government to cede back to Mexico the Gadsden Purchase, a nearly 30,000-square-mile portion of southern Arizona and New Mexico that once belonged to Mexico before being purchased by the United States in 1854 (American Patrol 2016).

American Border Patrol (ABT) was founded in 2002 by Spencer as a "shadow" border patrol to augment the efforts of the American government's border patrol. However, according to the Southern Poverty Law Center, which views the ABT as a "virulent anti-immigration group," the group's activities were actually meant to "embarrass the federal government into fully militarizing the border by capturing images of undocumented workers on film and uploading them to the American Border Patrol website for all to see."

In 2016, the group initially embraced Donald Trump's campaign and the attention it brought to the border issue with Mexico. However, because of Trump's focus on the issue, money flowed away from the group and toward more mainstream sources that supported the Trump presidential campaign.

See also: Spencer, Glenn

Further Reading

American Border Patrol. October 24, 2016. "Obama to Rescind Gadsden Purchase?" americanborderpatrol.com/2013-2014/161115.htm (link no longer active).

Southern Poverty Law Center. "American Border Patrol." https://www.splcenter.org/fighting-hate/extremist-files/group/american-border-patrolamerican-patrol (Accessed March 9, 2017).

Spencer, Glenn. "Trust but Verify." *American Border Patrol*. http://americanborderpatrol.com/ (Accessed March 9, 2017).

Wiegel, David. May 6, 2013. "The Fence Junkies." *Slate*. http://www.slate.com/articles/news_and_politics/politics/2013/05/glenn_spencers_american_border_patrol_is_waging_a_high_tech_campaign_to.html (Accessed March 9, 2017).

AMERICAN FREEDOM PARTY

Founded in 2009 as the American Third Position, or A3P, the American Freedom Party is a group of white nationalists who claim to represent the interests of white Americans, particularly as they relate to the immigration of non-Europeans. Like many white nationalist groups, the American Freedom Party has a noticeably racist element, believing that the current demographic makeup of the United States is no longer "recognizable" and puts white Americans in an inferior position.

The A3P was renamed in 2013 as the American Freedom Party, and the group has dedicated itself to raising awareness and funds in support of its causes. The group has attempted to court both Tea Party Republicans and Libertarians. In an Internet broadcast in 2010, a member of the group stated, "There's a great overlap in Patriot activities and Patriot causes, and we have, we will have a big effect on this much larger movement, the Ron Paul Revolution, that has millions of people engaged . . . we'll be pulling them from the right" (Southern Poverty Law Center).

Like many right-wing extremist groups, the American Freedom Party appeals to Americans who believe that the "white essence" of American political and social life is being eroded by governmental policies and the continuing influx of immigration from nonwhite countries. The tagline of the group's Web site proclaims, "Liberty, Sovereignty, Identity" (American Freedom Party). These "code" words are familiar to most within the patriot movement and other extremist groups; they symbolize the disaffection that many white Americans feel in their own country. The group has used statements such as "We . . . embrace principles that will secure the existence of our people and a future for our children," which is very similar to the passage known as "14 Words" from Hitler's *Mein Kampf* that has served as inspiration for neo-Nazis and other white supremacists: "We must secure the existence of our people and a future for white children" (Southern Poverty Law Center). The term "14 Words" was coined by David Lane, "a member of the white supremacist terrorist group known as The Order" (Anti-Defamation League). According to the Anti-Defamation League, the 14 Words reflect "the primary white supremacist worldview in the late 20th and early 21st centuries that unless immediate action is taken, the white race is doomed to extinction by an alleged rising tide of color purportedly controlled and manipulated by Jews."

The American Freedom Party takes issue with both Republicans and Democrats, seeing independents and libertarians as the base from which to draw new members. Pronouncements have stated that the party will rally to the banner of any group that best represents the "interests of white Americans."

See also: Fourteen Words

Further Reading

American Freedom Party. http://american3rdposition.com/ (Accessed August 12, 2016).
Anti-Defamation League. "14 Words." https://www.adl.org/education/references/hate-symbols/14-words.
Southern Poverty Law Center. "American Freedom Party." https://www.splcenter.org/fighting-hate/extremist-files/group/american-freedom-party (Accessed August 12, 2016).

AMERICAN JIHADIST TERROR ATTACKS

Since September 11, 2001, Americans have been increasingly aware of the threat posed by Islamic jihadists. Since 9/11, nearly 50 deadly terror attacks perpetrated in the United States have been attributed to Islamic jihadists (The Religion of Peace). Though some of these attacks have been carried out by foreign nationals acting on American soil, increasingly attacks have come at the hand of "homegrown" jihadists—American citizens who have become radicalized by jihadi propaganda and carry out "lone wolf" attacks in the name of Islam.

Islamic jihadism has manifested itself in many forms over the centuries. However, the current iteration can trace its beginnings to the success of the Iranian Revolution in 1979. From that time, the advent of groups whose terror activities are largely guided by their adherence to radical Islam has increased in the United States and around the world.

Many Americans see Islamic jihadi attacks as indicative of a religious philosophy that is committed to the destruction of all other religions besides Islam. This extremist interpretation by some followers of Islam both at home and abroad has raised mistrust and suspicion among many Americans who can clearly recall the callousness and brutality of the 9/11 attacks. Since that date, a wave of Islamophobia has swept the country with native-born Muslims increasingly the target of anti-Islamic attacks. Recent jihadi attacks—including the attack by a husband–wife pair in San Bernardino, California, in 2015 and an attack on a gay nightclub in Orlando, Florida, in 2016—have punctuated fears among Americans that even native-born Muslims are now becoming increasingly susceptible to radicalization that preaches the virtues of Islam as the only defense against an increasingly decadent and corrupt American political and social system.

See also: Boston Marathon Bombing; Orlando Nightclub Shooting; San Bernardino Shooting

Further Reading

New America. "Terrorism in America after 9/11." http://www.newamerica.org/in-depth /terrorism-in-america/ (Accessed October 27, 2016).

Religion of Peace. "Islamic Terror on American Soil." https://www.thereligionofpeace.com /attacks/american-attacks.aspx (Accessed October 27, 2016).

AMERICAN NAZI PARTY

Founded by George Lincoln Rockwell in 1959, the American Nazi Party exists to foster the goals of national socialism in the United States. The group claims to be guided by the so-called 14 Words: "We must secure the existence of our people and a future for white children" (American Nazi Party).

Like other national socialists, the American Nazi Party believes in the supremacy of the white race over all other races and holds that the American national system of government has been corrupted by Jewish influences. In examining what they stand for, their beliefs look much like other right-wing extremist groups. Though these beliefs appear benign in their expression, they become vitriolic in practice. The American Nazi Party professes the following principles:

1. Race—all Aryans in North America should be in union.
2. Citizenship—only those of Aryan blood should be citizens of the state.
3. Aryan community—society should be organized into racial communities that will fully recognize, and embrace, Aryanism as a separate race.
4. The family farm—the family farm should be protected, and there should be a stable market and fair prices for the farmer's goods.
5. Motherhood and family—the family should be recognized as indispensable to Aryan society, and motherhood should be elevated from a position of "low esteem" to one that is universally recognized as the "noblest position to which any Aryan woman can aspire."
6. A new education system—the education system should emphasize the physical and moral development of young people.
7. An honest economy—there should be an honest and debt-free economy based on the productive capacity of the Aryan worker.
8. Energy and environment—the state should be totally self-sufficient in terms of energy.
9. Culture and science—the state should promote every form of Aryan cultural expression, and "alien" influences should be removed from the cultural life of the community (i.e., modern art and modern music, such as rap).
10. Foreign policy and defense—foreign policy and defense should be based on the long-term interests of the Aryan race.
11. White self-defense—white people should have the absolute right to keep and bear arms.
12. A better race—the state should use eugenics to propagate the highest racial elements of the Aryan race and halt the spread of hereditary defects and "racially impure blood."
13. A spiritual rebirth—the state should take an active part in the spiritual life of the community and turn citizens away from "materialism, cynicism, and egoism."

In 2016, the American Nazi Party endorsed the candidacy of Donald Trump by stating:

> Trump has had the balls or the gall, to REACH OUT to the true feelings of most of what is left of White America, and "say the things they have longed to hear for decades"—he has brought them out from under the stones where they have been HIDING, and given them a VOICE to vent one last, long call of despair before they are subsumed in a sea of non-White creatures from every corner of planet earth, who are intent on TAKING from the hands of the pathetic Mighty Whiteys who shamble along like the Walking Dead Zombies, who have LOST their heritage/history of being willing to FIGHT, both tooth and nail to PRESERVE what is THEIRS! (American Nazi Party)

See also: National Socialist Movement; Rockwell, George Lincoln

Further Reading
American Nazi Party. "The Fourteen Words." http://www.americannaziparty.com/14words cards.pdf (Accessed October 25, 2016).

American Nazi Party. "News." http://www.americannaziparty.com/news/index.php (Accessed October 25, 2016).
American Nazi Party. "Platform." http://www.americannaziparty.com/platform/index.php (Accessed October 25, 2016).

AMERICAN PATRIOT PARTY

The American Patriot Party (APP) is a loose collection of individuals and groups who attempt to educate members about the "inalienable" rights of American citizens as well as the virtues of states' rights and local control (American Patriot Party). The APP was founded in 2011 at the height of the Tea Party movement, and its fundamental goal is to de-emphasize federal control in favor of state and local control. The APP is an organization whose official motto is "Inalienable Rights, States Rights, Local Control" (American Patriot Party). The APP has been designated as an active patriot and antigovernment group by the Southern Poverty Law Center. The platform of the APP is very much in line with other patriot and antigovernment groups that have organized themselves to resist perceived government overreach and intrusion into local matters of social and political importance. The fundamental belief of the APP is that the "United States Government and appointed officials need to respect the Constitution." The APP believes in upholding the rights of the states and individuals over that of the federal government (Patriot Party). The APP's platform is to

> Protect, defend and implement the intents set forth in the Originating Founders Letters which includes "The Absolute Rights of the Colonists of 1772" and the Declaration of Independence, the documents which define Freedom. This Platform may be amended as needed through the literal understanding of these documents that define and establish freedom and a free country. (American Patriot Party Platform, http://www.pacificwestcom.com/platform/)

The APP's goal is to have the federal government tie all of its platform statements into the standard interpretation of the Declaration of Independence, the U.S. Constitution, and other founding documents. The APP has divided its platform into 10 distinct subjects:

1. Origin of government
2. Limited federal government
3. Rights of the individual
4. Rights of the states
5. Responsibilities of the federal government
6. Rights of local communities over state, county, federal governments, entities, and outside intervention
7. Roles and duties within the federal government—the executive branch
8. Roles and duties within the federal government—the judicial branch
9. Roles and duties within the federal government—the legislative branch
10. Campaigns and elections

(American Patriot Party Platform, http://www.pacificwestcom.com/platform/)

Much of what is articulated by the American Patriot Party can be found in groups that have preceded it. For instance, the APP's emphasis on the rights of individuals and local communities over any state, county, or federal structure is very similar to the thought of the sovereign citizens movement and the Posse Comitatus. These groups, also seen as antigovernment in nature, believe that the federal government has usurped power and has gone far beyond the limited power that was ceded to it at the founding. For patriot and other antigovernment groups, the goal is to reduce the power of the federal government and bring it back in line with a more idealized version of limited government that, for most adherents of this view, is epitomized by the U.S. Constitution as it was originally constructed.

Today, the American Patriot Party has chapters in 27 states (Southern Poverty Law Center).

See also: Patriot Movement; Posse Comitatus; Sovereign Citizens Movement; Tea Party Movement

Further Reading

American Patriot Party. "American Patriot Party National Platform." http://www.american patriotparty.cc/platform/ (Accessed May 15, 2017).

Balleck, Barry J. 2015. *Allegiance to Liberty: The Changing Face of Patriots, Militias, and Political Violence in America.* New York: Praeger.

Patriot Party. http://thepatriotparty.org/ (Accessed May 15, 2017).

Southern Poverty Law Center. "Active Antigovernment Groups in the United States." https://www.splcenter.org/active-antigovernment-groups-united-states (Accessed May 15, 2017).

Southern Poverty Law Center. February 15, 2017. "Active Patriot Groups in the US in 2016." *Southern Poverty Law Center—Intelligence Report.* https://www.splcenter.org/fighting-hate/intelligence-report/2017/active-patriot-groups-us-2016 (Accessed May 15, 2017).

AMERICAN RENAISSANCE

American Renaissance is a magazine published by the New Century Foundation that puts forth questionable scientific studies that attempt to demonstrate what the organization claims is the supremacy of the white race over all others. The magazine was published monthly from October 1990 through January 2012, when it switched to an online version only (American Renaissance).

American Renaissance was founded by noted white supremacist Jared Taylor in 1990, and it conveys to readers "that race is an important aspect of the individual and group identity" (American Renaissance). Of the many issues that can be characterized as fault lines that punctuate the divisions in society, *American Renaissance* contends that the issue of race is the most important and the most divisive.

The Southern Poverty Law Center contends that *American Renaissance* is a front for the New Century Foundation, a white supremacist organization that hosts "suit-and-tie affairs" in order to attract a number of extremist groups to its conferences, including "neo-Nazis, white supremacists, Ku Klux Klan members, Holocaust deniers and eugenicists." However, unlike many other right-wing extremists, founder Jared Taylor is known for a less virulent brand of anti-Semitism and for encouraging Jews to participate in his events. In an interview with Phil Donahue on MSNBC-TV in 2003, Taylor said Jews "are fine by me" and "look white to me" (Southern Poverty Law Center). This attitude has put Taylor and *American Renaissance* at odds with other white supremacist groups and has led to conflict within the movement, particularly in terms of funding. In recent years, Taylor has taken up the cause of a "whites-only" homeland somewhere in the United States. Believing that whites will soon be a minority in the country, Taylor says that the U.S. government has been a traitor to its own people. He also points out that the desire among whites for a national homeland automatically labels them as "haters" of all other peoples.

See also: New Century Foundation; Taylor, Jared

Further Reading

American Renaissance. "What We Believe." http://www.amren.com/about/ (Accessed October 7, 2016).

American Renaissance. "Who We Are." http://www.amren.com/about/ (Accessed October 7, 2016).

Southern Poverty Law Center. "American Renaissance." https://www.splcenter.org/fighting -hate/extremist-files/group/american-renaissance (Accessed October 7, 2016).

ANARCHIST COOKBOOK

Published in 1971 by William Powell, the *Anarchist Cookbook* was a counterculture protest piece about U.S. involvement in Vietnam. In its original publication, the book was a rudimentary do-it-yourself exercise in the making of drugs, various weapons, and explosive devices, the instructions of which had been pieced together from a variety of military manuals and anarchist publications. A more recent version of the cookbook, published in 2000, includes articles on counterfeiting money, engaging in credit card fraud, obtaining free postage, picking locks, "phreaking" (hacking) cell phones, and hot-wiring cars (Anarchy Cookbook Version 2000).

Since its publication, the book, in one form or another, has been linked to dozens of terrorist attacks both in the United States and abroad, including

> the Croatian separatists who planted a bomb in Grand Central Terminal and hijacked TWA Flight 355 in 1976; a series of abortion clinic bombings in the 1980s; the Oklahoma City bombing in 1995; the Columbine High School massacre in 1999; the 7/7 London bombings; the 2011 Tucson shooting targeting U.S. Rep. Gabrielle Giffords; the Boston Marathon bombing; and the Aurora shooting in 2012 during *The Dark Knight Rises*. (Stern 2016)

As evidenced by the partial list above, since its publication, the *Anarchist Cookbook* has provided inspiration to extremists on both the left and right side of the political spectrum. When it was written, the book served as a handbook for anarchists and other revolutionaries who agitated for violent revolution but had to do so within the constraints of a budget. In later years, the book has provided inspiration to antigovernment extremists in the United States and elsewhere. The book has often been found at gun shows in the United States along with other antigovernment literature and publications such as *The Turner Diaries*, the apocalyptic novel about the destruction of the American political system. It has also become popular among survivalists and others wishing to protect themselves against either excessive government intrusion or the possibility of seizure of property during times of crisis or civil unrest.

Though the publication at one point opines, "respect must be earned by the spilling of blood," author William Powell insists that he wrote it only as a teenager disaffected by the senselessness of the Vietnam conflict. Powell claims never to have attempted any of the "recipes" outlined in the book, though others certainly did. In 2013, an 18-year-old, who friends say had been "consuming" the *Anarchist Cookbook* for years, entered a Colorado high school with a 12-gauge shotgun and Molotov cocktails that he had learned to construct by means of the *Cookbook*. Though he could not find his intended target (a debate coach who had dismissed him from the school's debate team), he ended up shooting a 17-year-old girl who later died from her wounds. When none of his Molotov cocktails ignited, the young man turned the gun on himself. Powell has admitted that "the *Cookbook* has been found in the possession of alienated and disturbed young people who have launched attacks against classmates and teachers. I suspect that the perpetrators of these attacks did not feel much of a sense of belonging, and the *Cookbook* may have added to their sense of isolation" (Stern 2016). In the case of the connection of his book with terror attacks, Powell later stated that the book should "quickly and quietly go out of print."

Unfortunately, the book remains in print and is still easily accessible in both print and digital forms. Its table of contents appeals to those who just want to get a high from hallucinogenic drugs, to those who want to commit acts of vandalism, to those who want to wreak havoc on society through violent and sometimes revolutionary means. As is the case in so many extremist publications, the *Anarchist Cookbook* is a source of inspiration to those looking for an outlet, hence the reason why it is found in the possession of so many people who have committed acts of violence.

When William Powell died on July 11, 2016, a documentary on the *Anarchist Cookbook* was in the final stages of completion. In his final remarks about the role that the book has played in so many acts of violence, Powell remarked, "It fills me with remorse. I grossly underestimated the controversy it would provoke. . . . I do feel responsible for the ways in which the book has been used" (Stern 2016).

See also: Colorado Theater Shooting; Columbine High School Shooting; Oklahoma City Bombing; *Turner Diaries, The*

Further Reading

Anarchy Cookbook Version 2000. "Table of Contents." http://bnrg.cs.berkeley.edu/~randy/Courses/CS39K.S13/anarchistcookbook2000.pdf (Accessed October 5, 2016).

Pierce, William (as Andrew Macdonald). 1978. *The Turner Diaries*. Mill Point, WV: National Vanguard Books.

Powell, William. 1971. *Anarchist Cookbook*. New York: Lyle Stuart.

Stern, Marlow. September 4, 2016. "'The Anarchist Cookbook' Author's Last Confession: 'It Fills Me with Remorse.'" *The Daily Beast*. http://www.thedailybeast.com/articles /2016/09/04/the-anarchist-cookbook-author-s-last-confession-it-fills-me-with -remorse.html (Accessed October 5, 2016).

ANIMAL LIBERATION FRONT

The Animal Liberation Front (ALF) is a direct action extremist organization committed to ending the abuse and exploitation of animals. ALF engages in clandestine direct acts of resistance against those who exploit animals "by removing animals from laboratories and farms, destroying facilities, arranging safe houses and veterinary care, and operating sanctuaries where the animals subsequently live" (ALF). There is no central leadership of ALF. Rather, various "cells" consist of small groups of individuals or friends, or even just one person, who are dedicated to the protection of animals. Though activists claim that the movement is nonviolent, they nevertheless engage in acts of vandalism and animal rescue that cause great economic damage to their victims. These acts are criminal in nature as they are "designed to cause economic loss and destroy the victim's company operations or property" (Federal Bureau of Investigation 2008). ALF claims that its activists intend no harm to any human or nonhuman life. This fact has been recognized by the Southern Poverty Law Center, which, although it characterizes ALF as an extremist group, notes that no human deaths can be attributed to the organization (Nelson 2011). In 2005, ALF was identified by the U.S. Department of Homeland Security as a domestic terror threat (Rood 2005). In 2006, the U.S. Department of Justice launched Operation Backfire and announced charges again nine Americans and two Canadians for a string of arson attacks between 1996 and 2001 that caused more than $40 million in damage (Federal Bureau of Investigation 2008). The incidents included "arson attacks against meat-processing plants, lumber companies, a high-tension power line, and ski centers in Oregon, Wyoming, Washington, California, and Colorado" (Department of Justice).

ALF was formed in 1971 in the United Kingdom by animal rights activists Ronnie Lee and Cliff Goodman, who determined that more militant tactics were needed in the defense of animals. The organization was originally known as the Band of Mercy. The first known act of vandalism occurred in 1973, when a building associated with a research laboratory for a pharmaceutical company was set on fire. In 1974, Lee and Goodman were arrested for raiding an Oxford animal laboratory. They were sentenced to three years in prison, during which they both engaged in a hunger strike, demanding vegan food and clothing. They were paroled after 12 months and gathered new activists to their cause. Deciding that the name Band of Mercy did not convey the revolutionary spirit they wished to engender, Lee and Goodman renamed the group the Animal Liberation Front (Molland 2004).

ALF activities began in the United States in the late 1970s (Federal Bureau of Investigation 2004). Groups and individuals associated with ALF engaged in "a multi-national campaign of harassment, intimidation and coercion against animal testing companies and any companies or individuals doing business with those targeted companies" (Federal Bureau of Investigation 2004). The most common tactic used by ALF is attacks on businesses or laboratories perceived as abusing animals. Employees of businesses involved in animal testing have had their homes spray-painted with "Puppy killer" and "We'll be back" notices (Southern Poverty Law Center). On September 20, 2001, a mere nine days after the events of 9/11, ALF set a $1 million fire at a primate lab in New Mexico, causing conservative commentators and the FBI to label the act "ecoterrorism" (Southern Poverty Law Center). Self-appointed ALF spokesperson David Barbarash disagreed, stating,

I mean, what was the Boston Tea Party, if not a massive act of property destruction? . . . Property damage is a legitimate political tool called economic sabotage, and it's meant to attack businesses and corporations who are profiting from the exploitation, murder and torture of either humans or animals, or the planet. . . . To call those acts terrorism is ludicrous." (Southern Poverty Law Center)

In 2011, ALF ramped up its harassment. A group associated with ALF called Negotiation Is Over has emerged; it "strives to be an instrument of defiance, disruption, disobedience, subversion, creative & aggressive grassroots action, and a catalyst for revolutionary change. Total liberation—human animals, nonhuman animals, and the earth—will not happen by politely asking abusers to be decent. Emotion and passion drive action . . . not sterile debate" (Nelson 2011). Negotiation Is Over went on to strike a more ominous tone, indicating that it might use more violent tactics in the defense of animal rights:

If you spill blood, your blood should be spilled as well. . . . We're no longer playing games. We will print your information. And we'll be at your homes. We'll be at your work. We'll be at your country clubs and golf courses. We'll see you at your manicurist and we'll be kneeling next to you when you take that next holy communion wafer on Sunday. If I have my way, you'll be praying to us for mercy. (Nelson 2011)

ALF's credo still maintains that "it is a nonviolent campaign, [with] activists taking all precautions not to harm any animal (human or otherwise)" (Animal Liberation Front). Unfortunately, with no centralized organization, and with the policy of direct action as the guiding modus operandi of the group, more radicalized members of the movement may emerge and take more drastic steps in their pursuit of animal rights.

See also: Earth Liberation Front

Further Reading

Animal Liberation Front. "The ALF Credo and Guidelines." http://www.animalliberationfront
.com/ALFront/alf_credo.htm (Accessed May 1, 2017).

Animal Liberation Front. "Mission Statement." http://www.animalliberationfront.com/ALFront/mission_statement.htm (Accessed May 1, 2017).

Department of Justice. "Eleven Defendants Indicted on Domestic Terrorism Charges." https://www.justice.gov/archive/opa/pr/2006/January/06_crm_030.html (Accessed May 1, 2017).

Federal Bureau of Investigation. May 18, 2004. "John E. Lewis: Testimony Before the Senate Judiciary Committee." https://archives.fbi.gov/archives/news/testimony/animal-rights-extremism-and-ecoterrorism (Accessed May 1, 2017).

Federal Bureau of Investigation. November 19, 2008. "Operation Backfire: Help Find Four Eco-Terrorists." https://archives.fbi.gov/archives/news/stories/2008/november/backfire_11908 (Accessed May 1, 2017).

Molland, Noel. 2004. "Thirty Years of Direct Action." In Steven Best and Anthony J. Nocella, editors. *Terrorists or Freedom Fighters? Reflections of the Liberation of Animals.* Lantern Books.

Nelson, Leah. November 3, 2011. "Animal Rights Activist: 'If You Spill Blood, Your Blood Should Be Spilled.'" *Southern Poverty Law Center—Hatewatch.* https://www.splcenter.org/hatewatch/2011/11/03/animal-rights-activist-if-you-spill-blood-your-blood-should-be-spilled (Accessed May 1, 2017).

Rood, Justin. March 25, 2005. "Animal Rights Groups and Ecology Militants Make DHS Terrorist List, Right-Wing Vigilantes Omitted." *Congressional Quarterly.*

Southern Poverty Law Center. "Stop Huntingdon Animal Cruelty Threatens Terrorist-Style Attack." *Southern Poverty Law Center—Intelligence Report.* https://www.splcenter.org/fighting-hate/intelligence-report/2002/stop-huntingdon-animal-cruelty-threatens-terrorist-style-attack?page=0%2C2 (Accessed May 1, 2017).

ANTI-DEFAMATION LEAGUE

The Anti-Defamation League (ADL) is a Jewish nongovernmental organization based in the United States that seeks to defend Jewish interests and dispel falsehoods that are spread about the Jewish people. The ADL claims to carry on the vision of its founder, Chicago attorney Sigmund Livingston, who "envisioned an America where those who seemed different were not targets of discrimination and threats, but were equals, worthy of shared opportunity and a place in the American dream" (ADL Mission). The ADL claims to be a civil rights/human relations agency that is committed to

1. combating anti-Semitism;
2. combating hate and protecting communities;
3. confronting discrimination and security justice;
4. standing up for Israel; and
5. promoting respectful schools and communities (ADL, What We Do).

Though the ADL aims to prevent the defamation of the Jewish people, recent critics have noted that the organization today seems to advocate more for Israeli policy in the United States than for protection of Jewish civil rights, as had originally been its cause (Pfeffer 2010). Others accuse the ADL of equating criticism of Israel with anti-Semitism and, as such, "manipulat[ing] our Jewish Citizens and the general population of America by applying the term 'anti-Semitic' to any and all opposition" (Hour of the Time).

According to its Web site, the purpose of the ADL is to campaign against

anti-Semitism and all forms of bigotry (in the United States) and abroad, combat
international terrorism, probe the roots of hatred, advocate before the United States
Congress, come to the aid of victims of bigotry, develop educational programs, and
serve as a public resource for government, media, law enforcement, and the public,
all towards the goal of countering and reducing hatred. (ADL)

Like another civil rights organization, the Southern Poverty Law Center, one of
the primary foci of the ADL is to monitor the activities of various extremist groups
and movements within the United States (ADL, What We Do). The organization
claims that it is the foremost authority on extremism, terrorism, and hate, both
foreign and domestic (ADL, What We Do). The ADL frequently produces reports
on incidences of anti-Semitism and other extremist activity that occurs on both the
far left and the far right of the political spectrum. In 2017, the ADL reported that
anti-Semitic incidents had spiked 86 percent in the first quarter of the year. Attrib-
uting the increase to the number of right-wing groups inspired by the election of
Donald Trump to the U.S. presidency in November 2016, the ADL reported that
there "has been a massive increase in the amount of harassment of American Jews,
particularly since November, and a doubling in the amount of anti-Semitic bullying and vandalism at non-denominational K-12 grade schools" (ADL).

The ADL also strives to call attention to the Holocaust in order to prevent the
reoccurrence of any similar event. As such, the ADL sponsors information events
and conferences that fight Holocaust denial and authors of revisionist histories
about the Holocaust. The inappropriate use of the term "Holocaust" can also draw
the ire of the ADL, as was demonstrated in 2003 when the People for the Ethical Treatment for Animals (PETA) initiated an advertising campaign in which the
organization equated meat eating with the horrors of the Holocaust. In a sharply
worded statement issued by the ADL, the organization stated that

PETA's effort to seek "approval" for their "Holocaust on Your Plate" campaign is outrageous, offensive and takes chutzpah to new heights. Rather than deepen our revul-
sion against what the Nazis did to the Jews, the project will undermine the struggle
to understand the Holocaust and to find ways to make sure such catastrophes never
happen again. (CNN 2003)

The ADL has been accused of being too slow to recognize genocides other than the
Holocaust when it suits its purposes. For years, the American Jewish community
refused to openly criticize Turkey for its part in the 1915 genocide of Armenians
under Ottoman rule. Leaders concede that they did it out of gratitude for Turkey
being a staunch Muslim ally of Israel (Arax 2010). In 2007, the ADL released a
statement referring to the Armenian genocide as a "massacre" and an "atrocity," but
not a genocide. Turkey denounced the statement, and the ADL was pressured to
use stronger language to identify the genocide but ultimately decided that it would
not revise its original statement (Woolhouse 2007). In 2016, the ADL finally recognized the Armenian genocide when Jonathan Greenblatt, CEO of ADL, stated,

When we teach about the Holocaust, we speak about the 2,000-year history of anti-Semitism that made the Shoah possible.

We have a similar responsibility to talk more broadly and recall that in our own lifetime the world did not stand up against the horrors happening in Cambodia, Bosnia and Rwanda. Too often, the response to genocide has been global silence.

So, let me be crystal clear: the first genocide of the 20th century is no different. What happened in the Ottoman Empire to the Armenians beginning in 1915 was genocide. The genocide began with the ruling government arresting and executing several hundred Armenian intellectuals. After that, Armenian families were removed from their homes and sent on death marches. The Armenian people were subjected to deportation, expropriation, abduction, torture, massacre and starvation.

What happened to the Armenian people was unequivocally genocide. (Greenblatt 2016)

The ADL was very vocal in 2016, calling out the anti-Semitic behavior of supporters of presidential candidate Donald Trump. When Trump chose former *Breitbart News* executive chairperson Steve Bannon as his senior advisor and chief strategist, the ADL wrote, "It is a sad day when a man who presided over the premier website of the 'alt-right'—a loose-knit group of white nationalists and unabashed anti-Semites and racists—is slated to be a senior staff member in the 'people's house'" (Zauzmer and Itkowitz 2016).

See also: Alt-Right Movement; *Breitbart News*; Holocaust Denial; Institute for Historical Review; Southern Poverty Law Center

Further Reading

Anti-Defamation League. April 24, 2017. "U.S. Anti-Semitic Incidents Spike 86 Percent So Far in 2017 After Surging Last Year, ADL Finds." https://www.adl.org/news/press-releases/us-anti-semitic-incidents-spike-86-percent-so-far-in-2017 (Accessed May 1, 2017).

Anti-Defamation League. "Our Mission." https://www.adl.org/who-we-are/our-mission (Accessed May 1, 2017).

Anti-Defamation League. "What We Do." https://www.adl.org/what-we-do (Accessed May 1, 2017).

Arax, Mark. June 16, 2010. "Suddenly, the Israel Lobby Discovers a Genocide." *Salon*. http://www.salon.com/2010/06/16/israel_lobby_genocide_armenia/ (Accessed May 1, 2017).

CNN. February 28, 2003. "Group Blasts PETA 'Holocaust' Project." http://edition.cnn.com/2003/US/Northeast/02/28/peta.holocaust/ (Accessed May 1, 2017).

Greenblatt, Jonathan. May 13, 2016. "ADL on the Armenian Genocide." *Anti-Defamation League*. https://www.adl.org/blog/adl-on-the-armenian-genocide (Accessed May 1, 2017).

Hour of the Time. "The Ugly Truth About the Anti-Defamation League (ADL)." http://www.hourofthetime.com/adltruth.htm (Accessed May 1, 2017).

Pfeffer, Anshel. August 27, 2010. "The ADL Has Lost Its Way Under Abe Foxman." *Haaretz*. http://www.haaretz.com/the-adl-has-lost-its-way-under-abe-foxman-1.310432 (Accessed May 1, 2017).

Woolhouse, Megan. December 5, 2007. "ADL's Regional Leader Resigns." *Boston.com*. http://archive.boston.com/news/local/articles/2007/12/05/adls_regional_leader_resigns/ (Accessed May 1, 2017).

Zauzmer, Julie and Colby Itkowitz. November 15, 2016. "Anti-Defamation League Decries Stephen Bannon, While Other Jewish Groups Stay Silent." *The Washington Post.* https://www.washingtonpost.com/news/acts-of-faith/wp/2016/11/15/anti-defamation -league-decries-stephen-bannon-while-other-jewish-groups-stay-silent/?utm_term= .a2631355df95 (Accessed May 1, 2017).

ANTIFASCIST MOVEMENT (ANTIFA)

The antifascist movement, otherwise known as Antifa, can trace its roots to the 1920s and 1930s when militant protestors from the left battled Nazi fascists in the streets of Germany. After World War II, the term reemerged in England as neo-Nazi skinheads began to infiltrate the punk rock scene that was then emerging in the country. By the late 1980s, the group took root in the United States and began a series of counterprotests to perceived right-wing inroads into the American political scene. Inasmuch as their roots stem from the communist left, Antifa also protests incidents of capitalism and globalism. The group burst onto the scene in 1999 when members descended on Seattle to protest meetings of the nascent World Trade Organization in that city. Major protests also occurred in Toledo in 2005, in New York City in 2012 (in support of the Occupy Wall Street movement), and most recently at Charlottesville, Virginia, in August 2017. Antifa is not an actual organization but a loose coalition of like-minded individuals who use direct action tactics to protest the messages of hate and racism preached by many extreme right-wing groups, such as the Ku Klux Klan, racist skinheads, neo-Nazis, and members of the new alt-right movement.

Antifa activists generally conceal themselves from public view by wearing head-to-toe black clothing and covering their faces. This anonymity, they feel, provides protection against the violent tendencies associated with the groups they protest. Antifa activists offer no apologies for confronting extremism with violence. Taking their cue from the lessons of the Holocaust, they believe that racism, hatred, and extremism—when it manifests itself in violence—must be confronted in a like manner. This tactic was on display in Charlottesville, Virginia, on August 11–12, 2017, when a group of right-wing protestors, calling themselves Unite the Right, descended on Charlottesville to protest the removal of a statue of Robert E. Lee. Carrying lighted torches reminiscent of the Nazi parades of the 1930s, the right-wing protestors shouted "white lives matter," "blood and soil," and "Jews will not replace us"—each phrase calculated to signal disdain for a particular group (Black Lives Matter adherents, for instance) or their fealty to the Nazi past that inspired their actions ("blood and soil" being a popular slogan of the Nazi era). The presence of the Unite the Right protestors was met with an Antifa presence that turned violent on both sides in the form of fist fights, assaults with clubs and other objects, and violent rhetoric hurled back and forth across police lines. Though President Donald Trump condemned hate and violence "on many sides" in the aftermath of the clashes, the media generally criticized his remarks, noting that Antifa members were in Charlottesville to counter the message of hate and racism being perpetrated by the extremists. As one Antifa member put it, "For the extreme right, politics is ultimately steeped in the irrational, powered by a mood of victimhood, fear of otherness and a racist vision of a 'purified' world" (Jackson 2017).

While Antifa's tactics have "elicited substantial support from the mainstream left," its use of violence makes supporters hesitant to fully embrace their presence at extreme right-wing events (Beinart 2017). Antifa activists contend that "anti-fascists promote acceptance of a diverse, multicultural world [whereas] right-wing extremists reject the diverse reality of modern life" (Jackson 2017). "Hate speech against vulnerable minorities leads to violence against vulnerable minorities" (Beinart 2017). Therefore, Antifa activists contend that they will continue to defend the weak and vulnerable, meet violence with violence, and protect the advancements of modern civilized society that they see threatened by the messages of individuals and groups on the extreme right wing of American politics.

See also: Alt-Right Movement; Ku Klux Klan; Neo-Nazis; White Nationalism; White Supremacist Movement

Further Reading

Beinart, Peter. September 2017. "The Rise of the Violent Left." *The Atlantic*. https://www
.theatlantic.com/magazine/archive/2017/09/the-rise-of-the-violent-left/534192/
(Accessed September 27, 2017).

Ganim, Sara and Chris Welch. August 22, 2017. "Unmasking the Leftist Antifa Movement." *CNN*.
http://www.cnn.com/2017/08/18/us/unmasking-antifa-anti-fascists-hard-left/index
.html (Accessed September 27, 2017).

Jackson, Paul. August 23, 2017. "If You Want to Understand Anti-Fascist Movements, You
Need to Know This History." *Huffington Post*. http://www.huffingtonpost.com/entry
/anti-fascist-movements_us_599b11b8e4b04c532f4348f4 (Accessed September 27,
2017).

ANTI-GOVERNMENT MOVEMENT GUIDEBOOK

The *Anti-Government Movement Guidebook* was copyrighted in 1999 by the National Center for State Courts. The *Guidebook* was developed under a government grant that was entitled, "The Rise of Common Law Courts in the United States: An Examination of the Movement, the Potential Impact on the Judiciary, and How the States Could Respond" (Family Guardian). The *Guidebook* was written in response to an increase in nuisance lawsuits filed by antigovernment individuals and/or groups that are known colloquially as "paper terrorists." "Paper terrorism" refers to "false liens, frivolous lawsuits, bogus letters of credit, and other legal documents lacking sound factual basis as a method of harassment, especially against government officials" (Chamberlain and Haider-Market 2005). Another method of paper terrorism is filing bankruptcy petitions against others in an effort to ruin their credit ratings. The individuals and groups who have employed paper terrorism are antigovernment in nature, believing that neither state nor federal governments have the power or authority to impose certain laws on citizens, taxation in particular. The tactic of using paper terrorism clogs the court system and makes it more difficult to process other cases.

The publication of *Anti-Government Movement Guidebook* occurred in recognition of the antigovernment sentiments that were arising among citizens as the new millennium dawned. The preface of the *Guidebook* reads,

> There is a movement afoot in this country today that is made up of disaffected and often dispossessed Americans who are seeking a better way through a wholesale return to their view of the past. This movement has been called many things: the antigovernment movement, the sovereignty movement, and the common law courts movement. Regardless of the name attached to the beliefs and the people who follow them, one common denominator exists: a feeling of despair, rooted in personal and pecuniary loss, and manifested in a new, defiant mistrust and spite for the ways of the current government. This guide focuses on the ways in which followers of these movements impact the operation of our state court systems. . . .
>
> The people who make up the movements that we are concerned with consistently speak out to say that our government today does not listen, it no longer serves the American people, it exists to serve its own ends. The merits of that argument are not within the purview of this guide. Rather, the authors wish to urge Justice Brandeis's warning upon those who administer our state courts. That is, while we do not advocate an ultra-sympathetic response at the expense of safety and the efficient operation of the courts, we do implore those charged with running our court system to do two things: learn the history behind the beliefs we are seeing spread across our land, and understand that these are not militia members or "Patriots" or "ultra-conservatives," but rather citizens who come before you seeking the same fair treatment that those without any label attached receive. (*Anti-Government Movement Guidebook*, Preface)

From the *Guidebook* preface, it is obvious that court officials are being instructed to deal compassionately with American citizens who feel they have been left behind in the legal system. Though such individuals, and the groups with which they associate (e.g., sovereign citizens movement, Posse Comitatus, Montana Freemen) attempt to clog up and slow the judicial system to their advantage, jurists should nevertheless be sensitive to the issues behind the paper terrorism and ensure that all citizens receive the care and attention from the court system that every citizen deserves.

Of course, antigovernment groups have dismissed the cautions to jurists provided in the preface and focused rather on the claim that the *Guidebook* is meant to instruct judges on how to ignore citizen rights by circumventing the Constitution. One organization, Family Guardian, which states that obedience to God's laws and man's laws (the U.S. Constitution) are "compelling state interests," has published a facsimile of the *Guidebook*'s title page, inserting the word "corrupt" over the word "government" on the title page. This sentiment is typical of individuals and groups who see themselves as oppressed by government rules, laws, and regulations. Such antigovernment sentiment rises and falls with society's perceptions of social, economic, and political conditions. In 2017, American society is rife with antigovernment sentiment as evidenced by the level of support demonstrated for the populist presidential candidacy of Donald Trump.

See also: Montana Freemen; Paper Terrorism; Posse Comitatus; Sovereign Citizens Movement

Further Reading

Balleck, Barry J. 2015. *Allegiance to Liberty: The Changing Face of Patriots, Militias, and Political Violence in America.* New York: Praeger.

Chamberlain, Robert and Donald P. Haider-Market. September 2005. "Lien on Me: State Policy Innovation in Response to Paper Terrorism." *Political Research Quarterly* 3: 449–460.

Family Guardian. "What Is the Anti-Government Movement Guidebook." http://famguardian .org/Publications/AntiGovernmentMvmt/whats_this.htm (Accessed May 4, 2017).

National Center for State Courts. 1999. "The Anti-Government Movement Guidebook." http://www.tulanelink.com/pdf/anti-gov_movement_guidebook.pdf (Accessed May 4, 2017).

ANTI-LGBT MOVEMENT

The issue of equal rights for LGBT people has mobilized members of the Christian right since the 1980s, a period that also witnessed the rise of a fundamentalist reinterpretation of American society as evidenced by the formation of such groups as the Moral Majority. For leaders on the Christian right, LGBT issues, particularly what is referred to as the "homosexual agenda," are considered the primary suspects in what those on the Christian right believe is the "destruction of American society and culture" (Southern Poverty Law Center). James Dobson, the founder of Focus on the Family, has likened the conservative battle against equality for LGBT peoples as a "second civil war" whereupon those who reject LGBT rights are fighting to ensure that the correct government (i.e., one that opposes any type of gay agenda) is placed and kept in power (Southern Poverty Law Center).

The most vocal anti-LGBT activists are generally those on the extreme fringe of the religious right (e.g., Westboro Baptist Church), and they increasingly use defamation as their main weapon. Many anti-LGBT leaders today use disparaging language to describe LGBT people, referring to them "as perverts with filthy habits who seek to snatch the children of straight parents and convert them to gay sex" (Southern Poverty Law Center). These tactics also include the dissemination of false facts about gays, including disinformation that gays are more likely to engage in bestiality, have been abused as children, and are themselves more likely to engage in abusive behavior toward their children than are heterosexual parents. These assertions "are remarkably reminiscent of the way white intellectuals and scientists once wrote about the 'bestial black man and his supposedly threatening sexuality'" (Southern Poverty Law Center).

Verbal attacks may not cause physical harm, but they undeniably cause emotional and mental anguish. According to the U.S. Center for Disease Control, LGBT youth "are more likely than their heterosexual peers to experience negative health and life outcomes" due to violent behaviors perpetrated upon them, such as "bullying, teasing, harassment, and physical assault" (Center for Disease Control and Prevention). LGBT youth are also "at greater risk for depression, suicide, substance use, and sexual behaviors that can place them at increased risk for HIV and other sexually transmitted diseases" (Center for Disease Control and Prevention). A national study of LGBT adolescents found that they were four times as likely to attempt suicide as their heterosexual peers (Chen 2016).

There are also hundreds of reports of gay bashing and deaths that occur because of antigay hate and bias (Schlatter 2010). The violence never seems to end and is constantly reinforced by groups that claim to be speaking on behalf of family values. Unfortunately, many right-wing extremist groups have taken up gay bashing and antigay activities as part of their overall patterns of hate against minorities and other groups that they deem undesirable. In the aftermath of the U.S. Supreme Court's ruling in *Obergefell v. Hodges* (2015), the case that held that same-sex couples in the United States have the same constitutionally guaranteed right to marry as heterosexual couples, conservative politicians and organizations lashed out, and physical attacks increased (New Civil Rights Movement). Perhaps the most infamous act against LGBT people was perpetrated in an Orlando, Florida, nightclub on June 12, 2016. In the attack, Omar Mateen, who claimed allegiance to the Islamic Sate of Iraq and Syria (ISIS), killed 49 people and wounded 53 others. Mateen purposely targeted the nightclub because it was known as a gay nightclub. The massacre was the deadliest incident of violence against LGBT people in U.S. history, at the time it was perpetrated. On October 1, 2017, the carnage was surpassed when Stephen Paddock opened fire on a music festival in Las Vegas, Nevada, killing 58 people and injuring more than 850.

As a significant number of American citizens long to return to a time in U.S. history when social and political values more closely mirrored "biblical values," the incidences of anti-LGBT sentiments and violence will continue (Bailey 2017). The rise of movements such as the alt-right will continue to foster such sentiments, and the predilection for citizens to elect officials that support an antigay-rights agenda will only lead to more violence against the LGBT community in the future.

See also: Alt-Right Movement; Cameron, Paul; Family Research Council; Family Research Institute; Focus on the Family

Further Reading

Bailey, Sarah Pulliam. January 5, 2017. "How Nostalgia for White Christian America Drove So Many Americans to Vote for Trump." *The Washington Post*. https://www.washingtonpost.com/local/social-issues/how-nostalgia-for-white-christian-america-drove-so-many-americans-to-vote-for-trump/2017/01/04/4ef6d686-b033-11e6-be1c-8cec35b1ad25_story.html?utm_term=.a42451b745eb (Accessed May 4, 2017).

Center for Disease Control and Prevention. "Lesbian, Gay, Bisexual, and Transgender Health." https://www.cdc.gov/lgbthealth/youth.htm (Accessed May 4, 2017).

Chen, Angela. August 11, 2016. "Queer Teens Are Four Times More Likely to Commit Suicide, CDC Reports." *The Verge*. https://www.theverge.com/2016/8/11/12438678/cdc-report-queer-teens-health-risk-suicide (Accessed July 3, 2017).

Hatewatch Staff. "Anti-LGBT Activities." *Southern Poverty Law Center—Hatewatch*. https://www.splcenter.org/hatewatch/2017/04/03/anti-lgbt-activities (Accessed May 4, 2017).

New Civil Rights Movement. "Violent Anti-LGBT Hate Crimes on the Rise After Marriage Equality Ruling." http://www.thenewcivilrightsmovement.com/ericrosswood/violent_lgbt_hate_crimes_on_the_rise_after_marriage_equality_ruling (Accessed May 4, 2017).

Potok, Mark. February 27, 2011. "Gays Remain Minority Most Targeted by Hate Crimes." *Southern Poverty Law Center—Intelligence Report*. https://www.splcenter.org/fighting -hate/intelligence-report/2011/gays-remain-minority-most-targeted-hate-crimes (Accessed May 4, 2017).

Rosswood, Eric. June 26, 2015. "These Conservative Leaders' Heads Exploded with the Supreme Court Marriage Equality Ruling." *The New Civil Rights Movement.com*. http:// www.thenewcivilrightsmovement.com/ericrosswood/these_conservative_leader_s _heads_exploded_with_today_s_marriage_equality_ruling (Accessed May 4, 2017).

Schlatter, Evelyn. October 7, 2010. "Suicides and Gay-Bashings: More Violence for LGBT People." *Southern Poverty Law Center—Hatewatch*. https://www.splcenter.org/hatewatch /2010/10/07/suicides-and-gay-bashings-more-violence-lgbt-people (Accessed May 4, 2017).

Schlatter, Evelyn. November 4, 2010. "18 Anti-Gay Groups and Their Propaganda." *Southern Poverty Law Center—Intelligence Report*. https://www.splcenter.org/fighting-hate /intelligence-report/2010/18-anti-gay-groups-and-their-propaganda (Accessed May 4, 2017).

Southern Poverty Law Center. "Anti-LGBT." https://www.splcenter.org/fighting-hate/extremist -files/ideology/anti-lgbt (Accessed May 4, 2017).

ARMY OF GOD

The Army of God is a Christian terrorist organization that perpetrates attacks on abortion clinics and abortion providers. The U.S. Department of Justice defines the group as an underground terrorist organization with no definable structure or leadership. Individuals who have perpetrated attacks on abortion providers have claimed to act on behalf of the Army of God. A Web site that purports to be part of the Army of God is full of biblical scriptures and graphic pictures of aborted fetuses. The Web site also celebrates the acts of several individuals who have perpetrated acts of violence, including murder, against doctors who perform abortions, abortion clinics, and the patrons of abortion or family-planning clinics.

The first known violent act claimed in the name of the Army of God was perpetrated in 1982 when a doctor who performed abortions and his wife were kidnapped and held captive for eight days. Subsequently, individuals either succeeded in killing their targets or severely injured those whom they attacked. Eric Robert Rudolph, the bomber of the Atlanta Olympics who also bombed two Atlanta abortion clinics and a lesbian nightclub, is held in high esteem by members of the Army of God. The Army of God claimed credit for Rudolph's actions and, after his arrest, encouraged others to take up his cause. On November 27, 2015, Robert Lewis Dear Jr. killed three individuals, including a University of Colorado at Colorado Springs police officer, in an attack on a Planned Parenthood clinic in Colorado Springs, Colorado. Claiming that he was engaged in "God's work," Dear praised the antiabortion activities of the Army of God and claimed that he was "killing the killers" (Loon 2015). In addition to three individuals killed by Robert Dear at the Planned Parenthood clinic, nine other individuals—including five police officers—were wounded in the standoff that followed the initial killings. Dear used a semiautomatic rifle and possessed hundreds of rounds of ammunition. Because of his actions, Robert Lewis Dear Jr. maintains a prominent position on the Web site dedicated to the Army of God.

See also: Rudolph, Eric Robert

Further Reading

Army of God. http://www.armyofgod.com/ (Accessed July 3, 2017).

Loon, Mick Van. November 28, 2015. "Equal Terrorism: Basic Christian Addresses Massacre at Abortion Clinic in Colorado." *Newsmonkey.* https://translate.google.com /translate?hl=en&sl=nl&u=http://newsmonkey.be/article/61273&prev=search (Accessed July 3, 2017).

ARYAN NATIONS

Aryan Nations (AN) is a white supremacist organization originally based in Hayden Lake, Idaho. It was founded in 1977 by Richard Butler, an adherent of Christian Identity, who preached a virulently racist and anti-Semitic message. During the 1980s and 1990s, AN was the most powerful organizing force for white supremacists in the United States and attracted neo-Nazis, racist skinheads, KKK members, and white nationalists. The organization also spawned other organizations, such as The Order, which became even more violent than AN. By 2000, AN began losing members and influence within extremist communities after losing a civil rights lawsuit brought by the Southern Poverty Law Center. The damages that were assessed to AN caused the group's compound and assets in Idaho to be sold to satisfy the judgment. In the aftermath of the defeat, AN fractured and lost all cohesion when founder Richard Butler died in 2004. Today, Aryan Nations still exists as an entity, but it has all but faded from the white supremacists' scene, with only a few dozen adherents scattered across the United States (Morlin 2015).

Though Richard Butler founded Aryan Nations, the roots of the organization are found in the "theology" of Christian Identity, an anti-Semitic and white supremacy organization that teaches that white people are God's chosen people and that Jews are the spawn of a union between Eve and Satan. Butler was introduced to Christian Identity by Wesley Swift, who founded a Christian Identity church— the Church of Jesus Christ Christian—in California in the 1940s. One of Swift's associates was William Potter Gale, a retired army colonel who had served on the staff of General Douglas MacArthur during World War II. At the end of the war and as the Cold War ramped up, Gale became a leading figure in various antitax and paramilitary movements until founding the antigovernment and anti-Semitic organization Posse Comitatus ("force of the county") in the 1960s. Gale introduced Butler to Posse Comitatus, and Butler began attending Christian Identity meetings and sermons. Around 1965, Butler became an ordained Christian Identity minister (Southern Poverty Law Center).

Butler had long expressed his admiration for Adolph Hitler and believed that white civilization could only be protected through the establishment of a whites-only homeland in the Pacific Northwest, the only portion of the country where

Richard Butler, founder of the white supremacist organization Aryan Nations, addresses the World Congress of the groups in Coeur d'Alene, Idaho, in 2004. Under Butler's leadership, Aryan Nations became the most powerful white supremacist organization in the United States, attracting neo-Nazis, racist skinheads, KKK members, and various other white nationalist groups. (Jerome Pollos/Getty Images)

blacks and minorities were not found in large numbers. Butler retired in 1973 from his position as an aeronautical engineer and purchased 20 acres of land near Hayden Lake, Idaho. There he established his own Christian Posse Comitatus group. In 1977, Butler opened a congregation of the Church of Jesus Christ Christian on his property and organized Aryan Nations as the congregation's political arm.

In 1981, Butler's church was bombed, causing more than $80,000 in damage. Butler then fortified his land with a two-story guard tower and posted armed guards all around the land (Southern Poverty Law Center). For the next 20 years, Butler would host gatherings of racists, white nationalists, white supremacists, anti-Semites, KKK members, and other extremists at the annual Aryan World Congress gatherings on his property. During the 1980s, Aryan Nations became the most powerful voice in the white supremacist movement, and its influence was felt across the breadth of the United States.

An acolyte of Butler's, Bob Mathews, believed that the white race was on the verge of extinction due to immigration and higher birth rates among minority groups. Mathews had attended several Aryan Nations meetings and had made many friends within the organization. In 1982, Mathews made an effort to attract white families—what he called the "White American Bastion"—to settle in the Pacific Northwest in order to create a "whites-only homeland." In a speech at a National Alliance convention the next year, Mathews called upon "yeoman farmers and independent truckers" to join his "White American Bastion" group (Martinez and Guinther 1999). At the time, the National Alliance was the leading neo-Nazi organization in the United States. As inspiration for his movement, Mathews drew upon the published material of William Pierce, the founder of the National Alliance. In *The Turner Diaries*, Pierce had imagined a future world in the United States where politicians, academics, and "race traitors" (the "System") are exterminated in a race war led by militants calling themselves The Order. Thus, "The Order" became Mathew's new organization. The group would go on to become one of the most notorious terror groups in the United States, purloining over $3.6 million in funds from armored car heists and assassinating Jewish talk show host Alan Berg in Denver, Colorado, in 1984. Mathews would die in a shootout with the FBI in December 1984.

Aside from Mathews, other AN members committed violent crimes, including the murder of a state trooper in Missouri in 1985 and conspiracy to commit murder of federal agents. In 1987, Butler and 13 others were charged as the "godfathers of a conspiracy hatched at the 1983 Aryan World Congress to commit a variety of crimes and violent acts across the country" (Southern Poverty Law Center). After a trial, the defendants were all acquitted.

In 1989, Butler celebrated the 100th anniversary of Adolph Hitler's birth by inviting racist skinheads and other extremist groups to the AN compound "for a celebration that included musical performances by white power skinhead bands. This was the beginning of Butler's attempts to recruit younger members into the Aryan Nations" (Southern Poverty Law Center).

By 1997, AN had lost half its membership, and Butler was seeking to appoint a successor. Butler appointed a fellow Christian Identity pastor, Neuman Britton, but he died before taking the reins of the organization. Eventually, Butler named Ray Redfeairn to replace him, even though Redfeairn would leave AN, return, and then leave again before eventually returning to take over the organization upon Butler's death.

In 1998, a former Aryan Nations guard fired dozens of rounds from a submachine gun at a Jewish community center in Los Angeles, California. He would confess that he perpetrated the attack because of his hatred for Jews. The same year, AN security guards accosted a woman and her son who were traveling in the vicinity of the AN compound. The security guards mistook the couple's car backfire as an attack on their compound. The AN guards ran down the car and forced it into a ditch. The mother and son were brutally assaulted before being released.

In 2000, the Southern Poverty Law Center brought a civil rights suit against Aryan Nations on behalf of Victoria and Jason Keenan, whom the AN guards had assaulted. Claiming that the assault was the result of the virulent hatred preached by Aryan Nations, a jury eventually awarded a $6.3 million judgment against AN, of which Butler was responsible for $4.8 million. In February 2001, "Aryan Nation's Hayden Lake compound and intellectual property, including the names of 'Aryan Nations' and 'Church of Jesus Christ Christian' were transferred to the Kennans who sold the property to an Idaho philanthropist" (*Keenan v. Aryan Nations*). Both the guard tower and the church on the property were burned down during firefighting drills. Butler remained in the Hayden Lake area after a sympathetic and "wealthy supporter bought him a house" (Southern Poverty Law Center).

Butler died in September 2004. After his death, the remaining membership of Aryan Nations split into two factions, with one group relocating to Pennsylvania and the other to Georgia. After several attempts to revive the organization, the last self-proclaimed leader of Aryan Nations, Morris Gulett, announced in November 15, 2015, that he was disbanding the organization, saying,

> I will never lose respect for the noble and honorable organization that Pastor Butler created 40 years ago, but our Holy White Race has evidently lost the will to live. Because of the degeneration of our people, the noble and honorable organization Aryan Nations no longer exists with the veracity that it once had. Therefore, it deserves to be respectfully laid to rest. No doubt some will continue to haul Aryan Nations through the mud by attaching its Christian standard to their filthy unwashed lives. (Morlin 2015)

Today, there is a movement afoot to resurrect Aryan Nations in the Hayden Lake, Idaho, area by those who were influenced by the "indelible ideological marks" that AN left on the region (Day 2016). Their numbers are small, however, and it is not apparent that the rejuvenation will last long.

See also: Butler, Richard; Gale, William Potter; Gulett, Morris; Mathews, Bob; National Alliance; Neo-Nazis; Order, The; Pierce, William; Posse Comitatus; Southern Poverty Law Center; *Turner Diaries, The*; White Nationalism; White Supremacist Movement

Further Reading

Anti-Defamation League. "Aryan Nations/Church of Jesus Christ Christian." https://www.adl.org/education/resources/profiles/aryan-nations (Accessed May 19, 2017).

Day, Meagan. November 4, 2016. "Welcome to Hayden Lake, Where the White Supremacists Tried to Build Their Homeland." *Timeline.com*. https://timeline.com/white-supremacist-rural-paradise-fb62b74b29e0 (Accessed May 19, 2017).

Kennan v. Aryan Nations. Case Number: CV-99-441. Southern Poverty Law Center. https://www.splcenter.org/seeking-justice/case-docket/keenan-v-aryan-nations (Accessed May 19, 2017).

Macdonald, Andrew (aka William Pierce). 1999. *The Turner Diaries*. 2nd ed. National Vanguard Books.

Martinez, Thomas and John Guinther. 1999. *Brotherhood of Murder*. iUniverse.

Morlin, Bill. December 17, 2015. "Aryan Nations Quickly Fading into Racist History." *Southern Poverty Law Center—Hatewatch*. https://www.splcenter.org/hatewatch/2015/12/17/aryan-nations-quickly-fading-racist-history (Accessed May 19, 2017).

Southern Poverty Law Center. "Aryan Nations." https://www.splcenter.org/fighting-hate/extremist-files/group/aryan-nations (Accessed May 19, 2017).

B

BANNON, STEVE

Steven Bannon (b. 1953) served as executive chair of *Breitbart News* before being named as chief strategist to President Donald Trump in 2016. *Breitbart News* is generally considered to be a news, opinion, and commentary Web site with far-right leanings and close ties to the alt-right movement. In August 2016, Bannon joined Donald Trump's campaign for the U.S. presidency, taking the post of chief executive officer (Acosta, Bash, and Kopan 2016). After Trump's surprise victory in November 2016, Bannon was named as Trump's primary political advisor and chief strategist. In this capacity, Bannon was a member of the "principals committee" on the U.S. National Security Council from January 28 to April 5, 2017 (Baker, Haberman, and Thrush 2017). Barely two months into this position, Bannon was purged from the post after complaints from National Security Council staffers and Bannon's conflicts with Trump's son-in-law, Jared Kushner (Suebsaeng 2017).

From the beginning, Bannon's role in the Trump administration was controversial. A former staffer at *Breitbart News* complained that Bannon ran meetings at the organization "like white supremacist rallies" (Hankes 2016). The staffer went so far as to claim that "under Bannon's leadership, *Breitbart* [became] the alt-right go-to website, with [Milo] Yiannopoulos pushing white ethno-nationalism as a legitimate response to political correctness, and the comment section turning into a cesspool for white supremacist mememakers" (Drum 2016). The Southern Poverty Law Center, Stephen Bannon claims that Bannon is unfit to have a place in the White House because of his overtly racist views. Aside from proclaiming *Breitbart News* as the "platform for the alt-right," Bannon has published extremist anti-Muslim literature and suggested that "rape culture" is "integral" in Islam. The Southern Poverty Law Center further contends that "Bannon presided over a news empire where he, according to former staffers, 'aggressively pushed stories against immigrants, and supported linking minorities to terrorism and crime.'" Moreover, "under Bannon, *Breitbart* published a call to 'hoist [the Confederate flag] high and fly it with pride' only two weeks after the Charleston massacre when the country was still reeling from the horrors of the murders" (Southern Poverty Law Center, Stephen Bannon).

When Bannon was named Trump's chief strategist in November 2016, Richard Spencer, the founder of the alt-right movement and the director of the far right-wing "think tank" National Policy Institute, commented that "strategist is the best possible position for Steve Bannon in the Trump White House. Bannon will answer directly to Trump and focus on the big picture, not get lost in the weeds" (Piggot 2016). Bannon's appointment to a senior position in the Trump administration was

Former chief strategist in the Trump Administration, Steve Bannon is a leading figure in the white nationalist movement. Bannon's editorship of *Breitbart News*, from which he resigned in January 2018, was embraced by a variety of white supremacist and white nationalist groups, including the alt-right movement. (Scott Olson/Getty Images)

also hailed by far-right-wing racist groups, as well as neo-Nazis, white supremacists, and white nationalists. *Stormfront*, the oldest neo-Nazi message board on the Web, published a post that exulted in Bannon's appointment:

> Stephen Bannon: racist, anti-homo, anti-immigrant, anti-Jewish, anti-establishment. Declared war on (((Paul Ryan))). Sounds perfect. Muhahahaha. The man who will have Trump's ear more than anyone else. Being anti-jewish is not illegal. Nothing you dirty stinking jews can do to keep him out. (Piggot 2016)

While serving as executive chairperson of *Breitbart News*, Bannon regularly published headlines that attracted headlines of their own. Calling one conservative a "renegade Jew" and comparing the reproductive rights activities of Planned Parenthood to the Holocaust, Bannon specialized in shock headlines in order to whip up sentiment and agitate disaffected white voters. Bannon struck at the liberal political agenda by criticizing everything from feminism to birth control. One headline on *Breitbart* read, "Would you rather your child had feminism or cancer?" while another stated, "Birth control makes women unattractive and crazy" (BBC 2017).

Under Bannon's leadership, *Breitbart News* became the mouthpiece for the alt-right movement, a reaction against mainstream American conservatism. The alt-right is composed mainly of young white males who embrace "white identity" while "rejecting progressive views on immigration, race, LGBT issues and gender equality" (BBC 2017). An acolyte of Bannon's, Milo Yiannopoulos, who served as a senior editor at *Breitbart*, became the "face" of the alt-right (Stein 2016). In a March 2016 column, *Breitbart* gushed that the alt-right had "a youthful energy and jarring, taboo-defying rhetoric" (BBC 2017).

On April 5, 2017, Bannon was pushed off the principals committee of the National Security Council, a post that he had held for just over two months. Reportedly, Bannon, who considered himself a "virulently anti-establishment" revolutionary out to destroy the "administrative state," frequently clashed with Donald Trump's son-in-law, Jared Kushner, who had become a key advisor to the president (Baker, Haberman, and Thrush 2017). Kushner is everything Bannon despised: well educated, polished, moderate, and well connected to the establishment. Bannon regularly called Kushner a "globalist"—an individual who believes in American engagement in the world—behind his back to distinguish his (Kushner's) views from Bannon's "nationalist" views. More sinisterly, Bannon often referred to Kushner as a "cuck," short for "cuckservative," a favorite racial slur of the right wing (Suebsaeng 2017). The term is a combination of the words "cuckold" and "conservative" and designates mainstream conservative (mostly Republican) politicians who are considered to be traitors to the American people inasmuch as they are willing to sell out their traditional ideals in order to support programs and policies related to globalism and certain liberal ideals (Southern Poverty Law Center). The phrase is racist and sexist in its overtones as the term "cuckold" implies that conservative politicians, who are viewed as part of the establishment, are like white men who allow black men to sleep with their wives (Southern Poverty Law Center, Alternative Right).

After his demotion from the principals committee of the National Security Council, there were reports that Bannon threatened to quit (Johnson, Vogel, and Dawsey 2017). However, he remained as Trump's chief strategist, though his public visibility was greatly reduced.

See also: Alt-Right Movement; *Breitbart News*; Charleston Church Shooting (in Roof, Dylann Storm entry); National Policy Institute; Spencer, Richard Bertrand; *Stormfront*; Yiannopoulos, Milo

Further Reading

Acosta, Jim, Dana Bash, and Tal Kopan. November 14, 2016. "Trump Picks Priebus as White House Chief of Staff, Bannon as Top Adviser." *CNN.* http://www.cnn.com/2016/11/13/politics/donald-trump-reince-priebus-white-house-chief-of-staff/index.html (Accessed May 20, 2017).

Baker, Peter, Maggie Haberman, and Glenn Thrush. April 5, 2017. "Trump Removes Stephen Bannon from National Security Post." *The New York Times.* https://www.nytimes.com/2017/04/05/us/politics/national-security-council-stephen-bannon.html (Accessed May 20, 2017).

BBC. April 13, 2017. "Steve Bannon: Who Is Trump's Key Adviser?" *BBC News.* http://www.bbc.com/news/election-us-2016-37971742 (Accessed May 20, 2017).

Drum, Kevin. November 14, 2016. "Is Steve Bannon Racist? Let's Find Out!" *Mother Jones.* http://www.motherjones.com/kevin-drum/2016/11/steve-bannon-racist-lets-find-out/ (Accessed July 6, 2017).

Green, Joshua. October 8, 2015. "This Man Is the Most Dangerous Political Operative in America." *Bloomberg Politics*. https://www.bloomberg.com/politics/graphics/2015 -steve-bannon/ (Accessed May 20, 2017).

Hankes, Keegan. August 25, 2016. "Whose Alt-Right Is It Anyway?" *Southern Poverty Law Center—Hatewatch*. https://www.splcenter.org/hatewatch/2016/08/25/whose-alt -right-it-anyway (Accessed May 20, 2017).

Johnson, Eliana, Kenneth P. Vogel, and Josh Dawsey. April 5, 2017. "Megadonor Urged Bannon Not to Resign." *Politico*. http://www.politico.com/story/2017/04/bannon -resign-mercer-trump-236939 (Accessed May 20, 2017).

Piggot, Stephen. November 14, 2016. "White Nationalists Rejoice at Trump's Appointment of Breitbart's Stephen Bannon." *Southern Poverty Law Center—Hatewatch*. https://www .splcenter.org/hatewatch/2016/11/14/white-nationalists-rejoice-trumps-appointment -breitbarts-stephen-bannon (Accessed May 20, 2017).

Southern Poverty Law Center. "Alternative Right." https://www.splcenter.org/fighting-hate /extremist-files/ideology/alternative-right (Accessed May 20, 2017).

Southern Poverty Law Center. "Stephen Bannon Has No Business in the White House." https:// www.splcenter.org/stephen-bannon-has-no-business-white-house (Accessed May 20, 2017).

Stein, Joel. September 15, 2016. "Milo Yiannopoulos Is the Pretty, Monstrous Face of the Alt-Right." *Bloomberg*. https://www.bloomberg.com/features/2016-america-divided/milo -yiannopoulos/ (Accessed May 20, 2017).

Suebsaeng, Asawin. April 6, 2017. "Steve Bannon Calls Jared Kushner a 'Cuck' and 'Globalist' Behind His Back." *The Daily Beast*. http://www.thedailybeast.com/articles /2017/04/06/steve-bannon-calls-jared-kushner-a-cuck-and-globalist-behind-his-back (Accessed May 20, 2017).

BAUM, GORDON

Gordon Baum (1940–2015) was the cofounder of the Council of Conservative Citizens (CCC), an organization that routinely identified African Americans as "genetically inferior," complained about the influence of "Jewish power brokers" in American business and government, called LGBT people "perverted sodomites," and stated that nonwhite immigration to the United States was turning the country into a "slimy brown mass of glop" (Lenz 2015). The CCC also once referred to the avowed champion of southern segregation, former Georgia governor Lester Maddox, as the "Patriot of the Century" (Lenz 2015).

Baum was a personal injury lawyer in St. Louis, Missouri, when he helped form the CCC in 1985. Baum, along with his confederates, culled the mailing lists of various white segregationist groups and organized the CCC into a group of individuals numbering over 15,000. The CCC labored in relative obscurity until 1998, when it was revealed that former U.S. House of Representatives member Bob Barr (R-GA) had delivered the keynote speech at the CCC's national convention in 1998. Later, it was revealed that Senate majority leader Trent Lott (R-MS), who was then the Senate majority leader, had spoken to the group at least five times and was, in fact, a member of the CCC, though Lott claimed to know very little about the group. In light of the scandal, the chairperson of the Republican National Committee asked all Republican Party members to immediately resign from the CCC because of its "racist views" (Southern Poverty Law Center).

Though quiet and unassuming, Baum openly supported former Grand Wizard of the Ku Klux Klan David Duke in his failed bid to be elected governor of Louisiana in 1991. Duke, a virulent racist, had once been a member of the American Nazi Party. Upon his death in 2015, Gordon Baum's son-in-law, Hunter Wallace, eulogized his father-in-law by stating,

> when the Civil Rights Act of 1964 was passed, when the Citizens' Councils movement collapsed, when George Wallace, Strom Thurmond, and all the rest repudiated segregation and proclaimed their newfound faith in "racial equality," when others quit, Gordon Lee Baum stood firm. As the world entered the present Dark Age, Gordon was there to keep up the fire of resistance. (Wallace 2015)

See also: Council of Conservative Citizens; Duke, David

Further Reading

Lenz, Ryan. March 6, 2015. "Breaking: Gordon Baum, Who Helped Found CCC, Has Died." *Southern Poverty Law Center—Hatewatch.* https://www.splcenter.org/hatewatch/2015/03/06/breaking-gordon-baum-who-helped-found-ccc-has-died (Accessed September 20, 2016).

Southern Poverty Law Center. https://www.splcenter.org/fighting-hate/extremist-files/individual/gordon-baum; https://www.splcenter.org/fighting-hate/extremist-files/individual/gordon-baum (Accessed September 20, 2016).

Wallace, Hunter. March 10, 2015. "In Memoriam, Gordon Lee Baum." http://www.occidentaldissent.com/2015/03/10/in-memoriam-gordon-lee-baum/ (Accessed September 20, 2016).

BEACH, HENRY LAMONT "MIKE"

Together with William Potter Gale (1917–1988), Henry Lamont ("Mike") Beach (1903–1989) is credited with the founding of the right-wing antigovernment group Posse Comitatus in the late 1960s. In the 1930s, Beach belonged to a pro-Nazi group in the United States known as the Silver Shirts. In 1969, Beach organized a group known as the Sheriff's Posse Comitatus, sometimes referred to as the Citizen's Law Enforcement Research Committee. The Posse Comitatus, or "power of the county," was organized on the principles of survivalism, vigilantism, and antigovernment activities (including the nonpayment of federal taxes). Its bylaws stated that no federal or state government had any legal standing to govern the people—only local and county governments (History Commons).

Beach perpetrated anti-Semitic views through Posse Comitatus, holding that the entire U.S. federal government was controlled by a vast Jewish conspiracy and therefore had no authority over the white race, the legitimate successor to the goals and principles of the Founding Fathers. Beach furthered the notion that "the U.S. Constitution was a divinely inspired document, but all amendments after the Bill of Rights were unconstitutional and void. Finally, the only individuals allowed to participate in this system [of governance] were white Christian males" (Atkins 2011).

The original policy manual for Posse Comitatus outlined Beach's belief in the supremacy of local law and the responsibilities of the highest law enforcement authority that he, or any citizen, should recognize—the county sheriff. The manual states:

> In some instances of record the law provides for the following prosecution of officials of government who commit criminal acts or who violate their oath of office. . . . He shall be removed by the posse to the most populated intersection in the streets in the township and, at high noon, be hung by the neck, the body remaining until sundown as an example to those who would subvert the law. (Atkins 2011)

Though Beach could claim to be the original founder of Posse Comitatus, it was William Potter Gale who would eventually merge his group, the U.S. Christian Posse Association, with Posse Comitatus to provide the group with its antigovernment, anti-Semitic, and anti-immigration ideology. Beach retired from his job as a dry-cleaning executive in 1969 and died in 1989.

See also: Common-Law Court Movement; Gale, William Potter; Posse Comitatus; Sovereign Citizens Movement

Further Reading

Atkins, Steven E. 2011. *Encyclopedia of Right-Wing Extremism in Modern American History*. ABC-CLIO.

History Commons. "Profile: Henry L. Beach." http://www.historycommons.org/entity.jsp?entity=henry_l__beach_1 (Accessed December 14, 2016).

Southern Poverty Law Center. June 15, 1998. "Hate Group Expert Daniel Levitas Discusses Posse Comitatus, Christian Identity Movement and More." https://www.splcenter.org/fighting-hate/intelligence-report/1998/hate-group-expert-daniel-levitas-discusses-posse-comitatus-christian-identity-movement-and more (Accessed December 14, 2016).

BEAM, LOUIS

Louis Beam (b. 1946) is an American white supremacist and a leading thinker in movements that are on the revolutionary right. Beam is credited with popularizing the idea of "leaderless resistance" among radical groups. This strategy generally involves small, independent groups (cells) or individuals ("lone wolves") that challenge existing political, social, and economic institutions. Beam is credited with helping to "guide the white supremacist movement into the computer age" (Southern Poverty Law Center).

Beam, born in Texas in 1946, was a helicopter gunner during the Vietnam War (Gardell 2003). When he returned to the United States in 1968, he was "full of rage at the communists and the [U.S.] government" (Southern Poverty Law Center). He joined the "Texas state chapter of the United Klans of America, the Alabama-based group that was behind much of the violence directed upon civil rights workers in the 1950s and 1960s" (Southern Poverty Law Center).

In 1976, Beam shifted his KKK allegiance to David Duke's Knights of the Ku Klux Klan (KKKK). Under Duke's direction, Beam quickly rose in the ranks of the KKKK and began recruiting active-duty personnel to the ranks of the KKKK and conducting workshops in guerilla warfare and paramilitary tactics. He instructed recruits on how to "get people in the kill zone" (Southern Poverty Law Center).

In 1981, Beam gave a fiery speech before U.S. fishers near Galveston Bay, Texas, who were "angry at having to compete with Vietnamese refugee shrimpers in the Gulf of Mexico" (Southern Poverty Law Center). In the aftermath of the speech, arsonists burned two Vietnamese fishing boats and lit crosses in the yards of several Vietnamese fishers. The Southern Poverty Law Center took up the case of the Vietnamese fishers and secured injunctions against Beam and the KKKK to cease and desist the intimidation tactics that were being employed against them. The Southern Poverty Law Center was also able to shut down five paramilitary camps (Southern Poverty Law Center).

Also in 1981, Beam traveled to Hayden Lake, Idaho, and attended meetings of Richard Butler's neo-Nazi Aryan Nations, which was located there. Beam was designated by Aryan Nations leader Richard Butler as "ambassador at large," a title that became moot the next year when Beam moved to Idaho and took up residence in the Aryan Nations compound.

Two months after Beam's relocation to Idaho, several members of the Aryan Nations broke away from the group and secretly formed The Order, the white supremacist revolutionary terrorist organization that operated in the United States in 1983 and 1984. Though Beam was not apparently a member of The Order, its leader, Bob Mathews, passed out copies of Beam's *Essays of Klansman*, and Mathews indicated that Beam, code named Lone Star, was designated to become the leader of the "western district" of the United States after the racial victory that would secure an all-white homeland (Southern Poverty Law Center).

In early 1987, Beam left the United States for fear that federal agents were about to arrest him. He and "13 other white supremacists were indicted by a federal grand jury in Arkansas for allegedly conspiring to overthrow the U.S. government" (Southern Poverty Law Center). After being arrested in Mexico and extradited back to the United States, Beam and several others who had been indicted were acquitted at trial of sedition, a victory that was widely celebrated by members of the radical right (Southern Poverty Law Center).

In 1992, Beam revised an earlier essay he had written on "leaderless resistance," saying that white revolutionaries needed to abandon plans to carry out activities against the government in large groups and instead concentrate on taking actions in small cells that numbered from one to six men. The idea was that infiltration of one cell by federal officials could not compromise an entire movement. Beam encouraged "lone wolves" to act "when they feel the time is ripe, or take their cues from others who precede them" (Southern Poverty Law Center). Beam's ideas cemented his place as a leading radical theorist in the white supremacist community.

Beam largely disappeared from the white supremacist scene after 1996, when he began complaining of the effects of his exposure to Agent Orange while in Vietnam. He continued to be a member of Aryan Nations and was designated as ambassador at large for the organization after moving back to his native Texas.

See also: Aryan Nations; Butler, Richard; Duke, David; Mathews, Bob; Order, The; White Supremacist Movement

Further Reading

Gardell, Mattias. 2003. *Gods of the Blood: The Pagan Revival and White Separatism.* Duke University Press.

Southern Poverty Law Center. "Louis Beam." https://www.splcenter.org/fighting-hate /extremist-files/individual/louis-beam (Accessed March 23, 2017).

BLACK, DON

Stephen Donald "Don" Black (b. 1953) is considered one of the most influential white nationalists and white supremacists in the United States. He founded one of the most popular Internet forums for white supremacist thought in the country, *Stormfront*. Black is a former Grand Wizard of the Ku Klux Klan, and he maintains a number of affiliations with individuals on the extreme right in American politics. Though Black's white nationalist credentials stretch back decades, in recent years it has come to light that his wife works for a Latin American sugar baron and that among her responsibilities is the advocacy of a charter school "to lift underprivileged black and Hispanic children out of poverty" (Fox News 2008). In 2013, Black's son, Derek, announced that he had forsaken his white supremacist attitudes and issued an apology to all those who had been hurt by his actions related to material he had authored and disseminated on the Internet (Potok 2013).

Black was born in Alabama and came of age during the civil rights movement in the South. He stated that his upbringing made him acutely aware of the "white" perspective, and he began distributing racist political literature while still in high school. When he was only 16, Black worked on the gubernatorial campaign of a noted segregationist and leader of the National States' Rights Party, J. B. Stoner. In 1975, he became affiliated with the Knights of the Ku Klux Klan just one year after the organization was taken over by David Duke. In 1981, Black and nine others—many recruited from among the ranks of the Knights of the Ku Klux Klan—were arrested when they attempted to board a boat that had been stocked with weapons and ammunition. The group's intention was to invade the island nation of Dominica—whose government leaders were black—and replace its leadership with an all-white delegation. Upon his conviction, Black would spend three years in federal prison. However, while in prison, he would learn computer programming, which aided him when he established *Stormfront* several years later.

Black very quickly recognized the reach and impact that the Internet afforded to those with extremist views. He believed that the advent of the Internet meant that white supremacists would no longer have to rely on the mainstream media to disseminate their ideas. Rather, online forums meant white supremacists could explore and share their ideas within the confines of their own homes without the fear of embarrassment or reproach. As he told a reporter in 1996, a year after he founded *Stormfront*, "The potential of the Net for organizations and movements such as ours is enormous. We're reaching tens of thousands of people who never before had access to our point of view" (Southern Poverty Law Center, Stormfront). By 1998, *Stormfront* had more than 133,000 registered users.

Stormfront's motto, "White Pride World Pride," fosters an atmosphere where white supremacists are encouraged to share their extremist ideas in articles and forum discussions. In a departure from *Stormfront's* early years, where racial slurs were the norm, members are now urged not to use such language. This tactic, which Black has modeled after David Duke's axiom to "get out of the cow pasture and into hotel meeting rooms," has continued to attract followers. But the message is anything but moderate. As noted by the Southern Poverty Law Center (Stormfront), "The talk is all about the evils of African Americans, homosexuals, non-white immigrants, and, above all, Jews, who are blamed for most of what's wrong in the world."

With Barack Obama's election in 2008, Black noted that *Stormfront's* usual Web traffic had seen a 600 percent increase, which Black attributed to "a lot of angry white people looking for answers" (Southern Poverty Law Center, Don Black). In March 2015, *Stormfront* celebrated its 20th year of existence. The Web site boasts over 300,000 members and sponsors a daily radio show that reaches a global audience. As a consequence, both Don Black and *Stormfront* are today among the most recognized actors in the white nationalist and white supremacist movement.

See also: Duke, David; *Stormfront*; White Nationalism; White Supremacist Movement

Further Reading

Anti-Defamation League. "Don Black/Stormfront." *Anti-Defamation League—Extremism in America.* http://archive.adl.org/learn/ext_us/don-black/ (Accessed January 4, 2017).

Fox News. July 30, 2008. "Woman with Ties to White Supremacists Represents School for Blacks and Hispanics." http://www.foxnews.com/story/2008/07/30/woman-with-ties-to-white-supremacists-represents-school-for-blacks-and.html (Accessed January 4, 2017).

PageSix.com. October 9, 2010. "Billionaire Won't Fire Assistant for KKK Link." *New York Post.* http://pagesix.com/2010/10/09/billionaire-wont-fire-assisant-for-kkk-link/ (Accessed January 4, 2017).

Potok, Mark. July 18, 2013. "Racists React with Shock, Anger to Fellow Activist's Renunciation." *Southern Poverty Law Center.* https://www.splcenter.org/hatewatch/2013/07/18/racists-react-shock-anger-fellow-activist's-renunciation (Accessed January 4, 2017).

Southern Poverty Law Center. "Don Black." https://www.splcenter.org/fighting-hate/extremist-files/individual/don-black (Accessed January 4, 2017).

Southern Poverty Law Center. "Stormfront." https://www.splcenter.org/fighting-hate/extremist-files/group/stormfront (Accessed January 4, 2017).

BLACK MUSLIMS

In the United States, black Muslims were among the first African Americans to call for a movement that advocated black separatism and black nationalism. Since the late 1970s, black Muslims have largely split into two groups: the American Society of Muslims and the Nation of Islam. Though a renewed African American religious movement that centered on Islam began in the United States in the 1930s, by the 1950s and 1960s, the Nation of Islam dominated the political and social landscape that had been created by the black Muslims. The Nation of Islam had only numbered about 8,000 when Elijah Muhammad assumed control of the group in 1934. With the ascension of Malcolm X, however, membership grew to include tens of thousands of black Muslims. Malcolm X's charisma and powerful speaking style attracted many adherents who believed in the message that black Muslims were preaching: that whites were a race of "devils," and black people were God's original people. As Elijah Muhammad had stated,

> The Blackman is the original man. From him came all brown, yellow, red, and white people. By using a special method of birth control law, the Blackman was able to produce the white race. This method of birth control was developed by a Black scientist known as Yakub, who envisioned making and teaching a nation of people who would be diametrically opposed to the Original People. A Race of people who would one day rule the original people and the earth for a period of 6,000 years. Yakub promised his followers that he would graft a nation from his own people, and he would teach them how to rule his people, through a system of tricks and lies whereby they use deceit to divide and conquer, and break the unity of the darker people, put one brother against another, and then act as mediators and rule both sides. (Blake 1991)

A break between Elijah Muhammad and Malcolm X weakened the black Muslim movement for a time, and the movement would suffer a severe blow when Malcolm X was assassinated in 1965. When Elijah Muhammad's son, Warith (W.) Deen Mohammed, took over from his father in 1976, he preached a less inflammatory and more accommodating version of black Islam than had his father. The younger Mohammed "aligned the organization with the international Islamic community, moving toward Sunni Islamic practice, and opened the group (renamed the World Community of al-Islam in the West, then the American Muslim Mission, and later the American Society of Muslims) to individuals of all races" (Encyclopedia.com).

In 1977, a disaffected member of the organization, Louis Farrakhan, split off from W. Deen Mohammed's organization because of his "integrationist ideals and lack of allegiance to his father's brand of Islam" and took dozens of black Muslims with him (Encyclopedia.com). The splinter group assumed the Nation of Islam name and sought to emulate the thoughts and teachings of Elijah Muhammad. In 1995, the Nation of Islam organized the Million Man March in Washington, D.C., to promote African American unity and family values. Under Farrakhan's leadership, the Nation of Islam tried to redefine the "black male stereotype" of individuals plagued by drug-related crimes and gang violence. Since assuming control of the Nation of Islam, Farrakhan has promoted social reform within African American communities and challenged African Americans to foster traditional forms of self-reliance and economic independence that focus on the family and not the government (Nation of Islam).

Farrakhan has continued preaching a message of black nationalism and black separatism. On April 13, 1997, he was a guest on NBC's *Meet the Press* and was interviewed by Tim Russert and David Broder. During the interview, Russert asked Farrakhan to clarify the Nation of Islam's teachings on race. He replied,

You know, it's not unreal to believe that white people—who genetically cannot produce yellow, brown or black—had a Black origin. The scholars and scientists of this world agree that the origin of man and humankind started in Africa and that the first parent of the world was black. The Qur'an says that God created Adam out of black mud and fashioned him into shape. So if white people came from the original people, the Black people, what is the process by which you came to life? That is not a silly question. That is a scientific question with a scientific answer. It doesn't suggest that we are superior or that you are inferior. It suggests, however, that your birth or your origin is from the black people of this earth: superiority and inferiority is determined by our righteousness and not by our color. (Final Call 2008)

When Russert asked Farrakhan if he agreed with Elijah Muhammad's teaching that whites are "blue-eyed devils," he responded,

Well, you have not been saints in the way you have acted toward the darker peoples of the world and toward even your own people. But, in truth, Mr. Russert, any human being who gives themself over to the doing of evil could be considered a devil. In the Bible, in the "Book of Revelation," it talks about the fall of Babylon. It says Babylon is fallen because she has become the habitation of devils. We believe that ancient Babylon is a symbol of a modern Babylon, which is America. (Final Call 2008)

In the late 1990s, the Nation of Islam began moving away from its overt message of racism to embrace more traditional Islamic practices. In 2000, Farrakhan and W. Deen Mohammed publicly declared an end to the rivalry between their two groups. In 2003, W. Deen Mohammed resigned as head of the American Society of Muslims (Encyclopedia.com).

Today, many black Muslims struggle not only with the stereotypes sometimes associated with blacks but also the hostilities and resentments that have been leveled at Muslims since 9/11. Black American Muslims are under intense scrutiny by law enforcement and vilified by the media. As one author has noted, "Efforts of anti-Islamophobia activism in Muslim communities seemed more about regaining the privilege of proximity to whiteness that Arab and South Asians enjoyed before 9/11, rather than about justice" (Hill 2016).

See also: Black Nationalism; Farrakhan, Louis; Malcolm X; Nation of Islam

Further Reading

Blake, Dorothy. 1991. *Yakub & the Origins of White Supremacy: Message to the White Man & White Woman in America.* Conquering Books.

Encyclopedia.com. "Black Muslims." http://www.encyclopedia.com/philosophy-and-religion/islam/islam/black-muslims (Accessed May 13, 2017).

Final Call. June 13, 2008. "Tim Russert's Interview with Minister Louis Farrakhan." http://www.finalcall.com/artman/publish/Perspectives_1/Tim_Russert_s_interview_with_Minister_Louis_Farrak_4842.shtml (Accessed May 13, 2017).

Hill, Margari. December 15, 2016. "Islamophobia and Black American Muslims." *Huffington Post*. http://www.huffingtonpost.com/margari-hill/islamophobia-and-black-am_b_8785814.html (Accessed May 13, 2017).

Nation of Islam. "Honorable Minister Louis Farrakhan." https://www.noi.org/hon-minister-farrakhan/ (Accessed May 13, 2017).

Southern Poverty Law Center. "Black Separatists." https://www.splcenter.org/fighting-hate/extremist-files/ideology/black-separatist (Accessed May 13, 2017).

BLACK NATIONALISM

Black nationalism was a political and social movement that arose in the United States during the 1960s and early 1970s. Many adherents to black nationalism hoped that the culmination of the movement would be the creation of a separate black nation populated by African Americans. The core of the black nationalism movement was a desire among blacks to maintain and promote their separate identity as people with black ancestry, as opposed to being assimilated into an American nation that was predominantly white. With such slogans as "black power" and "black is beautiful," the black nationalism movement and its adherents sought to instill a sense of pride among blacks in the United States at a time when the civil rights movement was seeking equal rights for blacks (Encyclopedia Britannica). Through black nationalist groups such as the Nation of Islam and charismatic individuals like Malcolm X, "proponents of black nationalism advocated economic self-sufficiency, race pride for African Americans, and black separatism" (King Encyclopedia). In the 1960s, black nationalists criticized the nonviolent, interracial activism advocated by Martin Luther King Jr. King once described himself as "standing between the forces of complacency and the hatred and despair of the black nationalist" (King Encyclopedia). There are many in the United States today who believe that the black nationalism of the 1960s has been resurrected in the form of the Black Lives Matter movement that emerged in 2013 (Williams 2016).

The roots of black nationalism date to the 19th century when Booker T. Washington and his adherents emphasized a message of "racial solidarity, economic self-sufficiency, and black self-help" (Digital History). After World War I, black leaders such as Martin Delaney believed that blacks would never be able to achieve true equality in the United States given the social and political impediments that they faced. Therefore, Delaney advocated for the repatriation of blacks back to Africa, "where they would settle and assist native Africans in nation-building" (King Encyclopedia).

The rise of black nationalism was revitalized during the economic depression of the 1930s, when Farrad Muhammad founded the Nation of Islam (NOI), which sought "to develop an intentionally separate and economically self-sufficient black community governed by a revised version of the Muslim faith" (King Encyclopedia). NOI's cause was later taken up by Farrad Muhammad's successor, Elijah

Muhammad, who became NOI's leader. Elijah Muhammad took up the cause of black separatism and black supremacism when he declared that "whites were doomed to destruction" and that

> the white devil's day is over. He was given six thousand years to rule. . . . He's already used up most trapping and murdering the black nations by the hundreds of thousands. Now he's worried, worried about the black man getting his revenge. Unless whites accede to the Muslim demand for a separate territory for themselves, your entire race will be destroyed and removed from this earth by Almighty God. And those black men who are still trying to integrate will inevitably be destroyed along with the whites. (Digital History)

The Nation of Islam and black Muslims preached a message that encouraged blacks to lift themselves up and engage in actions of self-help. The black Muslim movement called on black Americans to "wake up, clean up, and stand up in order to achieve true freedom and independence" (Digital History). To counteract the behaviors that they believed reinforced racist stereotypes, the black Muslims "forbade eating pork and cornbread, drinking alcohol, and smoking cigarettes" (Gprep.org). They also encouraged black entrepreneurship by supporting the creation of black businesses.

By the late 1950s, Malcolm X was recognized as the most eloquent spokesperson for the Nation of Islam and the cause of black nationalism. Malcolm X had been born Malcolm Little, but after a stint in prison in the early 1950s, he adopted the name Malcolm X to replace "the white slave-master name which had been imposed upon my paternal forebears by some blue-eyed devil" (Digital History). Malcolm X denounced alcohol, tobacco, and premarital sex. He rapidly became the face and voice of the black nationalist cause. However, his rhetoric and tactics ran afoul of the larger civil rights movement that was then being led by the Reverend Martin Luther King Jr. Whereas King preached nonviolent resistance to the segregationist policies found around the United States, Malcolm X declared, "If ballots won't work, bullets will" (Digital History). Malcolm X attacked King on several occasions, calling him a "chum" and an "Uncle Tom." He also directly challenged King's leadership of the cause for black civil rights when he stated, "If you're afraid of Black nationalism, you're afraid of revolution. And if you love revolution, you love black nationalism" (King Encyclopedia). After King's 1964 "I Have a Dream" speech, Malcolm X stated, "While King was having a dream, the rest of us Negroes are having a nightmare" (Cone 2012).

Malcolm X left the Nation of Islam in 1964 and established his own organization for the betterment of African Americans. He was assassinated by Nation of Islam members in 1965. By this time, many black activists had become skeptical of the power of nonviolent resistance, as preached by Martin Luther King Jr., to positively influence the white power structure in the United States. The death of student activists during the Freedom Summer in 1964 and the marginalization of the Mississippi Freedom Democratic Party at the Democratic National Convention that same year convinced many black activists that nonviolence was not working and would not further the black nationalist cause.

In 1966, two black civil rights organizations—the Student Nonviolent Coordinating Committee and the Congress on Racial Equality—embraced the tenets of black nationalism. Stokely Carmichael, who would eventually become an activist in the black power movement, was elected chairperson of the Student Nonviolent Coordinating Committee and proceeded to move away from a strategy of nonviolence to an all-black organization committed to black power. Carmichael stated that "integration is irrelevant. Political and economic power is what the black people have to have" (Digital History). He began using the ideal of black power to promote "racial self-respect and increased power for blacks in economic and political realms" and asserted that "the concern for black power addresses itself directly to . . . the necessity to reclaim our history and our identity from the cultural terrorism and depredation of self-justifying white guilt" (Carmichael 1966). In his statements, Carmichael reiterated the sentiments of the fallen Malcolm X, who had declared, "The worst crime the white man has committed has been to teach us to hate ourselves" (Digital History).

Of all the groups that advocated for racial separatism and black power, none was more influential than the Black Panther Party (BPP). The BPP was founded by Huey P. Newton and Bobby Seale in October 1966 as "an armed revolutionary socialist organization advocating self-determination for black ghettoes" (Digital History). As one member of the BPP declared, "Black men . . . must unite to overthrow their white oppressors, becoming 'like panthers'—smiling, cunning, scientific, striking by night and sparing no one!" (Digital History). Members of the BPP showed up armed at a California State Assembly Committee hearing in May 1967. Later that same month, the BPP would publish the "Ten Point Program," also known as "What We Want," which was a set of guidelines established by the BPP to direct their ideals and ways of operation.

By the early 1970s, the rhetoric of black nationalism had receded, but the advocacy of black nationalism had

> exerted a powerful and positive influence upon the Civil Rights Movement. In addition to giving birth to a host of community self-help organizations, supporters of black power spurred the creation of black studies programs in universities and encouraged black Americans to take pride in their racial background and to recognize that "black is beautiful." A growing number of black Americans began to wear "Afro" hairstyles and take African or Islamic surnames. Singer James Brown captured the new spirit: "Say it loud—I'm black and I'm proud." (Digital History)

In 2013, the Black Lives Matter movement was birthed after the acquittal of George Zimmerman in the shooting death of African American Trayvon Martin. Black Lives Matter demonstrations were held around the United States following the death of other African Americans in 2014. Because of their increased numbers and advocacy for black rights, the Black Lives Matter movement was criticized by those on the political right. At the 2016 Republican National Convention, the theme of "Make America Safe Again" was at least partly aimed at the Black Lives Matter movement, which right-wing citizens and politicians alike were blaming for the shooting deaths of police officers in Dallas, Texas, and New Orleans, Louisiana. Author Yohuru Williams (2016) stated,

> All of this rhetoric is part of a rising chorus after the Texas and Louisiana killings, an effort to define a new category in the war on extremism—so-called black-nationalist terrorism. Proponents struggle to manufacture a domestic equivalent for Al Qaeda. Efforts to link the violence against law enforcement to some mythical, larger black separatist movement, which has made retaliatory violence against police one of its chief aims, is weak at best and irresponsible at worst.

Williams (2016) would note that like the black nationalism movement of the 1960s and 1970s, the Black Lives Matter movement engages in activities of self-defense in order "to create a sense of security and belonging for people of color under oppressive circumstances—not retaliatory violence or unprovoked attacks against whites or police, as it is often erroneously portrayed."

See also: Black Muslims; Black Panther Party; Farrakhan, Louis; Malcolm X; Nation of Islam; Newton, Huey P.; Seale, Bobby

Further Reading

Carmichael, Stokely. 1966. *Toward Black Liberation*. Student Nonviolent Coordinating Committee.

Cone, James H. 2012. *Martin & Malcolm: A Dream or a Nightmare*. Orbis Books.

Digital History. "Black Nationalism and Black Power." http://www.digitalhistory.uh.edu/disp_textbook.cfm?smtid=2&psid=3331 (Accessed May 5, 2017).

Encyclopedia Britannica. "Black Nationalism." https://www.britannica.com/event/black-nationalism (Accessed May 5, 2017).

Gprep.org. "America in Ferment: The Tumultuous 1960s/The Civil Rights Movement Moves North." http://claver.gprep.org/fac/sjochs/black%20power-digital-2010.htm (Accessed July 7, 2017).

KingEncyclopedia. "Black Nationalism." http://kingencyclopedia.stanford.edu/encyclopedia/encyclopedia/enc_black_nationalism.1.html (Accessed May 5, 2017).

Williams, Yohuru. July 20, 2016. "The Coming War on 'Black Nationalists.'" *The Nation*. https://www.thenation.com/article/the-coming-war-on-black-nationalists/ (Accessed May 5, 2017).

BLACK PANTHER PARTY

The Black Panther Party (BPP or Black Panthers) was a black, left-wing socialist revolutionary organization founded in the 1960s during the height of the civil rights movement in the United States. It was active from its founding in 1966 to its official disbandment in 1982. The original goal of the BPP was to provide a protective force for black neighborhoods against police brutality during the unrest of the civil rights movement. Later, the philosophy and objectives of the Black Panthers would evolve to include demands relating to the place of blacks within American society and the American political system.

The BPP was founded in 1966 by Huey P. Newton and Bobby Seale. Soon after its founding, the Blank Panthers published the "Ten-Point Program," also known as the "The Black Panther Party for Self-Defense Ten-Point Platform and Program." The program became the guiding manifesto by which all Black Panther Party members were encouraged to live. The Ten-Point Program consisted of two sections entitled "What We Want Now!" and "What We Believe." The program was a statement about what the Black Panthers believed was the inherent right of every black American. Two points of particular note were the notion of monetary reparations for the centuries of slavery under which black Americans had been forced to labor (Point 3) and the end of conscription for black soldiers who, as the program noted, are "forced to fight in the military service to defend a racist government that does not protect us" (Point 6) (History of the Black Panther Party).

Throughout the early part of their existence, the Black Panthers were known for their militancy and their violent tactics against police (Pearson 1994). On May 2, 1967, members of the Black Panthers appeared at a hearing of the California State Assembly in Sacramento to protest contemplated changes to the Mulford Act, which allowed California residents to carry firearms as long as they were openly displayed and not pointed at anyone. By this time, the public display of guns had become a significant symbol for the Black Panthers. Portraying themselves

Members of the Black Panther Party (BPP) appear at a hearing of the California State Assembly in Sacramento on May 2, 1967. The BPP was protesting contemplated changes to a California gun law that allowed the open carry of firearms. Because public displays of weapons strengthened the BPP cause, the Black Panthers were determined to prevent what they perceived as a diminishment of their rights. (Bettmann/Getty Images)

as a self-defense movement against the brutality of predominantly white police forces, the Black Panthers openly displayed weapons both in private and in public. Moreover, they would regularly make open threats against police officers, chanting slogans such as "The revolution has come, it's time to pick up the gun. Off the pigs!" (Farber 1994). Author Linda Lumsden (2009) contends that such displays "reclaimed black masculinity and traditional gender roles." Indeed, several authors consider the Black Panthers' policy of armed resistance as a reaffirmation of black masculinity, "with the use of guns and violence affirming proof of manhood" (Williams 2012). Many female BPP members also participated in the self-defense movement and were often photographed playing with their children with guns noticeably displayed—thereby "serving as protectors of the home, the family, and the community" (Lumsden 2009). This visual imagery would play in stark contrast to many patriot/militia groups of later years, which made it a point never to include women in their organizations.

Thus, when the Black Panthers entered the California State Assembly in May 1967, they may have firmly believed that they were exercising their rights under California law, and under the protections of the United States Constitution, to keep and bear arms. However, the reaction to their presence in a legislative body was anything but cordial. All the members who entered the chamber, including Bobby Seale, who was a cofounder of the movement, were arrested on misdemeanor charges. As one newspaper of the time noted,

> In May 1967, the Panthers invaded the State Assembly Chamber in Sacramento, guns in hand, in what appears to have been a publicity stunt. Still, they scared a lot of important people that day. At the time, the Panthers had almost no following. Now, (a year later) however, their leaders speak on invitation almost anywhere radicals gather, and many whites wear "Honkeys for Huey" buttons, supporting the fight to free Newton, who has been in jail since last Oct. 28 (1967) on the charge that he killed a policeman. (St. Petersburg Times 1968)

The account above references an incident in which Huey Newton, who together with Seale founded the BPP, became involved in an altercation with Oakland police officer John Frey after a traffic stop. Frey was killed, and his backup officer was wounded, as was Newton. Newton was arrested after the incident and was charged with Frey's murder. The charge sparked a "free Huey" campaign both in California and around the world (Bloom and Martin 2014).

In February 1968, at a "Free Huey" rally, several Black Panther leaders spoke, one even declaring, "Huey Newton is our only living revolutionary in this country today. . . . He has paid his dues. He has paid his dues. How many white folks did you kill today?" (Pearson 1994). As the mostly black audience in attendance erupted into applause, another Black Panther arose and said,

> We must serve notice on our oppressors that we as a people are not going to be frightened by the attempted assassination of our leaders. For my assassination—and I'm the low man on the totem pole—I want 30 police stations blown up, one southern

governor, two mayors, and 500 cops, dead. If they assassinate Brother Carmichael, Brother Brown . . . Brother Seale, this price is tripled. And if Huey is not set free and dies, the sky is the limit! (Pearson 1994).

After three years in prison, Huey Newton was released from prison on appeal. He would later boast to Robert Trivers, one of the few white people to ever be a member of the Black Panthers, that he (Newton) had, in fact, murdered Officer John Frey (Pearson 1994).

A mere two months after a February 1968 gathering in Oakland, Martin Luther King Jr. was assassinated in Memphis, Tennessee, sparking grief and outrage in black communities around the country. Two days later, Eldridge Cleaver, the BPP member who served as minister of information for the organization, was joined by 17-year-old Bobby Hutton on what "Cleaver later admitted was an 'ambush' on Oakland police officers" (Coleman 1980). In the ensuing shootout, Bobby Hutton was killed, and two Oakland police officers and Cleaver were wounded. Though the Black Panthers would contend that Hutton and Cleaver were ambushed by the police, Cleaver would admit that it was, in fact, a provocation on his part to exacerbate the raw feelings between the black and white communities over the King assassination. In fact, author Kate Coleman, who interviewed Eldridge Cleaver in *New West Magazine* in 1980, noted that Cleaver's admission of guilt was startling given that "the Panthers had steadfastly maintained that they had never attacked first, that they armed only in self-defense. . . . But even the formidable array of weaponry recovered near the scene of the shootout—from repeating pump-action shotguns and M-16s to high caliber pistols—hardly seemed the stuff of self-defense" (Coleman 1980).

In the months following the Seal and Newton incidents, "nine police officers were killed and 56 were wounded" (Balleck 2015). Ten black members also died during this time, and other members sustained numerous injuries. In 1969, 348 Black Panthers were arrested for a "variety of crimes" (Pearson 1994). Perhaps the most galvanizing of the events in 1969 was the death of Fred Hampton, who served as deputy chairperson of the BPP in Illinois. Closely surveilled by the Federal Bureau of Investigation (FBI) since 1967, Hampton's activities were infiltrated by an FBI informant who had agreed to get close to Hampton in exchange for the dropping of felony charges against him. When the FBI informant, William O'Neal, reported that the Black Panthers were merely feeding breakfast to inner-city children, J. Edgar Hoover, the director of the FBI, wrote a scathing memo to O'Neal, reminding him that his future aspirations depended on supplying evidence to Hoover in support of his (Hoover's) belief that the Black Panthers were "a violence-prone organization seeking to overthrow the Government [of the United States] by revolutionary means" (Smitha 1998). On December 3, 1969, a raid of Hampton's apartment was conducted by the Cook County office of the state's attorney and resulted in Fred Hampton's death. Postmortem analysis revealed the presence of barbiturates in Fred Hampton's blood stream, though he was not known to be a drug user. Many believed that O'Neal had slipped the barbiturates to Hampton in an effort to keep him from reacting to the police raid. Hampton was shot twice in the head (Churchill and Wall 1988). Though a federal grand jury was convened in the matter of Hampton's death, no one associated with the raid was ever prosecuted (Bennett 1999).

As the 1970s dawned, the killing of Black Panther Party members by other members began the disaffection that many inside the party had begun to feel. Coupled with ideological differences over whether the party should continue its armed confrontation or whether it should emphasize self-defense tactics with a continued focus on community service led to an irreparable split in the Black Panther movement. By 1980, membership in the Black Panthers was only 27, whereas it had been nearly 10,000 at the end of the 1960s (Perkins 2000).

See also: Black Separatists; New Black Panther Party; Newton, Huey P.; Seale, Bobby

Further Reading

Balleck, Barry J. 2015. *Allegiance to Liberty: The Changing Face of Patriots, Militias, and Political Violence in America*. Praeger.

Bennett, Hans. 1999. "The Black Panthers and the Assassination of Fred Hampton." *Philadelphia Independent Media Center*. Originally published at www.TowardFreedom.com. http://www.phillyimc.org/en/black-panthers-and-assassination-fred-hampton (Accessed March 18, 2017).

"Black Panthers: A Taut, Violent Drama." St. Petersburg Times, Sunday, July 21, 1968 Special to the St. Petersburg Times from the New York Times.

Bloom, Joshua and Waldo E. Martin. 2014. *Black Against Empire: The History and Politics of the Black Panther Party*. University of California Press, pp. 71–72.

Churchill, Ward and Jim Vander Wall. 1988. *Agents of Repression: The FBI's Secret Wars Against the Black Panther Party and the American Indian Movement*. South End Press, pp. 69–70.

Coleman, Kate. 1980. "Souled Out: Eldridge Cleaver Admits He Ambushed Those Cops." *New West Magazine*. http://colemantruth.net/kate (Accessed March 18, 2017).

Farber, David. 1994. *The Age of Great Dreams: America in the 1960s*. Hill and Wang, p. 207.

History of the Black Panther Party. "Black Panther Party Platform and Program: What We Want, What We Believe." Stanford University. https://web.stanford.edu/group/blackpanthers/history.shtml (Accessed March 18, 2017).

Lumsden, Linda. 2009. "Good Mothers with Guns: Framing Black Womanhood in the Black Panther, 1968–1980." *J & MC Quarterly* 86(4) (Winter), pp. 900–922.

Pearson, Hugh. 1994. *In the Shadow of the Panther: Huey Newton and the Price of Black Power in America*. Perseus Books.

Perkins, Margo V. 2000. *Autobiography as Activism: Three Black Women of the Sixties*. University Press of Mississippi, p. 5.

Smitha, Frank. 1998. "Ruin for the Black Panther Party, 1968–89." *Macrohistory and World Timeline*. http://www.fsmitha.com/h2/ch28B-5.htm (Accessed March 18, 2017).

Williams, Jakobi. 2012. "'Don't No Woman Have to Do Nothing She Don't Want to Do:' Gender, Activism, and the Illinois Black Panther Party." *Black Women, Gender & Families* 6, no. 2 (Fall), pp. 29–54.

BLACK SEPARATISTS

The black separatist movement in the United States seeks to separate those of African descent into distinct economic, political, and cultural units. Black separatism is generally recognized as a subcategory of black nationalism that opposes attempts to integrate blacks with other racial groups and expresses disdain for interracial marriage. Most black separatists want a separate nation for blacks, apart from whites and other minority groups, and are virulently antiwhite and anti-Semitic, and they express a belief that blacks are God's chosen people. Black separatism teaches that blacks should seek their original cultural homeland because they are hindered in their advancement by a society that is dominated by a white majority (Hall 1978). The Southern Poverty Law Center recognizes that "black racism in America is, at least in part, a reaction to white racism," and hatred by blacks of whites can be traced to the white dominance of blacks over several centuries. However, the Southern Poverty Law Center also notes that white groups espousing beliefs similar to those of black separatists would be considered racist and would be designated as hate groups. Therefore, "the same criterion should be applied to all groups regardless of their color" (Southern Poverty Law Center).

According to the Southern Poverty Law Center, a prime example of black separatists is in the teachings of the Nation of Islam (NOI) and its current leader, Louis Farrakhan. One of NOI's early leaders, Elijah Mohammed, regularly expressed antiwhite, anti-Semitic, anti-Catholic, and antigay views. According to NOI beliefs articulated by Elijah Mohammed, an evil black scientist, Yacub, created whites as "blue-eyed devils." Because of the evil nature by which they came forth, whites are inherently evil and ungodly. After Elijah Mohammed's death, his successor, Louis Farrakhan, took up his mantra and decried the abuses heaped on black people by whites, particularly blaming Jews for their complicity in aiding and abetting the slave trade that brought black people to the United States. When a subordinate of Farrakhan's once called for the slaughtering of white South Africans, Farrakhan regretted the "tone" of the comments but "agreed with the message" and renewed NOI's call for "racial separatism" and an end to the evils of "interracial relationships" (Southern Poverty Law Center).

In 1996, the New Black Panther Party, a group that attempted to capture the enthusiasm in the black community that had been generated by the original Black Panther Party, held a protest in which its leader, Malik Zulu Shabazz, led the crowd in chants of "Fifty shots! Fifty cops! Kill the pigs who kill our kids!" (Beirich and Lenz 2016). In July 2016, black separatism was once again violently demonstrated when Micah Xavier Johnson was identified as the man who shot 14 law enforcement officers during protests in Dallas, Texas. According to the Dallas police chief, Johnson was upset about a rash of police shootings in which white police had killed black, sometimes unarmed, citizens. Because of these shootings, "the suspect said he was upset at white people. The suspect stated he wanted to kill white people, especially white officers" (Beirich and Lenz 2016). As a result of Johnson's actions, five police officers were killed and nine others injured. Immediately after the shootings, Johnson fled from the scene and was eventually cornered inside a building where, after a standoff with police, he was killed by a bomb attached to a bomb disposal robot. After Johnson's death, a police investigation showed that he had "liked" several Facebook groups of black separatist movements, including the Nation of Islam, the Black Riders Liberation Party, and the New Black Panther Party, all designated as hate groups by the Southern Poverty Law Center (Beirich and Lenz 2016).

See also: Farrakhan, Louis; Nation of Islam; New Black Panther Party; Shabazz, Malik Zulu

Further Reading

Beirich, Heidi and Ryan Lenz. July 8, 2016. "Dallas Sniper Connected to Black Separatist Hate Groups on Facebook." *Southern Poverty Law Center—Hatewatch*. https://www.splcenter.org/hatewatch/2016/07/08/dallas-sniper-connected-black-separatist-hate-groups-facebook (Accessed March 18, 2017).
Hall, Raymond. 1978. *Black Separatism in the United States*. Dartmouth.
Southern Poverty Law Center. "Black Separatist." https://www.splcenter.org/fighting-hate/extremist-files/ideology/black-separatist (Accessed March 18, 2017).

BOSTON MARATHON BOMBING

On April 15, 2013, two bombs exploded near the finish line of the annual running of the Boston Marathon. It was later discovered that the bombs were homemade constructions that had used kitchen pressure cookers packed with nails and other sharp debris to cause injury. The explosions killed three spectators who were watching the race and injured more than 260 others. In the following days, the U.S. Federal Bureau of Investigation (FBI) determined that two Chechen brothers had perpetrated the attacks in protest of U.S. actions in Iraq and Afghanistan. Tamerlan Tsarnaev, the older of the brothers, was considered the mastermind of the attack. He was described by acquaintances as a "very religious" Muslim, though he also apparently was very enamored with U.S. culture. The younger brother, Dzhokhar Tsarnaev, was only 19 at the time of the attack. He had become a U.S. citizen less than one year before the attack, and he was characterized by those who knew him as introverted and shy.

After the attack, the brothers were publicly identified by the FBI, and a manhunt ensued. On April 19, Tamerlan Tsarnaev was killed in a shootout with law enforcement officials in Watertown, a suburb of Boston. The brothers had killed an Massachusetts Institute of Technology police officer, hijacked an SUV, and engaged in a gun battle with police before the final shootout. Tamerlan Tsarnaev was shot several times by police and was run over in the stolen SUV by his brother as the younger Tsarnaev escaped. He would later die at a Boston hospital. A Boston police officer who was seriously wounded in the shootout would die nearly a year later from wounds sustained in the battle. Dzhokhar Tsarnaev was captured on April 19—four days after the attack—hiding beneath the covering of

Boston police officers react to a bomb being detonated near the finish line of the Boston Marathon in 2013. Two brothers, Tamerlan and Dzhokhar Tsarnaev, were responsible for the bombing that killed three bystanders and injured more than 250. (John Tlumacki/The Boston Globe via Getty Images)

a boat in a neighborhood backyard. At his trial, defense attorneys claimed that Dzhokhar had been manipulated and coerced into perpetrating the attacks by his older brother. Dzhokhar Tsarnaev received 30 charges related to domestic terrorism, including constructing weapons of mass destruction. On April 8, 2015, Tsarnaev was found guilty on all charges and was later sentenced to death for his crimes.

The Boston Marathon bombing was the first major terror attack in the United States since the events of September 11, 2001. But unlike the events of 9/11, which had been perpetrated by foreign nationals, the Tsarnaev brothers had lived in the United States for many years. Investigations determined that Tamerlan Tsarnaev, the older of the brothers, had been radicalized online and had taken up the cause of bringing death and destruction to the United States because of its policies in the Middle East, particularly as they applied to Muslim countries. For terror experts, the Boston Marathon bombing punctuated the fear of homegrown terrorism that would later be repeated in attacks in Las Vegas, Nevada, San Bernardino, California, and Orlando, Florida as well as New York, New Jersey, and Minnesota. The latter attacks used the same bomb-making technique of packing pressure cookers with explosive material.

See also: Orlando Nightclub Shooting; San Bernardino Shooting

Further Reading

CNN. "Boston Marathon Terror Attack Fast Facts." Updated March 29, 2017. http://www
.cnn.com/2013/06/03/us/boston-marathon-terror-attack-fast-facts/index.html
(Accessed January 23, 2018).

History.com. "Boston Marathon Bombing." http://www.history.com/topics/boston-marathon
-bombings (Accessed January 23, 2018).

Huffpost. "Boston Marathon Bombing." *Huffington Post.* https://www.huffingtonpost.com
/topic/boston-marathon-bombing (Accessed January 23, 2018).

BOYKIN, LIEUTENANT GENERAL WILLIAM G. "JERRY" (RET.)

William G. "Jerry" Boykin (b. 1949) is a retired lieutenant general and former U.S. deputy undersecretary of defense for intelligence under the presidential administration of George W. Bush from 2002 to 2007. Boykin spent 13 years of his 36-year military career as a commando in the elite Delta Force special forces group, which Boykin said God had commanded him to join (Gaffney 2016). In 2003, as President Bush's deputy undersecretary of defense, Boykin "came under fire for remarks he made at several churches where he appeared in full dress uniform" (Southern Poverty Law Center, Jerry Boykin). In these addresses, Boykin reiterated that the United States was a "Christian nation" and that it was engaged in a "spiritual" battle against Satan, couching Islam as the enemy and casting the "war on terror" declared by President Bush as a religious war of good versus evil (Leung 2004). Boykin has said that "Islamic extremists hate the United States" because it is a "Judeo-Christian" nation (Southern Poverty Law Center, Jerry Boykin). After retiring, Boykin was named the executive vice president of the Family Research Council, a Christian lobbying group opposed to an LGBT agenda as well as abortion, stem-cell research, and divorce (Southern Poverty Law Center, FRC). Boykin said he joined the organization to "restore the values that made America a great nation" and "preserve the future of his grandchildren" (Jeffrey 2012).

Despite his distinguished military career, Boykin's intimation of religious rhetoric with government policy often caused public controversy. Before being appointed to a position in George W. Bush's administration, Boykin stated, "Why is this man in the White House? The majority of Americans did not vote for him. He's in the White House because God put him there for a time such as this. . . . George Bush was not elected by a majority of the voters in the United States. He was appointed by God" (NNDB).

Since Boykin's retirement in 2007, he has made himself "a popular speaker on the Conservative Christian speaking circuit" (Terry 2014). In his work, "Boykin is constantly on the road, crisscrossing the country from pulpit to pulpit, recruiting a Christian army to battle the forces of Satan, hell-bent, he says, on destroying America with such weapons as same-sex marriage, radical Islamists, gun control, abortion, and a 'Marxist model' for world conquest" (Terry 2014).

In 2012, Boykin became executive vice president of the Family Research Council, an organization that "is feverishly obsessed with the LGBT community, and has regularly and baselessly made claims like LGBT people are promiscuous, unstable and dangerous to children and that gay men are prone to pedophilia" (Terry 2014). In his work with the Family Research Council, Boykin was tasked with explaining conservative opposition to President Barack Obama's military policies, particularly "Don't ask, don't tell," which allowed gays and lesbians to serve openly in the U.S. military (Southern Poverty Law Center, Boykin). The FRC had stated that the repeal of the policy would "encourage molestation of heterosexual service members" (McMorris-Santoro 2010).

Boykin insists that he is not anti-Muslim in his views, though he has stated publicly that "[Islam] should not be protected under the First Amendment, particularly given that those following the dictates of the Quran are under an obligation to destroy our Constitution and replace it with sharia law" (Southern Poverty Law Center, Family Research Council). In March 2014, Boykin claimed that "Islam is full of subliminal messages, and that President Obama engaged in them as a way to encourage Muslims" (Southern Poverty Law Center, Family Research Council). Boykin has also seemed to intimate that what he perceived to be President Obama's lack of a hard stance against "Islamic radicals" was actually providing support to the groups that opposed the United States (Southern Poverty Law Center, Boykin).

See also: Family Research Council; Gaffney, Frank, Jr.

Further Reading

Gaffney, Frank. April 7, 2016. "Lt. Gen. Jerry Boykin on Genocide, the SCLC, Military Readiness and More." Center for Security Policy. http://www.centerforsecuritypolicy .org/2016/04/07/lt-gen-jerry-boykin-on-genocide-the-SCLC-military-readiness-and -more/ (Accessed March 24, 2017).

Jeffrey, Terence P. July 13, 2012. "Green Beret General Joins Family Research Council to Fight 'Culture War' for America's Grandkids.'" *CNS News.* http://www.cnsnews.com /news/article/green-beret-general-joins-family-research-council-fight-culture-war -america-s-grandkids (Accessed March 24, 2017).

Leung, Rebecca. September 15, 2004. "The Holy Warrior: General Called a Religious Fanatic Finally Speaks Out." *CBS News.* http://www.cbsnews.com/news/the-holy -warrior/ (Accessed March 24, 2017).

McMorris-Santoro, Evan. November 24, 2010. "Family Research Council Labeled 'Hate Group' by SCLC Over Anti-Gay Rhetoric." *Talking Points Memo.* http://talkingpoints memo.com/dc/family-research-council-labeled-hate-group-by-SCLC-over-anti-gay -rhetoric?ref=tn (Accessed March 24, 2017).

NNDB. "Jerry Boykin." http://www.nndb.com/people/357/000058183/ (Accessed March 24, 2017).

Southern Poverty Law Center. "Family Research Council." https://www.splcenter.org/fighting -hate/extremist-files/group/family-research-council (Accessed March 24, 2017).

Southern Poverty Law Center. "Lieutenant General William G. 'Jerry' Boykin (Ret.)." https://www.splcenter.org/fighting-hate/extremist-files/individual/lieutenant-general -william-g-"jerry"-boykin-ret (Accessed March 24, 2017).

Terry, Don. November 21, 2014. "Warrior for God." *Southern Poverty Law Center—Intelligence Report.* https://www.splcenter.org/fighting-hate/intelligence-report/2014/'warrior-god' (Accessed March 24, 2017).

BREITBART NEWS

Breitbart News is a far-right American news Web site founded by Andrew Breitbart in 2007. Breitbart reportedly conceived of the idea for the Web site after a visit to Israel in mid-2007. Upon his return to the United States, he imagined a news service "that would be unapologetically pro-freedom and pro-Israel" (Solov 2015). Early on, *Breitbart News* would align with populist movements on the right in Europe and would embrace the American alt-right movement under executive chairperson Steve Bannon. *The New York Times* has described *Breitbart News* as an organization with "ideologically driven journalists" that generates controversy "over material that has been called misogynist, xenophobic and racist" (Grynbaum and Herrman 2016). During the U.S. presidential campaign of 2016, executive chairperson Steve Bannon "declared that the website was the platform of the alt-right," and *Breitbart News* voiced unwavering support for Trump's campaign (Roy 2016). After Donald Trump was elected, Steve Bannon became President Trump's chief strategist. *Breitbart News* has been accused of publishing a number of intentionally false and misleading stories, including perpetuating conspiracy theories, many of which showed up during the presidential campaign of 2016 (Krieg 2016).

Since its founding, *Breitbart News* has been a voice of the far right. However, during the U.S. presidential campaign of 2016, the news organization underwent "a noticeable shift toward embracing ideas on the extremist fringe of the conservative right," including "blatantly racist ideas" along with "anti-Muslim and anti-immigrant ideas" (Piggot 2016). These tenets align *Breitbart News* with the alt-right movement, "a loose set of far-right ideologies at the core of which is a belief that 'white identity' is under attack through policies prioritizing multiculturalism, political correctness and social justice and must be preserved, usually through white-identified online communities and physical ethno-states" (Piggot 2016). In the past, *Breitbart* has organized conferences featuring white nationalist speakers and "has published op-eds and interviews with movement leaders" (Amend and Morgan 2017). In May 2015, *Breitbart* defended Pamela Geller, a noted Islamophobe who hosted a "Draw Mohammed" cartoon contest in Garland, Texas, which provoked two individuals, who claimed ties to ISIS, to target the event (Piggot 2016). The two extremists were killed by police in an exchange of gunfire when they attempted to gain access to the event. *Breitbart News* later published an article entitled, "6 Reasons Pamela Geller's Cartoon Contest Is No Different from Selma." In the article, a picture of Geller was superimposed "alongside a photo of the late Martin Luther King, Jr.," drawing the comparison that the "notorious Muslim-basher" Geller belonged in the same category of civil rights activists as the revered Martin Luther King Jr. (Piggot 2016).

In February 2016, *Breitbart* produced a "short anti-Muslim video" about the introduction of an anti-sharia bill in South Carolina (Piggot 2016). The video "pieced together video of stoning executions and harsh punishments to warn that Shariah law would undercut American justice." The claim echoed "similar statements made by anti-Muslim activists who fear that 'creeping Shariah' will soon preempt the Constitution" (Piggot 2016). A month earlier, *Breitbart* had published a piece by a longtime anti-immigrant politician who equated Islam with a pervasive "rape culture," noting that rapes had become an "epidemic" in Europe as the result of increasing numbers of Muslim immigrants into European countries (Piggot 2016).

Breitbart's reach is troubling because it is one of the 250 most popular Web sites in the United States and "is one of the top 1,000 most popular websites on the Internet" (Piggot 2016). *Breitbart* has increasingly published stories that African American crimes against whites are on the rise. Stories such as these, published on the Web site of the Council of Conservative Citizens, a white nationalist group, were noted by Charleston Church shooter Dylann Roof as being his introduction into white nationalism.

Though *Breitbart* was founded ostensibly to be "pro-Israel," the Southern Poverty Law Center has noted that under Steve Bannon's executorship, comments on *Breitbart* articles have "increasingly reflected language specific to the white nationalist 'alt-right' movement, including anti-Semitic sentiment" (Amend and Morgan 2017). As noted by authors Amend and Morgan (2017),

> Comparing the language of Breitbart commenters to the language of the most aggressive far-right extremists online—e.g. language used by Twitter users who advocate for violence against minorities and are openly pro-Nazi—we can see a clear trend of increasing similarity over a three-year period, the bulk of it under [executive chairperson Steve] Bannon.

In 2013, rhetorical analysis published in *The Washington Post* noted that the term "Jewish" was generally found to be statistically similar to words such as "Muslim" and "Christian," "meaning that mainstream authors usually rely on the word 'Jewish' to describe someone or something religious" (Morgan 2016). Yet when tweets by white extremists are examined, the word "Jewish" usually is not used to denote a religious affiliation but is more commonly found in proximity to words such as "communist," "homosexual," "anti-white," and "satanic," "signify[ing] something they hate, rather than as a religious description" (Morgan 2016). Under Steve Bannon, *Breitbart News* has focused on the term "globalist elites," a traditional "anti-Semitic dog whistle used by the radical right" to appeal to right-wing populists in the United States (Amend and Morgan 2017).

Since Bannon's ascension to the Trump administration, *Breitbart* has continued its inflammatory coverage, echoing most of the hard-core sentiments of the Trump administration on issues such as immigration and terrorism. Indeed, many right-wing, white nationalist Web sites, such as VDARE and *Stormfront*, have seen their users turn to *Breitbart News* as the site is increasingly viewed as more mainstream since Donald Trump was elected president of the United States (Hankes 2017).

See also: Alt-Right Movement; Bannon, Steve; Geller, Pamela; Neo-Nazis; Roof, Dylann Storm; Spencer, Richard Bertrand; *Stormfront*; VDARE; White Nationalism

Further Reading
Amend, Alex and Jonathon Morgan. February 21, 2017. "Breitbart Under Bannon: Breitbart's Comment Section Reflects Alt-Right, Anti-Semitic Language." *Southern Poverty*

Law Center—Hatewatch. https://www.splcenter.org/hatewatch/2017/02/21/breitbart -under-bannon-breitbarts-comment-section-reflects-alt-right-anti-semitic-language (Accessed April 29, 2017).

Breitbart News Network. www.breitbart.com/.

Grynbaum, Michael M. and John Herrman. August 26, 2016. "Breitbart Rises from Outlier to Potent Voice in Campaign." *The New York Times.* https://www.nytimes.com/2016 /08/27/business/media/breitbart-news-presidential-race.html?_r=0 (Accessed April 29, 2017).

Hankes, Keegan. March 1, 2017. "Breitbart Under Bannon: How Breitbart Became a Favorite News Source for Neo-Nazis and White Nationalists." *Southern Poverty Law Center— Hatewatch.* https://www.splcenter.org/hatewatch/2017/03/01/breitbart-under-bannon-how-breitbart-became-favorite-news-source-neo-nazis-and-white (Accessed April 29, 2017).

Krieg, Gregory. August 24, 2016. "The New Birthers: Debunking the Hillary Clinton Health Conspiracy." *CNN Politics.* http://www.cnn.com/2016/08/22/politics/hillary-clinton -health-conspiracy-theory-explained/index.html (Accessed April 29, 2017).

Morgan, Jonathon. September 26, 2016. "These Charts Show Exactly How Racist and Radical the Alt-Right Has Gotten This Year." *The Washington Post.* https://www.washing tonpost.com/news/the-intersect/wp/2016/09/26/these-charts-show-exactly-how -racist-and-radical-the-alt-right-has-gotten-this-year/?utm_term=.09b25eabd12d (Accessed April 29, 2017).

Piggot, Stephen. April 28, 2016. "Is Breitbart.com Becoming the Media Arm of the 'Alt-Right.'" *Southern Poverty Law Center—Hatewatch.* https://www.splcenter.org/hatewatch /2016/04/28/breitbartcom-becoming-media-arm-alt-right (Accessed April 29, 2017).

Posner, Sarah. August 22, 2016. "How Donald Trump's New Campaign Chief Created an Online Haven for White Nationalists." *Mother Jones.* http://www.motherjones.com /politics/2016/08/stephen-bannon-donald-trump-alt-right-breitbart-news (Accessed April 29, 2017).

Roy, Jessica. November 14, 2016. "What Is the Alt-Right? A Refresher Course on Steve Bannon's Fringe Brand of Conservatism." *Los Angeles Times.* http://www.latimes.com /nation/politics/trailguide/la-na-trailguide-updates-what-is-the-alt-right-a-refresher -1479169663-htmlstory.html (Accessed July 10, 2017).

Solov, Larry. November 17, 2015. "Breitbart News Network: Born in the US, Conceived in Israel." *Breitbart.com.* http://www.breitbart.com/big-journalism/2015/11/17/breitbart -news-network-born-in-the-usa-conceived-in-israel/ (Accessed April 29, 2017).

Tuttle, Ian. April 5, 2016. "The Racist Moral Rot at the Heart of the Alt-Right." *National Review.* http://www.nationalreview.com/article/433650/alt-rights-racism-moral-rot (Accessed April 29, 2017).

Weigel, David. "July 29, 2015. "'Cuckservative'—The Conservative Insult of the Month Explained." *The Washington Post.* https://www.washingtonpost.com/news/the-fix/wp /2015/07/29/cuckservative-the-conservative-insult-of-the-month-explained/?utm _term=.116b1b82dfd4 (Accessed April 29, 2017).

BRIMELOW, PETER

Peter Brimelow (b. 1947) is an outspoken critic of U.S. immigration policy who believes that the country's policies have "choked off" immigration from traditionally white countries in favor of immigration from "third world countries," particularly Mexico. In 1999, Brimelow founded the Center for American Unity and established a Web site entitled VDARE. The name VDARE is an homage to Virginia Dare, the first white English child born to European colonists in the New World in 1587. VDARE is notorious for its anti-immigration articles that are often authored by noted anti-Semites, white supremacists, and others from the radical and extreme right wing. Brimelow commented in 2008 that "the way to win [a presidential election] is to get white votes. . . . If [Republicans] did that, even without actually cutting off immigration, they could continue to win national elections for quite a long time" (Southern Poverty Law Center, VDARE).

Brimelow once served as an editor of *Forbes* magazine and is also a past columnist of such conservative publications as the *Financial Post* and the *National Review*. He is perhaps best known for his 1995 book, *Alien Nation: Common Sense about America's Immigration Disaster*. In the book, Brimelow argues that the United States was founded as a white nation and that the American people and the government should take steps to keep it that way. Brimelow has labeled anything of a "multicultural" nature as subversive of white values and has written that if one was to walk into a waiting room of the Immigration and Naturalization Service, "it would be like walking into a New York City subway—you find yourself in an underworld that is not just teeming but also almost entirely colored" (Southern Poverty Law Center, Peter Brimelow). Forecasting Donald Trump's winning strategy in 2016, Brimelow commented on the defeat of John McCain to Barack Obama in the 2008 U.S. presidential campaign that the GOP would be "unable to compete in presidential elections in the future because the racial makeup of the country was being radically changed by non-white immigration" (Southern Poverty Law Center, Peter Brimelow). Thus, after McCain's defeat, Brimelow encouraged the Republican Party to pursue a strategy that would focus heavily on white voters, noting that the "backlash" against the Obama administration was "overwhelmingly white" (Southern Poverty Law Center, Peter Brimelow). This was almost precisely the strategy that the Trump campaign pursued as Donald Trump's message of anti-immigration and anti-Muslim sentiment was aimed almost exclusively at disaffected white voters.

Critics of Brimelow state that VDARE publishes the writings of self-avowed white nationalists, anti-Semites, and other race haters. The Southern Poverty Law Center, VDARE has noted that whereas VDARE was once a "relatively mainstream anti-immigration page," by 2003 it had degenerated into "a meeting place for the many on the radical right." Brimelow has denied that VDARE promotes white nationalism and views criticism from the SPLC as a "badge of honor" (VDARE). In recent years, Brimelow has publicly stated that states may have to consider "secession" in order to protect the rights of white citizens (Bean 2015).

See also: VDARE; White Nationalism

Further Reading

Bean, Mikayla. May 21, 2015. "Peter Brimelow: States Like Texas Must Consider Secession to Protect 'White Rights.'" *Right Wing Watch*. http://www.rightwingwatch.org/post

/peter-brimelow-states-like-texas-must-consider-secession-to-protect-white-rights/ (Accessed January 5, 2017).

Southern Poverty Law Center. "Peter Brimelow." https://www.splcenter.org/fighting-hate /extremist-files/individual/peter-brimelow (Accessed January 5, 2017).

Southern Poverty Law Center. "VDARE." https://www.splcenter.org/fighting-hate/extremist -files/group/vdare (Accessed January 5, 2017).

VDARE. "The Speech that Launched an SPLC 'Hate' Honor." http://www.vdare.com/articles /the-speech-that-launched-an-splc-hate-honor (Accessed January 5, 2017).

BUNDY RANCH STANDOFF

In April 2014, a standoff ensued between Nevada rancher Cliven Bundy, dozens of his armed supporters, and officials of the U.S. Bureau of Land Management (BLM) over delinquent grazing fees Bundy owed the federal government. Bundy had legally grazed his cattle on land near Bunkerville, Nevada, for decades, but in 1993, in a dispute over changes to the rules governing the grazing of cattle on federal land, Bundy declined to renew his permit with the BLM. In 1994, Bundy's permits were cancelled, but for the next two decades he continued to allow his cattle onto federal lands without paying the proper grazing fees. At the time of the standoff, Bundy owed the federal government more than $1 million in delinquent grazing fees (Pearce 2016).

Cliven Bundy's family has owned its ranch in Nevada since 1948. From that time until 1993, Bundy or his father grazed cattle on federal land with proper permits. However, when Bundy refused to renew his permits in 1993—claiming that he had inherited grazing rights from his maternal grandmother—and continued to graze his cattle on the land, the federal government brought suit against him. Bundy claimed that the federal government had no legal claim to the land on which his cattle were grazing, claiming instead that the land legally belonged to the state of Nevada and not the federal government, intimating that the federal government had no standing in the case (*United States v. Bundy*). Bundy's claims were dismissed, and he ignored a "decision order to remove" his cattle from the land. For over 15 years, Bundy flouted court orders and ignored government injunctions while he continued to allow his cattle to graze on federal lands without payment, though other ranchers in the area continued to pay the rightful fees to graze their cattle.

In March 2014, the Department of the Interior informed Nevada state officials of its intention to close a portion of public lands for the purpose of impounding illegally grazing cattle upon federal land. Within days, Bundy "sent letters entitled 'Range War Emergency Notice and Demand for Protection' to county, state, and federal officials" (Donahue 2014). Evoking the language of the sovereign citizen movement, Bundy appealed for help and eventually received support from a variety of militia groups, including the Oath Keepers. Bundy's son, Ryan, stated his family's position on the matter:

> This is an issue of state sovereignty. . . . These large tracts of land that Bureau of Land Management, Forest Service, monuments, parks and, you know, National Parks,

et cetera, et cetera, there is no constitutionality to them at all. . . . If they are going to be out in the hills stealing our property, we will put measures of defense. And they have always asked us, "What will you do, what will you do?" and our stance has always been we will do whatever it takes. Open-ended. And because of that, that's why they are scared, because they don't know to what level we will go to protect, but we will protect. (Hernandez and Langdon 2014)

By early April, dozens of armed militia group members from across the United States had converged on the Bundy ranch. As the cattle roundup by the BLM progressed, several confrontations arose between armed protestors and BLM officials. Though none were violent, there were reports of semiautomatic weapons being drawn down on federal officials and incidents of pushing and shoving. Bundy would claim that guns had been pointed at the protestors and that attack dogs had been used to harass and intimidate those present. Addressing the protestors at one point, Bundy said, "We definitely don't recognize [the BLM director's] jurisdiction or authority, his arresting power or policing power in any way" and "We're about ready to take the country over with force!" (Hernandez and Langdon 2014). Recognizing the possibility for an armed confrontation that would likely lead to casualties, the BLM relented, announcing that it would release Bundy's cattle and withdraw from the area. Over the course of the next few months, the BLM sent several certified letters to Bundy informing him of their intention to seek administrative and judicial proceedings to compel Bundy to pay the over $1 million he owed to the federal government in grazing fees.

In the aftermath of the standoff, armed groups remained in and around the Bundy ranch, often eliciting complaints from residents to local law enforcement officials that their (the armed groups) presence was menacing and intimidating. Bundy and his supporters reveled in the perceived victory and called the standoff the Battle of Bunkerville, drawing comparisons with the Battle of Bunker Hill, though there was never a shot fired (Gorman et al. 2014). Several supporters of the Tea Party stood in solidarity with the Bundys and initiated a protest outside of Las Vegas Police Headquarters claiming that Clark County, Nevada, "Sheriff Doug Gillespie had failed in his sworn duty to protect the citizens of his county" from the intrusions of the federal government, a claim oft repeated by adherents of the extremist group known as Posse Comitatus (Knightly 2014).

In February 2016, while on his way to assist his sons Ammon and Ryan, who were then involved in the occupation of the Malheur National Wildlife Refuge, Cliven Bundy was arrested by federal officials at Portland International Airport. He was later indicted by a federal grand jury on 16 felony charges relating to the armed standoff at his ranch in 2014. On January 8, 2018, a federal judge in Las Vegas dismissed all charges against Ammon and Ryan Bundy in connection with the standoff. The judge ruled that the federal government had withheld evidence that was prejudicial against the Bundys (Johnson 2018).

See also: Oath Keepers; Posse Comitatus; Sagebrush Rebellion; Sovereign Citizens Movement

Further Reading

Donahue, Mike. March 24, 2014. "Bundy Declares 'Range War', BLM to Impound Embattled Rancher's Cattle." *Desert Valley Times*.

Gorman, Ryan, Dan Miller, Meghan Keneally, and Jessica Jerreat. April 11, 2014. "Federal Agents Back Down in Stand-off with Armed Cowboys." *Daily Mail*.

Hernandez, Daniel and Joseph Langdon. April 13, 2014. "Federal Rangers Face Off Against Armed Protesters in Nevada Range War." *The Guardian*.

Johnson, Kirk. January 8, 2018. "Charges Against Bundys in Ranch Standoff Case Are Dismissed." *New York Times*. https://www.nytimes.com/2018/01/08/us/bundy-ranch-standoff-case-charges-dismissed.html (Accessed January 23, 2018).

Knightly, Arnold M. April 11, 2014. "Cliven Bundy Supporters Bring Cattle Roundup Protest to Las Vegas Police Headquarters." *Las Vegas Review-Journal*.

Pearce, Matt. January 7, 2016. "Cliven Bundy Still Owes the U.S. $1 Million. What Are the Feds Doing to Collect It?" *Los Angeles Times*. http://www.latimes.com/nation/la-na-cliven-bundy-fines-20160107-story.html (Accessed July 11, 2017).

Southern Poverty Law Center. "War in the West: The Bundy Ranch Standoff and the American Radical Right." https://www.splcenter.org/20140709/war-west-bundy-ranch-standoff-and-american-radical-right (Accessed November 22, 2016).

United States District Court for the District of Nevada. Decision and Order. *United States v. Bundy—1998*. http://dohiyimir.typepad.com/bundy-1998-court.pdf (Accessed November 22, 2016).

BUTLER, RICHARD

Richard Butler (1918–2004) founded the organization known as the Church of Jesus Christ Christian, a name he would later change to Aryan Nations. From its headquarters in Hayden Lake near Coeur d'Alene, Idaho, Aryan Nations would grow into one of the most powerful and influential white supremacist and neo-Nazi organizations in the United States. At its height, Aryan Nations attracted some of the most noted and infamous white supremacists of the time. At a 1982 weekend gathering, for instance, prominent members from several neo-Nazi, Ku Klux Klan, and other white supremacist and racist groups gathered at Butler's Hayden Lake compound (Anti-Defamation League, Richard Butler). A splinter group of Aryan Nations, known as The Order, would become one of the most infamous domestic terror groups in the history of the United States, robbing several banks and armored cars and assassinating Alan Berg, a popular radio talk show host in Denver, Colorado. Though Butler would be accused of plotting to overthrow the government in the late 1980s, an Arkansas jury was unconvinced, and Butler and his codefendants were acquitted. However, in 1998, members of Aryan Nations assaulted a mother and her teenage son near the Hayden Lake compound. With the help of the Southern Poverty Law Center, a judgment against Aryan Nations in the amount of $6.3 million was awarded to the victims. As a result of the judgment, Butler had to auction off the compound and all of its lands. By the time of his death in 2004, Butler had largely lost control of the remnants of Aryan Nations.

Richard Butler joined the U.S. military as a member of the Army Air Corps soon after the attack on Pearl Harbor in 1941. Though he never saw action, he recalled that he was "thrilled" to see newsreels of the precision with which the Germany army marched. He would later admit an admiration of Hitler because of his fierce anticommunism. Butler would later be a prominent advocate of Senator Joseph McCarthy and his anticommunist stance, even donating money to the senator's campaign. Butler himself joined the California Committee to Combat Communism in order to "expose" teachers of communism. It was here that Butler would come into contact with one of the most important influences in his life, William Potter Gale, the future founder of Posse Comitatus. (Posse Comitatus would provide the white supremacist and anti-Semitic ideology that would become the cornerstone of Aryan Nations.) Later, Butler would begin attending a Christian Identity church, a theology that taught "that whites are the true Israelites" and that Jews are "descended directly from a mating of Eve and the devil" (Southern Poverty Law Center). Butler would later take a correspondence course and become an ordained minister of Christian Identity.

Butler retired from Lockheed Aircraft Company in 1974 after having developed "a rapid repair system for the tubeless tire" (Southern Poverty Law Center). He moved to northern Idaho because he considered it to be the most "pure" white area in the United States. At his Hayden Lake compound, Butler began his own self-sustaining "township" after the order of such communities as had been modeled by his old friend and mentor William Potter Gale. In 1977, Butler formed the Church of Jesus Christ Christian. The political arm of the "church" would be known as Aryan Nations. In "church," Butler would teach a healthy dose of antigovernment sentiment, anti-Semitism, survivalism, and Hitler worship. Over the next 20 years, Butler's Aryan Nations would spawn the spin-off group The Order, led by Bob Mathews. This group was at one time deemed by the Federal Bureau of Investigation to be one of the most dangerous domestic terror groups in the country. Randy Weaver, who would confront federal agents at Ruby Ridge, Idaho, in 1993, was also an acquaintance and follower of Richard Butler.

By the beginning of the 1980s, Butler's Hayden Lake compound had become a fortress, patrolled by an armed security force and guard dogs. Beginning in 1982, Butler would each summer host white supremacist "festivals" known as the World Congress of Aryan Nations (Southern Poverty Law Center). The conference would attract as many as 200 participants of every ilk of the white supremacist movement. At the congresses, Aryan Nations would offer "paramilitary training in urban terrorism and guerrilla warfare as well as, more generally, a chance for like-minded extremists to address issues of common interest" (Anti-Defamation League, Aryan Nations).

Aryan Nations would wax and wane in influence throughout the 1980s and 1990s, but the real end of the groups began in 1998 when Aryan Nation guards assaulted a mother and her son near the Hayden Lake compound. With the assistance of the Southern Poverty Law Center, the two sued Aryan Nations. A jury later found Aryan Nations liable for their injuries, and the plaintiffs were awarded a $6.3 million judgment. To satisfy the judgment, in 2001 Butler was forced to auction off the Hayden Lake compound. Though Butler continued as Aryan Nations' titular head, the organization splintered into several different factions in 2002

(Anti-Defamation League, Aryan Nations). By this time, Butler was in failing health, and his influence among the growing patriot and militia movements was minimal. In the fall of 2003, Butler ran for mayor of Hayden, Idaho, but he garnered only 50 votes of the more than 2,000 cast. He died in his sleep in September 2004.

See also: Aryan Nations; Christian Identity; Gale, William Potter; Matthews, Bob; Order, The; Posse Comitatus; Ruby Ridge; Weaver, Randy

Further Reading

Anti-Defamation League. "Aryan Nations/Church of Jesus Christ Christian." *ADL Extremism in America.* http://archive.adl.org/learn/ext_us/aryan_nations.html (Accessed December 14, 2016).

Anti-Defamation League. "Richard Butler." *ADL Extremism in America.* http://archive.adl.org/learn/ext_us/butler.html (Accessed December 14, 2016).

Southern Poverty Law Center. "Richard Butler." https://www.splcenter.org/fighting-hate/extremist-files/individual/richard-butler (Accessed December 14, 2016).

C

CAMERON, PAUL

Paul Cameron (b. 1939) gained notoriety for being a research pioneer on the effects of second-hand smoke. In 1978, however, Cameron began his descent into antigay activism by publishing *Sexual Gradualism*, a tract that suggests "that parents allow their children to experiment with heterosexual sex, short of intercourse" (Southern Poverty Law Center). Though no parent wants their child to start the process of sexual awakening too young, for Cameron it is better "too young than homosexual" (Southern Poverty Law Center). In 1982, Cameron joined the Committee to Oppose Special Rights for Homosexuals, an antigay-rights pressure group that had begun to campaign against a gay-rights ordinance being proposed in Lincoln, Nebraska (Southern Poverty Law Center). In the same year, Cameron founded the Institute for the Scientific Study of Sexuality. The group was renamed the Family Research Institute in 2005. Cameron moved to Colorado Springs, Colorado, in 1992 "after supporters of a constitutional amendment barring gay rights legislation in the state distributed 100,000 copies of his study, 'What do Homosexuals Do?'" (Southern Poverty Law Center). The move paid off after Colorado voters approved the amendment in 1994, though the U.S. Supreme Court later invalidated the amendment in 1996, ruling it unconstitutional in the case of *Romer v. Evans*. Though Cameron maintains that "his research demonstrates a link between homosexuality and the perpetration of child sexual abuse and even reduced life expectancy, his work has been largely disavowed by the American Psychological Association (APA), the American Sociological Association, and the Canadian Psychological Association" (Schlatter and Steinback 2011).

Though largely discredited, Cameron's work continues to be cited by opponents of gay rights. In 2003, dissenting justices on the Massachusetts Supreme Court cited Cameron's research in the case that legalized same-sex marriage in that state (Southern Poverty Law Center). In 2004, the Florida Supreme Court, in a majority decision, quoted Cameron's research that "children raised by homosexuals disproportionately experience emotional disturbance and sexual victimization" (Southern Poverty Law Center). Cameron also maintains that his research "prove[s] that gays and lesbians are more likely to be criminals and child molesters," though such claims have been shown to be false (Southern Poverty Law Center; see also Schlatter and Steinback 2011).

In recent years, Cameron has extended his antigay "findings" beyond the United States. In 2011, he stated in Moldova that the country's declining birth rate was a "demographic disaster brought on by women's emancipation and the promotion of the rights of sexual minorities, particularly the LGBT [lesbian, gay, bisexual, and transgender] community" (Southern Poverty Law Center).

See also: Family Research Institute

Further Reading

Family Research Institute. http://www.familyresearchinst.org/ (Accessed January 11, 2017).

Schlatter, Evelyn and Robert Steinback. February 27, 2011. "10 Anti-Gay Myths Debunked." *Southern Poverty Law Center—Intelligence Report.* https://www.splcenter .org/fighting-hate/intelligence-report/2011/10-anti-gay-myths-debunked (Accessed January 11, 2017).

Southern Poverty Law Center. "Paul Cameron." https://www.splcenter.org/fighting-hate /extremist-files/individual/paul-cameron (Accessed January 11, 2017).

CARTO, WILLIS

Willis Carto (1926–2015) was a member of the far right wing who used political and mass communication means to foster his anti-Semitic views and racist attitudes toward other minorities. He also led the movement in the United States of individuals and groups who collectively became known as Holocaust deniers—those who held that the Holocaust was a fabrication and that there never was a systematic effort by Adolf Hitler and the Nazis to exterminate the Jewish race. Through his efforts, Carto "raised money to finance a right-wing military dictatorship in the United States," led efforts to "persuade blacks to voluntarily return to Africa," worked on George Wallace's failed 1968 presidential campaign, and founded the National Youth Alliance, an organization that would be reconstituted by William Pierce as the National Alliance and become the most important neo-Nazi organization in the United States (Martin 2015). Carto disseminated his views through the various organizations and publications that he helped found, such as the Institute for Historical Review, the Liberty Lobby, *Spotlight*, and *The Barnes Review.* Carto also "helped to found the far-right Populist Party, which soon became a haven for white supremacists and other racial extremists" (Southern Poverty Law Center). Twice, the Populist Party fielded candidates in the U.S. presidential election— David Duke in 1988 (a former Grand Wizard of the KKK) and former Green Beret and militia advocate Bo Gritz in 1992.

Carto began his activism in the 1950s. He founded the Liberty Lobby, a right-wing advocacy group, in 1955. At a time of anticommunist fervor, the Liberty Lobby marketed itself as staunchly conservative and anticommunist. However, very quickly after its founding, it became a haven for anti-Semitic activists and advocates of white supremacy. Carto began to promote the views of the Liberty Lobby through its publication, *Spotlight*, and he supported Governor George Wallace's presidential bid in 1968, stating that Wallace was the only candidate who was capable of "beating back 'Blacky' and the Communist-dominated federal government" (Southern Poverty Law Center). When Wallace was defeated, Carto embraced neo-Nazi views and reorganized the "Youth for Wallace" movement, renaming it the National Youth Alliance (NYA). The NYA became very secretive and were known only among each other by code names. They perpetrated the use of Nazi war relics, Nazi songs, Nazi symbols, and other Nazi-related paraphernalia. The NYA would eventually fall apart amid infighting, but it would rise again in the form of the National Alliance, which would become the most virulent neo-Nazi organization in the United States (Southern Poverty Law Center).

In 1978, Carto founded the Institute for Historical Review (IHR) "as a legitimate historical research group devoted to revisionism"—a term meant to convey the idea of the reinterpretation of ideas commonly accepted in the historic community (Southern Poverty Law Center). The IHR, however, was populated by white supremacists and Nazi sympathizers who pushed the idea that the Holocaust was a fabrication and had never happened. The goal of the IHR was to "erase" the holocaust from history—through distortion, misquotation, and outright falsification (Southern Poverty Law Center).

In 1996, over a dispute with the IHR, Carto was forced to declare bankruptcy, and the Liberty Lobby was officially shuttered. Soon after, Carto founded *The Barnes Review*, which "dedicated itself to historical revisionism" (Southern Poverty Law Center). Carto would later assert that the *Review* was one of the only patriotic and independent publications around the country, as the popular press was all literally controlled by Jews. A second publication of Carto's—*American Free Press*—carried stories on Zionism, "New World Order" conspiracy theories, and the views of Christian Identity, among them that Jews are the offspring of a union between Eve and Satan. Late in his life, Carto became an adherent of Christian Identity.

Carto died in October 2015 and was buried in Arlington National Cemetery, despite his controversial past.

See also: Christian Identity; Duke, David; Gritz, Bo; Holocaust Denial; Liberty Lobby; National Alliance; Pierce, William; White Supremacist Movement

Further Reading

Martin, Douglas. November 1, 2015. "Willis Carto, Far-Right Figure and Holocaust Denier, Dies at 89." *The New York Times.* https://www.nytimes.com/2015/11/02/us/willis-carto-far-right-figure-and-holocaust-denier-dies-at-89.html?_r=0 (Accessed January 13, 2017).

Southern Poverty Law Center. "Willis Carto." https://www.splcenter.org/fighting-hate/extremist-files/individual/willis-carto (Accessed January 13, 2017).

CATHEY, BOYD

According to the Southern Poverty Law Center, Boyd Cathey (b. 1950) has worked for over three decades to "bridge mainstream conservative politics and the far-right fringe worlds of Holocaust denial, extremist Catholicism, and racially tinged neo-Confederate causes." In his youth, Cathey studied "at institutions run by the Society of St. Pius X (SSPX), a radical traditionalist Catholic sect that was censured by the Vatican for refusing to comply with modern Catholic theological norms, including reconciliation with Jews and other religions" (Southern Poverty Law Center). These institutions were also associated with Opus Dei, a far-right-wing Catholic organization. Cathey was ordained to Opus Dei in 1979, but two years later he left to work for the state of North Carolina in the Department of Cultural Resources. Cathey is known for his association with Holocaust denial organizations, including the Institute for Historical Review and the neo-Confederate movement. In recent years, Cathey has been a frequent contributor to the writings associated with the Abbeville Institute, a group founded in 2002 at the University of Virginia to "acknowledge the achievements of the white people of the South." The institute maintains that contemporary American society's political, educational, and scholarly community have "worked overtime to purge the Southern tradition from the cultural and physical landscape, to banish it to one little, dark corner labeled slavery and treason" (Abbeville Institute).

After leaving the priesthood and taking his job in North Carolina, Cathey forged ties with far-right groups, including the Southern Partisan, a virulent neo-Confederate group that regularly "publishes rants against homosexuality, feminism, affirmative action and multiculturalism, all while painting a rosy picture of the quality of life for African-American slaves in the pre-Civil War South" (Southern Poverty Law Center). From 1984 until 1999, the mastheads of the magazine "identified Cathey as a contributor, editor, and senior adviser" (Southern Poverty Law Center).

In 1988, Cathey worked on the presidential campaign of Pat Robertson, a prominent Christian Coalition televangelist who frequently spouted antigay sentiments and the belief that God was punishing the United States for its sanctioning of drugs, homosexuality, illicit sex, and other "sins" against society. Robertson also frequently spoke about deep-seated conspiracies being perpetrated by Jewish bankers and Freemasons. In 1992, Cathey was part of the presidential campaign of Pat Buchanan, cofounder of *The American Conservative* magazine and a foundation named The American Cause. He had previously served as an advisor to various Republican presidents, including Nixon, Ford, and Reagan. It was during Cathey's association with the Buchanan campaign that his (Cathey's) ties to the Holocaust-denying Institute for Historical Review were exposed. Though Cathey later claimed that he had ended his affiliation with the institute, in 2003 his name still appeared very prominently on the group's Web site (Southern Poverty Law Center).

Cathey's extremist ties were accentuated when he became part of a group that attempted to wrest control of the Sons of Confederate Veterans heritage group. When new leadership purged members who criticized excessive racism within the group, Cathey was appointed to the group's executive council. In 2015, Cathey wrote a spirited defense of the Confederate battle flag after Dylann Roof, the lone gunman who killed nine black parishioners in an historic Charleston, South Carolina, Methodist church, was linked in his actions to the flag and his (Roof's) support of white nationalism. In 2015, in response to growing calls to remove the Confederate battle flag from the state capitol building in South Carolina, Cathey wrote,

If a rabid fox comes out of the woods and bites someone, you don't burn the woods down, you stop the fox. . . . It is a slippery slope, but an incline that in fact represents a not-so-hidden agenda, a cultural Marxism, that seeks to take advantage of the genuine horror at what happened in Charleston to advance its own designs which are nothing less than the remaking completely of what remains of the American nation.

In 2016, Cathey led an effort to distribute a list of intellectuals in support of the presidential candidacy of Donald Trump in an effort to demonstrate that "supporters of the Trump agenda are by no means limited to the badly educated and ill-informed" (Guttman 2016).

See also: Carto, Willis; Holocaust Denial; Neo-Confederates; Roof, Dylann Storm; White Nationalism

Further Reading

Abbeville Institute. "Purpose and Principles." https://www.abbevilleinstitute.org/principles/ (Accessed January 13, 2017).

Cathey, Boyd. August 4, 2015. "A Sickness in the Public Mind: The Battle Flag and the Attack on Western Culture." *The Abbeville Blog.* https://www.abbevilleinstitute.org /blog/a-sickness-in-the-public-mind-the-battle-flag-and-the-attack-on-western -culture/ (Accessed January 13, 2017).

Guttman, Nathan. October 31, 2016. "Holocaust-Denying Academic Organized List of Trump Endorsers." *Forward.com.* http://forward.com/news/national/353064/holocaust -denying-academic-organized-list-of-trump-endorsers/ (Accessed January 13, 2017).

Southern Poverty Law Center. "Boyd Cathey." https://www.splcenter.org/fighting-hate /extremist-files/individual/boyd-cathey (Accessed January 13, 2017).

CENTER FOR IMMIGRATION STUDIES

In February 2017, for the first time, the Southern Poverty Law Center (SPLC) "designated the Center for Immigration Studies (CIS) as a hate group" (Southern Poverty Law Center). According to the SPLC, CIS is a "nativist think tank that churns out a constant stream of fear-mongering misinformation about Latino immigrants" (Beirich 2009). The group was founded in 1985 as one of a network of anti-immigration groups by John Tanton, "an activist with white nationalist leanings and a fondness for extreme 'population control' measures" (Right Wing Watch). Tanton has been dubbed by the SPLC as the "racist architect of the modern anti-immigrant movement" (Southern Poverty Law Center). Predictably, the executive director of CIS, Mark Krikorian, condemned the designation, complaining that SPLC's designation of CIS as a hate group lumps the organization in with groups such as the KKK and that the designation was made simply because SPLC does not share CIS's beliefs. But the SPLC has stated that

hate has gone mainstream. Today, the purveyors of hate don't always burn crosses or use racial slurs. They might wear suits and ties. They might have sophisticated public relations operations. They might even testify before Congress.

They're also more likely to be animated by a nativist or white nationalist ideology that sees the "white race" as being under siege by immigrants of color across the Western world. Reflecting this trend, our annual list of hate groups has evolved to include more groups closely linked to white nationalism. (Beirich 2017)

The CIS has been criticized for periodically publishing reports deemed misleading and using poor or questionable methodology when reporting statistics on immigration. Though such reports have from time to time found their way into the mainstream media, they have been criticized as being misleading and skewing the argument to the CIS's point of view (Sherman 2017). The CIS regularly circulates pieces on its Web site (cis.org) that have been authored "by white nationalists, Holocaust deniers, and other material from explicitly racist websites" (Piggott 2016). In the past, CIS has circulated pieces from the white nationalist Web site *American Renaissance* (AmRen), which is run by Jared Taylor, "one of America's most prominent and outspoken racists" (Piggott 2016). Taylor has stated that "blacks and whites are different. When blacks are left entirely to their own devices, Western civilization—any kind of civilization—disappears" (Piggott 2016). In October 2016, AmRen published an article of a CIS event that featured Charles Murray, author of the controversial text *The Bell Curve*, which "uses racist pseudoscience and misleading statistics to argue that social inequality is caused by the genetic inferiority of black and Latino communities" (Piggott 2016). CIS has also circulated links to the anti-immigrant and nationalist hate site VDARE. Run by white nationalist Peter Brimelow, who has argued that the United States is a historically white-dominated society and should remain that way, VDARE is a hub for white nationalist and anti-Semitic authors (Beirich 2009).

Though one commentator has stated that CIS's designation as a hate group is based more on "its associations rather than its current work" (Sherman 2017), the director of SPLC's Intelligence Project articulated why CIS landed on SPLC's "hate radar":

> CIS has a long history of bigotry, starting with its founder, white nationalist John Tanton, but in 2016, the group hit a new low. CIS commissioned Jason Richwine, a man who's [sic] Ph.D. dissertation endorses the idea of IQ differences between the races, to write multiple reports and blog pieces for the organization. The group also continued to circulate racist and anti-Semitic authors to its supporters, and finally, staffer John Miano attended the white nationalist group VDARE's Christmas party in December. (Sherman 2017)

SPLC has stated that CIS also circulates a weekly e-mail listerv with dozens of links to articles about immigration. These e-mails highlight articles

> by "white nationalists" such as Paul Weston, a Holocaust denier, and articles by American Renaissance, run by Jared Taylor, who has made racist statements about blacks. One article entitled "Voting for Hillary equals more Muslim killings of Americans" claimed that Clinton's assistant "works fervently for Sharia law in America" and that Trump would give the United States a chance to "survive this immigration invasion." (Sherman 2017)

In March 2017, CIS executive director Mark Krikorian wrote an op-ed piece in *The Washington Post* in which he complained of the "poison of the blacklist" that accompanies the "hate designation" affixed to CIS by the SPLC (Krikorian 2017). While Krikorian did not articulate exactly what CIS believes, he did state that the organization's views regarding immigration are "held by a large share of the American public" (Letters to the Editor 2017). Heidi Beirich of the SPLC, who wrote the op-ed, retorted, "So? At one time a 'large share' of the American public thought slavery was okay. Today, a large share of Americans believe white people are superior to others and that any religion besides Christianity is evil. Just because a large share of people believe something doesn't make it right or moral" (Letters to the Editor 2017). Beirich concluded that CIS certainly is not an organization that "promotes love and acceptance."

See also: American Renaissance; Brimelow, Peter; Federation for American Immigration Reform; Holocaust Denial; MacDonald, Kevin; Murray, Charles; *Occidental Observer*; Tanton, John; Taylor, Jared; VDARE; White Nationalism

Further Reading

Beirich, Heidi. January 31, 2009. "The Nativist Lobby: Three Faces of Intolerance." *Southern Poverty Law Center—Hatewatch*. https://www.splcenter.org/20090201/nativist-lobby-three-faces-intolerance (Accessed May 22, 2017).

Beirich, Heidi. March 23, 2017. "Hate Groups Like Center for Immigration Studies Want You to Believe They're Mainstream." *Southern Poverty Law Center—Hatewatch*. https://www.splcenter.org/hatewatch/2017/03/23/hate-groups-center-immigration-studies-want-you-believe-they're-mainstream (Accessed May 22, 2017).

Krikorian, Mark. March 17, 2017. "How Labeling My Organization a Hate Group Shuts Down Public Debate." *The Washington Post*. https://www.washingtonpost.com/opinions/how-labeling-my-organization-a-hate-group-shuts-down-public-debate/2017/03/17/656ab9c8-0812-11e7-93dc-00f9bdd74ed1_story.html?utm_term=.8eaa240cb60e (Accessed May 22, 2017).

Letters to the Editor. March 24, 2017. "Does the Center for Immigration Studies Deserve to Be Labeled a 'Hate Group.'" *The Washington Post*. https://www.washingtonpost.com/opinions/does-the-center-for-immigration-studies-deserve-to-be-labeled-a-hate-group/2017/03/24/89ab4cda-0f38-11e7-aa57-2ca1b05c41b8_story.html?utm_term=.1ed5f21cb565 (Accessed May 22, 2017).

Piggott, Stephen. November 7, 2016. "Anti-Immigrant Center for Immigration Studies Continues to Promote White Nationalists." *Southern Poverty Law Center—Hatewatch*. https://www.splcenter.org/hatewatch/2016/11/07/anti-immigrant-center-immigration-studies-continues-promote-white-nationalists (Accessed May 22, 2017).

Right Wing Watch. "Center for Immigration Studies." http://www.rightwingwatch.org/organizations/center-for-immigration-studies/ (Accessed May 22, 2017).

Sherman, Amy. March 22, 2017. "Is the Center for Immigration Studies a Hate Group, as the Southern Poverty Law Center Says?" *PolitiFact.com*. http://www.politifact.com/florida/article/2017/mar/22/center-immigration-studies-hate-group-southern-pov/ (Accessed May 22, 2017).

Southern Poverty Law Center. "John Tanton." https://www.splcenter.org/fighting-hate/extremist-files/individual/john-tanton (Accessed May 22, 2017).

CENTER FOR SECURITY POLICY

The Center for Security Policy (CSP) was founded by Frank Gaffney Jr., a neo-conservative who had served as a government official in the Ronald Reagan administration. The CSP was founded as a think tank, "to identify challenges and opportunities likely to affect American security, broadly defined, and to act promptly and creatively to ensure that they are the subject of focused national examination and effective action" (Center for Security Policy). From its founding through the mid-2000s, CSP was seen as a mainstream, though hawkish, organization that followed the neoconservative ideal of "peace through strength." Like many neoconservative organizations, however, with the end of the Cold War, CSP struggled to justify its existence. Communism had been defeated, and the United States was the lone remaining superpower. With 9/11 and subsequent U.S. wars in Iraq and Afghanistan, CSP was able to shift its focus from fighting communism to fighting Islam. When the anti-Muslim movement ratcheted into high gear in the late 2000s, CSP was ready and had extensive Washington roots to draw upon.

CSP focuses on claims that American Muslims are engaging in a vast conspiracy to overthrow the U.S. government from within. Much of what CSP publicizes is conspiratorial in nature, like the notion that Muslims intend to establish sharia law under the guise of constitutional protections regarding freedom of religion. CSP has called the imposition of sharia law as the "preeminent totalitarian threat of our time: the legal-political-military doctrine known within Islam as shariah" (Southern Poverty Law Center). Much of what CSP publishes intends to show that prominent Muslim organizations in the United States are actually fronts for the Muslim Brotherhood, an organization whose goal is to instill the Quran (holy book of Islam) and Sunnah (teachings and sayings of Muhammad) as the "sole reference point for . . . ordering the life of the Muslim family, individual, community . . . and state" (Kull 2011).

In 2010, CSP produced a report about the Muslim threat in the United States in which it called for a halt to all government outreach–related efforts to Muslim communities, warnings to imams that they would be charged with sedition if they spoke of imposing sharia law in the United States, and the dismantling of so-called "no-go zones," neighborhoods that law enforcement is unable to police because they are so overwhelmingly Muslim. In 2015, Donald Trump, who was then running for president, picked up on this CSP claim and used it in campaign material (Gunter 2015). A prominent member of CSP, retired lieutenant general Jerry Boykin—a former U.S. deputy undersecretary of defense for intelligence under President George W. Bush—stated in 2010 that "[Islam] should not be protected under the First Amendment, particularly given that those following the dictates of the Quran are under an obligation to destroy our Constitution and replace it with sharia law" (Southern Poverty Law Center).

In 2015, CSP devoted itself to creating a climate of fear in the United States around Syrian refugees entering the country. In stoking the anti-immigrant and anti-Muslim fires, CSP's founder, Frank Gaffney, invited Jared Taylor, the white nationalist who founded the virulently racist Web site *American Renaissance*, onto CSP's radio show. During the interview, Gaffney called *American Renaissance* "wonderful" and tried to tie the flow of Syrian refugees into Europe as hastening the "death" of that continent.

CSP teamed up with Donald Trump and Ted Cruz for an anti-Iran rally in Washington, D.C., in September 2015. In December 2015, Donald Trump issued a press release that urged the U.S. government to ban Muslims from entering the United States. Trump cited statistics from a CSP poll that indicated that "25% of those polled agreed that violence against Americans here in the United States is justified as a part of the global jihad." However, as was later noted, the poll was an opt-in online survey that "cannot be considered representative of the intended population, which was, in this case, Muslims" (Southern Poverty Law Center).

See also: American Renaissance; Taylor, Jared; White Nationalism

Further Reading

Center for Security Policy. "About Us." http://www.centerforsecuritypolicy.org/about-us/ (Accessed January 13, 2017).

Gunter, Joel. December 8, 2015. "Trump's 'Muslim Lockdown;' What Is the Center for Security Policy?" *BBC News*. http://www.bbc.com/news/world-us-canada-35037943 (Accessed January 13, 2017).

Kull, Steven. 2011. *Feeling Betrayed: The Roots of Muslim Anger at America*. Brookings Institution Press.

Southern Poverty Law Center. "Center for Security Policy." https://www.splcenter.org/fighting -hate/extremist-files/group/center-security-policy (Accessed January 13, 2017).

CHRISTIAN IDENTITY

Christian Identity is an anti-Semitic and racist pseudotheology that rose in prominence among adherents of the racist right in the 1980s and 1990s. Christian Identity teaches that all nonwhite peoples will eventually be exterminated or compelled to serve the master white race in a heavenly kingdom that will be ruled over by Jesus Christ himself. Christian Identity has spawned some of the most virulently racist extremist groups and individuals in the United States, but its influence has extended to other countries as well (Southern Poverty Law Center, Christian Identity). Christian Identity is estimated to have perhaps as many as 25,000 adherents (Anti-Defamation League).

Christian Identity espouses a white supremacist philosophy, justifying their beliefs on specific interpretations of the Bible and influences from elsewhere. Some adherents of Christian Identity (e.g., Aryan Nations) couple a strongly held anti-government sentiment with their theological beliefs. Christian Identity "theology" consists of several tenets:

1. Adam and Eve were the progenitors of the white race, and all other races are pre-Adamic or beasts that evolved into human form.
2. Contemporary Jews are not the true descendants of the tribe of Judah but are descendants of Esau, Isaac's oldest son, who sold his birthright.
3. There will be an "end times" and the epic battle of Armageddon, which will herald the Second Coming of Jesus Christ.

4. Interracial marriage, homosexuality, and any "deviant" behavior is not of God and is, therefore, beastly and deserving of eradication.
5. There is general suspicion of the federal government and, in particular, anything pertaining to a "new world order." (Balleck)

Christian Identity posits what is known as "two house theology," which is that the ancient kingdom of Israel was split into two houses—Israel and Judah—about 931 BCE. Approximately 722 BCE, most of those living in the northern portion of what had been the Kingdom of Israel were conquered by the Assyrians, taken into captivity, and scattered about. The southern part of the kingdom, including Judah, largely survived to constitute modern-day Jews. However, whereas British Israelism held that Jews were descended from the tribe of Judah, Christian Identity in its American "bastardization" believes that the true descendants of Judah (and Israel) are instead white Europeans. These were members of the original 10 lost tribes, which had been "scattered" but had settled in Scotland, Germany, and other European countries. These "true Israelites" are "Anglo-Saxon, Celtic, Germanic, Nordic, and kindred peoples" (Roberts 2003).

In the theology of Christian Identity, contemporary Jews are the descendants of Esau (son of Isaac), who sold his God-given birthright for a bowl of pottage (Genesis 25: 29–34). Jacob, his younger brother, who would become Israel (and would have 12 sons), thus became the recipient of the promises made to Abraham and his posterity. The "dual seedliner" strain of Christian Identity thought holds that the Jews are actually the spawn of Satan through Adam and Eve's son, Cain. In this belief, Satan seduced Eve, and she gave birth to Cain, while Abel, whom Cain would slay, was the "pure" progeny of Adam and Eve. This line of reasoning was originally fostered by a 1900 book by Charles Carroll entitled *The Negro: A Beast or in the Image of God?* In his treatise, Carroll (1900) concluded that only the white race was the true offspring of Adam and Eve, "while Negros are pre-Adamite beasts and could not possibly have been made in God's image and likeness because they are beastlike, immoral and ugly," that blacks did not have souls, and that the mixing of the races led to the blasphemous ideas of atheism and evolutionism. Variants on these themes have led many Christian Identity adherents to fiercely defend such policies as the separation of the races, while other Christian Identity adherents go so far as to suggest that the mixing of the races is a defilement of the white race and that the penalty for this and other "beastly" behaviors (e.g., homosexuality) should be death (Ago 1995).

In addition to racism, Christian Identity teaches that there will be an end of times and that the biblically foretold battle of Armageddon, in which the forces of good will battle the forces of evil, will be fought. This "end times" scenario makes Christian Identity members very extremist in their interpretation of events. For instance, adherents view the United Nations as an organization controlled by a Jewish-backed conspiracy that aims at overthrowing the United States of America (Kaplan 2002). Jews also play prominently in their control of the world banking system and their control of the "root of all evil" (i.e., paper money). As noted by author James Alfred Ago (1995), "The creation of the Federal Reserve System in 1913 shifted control of money from Congress to private institutions and violated the Constitution. The money system encourages the Federal Reserve to take out loans, creating trillions of dollars of government debt and allowing international bankers to control America." Christian Identity preacher Sheldon Eery similarly claims that "most of the owners of the largest banks in America are of Eastern European (Jewish) ancestry and connected with the (Jewish) Rothschild European banks." Thus, in the doctrine of Christian Identity, "the global banking conspiracy is led and controlled by Jewish interests" (Ago 1995).

A leading figure in the cause of Christian Identity was William Potter Gale (1917–1988), a former aide to General Douglas MacArthur. Gale was an antitax advocate during the 1970s and 1980s and was a leading figure in the paramilitary and militia movements of the same time, including the Posse Comitatus (History Commons). Several past and current patriot/militia groups identify with Christian Identity ideas, including "The Covenant, Sword, and the Arm of the Lord; the Faience Priesthood; the Aryan Republican Army; the Church of Jesus Christ, Christian; Church of Israel; and, Kingdom Identity Ministries" (Southern Poverty Law Center, Christian Identity).

Perhaps the most "successful" of the groups associated with Christian Identity theology is Aryan Nations. Aryan Nations adheres to most of the regular tenets of Christian Identity, but they differ in the zeal with which they profess antigovernment sentiments. The ultimate goal of Aryan Nations is to establish a "whites only homeland in five northwestern states—Oregon, Idaho, Wyoming, Washington, and Montana" (Southern Poverty Law Center, Christian Identity). If relinquished by their governments, these states would become the base of the "white power" movement and would be known as the Northwest Territorial Imperative. The headquarters of Aryan Nations was Hayden Lake, Idaho, from the late 1970s until the early 2000s. The group was founded by Richard Butler, who had been inspired by William Potter Gale's association with the Posse Comitatus movement. Butler was a great admirer of Adolph Hitler and strove to establish a "whites-only homeland in the Pacific Northwest" (Southern Poverty Law Center, Aryan Nations). In 1981, Butler held the first Aryan World Conference at his Hayden Lake compound. These "confabs" would attract

> almost every nationally significant racist leader around. Among them: Tom Metzger, former Klansman and leader of White Aryan Resistance; Louis Beam, another onetime Klansman who promoted the concept of leaderless resistance; Don Black, the former Klansman who created Stormfront, the oldest and largest white nationalist forum on the Web; and Kirk Lyons, a lawyer who has represented several extremists and who was married on the compound by
> Butler. (Southern Poverty Law Center, Aryan Nations)

William Butler died in September 2004, but by this time his legacy had already become bloodied. Butler's most loyal and committed follower was Robert J. "Bob" Mathews, who founded The Order. Mathews and his organization would go on to be dubbed by the Federal Bureau of Investigation one of the most dangerous domestic terror groups in the United States. Today, Christian Identity continues to provide the ideological foundation for dozens of extremist groups.

See also: Aryan Nations; Black, Don; Butler, Richard; Gale, William Potter; Gritz, Bo; Metzger, Tom; Posse Comitatus; *Stormfront*; Wickstrom, James

Further Reading

Ago, James Alfred. 1995. *The Politics of Righteousness: Idaho Christian Patriotism.* University of Washington Press, p. 86.

Anti-Defamation League. "Christian Identity." https://www.adl.org/education/resources /backgrounders/christian-identity (Accessed March 27, 2017).

Balleck, Barry J. 2015. *Allegiance to Liberty: The Changing Face of Patriots, Militias, and Political Violence in America.* Praeger.

Barkun, Michael. 1996. *Religion and the Racist Right: The Origins of the Christian Identity Movement.* University of North Carolina Press.

Carroll, Charles. 1900. *The Negro a Beast . . . or . . . In the Image of God.* American Book and Bible House.

History Commons. "Profile: William Potter Gale." http://www.historycommons.org/entity .jsp?entity=william_potter_gale_1 (Accessed March 27, 2017).

Kaplan, Jeffrey. 2002. *Millennial Violence: Past, Present, and Future.* Routledge, p. 38.

Quarles, Chester L. 2004. *Christian Identity: The Aryan American Bloodline Religion.* McFarland & Company.

Roberts, Charles H. 2003. *Race Over Grace: The Racialist Religion of the Christian Identity Movement.* iUniverse Press, pp. 40–60.

Southern Poverty Law Center. "Aryan Nations." https://www.splcenter.org/fighting-hate /extremist-files/group/aryan-nations (Accessed March 27, 2017).

Southern Poverty Law Center. "Christian Identity." https://www.splcenter.org/fighting-hate /extremist-files/ideology/christian-identity (Accessed March 27, 2017).

COE, BARBARA

Barbara Coe (1933–2013) founded the California Coalition for Immigration Reform (CCIR) in 1994, an organization that became noted for its opposition to Mexican immigration into the United States. After Coe's death in 2013, the CCIR was renamed the National Coalition for Immigration Reform (NCIR). Coe was infamous for her rants against illegal immigration and her racist rhetoric, often calling Mexicans "savages" and "invaders" who were out to reconquer and destroy the United States. Coe also perpetuated myths of a "new world order" that was being forced upon the United States by "globalists" intent on subjugating the country and destroying its independence and freedom. Later in life, Coe admitted to being a member of the Council of Conservative Citizens, a far-right political organization dedicated to white nationalism and white separatism. Coe helped write and push through California's Prop. 187, a piece of legislation that intended to "cut off undocumented immigrants from social services like public school and hospital care" (Southern Poverty Law Center, Barbara Coe). Coe often referred to President Barack Obama as a "lying Muslim."

Coe did not demonstrate her prejudices throughout her life. When she was in her fifties, she became concerned about the number of illegal immigrants that were making their way to California. Coe said that everything changed for her in 1991 when she and an older friend walked into a social services center in Orange County, California: "I walked into this monstrous room full of people, babies and little children all over the place, and I realized nobody was speaking English. . . . I was overwhelmed with this feeling: 'Where am I? What's happened here?'" (Woo 2013).

After her experience, Coe helped craft legislation that would become California Proposition 187 (Prop. 187). Prop. 187 would appear on the November 1994 ballot in California and eventually be passed by California voters, 59 percent to 41 percent. The initiative prohibited those designated as "illegal aliens" from using health care services (except in the case of emergencies), barred them from public education, and blocked their access to other public services in the state of California. The law was challenged in federal court and found to be unconstitutional in 1999. California governor Gray Davis eventually ordered a halt to all state appeals of the ruling, prompting Coe to label Davis a communist and organize efforts to recall him from the governorship (Southern Poverty Law Center).

In 2003, Coe responded to an initiative by immigrant workers, known as the Immigrant Workers Freedom Ride, which sought a path to citizenship for all immigrant workers, by urging members of CCIR "to flood Congress and the White House with calls to arrest the riders" (Southern Poverty Law Center). Coe stated:

These people are criminals. . . . As such, they have NO "RIGHTS" other than emergency medical care and humane treatment as they are being DEPORTED! We can only wonder how many in this group of foreign invaders have robbed, raped and possibly murdered law-abiding American citizens and legal residents [emphasis in original]. (Southern Poverty Law Center, National Coalition)

In May 2005, Coe claimed to have exposed a Mexican plan to reconquer the American Southwest. In 2007, she jumped on the "globalist conspiracy" bandwagon and claimed that illegal immigration was an effort being imposed by the New World Order on the United States. Coe declared that "illegal aliens are the ground troops needed by Bush Jr. [President George W. Bush] and his globalist buddies for the ultimate death of America." She went on to charge that "globalists have a plan to take control of America by encouraging illegal immigration and then exploiting their herd mentality to win elected offices" (Southern Poverty Law Center, Barbara Coe).

Coe died at age 79 on August 31, 2013.

See also: Council of Conservative Citizens

Further Reading

Southern Poverty Law Center. "Barbara Coe." https://www.splcenter.org/fighting-hate/extremist-files/individual/barbara-coe (Accessed January 14, 2017).

Southern Poverty Law Center. "National Coalition for Immigration Reform." https://www.splcenter.org/fighting-hate/extremist-files/group/national-coalition-immigration-reform (Accessed January 14, 2017).

Woo, Elaine. September 4, 2013. "Barbara Coe Dies at 79; Foe of Services for Those in U.S. Illegally." *Los Angeles Times.* http://articles.latimes.com/2013/sep/04/local/la-me-barbara-coe-20130905 (Accessed January 14, 2017).

COLORADO THEATER SHOOTING

The Colorado (Aurora) theater shooting was a mass shooting of theatergoers perpetrated by James Eagan Holmes on July 20, 2012. Holmes killed 12 people in the shooting and injured more than 70 others. The shooting was responsible for the largest number of mass casualties in a nonschool shooting until the Orlando nightclub shooting four years later. Holmes, who had no criminal record prior to the shooting, surrendered to police shortly after the crime. His motivation for the crime, as later learned in court, was to "kill as many people as possible" (La Ganga 2015). This motivation was reinforced when, soon after the shooting, it was learned that Holmes had "booby-trapped his apartment" with explosives, intending to kill law enforcement officers after the fact (Bolton 2015). Holmes pleaded not guilty to the shootings by reason of insanity. In August 2015, Holmes was found guilty and "sentenced to 12 consecutive life sentences, plus 3,318 years without parole" (Healey 2015).

Holmes was born in 1987 in San Diego, California. Prior to the shooting, he had been under psychiatric care and was reported by a University of Colorado psychiatrist to be making "homicidal statements" (Winter 2013). Holmes "was a fan of superheroes, including Batman, and had his apartment decorated with Batman paraphernalia" (Quinones, Murphy, and Mozingo 2012). On July 19, 2012, Holmes attended the midnight premier of *The Dark Knight Rises* at the Century Aurora 16 Multiplex in Aurora, Colorado. He "entered theater #9 but exited soon after through a rear door leading to the parking lot leaving the door propped open" (CNN 2016).

Around 12:30 a.m., Holmes "reentered the theater dressed in black and wearing a gas mask, a load-bearing vest (not to be confused with a bulletproof vest), a ballistic helmet, bullet-resistant leggings, a bullet-resistant throat protector, a groin protector, and tactical gloves" (CNN 2016). Though some believed Holmes to be perpetrating a prank, he threw two tear gas grenades into the audience and then began firing at the stunned patrons. Holmes fired "a 12-gauge Remington 870 Express Tactical shotgun, first at the ceiling and then at the audience. He also fired a Smith & Wesson M&P15 semi-automatic rifle with a 100-round drum magazine, which eventually malfunctioned" (Parker 2012). Finally, Holmes fired a Glock 22 .40 caliber handgun. In a matter of minutes, Holmes fired "76 shots in the theater: six from the shotgun, 65 from the semi-automatic rifle, and five from the .40-caliber handgun" (Tenser 2015).

Holmes was arrested at about 12:45 a.m. in his car, after initially being mistaken for a police officer who was responding to the scene because of the tactical gear he was wearing (Wian, Spellman, and Pearson 2013). Prior to the shooting, he "had dyed his hair red and had referred to himself as 'The Joker'" (Wian, Spellman, and Pearson 2013). When taken into custody, Holmes informed police that his apartment was "booby-trapped." The next day, investigators disarmed all of Holmes' makeshift bombs using "controlled detonation" to disable secondary triggering devices. In all, investigators removed "more than 30 homemade grenades from Holmes' apartment and 10 gallons of gasoline" (CNN 2016).

After pleading not guilty to the shooting by reason of insanity, Holmes was tried in 2015. On July 16, 2015, he was "found guilty of all 165 counts against him, making him eligible for the death penalty" (CNN 2016). Holmes had earlier agreed to plead guilty to all the charges in exchange for a life sentence, but the prosecutor in the case rejected this (CNN 2016). On August 7, 2015, Holmes "was sentenced to life in prison when the jury was unable to reach a unanimous sentencing verdict" as to whether Holmes should receive the death penalty or be incarcerated for the rest of his life (CNN 2016). Later that month, Holmes was sentenced "to 12 life sentences, one life term for each person he killed, plus 3,318 years in prison for the attempted murders of those he wounded and for rigging his apartment with explosives" (CNN 2016).

After the shooting, "the political debate on gun control reignited, with one issue being the easy access" Holmes had to semiautomatic rifles and high-capacity magazines, "which were federally banned from 1994 to 2004" (Jervis and McAuliff 2012). Gun sales in Colorado spiked after the shooting, as did gun sales "in Washington, Florida, California, and Georgia" (New York Post 2012). As has been typical in the aftermath of many mass shootings in the United States, citizens, fearful that the federal government will impose new gun restrictions in the wake of such tragedies, buy guns in greater numbers to "stockpile" weapons against the eventuality. Gun-rights organizations like the National Rifle Association also use such events to warn the government about imposing restrictions on the gun-owing rights of Americans as guaranteed by the Second Amendment. Following the Colorado theater shooting, a survey conducted by the Pew Research Center (2012) "suggested that the shooting did not significantly change Americans' views on the issue of gun control."

After the shooting, more than two dozen lawsuits were filed against the theater's owner, Cinemark. The lawsuits focused mainly on the lack of security at the theater. In May 2016, a jury ruled that "Cinemark was not liable for the shooting and many survivors accepted a small settlement." Four survivors who refused the settlement were ordered by a judge to pay Cinemark $700,000 for legal bills (Fox59 2016).

See also: Orlando Nightclub Shooting; Second Amendment

Further Reading

Bolton, Anastasiya. September 10, 2015. "Inside Colo. Theater Shooter James Holmes' Booby-Trapped Apartment." *USA Today.* https://www.usatoday.com/story/news/nation -now/2015/09/10/james-holmes-aurora-theater-shooting-booby-trapped-apartment /71996544/ (Accessed May 29, 2017).

CNN. July 4, 2016. "Colorado Theater Shooting Fast Facts." http://www.cnn.com /2013/07/19/us/colorado-theater-shooting-fast-facts/ (Accessed May 29, 2017).

Fahrenthold, David A., Thomas Heath, and Joel Achenbach. July 22, 2012. "Aurora, Colo., Shooting Spree: A Day of Tears for Victims and Twists in Case." *The Washington Post.* https://www.washingtonpost.com/national/explosives-removed-from-james-holmess -apartment-and-destroyed-officials-say/2012/07/22/gJQAL9XN2W_story.html?utm _term=.4a4decafe451 (Accessed May 29, 2017).

Fox59. September 1, 2016. "Judge Rules Four Survivors of Colorado Theater Shooting Must Pay Cinemark $700K." http://fox59.com/2016/09/01/judge-rules-four-survivors -of-colorado-theater-shooting-must-pay-cinemark-700k/ (Accessed May 29, 2017).

Frosch, Dan and Kirk Johnson. July 20, 2012. "Gunman Kills 12 in Colorado, Reviving Gun Debate." *The New York Times*. http://www.nytimes.com/2012/07/21/us/shooting -at-colorado-theater-showing-batman-movie.html (Accessed May 29, 2017).

Healey, Jack. August 7, 2015. "Life Sentence for James Holmes, Aurora Theater Gunman." *The New York Times*. https://www.nytimes.com/2015/08/08/us/jury-decides-fate-of -james-holmes-aurora-theater-gunman.html (Accessed May 29, 2017).

Jervis, Rick and John McAuliff. July 25, 2012. "Colo. Rampage Adds Fuel to Gun-Control Debate." *USA Today*. https://usatoday30.usatoday.com/news/nation/story/2012-07-24 /aurora-gun-control-debate/56465980/1 (Accessed May 29, 2017).

La Ganga, Maria L. June 2, 2015. "James Holmes Wanted to Kill 'as Many People as Possible' in Colorado Theater Rampage." *Los Angeles Times*. http://www.latimes.com/nation /la-na-james-holmes-20150602-story.html (Accessed July 25, 2017).

New York Post. July 25, 2012. "Gun Sales Surging in Wake of 'Dark Knight Rises' Shooting." http://nypost.com/2012/07/25/gun-sales-surging-in-wake-of-dark-knight-rises-shooting/ (Accessed May 29, 2017).

Parker, Mike. July 23, 2012. "Rifle Failure That Stopped Yet More Batman Carnage." *Express*. http://www.express.co.uk/news/world/334642/Rifle-failure-that-stopped-yet -more-Batman-carnage (Accessed May 29, 2017).

Pew Research Center. July 30, 2012. "View on Gun Laws Unchanged After Aurora Shooting." http://www.people-press.org/2012/07/30/views-on-gun-laws-unchanged-after-aurora -shooting/ (Accessed May 29, 2017).

Quinones, Sam, Kim Murphy, and Joe Mozingo. July 23, 2012. "Aurora Suspect's Profile Grows Murkier." *Los Angeles Times*. http://articles.latimes.com/2012/jul/23/nation/la -na-colorado-shooting-sider-20120723 (Accessed May 29, 2017).

Tenser, Phil. May 14, 2015. "Aurora Police Testify in James Holmes's Trial: 240 Ballistic Impacts Found After Theater Shooting." *KJRH.com*. http://www.kjrh.com/news /national/aurora-police-testify-in-james-holmes-trial-240-ballistic-impacts-found -after-theater-shooting (Accessed May 29, 2017).

Wian, Casey, Jim Spellman, and Michael Pearson. January 8, 2013. "New Details Emerge in Hearing for Colorado Theater Shooting Suspect." *CNN*. http://www.cnn .com/2013/01/07/justice/colorado-theater-shooting/ (Accessed May 29, 2017).

Winter, Michael. April 4, 2013. "Holmes' Doctor Warned Police Before Colo. Theater Attack." *USA Today*. https://www.usatoday.com/story/news/nation/2013/04/04/colorado -theater-james-holmes-records/2054753/ (Accessed May 29, 2017).

COLUMBINE HIGH SCHOOL SHOOTING

The Columbine High School shooting occurred in Littleton, Colorado, on April 20, 1999. The perpetrators of the attacks, Eric Harris and Dylan Klebold, had planned for nearly a year to firebomb the school and then shoot first responders who arrived at the scene, as well as faculty, staff, and students who survived the blasts (Cullen 2004). In addition to a stockpile of weapons, Harris and Klebold had secured propane tanks and converted them into bombs, placing them in the school cafeteria. They had also constructed several car bombs. In all, Harris and Klebold had prepared 99 explosive devices in an effort to perpetrate an attack that would "dwarf" the Oklahoma City bombing, and they had prepared the attack to coincide with that event's fourth anniversary, though it actually took place one day later (Cullen 2004). When the homemade bombs they previously placed failed to detonate, Harris and Klebold began shooting students outside of the high school, moving in to the school and shooting most of their victims in the school's library. In all, Harris and Klebold massacred 12 students and 1 teacher and injured more than 20. The pair committed suicide before police were able to engage or apprehend them. At the time, the shooting was the deadliest school shooting in American history. It would later be dwarfed in its carnage by the Virginia Tech University shooting as well as the Sandy Hook Elementary School shooting (Shen 2012). The massacre would once again spark debates over gun control laws, but it would also bring to the forefront issues about high school bullying, cliques, and subcultures. The shooting "resulted in an increased emphasis on school security with zero tolerance policies regarding guns, drugs, clothing, and speech" (Cullen 2009).

Eric Harris, 18, and Dylan Klebold, 17, considered themselves outsiders at their school, resenting the cliques of cheerleaders, athletes, and other "cool kids." They were part of what became known at Columbine High School as the "Trench Coat Mafia," a group of goth kids that wore long, black trench coats to school to distinguish themselves from the rest of the groups that naturally formed at any American high school. Harris was described as "the callously brutal mastermind" of the massacre, while Klebold was a "quivering depressive who journaled obsessively about love and attended the Columbine prom three days before opening fire" (Cullen 2010).

Surveillance video captures Eric Harris (left) and Dylan Klebold during their shooting rampage at Columbine High School in Littleton, Colorado, on April 20, 1999. The two students moved throughout the school with various weapons, eventually murdering 12 students and one teacher. The pair took their lives when finally confronted by police. (Jefferson County Sheriff's Department/Getty Images)

The shooters, however, had dreams of immortality. Like Timothy McVeigh, who was famous as the Oklahoma City bomber, Harris and Klebold dreamed of perpetrating an attack far bigger than Oklahoma City. While "school shooters tend to act impulsively and attack the targets of their rage"—students and faculty—for Harris and Klebold,

> the school served as means to a grander end, to terrorize the entire nation by attacking a symbol of American life. Their slaughter was aimed at students and teachers, but it was not motivated by resentment of them in particular. Students and teachers were just convenient quarry, what Timothy McVeigh described as "collateral damage."
>
> The killers, in fact, laughed at petty school shooters. They bragged about dwarfing the carnage of the Oklahoma City bombing and originally scheduled their bloody performance for its anniversary. Klebold boasted on video about inflicting "the most deaths in U.S. history." Columbine was intended not primarily as a shooting at all, but as a bombing on a massive scale. If they hadn't been so bad at wiring the timers, the propane bombs they set in the cafeteria would have wiped out 600 people. After those bombs went off, they planned to gun down fleeing survivors. An explosive third act would follow, when their cars, packed with still more bombs, would rip through still more crowds, presumably of survivors, rescue workers, and reporters. The climax would be captured on live television. It wasn't just "fame" they were after . . . they were gunning for devastating infamy on the historical scale of an Attila the Hun. Their vision was to create a nightmare so devastating and apocalyptic that the entire world would shudder at their power. (Cullen 2004)

Harris and Klebold had arrived at school the morning of April 20, 1999, at around 11:10 a.m. They "walked into the school cafeteria where they placed two duffel bags each containing a 20-pound propane bomb set to explode at 11:17 a.m." (History.com). The two killers "then went back outside to their cars to wait for the bombs to go off. When the bombs failed to detonate, Harris and Klebold began their killing spree" (History.com).

Dressed in trench coats, Harris and Klebold began shooting students at approximately 11:19 a.m. outside the high school before moving inside. The majority of their victims were gunned down in the school library before the two moved to the cafeteria. Roaming up and down the halls looking for victims, and even firing at one of the bombs they had planted in the hopes of detonating it, at approximately 12:08 p.m., both Harris and Klebold killed themselves—"Harris by firing his shotgun through the roof of his mouth and Klebold by shooting himself in the left temple with his TEC-9 semi-automatic handgun" (Anonymous). During the shooting spree, Harris and Klebold "had killed 12 students and one teacher. More than 20 other individuals had been injured" (CNN 2017).

Harris and Klebold "had constructed a total of 99 improvised explosive devices (IEDs) of various shapes and sizes. Additionally, they had sawed the barrels off of their shotguns to make them easier to conceal" (Anonymous). The weapons they used were "Intratec TEC-DC9 assault pistol, Hi-Point 9mm Carbine, Savage 67H pump-action shotgun, and a Savage 311-D 12-gauge shotgun" (Violence Policy Center). Robyn Anderson, a friend of Klebold and Harris, had bought the shotguns and the Hi-Point 9mm Carbine at The Tanner Gun Show in December of 1998 from unlicensed sellers. Because Anderson purchased the guns for someone else, the transition constituted an illegal straw purchase. Klebold and Harris bought the TEC-DC9 from a pizza shop employee named Mark Manes, who knew they were too young to purchase the assault pistol, but nevertheless sold it to them for $500. (Violence Policy Center)

In November 1999, Manes would be sentenced to six years in prison for selling the gun to minors Harris and Klebold (CNN 2017).

The massacre resulted in a call for more gun-control measures, though legislation suggesting that background checks be run at gun shows generated considerable controversy. As expected, the gun lobby expressed concern about the impact of such a restriction on Second Amendment rights (Araya 2000).

Though the initial reports that Harris and Klebold may have perpetrated the attacks because of bullying, depression, and isolation, anger at high school cliques, access to violent video games, or other motivations, Dave Cullen, who wrote a best-selling book about the massacre entitled *Columbine*, suggests that it was, in the end, Harris and Klebold's quest for infamy and their goal of "eclipsing the world's greatest mass murderers" that drove them to perpetrate the massacre (Cullen 2004).

According to Cullen (2009), these were the four most important lessons learned from Columbine:

1. "There isn't a distinct psychological profile of high school killers. Shooters come from all ethnic, economic, and social classes. Most have exhibited some history of violence, though they came from solid, two-parent homes." But shooters did have some things in common: "All were male. Ninety-eight percent had suffered a recent loss or failure. It could be as minor as blowing a test or getting dumped, yet they perceived it as serious. But they didn't lash out in a fit of passion: That notion is another insidious myth. Ninety-three percent planned their attacks in advance."
2. "Leakage. . . . Gunfire in the classroom is the final stage of a long-simmering attack. The Secret Service found that 81 percent of shooters had explicitly revealed their intentions. Most told two people. Some told more. Kids are bad at secrets. The grander the plot, the more likely to sprout leaks."
3. "We need to prepare students and teachers better for an emergency. . . . Harris and Klebold caught their high school unprepared. We're less naive now. Most kids and their teachers are now drilled on lockdowns and evacuations."
4. "A revolution in police response tactics. . . . Cops followed the old book at Columbine: surround the building, set up a perimeter, contain the damage. That approach has been replaced by the 'active shooter protocol.'"

Though there may have been lessons learned at Columbine, it did not prevent school shooting from occurring. In April 2007, the deadliest school shooting in history in the United States occurred at Virginia Tech University in Blacksburg, Virginia. In all, 32 people were killed and more than 17 wounded. At the Sandy Hook Elementary School shooting in December 2012, 26 people were killed, including 20 children. Though these shootings occurred after Columbine, Cullen (2009) believes that the "active shooter protocol" developed in the aftermath of Columbine probably saved dozens of lives at Virginia Tech and elsewhere.

See also: Oklahoma City Bombing; Sandy Hook Elementary School Shooting; Second Amendment; Virginia Tech Shooting

Further Reading

Anonymous. April 20, 1999. "Columbine Shooting Site." http://www.acolumbinesite.com/event/event2.php (Accessed May 29, 2017).

Araya, Alberto. February 16, 2000. "Colorado Kills Gun Laws." *CBS News.* http://www.cbsnews.com/news/colorado-kills-gun-laws/ (Accessed May 29, 2017).

CNN. April 5, 2017. "Columbine High School Shootings Fast Facts." http://www.cnn.com/2013/09/18/us/columbine-high-school-shootings-fast-facts/ (Accessed May 29, 2017).

Cullen, Dave. April 20, 2004. "The Depressive and the Psychopath." *Slate.* http://www.slate.com/articles/news_and_politics/assessment/2004/04/the_depressive_and_the_psychopath.html (Accessed May 29, 2017).

Cullen, Dave. April 29, 2009. "The Four Most Important Lessons of Columbine." *Slate.* http://www.slate.com/articles/news_and_politics/history_lesson/2009/04/the_four_most_important_lessons_of_columbine.html (Accessed May 29, 2017).

Cullen, Dave. 2010. *Columbine.* Twelve Publishers.

History.com. "Columbine High School Shootings." http://www.history.com/topics/columbine-high-school-shootings (Accessed May 29, 2017).

Manson, Marilyn. June 24, 1999. "Columbine: Whose Fault Is It?" *Rolling Stone.* http://www.rollingstone.com/culture/news/columbine-whose-fault-is-it-19990624 (Accessed May 29, 2017).

Shen, Aviva. December 14, 2012. "A Timeline of Mass Shootings in the US Since Columbine." *ThinkProgress.org.* https://thinkprogress.org/a-timeline-of-mass-shootings-in-the-us-since-columbine-f33162dd2ea7 (Accessed May 29, 2017).

Violence Policy Center. "Where'd They Get Their Guns." http://www.vpc.org/studies/wgun990420.htm (Accessed May 29, 2017).

COMMON-LAW COURT MOVEMENT

The common-law court (CLC) movement is an outgrowth of a sentiment among some Americans that the government has become illegitimate and they must create their own political and judicial institutions to promote governance. Such individuals generally proclaim themselves to be sovereign citizens, and they are "determined to wrest control of their lives back from all forms of government or authority" (National Center for State Courts 1999). The first examples of common-law courts originally arose in rural areas in Texas and Florida in the 1970s, but the notion of common-law courts soon "spread to Kansas and other farm states in the 1980s and then quickly moved across the nation" (National Center for State Courts). The common-law court movement now "exists in some form in every state in the country. In some states, activity is minimal; in others, common law courts are a serious nuisance; in some, they have become a plague on the judicial system" (National Center for State Courts 1999).

In 1997, "27 judges, court clerks, court administrators, and prosecutors met in Scottsdale, Arizona" to more closely examine the so-called common-law court movement. The goal of this group was to "make recommendations for establishing a curriculum for judicial educators to train judges and court officials on how to deal with CLC activities in their own jurisdictions" (National Center for State Courts). The result of their efforts was the publication of the *Anti-Government Guidebook*. The preface of the guidebook states that the CLC movement was an outgrowth of a phenomenon that had been growing in the United States over the course of three decades:

> There is a movement afoot in this country today that is made up of disaffected and often dispossessed Americans who are seeking a better way through a wholesale *return to their view of the past* [emphasis added]. This movement has been called many things: the anti-government movement, the sovereignty movement, and the common law courts movement. Regardless of the name attached to the beliefs and the people who follow them, one common denominator exists: a *feeling of despair* [emphasis added], rooted in personal and pecuniary loss, and manifested in a new, defiant mistrust and spite for the ways of the current government. This guide focuses on the ways in which followers of these movements impact the operation of our state court systems. . . .
>
> The people who make up the movements that we are concerned with consistently speak out to say that our government today does not listen, it no longer serves the American people, it exists to serve its own ends. The merits of that argument are not within the purview of this guide. . . . [But] while we do not advocate an ultra-sympathetic response at the expense of safety and the efficient operation of the courts, we do implore those charged with running our court system to do two things: learn the history behind the beliefs we are seeing spread across our land, and understand that these are not militia members or "Patriots" or "ultra-conservatives," but rather citizens who come before you seeking the same fair treatment that those without any label attached receive. (National Center for State Courts)

Common-law courts are used by self-proclaimed patriots and other individuals who have become disenchanted with the current political and legal system of the United States. Such individuals generally consider themselves sovereign citizens, meaning that they are answerable to no one but themselves. Common-law courts, therefore, are set up among such individuals and groups, though they have absolutely no legal authority. They do, however, satisfy a visceral need on the part of many recalcitrant and dispossessed individuals who long for the justice they feel has been denied to them by the government-sanctioned judicial system. Such self-styled courts demonstrate the willingness of their members "not only to oppose local or federal government, but to go so far as to set up parallel governments of their own" (Pitcavage 1997). In the 1980s, this resulted in the establishment of so-called "townships," where patriots and others would establish a local government and court system outside the established norms of local, state, and federal law. The desire in these townships was that the individuals could live free from the constraints that were imposed by existing government structures.

For many adherents of the CLC movement, there is a very real belief that "common law," the judicial system set up by the Founding Fathers,

> was secretly replaced by a new government system based on admiralty law, the law of the sea and international commerce. Under common law, or so they believe, the sovereigns would be free men. Under admiralty law, they are slaves, and secret government forces have a vested interest in keeping them that way. Some sovereigns believe this perfidious change occurred during the Civil War, while others blame the events of 1933, when the U.S. abandoned the gold standard. Either way, they stake their lives and livelihoods on the idea that judges around the country know all about this hidden government takeover but are denying the sovereigns' motions and filings out of treasonous loyalty to hidden and malevolent government forces. (Southern Poverty Law Center)

Common-law courts are often used today to "convict" government officials in absentia, often "sentencing" them to death for treasons that they have committed against the people. When sovereign citizens do use the legitimate courts, they often clog up the judicial system by filing false liens, false claims of tax evasion, and nuisance lawsuits. County clerks, police, and judges must deal with them and their disdain for the established political order.

See also: Monkeywrenching; Paper Terrorism; Posse Comitatus; Sovereign Citizens Movement

Further Reading

Hollow Earth Network. "Common Law Courts at Work." http://www.hollowearthnetwork.com/page/488075584 (Accessed December 14, 2016).

Levin, Daniel Lessard and Michael W. Mitchell. 1999. "A Law Unto Themselves: The Ideology of the Common Law Court Movement." *South Dakota Law Review. 44 S.D. L Rev. 9.*

National Center for State Courts. 1999. "Anti-Government Movement Guidebook." http://www.tulanelink.com/pdf/anti-gov_movement_guidebook.pdf (Accessed December 14, 2016).

Pitcavage, Mark. July 25, 1997. "Common Law and Uncommon Courts: An Overview of the Common Law Court Movement." *Anti-Defamation League: The Militia Watchdog.* http://archive.adl.org/mwd/common.html (Accessed December 14, 2016).

Southern Poverty Law Center. "Sovereign Citizens Movement." https://www.splcenter.org/fighting-hate/extremist-files/ideology/sovereign-citizens-movement (Accessed December 14, 2016).

CONSTITUTIONAL TOWNSHIP OF TIGERTON DELLS

In 1982, after losing an election for local office, James Wickstrom established the Constitutional Township of Tigerton Dells on the banks of the Embarrass River in eastern Wisconsin. Wickstrom established himself as clerk and municipal judge of the township and began taking applications for liquor and cigarette licenses for the township's businesses. Wickstrom believed he was acting as a sovereign citizen and that it was his inherent right to establish a town based on his status as an American citizen. As an advocate of Posse Comitatus, Wickstrom believed that Tigerton Dells did not have to be sanctioned by the state or the federal government. Rather, as a sovereign citizen, Wickstrom could establish a sanctuary away from government influence. Indeed, Tigerton Dells was envisioned to be a "paramilitary settlement for white supremacists, a haven from governmental regulations and taxes" (Imrie 1990).

Wickstrom and others vowed that there was an inevitable confrontation between themselves and the federal government in the offing. At the time, farmers were losing their livelihoods to banks, and the federal government was increasingly imposing stringent land-use and environmental standards. The "citizens" of Tigerton Dells trained with guns, built underground shelters, and prepared themselves for a showdown with the federal government (Imrie 1990). Wickstrom threatened local officials with violent action if they did not recognize his legal right to establish the Constitutional Township of Tigerton Dells. In response, the state of Wisconsin arrested him for "assuming to act as [a] public officer" (*Wickstrom v. Schardt*). During his trial, Wickstrom stated his intentions to establish similar townships in other states and issued a "subpoena" to the presiding judge in his trial to appear before a "citizens grand jury" (*Wickstrom v. Schardt*). Wickstrom was eventually found guilty and served 13 months in prison. Upon his release, he left Wisconsin and moved to Pennsylvania.

In 1985, the Constitutional Township of Tigerton Dells ceased to exist when government officials moved in on the compound and removed several mobile homes that had been placed on the land in violation of county zoning laws. Though Tigerton Dells was gone, the sentiment behind its establishment continued to linger in Posse Comitatus circles and was inspiration for succeeding patriot and militia groups that would be established throughout the 1980s, 1990s, and 2000s.

See also: Christian Identity; Posse Comitatus; Sovereign Citizens Movement; Wickstrom, James

Further Reading

Imrie, Robert. September 23, 1990. "With Leaders in Jail, Posse Comitatus' Fate Is Uncertain." *Los Angeles Times*. http://articles.latimes.com/1990-09-23/news/mn -1546-1-posse-leaders-comitatus (Accessed December 13, 2016).

Southern Poverty Law Center. "James Wickstrom." https://www.splcenter.org/fighting -hate/extremist-files/individual/james-wickstrom (Accessed December 13, 2016).

Wickstrom v. Schardt. 798 F.2d 268; No. 85-3224, United States Court of Appeals, Seventh Circuit. Submitted July 8, 1986; Decided August 19, 1986.

COUNCIL OF CONSERVATIVE CITIZENS

The Council of Conservative Citizens (CCC) is an organization that "opposes all efforts to mix the races" and publicly supports causes related to white nationalism, white supremacism, and white separatism. The political and ideological roots of the CCC lay in the original Citizens' Councils of America (CCA, originally configured as White Citizens' Councils) "which was an overtly racist organization formed in the 1950s in opposition to the U.S. Supreme Court's decision in *Brown v. Board of Education* that outlawed public school segregation" (Southern Poverty Law Center). The CCA celebrated the "Southern way of life," and the group "used a traditionalist rhetoric that appealed to better-mannered, more discreet racists; while the Klan burned crosses, the CCA relied on political and economic pressure" (Anti-Defamation League). By the 1970s, when the CCA had lost the cultural struggle of segregation, the group faded from public view, though many former members retained their racist views—a fact that would lead to the group's rebirth in the 1980s and its influence into the 21st century.

Rising from the ashes of the CCA, the CCC was founded in 1985 by Gordon Baum, a former CCA field organizer in the Midwest. Baum and 29 others gathered in Atlanta, Georgia, over their collective frustration with government "giveaway programs, special preferences and quotas, crack-related crime and single mothers and third generation welfare mothers dependent on government checks and food stamps" (Anti-Defamation League). Using old CCA mailing lists, the CCC was established with Baum appointed as the chief executive of the new organization. The group rapidly gained members, and by 1999, the CCC had 15,000 members in more than 20 states, with the majority of adherents located in just three states—Mississippi, Alabama, and Georgia (Anti-Defamation League).

The beliefs of the CCC reflected those of the CCA, but the CCC played on the collective fears of its new membership by focusing on issues like "interracial marriage, black-on-white violence, and the demise of white Southern pride and culture—best exemplified by the debate over the display of the Confederate battle flag" (Anti-Defamation League). In addition, the CCC picked up on themes of antigovernment distrust with its inflammatory rhetoric regarding the New World Order and its contention that states' rights were being subverted by the federal government. By illuminating these issues, the CCC found many sympathizers among those in the patriot and militia movements, who expressed the same angst about the power of the federal government.

The CCC first gained national notoriety in 1998 when a scandal erupted after it became public knowledge that several prominent Southern politicians had intimate ties with the group. In 1998, Bob Barr (R-GA), a former member of Congress, gave the keynote address at the CCC's national convention. It was later revealed "that then-Senate majority leader Trent Lott (R-MS) had spoken to the group five times" (Southern Poverty Law Center). Both Barr and Lott claimed ignorance of the CCC's racist agenda, "though an *Intelligence Report* published by the Southern Poverty Law Center (SPLC), and publicized by national television and newspaper reports," definitely demonstrated that the CCC was, in fact, a hate group

> that routinely denigrated blacks as "genetically inferior," complained about "Jewish power brokers," called LGBT people "perverted sodomites," accused immigrants of turning America into a "slimy brown mass of glop," and named Lester Maddox, the now-deceased, ax handle-wielding, arch-segregationist former governor of Georgia, "Patriot of the Century." (Southern Poverty Law Center)

However, Barr and Lott were only the most visible supporters of the CCC. After the SPLC's report, it became public knowledge that the former governors of both

Mississippi and Alabama had ties to the group, as well as 34 members of the Mississippi state legislature (Anti-Defamation League). Also in Mississippi, "all five members of the Lamar County Supervisors Board attended a meeting of the CCC in which the ongoing battle to save our beloved state flag" was discussed (the Mississippi flag displays the Confederate battle flag as part of its design) (Anti-Defamation League). Other prominent state and national figures included former politicians from Tennessee, South Carolina, and Arkansas.

In January 1999, a resolution was introduced into Congress "that condemned the racism and bigotry espoused by the Council of Conservative Citizens" (Anti-Defamation League). The resolution was modeled after a 1994 House resolution that had passed criticizing former Nation of Islam member Khalid Muhammad "for racist and anti-Semitic remarks, while also condemning any manifestations or expressions of racial and religious intolerance, wherever they were found." But whereas the resolution against Muhammad passed through both houses of Congress in 20 days, "the criticism of the CCC never even made it to the floor, due largely to the reluctance of Republicans to accept what amounted to an indirect censure of their leadership" (Anti-Defamation League).

The public exposure of politicians and their connections to the CCC did not end with the revelations of 1998. In 2004, an *Intelligence Report* published by the SPLC noted that no fewer than 38 Southern politicians from the "federal, state, and local areas of government had attended CCC events between 2000 and 2004, most of them giving speeches to local chapters of the organization" (Southern Poverty Law Center). *Right Wing Watch* also reported that "a number of figures on the religious right have spoken before CCC conventions or defended them in the press," a signal of "uneasy and often hidden alliances between the Religious Right and racist groups" (Right Wing Watch). Among those singled out by *Right Wing Watch* were Mike Huckabee, former governor of Arkansas; Tony Perkins, president of the Family Research Council; Roy Moore, the Alabama chief justice who defied federal orders to remove a monument to the Ten Commandments; John Eidsmoe, "the intellectual godfather of a strain of Christian nationalism that takes to an extreme the idea that 'God's law' must always be put before 'man's law;'" and Ann Coulter, the anti-immigrant pundit for *Fox News* (Right Wing Watch).

The danger of "race mixing" continues to be a major theme for the CCC. On the CCC's Web site in 2001, a story appeared that declared, "God is the author of racism. God is the One who divided mankind into different types. . . . Mixing the races is rebelliousness against God" (Southern Poverty Law Center). The CCC's publication, the *Citizens Informer*, has also "published numerous stories detailing scientific evidence for the superiority of whites over any other race" (Counter Extremism Project). In a 2004 article that discussed how striking down public school segregation still left the United States "short of racial equality," a *Citizens Informer* contributor stated that the lack of progress "should surprise no one, because racial inequality is genetic and cannot be changed by social programs. . . . Blacks are on average probably less intelligent than Whites and more aggressive, impulsive and prone to psychopathologies" (Southern Poverty Law Center). To emphasize this point, another article in the *Citizens Informer* in the aftermath of Hurricane Katrina described "accounts of little children—girls and boys—being gang raped, rescue vans and copters being repeatedly fired upon by mobs of violent blacks, anarchy, chaos, confusion, looting even by black police officers" (Southern Poverty Law Center).

As illegal immigration came to the forefront in American politics, the CCC was there to prime the pump of hysteria regarding the issue. The CCC has prominently supported the rhetoric of "major nativist group leaders," such as Barbara Coe and Glenn Spencer, "both of whom worked to pass the anti-immigration California Proposition 187" (Southern Poverty Law Center). The CCC has also invited prominent racist leaders, including Jared Taylor and Don Black, to its annual conferences. Both Taylor and Black are leaders in white supremacist communities.

Longtime leader Gordon Baum died in March 2015, just prior to the CCC bursting on the national scene once more when Dylann Roof, a 21-year-old white supremacist, entered the historic Emanuel African American Episcopal Church in downtown Charleston, South Carolina, and shot 12 parishioners, killing 9. After the massacre, it was discovered that he had been inspired by the CCC's messages of "black-on-white" crime:

> The event that truly awakened me was the Trayvon Martin case. I kept hearing and seeing his name, and eventually I decided to look him up. I read the Wikipedia article and right away I was unable to understand what the big deal was. It was obvious that Zimmerman was in the right. But more importantly this prompted me to type in the words "black on White crime" into Google, and I have never been the same since that day. The first website I came to was the Council of Conservative Citizens. There were pages upon pages of these brutal black on White murders. I was in disbelief. At this moment I realized that something was very wrong. How could the news be blowing up the Trayvon Martin case while hundreds of these black on White murders got ignored? (NPR 2017)

In the aftermath of Roof's revelations about the CCC's influence on him, the CCC issued a statement defending Roof, stating that he had "legitimate grievances." In the statement, the CCC "condemned Roof's murderous actions" but warned that

> our society's silence about [such] crimes—despite enormous amounts of attention to "racially tinged" acts by whites—only increase the anger of people like Dylann Roof. This double standard *only makes acts of murderous frustration more likely* [emphasis by the council]. In his manifesto, Roof outlines other grievances felt by many whites. Again, we utterly condemn Roof's despicable killings, but they do not detract in the slightest from the legitimacy of some of the positions he has expressed. (Gross 2015)

As the investigation into the Charleston shooting progressed, Roof was found to have photographed himself several times with the Confederate battle flag and many other white supremacist symbols. Later investigations continually linked Roof with the CCC. Attempting to portray the organization as a mainstream political group, the CCC's president, Earl Holt III, pointed out that he had donated money to the campaigns of several GOP politicians, including Ted Cruz, Rick Santorum, Mitt Romney, and Rand Paul. Because of the embarrassment of being linked with a notorious hate group that had inspired Roof's rampage, a spokesperson for Ted Cruz's presidential campaign later reported that it had returned the CCC's money (Gross 2015).

See also: Baum, Gordon; Black, Don; Coe, Barbara; Militia Movement; Patriot Movement, Roof, Dylann Storm; Spencer, Glenn; Taylor, Jared; White National-ism; White Supremacist Movement

Further Reading

Anti-Defamation League. "Council of Conservative Citizens." https://www.adl.org/sites /default/files/documents/assets/pdf/combating-hate/Council-of-Conservative-Citizens -Extremism-in-America.pdf (Accessed May 27, 2017).

Blue, Miranda. June 24, 2015. "The Religious Right's Council of Conservative Citizens Connection." *Right Wing Watch.* http://www.rightwingwatch.org/post/the-religious -rights-council-of-conservative-citizens-connection/ (Accessed May 27, 2017).

Counter Extremism Project. "Council of Conservative Citizens." https://www.counterex tremism.com/threat/council-conservative-citizens (Accessed May 27, 2017).

Graham, David A. June 22, 2015. "The White Supremacist Group that Inspired a Racist Manifesto." *The Atlantic.* https://www.theatlantic.com/politics/archive/2015/06/council -of-conservative-citizens-dylann-roof/396467/ (Accessed May 27, 2017).

Gross, Allie. June 21, 2015. "White Nationalists Group Defends Dylann Roof's 'Legitimate Grievances.'" *Mother Jones.* http://www.motherjones.com/politics/2015/06/council -conservative-citizens-dylann-roof (Accessed May 27, 2017).

NPR. January 10, 2017. "What Happened When Dylann Roof Asked Google for Information About Race?" http://www.npr.org/sections/thetwo-way/2017/01/10/508363607/what -happened-when-dylann-roof-asked-google-for-information-about-race (Accessed May 27, 2017).

Southern Poverty Law Center. "Council of Conservative Citizens." https://www.splcenter .org/fighting-hate/extremist-files/group/council-conservative-citizens (Accessed May 27, 2017).

THE COVENANT, THE SWORD, AND THE ARM OF THE LORD

The Covenant, the Sword, and the Arm of the Lord (CSA) was a white supremacist paramilitary group based in Arkansas in the late 1970s and 1980s. CSA became associated with a number of high-profile crimes and suspected terror plots, includ-ing a plot to bomb the Alfred P. Murrah Federal Building in Oklahoma City, Okla-homa. The group dissolved after federal agents besieged its compound for four days in 1985 (Egan 2016).

The CSA was founded by Texas minister James Ellison near Elijah, Missouri, in 1970. In 1976, Ellison purchased 220 acres in Marion County, Arkansas, and established an organization that he called Zarephath-Horeb. According to the *Encyclopedia of Arkansas History and Culture,*

The CSA was true to its ideological rhetoric when selecting the name of their com-pound: Mount Horeb was the mountain to which Moses moved the Hebrews during the Exodus from Egypt, and Zarephath is listed in the Bible as the city to which God ordered Elijah to move in order to undergo a crucible for his faith. This isolated portion of the state was suitable for Ellison's intentions because it is demographically concentrated with a predominantly white population, is secluded in rural terrain that makes monitoring by law enforcement agencies difficult, and is positioned on the border between two states, complicating jurisdictional responsibilities.

Until 1979, racism was not a major tenet of CSA's ideology. However, in that year Ellison adopted the beliefs of Christian Identity, a white supremacist ideology that espouses that the white race is God's chosen people and that Jews are the offspring of a union between Eve and Satan. Under Ellison, CSA became an organization that believed that doomsday was inevitable and that an armed confrontation between the forces of good (CSA) and evil (the federal government) would soon come to pass. Members of CSA believed that the government of the United States was under the control of Jewish interests intent on controlling the world, known as the Zionist Occupation Government. As such, Ellison "intensified paramilitary training at his compound and changed the name of the group to the Covenant, the Sword, and the Arm of the Lord (CSA) to reflect the group's new militant outlook" (Encyclopedia of Arkansas History & Culture). Ellison explained that CSA was establishing an "Ark for God's people" for the coming race war (Encyclopedia of Arkansas History & Culture). As CSA gained prominence, "members of other white supremacist groups, including Aryan Nations and The Order, began to visit CSA's compound to engage in paramilitary training" (Egan 2016).

CSA began to construct terror plots after the death of Gordon Kahl, "a white supremacist who had killed two U.S. marshals and was later killed in a federal raid, making him a martyr for the extreme right" (Egan 2016). CSA members had plans to "assassinate government officials that had prosecuted Kahl before his death, including a judge, an FBI agent, and a U.S. attorney" (Egan 2016). The planned assassinations never occurred, though a CSA member, Richard Snell, did mistakenly kill an individual he believed to be a Jew as well as an African American state trooper.

Beginning on April 19, 1985, more than 300 federal agents from the Federal Bureau of Investigation and the Bureau of Alcohol, Tobacco, and Firearms, as well as state and local law enforcement officials, surrounded the Zarephath-Horeb compound. After a four-day standoff, "law enforcement officials entered the compound, without shots being fired, and seized weapons, ammunition, explosives, gold, and thirty gallons of potassium cyanide," which was intended to poison the water supply of several major cities "in an effort to expedite the Second Coming of the Messiah" (Encyclopedia of Arkansas History & Culture). James Ellison, along with other key members of the CSA, were indicted on charges of "conspiring to overthrow the U.S. government" (Encyclopedia of Arkansas History & Culture). Neither Ellison nor any of his compatriots were convicted on this charge, but they were convicted on various weapons charges as well as for violations related to the Racketeer Influence and Corrupt Organizations statute. Ellison faced a maximum sentence of 20 years in prison, but he was released after agreeing to testify against senior members of the Aryan Nations (Encyclopedia of Arkansas History &

Culture). After his release, the CSA disbanded, and Ellison moved to Elohim City ("City of God"), Oklahoma, where founder Robert Millar had established a community that had rejected mainstream American life (Southern Poverty Law Center). Several years after the dissolution of the CSA, it was revealed that members of the group may have plotted to blow up the Alfred P. Murrah Federal Building in Oklahoma City, Oklahoma, in 1983 (Thomas 1995).

See also: Aryan Nations; Christian Identity; Kahl, Gordon; Oklahoma City Bombing; Order, The; White Supremacist Movement

Further Reading

Egan, Nancy. May 29, 2016. "The Covenant, the Sword, and the Arm of the Lord." *Encyclopedia Britannica.* https://www.britannica.com/topic/The-Covenant-the-Sword-and-the-Arm-of-the-Lord (Accessed March 14, 2017).

Encyclopedia of Arkansas History and Culture. "Covenant, the Sword and the Arm of the Lord." http://www.encyclopediaofarkansas.net/encyclopedia/entry-detail.aspx?entryID=4031 (Accessed March 14, 2017).

History Commons. "Profile: Covenant, Sword, and Arm of the Lord (CSA)." http://www.historycommons.org/entity.jsp?entity=covenant_sword_and_arm_of_the_Lord_1 (Accessed March 14, 2017).

Southern Poverty Law Center. August 29, 2001. "Changing of the Guard." *Southern Poverty Law Center—Intelligence Report.* https://www.splcenter.org/fighting-hate/intelligence-report/2001/changing-guard (Accessed March 14, 2017).

Thomas, Jo. May 20, 1995. "Oklahoma City Building Was Target of Plot as Early as '83, Official Says." *The New York Times.* http://www.nytimes.com/1995/05/20/us/oklahoma-city-building-was-target-of-plot-as-early-as-83-official-says.html?pagewanted=all&src=pm (Accessed March 14, 2017).

CREATIVITY MOVEMENT

The Creativity Movement is a white separatist religious movement that was founded in 1973 by Ben Klassen, a virulent racist, as the Church of the Creator (COTC). Adherents of the Creativity Movement believe that "race, not religion, is the embodiment of absolute truth and that the white race is the highest expression of culture and civilization" (Southern Poverty Law Center). COTC adherents believe that "Jews and non-whites" are "mud races" who "conspire to subjugate whites and destroy their culture and civilization" (Southern Poverty Law Center).

Creators, as members of the Creativity Movement have sometimes called themselves, advocate RAHOWA, or "racial holy war," and some have "been arrested and imprisoned for violent, race-based crimes" (Southern Poverty Law Center). After Klassen's death in 1993, Matt Hale took over the group and changed its name to the World Church of the Creator (WCOTC) and declared himself to be the Pontifex Maximus, or "great high priest." Under Hale's leadership, the WCOTC attracted hard-core neo-Nazis and racist skinheads and grew from 14 chapters in 1996 to 88 by 2002 (Southern Poverty Law Center). After soliciting an undercover federal agent to kill a federal judge in 2004, Hale was convicted and sentenced to a

40-year federal prison sentence. As a result of Hale's conviction, membership in the WCTOC fell from 88 chapters to just 5. Though attempts were made to revive the organization, they were never able to replicate the success that had been achieved under Hale.

Members of the Creativity Movement "do not believe in God, heaven, hell or eternal life" (Southern Poverty Law Center). To "creators," "race is everything: the white race is 'nature's highest creation,' 'white people are the creators of all worthwhile culture and civilization,' 'every issue, whether religious, political or racial . . . [should be] viewed through the eyes of the White Man and exclusively from the point of view of the White race as a whole'" (Anti-Defamation League). Ultimately, the Creativity Movement hopes to organize white people to achieve world domination, "free from alien control and free from pollution of alien races. . . . Only on the basis of recognizing our enemies, destroying and/or excluding them and practicing racial teamwork can a stable lasting government be built" (Anti-Defamation League).

While still under the control of Klassen, Creativity "reverend" George Loeb "was convicted of the racially-motivated killing of a black sailor and Gulf War veteran—Harold Mansfield" (Southern Poverty Law Center). In 1993, "eight individuals with ties to the COTC were arrested for plotting to bomb a black church in Los Angeles, California as well as assassinate Rodney King, whose videotaped beating by L.A. police officers in 1991 had sparked the L.A. riots in 1992" (Southern Poverty Law Center).

In anticipation of a civil rights lawsuit being brought by the Southern Poverty Law Center (SPLC) against COTC for the Mansfield murder, Klassen sold most of the assets associated with COTC to the neo-Nazi National Alliance, headed by William Pierce. After selling his assets, Klassen committed suicide. The SPLC did bring a lawsuit against the COTC on behalf of Mansfield, but Klassen's successor failed to defend the COTC against the charges, resulting in a default judgment of $1 million. The assets sold to the National Alliance had been resold by Pierce at a profit of $85,000. The SPLC later sued Pierce "for engaging in a scheme to defraud Mansfield's estate and Pierce was forced to give up the profit he had made on the resale of Klassen's assets" (Southern Poverty Law Center).

In 1995, Matt Hale joined COTC; he seized control of the organization in 1996, renaming it from the Church of the Creator to the World Church of the Creator (WCOTC). Hale dubbed himself Pontifex Maximus ("great high priest") and began recruiting avowed neo-Nazis and racist skinheads into the organization. Under Hale's leadership, WCOTC grew rapidly and boasted 88 chapters in 2002, "making it the largest neo-Nazi organization in the United States at the time" (Southern Poverty Law Center).

In 1999, WCOTC came into the national spotlight when "creator" Ben Smith went on a three-day rampage in Illinois and Indiana that left two nonwhites dead and nine wounded. Smith had undertaken the killing spree "after the Illinois Bar Association had refused to grant Hale a law license" (Southern Poverty Law Center). In the fall of 2002, another of Hale's followers was convicted of a plot that targeted the destruction of landmarks on the east coast of the United States (Southern Poverty Law Center).

Hale's downfall began when the "TE-TA-MA Truth Foundation, a peace-loving multicultural church in Oregon sued WCOTC over the name 'Church of the Creator'" (Southern Poverty Law Center). In 1987, the foundation had copyrighted the name with the U.S. Patent and Trademark Office. After the violence associated with WCOTC hit national headlines, the Truth Foundation sued WCOTC for copyright infringement, demanding that the racist and neo-Nazi organization cease using the copyrighted name. Hale initially won the suit when a U.S. district court judge ruled in his favor. However, an appeals court reversed the decision and sent the case back to the district judge, Joan Humphrey Lefkow, for reconsideration. Abiding by the appeals court decision, "Lefkow ruled against Hale and ordered WCOTC to give up all use of the 'Church of the Creator' name" (Southern Poverty Law Center).

Outraged by the ruling, Hale attempted to solicit the murder of Judge Lefkow, confiding his plan to an individual who turned out to be an undercover federal agent. In 2004, "Hale was found guilty of one count of solicitation of murder and three counts of obstruction of justice" (Southern Poverty Law Center). A year later, he was sentenced to a federal prison for the maximum sentence allowed: 40 years (Southern Poverty Law Center). In Hale's absence, WCOTC collapsed, losing nearly 90 percent of its membership, and, because of the copyright suit, the group was forced to change its name to the Creativity Movement.

After Hale's departure, the Creativity Movement was racked with schisms, defections, and the lack of a centralized leadership to provide meaningful direction. In 2011, the Creativity Movement showed signs of life when Allen Goff, an 18-year-old neo-Nazi from Montana with a criminal record, began to attract new followers to the movement. The resurgence coincided with other white supremacist and neo-Nazi activity in Montana at the time (Keller 2011). In 2017, the FBI arrested a Georgia man with ties to the Creativity Movement after he sought medical attention for exposure to the deadly poison ricin. The FBI launched a formal investigation into the matter after finding that the individual's car tested positive for ricin (Morlin 2017).

See also: Hale, Matt; National Alliance; Neo-Nazis; Pierce, William; White Nationalism; White Supremacist Movement

Further Reading

Anti-Defamation League. "Creativity Movement (Formerly World Church of the Creator)." https://www.adl.org/education/resources/profiles/creativity-movement (Accessed May 22, 2017).

Keller, Larry. February 27, 2011. "Neo-Nazi Creativity Movement Is Back." *Southern Poverty Law Center—Intelligence Report.* https://www.splcenter.org/fighting-hate/intelligence-report/2015/neo-nazi-creativity-movement-back (Accessed May 22, 2017).

Morlin, Bill. February 9, 2017. "FBI Investigates White Supremacist for Deadly Poison." *Southern Poverty Law Center—Hatewatch.* https://www.splcenter.org/hatewatch/2017/02/09/fbi-investigates-white-supremacist-deadly-poison (Accessed May 22, 2017).

Southern Poverty Law Center. "Creativity Movement." https://www.splcenter.org/fighting-hate/extremist-files/group/creativity-movement-0 (Accessed May 22, 2017).

CYBERHATE

Cyberhate is hatred that is expressed by means of computer networks. It has been defined as

> Any use of electronic communications technology that attacks people based on their actual or perceived race, ethnicity, national origin, religion, sex, gender, sexual orientation, disability or disease to spread bigoted or hateful messages or information. These electronic communications technologies include the Internet (i.e., websites, social networking sites, user-generated content, dating sites, blogs, online games, instant messages and email) as well as other information technologies. (Anti-Defamation League-2)

Since the advent of the Internet and home computers, it has become an axiom that "the internet is the greatest thing to ever happen to hate" (Southern Poverty Law Center). Today, sites like *American Renaissance*, *InfoWars*, and *Stormfront* post vitriolic hate pieces about minorities, LGBT people, immigrants, government policies, and politicians. Sites such as these also create, nurture, and disseminate conspiracy theories that perpetrate stereotypes, create misperceptions, and foster hatred against individuals, groups, and entire nations.

Although cyberhate has been recognized as an undeniable by-product of the Internet since the early 1990s, cyberbullying is a more recent phenomenon that has invaded social media networks and has been a major factor in teenage suicides (Cyber Bully Hotline). In the modern technological age, people's fears, prejudices, and expressions of hate have found a voice on the Internet, and individuals are much more likely to express their feelings in virtually anonymous cyberspace. Some organizations, like the Anti-Defamation League (ADL), are attempting to respond to cyberhate with practical solutions and measures that can be implemented by individuals, families, communities, and even states (Anti-Defamation League-3). The ADL also publishes the "Cyber-Safety Action Guide," which outlines the policies of various online companies regarding hate speech or cyberbullying and/or harassment (Anti-Defamation League-4).

As noted by the ADL,

> The Internet is the largest marketplace of ideas the world has ever known. It enables communications, education, entertainment and commerce on an incredible scale. The Internet has helped to empower the powerless, reunite the separated, connect the isolated and provide new lifelines for the disabled. By facilitating communication around the globe, the Internet has been a transformative tool for information-sharing, education, human interaction and social change. We treasure the freedom of expression that lies at its very core.
>
> Unfortunately, while the Internet's capacity to improve the world is boundless, it also is used by some to transmit anti-Semitism, anti-Muslim bigotry, racism, homophobia, misogyny, xenophobia and other forms of hate, prejudice and bigotry. This hate manifests itself on websites and blogs, as well as in chat rooms, social media, comment sections and gaming. In short, hate is present in many forms on the Internet. This diminishes the Internet's core values, by creating a hostile environment

and even reducing equal access to its benefits for those targeted by hatred and intimidation. (Anti-Defamation League-1)

The Anti-Defamation League has published a list of best practices for addressing cyberhate (Anti-Defamation League-1). These best practices are aimed at providers (Internet sites, blogs, chat rooms, social media, etc.) and individuals inhabiting the world of the Internet and encourage them to

1. Take reports about cyberhate seriously, mindful of the fundamental principles of free expression, human dignity, personal safety and respect for the rule of law.
2. Offer users a clear explanation of their approach to evaluating and resolving reports of hateful content, highlighting their relevant terms of service.
3. Offer user-friendly mechanisms and procedures for reporting hateful content.
4. Respond to user reports in a timely manner.
5. Enforce whatever sanctions their terms of service contemplate in a consistent and fair manner. (Anti-Defamation League-1)

Best practices encourage the Internet community (individuals) to

1. Work together to address the harmful consequences of online hatred.
2. Identify, implement and/or encourage effective strategies of counter-speech—including direct response; comedy and satire when appropriate; or simply setting the record straight.
3. Share knowledge and help develop educational materials and programs that encourage critical thinking in both proactive and reactive online activity.
4. Encourage other interested parties to help raise awareness of the problem of cyberhate and the urgent need to address it.
5. Welcome new thinking and new initiatives to promote a civil online environment. (Anti-Defamation League-1)

In an ideal world, "people and organizations would not choose to communicate their hate" (Anti-Defamation League-1). Unfortunately, "in the real world, they all too often do" (Anti-Defamation League-1). As evidenced by the daily news, hate expressed online can motivate those with nascent fears and prejudices, can urge them to action, and can result in violence that comes in many forms. As long as there is an Internet, there will be cyberhate. The challenge, therefore, is to "find effective ways to confront online hate, to educate about its dangers, to encourage individuals and communities to speak out when they see it, and to find and create tools and means to deter it and to mitigate its negative impact" (Anti-Defamation League-1).

See also: American Renaissance; Black, Don; Jones, Alex; *Stormfront*; Taylor, Jared

Further Reading

Anti-Defamation League-1. "Cyberhate Response: Best Practices for Responding to Cyberhate." https://www.adl.org/cyberhate-response (Accessed May 27, 2017).
Anti-Defamation League-2. "Responding to Cyberhate." https://www.adl.org/education/resources/tools-and-strategies/table-talk/cyberhate (Accessed May 27, 2017).

Anti-Defamation League-3. "Responding to Cyberhate: Toolkit for Action." https://www
.adl.org/sites/default/files/documents/assets/pdf/combating-hate/ADL-Responding-to
-Cyberhate-Toolkit.pdf (Accessed May 27, 2017).

Anti-Defamation League-4. "Cyber-Safety Action Guide." https://www.adl.org/cyber-safety
-action-guide (Accessed May 27, 2017).

Cyber Bully Hotline. "Cyberbullying Rampant on the Internet." http://www.cyberbullyhotline
.com/07-10-12-scourge.html (Accessed May 27, 2017).

Inach. "Profile, Vision and Mission." http://www.inach.net/mission-statement.html
(Accessed May 27, 2017).

Southern Poverty Law Center. March 21, 2001. "Harvard Law School Librarian Discusses
Cyberhate." *Southern Poverty Law Center—Intelligence Report.* https://www.splcenter
.org/fighting-hate/intelligence-report/2001/harvard-law-school-librarian-discusses
-cyberhate (Accessed May 27, 2017).

Williams, Matthew L. and Pete Burnap. June 25, 2015. "Cyberhate on Social Media in
the Aftermath of Woolwich: A Case Study in Computational Criminology and Big
Data." *The British Journal of Criminology* 56, no. 2. https://academic.oup.com/bjc
/article/56/2/211/2462519/Cyberhate-on-Social-Media-in-the-aftermath-of (Accessed
May 27, 2017).

D

DE LA BECKWITH, BYRON

Byron De La Beckwith (1920–2001) was a virulent segregationist and a member of the Ku Klux Klan. He is infamous as the killer of National Association for the Advancement of Colored People (NAACP) field secretary Medgar Evers on June 12, 1963. Although two all-white, all-male juries tasked with determining De La Beckwith's guilt in 1964 could not reach a verdict, he was finally convicted of murder in 1994—30 years after the fact. He was given a life sentence with no possibility for parole, which he appealed, but his appeal was denied. He died in prison on January 21, 2001.

De La Beckwith was born in 1920 in California. He joined the marines and served during World War II, being awarded the Purple Heart for being wounded in the service. De La Beckwith married in 1945 and later joined the Ku Klux Klan. After the ruling by the U.S. Supreme Court in 1954's *Brown v. Board of Education*, the segregationist organization Citizens' Council (also referred to as White Citizens' Council and later Council of Conservative Citizens) formed across the South to resist the desegregation of schools. De La Beckwith joined a chapter of the Citizens' Council soon after it came to Mississippi. Members of the Citizens' Council employed a variety of political and economic tactics to discourage black activism and to maintain the segregationist policies that existed in Mississippi. The council "applied severe pressure through boycotts of black businesses, denial of loans and credit to African Americans, firing people from jobs, and other means. In Mississippi they prevented school integration until 1964" (Dittmer 2010).

Medgar Evers was the embodiment of a white supremacist's worst fears. Evers became a prominent spokesperson for civil rights in Mississippi, and, as field secretary for the NAACP, he advocated for equal economic, social, and political rights for African Americans. Despite threats to both him and his family, Evers continued to reside in Jackson, Mississippi, in spite of the growing Klan activity. In the early morning of June 12, 1963, Evers was shot in the back as he exited his car at his home. De La Beckwith was arrested after his rifle and fingerprints were found at the scene (Biography).

In 1963, Mississippi was a hotbed of activity in the civil rights movement. Just over a year after Evers's death, Mississippi would again make national headlines with the murder of three civil rights workers working the Freedom Summer, a volunteer campaign to register African American voters in Mississippi.

After De La Beckwith's arrest, he received donations for his defense and many letters of support. When his case went to trial, two all-white, all-male juries were unable to reach a verdict in two separate trials, allowing De La Beckwith to go free. Blacks were excluded from serving on juries in Mississippi at that time.

In 1973, informants alerted the Federal Bureau of Investigation that De La Beckwith was planning to murder the director of the New Orleans–based Anti-Defamation League (ADL) in retaliation for his disparaging remarks about white Southerners. When New Orleans police arrested De La Beckwith, they found several loaded firearms in his vehicle, a map with highlighted directions to his intended victim's home, and a timer attached to dynamite. In August 1975, De La Beckwith was convicted of conspiracy to commit murder. After serving nearly three years in prison, he was released in 1980. Before he entered prison, De La Beckwith had been ordained as a Christian Identity minister (Lloyd 1995).

In the 1980s, the Jackson, Mississippi, *Clarion Ledger* found that the Mississippi State Sovereignty Commission, a prosegregation state agency supported by taxpayer dollars, had helped De La Beckwith and his defense team screen potential jurors at both of his trials in 1964 (Stout 2001). Armed with this evidence, Evers's widow, Myrlie Evers Williams, lobbied local prosecutors to conduct a new trial. As De La Beckwith's previous trials had resulted in mistrials due to deadlocked juries, and not acquittals, De La Beckwith could not claim double jeopardy.

In 1990, De La Beckwith was again indicted for Evers's death. After various legal maneuvers, he was finally put on trial in January 1994. The physical evidence against him was the same as it had been in 1964. New evidence included the testimony of those who claimed that De La Beckwith had boasted of killing Evers at Ku Klux Klan meetings. De La Beckwith was found guilty of Evers's murder and sentenced to life in prison with no possibility for parole. He appealed his sentence to the Mississippi Supreme Court, but they upheld his conviction. The U.S. Supreme Court later denied his petition to have his case reviewed, allowing the life sentence to stand.

De La Beckwith died on January 21, 2001. He was 80 years old.

See also: Anti-Defamation League; Christian Identity; Council of Conservative Citizens; Ku Klux Klan; White Supremacist Movement

Further Reading

Biography. "Byron De La Beckwith." http://www.biography.com/people/byron-de-la-beckwith-21442573 (Accessed May 4, 2017).

Dittmer, John. December 22, 2010. "'Barbour Is an Unreconstructed Southerner:' Prof. John Dittmer on Mississippi Governor's Praise of White Citizens' Councils." *Democracy Now!* https://www.democracynow.org/2010/12/22/barbour_is_an_unreconstructed _southerner_prof (Accessed May 4, 2017).

Lloyd, James B., editor. November 1, 1995. "Tennessee, Racism, and the New Right: The Second Beckwith Collection." *The Library Development Review*, pp. 3–5. http://trace .tennessee.edu/cgi/viewcontent.cgi?article=1106&context=utk_libdevel   (Accessed May 4, 2017).

Stout, David. January 23, 2001. "Byron De La Beckwith Dies; Killer of Medgar Evers Was 80." *The New York Times.* http://www.nytimes.com/2001/01/23/us/byron-de-la -beckwith-dies-killer-of-medgar-evers-was-80.html (Accessed May 4, 2017).

DEPUGH, ROBERT

Robert DePugh (1923–2009) founded the Minutemen, an anticommunist organization, in 1961. The Minutemen became "a secretive, extreme right-wing group that perceived an impending Communist takeover of the U.S. and organized violent 'counteraction' to prevent the alleged takeover" (Nizkor Project). The Minutemen believed that an attempted communist takeover of the United States was imminent, and they stockpiled weapons and engaged in paramilitary training in preparation for this eventuality. DePugh published instructions about how to conduct guerilla warfare in the group's newsletter, *On Target*, and he later founded the Patriotic Party in 1966. DePugh was a member of the John Birch Society and stated that he had been heavily influenced in his anticommunist views by the activities of the House Un-American Activities Committee (Nizkor Project). In the 1980s, DePugh became involved in the virulently anti-Semitic Christian Identity movement. In the early 1990s, he was tried on pornography charges stemming from an incident with an underage girl, but he was acquitted of the charges (Greaney 2009). DePugh died in June 2009.

DePugh was born in Independence, Missouri, in 1923. During World War II, he enlisted in the U.S. Army but was discharged after exhibiting signs of nervousness and depression. He enrolled at Kansas State University but dropped out after a few months. In 1953, he founded a veterinary firm and later BioLab, another veterinary drug firm that, in addition to veterinary products, produced a malt-flavored food storage tablet that was promoted as a necessary food product for survivalists and those wishing to protect themselves against food shortages due to war, famine, or disease. The tablets were known as Minutemen Survival Tabs (Hamilton 2002).

In 1961, DePugh founded the Minutemen and envisioned it as a guerilla warfare group ready to fight communists, a nationwide spy network reporting on un-American and treasonous activities, and a propaganda group that would distribute literature about the international communist conspiracy (Hamilton 2002). DePugh said that he wanted to "provoke the federal government—which he considered to be dominated by communist sympathizers—into repressive measures that would, in turn, cause the people to rise up against it" (Hamilton 2002). He organized the Minutemen into small cells to avoid compromise, and the group "stockpiled weapons and trained together to defend the country against what they deemed 'subversives'" (Nizkor Project). In October 1966, 19 New York Minutemen were arrested for conspiracy when it was discovered that they had plans to bomb summer camps in New York that were reportedly used by "Communist, left-wing, and liberal" individuals. Law enforcement authorities found "huge supplies of weapons and explosives—including rifles, pipe bombs, mortars, machine guns, grenade launchers and a bazooka" (Nizkor Project). Due to improperly served search warrants, all charges against the Minutemen were eventually dropped.

DePugh also used the Minutemen to threaten the group's enemies. In one incident, he "published the names of 20 Congressmen who had criticized the activities of the House Committee on Un-American Activities and warned them, 'Traitors beware! Even now the cross hairs are on the back of your necks'" (Nizkor Project).

The image of crosshairs became a favorite trope for DePugh. As one author noted,

> In the 1960s if you entered a restroom or a phone booth, there's a chance you might have noticed a three-inch-square sticker at eye level. A closer look might show the image of a rifle crosshairs superimposed over a menacing text:
> "See that old man at the corner where you buy your papers?" the sticker read. "He may have a silencer equipped pistol under his coat. That fountain pen in the pocket of the insurance salesman that calls on you might be a cyanide gas gun. What about your milkman? Arsenic works slow but sure. . . . Traitors, beware! Even now the crosshairs are on the back of your necks." (Greaney 2009)

In February 1968, DePugh disappeared from public view after he and other Minutemen were charged with conspiring to rob a bank. Seventeen months after the indictments were handed down, federal agents captured DePugh. He was eventually tried, convicted, and sentenced to 11 years in prison "for firearms violations, bond jumping, and breaking Federal fugitive gun control laws" (Nizkor Project).

Following his release from prison in 1973, DePugh attempted to revive his standing in the extremist community by associating himself with the Liberty Lobby, a group known for its anti-Semitic conspiracy theories and Holocaust denial.

In 1991, he was arrested on child pornography charges. He was later acquitted, but his role in the extremist right was over. As a result of the charges, he and his wife divorced and his children became estranged from him. In his later years, his political views became "bizarre and often contradictory. . . . His writings were anti-Bush, pro-Obama and anti-Semitic, all at the same time" (Greaney 2009). DePugh would later tell a journalist, "I've done some really interesting things in my life, but I just wish it hadn't hurt so many people" (Greaney 2009).

DePugh died on June 30, 2009, at the age of 86. Though "he had at one time appeared on the front page of *The New York Times*, his passing warranted scant coverage, with only a two-line obituary in the *Kansas City Star* that misspelled his middle name" (Greaney 2009).

See also: Christian Identity; John Birch Society; Liberty Lobby

Further Reading

Greaney, T. J. August 6, 2009. "Minuteman Outlasted Notoriety, Died with Regrets." *Columbia Daily Tribune*. http://www.columbiatribune.com/bc69cd47-d0a5-53b5-a190-bc17f7d6512c.html (Accessed May 3, 2017).

Hamilton, Neil A. 2002. *American Social Leaders and Activists*. Facts on File, pp. 107–108.

Nizkor Project. "Robert DePugh and the Minutemen." http://www.nizkor.org/hweb/orgs/american/adl/paranoia-as-patriotism/minutemen.html (Accessed May 3, 2017).

DUKE, DAVID

David Duke (b. 1950) is an American white nationalist, white supremacist, Holocaust denier, neo-Nazi, anti-Semitic conspiracy theorist, and former Grand Wizard of the

Ku Klux Klan (KKK). Duke may be "America's most well-known racist and anti-Semite as he has been active in the white supremacy movement for more than nearly 50 years" (Southern Poverty Law Center).

Though a member of the KKK, Duke has tried to portray himself to the general public as a "respectable racist," eschewing the regalia and rituals of the Klan in favor of a business suit and tie. Duke is credited with leading a resurgence in the Klan during the 1970s as changing social, economic, cultural, and political dynamics were displacing the traditional power and dominance of white males. Duke ran for political office on several occasions, including campaigns for state legislator, governor, U.S. House, U.S. Senate, and even president of the United States. He served one term in the Louisiana State House of Representatives after winning a special election. Though Duke began his political life as a Democrat, he switched his political party affiliation to the Republican side in December 1988 (Zatarain 1990). In 2016, Duke, hoping Donald Trump's populist rise to power would resurrect his political career, received "only three percent of the vote in a 24-candidate field" for a U.S. Senate seat from Louisiana (Murphy 2016). Duke continues to promote his racist and anti-Semitic views through "the white supremacist European American Unity and Rights Organization," and, in recent years, "has promoted his anti-Jewish ideology in Europe and the Middle East, devoting particular attention to Russia and the Ukraine" (Anti-Defamation League).

Duke was born in 1950. As a young teenager, he attended meetings of the Citizens Councils of America, a forerunner to today's racist Council of Conservative Citizens (Southern Poverty Law Center). He joined the KKK in 1967 and later met William Pierce, "the leader of the white nationalist and anti-Semitic National Alliance" (Zatarain 1990). In 1968, Duke enrolled at Louisiana State University (LSU), and in 1970 "he formed a white student group known as the White Youth Alliance, a student group affiliated with the National Socialist White People's Party (NSWPP), a hard-line descendent of George Lincoln Rockwell's American Nazi Party" (Southern Poverty Law Center). Duke became notorious on LSU's campus for holding parties on the anniversary of Adolf Hitler's birth and for wearing a Nazi uniform on campus (Bridges 1995). Duke graduated from LSU in 1974 and soon after founded the Knights of the Ku Klux Klan (KKKK) (DavidDuke.com).

In founding the KKKK, Duke envisioned a new type of Klan, one that forsook the traditional garb and rhetoric of the old Klan for the suits, ties, and polished racist propaganda of the new Klan. During the first few years of its existence, membership in the KKKK soared. However, Duke's inability to retain top leaders hampered the group's ability to sustain its gains. Many of Duke's associates were "frustrated by what they saw as Duke's boundless ego, his well-known womanizing, and repeated accusations that he was embezzling Klan funds" (Southern Poverty Law Center). As a result, "several high-level resignations crippled the organization in the late 1970s," including Tom Metzger, who remains critical of Duke today, calling him a "fraud, egomaniac, and ripoff artist" (Southern Poverty Law Center). In 1979, Duke made public attempts to disassociate himself from the Klan, and he left the group altogether in 1980 when he made a halfhearted run for president.

Former Grand Wizard of the Ku Klux Klan, David Duke, addresses reporters after founding the National Association for the Advancement of White People (NAAWP) in 1980. Duke is widely recognized as a white supremacist, anti-Semitic conspiracy theorist, Holocaust denier, neo-Nazi, and white nationalist. (Bettmann/Getty Images)

In 1981, Duke founded the National Association for the Advancement of White People (NAAWP), an organization that he billed as a "Klan without the sheets." Duke attempted to build the character and reputation of the NAAWP by denigrating the Klan as a bunch of "simple-minded n****r haters" with no positive agenda or intellectual direction (Southern Poverty Law Center). This, however, did not stop Duke from recruiting former Klan members into his new organization.

Between 1980 and 1987, Duke appeared infrequently in the national media, in contrast to his days during the 1970s while in the KKKK. Duke's ideology became more conspiratorial based, and he also gambled heavily. The NAAWP never achieved membership numbers of more than about 1,000 (Southern Poverty Law Center).

In 1988, Duke made a determined run for the presidency. He received less than 5 percent of the vote in his home state of Louisiana and only "a negligible amount nationally." The following year, "Duke ran in a special election for the Louisiana State House. Running as an anti-tax, anti-busing Republican, Duke toned down his anti-Semitism and dodged questions about his neo-Nazi and Klan past" (Southern Poverty Law Center). In an unusually high turnout due to the number of candidates in the race, Duke won 33 percent of the vote. In the runoff that followed between himself and the next highest vote getter, Duke beat his opponent by 227 votes (Southern Poverty Law Center). According to his colleagues, Duke had no significant legislative achievements during his time in office (Gomez 2006).

In 1990, Duke ran for the U.S. Senate from Louisiana, gaining 60 percent of the white vote but losing the primary. In 1991, he ran for governor of Louisiana and was neck and neck with the Democratic incumbent, who was "a scandal-dogged, Huey Long–style populist" (Southern Poverty Law Center). Duke would go on to lose the primary challenge, and his dreams of electoral success were largely dashed.

In 1998, Duke published his autobiography, *My Awakening: A Path to Racial Understanding*. In the book, Duke details his philosophies, "particularly his reasoning behind his support of racial separation":

> We [Whites] desire to live in our own neighborhoods, go to our own schools, work in our own cities and towns, and ultimately live as one extended family in our own nation. We shall end the racial genocide of integration. We shall work for the eventual establishment of a separate homeland for African Americans, so each race will be free to pursue its own destiny without racial conflicts and ill will. (Duke 1998)

During most of the 2000s, Duke traveled the world in support of his anti-Semitic ideals and beliefs. In 2003, he published *Jewish Supremacism: My Awakening to the Jewish Question*. The Anti-Defamation League deemed the book anti-Semitic, though Duke denied this (Anti-Defamation League). Duke found an audience for his ideas in former communist countries in Eastern Europe and in the Middle East. When the Cold War ended, he began cultivating a close relationship with far-right nationalists in Russia. In June 2006, for instance, Duke traveled to Moscow for a conference on "The White World's Future," where he "praised the host city for having the largest number of White people of any city in the entire world" (Southern Poverty Law Center).

Duke considered running for the U.S. presidency on the Republican ticket in 2012 after "thousands of Tea Party activists urged him to run" (Southern Poverty Law Center). He intimated that his presidential platform would include calls to "prosecute the criminal International banks, end affirmative action, and end foreign control over our foreign policy by the Israeli lobby" (Southern Poverty Law Center). Duke continued to post articles on his Web site about Jewish influence on the U.S. Federal Reserve Bank, that Jews own Hollywood and the U.S. media, and that Jews promote homosexuality (DavidDuke.com). In the end, Duke decided against a run for president.

In 2016, Duke once again entered the political fray by running for the U.S. Senate in Louisiana. The rise of Donald Trump encouraged Duke's return to politics:

> For his part, Duke is desperate to link himself to Trump. He specifically credited Trump for his return to politics, claiming that he was the originator of many of the "America-first" policy ideas Trump is pushing. Duke's campaign website features videos with titles like "Duke & Trump: The Supreme Court Does Matter" and "Never Trump & Never Duke Exposed as GOP Traitors." And Duke's Twitter feed is a scary mish-mash of ravings about anti-white bigotry and the decline of "Euro Americans," broadsides against more mainstream Republicans, and lamentations about the mistreatments and misrepresentations Trump has allegedly suffered. (Cottle 2016)

Duke intimated that he would be a staunch supporter of Donald Trump if he were elected to the Senate from Louisiana and if Trump were elected president. Duke linked his ideas, and those of his voters, with those being espoused by Trump (Domonoske 2016). Upon hearing of Duke's support, Trump on several occasions refused to condemn either Duke or the KKK (Appelbaum 2016). Finally, after several weeks of dodging the question, Trump finally rebuked Duke and the KKK, but only after stating "I don't know anything about what you're even talking about with white supremacy or white supremacists. So I don't know. I don't know—did he endorse me, or what's going on? Because I know nothing about David Duke; I know nothing about white supremacists" (Bradner 2016).

Trump's protestations were hollow as three months before fact checkers had found that Trump knew very well who David Duke was and the essence of his policies (Kessler 2016). Fortunately, Duke lost his bid for the Louisiana Senate seat, but history suggests that he may yet return to the political arena (Murphy 2016).

See also: Holocaust Denial; Ku Klux Klan; Metzger, Tom; National Alliance; Neo-Nazis; Pierce, William; Rockwell, George Lincoln; White Nationalism; White Supremacist Movement

Further Reading

Anti-Defamation League. "David Duke." https://www.adl.org/education/resources/profiles/david-duke (Accessed May 30, 2017).

Appelbaum, Yoni. February 28, 2016. "Why Won't Donald Trump Repudiate the Ku Klux Klan?" *The Atlantic.* https://www.theatlantic.com/politics/archive/2016/02/why-wont-donald-trump-repudiate-the-ku-klux-klan/471345/ (Accessed May 30, 2017).

Bradner, Eric. July 24, 2016. "Trump Rebukes David Duke 'as Quick as You Can Say It.'" *CNN.* http://www.cnn.com/2016/07/24/politics/donald-trump-david-duke-louisiana-senate/ (Accessed May 30, 2017).

Bridges, Tyler. 1995. *The Rise of David Duke.* University Press of Mississippi.

Cottle, Michelle. August 8, 2016. "How Donald Trump Opened the Way for David Duke's Return." *The Atlantic.* https://www.theatlantic.com/politics/archive/2016/08/duke-it-out/494855/ (Accessed May 30, 2017).

DavidDuke.com. https://davidduke.com/ (Accessed May 30, 2017).

Domonoske, Camila. August 5, 2016. "Former KKK Leader David Duke Says 'of Course' Trump Voters Are His Voters." *NPR.* http://www.npr.org/sections/thetwo-way/2016/08/05/488802494/former-kkk-leader-david-duke-says-of-course-trump-voters-are-his-voters (Accessed May 30, 2017).

Duke, David. 1998. *My Awakening: A Path to Racial Understanding.* Free Speech Books.

Duke, David. 2003. *Jewish Supremacism: My Awakening to the Jewish Question.* Free Speech Books.

Gomez, Ron. 2006. *My Name Is Ron, and I'm a Recovering Legislator: Memoirs of a Louisiana State Representative.* iUniverse, Inc.

Kessler, Glenn. March 1, 2016. "Donald Trump and David Duke: For the Record." *The Washington Post.* https://www.washingtonpost.com/news/fact-checker/wp/2016/03/01/donald-trump-and-david-duke-for-the-record/?utm_term=.0f041bcb124e (Accessed May 30, 2017).

Murphy, Tim. November 8, 2016. "Reviled White Nationalist David Duke Just Lost His Senate Bid." *Mother Jones.* http://www.motherjones.com/politics/2016/11/white-nationalist-david-duke-loses-senate-bid (Accessed May 30, 2017).

Southern Poverty Law Center. "David Duke." https://www.splcenter.org/fighting-hate/extremist-files/individual/david-duke (Accessed May 30, 2017).

Zatarain, Michael. 1990. *David Duke: Evolution of a Klansman.* Pelican Publishing.

E

EARTH LIBERATION FRONT

The Earth Liberation Front (ELF) is the collective name given to autonomous individuals and covert cells of individuals who perpetrate acts of vandalism and economic sabotage to stop the exploitation and destruction of the earth's environment. Adherents sometimes refer to themselves as "Elves." John Hanna, an environmental activist, founded the "original ELF," which he called Environmental Life Force, in 1977 (Earth Liberation Front). Hanna intended ELF to be a guerilla force that would use a variety of violent tactics to protect the earth. However, after dialogue with other environmental activists, a consensus was reached in which "terrorist actions were clearly counter-productive to the environmental movement—regardless of the perceived righteousness of a given cause" (Earth Liberation Front).

ELF was disbanded in 1978 and was replaced the following year by the Earth First! movement, founded by Dave Foreman. Earth First! was a radical environmental advocacy group that used direct action to disrupt what was perceived as incidences of environmental destruction. Earth First! adherents engaged in protests, tree sitting, road blockades, and sabotage. Later actions became more costly as members engaged in the practice of tree spiking and monkeywrenching (sabotage in the name of environmental defense). By 1992, Earth First! was moving much more into the mainstream of political action. This led to the creation of the Earth Liberation Front (ELF) in 1992. The new ELF, like John Hanna's of 15 years before, was committed to extremism in defense of the environment. Members of ELF engaged in arson, direct destruction of property, and other acts of economic sabotage in order to thwart corporate actions deemed to be harmful to the environment. In 2001, the FBI designated ELF as "ecoterrorists" and classified the group as the top "domestic terror threat in the United States" (Jarboe 2002). The group was highlighted in a *60 Minutes* exposé in 2005 and "was further highlighted in a 2011 Academy Award nominated documentary, *If a Tree Falls: A Story of the Earth Liberation Front*" (Anderson 2011).

The Earth Liberation Front, like its companion organization the Animal Liberation Front (ALF), has no formal leadership, membership, or hierarchy. Direct action engaged in by individuals, or actions by small cells of people, are usually self-funded and are intended not to harm people, animals, or the environment as a whole. Rather, in what is sometimes called "ecotage" (economic sabotage), ELF (and ALF) members engage in acts "against facilities and companies involved in logging, genetic engineering, GMO crops, deforestation, sport utility vehicles (SUVs) sales, urban sprawl, rural cluster, developments with larger homes ("mcmansions"), energy production and distribution, and a wide variety of other activities" (Best and Nocella 2006). Known as "monkeywrenching," acts of "ecotage"

> describe the unlawful sabotage of industrial extraction and development equipment, as a means of striking at the Earth's destroyers where they commit their crimes and hitting them where they feel it most—in their profit margins.
>
> Monkeywrenching is a step beyond civil disobedience. It is nonviolent, aimed only at inanimate objects. It is one of the last steps in defense of the wild, a deliberate action taken by an Earth defender when almost all other measures have failed. (Earth First!)

In 2005, it was estimated that the ecoterrorists of ELF and ALF had been responsible for nearly 1,000 incidents of ecotage, resulting in damages of more than $100 million (Schorn 2005). Two of the most famous acts of ecotage perpetrated by ELF were the setting of fires at the Vail Mountain Ski Resort in Colorado in 1998— which burned several buildings, destroyed four chairlifts, and caused $12 million in damage—and the arson in 2003 that destroyed a nearly completed $23 million apartment just outside of San Diego, California. The fire was set to protest urban sprawl (Schorn 2005).

In late 2005 and early 2006, as part of Operation Backfire, U.S. grand juries, with the assistance of the Bureau of Alcohol, Tobacco, and Firearms and the Federal Bureau of Investigation, indicted six women and seven men on a total of 65 charges. Known collectively as The Family, the individuals were believed to have been responsible for the fire set at the Vail Mountain Ski Resort in 1998. According to law enforcement, at least 11 of the individuals had taken an oath to protect each other (Harden 2006). The case was broken open when an informant was found.

Daniel G. McGowan, one of those charged in Operation Backfire, was arrested and charged with multiple counts of arson and conspiracy in federal court. McGowan had reportedly been involved in the arson of a lumber company in Glendale, Oregon, and a poplar (tree) farm in Clatskane, Oregon. Because of increased sentencing guidelines related to terrorism prompted by the Oklahoma City bombing in 1995, McGowan faced a minimum of life in prison if convicted. He was informed, "If you use violence or the threat of violence to further your ideological goals, you're guilty of terrorism" (Anderson 2011). He later accepted "a non-cooperation plea deal" and was sentenced to seven years in prison on November 9, 2006 (Anderson 2011), and released on parole in June 2013. McGowan's actions were the subject of an Academy Award–nominated documentary, *If a Tree Falls: A Story of the Earth Liberation Front* (Anderson 2011).

As of 2017, ELF is still an active organization. However, the group's Web site (earth-liberation-front.com) rails against those ELF members who caved and "turned snitches" in the case of Operation Backfire. The site calls out some 19 activists by name, stating that "more than twenty [other] ELF activists did not have to lose their freedom in order to wage an effective battle defending the Earth" (Earth Liberation Front). The introduction on the Web site also announced that the domain name at which it was located would "cease to exist in July, 2017." In what

FAIRBURN, ERIC "THE BUTCHER"

Eric Fairburn (b. 1974), nicknamed "the Butcher," was the founder of the Vinlanders Social Club, a coalition of independent state skinhead groups. Fairburn was a particularly violent skinhead and "served time in prison for beating a homeless black man in Indianapolis, Indiana" (Southern Poverty Law Center, Eric Fairburn). He was unmistakable in the skinhead movement for having the word "murder" tattooed across his neck. He was also a member of the hate rock group RAHOWA (RAcial HOly WAr). In 2010, Fairburn walked into a police station in Indianapolis and confessed to committing a murder. He is now serving a life sentence after having been convicted of that crime (Southern Poverty Law Center, Eric Fairburn).

Fairburn was the one-time marketing director for Resistance Records, a label that featured the music of neo-Nazis and white separatists. When Michigan tax authorities audited Resistance's office in 1997, Fairburn left the company and "went to work for Holocaust denier Willis Carto's extreme-right political advocacy organization" (Southern Poverty Law Center, Eric Fairburn). Fairburn was deemed to have "poor impulse control." When he went to collect a debt from one of Carto's business partners, Fairburn, in finding the debtor absent from his home, broke in to the garage and "stole a chainsaw and subsequently cut down every single tree and shrub on the individual's property" (Southern Poverty Law Center, Eric Fairburn).

In 2000, Fairburn joined the Outlaw Hammerskins, a loose association of skinhead groups formed in Indiana. In 2002, he joined another group known as the Hoosier State Skinheads. After seeing the movie *Gangs of New York*, Fairburn renamed himself "the Butcher" after the character in the film, William "Bill the Butcher" Cutting, "a crime lord and sadist who hated all non-whites and Irish immigrants" (Southern Poverty Law Center, Eric Fairburn). To cultivate his image, Fairburn began to carry a large sledgehammer and became known for his "unpredictable and abusive conduct, especially toward women" (Southern Poverty Law Center, Eric Fairburn). In one instance, he tossed a girlfriend's dog out of a moving car during heavy traffic while the car was traveling in excess of 70 mph. Fairburn would later comment that a truck hit the dog and it "exploded," to which Fairburn exclaimed, "Great stuff" (Southern Poverty Law Center, Eric Fairburn).

In 2003, Fairburn and others formed the Vinlanders Social Club in reaction to the waning authority of the Hammerskin Nation, a white supremacist group that had been formed in 1988. In March 2007, Fairburn and two other Vinlanders severely beat a homeless black man in Indianapolis, Indiana. Fairburn served two years of a five-year sentence and vowed upon his release he would no longer associate himself with the skinhead movement, stating, "I'm 34 years old seemed an official farewell, and a continued call for action, the Web site stated that the "domain name will be up for grabs" and

> maybe earth_liberation_front.com will be commandeered by some greed-head and become a sales platform for a blue sex-enhancing pill. Maybe some enterprising ELF activist will take the reins. If so, good luck! It's been a good run but it's time for this webmaster to pass the ball. Thankfully, no one has gone to jail for a while. Remember, act alone and don't conspire. Focus on one problem and put your heart and soul into that one thing. Don't rat out your comrades and do no harm to all living beings; that includes Mother Earth. If you do choose to practice civil disobedience, be prepared to go to jail if you're busted. But keep in mind, you won't be an effective "ecommando" or activist behind bars. Think for yourself! Don't follow leaders. Good luck. (Earth Liberation Front)

See also: Animal Liberation Front; Monkeywrenching

Further Reading

Anderson, John. June 8, 2011. "Activist or Terrorist, Rendered in Red, White, and Green." *The New York Times.* http://www.nytimes.com/2011/06/12/movies/if-a-tree-falls-documentary-by-marshall-curry.html (Accessed May 6, 2017).

Best, Steven and Anthony J. Nocella II. 2006. *Igniting a Revolution: Voices in Defense of the Earth.* AK Press.

Earth First! "Monkeywrenching." *Earth First! Journal.* http://earthfirstjournal.org/monkey wrenching/ (Accessed May 6, 2017).

Earth Liberation Front. http://earth-liberation-front.com/ (Accessed May 6, 2017).

ELF (the original). http://www.originalelf.com/ (Accessed May 6, 2017).

Harden, Blain. January 21, 2006. "11 Indicted in 'Eco-Terrorism' Case.'" *The Washington Post.* http://www.washingtonpost.com/wp-dyn/content/article/2006/01/20/AR20060 12001823.html (Accessed May 6, 2017).

Jarboe, James F. February 12, 2002. "The Threat of Eco-Tourism." *Federal Bureau of Investigation.* https://web.archive.org/web/20040714065542/http://www.fbi.gov/congress /congress02/jarboe021202.htm (Accessed May 6, 2017).

Schorn, Daniel. November 10, 2005. "Burning Rage." *CBS News.* http://www.cbsnews.com /news/burning-rage/ (Accessed May 6, 2017).

and I've got too much going on in my life to waste any more of it" (Southern Poverty Law Center, Vinlanders). In September 2010, Fairburn walked into a police station in Indianapolis, Indiana, and confessed to the 2004 murder of William McDaniel, an individual who was charged in a car/motorcycle accident that had claimed the life of one of Fairburn's friends (Baird 2009). After his extradition to Springfield, Missouri, the site of the crime, Fairburn was sentenced to life in prison (OzarksFirst.com).

See also: Carto, Willis; Holocaust Denial; Neo-Nazis; White Supremacist Movement

Further Reading

Baird, Kathee. September 2009. "Skinhead Confesses to 2004 Springfield Murder." *The Crime Scene.* http://crimesceneinvestigations.blogspot.com/2010/09/skinhead -confesses-to-2004-murder-in.html (Accessed April 19, 2017).

OzarksFirst.com. "Admitted Killer Sentenced to Life in Prison." http://www.ozarksfirst .com/news/admitted-killer-sentenced-to-life-in-prison/69924058 (Accessed April 19, 2017).

Southern Poverty Law Center. "Eric 'The Butcher' Fairburn." https://www.splcenter.org /fighting-hate/extremist-files/individual/eric-butcher-fairburn (Accessed April 19, 2017).

Southern Poverty Law Center. "Vinlanders Social Club." https://www.splcenter.org/fighting -hate/extremist-files/group/vinlanders-social-club (Accessed April 19, 2017).

FAMILY RESEARCH COUNCIL

The Family Research Council (FRC) is a nonprofit organization that was founded in 1981 to promote traditional family values in American society by lobbying on behalf of American Christian conservative values and advocating for socially conservative policies. FRC "opposes and lobbies against equal rights for LGBT people (such as same-sex marriage, same-sex civil unions, and LGBT adoption), abortion, divorce, embryonic stem-cell research, and pornography" (Hernson, Shaiko, and Wilcox 2005). In 2010, the FRC was designated as a hate group by the Southern Poverty Law Center (SPLC). FRC's president, Tony Perkins, labeled the designation a smear by a "liberal organization" and called the SPLC an intolerant organization that simply did not agree with the FRC's belief that marriage should be between a man and a woman (Thompson 2010). A columnist for *The Washington Post* called the designation "reckless" as it characterized the FRC "in the same category as groups such as Aryan Nations, Knights of the Ku Klux Klan, Stormfront, and the Westboro Baptist Church" (Brydum 2012).

In an effort to combat LGBT civil rights measures, the FRC strongly promotes the belief that LGBT people can be "cured" of their affliction, although in 2009 the American Psychological Association issued a report stating that there are no credible studies that "provide evidence of sexual orientation change." The SPLC contends that "the FRC's strategy is to pound home the false claim that gays and lesbians are more likely to sexually abuse children than heterosexual people" (Southern Poverty Law Center, Family Research Council). However, the American Psychological Association has concluded that "homosexual men are not more likely to sexually abuse children than heterosexual men are." FRC's president, Tony Perkins, has labeled gay men as "pedophiles."

The FRC "supports a federal conscience clause that would allow medical workers to refuse to provide certain treatments or medications to patients such as abortions, blood transfusions, or birth control" (Family Research Council). The FRC also opposes same-sex marriage, same-sex unions, and gambling and has questioned whether humans are responsible for climate change (CNN 2007).

In 2010, the FRC "paid $25,000 to lobbyists" to sink a resolution in the U.S. Congress denouncing legislation in Uganda that included the death penalty for homosexual acts (McEwen 2010). In the same year, a spokesperson for the FRC stated on Chris Matthew's *Hardball* program on NBC that gay behavior should be outlawed in the United States and that "criminal sanctions against homosexual behavior should be enforced." The FRC also took a very public stance against the repeal of the "don't ask, don't tell" policy, stating that the repeal of the policy "would encourage molestation of heterosexual service members" (McMorris-Santoro 2010). "Don't ask, don't tell" was the Clinton-era directive that specified that gays, bisexuals, and lesbians could serve in the U.S. military. Those recruiting such individuals were directed to "don't ask" about an individual's sexual orientation, while those serving were directed to "don't tell" their sexual orientation to anyone. "Don't ask, don't tell" was repealed by the U.S. government in 2011.

In 2012, the FRC extended its attacks to include Islam and Muslim immigration to the United States. The FRC enlisted the support of retired Lieutenant General William G. "Jerry" Boykin as executive vice president of the organization. Boykin had previously served as the undersecretary for defense under President George W. Bush. He has stated that the United States is in a "spiritual battle" against Satan and intimated that Islam was the greatest evil and the war on terror was a religious battle that had to be won. According to the SPLC (Family Research Council),

> Boykin has also claimed that Islam is evil because it calls for innocent blood. He has said that the U.S. government is infiltrated by the Muslim Brotherhood and that the continent of Europe is lost to it. He has even claimed that there is a "cabal, a group of very nefarious people, who very much want to create a global government," and that American billionaire George Soros is part of it—a prevalent conspiracy theory on the right.

In 2013, FRC president Tony Perkins accused President Barack Obama of working the "totalitarian homosexual lobby" and stated that Obama's agenda would destroy freedom of religion (Southern Poverty Law Center, Family Research Council). After the 2015 U.S. Supreme Court ruling in *Obergefell v. Hodges*, which recognized the legality of same-sex marriages in the United States, the FRC began to work furiously with other groups and state legislatures to support "religious liberty" laws that would allow those who object to same-sex marriage to refuse goods and services to same-sex couples (Southern Poverty Law Center 2016).

In 2016, Perkins was a delegate from Louisiana for the Republican National Convention. He helped craft "the most anti-LGBT platform in the party's history," a platform that affirmed the "right of parents to determine the proper medical treatment and therapy for their minor children" as well as "issuing a call for the overturning of marriage equality" (Southern Poverty Law Center 2016).

After the election of Donald Trump, an FRC senior fellow, Ken Blackwell, was on Trump's transition team as head of domestic policy (Blue 2016). The FRC thus worked to undo progress that had been made by LGBT people by recommending that President Trump issue a list of executive orders rescinding LGBT-friendly policies that had been put in place by the Obama administration (Blue 2016).

See also: Boykin, Lieutenant General William G. "Jerry" (Ret.); Perkins, Tony; Southern Poverty Law Center

Further Reading

American Psychological Association. August 5, 2009. "Insufficient Evidence that Sexual Orientation Change Efforts Work, Says APA." http://www.apa.org/news/press/releases/2009/08/therapeutic.aspx (Accessed March 24, 2017).

Blue, Miranda. November 10, 2016. "Religious Right Activist Ken Blackwell Leading Domestic Policy for Trump's Transition Team." *Right Wing Watch*. http://www.rightwingwatch.org/post/religious-right-activist-ken-blackwell-leading-domestic-policy-for-trumps-transition-team/ (Accessed July 26, 2017).

Brydum, Sunnivie. August 17, 2012. "Washington Post Writers: Putting FRC in Same Club as KKK Is Unfair." *Advocate*. http://www.advocate.com/crime/2012/08/17/washington-post-columnists-continue-blaming-hate-group-classification-frc-shooting (Accessed March 24, 2017).

CNN. March 14, 2007. "Global Warming Gap Among Evangelicals Widens." http://www.cnn.com/2007/POLITICS/03/14/evangelical.rift/index.html?eref=rss_politics (Accessed March 24, 2017).

Family Research Council. May 4, 2011. "FRC Action Praises Bipartisan House Majority for Approving a 'No Taxpayer Funding for Abortion Act.'" *FRC Action*. https://www.frcaction.org/action/frc-action-praises-bipartisan-house-majority-for-approving-no-taxpayer-funding-for-abortion-act (Accessed March 24, 2017).

Hernson, Paul S., Ronald G. Shaiko, and Clyde Wilcox. 2005. *The Interest Group Connection: Electioneering, Lobbying, and Policymaking in Washington*. CQ Press.

McEwen, Alvin. June 3, 2010. "Family Research Council Accused of Undermining Support for Resolution Against Uganda's Anti-Gay Bill." *Huffington Post*. http://www.huffingtonpost.com/alvin-mcewen/family-research-council-a_b_600171.html (Accessed March 24, 2017).

McMorris-Santoro, Evan. November 24, 2010. "Family Research Council Labeled 'Hate Group' by SPLC Over Anti-Gay Rhetoric." *Talking Points Memo*. http://talkingpointsmemo.com/dc/family-research-council-labeled-hate-group-by-splc-over-anti-gay-rhetoric?ref=tn (Accessed March 24, 2017).

Sanchez, Casey. January 1, 2003. "Memphis Area Love in Action Residential Program to 'Cure' Homosexuality." *Southern Poverty Law Center—Intelligence Report*. https://www.splcenter.org/fighting-hate/intelligence-report/2003/memphis-area-love-action-offers-residential-program-"Ccure"-homosexuality (Accessed March 24, 2017).

Southern Poverty Law Center. "Family Research Council." https://www.splcenter.org/fighting-hate/extremist-files/group/family-research-council (Accessed March 24, 2017).

Southern Poverty Law Center. February 11, 2016. "'Religious Liberty' and the Anti-LGBT Right." https://www.splcenter.org/20160211/religious-liberty-and-anti-lgbt-right (Accessed March 24, 2017).

Thompson, Krissah. November 24, 2010. "'Hate Group' Designation Angers Same-Sex Opposition Opponents." *The Washington Post.* http://www.washingtonpost.com/wp-dyn/content/article/2010/11/24/AR2010112405573.html (Accessed March 24, 2017).

Tripodi, Paul. August 16, 2012. "Lobbying Report." Lobbying Disclosure. US House of Representatives. http://disclosures.house.gov/ld/pdfform.aspx?id=300256072 (Accessed March 24, 2017).

FAMILY RESEARCH INSTITUTE

The Family Research Institute (FRI) is a nonprofit organization based in Colorado Springs, Colorado, that states that is has "one overriding mission: to generate empirical research on issues that threaten the traditional family, particularly homosexuality, AIDS, sexual social policy, and drug abuse" (Family Research Institute, About FRI). The FRI is often associated with the Christian right movement in the United States, which seeks to shape and influence political debate, particularly on issues that have biblical connections. The FRI seeks "to restore a world where marriage is upheld and honored, where children are nurtured and protected, and where homosexuality is not taught and accepted, but instead is discouraged and rejected at every level" (Family Research Institute, About FRI). The FRI was founded by Paul Cameron in 1982 as the "Institute for the Scientific Investigation of Sexuality. He later changed the name to the Family Research Institute" (Kranish 2005). Cameron received a PhD in psychology from the University of Colorado at Boulder in 1966, but his methods and research into gay psychology have largely been debunked and discredited by more respected researchers (Southern Poverty Law Center 2006).

In 1978, Cameron "made his first foray into anti-gay activism with the publication of *Sexual Gradualism,* a book in which Cameron suggested that parents should allow their children to experiment with heterosexual sex, short of intercourse, as a means of preventing homosexuality" (Southern Poverty Law Center). Cameron defended his suggestion by pointing out that "while no parent wants his child starting the process 'too young,' better too young than homosexual" (Southern Poverty Law Center, Paul Cameron). Under the auspices of the Institute for the Scientific Investigation of Sexuality, which Cameron founded in 1982, he "began to disseminate anti-gay propaganda in 'pay-to-publish' journals" (Southern Poverty Law Center, Paul Cameron). As the AIDS crisis advanced during the 1980s, Cameron "advocated establishing concentration camps for sexually active homosexuals" (Southern Poverty Law Center, Paul Cameron).

In 1987, Cameron moved to Washington, D.C., and changed the name of his organization to the Family Research Institute. In 1992, Cameron and his group moved to Colorado Springs, Colorado, after supporters of an antigay amendment in Colorado (Amendment 2) "distributed 100,000 copies of his study," "What Do Homosexuals Do?" (Southern Poverty Law Center, Paul Cameron). Among many false claims in the publication, Cameron said that "17% of LGBT people enjoy consuming human feces" (Southern Poverty Law Center). Amendment 2 was eventually passed by Colorado voters in 1994 but was later overturned by the U.S. Supreme Court in *Romer v. Evans* (1996).

Cameron and the Family Research Institute continue to publish pseudoscientific studies purporting that "gays and lesbians are more prone than heterosexuals to commit murder, die young and molest children" (Southern Poverty Law Center 2006). A March 2014 article by the Family Research Institute even suggested that gay parents are more apt to commit incest (Family Research Institute). Among other claims supported by the Family Research Institute are that "children raised by homosexuals disproportionately experience emotional disturbance and sexual victimization" and that homosexuality promotes "demographic suicide" as areas where homosexuality is tolerated or legalized show declining birth rates that threaten civil society (Southern Poverty Law Center 2006).

Cameron and the work of the Family Research Institute remain central to anti-LGBT groups on the extreme right of the political spectrum, "even though such work has been discredited by the American Psychological Association and the American Sociological Association" (Southern Poverty Law Center 2006). Despite repudiations of claims put forward by Cameron and the FRI, however, Cameron's "junk science" is continually cited by campaigns that work against civil rights for LGBT people (Southern Poverty Law Center 2006).

See also: Cameron, Paul

Further Reading

Brooke, James. October 11, 1995. "Colorado Is Engine in Anti-Gay Uproar." *The New York Times*. http://www.nytimes.com/1995/10/11/us/colorado-is-engine-in-anti-gay-uproar.html (Accessed April 29, 2017).

Family Research Council. January 18, 2012. "Saving Society from Demographic Suicide." http://www.familyresearchinst.org/category/public-policy/ (Accessed April 29, 2017).

Family Research Institute. "About FRI." http://www.familyresearchinst.org/ (Accessed July 26, 2017).

Family Research Institute. March 2014. "Are Gay Parents More Apt to Commit Incest?" http://www.familyresearchinst.org/2014/04/frr-mar-2014-are-gay-parents-more-apt-to-commit-incest/ (Accessed April 29, 2017).

Kranish, Michael. July 31, 2005. "Beliefs Drive Research Agenda of New Think Tanks." *The Boston Globe*. http://archive.boston.com/news/nation/articles/2005/07/31/beliefs_drive_research_agenda_of_new_think_tanks/?page=full (Accessed April 29, 2017).

Schlatter, Evelyn. September 20, 2012. "Anti-LGBT Propagandist Published Again in Academic Journal." *Southern Poverty Law Center—Hatewatch*. https://www.splcenter.org/hatewatch/2012/09/20/anti-lgbt-propagandist-published-again-academic-journal (Accessed April 29, 2017).

Southern Poverty Law Center. "Paul Cameron." https://www.splcenter.org/fighting-hate/extremist-files/individual/paul-cameron (Accessed April 29, 2017).

Southern Poverty Law Center. January 31, 2006. "UC-Davis Psychology Professor Gregory Herek Aims to Debunk Anti-Gay Extremist Paul Cameron." *Southern Poverty*

Law Center—Intelligence Report. https://www.splcenter.org/fighting-hate/intelligence
-report/2006/uc-davis-psychology-professor-gregory-herek-aims-debunk-anti-gay
-extremist-paul-cameron (Accessed April 29, 2017).

FARAH, JOSEPH FRANCIS

Joseph Francis Farah (b. 1955) is editor in chief and CEO of *WorldNetDaily* (WND, About), a far-right "news" Web site he founded in 1997 with the stated intent of "exposing wrongdoing, corruption and abuse of power" (WND, About). *WorldNet-Daily* specializes in conspiracy theories and has become a leading platform for Tea Party activists and end times prophets (Right Wing Watch). One of WND's most prominent conspiracy theories was the discredited "birther" claim about President Barack Obama's birth certificate. WND worked very closely with Donald Trump, before he was elected president, to spread the false allegations that President Obama had not been born in the United States (Parker and Eder 2016). At one point, Farah had pledged $15,000 for the "long form" birth certificate that proved Obama's birth in Hawaii (WND 2010). After the White House posted the certificate in April 2011, Farah called it "fraudulent" and reneged on the pledge (Elliott 2011). Farah's *WorldNetDaily* "frequently makes accusations against LGBT people, perpetrates anti-Muslim rhetoric, and publishes fringe claims, such as WND's six-part series that claimed that eating soy causes homosexuality" (Southern Poverty Law Center, World Net Daily).

Farah was a long-haired activist in the 1970s. He claims to have voted for George McGovern and Jimmy Carter and describes himself as a "former communist." After graduating with a BA in communications from William Paterson University, Farah said that the 1980s led him to experience the two forces that would shape the remainder of his life: Ronald Reagan and Jesus. Farah adopted a Christian world view and became a journalist in response to the oft-repeated question, "What would Jesus do?" (Southern Poverty Law Center, Joseph Farah). Though Farah described Reagan as "the greatest American president of the 20th century," he stated that Reagan hadn't gone far enough:

> He still left us with bigger government. He didn't eliminate the Department of Education. He didn't eliminate the Internal Revenue Service. He didn't eliminate the Federal Reserve. He didn't eliminate many of the most destructive, immoral and lawless institutions that knocked America from its pedestal as a shining city on a hill. (Southern Poverty Law Center, Joseph Farah)

In 1990, Farah took over *The Sacramento Union.* What was already a conservative newspaper became even more so under Farah. Under his editorship, the *Union,* which was already struggling, lost an additional 25 percent of its circulation. Commentators said that the paper became "a mouthpiece for the fundamentalist Christian right, preoccupied with abortion, homosexuals and creationism" (Southern Poverty Law Center, Joseph Farah). Less than two years after taking the reins at the *Union,* Farah resigned, and the paper folded for good two years later. However, Farah believes that the experience helped him find his journalistic voice.

In 1997, Farah founded *WorldNetDaily*, a Web site that the Southern Poverty Law Center, World Net Daily states is "devoted to manipulative fear-mongering and outright fabrications designed to further the paranoid, gay-hating, conspiratorial and apocalyptic visions of Farah and his hand-picked contributors from the fringes of the far-right and fundamentalist worlds." Under Farah's leadership, *WorldNetDaily* has published stories claiming that "soybean consumption leads to homosexuality, gay men orchestrated the Holocaust, Satan was the first 'leftist,' Muslims have a 20-point plan for conquering the United States by 2020, and readers should invest all of their assets in gold as the world is inevitably coming to an end, sooner rather than later" (WND, About). Despite publishing these questionable stories, Farah maintains that WND is "America's Independent News Network" and that the Web site boasts "the broadest ideological forum of commentators in any news or opinion publication or website anywhere on the planet" (Southern Poverty Law Center, World Net Daily).

Farah has accused the American Civil Liberties Union of "waging a war on Christmas," has encouraged Americans to buy guns, "more than you think you need," and has suggested American parents withdraw their children from public schools, which are nothing but "indoctrination centers and brainwashing hubs run by individuals that wish to steal America's youth and make a mockery of the American family" (Southern Poverty Law Center, Joseph Farah).

In 2013, Farah stated that the "9/11 terror attacks were God's judgment on the United States," and he called for 9/11 to be designated a national day of prayer and repentance (Southern Poverty Law Center, Joseph Farah). In 2015, Farah demonized the Supreme Court's ruling on same-sex marriage, stating,

> What's happening in our society today is nothing short of the active recruitment of children into aberrant sexual lifestyles. We once called this child abuse. But today it's official state policy. The next step, which may have been unimaginable a few years ago, is to ensure there's no way out for those recruits. (Southern Poverty Law Center, Joseph Farah)

See also: Alt-Right Movement

Further Reading

Elliott, Justin. April 27, 2011. "Joseph Farah Owes $15,000 to Kapi'olani Medical Center." *Salon.* http://www.salon.com/2011/04/27/farah_birth_hospital/ (Accessed April 19, 2017).

Parker, Ashley and Steve Eder. July 2, 2016. "Inside the Six Weeks Donald Trump Was a Nonstop 'Birther.'" *The New York Times.* https://www.nytimes.com/2016/07/03/us/politics/donald-trump-birther-obama.html (Accessed July 26, 2017).

Right Wing Watch. "WorldNetDaily." http://www.rightwingwatch.org/organizations/worldnetdaily/ (Accessed April 19, 2017).

Southern Poverty Law Center. "Joseph Francis Farah." https://www.splcenter.org/fighting-hate/extremist-files/individual/joseph-francis-farah (Accessed April 19, 2017).

Southern Poverty Law Center. "WorldNetDaily." https://www.splcenter.org/fighting-hate/extremist-files/group/worldnetdaily (Accessed April 19, 2017).

WorldNetDaily. "About WND." http://go.wnd.com/aboutwnd/ (Accessed April 19, 2017).

WorldNetDaily. January 9, 2010. "$10,000, No $15,000 for Proof of Obama's Birth Hospital." http://www.wnd.com/2010/01/121395/ (Accessed April 19, 2017).

FARRAKHAN, LOUIS

Louis Farrakhan (b. 1933) is the leader of the Nation of Islam (NOI). Farrakhan preaches that white people are "devils" and that Jews have been manipulating governments for generations in an attempt to take over the world. Farrakhan also preaches against gays and Catholics. In June 2010, Farrakhan sent a letter to leaders of the Jewish community in the United States "demanding that they realize the evils that they have perpetrated and that they commit themselves to work to further Farrakhan's goals" (Southern Poverty Law Center, Farrakhan). The letter ended with a threat to "ruin and destroy your power and influence here and throughout the world if his terms were not met" (Southern Poverty Law Center, Farrakhan).

Farrakhan was born Louis Eugene Walcott in 1933 in New York City. In the early 1950s, he had a brief career singing calypso music and also performed as a dancer and cabaret singer. After hearing a speech by NOI's leader, Elijah Muhammad, Farrakhan joined NOI and became a member of the NOI congregation in Harlem led by Malcolm X, then the NOI's national spokesperson. Under Malcolm X's tutelage, Farrakhan rose quickly through the NOI ranks. He was drawn to NOI's message of a black separatist agenda—in other words, that blacks should have their own separate nation apart from white America. NOI preached that "all humans were made black and that God, a black man, created them. White people were not created by God but by the evil black scientist, Yakub" (Southern Poverty Law Center, Black Separatist). Because of the evil manner in which they were created, "NOI teaches that white people are inherently deceitful and murderous" (Southern Poverty Law Center, Louis Farrakhan). Whites are currently not allowed to be members of NOI.

NOI members believe that God is Allah, but they have very little in common with mainstream Islam. When Malcolm X left NOI in 1964 because he believed Elijah Muhammad was a fallen prophet, Farrakhan wrote,

> the die is set, and Malcolm shall not escape, especially after such evil foolish talk about his benefactor, Elijah Muhammad. Such a man as Malcolm is worthy of death, and would have met with death if it had not been for Muhammad's confidence in Allah for victory over the enemies. (Southern Poverty Law Center, Farrakhan)

After leaving NOI, Malcolm X had condemned the group's racist teachings and called for a reconciliation with civil rights groups. Two months after Farrakhan issued his warning, Malcolm X was assassinated in Manhattan, and three NOI members were convicted of his murder.

In 1967, Farrakhan assumed Malcolm X's former role as national spokesperson for NOI. From this point forward, he ramped up his personal attacks against Jews, blaming them for control of the media and manipulation of the government. After Elijah Muhammad died in 1975, Farrakhan split with Elijah Muhammad's son, who succeeded him as leader of NOI, and organized what he called a "resurrected" NOI.

Farrakhan came to national prominence in 1984 as a spokesperson for the presidential campaign of Jesse Jackson. Farrakhan's vitriol toward Jews, however, caused a split with Jackson. In a speech before an audience of 10,000 in Washington, D.C., in July 1985, Farrakhan said that the Jewish state (Israel) would never be accepted because

> there can never be any peace structured on injustice, thievery, lying, deceit and using God's name to shield your dirty religion . . . you cannot tell me your religion is what you profess; your religion is what you practice, and if you practice lying and stealing and cheating and murder and whoremongering then your religion is a dirty religion. (Southern Poverty Law Center, Farrakhan)

Farrakhan believes "the theory that Jews were largely responsible for the slave trade to the United States" and even tasked the NOI with finding evidence of Jewish complicity in the slave trade (Southern Poverty Law Center, Farrakhan). Farrakhan's anti-Semitism has won him allies among white supremacists and former Ku Klux Klan members. Farrakhan also associated with known anti-Semites abroad. In March 2011, he praised Libyan leader Muammar Gaddafi for his role in standing up to Jewish interests in the Middle East. Farrakhan also called U.S. president Barack Obama "the first Jewish president" for Obama's reliance on the Jewish community to secure his election (Southern Poverty Law Center, Farrakhan).

Farrakhan's hate also extends to gays. In 1996, he told a crowd in Kansas City, Missouri, "God don't like men coming to men with lust in their hearts like you should go to a female" (Southern Poverty Law Center, Farrakhan).

In 2016, Farrakhan "made a trip to Iran to take part in the 37th Anniversary of the Iranian Revolution" (Southern Poverty Law Center, Farrakhan). While attending a news conference in Iran, he stated, "Whenever America wants to destroy a nation, a people, they must first demonize them, and the Zionist controlled media in America has chosen to demonize Iran" (Southern Poverty Law Center, Farrakhan).

See also: Black Nationalism; Malcolm X; Nation of Islam

Further Reading

Southern Poverty Law Center. "Black Separatist." http://www.splcenter.org/fighting-hate /extremist-files/ideology/black-separatist (Accessed March 18, 2017).

Southern Poverty Law Center. "Louis Farrakhan." http://www.splcenter.org/fighting-hate /extremist-files/individual/louis-farrakhan (Accessed March 18, 2017).

Southern Poverty Law Center. "Nation of Islam." http://www.splcenter.org/fighting-hate /extremist-files/group/nation-islam (Accessed March 18, 2017).

FEDERATION FOR AMERICAN IMMIGRATION REFORM

The Federation for American Immigration Reform (FAIR) is an anti-immigrant organization whose mission is to limit both legal and illegal immigration into the United States. Specifically, FAIR seeks to overturn the 1965 Immigration and Nationality Act, "which ended a decades-long, racist quota system that limited immigration mostly to northern Europeans" (Southern Poverty Law Center, FAIR). Representatives from FAIR have testified before the U.S. Congress on many occasions, but many of its adherents express racist and eugenicist thoughts that betray its true intentions. Dan Stein, president of FAIR, has stated,

> I blame ninety-eight percent of responsibility for this country's immigration crisis on Ted Kennedy and his political allies, who decided some time back in 1958, earlier perhaps, that immigration was a great way to retaliate against Anglo-Saxon dominance and hubris, and the immigration laws from the 1920s were just this symbol of that, and it's a form of revengism, or revenge, that these forces continue to push the immigration policy that they know full well are creating chaos and will continue to create chaos down the line. (Berrier 2011)

John Tanton founded FAIR in 1979 in Washington, D.C. He was originally interested in the effects of population growth on the environment. He had been a member of the Sierra Club and was the president of Zero Population Growth, a group founded by Paul Ehrlich, a biologist and author of the best-selling novel *The Population Bomb*. With the founding of FAIR, Tanton became convinced that one crucial element to prevent unchecked population growth was to set immigration quotas and to prevent illegal immigration.

In 1988, secret memos published by the *Arizona Republic* revealed Tanton's, and FAIR's, agenda. The memos revealed Tanton's warnings of a "Latin onslaught" and complained of the "low educability" of Latinos. Tanton also speculated about the role of the Catholic Church in the United States, and he worried that increasing Latino immigration into the United States would give the church more political influence in the country. Linda Chavez, a prominent Reagan administration official and executive director of U.S. English, one of Tanton's groups, resigned her position over the memos, calling them "repugnant and not excusable," and "anti-Catholic and anti-Hispanic" (Southern Poverty Law Center, Tanton).

But the memos were not the full extent of Tanton's extremism. He also had associations with Holocaust deniers and leading white nationalist thinkers, such as Jared Taylor—founder and editor of the white nationalist magazine *American Renaissance*—and radical anti-Semitic professor Kevin MacDonald. In a 1993 memo to FAIR, Tanton stated his desire to limit nonwhite immigration into the United States, saying, "Projections by the U.S. Census Bureau show that midway into the next century, the current European-American majority will become a minority. . . . This is unacceptable; we decline to bequeath to our children minority status in their own land" (Southern Poverty Law Center, Tanton).

Between 1985 and 1994, more than $1.2 million in grants was given to FAIR by the Pioneer Fund, a eugenicist organization that devotes itself to "race betterment" through promoting studies that purportedly demonstrate the racial superiority of the white race (Southern Poverty Law Center, FAIR). From 1996 to 1997, FAIR produced a television program called *Borderline* that featured "a number of white nationalists including Sam Francis, Jared Taylor, and Peter Brimelow, who founded the anti-immigrant hate site VDARE" (Southern Poverty Law Center,

FAIR). *Borderline* "often advanced ideas popular in white nationalist circles; particularly popular was the idea that immigrants are destroying American culture or displacing Western civilization with degenerate, Third World ways" (Southern Poverty Law Center, FAIR).

In the late 2000s, FAIR began actively lobbying both state and local governments to enact stricter immigration laws. FAIR has also been an advocate for ending the birthright citizenship provision of the 14th Amendment, "which provides that all children born on U.S. soil are automatically granted U.S. citizenship" (Southern Poverty Law Center, FAIR). FAIR has also targeted organizations that attempt to aid those fleeing violence in other countries. In 2014, FAIR named locales where refugees were being resettled and the organizations that were helping them in the effort. FAIR helped organize protests against such efforts in states such as California and Michigan.

In 2015, Julie Kirchner, FAIR's executive director, left the organization to become an immigration advisor to Donald Trump's campaign (Piggott 2017). In February 2017, Kirchner was named the "chief of staff of U.S. Customs and Border Protection (CBP), the federal agency that oversees Border Patrol" (Vasquez 2017). A headline in *Rewire* magazine announcing the appointment trumpeted, "Trump's New Immigration Official Used to Lead Hate Group" (Vasquez 2017).

See also: American Renaissance; Brimelow, Peter; Holocaust Denial; MacDonald, Kevin; Pioneer Fund; Stein, Dan; Tanton, John; Taylor, Jared; VDARE; White Nationalism

Further Reading

Berrier, Justin. August 19, 2011. "CNN Turns to Anti-Immigrant Hate Group FAIR for Immigration Commentary." *MediaMatters*. https://mediamatters.org/blog/2011/08/19/cnn-turns-to-anti-immigrant-hate-group-fair-for/183858 (Accessed March 13, 2017).

Piggott, Stephen. January 23, 2017. "Former Executive Director of Anti-Immigrant Hate Group FAIR Joins Trump Administration." *Southern Poverty Law Center—Hatewatch*. https://www.splcenter.org/hatewatch/2017/01/23/former-executive-director-anti-immigrant-hate-group-fair-joins-trump-administration (March 13, 2017).

Smith, Laura. February 2, 2017. "Could This Anti-Immigrant Hardliner Grab a Top Border Patrol Spot." *Mother Jones*. http://www.motherjones.com/politics/2017/01/trump-customs-border-protection-julie-kirchner (March 13, 2017).

Southern Poverty Law Center. "Federation for American Immigration Reform." https://www.splcenter.org/fighting-hate/extremist-files/group/federation-american-immigration-reform (Accessed March 13, 2017).

Southern Poverty Law Center. "John Tanton Is the Mastermind Behind the Organized Anti-Immigration Movement." June 18, 2002. *Southern Poverty Law Center—Intelligence Report*. https://www.splcenter.org/fighting-hate/intelligence-report/2002/john-tanton-mastermind-behind-organized-anti-immigration-movement (Accessed March 13, 2017).

Vasquez, Tina. January 26, 2017. "Trump's New Immigration Official Used to Lead Hate Group." *Rewire*. https://rewire.news/article/2017/01/26/trumps-new-immigration-official-used-lead-hate-group/ (Accessed March 13, 2017).

FINICUM, ROBERT "LAVOY"

Robert "LaVoy" Finicum (1961–2016) was an Arizona cattle rancher who gained notoriety during the Malheur National Wildlife Refuge standoff in January 2016. Finicum became the unofficial spokesperson for the Citizens for Constitutional Freedom, the name the occupiers chose to portray their cause to the media. After nearly four weeks of occupation, Finicum attempted to run a roadblock that was set up by agents of the Federal Bureau of Investigation (FBI) and the Oregon State Police as he traveled to a nearby town for a rally. He was subsequently shot and killed as he attempted to reach for a handgun that he had hidden in his coat. His death reignited conspiracy theories as video evidence of the shooting left lingering questions about Finicum's death.

Finicum had protested alongside of Cliven Bundy during the Bundy ranch standoff in April 2014 (Southern Poverty Law Center). In August 2015, like Bundy, Finicum ceased to pay grazing fees to the federal government for the right to graze his cattle on federal lands. Finicum subsequently posted a YouTube video in which he stated that he was inspired to action by the Bundy ranch standoff and that it was "unconstitutional" for the Bureau of Land Management to assess fees for land to which it had no title (Finicum 2015). In the six months from Finicum's declaration to his death, he accrued more than $12,000 in fees and fines (Taylor 2016).

Finicum joined Ammon Bundy, son of Cliven Bundy, and other armed individuals on January 2, 2016, in an occupation of the Malheur National Wildlife Refuge in Harney County, Oregon. Over the next several days, Finicum appeared before reporters on several occasions stating the reasons for the occupation, which included a demand for the immediate release of Dwight and Steve Hammond, who had been incarcerated for setting fire to federal lands, and the return of all federal lands, including Malheur, to the respective states in which they were found. On one occasion, when asked if he would go to jail for his actions, Finicum replied, "I have no intention of spending my days in a concrete box" (Dokoupi 2016).

On January 26, 2016, Finicum and several other "protestors," including Ammon Bundy, left the Malheur Refuge to travel to John Day, Oregon, where they had been invited to speak at a public meeting. State and federal authorities had become aware of the trip and had set up roadblocks to take the occupiers into custody. Though several members of the group surrendered when confronted by law enforcement, Finicum sped off in his pickup truck and later crashed it into a snowbank. As he exited the vehicle, he was ordered to surrender. However, Finicum appeared twice to be attempting to reach inside his coat. During a verbal exchange with officers, Finicum apparently shouted, "You back down or you kill me now. Go ahead. Put the bullet through me. I don't care. I'm going to go meet the sheriff. You do as you damned well please" (Zaitz 2016). One of the passengers in Finicum's truck, Ryan Bundy, took cellphone footage that showed Finicum taunting officers and suggesting that they shoot him (Rollins 2016). Finicum may have believed that a high-profile killing by federal officials, like those at Ruby Ridge, would ignite the cause for which he was fighting.

In the aftermath of the shooting, Finicum was found to have a handgun in his coat. Though only two shots were believed to have been fired at Finicum by a member of the Oregon State Police, later investigations indicated that at least two additional shots had been fired. These shots were later determined to have been fired by members of the FBI's Hostage Rescue Team, though members of that team initially denied that they had discharged any shots. In August 2016, Finicum's widow, Jeanette, stated that her husband was "executed in cold blood" and that she would file a federal lawsuit that would claim that her husband's civil rights had been violated (Siemaszko 2016).

See also: Bundy Ranch Standoff; Malheur National Wildlife Refuge Standoff; Ruby Ridge

Further Reading

Dokoupil, Tony. January 6, 2016. "Oregon Occupier LaVoy Finicum Warns FBI He'd Take Death Over Jail." *NBC News.* https://www.nbcnews.com/news/us-news/oregon-occupier-lavoy-finicum-warns-fbi-he-d-take-death-n491056 (Accessed November 23, 2016).

Finicum, LaVoy. August 14, 2015. "LaVoy vs. BLM part 1, 8-14-15." *YouTube* (Accessed November 23, 2016).

Rollins, Michael. April 6, 2016. "New Video of Lavoy Finicum Stop Released." *KGW8.* http://www.kgw.com/article/news/local/eastern-oregon/new-video-of-lavoy-finicum-stop-released/122667003 (Accessed November 23, 2016).

Siemaszko, Corky. August 29, 2016. "Wife of Slain Oregon Occupier Robert Lavoy Finicum to File Civil Rights Lawsuit." *NBC News.* http://www.nbcnews.com/news/us-news/wife-slain-oregon-occupier-robert-lavoy-finicum-file-civil-rights-n639391 (Accessed November 23, 2016).

Southern Poverty Law Center. May 3, 2016. "In the Aftermath of LaVoy Finicum's Death, Growing Number of Rallies Push Martyrdom Narrative." https://www.splcenter.org/hatewatch/2016/05/03/aftermath-lavoy-finicums-death-growing-number-rallies-push-martyrdom-narrative (Accessed November 23, 2016).

Taylor, Phil. February 5, 2016. "Why LaVoy Finicum Spurned the Government." *E&E News.* Environment & Energy Publishing. https://www.eenews.net/stories/1060031902 (Accessed November 23, 2016).

Zaitz, Les. March 8, 2016. "LaVoy Finicum Shot 3 Times as He Reached for Gun, Investigators Say." *The Oregonian/OregonLive.com.* Advance Publications.

FOCUS ON THE FAMILY

Focus on the Family is an anti-LGBT organization based in Colorado Springs, Colorado. It was founded in 1977 by James Dobson as a conservative Christian lobbying organization intent on articulating its "socially conservative views on public policy" (Focus on the Family). Focus on the Family's stated mission is "nurturing and defending the God-ordained institution of the family and promoting biblical truths worldwide" (Focus on the Family). Focus on the Family promotes traditional and socially conservative values consistent with staunchly evangelical Christian organizations, such as "abstinence-only sexual education; creationism; adoption by married, opposite-sex parents; school prayer; and traditional gender roles" (Focus on the Family). The Southern Poverty Law Center considers the group an anti-LGBT group because of its virulent rhetoric and opposition to issues such as "LGBT rights, particularly LGBT adoption, and same-sex marriage" (Southern Poverty Law Center, Anti-LGBT). Founder James Dobson stated that "the battle against LGBT rights is essentially a 'second civil war' to put control of the U.S. government in the right hands, meaning those who reject LGBT rights" (Southern Poverty Law Center, Anti-LGBT). Focus on the Family has stated that homosexuality is "preventable and treatable" and has conducted programs to spread "reparative therapy," or conversion therapy, where LGBT people are psychologically treated or spiritually counseled "to change their sexual orientation from homosexual or bisexual to heterosexual" (Southern Poverty Law Center, Focus on the Family). Focus on the Family has asserted that the U.S. federal government has a "gay agenda" in order to "sneak homosexuality lessons into [public] classrooms" (Costello 2010).

Perhaps Focus on the Family's most controversial program has been its Love Won Out initiative, which focused on reparative or conversion therapies of gay individuals. The organization founded "Love Won Out in 1998 and eventually sold it to Exodus International," an exgay Christian organization, in 2009 (Southern Poverty Law Center, Anti-LGBT). Love Won Out was to "provide a Christ-centered, comprehensive conference which will enlighten, empower and equip families, church and youth leaders, educators, counselors, policy-makers, and the gay community on the truth about homosexuality and its impact on culture, family, and youth" (Burack and Josephson 2004). In 2013, Exodus International ceased activities. Its leader, John Paulk, a "former" gay man, apologized to the LGBT community, saying,

> From the bottom of my heart I wish I could take back my words and actions that caused anger, depression, guilt and hopelessness. In their place I want to extend love, hope, tenderness, joy and the truth that gay people are loved by God.
>
> Today, I see LGBT people for who they are—beloved, cherished children of God. I offer my most sincere and heartfelt apology to men, women, and especially children and teens who felt unlovable, unworthy, shamed or thrown away by God or the church.
>
> I want to offer my sincere thanks to everyone who encouraged me to take this initial step of transparency. Even while promoting "ex-gay" programs, there were those who called me on my own words and actions. I'm sure I didn't appreciate it at the time, but they have helped me to realize this truth about who I am. (Baldock 2013)

Critics of the Love Won Out initiative believed that the program really wasn't interested in "converting" people from gay to straight. Rather, they believe it was actually a veiled attempt to deny gay people equal rights. As a spokesperson for the National Organization of Women stated, "Their message is simple: Since gay people can 'change,' they do not deserve protection from discrimination" (Anonymous).

One month before the U.S. presidential election in 2008, "Focus on the Family began distributing a 16-page letter titled, *Letter from 2012 in Obama's America*" (Southern Poverty Law Center, Anti-LGBT). The letter described "an imagined American future in which 'many of our freedoms have been taken away by a liberal Supreme Court of the United States and a majority of Democrats in both the House of Representatives and the Senate" (Southern Poverty Law Center, Anti-LGBT). According to *USA Today*, the letter was part of an escalation in rhetoric from Christian right activists "trying to paint Democratic Party presidential nominee Senator Barack Obama in a negative light" (White 2008).

In 2010, an unnamed "educational analyst" for Focus on the Family suggested that antibullying efforts in public schools were meant to draw attention to LGBT students as part of a "gay agenda" being perpetrated by the federal government to "sneak homosexuality into classrooms" (Costello 2010). For critics, Focus on the Family's goal in this case was "to make schools less safe for LGBT students and more safe for their harassers" (Costello 2010).

The Southern Poverty Law Center (2005) has described Focus on the Family as one of a "dozen major groups [that] help drive the religious right's anti-gay crusade."

See also: Cameron, Paul; Family Research Council

Further Reading

Anonymous. "10 Things You Should Know about Focus on the Family." *Human Rights Campaign.* http://www.hrc.org/resources/10-things-you-should-know-about-focus-on-the-family (Accessed June 2, 2017).

Baldock, Kathy. April 24, 2013. "John Paulk, Former Exodus & Love Won Out Leader Apologizes." *Canyonwalker Connections.* http://canyonwalkerconnections.com/john-paulk-former-exodus-love-won-out-leader-apologizes/ (Accessed June 2, 2017).

Burack, Cynthia and Jyl J. Josephson. September 18, 2004. "A Report from 'Love Won Out: Addressing, Understanding, and Preventing Homosexuality.'" National Gay and Lesbian Task Force Policy Institute. http://www.thetaskforce.org/static_html/downloads/reports/reports/LoveWonOut.pdf (Accessed June 2, 2017).

Costello, Maureen. September 3, 2010. "Focus on the Family Goes After LGBT Students." Southern Poverty Law Center. https://www.splcenter.org/news/2010/09/03/focus-family-goes-after-lgbt-students (Accessed June 2, 2017).

Focus on the Family. "Foundational Values." http://www.focusonthefamily.com/about/foundational-values (Accessed June 2, 2017).

Gryboski, Michael. September 13, 2013. "Focus on the Family Cutting 40 More Staff as Part of Restructuring." *The Christian Post.* http://www.christianpost.com/news/focus-on-the-family-cutting-more-staff-as-part-of-restructuring-104516/ (Accessed June 2, 2017).

Southern Poverty Law Center. "Anti-LGBT." https://www.splcenter.org/fighting-hate/extremist-files/ideology/anti-lgbt (Accessed June 2, 2017).

Southern Poverty Law Center. "Family Research Council." https://www.splcenter.org/fighting-hate/extremist-files/group/family-research-council (Accessed June 2, 2017).

Southern Poverty Law Center. April 28, 2005. "A Dozen Major Groups Help Drive the Religious Right's Anti-Gay Crusade." *Southern Poverty Law Center—Intelligence Report.* https://www.splcenter.org/fighting-hate/intelligence-report/2005/dozen-major-groups-help-drive-religious-right's-anti-gay-crusade?page=0%2C0 (Accessed June 2, 2017).

White, Chet. October 27, 2008. "Christian Right's Mailings Depict Disastrous Future Under Obama." *USA Today.* https://usatoday30.usatoday.com/news/religion/2008-10-27-christian-right-obama_N.htm (Accessed June 2, 2017).

FORT HOOD SHOOTING

On November 5, 2009, a U.S. Army major and Army psychiatrist, Nidal Malik Hasan, opened fire on U.S. Army soldiers at Fort Hood, Texas, killing 13 people and wounding more than 30 in his rampage. Though not the most deadly shooting in U.S. history, the act nevertheless was the worst mass shooting at a U.S. military installation. Though concerns had been raised about Hasan because of his past statements and behaviors, he was nevertheless continually promoted up the ranks. Hasan claimed after the shooting that he had perpetrated the attack because of U.S. actions in the global war on terror. Hasan, who was scheduled to be deployed to Afghanistan, had publicly expressed reservations about the U.S. presence in both Iraq and Afghanistan, stating that the U.S. presence in those two countries was ostensibly a war on Islam. Prior to the shootings, Hassan had exchanged a number of e-mails with Yemen-based Imam Anwar al-Awlaki, who was under surveillance by the U.S. National Security Agency as a security threat. Al-Awlaki, an affiliate of Osama bin Laden's al Qaeda organization, praised Hasan after the attacks, stating, "Nidal Hasan is a hero, the fact that fighting against the U.S. army is an Islamic duty today cannot be disputed. Nidal has killed soldiers who were about to be deployed to Iraq and Afghanistan in order to kill Muslims" (Isikoff 2009). Hasan, who was shot in the rampage and paralyzed from the waist down, was tried and sentenced to death in the shootings (Kenber 2013). In 2017, Hasan declared that he is still an "SoA," or "Soldier of Allah" (Browne and Herridge 2017).

Hasan was born in Virginia, "the son of Palestinian immigrants who ran a Roanoke restaurant and convenience store. He graduated from Virginia Tech University and completed his psychiatry training at the Uniformed Service University of Health Science in Bethesda, Maryland in 2003" (History.com). He went on to work at Walter Reed Medical Center in Washington, D.C., "treating soldiers returning from the war with post-traumatic stress disorder" (History.com).

Prior to the shootings, Hasan had requested of his superiors that "some of his patients be prosecuted for war crimes based on the statements that they had made to him during psychiatric sessions" (Egerton 2009). Hasan also made it known to several people that he did not want to be deployed to either Iraq or Afghanistan, as he said, "Muslims shouldn't be in the U.S. military, because obviously Muslims shouldn't kill Muslims" (Drogin and Fiore 2009).

About three and a half months prior to the shootings, Hasan purchased an FN Five-seven semi-automatic pistol. According to a regular customer at a Guns Galore store in Killeen, Texas, Hasan had entered the store in late July 2009 asking for "the most technologically advanced weapon on the market and the one with the highest standard magazine capacity" (Huddleston 2010). Over the course of the next three months, Hasan purchased several additional magazines as well as more than 3,000 rounds of ammunition. He also "visited an outdoor shooting range where he became adept at hitting silhouette targets at distances up to 100 yards" (Huddleston 2010).

On November 5, 2009, at approximately 1:34 p.m. local time, Hasan entered the Soldier Readiness Process Center at Fort Hood, where personnel "receive

President Barack Obama and first lady Michelle Obama pay tribute to 13 soldiers killed by Army major Nidal Malik Hasan at Fort Hood, Texas, in November 2009. Hasan, who had expressed reservations about the United States' presence in Iraq and Afghanistan, perpetrated the worse mass shooting on a military installation in U.S. history. (U.S. Army)

routine medical treatment immediately prior to and upon return from deployment" (History.com). After entering the facility and asking for an officer who a staffer then went to retrieve, Hasan "bowed his head for several seconds and then suddenly stood up and shouted 'Allahu Akbar' ('God is great') and opened fire" (The Telegraph 2009).

During the shootings, Hasan passed by civilians and targeted only soldiers in uniform (Zucchino 2010). Hasan was finally stopped when he "was shot by a civilian police officer" (Browne and Herridge 2017). The shooting left Hasan partially paralyzed. At the end of the massacre, investigators found that Hasan had fired a total of 214 rounds from his semiautomatic pistol. A medic who treated Hasan "stated that his pockets were full of magazines, and that when the shooting ended, Hasan still was carrying 177 rounds of unfired ammunition in both 20- and 30-round clips" (Keyes 2010). The massacre left "12 service members dead and one Department of Defense employee" (History.com).

Hasan was finally tried for the shooting in 2013. During his opening statement, "he admitted that he was the shooter and that he had gunned down soldiers who were being deployed to Afghanistan to prevent them from killing Muslims" (History.com). On August 23, 2013, "a jury found Hasan guilty of 45 counts of premeditated murder and attempted premeditated murder for which Hasan was sentenced to death" (History.com).

Controversy swirled after the shootings as to whether the act was one of Islamic terrorism or even domestic terrorism. If the shooting had been classified as a terrorist attack, it would have accorded the victims benefits equal to their injuries had they been sustained in combat (Brown 2012). The Federal Bureau of Investigation "found no evidence to indicate that Hasan had any co-conspirators or was part of a broader terrorist plot, classifying him as a homegrown violent extremist" (Giuliano 2011). Conversely, the U.S. Defense Department "classified Hasan's attack as an act of workplace violence" and not a terrorist attack (AP 2012).

If Hasan is eventually executed for the Fort Hood shooting, he will be the first active-duty service member to be executed by the U.S. government since 1961. Hasan currently resides on military death row with five other inmates at Fort Leavenworth, Kansas (Kenber).

See also: Orlando Nightclub Shooting; San Bernardino Shooting

Further Reading

AP. October 19, 2012. "Victims Want 2009 Fort Hood Shooting Deemed Terror Act." *Fox News.* http://www.foxnews.com/us/2012/10/19/victims-want-200-fort-hood-shooting -deemed-terror-act.html (Accessed June 5, 2017).

Brown, Angela K. October 19, 2012. "Fort Hood Shooting Victims Seek Added Benefits." *CNS News.com.* http://www.cnsnews.com/news/article/fort-hood-shooting-victims-seek -added-benefits (Accessed June 5, 2017).

Browne, Pamela K. and Catherine Herridge. March 31, 2017. "Fort Hood Shooter Says He's Going on 'Hunger Strike.'" *Fox News.* http://www.foxnews.com/politics/2017/03/31 /fort-hood-shooter-says-hes-going-on-hunger-strike.html (Accessed June 5, 2017).

CBS News. "Tragedy at Fort Hood." http://www.cbsnews.com/feature/tragedy-at-fort-hood / (Accessed June 5, 2017).

Drogin, Bob and Faye Fiore. November 7, 2009. "Retracing Steps of Suspected Fort Hood Shooter, Nidal Malik Hasan." *Los Angeles Times.* http://articles.latimes.com/2009 /nov/07/nation/na-fort-hood-hasan7 (Accessed June 5, 2017).

Egerton, Brooks. November 2009. "Fort Hood Captain: Hasan Wanted Patients to Face War Crimes Charges." *Dallas Morning News.* https://www.dallasnews.com/news/news /2009/11/17/Fort-Hood-captain-Hasan-wanted-9439 (Accessed June 5, 2017).

Fernandez, Manny, Serge F. Kovaleski, and Eric Schmitt. April 3, 2014. "Soldier's Attack at Base Echoed Rampage in 2009." *The New York Times.* https://www.nytimes.com /2014/04/04/us/fort-hood-security-problems.html?_r=0 (Accessed June 5, 2017).

Giuliano, Mark F. April 14, 2011. "The Post 9/11 FBI: The Bureau's Response to Evolving Threats." FBI. https://archives.fbi.gov/archives/news/speeches/the-post-9-11-fbi-the -bureaus-response-to-evolving-threats (Accessed June 5, 2017).

History.com. "Army Major Kills 13 People in Fort Hood Shooting Spree." http://www .history.com/this-day-in-history/army-major-kills-13-people-in-fort-hood-shooting -spree (Accessed June 5, 2017).

Huddleston, Scott. October 21, 2010. "Hasan Sought Gun with 'High Magazine Capacity.'" *My San Antonio.com.* http://blog.mysanantonio.com/military/2010/10/hasan-sought -gun-with-high-magazine-capacity/ (Accessed June 5, 2017).

Isikoff, Michael. November 9, 2009. "Imam Anwar Al Awlaki Calls Hasan 'Hero.'" *Newsweek.* http://www.newsweek.com/imam-anwar-al-awlaki-calls-hasan-hero-216742 (Accessed June 5, 2017).

Kenber, Billy. August 28, 2013. "Nidal Hasan Sentenced to Death for Fort Hood Shooting Rampage." *The Washington Post.* https://www.washingtonpost.com/world/national-security/nidal-hasan-sentenced-to-death-for-fort-hood-shooting-rampage/2013/08/28/aad28de2-0ffa-11e3-bdf6-e4fc677d94a1_story.html?utm_term=.8521e49c788c (Accessed June 5, 2017).

Keyes, Charley. October 20, 2010. "Fort Hood Witness Says He Feared There Were More Gunmen." *CNN.* http://www.cnn.com/2010/CRIME/10/20/texas.fort.hood.shootings/index.html?hpt=T1 (Accessed June 5, 2017).

Mackey, Robert. November 5, 2009. "Mass Shooting at Fort Hood." *The New York Times.* https://thelede.blogs.nytimes.com/2009/11/05/reports-of-mass-shooting-at-fort-hood/ (Accessed June 5, 2017).

The Telegraph. November 6, 2009. "Fort Hood Shootings: The Meaning of 'Allahu Akbar.'" http://www.telegraph.co.uk/news/worldnews/northamerica/usa/6516570/Fort-Hood-shootings-the-meaning-of-Allahu-Akbar.html (Accessed June 5, 2017).

Zucchino, David. October 21, 2010. "Police Officers Describe Fort Hood Gunfight." *Los Angeles Times.* http://articles.latimes.com/2010/oct/21/nation/la-na-fort-hood-20101021 (Accessed June 5, 2017).

FOURTEEN WORDS

The 14 Words, or simply 14, references a slogan used by white supremacists and white nationalists to indicate their goals. The 14 words are "We must secure the existence of our people and a future for white children" (Palmer 2008). Alternatively, the 14 Words have been expressed as, "Because the beauty of the White Aryan woman must not perish from the earth" (Gardell 2003). Both slogans were coined by David Lane, a member of the white supremacist group The Order. Lane was convicted of racketeering and conspiracy for his activities with The Order, but also for violating the civil rights of Alan Berg, a Jewish radio talk show host who Lane conspired to murder on June 18, 1984. For his crimes, Lane was sentenced to 190 years in prison. He died in 2007 after serving more than 20 years of his time.

The first slogan was supposedly inspired by a statement, 88 words in length, from chapter 8 of Adolf Hitler's *Mein Kampf:*

> What we must fight for is to safeguard the existence and reproduction of our race and our people, the sustenance of our children and the purity of our blood, the freedom and independence of the fatherland, so that our people may mature for the fulfillment of the mission allotted it by the creator of the universe. Every thought and every idea, every doctrine and all knowledge, must serve this purpose. And everything must be examined from this point of view and used or rejected according to its utility.

Though Lane never made the claim that this passage from Hitler's book is the origin of the 14 Words, he was undoubtedly influenced by this passage as he had read it dozens of times. The number 88 is also highly significant in racist, white supremacist circles. The number eight represents the eighth letter of the alphabet, or "H." Thus, 88 represents "HH," or "Heil Hitler" (Spiegel Online 2011). For Lane, 88 also referred to his 88 Precepts, or his treatise on natural law, religion, and politics. Lane also believed that the 88 Precepts provided guidelines for "securing, protecting, preserving and establishing white territorial imperatives" (Anti-Defamation League).

The pairing of 14 and 88 has also been used by other white supremacists, such as Dylann Roof, the individual convicted of massacring nine people in a Charleston, South Carolina, church in 2015 (Siemaszko 2016). The numbers also figured prominently in a plot to assassinate Barack Obama in 2008. In this instance, two individuals with strong white supremacist beliefs planned to kill 88 African Americans in Tennessee, including Obama, and behead 14 of the victims (Lichtblau 2008). The pair was arrested before they could carry out their plans.

See also: Lane, David; Neo-Nazis; Order, The; White Nationalism; White Supremacist Movement

Further Reading

Anti-Defamation League. "14 Words." https://www.adl.org/education/references/hate -symbols/14-words#.VfCCOM5Z9pk (Accessed March 24, 2016).

Dunbar, Edward, Amalio Blanco, and Desirée A. Crèvecoeur-MacPhail. 2016. *The Psychology of Hate Crimes as Domestic Terrorism: U.S. and Global Issues.* ABC-CLIO, p. 91.

Gardell, Mattias. 2003. *Gods of the Blood: The Pagan Revival and White Separatism.* Duke University Press Books, p. 69.

Lichtblau, Eric. October 27, 2008. "Arrests in Plan to Kill Obama and Black Schoolchildren." *The New York Times.* http://www.nytimes.com/2008/10/28/us/politics/28plot .html?em (Accessed March 25, 2017).

Palmer, Brian. October 29, 2008. "White Supremacists by the Numbers." *Slate.* http:// www.slate.com/articles/news_and_politics/explainer/2008/10/white_supremacists _by_the_numbers.html (Accessed March 24, 2017).

Schechter, Asher. January 6, 2017. "What Are the '14 Words' Everyone's Been Freaking Out About?" *Haaretz.* http://www.haaretz.com/us-news/1.763410 (Accessed March 14, 2017).

Siemaszko, Corky. December 9, 2016. "Dylann Roof's Videotaped Confession Stuns Courtroom." *NBC News.* http://www.nbcnews.com/news/us-news/dylann-roof-s -videotaped-confessions-stuns-courtroom-n694036 (Accessed March 25, 2017).

Southern Poverty Law Center. "David Lane." https://www.splcenter.org/fighting-hate /extremist-files/individual/david-lane (Accessed March 24, 2017).

Southern Poverty Law Center. "Racist Skinhead Glossary." *Southern Poverty Law Center— Intelligence Report.* https://www.splcenter.org/fighting-hate/intelligence-report/2015 /racist-skinhead-glossary (Accessed March 24, 2017).

Spiegel Online. June 27, 2011. "The Truth About 88: New Book Reveals Secret Meaning of Neo-Nazi Codes." http://www.spiegel.de/international/germany/the-truth-about -88-new-book-reveals-secret-meaning-of-neo-nazi-codes-a-770820.html   (Accessed March 24, 2017).

FROMM, PAUL

Paul Fromm (b. 1949) is a neo-Nazi and white supremacist and the international director of the far-right, white nationalist Council of Conservative Citizens (CCC), an organization that supports the cause of white separatism (Southern Poverty Law Center). Fromm and the CCC have been accused of influencing the actions of Dylann Roof, the individual who killed nine African American parishioners in an historic black church in Charleston, South Carolina, in 2015 (Quan 2015). Fromm "has hosted a radio show on the *Stormfront*, a white nationalist, white supremacist, and neo-Nazi website, widely regarded as the internet's first major racial hate site" (Levin 2003). Fromm also has close associations with Ku Klux Klan members David Duke and Don Black.

While a student at the University of Toronto in the 1960s, Fromm "co-founded the ultra-conservative, anti-communist Edmund Burke Society (EBS) that precipitated confrontations with New Left and anti-Vietnam war groups" (Southern Poverty Law Center). In 1981, Fromm "founded the Canadian Association for Free Expression (CAFÉ), . . . which works against the Canadian Human Rights Commission to defend anti-Semites, racists and Holocaust deniers from persecution under hate crime and human rights legislation" (Southern Poverty Law Center).

From 1974 until 1997, Fromm taught public school, but he was fired after speaking at several Heritage Front events that promoted neo-Nazi and white supremacist ideals. A video of Fromm at one of these events showed him in front of a Nazi flag speaking to a crowd shouting "Siege Heil!," "white power," "Hail The Order," and shouting various racial epithets (Southern Poverty Law Center). In 1998, Fromm attended a CCC anti-immigration rally at which a Mexican flag was burned. The rally was also attended by Glenn Spencer, an American anti-illegal immigration advocate who serves as the president of the American Border Patrol.

In 2006, Fromm "helped found the Aryan Guard (AG), a neo-Nazi organization linked to assaults on different minority groups" (Southern Poverty Law Center). At the CCC annual conference in Greenville, South Carolina, in 2007, Fromm gave a speech entitled "Turning America Upside Down: From Karl Marx to Hillary Clinton and Barack Obama." In the speech, Fromm characterized the United States as "feminized, de-christianized, and deracialized," eventually referring to it as "Absurd-istan" (Southern Poverty Law Center). In 2012, Fromm spoke at the Annual Conference of American Renaissance, where he shared a stage with Jared Taylor and Richard Spencer, both well known in the neo-Nazi, white supremacist, and white nationalist circles.

At a CCC event in 2015, Fromm called the "creation of police hate-crime units an 'abomination,' denounce[d] those who malign the Confederate flag, and labelled a clothing company's diversity-centered branding as 'mind rape'" (Quan 2015). In Dylann Roof's online manifesto that surfaced after his killing of nine black church parishioners in 2015, Roof "credited the Council of Conservative Citizens (CCC) website" for drawing his attention to "black on white crime" (Quan 2015). In 2016, the Supreme Court of Canada invalidated a request to allow an American neo-Nazi's bequest to the National Alliance—a white nationalist, anti-Semitic, and white separatist organization—to be honored. The court also ordered "the would-be appellant—the Canadian Association for Free Expression (CAFÉ), led by white supremacist Paul Fromm—to pay the court costs, earlier estimated at $9,000, of those who originally sought to halt the bequest" (Potos 2016).

See also: American Border Patrol/American Patrol; Black, Don; Council of Conservative Citizens; Duke, David; Ku Klux Klan; National Alliance; Neo-Nazis; Order, The; Roof, Dylann Storm; Spencer, Glenn; White Nationalism; White Supremacist Movement

Further Reading

Levin, Brian. August 21, 2003. "Cyberhate: A Legal and Historical Analysis of Extremists' Use of Computer Networks in America." In Barbara Perry, editor, *Hate and Bias Crime: A Reader*. Routledge.

Potos, Mark. June 9, 2016. "Final Ruling: National Alliance Will Not Receive Bequest." *Southern Poverty Law Center—Hatewatch*. https://www.splcenter.org/hatewatch/2016/06/09 /final-ruling-national-alliance-will-not-receive-bequest (Accessed March 7, 2017).

Quan, Douglas. June 23, 2015. "Ex-Ontario Teacher Is International Director of American 'White Nationalist' Group that Influenced Dylann Roof." *National Post*. http:// news.nationalpost.com/news/canada/ex-ontario-teacher-is-international-director-of -american-white-nationalist-group-that-influenced-dylann-roof (Accessed March 7, 2017).

Southern Poverty Law Center. "Paul Fromm." https://www.splcenter.org/fighting-hate /extremist-files/individual/paul-fromm (Accessed March 7, 2017).

G

GAEDE, APRIL

April Gaede (b. 1966) gained fame in the extremist community as a white nationalist and neo-"Nazi stage mom." Gaede is the mother of twin daughters Lynx and Lamb, "who for years performed folk music at white supremacist festivals and gatherings under the name of 'Prussian Blue'" (Southern Poverty Law Center, April Gaede). Gaede reportedly selected her first husband because of his "Aryan" looks. Her twins, born several years later, were both blonde and blue-eyed, the supposed characteristics of true Aryans. Gaede is also famous for being given the "honor" of "disposing of the ashes of David Lane, a member of the terrorist organization The Order who was involved in the assassination of Jewish radio talk show host Alan Berg in 1984" (Southern Poverty Law Center, April Gaede).

Gaede grew up on a ranch in California where her father used to brand the family's horses and cattle with swastikas (Southern Poverty Law Center, April Gaede). Eight years after her marriage to her "Aryan-looking" husband in 1986, Gaede gave birth to twins Lynx and Lamb. She reportedly home-schooled her children using her own curriculum drawn from books from the 1950s—"from the years before 'civil rights' and feminism became so evident" (Buchanan 2005). In 2003, when the twins turned nine, Gaede begin to promote them as "new faces on the neo-Nazi music scene in an attempt to attract mainstream audiences to the white nationalist cause" (Southern Poverty Law Center 2011). As the twins grew older and their music career soared, Gaede said, "What young, red-blooded American boy isn't going to find two blonde twins . . . singing about white pride and pride in your race . . . very appealing?" (Southern Poverty Law Center 2011). Gaede and her twins named the singing duo Prussian Blue, the color of the residue of Zyklon B, the gas the Nazis used to exterminate millions of Jews during the Holocaust. At the height of their fame, Lynx and Lamb Gaede were described as the "neo-Nazi version of the Olsen twins" (Southern Poverty Law Center 2011).

When Gaede married for a third time in 2003, the marriage produced a third daughter whom Gaede named Dresden Hale—"Dresden after the German city nearly bombed out of existence in World War II, and Hale after then-imprisoned neo-Nazi leader Matt Hale, pastor of the virulent World Church of the Creator" (Southern Poverty Law Center, April Gaede). Gaede later lamented that she hadn't had more children during her prime childbearing years, stating, "I could have produced four to six more children with that ideal eugenic quality that [Lynx and Lamb] possess" (Southern Poverty Law Center, April Gaede).

In 2007, Gaede was given the "honor" of "disposing of the ashes of David Lane," one of the members of the terror group The Order who had assassinated Alan

Berg, a Denver-based Jewish radio talk show host, in 1984. During his imprisonment, Lane had become enamored with the Gaede twins, calling them his "fantasy sweethearts" (Southern Poverty Law Center April Gaede,). Gaede's credibility in the neo-Nazi community was damaged in 2011 when Lynx and Lamb renounced their extremist views "in favor of marijuana-fueled love and positivity" (Southern Poverty Law Center 2011). Gaede tried to downplay the defection when she portrayed the twins' announcement as "less than sincere saying, 'The girls are using the Jews [media] to make bank as usual. If they had done anything else they would not have gotten any attention'" (Southern Poverty Law Center 2011).

See also: Hale, Matt; Lane, David; Neo-Nazis; Order, The; White Nationalism

Further Reading

Buchanan, Susy. April 28, 2005. "Neo-Nazi April Gaede Pushes Twin Daughters Lynx and Lamb into Spotlight." *Southern Poverty Law Center Intelligence Report.* https://www.splcenter.org/fighting-hate/intelligence-report/2005/neo-nazi-april-gaede-pushes-twin-daughters-lynx-and-lamb-spotlight (Accessed January 5, 2017).

Potok, Mark and Laurie Wood. "Leaving White Nationalism." *Southern Poverty Law Center Intelligence Report.* https://www.splcenter.org/fighting-hate/intelligence-report/2013/leaving-white-nationalism (Accessed January 5, 2017).

Southern Poverty Law Center. "April Gaede." https://www.splcenter.org/fighting-hate/extremist-files/individual/april-gaede (Accessed January 5, 2017).

Southern Poverty Law Center. November 15, 2011. "Pop-Singing Gaede Twins Renounce Racism." *Southern Poverty Law Center Intelligence Report.* https://www.splcenter.org/fighting-hate/intelligence-report/2011/pop-singing-gaede-twins-renounce-racism (Accessed January 5, 2017).

GAFFNEY, FRANK, JR.

Frank Gaffney Jr. (b. 1953) is a recognized Islamophobe and conspiracy theorist (Southern Poverty Law Center). He is the founder and president of the "Center for Security Policy (CSP), a conservative, Washington, D.C.–based think tank that has been accused of engaging in the propagation of conspiracy theories involving a range of individuals, media outlets, and other organizations" (Gunter 2015). The CSP has been described by the Southern Poverty Law Center as an "anti-Muslim think tank." Gaffney's penchant for conspiracy theories has led to his calls for congressional hearings in order to "unmask" the Muslim conspirators that are embedded in the U.S. government. Gaffney is convinced that the United States is being "Islamified" and that the implementation of Islamic law (sharia) is imminent (Anti-Defamation League). In 2011, Gaffney was banned from the Conservative Political Action Conference by the American Conservative Union (ACU). The ACU chairperson stated in a press release that Gaffney "has become personally and tiresomely obsessed with his weird belief that anyone who doesn't agree with him on everything all the time or treat him with the respect and deference he believes is his due, must be either ignorant of the dangers we face or, in extreme case, dupes of the nation's enemies" (Reilly 2014).

Gaffney was once a respected policy maker. He "graduated from the Edmund A. Walsh School of Foreign Service at Georgetown University in 1975, and subsequently received a degree from John Hopkins University's Paul H. Nitze School of Advanced International Studies" (Southern Poverty Law Center). In 1983, Gaffney became the deputy assistant secretary of defense for nuclear forces and arms control policy in the Reagan administration, and he was later nominated for assistant secretary of defense for international security affairs in 1987, though he was never confirmed in the post by the U.S. Senate. In 1988, Gaffney founded the Center for Security Policy, "a hawkish think-tank that became a bastion of neo-conservative thought" (Southern Poverty Law Center).

It is generally believed that Gaffney's obsession with the "Islamification" of the United States stems from one source, "a 1991 fantasy written by a lone Muslim Brotherhood member that was introduced into evidence at the 2008 Holy Land Foundation Trial in Dallas Federal Court" (Clarion Project). In 2011, Gaffney said,

> When it is impracticable to engage in violence, Shariah-adherent Muslims are still obliged to engage in jihad through stealthy techniques or, in the words of the Muslim Brotherhood, 'civilization jihad.' . . . They are doing it through influence operations, the target set of which is comprehensive—government, law enforcement, intelligence agencies, the military, penal institutions, media think tanks, political entities, academic institutions. And they are very aggressively targeting non-Muslim religious communities in the name of ecumenicalism. (Southern Poverty Law Center)

When Barack Obama was running for the presidency in 2008, Gaffney claimed that Obama hoped to attract the "Jihadist vote." Gaffney also stoked the "birther" conspiracy theory by questioning whether Obama was a "natural born citizen of the United States" (Anti-Defamation League). In a 2009 *Washington Times* article, Gaffney reacted to President Obama's trip to Saudi Arabia and Egypt by claiming that "here is mounting evidence that the president not only identifies with Muslims, but actually may still be one himself" (Anti-Defamation League).

According the SPLC, Gaffney's rhetoric indicated that he would most likely favor the resurrection of the Cold War–era House Un-American Activities Committee in order to expose subversives in the U.S. government who are working to undermine the United States' political and religious institutions by implementing sharia religious law throughout the land (Southern Poverty Law Center). Gaffney's charges of organized subterfuge (e.g., "that Hillary Clinton's aide Huma Abedin was part of a 'Muslim Brotherhood' conspiracy") have been picked up by the likes of Representative Michele Bachmann (R.-Minn.), though they have been roundly denounced by more respected members of Congress. He was banished from the Conservative Political Action Committee in 2011 because of his claim that two prominent board members, Grover Norquist and Suhail Khan, "were Muslim Brotherhood subversives." The allegations were based on the fact that Norquist's wife is a Palestinian American and Khan is a Muslim (Southern Poverty Law Center).

In 2013 and 2014, Gaffney appeared at panels organized by Steve Bannon's *Breitbart News* that featured titles such as "Amnesty and Open Borders: The End of America—and the GOP," and "Benghazigate: The Ugly Truth and the Cover-up" (Southern Poverty Law Center). Among the participants at the panels were Representative Steven King (R-Iowa), "a noted anti-immigrant and anti-Muslim talking head," as well as Senator Ted Cruz (R-Texas), who would run for the U.S. presidency in 2016.

In 2015, Gaffney teamed up with Cruz and Donald Trump, who would eventually be elected to the U.S. presidency in November 2016, and organized three National Security Action Summits that featured anti-immigrant and anti-Muslim speakers (Southern Poverty Law Center). In the same year, Jeff Sessions, who was destined to become Donald Trump's attorney general, received the Keeper of the Flame award from CSP (Piggott 2016). In September 2015, to bolster his arguments against Syrian refugees, Gaffney invited Jared Taylor, a white supremacist and editor of *American Renaissance*, a white supremacist publication, on his radio program, *Secure Freedom Radio* (Hatewatch Staff 2015). The Southern Poverty Law Center described Gaffney's interview of Taylor as a "new low for a man who is used to rubbing shoulders with elected officials including a number of the GOP presidential candidates" (Hatewatch Staff 2015).

See also: Center for Security Policy

Further Reading

Anti-Defamation League. "Frank Gaffney Jr. and the Center for Security Policy." https://www.adl.org/education/resources/profiles/frank-gaffney-jr-and-the-center-for-security-policy (Accessed March 24, 2017).

Clarion Project. "The Muslim Brotherhood's Strategic Plan for America—Court Document." https://clarionproject.org/muslim_brotherhood_explanatory_memorandum/ (Accessed March 24, 2017).

Gunter, Joel. December 8, 2015. "Trump's 'Muslim Lockdown': What Is the Center for Security Policy?" *BBC News.* http://www.bbc.com/news/world-us-canada-35037943 (Accessed March 24, 2017).

Hatewatch Staff. September 30, 2015. "Anti-Muslim Activist Frank Gaffney Interviews White Nationalist Jared Taylor on His Radio Show." *Southern Poverty Law Center— Hatewatch.* https://www.splcenter.org/hatewatch/2015/09/30/anti-muslim-activist-frank-gaffney-interviews-white-nationalist-jared-taylor-his-radio-show (Accessed March 24, 2017).

Piggott, Stephen. November 18, 2016. "Jeff Sessions: Champion of Anti-Muslim and Anti-Immigrant Extremists." *Southern Poverty Law Center—Hatewatch.* https://www.splcenter.org/hatewatch/2016/11/18/jeff-sessions-champion-anti-muslim-and-anti-immigrant-extremists (Accessed March 24, 2017).

Reilly, Ryan J. February 15, 2014. "CPAC Banned Frank Gaffney Over Baseless Anti-Muslim Charges." *Talking Points Memo.* http://talkingpointsmemo.com/muckraker/cpac-banned-frank-gaffney-over-baseless-anti-muslim-charges (Accessed March 24, 2017).

Southern Poverty Law Center. "Frank Gaffney Jr." https://www.splcenter.org/fighting-hate/extremist-files/individual/frank-gaffney-jr (Accessed March 24, 2017).

GALE, WILLIAM POTTER

William Potter Gale (1917–1988) served as a military aide to General Douglas MacArthur in the Philippines during World War II. However, he is best known (together with Mike Beach) for being the founder of Posse Comitatus ("power of the county") in the late 1960s. Gale's right-wing, antigovernment sentiments helped spawn the sovereign citizens movement, a loose collection of individuals who reject all government authority and do not believe themselves to be bound by the laws of a federal government that they deem to be illegitimate.

Gale met Richard Butler in the early 1970s and introduced him to Posse Comitatus, which, aside from being an antigovernment and paramilitary organization, was virulently racist and anti-Semitic. Butler would eventually recast the centuries-old ideas of Christian Identity into a new organization known as Aryan Nations. As noted by the Southern Poverty Law Center, "which tracks racist and hate groups," though Richard Butler may have founded Aryan Nations, William Potter Gale was its inspiration.

In the mid-1970s, Gale established the Identity Church on his ranch near Mariposa, California. Gale, who preferred to be called "Reverend Gale," would deliver blistering attacks on blacks and Jews from behind a pulpit backed by an enormous Confederate flag (Los Angeles Times 1988). Gale had become a follower of Christian Identity theology in the mid-1950s. For more than 30 years, he "warned the world that a satanic Jewish conspiracy disguised as communism was corrupting public officials and the courts, undermining the United States and wrecking its divinely inspired Constitution" (Levitas 2002). Like so many in his generation, "Gale was drawn to the extremely conservative, anti-Communist politics that pervaded the United States in the 1950s" (Southern Poverty Law Center). His anti-Semitism went hand in hand with his stubborn opposition to racial integration and the civil rights policies of the American government during the 1950s and 1960s. Gale would publicly state that Jews were the "offspring of the devil, while non-whites were 'mud people' and whites were the real Hebrews of the Bible" (Levitas 2002). Ironically, William Potter Gale was later found to have Jewish blood "on his father's side from a long line of devout Jews" (Levitas 2002).

In 1984, Gale was instrumental in the formation of the tax protest group known as the Committee of the States, "a right-wing organization that rejected all federal authority" (Nizkor Project). In March 1986, the Committee of the States "sent letters to dozens of sheriffs in Georgia." The letter declared, "The sheriff is duty-bound to preserve and protect private rights of county residents against tyranny of public wrongs by public administrators" (Nizkor Project). In January 1988, "Gale and four other members of the 'Committee' were sentenced to one year and one day in jail" for sending death threats to agents of the Internal Revenue Service as well as to a Nevada state judge (Southern Poverty Law Center). The federal judge in the case suspended Gale's sentence because of his poor health. Four months later, in May 1988, Gale died of complications from emphysema.

See also: Aryan Nations; Beach, Henry Lamont "Mike"; Butler, Richard; Christian Identity; Posse Comitatus; Sovereign Citizens Movement

Further Reading

Levitas, Daniel. December 18, 2002. "Exploring What Is Behind the Rare Phenomenon of Jewish Anti-Semites." *Southern Poverty Law Center Intelligence Report*. https://www .splcenter.org/fighting-hate/intelligence-report/2002/exploring-what-behind-rare -phenomenon-jewish-anti-semites (Accessed December 14, 2016).

Los Angeles Times. May 4, 1988. "William P. Gale; Led Several Racist Groups." http://articles .latimes.com/1988-05-04/news/mn-1880_1_other-racist-groups (Accessed December 14, 2016).

Nizkor Project. "Paranoia as Patriotism: Far-Right Influences on the Militia Movement; Report on the Committee of the States." http://www.nizkor.org/hweb/orgs/american/adl /paranoia-as-patriotism/committee-of-the-states.html (Accessed December 14, 2016).

Southern Poverty Law Center. "Aryan Nations." https://www.splcenter.org/fighting-hate /extremist-files/group/aryan-nations (Accessed December 14, 2016).

GELLER, PAMELA

Pamela Geller (b. 1958) is a political activist and commentator whose rhetoric and activities focus on anti-Islamic causes. Her Islamophobic stance first came to the public's attention when she publicly stated her opposition to an Islamic community center that Muslim leaders hoped to build on land near the former World Trade Center in Lower Manhattan. Geller is also known for her association with the American Freedom Defense Initiative, an anti-Muslim hate group that she helped cofound with noted Islamophobe Richard Spence (Southern Poverty Law Center). The group helped sponsor the "Draw the Prophet" cartoon contest in Garland, Texas, that drew an attack by two Islamic extremists in May 2015. Though the attack was thwarted by security guards, "the Islamic State of Iraq and the Levant (ISIL) claimed responsibility for the attack" (Southern Poverty Law Center). U.S. officials did not verify that the attack was directed by ISIL, saying only that the attacks were "inspired" by ISIL, not necessarily directed by that organization. Geller consistently blogs about "creeping Sharia" in the United States, a reference to Islamic sharia law that Geller and other anti-Islamic groups claim Muslims want to impose in the United States. The Southern Poverty Law Center characterizes Geller as "relentlessly shrill and coarse in her broad-brush denunciations of Islam."

Geller was born in 1958 and became an associate editor of the *New York Observer* in 1989. She left her position in 1994 and spent most of the rest of the 1990s and the 2000s as a "well-to-do Long Island housewife" (Southern Poverty Law Center). Geller stated that her views and attitudes changed after the terror attacks of 9/11. After the attacks, she contributed several essays to various outlets in which she examined Muslim militancy (Howard 2012). Eventually, she would begin her own blogs (Atlas Shrugs), which consisted of "unvarnished anti-Muslim stridency" that won her many followers (Southern Poverty Law Center).

Geller's "evolution from blogger to activist began in 2007 when she joined Stop the Maddrassa," an initiative meant "to stop the opening of a secular public Arabic-English school in Brooklyn, New York" (Southern Poverty Law Center). In December 2009, Geller became more widely known when she blogged about the

Park51 project, "a proposal by a New York City imam to renovate an abandoned building in lower Manhattan into a 13-story mosque and community center, not far from the site of the former World Trade Center" (Left Alternatives).

In 2010, Geller teamed up with "radical Muslim alarmist Robert Spencer and took over the Stop Islamization of America (SIOA)" organization (also known as the American Freedom Defense Initiative) (Southern Poverty Law Center). The focal point of SIOA's initial projects was to demonstrate against the Park51 project. Thousands of protestors flocked to the demonstration, and Geller and Spencer depicted the project's planners as radical extremists. The project was even described as an "Islamic victory mosque to celebrate the 9/11 attacks," though no Muslim had ever used the term in any public way (Southern Poverty Law Center). After the scuttling of the Park51 project,

Pamela Geller is widely known as an anti-Islamic political activist and commentator. Geller is best known for her public opposition to a proposed Islamic community center that was to be built near the former site of the World Trade Center in New York City. (Jason Andrew/Getty Images)

Geller became a media darling, particularly for outlets on the conservative right. Indeed, for months afterwards, she was a fixture on *Fox News*, where she propagated her claims that Muslims intended to impose sharia law throughout the United States.

By means of her Web site, Geller has perpetuated conspiracy theories popular among adherents of the extreme right,

> including claims that President Obama is the love child of Malcolm X, that Obama was once involved with a "crack whore," that his birth certificate is a forgery, that his late mother posed nude for pornographic photos, and that he was a Muslim in his youth who never renounced Islam. She has described Obama as beholden to his "Islamic overlords" and said that he wants jihad to be victorious in America. (Southern Poverty Law Center)

Geller has been willing to "ally with any individual or movement that expresses anti-Muslim sentiments" (Southern Poverty Law Center). Thus, she has found confederates among neo-Nazis and white nationalists on the extreme right—"a rather remarkable feat, considering she is Jewish" (Southern Poverty Law Center). Geller "has been the subject of several positive postings on racist websites such as *Stormfront*, VDARE, *American Renaissance*, and the League of the South" (Southern Poverty Law Center). Geller's anti-Muslim activity was included among several references that Anders Breivik—the Norwegian terrorist who killed 77 people, most teenagers, at a left-wing youth camp in 2011—cited in his manifesto as justification for his attacks. Geller and her SIOA partner, Richard Spencer, were cited by Breivik 64 times (Southern Poverty Law Center).

Though Geller makes no pretense about being learned in Islamic studies, she nevertheless has garnered many followers through her belief that Muslims are infiltrating every level of the U.S. government. In 2013, she was forbidden from appearing at the Conservative Political Action Conference (CPAC) because she accused "CPAC board members Grover Norquist and Suhail Khan of being 'members of the Muslim Brotherhood and secret Islamist agents'" (Seitz-Wald 2013).

In 2015, Geller was the object of an assassination plot by an individual who had been radicalized by ISIL. The individual had planned to assassinate Geller by beheading for her role in the Draw the Prophet cartoon contest (Perez and Prokupecz 2015).

See also: American Renaissance; League of the South; Spencer, Robert Bertrand; *Stormfront*; VDARE

Further Reading

Bernard, Anne and Alan Feuer. October 8, 2012. "Outraged and Outrageous." *The New York Times*. http://www.nytimes.com/2010/10/10/nyregion/10geller.html?pagewanted=all (Accessed March 25, 2017).

Howard, Greg. November 28, 2012. "Pamela Geller's War." *The Village Voice*. http://www.villagevoice.com/news/pamela-gellers-war-6436870 (Accessed March 25, 2017).

LeftAlternatives. July 24, 2011. "Jihad Against Islam: The Anti-Muslim Inner Circle." *MyFineForum.org*. http://leftalternatives.myfineforum.org/Norway_s_tragedy_racism_and_zionism_about278.html (Accessed July 27, 2017).

Perez, Evan and Shimon Prokupecz. June 3, 2015. "Boston Shooting: Suspect Plotted to Behead Pamela Geller, Sources Say." *CNN*. http://www.cnn.com/2015/06/03/us/boston-police-shooting/index.html (Accessed March 25, 2017).

Seitz-Wald. March 16, 2013. "Pam Geller: CPAC Board Member Is 'Worse' Than Anwar al-Awlaki." *Salon*. http://www.salon.com/2013/03/16/pam_geller_cpac_board_member_is_worse_than_anwar_al_awlaki/ (Accessed March 25, 2017).

Southern Poverty Law Center. "Pamela Geller." https://www.splcenter.org/fighting-hate/extremist-files/individual/pamela-geller (Accessed March 25, 2017).

Steinback, Robert. May 5, 2011. "Muslim-Basher Pamela Geller Pushes Another Obama Fairy Tale, Proudly." *Southern Poverty Law Center—Hatewatch*. https://www.splcenter.org/hatewatch/2011/05/05/muslim-basher-pamela-geller-pushes-another-obama-fairy-tale-proudly (Accessed March 25, 2017).

Steinback, Robert. June 17, 2011. "The Anti-Muslim Inner Circle." *Southern Poverty Law Center—Intelligence Report*. https://www.splcenter.org/fighting-hate/intelligence-report/2011/anti-muslim-inner-circle (Accessed March 25, 2017).

GLIEBE, ERICH

Erich Gliebe (b. 1963) was a prominent figure in the neo-Nazi movement in the United States, having led the National Alliance (NA) after the death of its founder, William Pierce. Gliebe was innovative in attracting young recruits to the organization through "hate rock music and racist events such as European-American cultural festivals" (Southern Poverty Law Center). A former boxer, Gliebe was sometimes called the "Aryan Barbarian," a reference to his German heritage and that his father had been a soldier in the Germany Wehrmacht during World War II. Gliebe left the NA in 2014 and appears to have dropped out of the contemporary neo-Nazi movement (Southern Poverty Law Center).

Gliebe grew up in a Cleveland, Ohio, suburb. As he grew older, he disdained the lack of "honor and discipline" exhibited by his classmates. Gliebe idolized his father, who had fought for Germany in World War II, saying, "My father was my hero and I decided that one day I would give my all to fight for my race" (Southern Poverty Law Center).

In 1990, Gliebe joined the National Alliance, the white nationalist, anti-Semitic, and neo-Nazi organization founded by William Pierce in 1974. Gliebe proved himself to be an aggressive recruiter for the organization through his use of "cultural festivals" that catered to white pride and were billed as "family affairs." Gliebe also harnessed the growing affinity for hate rock music among extremist groups and organized concerts under the guise of Life Rune Records. These concerts had the effect of expanding membership in the NA, particularly among teenagers and young adults. Gliebe was so successful in his efforts that Pierce, in 1999, bought Resistance Records, a floundering record label that Gliebe was chosen to lead (Southern Poverty Law Center). Gliebe managed to turn a profit with the endeavor and gushed that "hate rock" could be used to "heighten Aryan racial consciousness—both in ourselves and in others." By 2002, Resistance Records was bring $1 million annually to the coffers of the NA (Southern Poverty Law Center).

William Pierce died unexpectedly in July 2002. Because of his success with Resistance Records, Gliebe was appointed the new chairperson of NA by the board of directors, but opposition to his leadership began to emerge. Gliebe alienated many white nationalists when he delivered a speech "a few months before Pierce's death in which he described members of hate groups other than NA as 'morons' and 'hobbyists'" (Southern Poverty Law Center). The reporting of the speech by the Southern Poverty Law Center caused many customers of Resistance Records to take their business elsewhere. The resulting internal dispute caused a split in NA, and Gliebe ended up firing Billy Roper, the organization's membership coordinator. Roper, who had advocated closer associations with other racist groups, took several hundred NA members with him when he left the organization.

As memberships and revenues declined under Gliebe's leadership, the NA board of directors soured on Gliebe's management style. Several prominent white nationalist and neo-Nazi groups began to openly criticize Gliebe. In 2005, Kevin Strom, a close ally of Gliebe's and editor of NA's magazine *National Vanguard*, openly questioned Gliebe's leadership, after which Gliebe fired Strom. Strom left NA to form his own neo-Nazi group and took with him the rights to the magazine and its name—*National Vanguard* (Southern Poverty Law Center).

A mere two days after Strom's departure, Gliebe left NA, "handing the reins over to one of his staunchest supporters, Shaun Walker" (Southern Poverty Law Center). However, Gliebe would reassume the leadership just over a year later when Walker "was convicted on federal civil rights charges related to several bar assaults" that he had perpetrated in Salt Lake City, Utah (Southern Poverty Law Center).

As NA's membership and revenue continued to decline, a group of former NA leaders—the National Alliance Reform and Restoration Group (NARRG)—sued Gliebe and the NA in an attempt to wrest control of the NA from Gliebe. The $2-million civil lawsuit accused Gliebe of "a myriad of instances of malfeasance, misfeasance, illegalities and irregularities" (Terry 2014). Rather than fight the charges, Gliebe stepped down, pleading for a case of "no mas," or "no more." Instead of ceding control of NA to the NARRG, however, Gliebe turned the organization over to 66-year-old William Williams. Gliebe's resignation shocked the racist world and left the NA—once the largest and best-financed neo-Nazi organization in the United States—on its last legs (Terry 2014).

In 2016, the NA had only about three dozen members. Gliebe disappeared from the white nationalist scene and appears to have given up his extremist tendencies.

See also: National Alliance; National Vanguard; Neo-Nazis; Pierce, William; Strom, Kevin; White Nationalism; White Supremacist Movement

Further Reading

Southern Poverty Law Center. "Erich Gliebe." https://www.splcenter.org/fighting-hate/extremist-files/individual/erich-gliebe (Accessed March 25, 2017).

Terry, Don. October 24, 2014. "In Major Surprise, Erich Gliebe Steps Down as National Alliance Chairman." *Southern Poverty Law Center—Hatewatch.* https://www.splcenter.org/hatewatch/2014/10/24/major-surprise-erich-gliebe-steps-down-national-alliance-chairman (Accessed March 25, 2017).

GOTTFREDSON, LINDA

Linda Gottfredson (b. 1947) is a longtime advocate of "scientific racism," arguing that racial inequality, especially in employment, is not the result of racism or long-standing hiring practices that have disadvantaged blacks and other minorities. Rather, she argues, it is the direct result of racial differences in intelligence. Gottfredson has been a tireless advocate against any program that attempts "to reduce racial inequality in either the workplace or society as a whole," arguing that social equality between black and white Americans is neither possible nor desirable (Southern Poverty Law Center, Linda Gottfredsom). Over the course of her career, Gottfredson has accepted at least $267,000 in grants from the Pioneer Fund, an American nonprofit group labeled by the Southern Poverty Law Center, Linda Gottfredsom, as a racist and white supremacist group that was established "to advance the scientific study of heredity and human differences" (Potok 2007). Gottfredson also opposed the 1991 Civil Rights Act because it fails to recognize "innate difference in intelligence." Gottfredson has been a strong opponent of affirmative action, arguing that it is neither possible nor desirable to have complete inequality in any realm of social of existence and that it is naive to believe "the egalitarian fiction that all groups are equal in intelligence" (Potok 2007).

Gottfredson was born in San Francisco and graduated with a bachelor's degree in psychology from the University of California at Berkeley and a PhD in sociology from Johns Hopkins University. Gottfredson spent her career largely working to fight efforts at workforce equality, stating that the United States has promulgated public policy based on the false premise that all racial groups are equal in intelligence. She believes that more problems are created by enacting policies that work to provide equality in numbers of racial groups in the workplace than the problems the policies were meant to solve. Gottfredson holds that "differences in intelligence have real world effects, whether we think they're there or not, whether we want to wish them away or not. And we don't do anybody any good, certainly not the low-IQ people, by denying that those problems exist" (Gottfredson).

In addition to her efforts to oppose workplace equality, Gottfredson has defended "some of the most egregious figures in academic racism" such as Arthur Jensen and J. Philippe Rushton (Southern Poverty Law Center, Arthur Jensen). Jensen, who was called the "father of modern academic racism," was largely responsible for "resurrecting the idea that the black population is inherently and immutably less intelligent than the white population" (Southern Poverty Law Center, Jensen). On the other hand, the Southern Poverty Law Center, Arthur Jensen, has called Rushton "probably the most important race scientist at work today."

In 1994, Gottfredson was one of 52 scientists who published a 1994 *Wall Street Journal* op-ed piece entitled, "Mainstream Science on Intelligence." The piece was a defense of Charles Murray and Richard Herrnstein's book, *The Bell Curve*, "which used arguments recycled from eugenicists, white supremacists, and neo-Nazis to claim that social inequality is caused by black genetic inferiority, especially in intelligence" (Southern Poverty Law Center, Linda Gottfredson). Through her own research, Gottfredson believes that an inherent IQ gap between blacks and whites means that "black 17-year-olds perform, on the average, more like white 13-year-olds" (Southern Poverty Law Center, Linda Gottfredsom). Therefore, since IQ largely determines social outcomes, and because racial disparities in IQ are innate and immutable, "policies intended to reduce racial inequality are doomed to fail, and may even exacerbate the problems they're intended to remedy" (Southern Poverty Law Center, Linda Gottfredsom). Barry Mehler, who founded the Institute for the Study of Academic Racism, has stated that Gottfredson attempts "to promote racial theories used by the Nazis":

Thus we see that Gottfredson's opposition to affirmative action is based not in any such claimed "objectivity," but in a sanitized resurrection of ideas put forward by Nazi racial theorists. Under the false pretense of intellectual honesty, she has endorsed the same poisonous ideology that half a century ago led to the Holocaust. (Mehler 1999)

Like many "race realists," Gottfredson believes that there is a global conspiracy to repress the truth about racial differences. This global conspiracy dominates discourse in the media, the academy, and all public discussion. The conspiracy is allegedly based in political interests on the left, but its chief villains are "duplicitous social scientists whose control over racial arguments mirrors the suppression of dissent under the Soviet regime." As such, IQ researchers, such as herself, are "coerced into 'living a lie' like peasants under Communist rule who were 'complicit in their own tyranny'" (Southern Poverty Law Center, Linda Gottfredsom).

See also: Jensen, Arthur; Pioneer Fund; Rushton, Jean-Philippe

Further Reading

Gottfredson, Linda. "Race, IQ, Success and Charles Murray." *Samtiden.com.* https://www.samtiden.com/tbc/las_artikel.php?id=63 (Accessed April 29, 2017).

Mehler, Barry. March 15, 1999. "Academia at Forefront of Racist Ideals, White Supremacy." *Southern Poverty Law Center—Intelligence Report.* https://www.splcenter.org/fighting-hate/intelligence-report/1999/academia-forefront-racist-ideals-white-supremacy (Accessed April 29, 2017).

Potok, Mark. December 9, 2007. "Academic Racism: Into the Muck." *Southern Poverty Law Center—Hatewatch.* https://www.splcenter.org/hatewatch/2007/12/09/academic-racism-muck (Accessed April 29, 2017).

Southern Poverty Law Center. "Arthur Jensen." https://www.splcenter.org/fighting-hate/extremist-files/individual/arthur-jensen (Accessed April 29, 2017).

Southern Poverty Law Center. "Linda Gottfredson." https://www.splcenter.org/fighting-hate/extremist-files/individual/linda-gottfredson (Accessed April 29, 2017).

Southern Poverty Law Center. "Pioneer Fund." https://www.splcenter.org/fighting-hate/extremist-files/group/pioneer-fund (Accessed April 29, 2017).

GRIFFIN, MICHAEL

Michael Frederick Griffin (b. 1961) is described as a "fundamentalist Christian and a loner with a bad temper" (Rimer 1993). On March 10, 1993, Griffin murdered Dr. David Gunn in Pensacola, Florida. The crime is believed to have been the first documented murder of an OB-GYN where the murderer's stated intention was to prevent a doctor from performing abortions (Kushner 2002). The murder prompted the federal government to enact the Federal Freedom of Access to Clinic Entrances Act, an act that makes it a federal crime to interfere with, or obstruct, any individual seeking reproductive health services. The act prompted Paul Jennings Hill, a former minister and adherent of the Army of God, to issue the "First Defense Action Statement," a document signed by 30 antiabortion leaders, that proclaimed that "whatever force is legitimate to defend the life of a born child is legitimate to defend the life of an unborn child" (Army of God). Griffin was convicted of murder in 1994 and is currently serving a life sentence in a correctional institution in Florida.

David Gunn had earned his MD from the University of Kentucky and was determined to practice in areas of the United States underserved by health services.

After his residency, Gunn moved to a rural area of Alabama because "no other doctor would do the job" (Rimer 1993). Because of his work, "Dr. Gunn received hate mail, death threats, and was constantly harassed by protestors who called him a murderer" (Rimer 1993). On the day that Michael Griffin killed Dr. Gunn, he waited for Gunn outside of his clinic in Pensacola, Florida—the Pensacola Women's Medical Services Clinic—and fired three shots into his (Gunn's) back. Gunn "died during surgery at a local hospital" (Booth 1993).

Griffin claimed to be "acting for God," but his defense lawyers claimed "that he had been brainwashed by another anti-abortion activist, John Burt" (Rohter 1994). Burt, a minister and former Ku Klux Klan member, allegedly influenced Griffin by exposing him to "videos, books, prayer sessions, [the] use of an effigy of Dr. Gunn and even a funeral for a pair of aborted fetuses" (Rohter 1994). Burt compared Griffin to a soldier who follows orders, comparing himself to a "general who sends out the orders to the troops. . . . I can't control if one goes bad. I can't be responsible" (Rimer 1993). Burt went on to say that "I've shown those videos and literature to thousands of people who never killed anyone. I would respect Michael a lot more if he had stuck with his original defense, which was that he acted for God when he shot Dr. Gunn" (Rohter 1994).

From Griffin's murder of Gunn in March 1993 to May 2009, three additional abortion providers were murdered by killers proclaiming pro-life motivation. Paul Jennings Hill was convicted of murdering Dr. John Britton in July 1994, was sentenced to death for his actions, and died by lethal injection in September 2003.

Upon the passage of Griffin's life sentence for killing Dr. Gunn, Paul Burt stated, "You're going to see more bombings and shootings. It's an extreme thing to tear a baby apart. It's an extreme thing to kill a doctor. We don't want either one" (Times Wire Services 1994). Burt pointed out that "Jesus was zealous. . . . Some people believe you should sit in church and pray for abortion to stop. I believe in putting feet on my prayers" (Rohter 1994). When asked if this meant "continued attacks on abortion clinics, bombings, and other acts of violence against abortion providers and the clinics in which they practice," Burt replied, "Whatever it takes" (Rohter 1994).

See also: Rudolph, Eric Robert

Further Reading

Army of God. "Defensive Action Statement." http://www.armyofgod.com/defense.html (Accessed April 26, 2017).

Booth, William. March 11, 1993. "Doctor Killed During Abortion Protest." *The Washington Post.* http://www.washingtonpost.com/wp-srv/national/longterm/abortviolence/stories /gunn.htm (Accessed April 26, 2017).

Kushner, Harvey. 2002. *Encyclopedia of Terrorism.* SAGE Publications.

Rimer, Sara. March 14, 1993. "The Clinic Gunman and the Victim: Abortion Fight Reflected in 2 Lives." *The New York Times.* http://www.nytimes.com/1993/03/14/us/the-clinic -gunman-and-the-victim-abortion-fight-reflected-in-2-lives.html?pagewanted=all (Accessed April 26, 2017).

Rohter, Larry. March 5, 1994. "Towering Over Abortion Foe's Trial: His Leader." *The New York Times.* http://www.nytimes.com/1994/03/05/us/towering-over-the-abortion-foe-s-trial-his-leader.html (Accessed April 26, 2017).

Times Wire Services. March 6, 1994. "Activist Gets Life for Killing Abortion Doctor." *Los Angeles Times.* http://articles.latimes.com/1994-03-06/news/mn-30794_1_abortion-clinic (Accessed April 26, 2017).

GRITZ, BO

Bo Gritz (b. 1939) is a decorated Vietnam War veteran who is perhaps best known for intervening on behalf of Randy Weaver, a white supremacist, who retreated to his home in Ruby Ridge, Idaho, after failing to appear in court on weapons charges in 1992. The Ruby Ridge standoff between Weaver and the Federal Bureau of Investigation lasted 11 days and resulted in the death of Weaver's wife and son as well as a U.S. Marshal. Gritz's offer to intervene in the standoff was based on his sympathies for Weaver as a white supremacist, Christian patriot, and survivalist. Gritz's ability to successfully convince Weaver to surrender himself and trust in the court system made Gritz a hero among many patriot and white supremacist groups. In 1996, Gritz attempted again to intervene on behalf of a Christian patriot group known as the Montana Freemen, who were wanted on federal charges related to counterfeiting and bank fraud. Gritz was unsuccessful in this attempt and left the Freemen compound frustrated by what he called the "legal mumbo-jumbo" that the Freemen were using to support their claims (Snow 2002). The Montana Freemen finally surrendered after an 81-day standoff with federal authorities. Gritz's penchant for spreading conspiracy theories, and his warnings about the dangers of the "New World Order," have made him a favorite in extremist circles.

Gritz was an active service member of the U.S. Army for 22 years and had been a member of the elite Special Forces unit. After the Vietnam War, Gritz made headlines when he made a series of trips to Southeast Asia in search of Vietnam War POWs. The missions were heavily publicized but were criticized as haphazard (Keating 1994). In 1988, Gritz had run as the vice presidential candidate on the presidential ticket of David Duke, a former Grand Wizard of the Ku Klux Klan. Gritz was a vocal proponent of racial segregation and advocated that states should have the right to reinstitute segregationist policies if they saw fit. In 1992, Gritz ran for political office on the U.S. Taxpayer's Party platform under the slogan, "God, Guns and Gritz" and "published a manifesto extolling the virtues of isolationism and survivalism" (Southern Poverty Law Center). In the manifesto—"The Bill of Gritz"—"Gritz called for a complete closing of the border with Mexico and the dismantling of the Federal Reserve" (Bringhurst and Foster 2008). Gritz opposed the New World Order and taught military and survivalist skills because he believed that the United States was headed toward total sociopolitical and economic collapse (Southern Poverty Law Center). For a time, Gritz associated with the Christic Institute, a group that pursued lawsuits against the U.S. government over charges that the government "helped foster drug trafficking in both Southeast Asia and Central America" (Berlet and Lyons 2000). Gritz had also been associated with the Christian Patriot and Christian Identity movements (Bringhurst and Foster 2008).

Gritz has consistently warned anyone who would listen about "pernicious federal activities and God's call to citizen action" and the dangers of "faggots, feminists, and the omnipresent Jew" (Southern Poverty Law Center).

In 1999, Gritz told a crowd of hundreds in Kansas City, Missouri, that "Y2K could bring chaos to the nation and the world. . . . For the general good, regulations could be imposed that turn you into less than an American" (Anti-Defamation League). Gritz also established SPIKE—Specially Prepared Individuals for Key Events—"where he taught participants all manner of survival skills and techniques" (Southern Poverty Law Center). He also attempted "to sell plots of land in a common-law community called 'Almost Heaven,' offering buyers an escape from cities where the effects of Y2K would no doubt be the worst" (Southern Poverty Law Center) and sold dozens of different survival products, ranging in cost from a few dollars to several hundred dollars (Anti-Defamation League). Also in 1999, Gritz married his second wife, and through her, accepted a milder version of Christian Identity, an ideology that holds that Jews are the descendants of Eve and Satan (Southern Poverty Law Center). Through his organization, The Center for Action, which has attempted to renew American values, Gritz has adopted a spiritual emphasis encouraging Christian "warriors" to "lead the fight against a satanic world order" (Southern Poverty Law Center).

In 2005, Gritz traveled to Florida to intervene in the case of Terri Schiavo, "a woman who had been in a persistent vegetative state for 15 years" and had been ordered to be removed from her feeding tube by a Florida judge (Southern Poverty Law Center). By going to Florida, Gritz intended to conduct a "citizen's arrest" of the judge and Schiavo's husband, who had requested the removal of the feeding tube. Reportedly, Gritz also carried a "citizen's arrest warrant" for then Florida governor Jeb Bush and Florida attorney general Charlie Crist (Southern Poverty Law Center).

Gritz now broadcasts a radio program known as *Freedom Call* on the American Voice Radio Network.

See also: Christian Identity; Duke, David; Montana Freemen; Ruby Ridge; Weaver, Randy

Further Reading

Anti-Defamation League. "James 'Bo' Gritz.'" https://www.adl.org/sites/default/files/documents/assets/pdf/combating-hate/Gritz-James-Bo-EIA.pdf (Accessed March 22, 2017).

Berlet, Chip and Matthew N. Lyons. 2000. *Right-Wing Populism in America: Too Close for Comfort*. Guilford Press, p. 340.

Bringhurst, Newell G. and Craig L. Foster. 2008. *The Mormon Quest for the Presidency*. John Whitmer Books, pp. 208–226.

Colonel Bo Gritz. http://bogritz.org/broadcastpage.htm (Accessed January 30, 2018).

Keating, Susan Katz. 1994. *Prisoners of Hope: Exploiting the POW/MIA Myth in America*. Random House.

Snow, Robert J. 2002. *Terrorists Among Us: The Militia Threat*. Perseus Books Group, p. 216.

Southern Poverty Law Center. "Bo Gritz." https://www.splcenter.org/fighting-hate/extremist-files/individual/bo-gritz (Accessed March 22, 2017).

GULETT, MORRIS

Morris Gulett (b. 1956) is a one-time member of Richard Butler's Aryan Nations movement and has been trying since Butler's death in 2004 to succeed him as the leader of Aryan Nations. When Butler died, leaving no clear successor to his neo-Nazi, anti-Semitic group, several individuals stepped forward and claimed that they were the rightful heirs to Butler's organization. What emerged was a turf war among former Butler followers and Aryan Nations members to be the rightful claimant to Butler's racist views. In 2010, Gulett emerged from prison, where he had been since 2005 on federal conspiracy charges, to establish what he called the "true" Aryan Nations in Converse, Louisiana. After assuming control of the group, Gulett made several sensational claims, including calling it the "most-feared and revered white supremacist organization the world has ever known" (Southern Poverty Law Center). Gulett currently claims to be the senior pastor of the Church of Jesus Christ Christian, an American white supremacist church associated with Christian Identity theology, though some former Aryan Nations members indicate that Paul Mullet, another former Butler follower, claims that title.

In 2012, Gulett announced his plans to build a church that would be the world headquarters for Aryan Nations. He released a statement that read,

> Nothing has changed about our plans. I still intend to build a church building and the World Headquarters for Aryan Nations WILL continue to be right here in Louisiana. This is my home. I am here to stay till death do I part from this earth. I will not be swayed from my job as the Senior Pastor of the Church of Jesus Christ Christian or the World Leader of Aryan Nations. And I or Aryan Nations will not be run off or discouraged by the Jews, Negros, Queers, Mestizos or Mulattoes of the diversity cult. As I said of this once great Christian Republic in the interview, diversity is NOT our greatest strength, but our greatest weakness. Diversity is what will be the demise and total destruction of this nation and the chief purveyors of tolerance, diversity and multiculturalism know that too. (Gulett 2012)

In April 2016, not many months after shuttering his "true" Aryan Nations group in Louisiana, Gulett announced that he was leaving Aryan Nations and the extremist scene. However, not long after, Gulett formed a new racist church based on the Christian Identity theology called The Church of the Sons of Yaheweh (Morlin 2016. He said, "We believe that the White, Anglo-Saxon, Germanic and kindred peoples are the direct descendants of the Adamic man made in the image of YHVH, and were placed here to be the light bearers and supreme ruling race of this lost and dying world" (Morlin 2016. Gulett went on to state that he saw Donald Trump as an ally in his cause and someone who "sounds committed and sincere and at this point in our political quagmire we can only hope that he is serious about freeing our nation from the parasites of the Republican and Democratic parties. We can only hope that he is a man sent by God to lead us out of the wilderness. But do not expect perfection" (Morlin 2016).

See also: Aryan Nations; Butler, Richard; Christian Identity; Neo-Nazis; White Supremacist Movement

Further Reading

Gulett, Morris L. February 21, 2012. "Full Statement from Pastor Morris L. Gulett." *KSLA News*. http://www.ksla.com/story/16974738/full-statement-from-pastor-morris-l-gulett (Accessed March 28, 2017).

Morlin, Bill. April 13, 2016. "White Supremacist Morris Gulett Launches New Racist Church." *Southern Poverty Law Center—Hatewatch*. https://www.splcenter.org/hatewatch /2016/04/13/white-supremacist-morris-gulett-launches-new-racist-church (Accessed March 28, 2017).

Southern Poverty Law Center. "Morris Gulett." https://www.splcenter.org/fighting-hate /extremist-files/individual/morris-gulett (Accessed March 28, 2017).

H

HALE, MATT

Matt Hale (b. 1971) is a white supremacist who, in 2005, was sentenced to 40 years in prison "for soliciting the murder of a federal judge" (Southern Poverty Law Center, Matt Hale). At age 11, Hale declared that he was a white supremacist after reading books about national socialism (*The Rise and Fall of the Third Reich*) and Adolf Hitler's *Mein Kampf*. Over the next two decades, Hale would become "one of the most effective and well-known leaders of the extremist right and the head of the World Church of the Creator" (later known as the Creativity Movement), a neo-Nazi organization that was once one of the most powerful organizations of its kind in the country (Southern Poverty Law Center, Matt Hale). Hale spent years "pumping out violent and aggressive propaganda" from his childhood bedroom in East Peoria, Illinois (Southern Poverty Law Center, Matt Hale). Once known by his followers in the World Church of the Creator as "Pontifex Maximus" ("highest priest"), Hale and hundreds of mostly young male followers spread tracts that denigrated nonwhites and promoted "conspiracy theories about Jewish control of the media and of the Atlantic slave trade, about the 'Kosher Food Tax,' as well as material allegedly demonstrating the biological superiority of whites" (Anti-Defamation League). After Hale was denied a law license in Illinois in 1999, one of his associates "went on a rampage targeting religious and racial minorities" (Southern Poverty Law Center, Matt Hale). Two people were killed and nine were wounded before Hale's compatriot committed suicide as police closed in on him. In 2000, Hale lost a copyright lawsuit over the name "Church of the Creator," which was under the legal ownership of another entity. Hale railed against the judge who handed down the decision and later solicited an undercover FBI agent to murder the judge. He was convicted for that crime and sentenced to 40 years in prison.

After Hale's self-proclaimed "racial awakening" at age 11 in which he discovered that "white people had been responsible for the vast majority of progress in the world," and as such, the "idea that the races were 'equal' to one another seemed incorrect," he attended Bradley University in Peoria, Illinois, where he double majored in political science and music (Anti-Defamation League). In 1990, while at Bradley University, Hale founded the American White Supremacist Party (AWSP). The AWSP never had more than seven or eight members, so Hale dissolved the group and "tried to open a chapter of the National Association for the Advancement of White People (NAAWP), a group founded by KKK member David Duke" (Southern Poverty Law Center, Matt Hale). This effort also failed. But in 1992, Hale declared himself the national leader of the National Socialist White Americans Party. As in his previous efforts, the group attracted few members and Hale disbanded it in 1995.

By this time, Hale had become associated with the Church of the Creator (COTC), a hate group that had been around since 1973. But after the group's founder and leader committed suicide in 1993, a void was left in the COTC's leadership that Hale was happy to fill (Anti-Defamation League). On July 27, 1996— Matt Hale's 25th birthday—the COTC's Guardians of the Faith Committee named Hale "Pontifex Maximus" ("highest priest") and rechristened the organization the World Church of the Creator (WCOTC) (Anti-Defamation League).

Before his association with the WCOTC, Hale's previous attempts to promote neo-Nazi ideals and white supremacism had been "limited to organizations that he had founded and leadership positions [that] he had bestowed upon himself" (Southern Poverty Law Center, Matt Hale). With WCOTC, Hale had inherited a group with a "developed philosophy"—"the idea that whites had created everything worthwhile in the civilized world. Race became the sole religious doctrine of the 'Church'" (Southern Poverty Law Center, Matt Hale).

Under Hale's leadership, "WCOTC chapters and memberships grew, populated by large numbers of racist skinheads and an unusually large number of female adherents" (Southern Poverty Law Center, Matt Hale). Hale actively reached out to women, stating, "While the Church first and foremost views women's most natural and important role to be that of mother to beautiful White children and loving wives to our glorious White men, our women members, just as our male Creators, can become ordained Reverends and rise to positions of influence" (Anti-Defamation League). Hale often criticized mainstream Christianity as a religion "concocted by Jews" (Anti-Defamation League).

In 1999, the Illinois State Bar Association denied Hale a law license on "ethical grounds." Although Hale had "earned a law degree from Southern Illinois University and successfully passed the bar exam, the Illinois Bar deemed Hale unfit for legal practice due to his racial activism" (Southern Poverty Law Center, Matt Hale). A friend and close confidant of Hale's, Benjamin Smith, sought revenge for the Illinois Bar's ruling and went on a rampage, intent on killing religious and racial minorities. Smith killed two individuals and wounded nine others before committing suicide. Hale's association with Smith reflected badly on him and WCOTC, but the killings allowed Hale to appear in the national media on several occasions, thereby providing him with a platform to espouse WCOTC's "theology."

In May 2000, "a lawsuit was brought against WCOTC by the TE-TA-MA Truth Foundation, a multicultural religious group that owned the copyright for 'Church of the Creator'" (Southern Poverty Law Center, Matt Hale). The attention that had come to Hale and the WCOTC over the Smith rampage "caused the Truth Foundation to take action for copyright infringement" (Southern Poverty Law Center, Matt Hale.

In a subsequent ruling, Judge Joan Humphrey Lefkow of Chicago barred the WCOTC from using the words "Church of the Creator." After Hale refused to comply with the judge's orders, he announced a "state of war" with Judge Lefkow. Hale denounced Lefkow because she was married to a Jew. Soon after, "death threats against Lefkow appeared on the white nationalist online forum *Stormfront*" (Southern Poverty Law Center, Matt Hale). Hale later solicited an undercover FBI informant to murder Judge Lefkow. The informant "had been embedded in the WCOTC soon after the Smith rampage" (Southern Poverty Law Center, Matt Hle). Hale was arrested on January 8, 2003, and charged with solicitation of murder. On April 6, 2005, he was sentenced to 40 years in prison. During the trial, "jurors heard more than a dozen tapes of Hale using racial slurs, including one in which he joked about Benjamin Smith's murderous shooting spree" (Southern Poverty Law Center 2005).

In 2014, Hale filed a "$19 million civil rights lawsuit against prison officials for not allowing him to play his violin in his cell." Hale's lawsuit also alleged "a host of civil rights violations by prison officials, including barring him from sending and receiving mail and keeping him from delivering sermons to his followers. The prison has also refused to provide him with his religious diet, which consists largely of raw fruits, vegetables, nuts and seeds" (Meisner 2014).

Hale's projected release date is December 2037. By that time, he will be 66 years old.

See also: Creativity Movement; Duke, David; Neo-Nazis; *Stormfront*; White Supremacist Movement

Further Reading

Anti-Defamation League. "Matt Hale." https://www.adl.org/sites/default/files/documents /assets/pdf/combating-hate/Hale-Matt-EIA.pdf (Accessed May 6, 2017).

Meisner, Jason. September 16, 2014. "White Supremacist Matthew Hale Wants to Play Violin in Solitary." *Chicago Tribune.* http://www.chicagotribune.com/news/local/breaking /chi-imprisoned-white-supremacist-government-violin-deal-20140916-story.html (Accessed May 6, 2017).

Southern Poverty Law Center. "Matt Hale." https://www.splcenter.org/fighting-hate /extremist-files/individual/matt-hale (Accessed May 6, 2017).

Southern Poverty Law Center. April 7, 2005. "Matthew Hale Gets Maximum 40-Year Sentence." *Southern Poverty Law Center—Intelligence Project.* https://web.archive.org /web/20060214090434/http://www.splcenter.org/intel/news/item.jsp?site_area =1&aid=102 (Accessed May 6, 2017).

HARPENDING, HENRY

Henry Harpending (1944–2016) was an American anthropologist and population expert whose research purportedly confirmed the notion that some races are superior to others, making him a hero of the racist right. Harpending was known for his controversial views on race, and his works have been associated with the notion of scientific racism, the belief that racism is justified within societies based on the racial superiority of some groups and the racial inferiority of other groups. Harpending often noted that "Africans, Papua New Guineans, and 'Baltimore' (African-Americans) possess the same genetic temperamental predispositions," which are characterized by "violence, laziness, and a preference for 'mating instead of parenting'" (Southern Poverty Law Center). Harpending's most famous book, which he coauthored with Gregory Cochran, was *The 10,000 Year Explosion: How*

Civilization Accelerated Human Evolution. The thesis of the book is that human evolution is currently on an accelerating curve, but demonstrable evolutionary change did not occur until modern Europeans left Africa. The Southern Poverty Law Center characterized Harpending as a eugenicist who believed that "medieval Europeans intuitively adopted eugenic policies" and pointed out that Harpending emphasized the importance of eugenics in American society. Before his death in 2016, Harpending's views made him a popular speaker at white supremacist conferences and were widely published on white supremacist Web sites, such as *Stormfront* and the *Vanguard News Network.*

Harpending believed that identifiable differences between the races define human society. Variations "between racial and ethnic groups—including cultural differences, social and economic disparities, and achievement gaps—are the result of recent and ongoing human evolution" (Southern Poverty Law Center). These differences have been accelerated, according to Harpending, because of the "new kind of human" that is found only in the populations of Western European and East Asian descent. Once humans left the primordial breeding ground of Africa and ventured into the rest of the world, evolution accelerated. Harpending contended that present-day hunter-gatherer societies represent the "old kind" of humans that are "impulsive, violent, innumerate, illiterate, and lazy" (Southern Poverty Law Center). On the other hand, the "new human" is the product of "medieval Europeans invented institutions like governments, courts, and contracts," which Harpending apparently believes "had never existed anywhere before being introduced in 11th century England" (Southern Poverty Law Center). Medieval Europe was able to further refine the breed of "new humans" through "genetic pacification" as the introduction of the death penalty resulted in "the steady removal of individuals who were more genetically prone to personal violence" (Southern Poverty Law Center).

In 2009, Harpending participated in a conference on "Preserving Western Civilization." During the conference, he appeared on the program with Peter Brimelow, president and chief contributor of the white nationalist Web site VDARE.com, and Jean-Philippe Rushton, president of the eugenicist Pioneer Fund (Burhgart 2009). The statement of purpose from the conference read,

> We believe that America's Judeo-Christian heritage and European identity must be defended. Today, our glorious Western civilization is under assault from many directions. Three such threats will be discussed at this conference. First, the massive influx to the United States and Europe of Third-World immigrants who do not share our fundamental political and cultural values. Second, the threat from Islam, a militant ideology that is hostile to our society and, in principle, committed to destroying it. Third, because of the persistent disappointing performance of blacks (which many whites mistakenly blame on themselves) many whites have guilt feelings that undermine Western morale and deter us from dealing sensibly with the other threats. (Southern Poverty Law Center)

At the conference, Harpending presented a "full-throated defense of scientific racism." He claimed that many of African descent were violent, lazy, and preferred "mating instead of parenting" (Southern Poverty Law Center). Harpending went on to say that

> the reason the Industrial Revolution happened in 1800, rather than the year one thousand, or zero, which it could have, the Romans certainly could have done it, is that a new kind of human evolved in northern Europe, and probably northern Asia. And that this led to the Industrial Revolution—this new kind of human was less violent, had an affinity for work. When you view your parents or grandparents, and you know that they're retired, they could relax. But afterwards they can't just sit on the couch and relax, they've got to go and get a shop and work on a cradle for their grandchildren. . . . I've never seen anything like that in an African. I've never seen anyone with a hobby in Africa. They're different. (Hart 2009)

Harpending's view that "old" humans are "impulsive, violent, innumerate, illiterate, and lazy," as opposed to "new" humans, who are "peaceful, diligent, and intelligent," are realities that "everyone knows to be true," but "anthropologists aren't allowed to say so because these are considered 'hate facts.' Instead, academics are forced to pretend 'that these are really all charming, lovely people who are just the victims of capitalism'" (Southern Poverty Law Center).

Harpending died on April 3, 2016.

See also: Brimelow, Peter; Pioneer Fund; Rushton, Jean-Philippe; *Stormfront; Vanguard News Network*; VDARE; White Nationalism; White Supremacist Movement

Further Reading

Burhgart, Devin. April 1, 2009. "Inside the Preserving Western Civilization Conference." Institute for Reach & Education on Human Rights. http://www.irehr.org/2009/04/01/inside-the-preserving-western-civilization-conference/ (Accessed April 22, 2017).

Cochran, Gregory and Henry Harpending. 2010. *The 10,000 Year Explosion: How Civilization Accelerated Human Evolution*. Basic Books.

Hart, Michael H. August 2009. *Preserving Western Civilization*. Washington Summit Publishers.

Southern Poverty Law Center. "Henry Harpending." http://www.splcenter.org/fighting-hate/extremist-files/individual/henry-harpending (Accessed April 22, 2017).

HEIMBACH, MATTHEW

Matthew Heimbach (b. 1991) is a white nationalist who was an active organizer of white nationalist groups during his years at Towson University in Maryland. While at Towson, Heimbach founded a chapter of Youth for Western Civilization (YWC) and later started a White Student Union (WSU) (Southern Poverty Law Center). Heimbach has been associated with such white nationalist, white supremacist, and neo-Nazi groups as the neo-Confederate League of the South, the Council of Conservative Citizens, the Sons of Confederate Veterans, and the American Freedom Party. After Heimbach graduated from Towson University in 2013, WSU was folded into a new organization, the Traditionalist Youth Network, which cloaked itself in "traditionalism" as a method to protect Western civilization from the effects of rampant multiculturalism and illegal immigration. In 2016, Heimbach appeared at several rallies in support of presidential candidate Donald Trump. In one incident in Louisville, Kentucky, Heimbach shoved and punched a black protestor. In 2017, the victim sued Heimbach and others for their actions. Heimbach replied that he had been responding to Trump's direction to those in attendance to "get 'em [the protestors] out of here" (Hensley 2017).

Heimbach cut his white nationalist teeth while a student at Maryland's Towson University. In 2011, the Youth for Western Civilization group that he founded stood for "stopping rampant multiculturalism" and was "against illegal immigration" (Southern Poverty Law Center). In early 2012, Heimbach issued a YWC report in which he stated that "the death of apartheid in South Africa orchestrated the systematic slaughter of the white community" (Southern Poverty Law Center). Later in 2012, YWC "executed a series of inflammatory events at Towson University, including chalking messages like 'white pride' and 'white guilt is over' on campus sidewalks" (Southern Poverty Law Center). YWC's actions "led to the resignation of the group's faculty sponsor and the ultimate loss of the group's official status on campus" (Southern Poverty Law Center). Heimbach stated that the chalked messages were simply an expression of "traditional conservative values and not racist" (Southern Poverty Law Center).

After YWC's dissolution, Heimbach formed the White Student Union. He claimed that the group was founded so that white people would be treated equally with every other group on campus, though he pointed out that "demanding equality for white people on campus apparently isn't very popular" (Southern Poverty Law Center).

One of WSU's first official events was inviting "race realist" Jared Taylor to speak on campus. Taylor is the founder of the white nationalist New Century Foundation and editor of *American Renaissance*, a "pseudo-academic journal that regularly publishes articles by proponents of eugenics and blatant anti-black and anti-Latino racists" (Southern Poverty Law Center). In the spring of 2013, Heimbach's last semester, WSU organized student night patrols "to combat a black crime wave" with Heimbach claiming that "every single day black predators prey upon the majority white Towson University student body" (Southern Poverty Law Center). After graduation, Heimbach merged WSU with the Traditionalist Youth Network in order to take the message of WSU to a larger audience outside of Towson. Upon its founding, Heimbach became the national director for the group.

In June 2013, Heimbach spoke at the annual conference of the Council of Conservative Citizens, a virulently racist organization that rails against black-on-white crime. Wearing a pistol on his hip, Heimbach claimed that "white people haven't had a true vote since 1860" and called for Southern secession from the Union, stating that the government could not be reformed. Heimbach closed his remarks with David Lane's "14 Words," the white nationalist motto and manifesto: "We must secure the existence of our people and a future for white children" (Southern Poverty Law Center).

Later in the summer of 2013, Heimbach spoke at an annual Stormfront gathering in Tennessee, "singing the praises of former Klan member David Duke" (Southern

Poverty Law Center). He would speak again before a Stormfront gathering in the summer of 2014 entitled "Death to America." Heimbach's remarks contained many white nationalist hot-button issues, including claims about the undo influence of Jews on the federal government.

Heimbach made headlines in March 2016 when he was caught on camera shoving a black woman and screaming in her face at a rally for presidential candidate Donald Trump. Wearing a "red baseball cap with the words 'Make America Great Again,'" Heimbach was urged on by fellow rally goers as he shoved and berated the black woman who had come to protest against the Trump campaign. When Heimbach came forward as the individual in the video, the media quickly seized on his white nationalist credentials. Ryan Lenz, the editor of the Southern Poverty Law Center's *Hatewatch* blog, calls Heimbach the "next David Duke." Lenz describes Heimbach as "a media-savvy millennial who has forged relationships with Stormfront, the League of the South, the Aryan Terror Brigade, the National Socialist Movement and other white-supremacist organizations. . . . He's the affable, youthful face of hate in America, and in many ways, he's the grand connector between all of these groups" (Helm 2016).

In April 2017, the victim of Heimbach's assault, Kashiya Nwanguma, "a public health major at the University of Louisville, was joined by two others in suing Trump and others, including Heimbach" (Hensley 2017). Heimbach responded that he "relied on Trump's authority to order disruptive persons removed" as the permission that he needed to act (Hensley 2017). Heimbach's claims followed another protestor who was at the rally who acted under Trump's "urging and inspiration." Heimbach believes that Trump, or his campaign, should pay his legal costs, citing a 2016 rally in Cedar Rapids, Iowa, in which Trump promised those who forced out protestors at his events, "I promise you. I will pay for the legal fees" (Hensley 2017).

See also: American Freedom Party; *American Renaissance*; Council of Conservative Citizens; Duke, David; Fourteen Words; Lane, David; League of the South; Neo-Confederates; Neo-Nazis; Taylor, Jared; White Nationalism

Further Reading

Helm, Joe. April 12, 2016. "This White Nationalist Who Shoved a Trump Protestor May Be the Next David Duke." *The Washington Post.* https://www.washingtonpost.com /local/this-white-nationalist-who-shoved-a-trump-protester-may-be-the-next-david -duke/2016/04/12/7e71f750-f2cf-11e5-89c3-a647fcce95e0_story.html?utm_term =.b8b735dc9fc6 (Accessed April 22, 2017).

Hensley, Nicole. April 18, 2017. "Matthew Heimbach Claims He Acted on Trump's 'Get 'Em Out of Here' Order to Remove Protestor at Louisville Rally." http://www.nydailynews .com/news/politics/matthew-heimbach-trump-authority-remove-ky-protester-article -1.3067679 (Accessed April 22, 2017).

Lenz, Ryan. April 18, 2017. "White Nationalist Matthew Heimbach Claims Trump Directed Supporters to Remove Protestors." *Southern Poverty Law Center—Hatewatch.* https:// www.splcenter.org/hatewatch/2017/04/18/white-nationalist-matthew-heimbach -claims-trump-directed-supporters-remove-protesters (Accessed April 22, 2017).

Southern Poverty Law Center. "Matthew Heimbach." https://www.splcenter.org/fighting -hate/extremist-files/individual/matthew-heimbach (Accessed April 22, 2017).

HILL, MICHAEL

Michael Hill (b. 1951) is a former professor of British history and Celtic culture at the historically black Stillman College in Tuscaloosa, Alabama. In 1994, Hill, along with other Southern intellectuals, founded the League of the South (LOS), a "Southern Nationalist organization that seeks the survival, well being, and independence of the Southern people" (League of the South, Welcome). LOS is dedicated to restoring the Old South (the states of the former Confederacy) and its gentility through the establishment of a theocratic Christian country apart from the rest of the United States. Thus, LOS advocates for secession and to that end has issued a call for the formation of a Southern defense force to "plan for contingencies—natural or man-made—that might affect the Southern people" (Hatewatch Staff, February 6, 2017). Hill has made it clear that he is first and foremost a "Southern nationalist." As he stated in March 2017, "the South must be free and independent of the American empire" (Hill 2017).

The evolution of Hill's ideas about the Confederate South started in the 1970s while he was a graduate student studying under his conservative mentors at the University of Alabama. Hill's mentors "argued that the South had been settled primarily by 'Anglo-Celts' (i.e., whites) while the North had been settled by British Protestants" (Southern Poverty Law Center). Though the distinction may seem nominal, Hill was convinced that the North and South were different due to the overarching "Celtic" influence in the South. To highlight the distinction, Hill and others founded the League of the South in 1994. The LOS "envisioned a seceded South that would be run, basically, as a theocratic state marked by medieval legal distinctions between different types of citizens, with white males at the top of the hierarchy" (Southern Poverty Law Center). The LOS started ostensibly to complain about media portrayals of the South, but it degenerated into a racist organization and began calling for a second secession of Southern states "while attacking egalitarianism, describing slavery as God-ordained, opposing racial intermarriage, and defending the segregationist policies of Southern governments" (Southern Poverty Law Center).

In 2000, LOS was designated as a hate group by the Southern Poverty Law Center based on its white supremacist ideology. Forrest McDonald, one of Hill's mentors at the University of Alabama that had helped found the group, denounced Hill's racist rants and said that Hill's racism had destroyed LOS. From this point on, Hill became even more virulent in his racially charged rhetoric, decrying a U.S. Supreme Court ruling in 2003 that struck down antigay sodomy laws as helping to advance what he called the "sodomite and civil rights agenda" (Southern Poverty Law Center). Hill also intoned that the Civil War was not about slavery but about the godless materialism and industrial capitalism of the Yankee North, and he complained that the elites of the Yankee Northeast had allowed the country to be "overrun by hordes of non-white immigrants" (Southern Poverty Law Center). In a 2012 essay, Hill claimed "that white people are endowed with 'God-ordained superiority' and that slavery was only ended in the name of 'equality' and misappropriated Christian ethics" (Southern Poverty Law Center).

By 2011, Hill was inciting his followers to violence "as he urged members to stock up on AK-47s, hollow-point bullets and tools to derail trains" (Southern Poverty

Law Center). Hill also began to voice rhetoric that aligned with the antigovernment patriot movement when he declared that "the federal government was an organized criminal enterprise" led by "domestic terrorists" (Southern Poverty Law Center). Hill also advised followers to not recognize any legal authority above that of the county sheriff, reminiscent of the ideology of the "Posse Comitatus, a racist, anti-Semitic group in the U.S. during the 1970s and 1980s" (Smith and Lenz 2011).

In May 2015, Hill published a provocative essay in which he discussed "the possibility of an American race war" and "warned black Americans that they were in for a rude awakening if such a war developed" (Hill 2015). In January 2017, Hill threw his weight behind an initiative to begin an "alt-South" movement, modeled after the success of the alt-right movement in mobilizing young people to accept alternative interpretations of conservatism. In February 2017, Hill announced the formation of the Southern Defense Force to combat the "leftist menace to our historic Christian civilization" (Hatewatch Staff, February 6, 2017).

Some have believed that Hill's activity after the election of Donald Trump in November 2016 was meant to drum up interest in his movement. After all, Hill, like many others, expected Hillary Clinton to capture the presidency. Under a Clinton administration, Hill believed that he could have "sown the seeds of discontent in fertile soil" (Hatewatch Staff, January 20, 2017). But with the advent of a Trump administration, which had been endorsed and supported by several extremist groups, Hill saw the possibilities for growth of LOS to be greatly diminished. Nevertheless, Hill has continued to position himself as a true "Southern nationalist," in opposition to Donald Trump, whom he called "a civic nationalist who still panders to the 'we all bleed the same color' malarkey that elevates blacks, Jews, feminists, and other minorities above the white founding stock of America" (Hill 2017).

See also: Alt-Right Movement; League of the South; Neo-Confederates; Patriot Movement; Posse Comitatus; White Nationalism; White Supremacist Movement

Further Reading

Hatewatch Staff. January 20, 2017. "The League of the South's Michael Hill Is Having a Bad Year." *Southern Poverty Law Center—Hatewatch.* https://www.splcenter.org/hatewatch/2017/01/20/league-souths-michael-hill-having-bad-year (Accessed March 16, 2017).

Hatewatch Staff. January 31, 2017. "Amid Growing Neo-Confederate Rifts, Brad Griffin Advocates for New 'Alt-South' Movement." *Southern Poverty Law Center—Hatewatch.* https://www.splcenter.org/hatewatch/2017/01/31/amid-growing-neo-confederate-rifts-brad-griffin-advocates-new-alt-south-movement (Accessed March 16, 2017).

Hatewatch Staff. February 6, 2017. "League of the South Announces Formation of 'Southern Defense Force.'" *Southern Poverty Law Center—Hatewatch.* https://www.splcenter.org/hatewatch/2017/02/06/league-south-announces-formation-'southern-defense-force' (Accessed March 16, 2017).

Hill, Michael. May 6, 2015. "A Few Notes on an American Race War." *League of the South.* http://leagueofthesouth.com/a-few-notes-on-an-american-race-war/ (Accessed March 16, 2017).

Hill, Michael. March 1, 2017. "A Southern Nationalist Response to Trump's Speech." *League of the South.* http://leagueofthesouth.com/a-southern-nationalist-response-to-trumps-speech/ (Accessed March 16, 2017).

League of the South. "Welcome to the New League of the South Website." http://league ofthesouth.com/ (Accessed March 16, 2017).

Smith, Janet and Ryan Lenz. November 15, 2011. "League of the South Rhetoric Turns to Arms." *Southern Poverty Law Center—Intelligence Report*. https://www.splcenter.org /fighting-hate/intelligence-report/2011/league-south-rhetoric-turns-arms (Accessed March 16, 2017).

Southern Poverty Law Center. "Michael Hill." https://www.splcenter.org/fighting-hate /extremist-files/individual/michael-hill (Accessed March 16, 2017).

HOLOCAUST DENIAL

Holocaust denial is a modern form of anti-Semitism, an intense hatred of Jews, that is intended to distort, misuse, and deny strategies meant to elicit public sympathy for the enormity of crimes committed against Jews and others during World War II and "to undermine the legitimacy of the State of Israel . . . which some believe was created as compensation for Jewish suffering during the Holocaust—to plant seeds of doubt about Jews and the Holocaust, and to draw attention to particular issues or viewpoints" (United States Holocaust Memorial Museum). Through the Internet and the ease with which individuals and groups can access information, both real and fabricated, Holocaust denial can be conducted in anonymity or with seeming authoritative credentials. Key Holocaust denial assertions include

> that the murder of approximately six million Jews during World War II never occurred, that the Nazis had no official policy or intention to exterminate the Jews, and that the poison gas chambers in Auschwitz-Birkenau death camp never existed. Common distortions include, for example, assertions that the figure of six million Jewish deaths is an exaggeration and that the diary of Anne Frank is a forgery. (United States Holocaust Memorial Museum)

Scholars use the term "denial" to distinguish the views and methodologies of those who contend the Holocaust never happened "from legitimate historical revisionists who challenge orthodox interpretations of history using established historical methodologies" (McFee). Holocaust deniers don't usually identify themselves as deniers (just as terrorists rarely identify themselves as terrorists). Rather, they prefer to be known as revisionists, though revisionism is the reinterpretation of known and accepted facts. Holocaust deniers generally fall into the category of "negationism," in that "they attempt to rewrite history by minimizing, denying, or simply ignoring widely documented and accepted facts":

> Negationism means the denial of historical crimes against humanity. It is not a reinterpretation of known facts, but the denial of known facts. The term negationism has gained currency as the name of a movement to deny a specific crime against humanity, the Nazi genocide on the Jews in 1941–45, also known as the holocaust (Greek: complete burning) or the Shoah (Hebrew: disaster). Negationism is mostly identified with the effort at re-writing history in such a way that the fact of the Holocaust is omitted. (Elst 2014)

Harry Elmer Barnes (1889–1968) epitomizes Holocaust denial in the post–World War II era. Barnes, once considered a legitimate historian, "became convinced that allegations made against Germany and Japan, including the Holocaust, were fabrications used as wartime propaganda to justify U.S. involvement in World War II" (Shah 2012). Several protégés of Barnes began to follow up on this theme and constructed elaborate theories and alternative explanations to the widely accepted facts associated with the Holocaust. The publication of Arthur Butz's *The Hoax of the Twentieth Century: The Case Against the Presumed Extermination of European Jewry* (1976) and David Irving's *Hitler's War* (1977) "brought other Holocaust deniers into the fold" (Lipstadt 1994).

In 1996, Irving defended himself against accusations of Holocaust denial by filing a libel lawsuit against Deborah Lipstadt and her publisher after the publication of her book, *Denying the Holocaust: The Growing Assault on Truth and Memory*. The trial, held in Great Britain, featured several witnesses for the defense who provided compelling evidence of the reality of the Holocaust. Moreover, the witnesses were able to demonstrate that Irving had misrepresented and mischaracterized factual information in his writings "as well as knowingly using forged documents as source material. The judge in the case ultimately delivered a verdict in favor of Lipstadt and referred to Irving as a 'Holocaust denier' and 'right-wing pro-Nazi polemicist'" (Lipstadt 2006).

In 1978, Willis Carto, another well-known Holocaust denier, founded the Institute for Historical Review (IHR). Though critics of the organization designate the IHR as engaged in Holocaust denial, the IHR contends that it "does not 'deny' the Holocaust. Indeed, the IHR as such has no 'position' on any specific event or chapter of history, except to promote greater awareness and understanding, and to encourage more objective investigation" (IHR). Despite the IHR's protestations, a careful reading of its mission reveals that it wished to "provide factual information" and "sound perspective" on "the Jewish-Zionist role in cultural and political life" (IHR). In 1980, the IHR offered $50,000 for definitive proof that Jews were gassed at Auschwitz. When individuals came forward with the requested proof, including eyewitnesses who had lost family members in the camp, IHR refused to pay the amount. Lawsuits were instigated against IHR, and a judgment against it in the amount of $90,000 ruled that "the existence of gas chambers at Auschwitz was common knowledge" and therefore did not require evidence that gas chambers, in fact, existed (Nizkor Project). The judge in the case ruled that in addition to the monetary judgment, IHR had "to issue a letter of apology to the plaintiff, a survivor of Auschwitz-Birkenau and Buchenwald, and all other survivors of Auschwitz for 'pain, anguish and suffering' caused to them" (Nizkor Project).

Despite the rebuke, IHR continued to propagate Holocaust denial. In 1989, IHR published a piece by Lutheran pastor Herman Otten in which he wrote,

> There is no dispute over the fact that large numbers of Jews were deported to concentration camps and ghettos, or that many Jews died or were killed during World War II. Revisionist scholars have presented evidence, which Exterminationists have not been able to refute, showing that there was no German program to exterminate Europe's Jews and that the estimate of six million Jewish wartime dead is an irresponsible exaggeration.

> The Holocaust, the alleged extermination of some six million Jews (most of them by gassing) is a hoax and should be recognized as such by Christians and all informed, honest and truthful men everywhere.

Holocaust denial is not just a phenomenon among Western deniers. Denials of the Holocaust "have been publicly perpetrated by various Middle Eastern figures and media" (Havardi 2012). In 1983, Mahmoud Abbas, cofounder of Fatah and president of the Palestinian National Authority, published a book entitled *The Other Side: The Secret Relationship Between Nazism and Zionism* based on his dissertation. Abbas "denied that six million Jews had died in the Holocaust; dismissing it as a 'myth' and a 'fantastic lie.' At most, he wrote, 890,000 Jews were killed by the Germans" (Havardi 2012). Organized Holocaust denial institutes have also been identified in Egypt, Qatar, and Saudi Arabia (Satloff 2006). Former Iranian president Mahmoud Ahmadinejad is also a frequent Holocaust denier, formally questioning the wealth of widely accepted facts related to the Holocaust. In December 2005, Ahmadinejad stated,

> They have fabricated a legend, under the name of the Massacre of the Jews, and they hold it higher than God himself, religion itself and the prophets themselves. . . . If somebody in their country questions God, nobody says anything, but if somebody denies the myth of the massacre of Jews, the Zionist loudspeakers and the governments in the pay of Zionism will start to scream.

Holocaust denial "is explicitly or implicitly illegal in 17 countries: Austria, Belgium, Czech Republic, France, Germany, Hungary, Israel, Liechtenstein, Lithuania, Luxembourg, Netherlands, Poland, Portugal, Romania, Russia, Slovakia, and Switzerland" (Bazyler). In January 2007, "the United Nations General Assembly condemned without reservation any denial of the Holocaust, though Iran disassociated itself from the resolution" (UN).

As noted by author Deborah Lipstadt (2006), "Holocaust denial is a virulent form of anti-Semitism. But it is not only that. It is also an attack on reasoned inquiry and inconvenient history. If this history can be denied any history can be denied." Lipstadt (2011) goes on to say that,

> Holocaust deniers have, thus far, been decidedly unsuccessful in convincing the broader public of their claims—although many people worry that after the last of the Holocaust survivors has died (most are now in their 80s) deniers will achieve greater success. However, historians, carefully relying on a broad array of documentary and material evidence . . . can and already have demonstrated that Holocaust denial is a tissue of lies.

See also: Carto, Willis; Duke, David; Institute for Historical Review; Irving, David; Rockwell, George Lincoln

Further Reading

Al Jazeera. December 14, 2005. "Ahmadinejad: Holocaust a Myth." http://www.aljazeera .com/archive/2005/12/200849154418141136.html (Accessed June 2, 2017).

Anti-Defamation League. "The Holocaust—Global Awareness and Denial." *Anti-Defamation League—Global 100*. http://global100.adl.org/info/holocaust_info (Accessed June 2, 2017).

Bazyler, Michael J. "Holocaust Denial Law and Other Legislation Criminalizing Promotion of Nazism." *Yad Vashem*. http://www.yadvashem.org/holocaust/holocaust-antisemitism /articles/holocaust-denial-laws (Accessed June 2, 2017).

Elst, Koenraad. 2014. *Negationism in India: Concealing the Record of Islam*. Voice of India.

Green, Emma. May 14, 2014. "The World Is Full of Holocaust Deniers." *The Atlantic*. https:// www.theatlantic.com/international/archive/2014/05/the-world-is-full-of-holocaust -deniers/370870/ (Accessed June 2, 2017).

Havardi, Jeremy. August 14, 2012. "Holocaust Denial Undermines the Palestinian Cause." *The Commentator*. http://www.thecommentator.com/article/1524/holocaust_denial _undermines_the_palestinian_cause (Accessed June 2, 2017).

Institute for Historical Review. "About the IHR: Our Mission and Record." http://www.ihr .org/main/about.shtml (Accessed June 2, 2017).

Jewish Virtual Library. "Holocaust Denial: Background & Overview." https://www.jewishvir tuallibrary.org/background-and-overview-of-holocaust-denial (Accessed June 2, 2017).

Lipstadt, Deborah. 1994. *Denying the Holocaust: The Growing Assault on Truth and Memory*. Plume.

Lipstadt, Deborah. 2006. *History on Trial: My Day in Court with a Holocaust Denier*. Harper Perennial.

Lipstadt, Deborah. February 17, 2011. "Denying the Holocaust." *BBC*. http://www.bbc .co.uk/history/worldwars/genocide/deniers_01.shtml (Accessed June 2, 2017).

McFee, Gord. "Why Revisionism Isn't." *PHDN.org*. http://phdn.org/archives/holocaust-history .org/revisionism-isnt/ (Accessed June 2, 2017).

Nizkor Project. "Shofar FTP Archive File: people/m/mermelstein.mel//mermelstein.order .072285." http://www.nizkor.org/ftp.cgi/people/m/mermelstein.mel/ftp.py?people/m /mermelstein.mel//mermelstein.order.072285 (Accessed June 2, 2017).

Otten, Herman. "Christianity, Truth and Fantasy: The Holocaust, Historical Revisionism and Christians Today." Institute for Historical Review. http://www.ihr.org/jhr/v09 /v09p321_otten.html (Accessed June 2, 2017).

Satloff, Robert. October 8, 2006. "The Holocaust Arab Heroes." *The Washington Post*. http:// www.washingtonpost.com/wp-dyn/content/article/2006/10/06/AR2006100601417 .html (Accessed June 2, 2017).

Shah, Zia H. September 18, 2012. "Holocaust Denial—Limits of Free Speech?" *The Muslim Times*. https://themuslimtimes.info/2012/09/18/holocaust-denial-limits-of-free-speech/ (Accessed July 27, 2017).

Southern Poverty Law Center. "Holocaust Denial." https://www.splcenter.org/fighting-hate /extremist-files/ideology/holocaust-denial (Accessed June 2, 2017).

UN. "UN General Assembly Condemns Holocaust Denial by Consensus; Iran Disassociates Itself." *UN News Centre*. http://www.un.org/apps/news/story.asp?NewsID=21355&Cr= holocaust&Cr1#.WTGTWNy1vRY (Accessed June 2, 2017).

United States Holocaust Memorial Museum. "Holocaust Denial and Distortion." https:// www.ushmm.org/confront-antisemitism/holocaust-denial-and-distortion (Accessed June 2, 2017).

INSTITUTE FOR HISTORICAL REVIEW

The Institute for Historical Review (IHR) was founded in 1978 by Willis Carto, "an individual infamous for his pro-Nazi and rabidly anti-Jewish views" (Southern Poverty Law Center, Willis Carto). According to its Web site, the IHR claims to "provide factual information and sound perspective on US foreign policy, World War Two, the Israel-Palestine conflict, war propaganda, Middle East history, the Jewish-Zionist role in cultural and political life, and much more" (IHR). The IHR "comments on a variety of subjects, but it is most noted (and criticized) for its positions regarding Holocaust denial. IHR is widely regarded as anti-Semitic and as having links to neo-Nazi organizations" (Southern Poverty Law Center, Institute for Historical Review). Many writers who post their pieces on the IHR Web site state that their primary focus is to deny or reinterpret key facts related to Nazism and the genocide of the Jews. The IHR insists that its work tends toward "revisionism" of Holocaust material, opposed to denial of such material:

> The Institute does not "deny the Holocaust." Every responsible scholar of twentieth century history acknowledges the great catastrophe that befell European Jewry during World War II. All the same, the IHR has over the years published detailed books and numerous probing essays that call into question aspects of the orthodox, Holocaust-extermination story, and highlight specific Holocaust exaggerations and falsehoods. (IHR)

Barbara Kulaszka, a contributor to IHR, "defends the distinction between 'denial' and 'revisionism' by arguing that considerable revisions have been made over time of most historical material" and concludes: "For purposes of their own, powerful, special-interest groups desperately seek to keep substantive discussion of the Holocaust story taboo. One of the ways they do this is by purposely mischaracterizing revisionist scholars as 'deniers.'"

The IHR was spun off from Willis Carto's blatantly anti-Semitic Liberty Lobby. The IHR presented itself as a legitimate historical research group by hijacking the "revisionist" term that was being used by historians at the time to reinterpret the origins of World War I (Southern Poverty Law Center, Institute for Historical Review). But the revisionist movement associated with studies of the Holocaust supported by the IHR "was made up of white supremacists and neo-Nazis, and it would draw expertise from the like-minded around the world. Its mission was to erase the Holocaust by any means at its disposal—including distortion, misquotation and outright falsification" (Southern Poverty Law Center, Institute for Historical Review).

The first annual conference of the IHR in 1979 attracted Holocaust deniers from around the world. David Duke, then the leader of the Knights of the Ku Klux Klan, was so enamored with the IHR's historical revisionist mission that he devoted a special issue of his publication, *The Crusader*, to the question. Moreover, the leader of the National Socialist Party of America embraced the IHR's mission by stating, "There was no Holocaust, but they deserve one—and will get it" (Southern Poverty Law Center, Institute for Historical Review).

Though the IHR was to outside observers blatantly anti-Semitic, it attempted to soften its views by applying a pseudoacademic gloss to its reports. In the *Journal of Historical Review*, the IHR published a number of Holocaust denial claims, including ones that Anne Frank's diary was a fraud, that death camp ovens were incapable of burning the volume of bodies claimed by the allies, and that the "Zyklon B gas used to kill the Jews was not of high enough quality to exterminate in the numbers claimed." Through it all, "IHR sought to give the appearance that its writers were honest, if skeptical, students of history" (Southern Poverty Law Center, Institute for Historical Review).

In 1993, Mark Weber, who had edited the National Alliance's neo-Nazi publication, the *National Vanguard*, wrested control of the IHR from Carto. Carto was eventually sued by Weber and other IHR leaders, contending that Carto had embezzled some $10 million from the IHR. In 1996, "IHR won a $6.4 million judgment against Carto" (Granberry 1996). Carto would go on to found other publications in which he referred to Weber as a "rat," "cockroach," and the "devil" (Southern Poverty Law Center, Willis Carto).

The fight between the IHR and Carto took a toll on the organization. By 2003, the organization's *Journal of Historical Review* ceased publication, and the annual conferences hosted by the IHR were reduced from lavish, multiday affairs with dozens of speakers, to "small, one-day affairs" with a much smaller roster. In 2009, the IHR received a major blow when "Weber decided to downgrade Holocaust denial in favor of criticizing Jews and Israel. Weber was viciously attacked by several important revisionists, many of whom called for his resignation from IHR" (Southern Poverty Law Center, Institute for Historical Review). Today, Weber maintains control of IHR, but the organization clearly does not have the influence among extremists as it once had.

See also: Carto, Willis; Holocaust Denial; Neo-Nazis; Weber, Mark; White Supremacist Movement

Further Reading

Anti-Defamation League. "Willis Carto." https://www.adl.org/sites/default/files/documents/assets/pdf/combating-hate/Willis-Carto-Extremism-in-America.pdf (Accessed April 29, 2017).

Granberry, Michael. November 16, 1996. "Judge Awards 6.4 Million to O.C. Revisionist Group." *Los Angeles Times*. http://articles.latimes.com/1996-11-16/local/me-65105_1_judge-awards (Accessed April 29, 2017).

Institute for Historical Review. "About the IHR: Our Mission and Record." http://www.ihr.org/main/about.shtml (Accessed April 29, 2017).

Kulaszka, Barbara. "What Is 'Holocaust Denial?'" *Institute for Historical Review.* http://www.ihr.
org/leaflets/denial.shtml (Accessed April 29, 2017).

Southern Poverty Law Center. "Institute for Historical Review." https://www.splcenter.org
/fighting-hate/extremist-files/group/institute-historical-review (Accessed April 29, 2017).

Southern Poverty Law Center. "Willis Carto." https://www.splcenter.org/fighting-hate/extremist
-files/individual/willis-carto (Accessed April 29, 2017).

IRVING, DAVID

David Irving (b. 1938) is recognized as one of the most prominent Holocaust deniers in the world. From his beginnings as a serious historian of the events of World War II, his career has spiraled downward as he perpetuates myths that Adolf Hitler knew nothing of the atrocities committed against Jews, or, if he did, actively opposed such efforts (Evans 2001). In 2000, Irving "sued Penguin Books and American scholar Deborah Lipstadt for libel after Lipstadt had written that Irving was a holocaust denier and a pro-Nazi ideologue" (Southern Poverty Law Center, David Irving). In a stunning verdict, the British judge in the case found for the defendants and condemned Irving for his anti-Semitic "political agenda" (Southern Poverty Law Center, David Irving).

Irving "never earned a degree in history, but took courses at Imperial College in London" (Southern Poverty Law Center, David Irving). In 1963, at the age of 25, he published *The Destruction of Dresden*, which gave him a "reputation as a World War II historian." Though the book was well received, Irving admitted that he "had based his figures on the word of Dresden's Deputy Chief Medical Officer, who himself said that he was just repeating rumors" (Southern Poverty Law Center, David Irving). In all, Irving would write almost 30 books on World War II, most of them from a German perspective. His most controversial book, *Hitler's War*, was published in 1977 and promoted the idea "that Hitler had no knowledge of the Holocaust," even if it had occurred. Later works increasingly manifested Irving's anti-Semitism, and he became increasingly isolated from the mainstream historical community, though he was drawing the attention of neo-Nazis and white supremacists (Southern Poverty Law Center, David Irving).

In 1983, Irving "gave a talk at a Los Angeles gathering of the Institute for Historical Review (IHR), a group dedicated to disproving the existence of the Holocaust" (Southern Poverty Law Center, David Irving). Though challenged at the event because he claimed that Hitler knew nothing of the Holocaust, Irving would later claim to have an "epiphany" that the Holocaust was indeed fabricated. When a report by a "self-styled" engineer claimed to have found "no traces of cyanide residue on the walls of Auschwitz's gas chambers," Irving stated, "That's what converted me. When I read that report in the courtroom of Toronto, I became a hardcore disbeliever" (Southern Poverty Law Center, David Irving).

Though he denied being a racist or anti-Semite, Irving became associated with the virulently racist and neo-Nazi National Alliance in the early 1990s (Southern Poverty Law Center, David Irving). His views were also garnering the attention of European states that had strict laws against Holocaust denial. In 1989, an arrest warrant for Irving was issued in Austria "after he gave two speeches in that country denying the existence of gas chambers at Auschwitz. In 1992, he was fined several thousand dollars by the German government for denying the existence of the Holocaust" (Southern Poverty Law Center, David Irving). The following year, he was banned from Germany, and he would later be banned from Canada, Australia, New Zealand, and Austria (Southern Poverty Law Center, David Irving).

Irving's reputation as a Holocaust denier would be cemented in 2000 when he brought suit "against Penguin Books and the American scholar Deborah Lipstadt over Lipstadt's portrayal of him [Irving] in her 1994 book, *Denying the Holocaust: The Growing Assault on Truth and Memory*" (Southern Poverty Law Center, 2000). Irving chose to bring suit against Lipstadt and Penguin Books in Great Britain "since British common law put the burden of proof on the defendant and not the plaintiff" (Southern Poverty Law Center, 2000). But the "London judge sided with Penguin and Lipstadt," calling Irving a "Holocaust denier" who displays a "distinctly pro-Nazi and anti-Jewish bias" (Southern Poverty Law Center, 2000). The judge went on to say that "no objective, fair-minded historian would have serious cause to doubt that there were gas chambers at Auschwitz and that they were operated on a substantial scale to kill hundreds of thousands of Jews" (Southern Poverty Law Center, 2000).

As a result of the judgment, Irving was ordered "to pay Lipstadt's court costs—estimated at $5 million" (Southern Poverty Law Center, 2000). Though he was nearly ruined, Irving remains solvent by giving speaking tours in the countries in which he has not been banned, including the United States.

See also: Holocaust Denial; National Alliance; Neo-Nazis; White Supremacist Movement

Further Reading

Evans, Richard J. 2001. *Lying About Hitler: History, Holocaust, and the David Irving Trial*. Basic Books.

Southern Poverty Law Center. "David Irving." http://www.splcenter.org/fighting-hate/extremist-files/individual/david-irving (Accessed January 16, 2017).

Southern Poverty Law Center. June 13, 2000. "It's Official: David Irving Is 'Pro-Nazi.'" *Southern Poverty Law Center—Intelligence Report*. http://www.splcenter.org/fighting-hate/intelligence-report/2000/its-official-david-irving-pro-nazi (Accessed January 16, 2017).

J

JENSEN, ARTHUR

Arthur Jensen (1923–2012) was, according to the Southern Poverty Law Center, "the father of modern academic racism." He was also an "educational psychologist at the University of California, Berkeley and was the author of over 400 scientific papers that were published in refereed journals" (Debate.org). In addition, Jensen sat on the "editorial boards of several scientific journals devoted to the topics of intelligence and personality" (Southern Poverty Law Center). Yet Jensen's theories about black inferiority made him a favorite of the racist right-wing and white nationalist circles. His basic premise was "that the black population was inherently less intelligent than the white population, an ideology that became known as 'Jensenism'" (Southern Poverty Law Center).

In 1969, Jensen published an article entitled, "How Much Can We Boost IQ and Scholastic Achievement?" in the *Harvard Educational Review*. What appeared on the surface to be an innocuous inquiry into methods for achieving increases in scholastic achievement in the American student population turned into a thesis that put forth the idea that race was the deciding biological factor that could explain differences in intelligence. As noted by Graham Richards, a historian of psychology, what should have long been decided by the middle of the 20th century—that there was no demonstrably scientific evidence to support that race differences accounted for intelligence scores—was resurrected by Jensen's work. Indeed, Jensen asserted that "differences in scholastic achievement between white and black students were due almost entirely to innate, genetic differences in intelligence" (Southern Poverty Law Center). This conclusion was drawn from Jensen's study of the Head Start program, which was intended to boost educational achievement among black students, but which, Jensen claimed, had failed. Jensen concluded that 80 percent of the variance in IQ "was the result of genetic factors, with the remainder due to environmental influences" (Current Comments 1978). This conclusion provided fuel to the racist right and white nationalist movements in the United States that had been on the defensive since the beginnings of the civil rights era in the early 1950s.

Throughout his career, Jensen never thought of himself as a racist. Yet his protestations against those who leveled claims of racism against him were confounded when, in 1992, "he gave an interview to the white nationalist magazine *American Renaissance*" (Southern Poverty Law Center). In the interview, Jensen intimated that the black population in the United States was "incapable of functioning in a civilized society" because a large proportion of the black population had low IQs, making them unsuitable for some jobs in the modern economy (American Renaissance 1992). Jensen stated that "the best thing the black community could do would be to limit the birth-rate among the least able members, which is of course a eugenic proposal" (American Renaissance 1992).

In 1994, Jensen received a $1.1 million grant from the Pioneer Fund, an organization described as white supremacist in nature, for the furtherance of his work (Tucker 2002). The Pioneer Fund also donated more than $3.5 million to a number of researchers who had contributed to the publication of *The Bell Curve* (1994), the controversial text by psychologist Richard J. Herrnstein and political scientist Charles Murray that argued that human intelligence is substantially influenced by inherited factors. Though Jensen himself did not directly contribute to the publication of *The Bell Curve*, his professional works were cited more than 20 times in the book's bibliography (Montagu 2002).

Jensen died in October 2012 at the age of 89.

See also: American Renaissance; Pioneer Fund; White Nationalism; White Supremacist Movement

Further Reading

American Renaissance. August and September 1992. "A Conversation with Arthur Jensen." Reposted on October 29, 2012. https://www.amren.com/news/2012/10/arthur-jensen -has-died/ (Accessed February 11, 2017).

Current Comments. October 9, 1978. "High Impact Science and the Case of Arthur Jensen." *Essays of an Information Scientist* 3, pp. 652–662. http://www.garfield.library.upenn .edu/essays/v3p652y1977-78.pdf (Accessed February 11, 2017).

Debate.org. "Racial IQ Differences: Social or Genetic?" http://www.debate.org/debates/Racial -IQ-Differences-Social-or-Genetic/1/ (Accessed July 31, 2017).

Herrnstein, Richard J. and Charles Murray. 1994. *Bell Curve: Intelligence and Class Structure in American Life*. Free Press.

Montagu, Ashley. 2002. *Race and IQ*. 2nd ed. Oxford University Press.

Southern Poverty Law Center. "Arthur Jensen." https://www.splcenter.org/fighting-hate /extremist-files/individual/arthur-jensen (Accessed February 11, 2017).

Tucker, William. 2002. *The Funding of Scientific Racism: Wickliffe Draper and the Pioneer Fund*. University of Illinois Press.

JEWISH DEFENSE LEAGUE

The Jewish Defense League (JDL) is a far-right religious-political organization in the United States whose primary purpose is to protect Jews from anti-Semitism by whatever means necessary (Anti-Defamation League). The group was founded by Rabbi Meir Kahane in 1968 and preaches violence against Arabs and Palestinians while supporting extreme forms of Jewish nationalism. The JDL's stated political position is to deny any Palestinian claims to land in Israel, and it calls "for the removal of all Arabs from Jewish soil" (Southern Poverty Law Center). The group has been responsible for terror attacks both "in the United States and abroad, and has engaged in intense harassment of foreign diplomats, Muslims, Jewish scholars and community leaders, and officials" (Southern Poverty Law Center). The JDL's five principles of action are as follows:

1. Love of Israel and Judaism
2. Dignity and pride in Jewish traditions, faith, culture, land, history, and peoplehood
3. Iron, or the need to help Jews everywhere project a strong and forceful image
4. Discipline and unity
5. Faith in the indestructibility of the Jewish people

The JDL was characterized as a right-wing extremist group by the U.S. Federal Bureau of Investigation in 2001 and is considered a hate group by the Southern Poverty Law Center.

The JDL was founded to protect Jews from the backlash that occurred because of a teacher's union strike in New York City in 1968. The strikes "brought to the surface racial tensions between the predominantly Jewish teachers unions and black residents who were seeking greater control over neighborhood schools" (Southern Poverty Law Center). The rising tensions that existed at the time because of black nationalism and black militantism caused many Jews to fear for their lives. Kahane even warned of a "second Holocaust." Kahane organized the JDL to protect Jews from violence, establishing neighborhood watches and roaming patrols of neighborhoods. The JDL's actions increased ethnic polarization in neighborhoods and contributed to many street clashes (Anti-Defamation League).

By 1970, "the JDL changed its focus from neighborhood protection to the plight of Soviet Jews." From this point on, "the JDL's main objective was to terrorize Soviet establishments in the United States to compel the Soviet Union to change its anti-Semitic policies—specifically its ban on allowing Russian Jews to emigrate to Israel" (Southern Poverty Law Center). In 1970, "the JDL committed five acts of terrorism" against Soviet interests (Southern Poverty Law Center). The violence became so intense that President Richard Nixon believed that the JDL's action would scuttle the Strategic Arms Limitation Talks that were then under way between the United States and the Soviet Union. Though the JDL's actions did not cause any loss of life, the actions were nevertheless viewed as terroristic in nature. After every incident, "the JDL would claim responsibility by phoning in its official slogan"—"Never Again"—a reference that indicated that the Jews would *never again* allow themselves to be slaughtered as they were during the Holocaust (Southern Poverty Law Center).

Though the Soviets were the primary targets of the JDL's actions, the group targeted anyone that it considered a threat to Jewish nationalism. This included "U.S. and foreign diplomats, domestic radical-right organizations, Arab and Muslim activists, journalists and scholars, and Jewish community members who are simply not 'Jewish enough'" (Southern Poverty Law Center). When the United Nations General Assembly "voted for a resolution equating Zionism with racism" in 1975, the JDL began targeting diplomats of all countries who had voted in favor of the resolution (Southern Poverty Law Center).

JDL's founder, Rabbi Meir Kahane, emigrated to Israel in 1971. His successor in the United States "could not maintain unity in the organization in succeeding years, so Kahane returned to the U.S. in 1974 and appointed Russel Kelner as the international chairman of JDL" (Southern Poverty Law Center). Kelner, who had been a lieutenant in the U.S. Army, where he had become a guerilla warfare expert, was determined to use paramilitary tactics in the furtherance of JDL's goals.

In 1990, Kahane was assassinated in the United States by an Arab after he (Kahane) had delivered a speech at a Zionist conference in New York City. In 1994, "a JDL member, Baruch Goldstein, massacred 29 Palestinian Muslims worshiping at the Ibrahimi Mosque in the West Bank City of Hebron." The JDL's Web site justified "Goldstein's mass murder by stating that Goldstein took a preventative measure against yet another Arab attack on Jews" (Southern Poverty Law Center).

The JDL continues its strategy of confrontation against those it deems as being in opposition to its causes. In March 2017, two JDL members were arrested as they confronted protestors outside of a policy conference that was conducted by the American Israel Public Affairs Committee. Heidi Beirich, director of the Intelligence Project at the Southern Poverty Law Center, said that these tactics are typical of JDL: "The JDL's position and activities have always been violent counter-protests. Their attitude is to take it to the streets and do in-your-face protest actions" (Altshuler 2017).

See also: Kahane, Meir David

Further Reading

Altshuler, George. March 27, 2017. "Jewish Defense League Counter-Protests Turn Violent Outside AIPAC Conference." *Washington Jewish Week.* http://washingtonjewishweek .com/37612/jewish-defense-league-counter-protests-turn-violent-outside-aipac -conference/news/ (Accessed May 23, 2017).

Anti-Defamation League. "The Jewish Defense League." https://www.adl.org/education /resources/profiles/jewish-defense-league (Accessed May 23, 2017).

Jewish Defense League. "About." http://www.jdl.org/about.html (Accessed May 23, 2017).

Southern Poverty Law Center. "Jewish Defense League." https://www.splcenter.org/fighting -hate/extremist-files/group/jewish-defense-league (Accessed May 23, 2017).

JOHN BIRCH SOCIETY

The John Birch Society (JBS) is an anticommunist, radical-right-wing organization founded by Robert W. Welch Jr. in 1958. With the perception of a growing communist menace in the United States, and communist infiltration of all levels of the U.S. government, the JBS was intended to serve as a last line of defense against an all-out communist takeover of the country. Welch authored a book, *The Politician* (1975), that was known only to "Birchers" as the "Blue Book" because of its blue cover. In the book, Welch accused Republican president Dwight Eisenhower of being a dedicated communist (Perlstein 2013).

In its heyday, the organization perpetrated calls for limited government, opposition to wealth redistribution, as well as government economic interventionism—all by-products of the liberal, New Deal agenda that had taken root in the United States. For all of its history, the JBS has been a stringent opponent of collectivism, totalitarianism, socialism, and communism. Its rabid pursuit of communists in the economic, social, cultural, and political sphere of American life won it many converts in the early years. After a rise in its membership after its initial founding, JBS became a pariah among conservatives as the organization "was identified as a fringe element of the conservative movement" and a radicalized version of the American political right (Regnery 2008). As the 21st century dawned, the JBS enjoyed a resurgence of sorts, as a new generation of conservatives began to see threats to American society and culture based on illegal immigration, rampant liberalism, and threats of a new world order.

Members of the John Birch Society (JBS) pledge allegiance to the flag. The JBS is widely recognized as a radical right-wing organization dedicated to stamping out all communist influence and infiltration within the United States. (Francis Miller/The LIFE Picture Collection/Getty Images)

JBS was founded in December 1958 by Robert W. Welch Jr., a retired business executive from Belmont, Massachusetts. Welch named the organization after John Birch, a 27-year-old U.S. military intelligence officer who had once been an American missionary and was killed by soldiers of Mao Zedong's Red Army in August 1945. Birch's mother gave Welch permission to use her deceased son's name, hoping "to see her son accorded a religious rather than a political martyrdom" (Mallon 2016). Welch considered Birch the "first casualty of the Cold War" and decided to honor him with the name of his new organization. Welch had not discovered Birch's story until 1953 because he contended that the circumstances of Birch's death had been suppressed as the result of a "Communist conspiracy within the American government." In the same manner in which Welch believed that Birch had been betrayed, both of Welch's heroes, Robert Taft and Joseph McCarthy, had also been betrayed "by the Republican political establishment" that Welch believed was riddled with communist sympathizers (Mallon 2016).

At the height of its popularity in the early 1960s, the JBS "may have had as many as 100,000 members, well short of Welch's goal of one million members" (Terry 2013). Members were attracted by the organization's rabid opposition to communism and its oft-repeated claims that the United Nations intended to establish a new world order and subvert American freedoms, liberties, and sovereignty. JBS "opposed civil rights legislation in the 1960s saying the African-American freedom movement was being manipulated from Moscow with the goal of creating a 'Soviet Negro Republic' in the Southern United States" (Terry 2013). The society "was a close ally of segregationist Alabama Governor George Wallace, and reportedly had 100 chapters in and around Birmingham, Alabama's capital and largest city" (Terry 2013).

In 1962, conservative commentator William F. Buckley Jr., editor of the mainstream conservative magazine the *National Review*, "denounced Welch and the John Birch Society as far removed from common sense" and urged the GOP to purge itself of Welch's and the JBS's influence (Buckley 2008). The JBS "was rejected by most conservatives mainly because of Welch's penchant for conspiracy theories" (Terry 2013). During the 1960s, for instance, "Welch insisted that the Johnson administration's fight against communism in Vietnam was part of a communist plot aimed at taking over the United States. Welch demanded that the United States get out of Vietnam, thus aligning the Society with the left" (Bennett 1971). The JBS "also opposed water fluoridation, which it called 'mass medicine,'" a belief parodied in the 1964 movie *Dr. Strangelove* (Lefler 2012). Though critics accused Welch and the JBS of harboring various prejudices against various groups, Welch rejected these accusations by stating, "All we are interested in here is opposing the advance of the Communists, and eventually destroying the whole Communist conspiracy, so that Jews and Christians alike, and Mohammedans and Buddhists, can again have a decent world in which to live" (Welch 1963).

In 1964, Welch and the JBS supported archconservative and anticommunist Barry Goldwater, who was vying for the 1964 Republican presidential nomination. The revelation that Welch considered Eisenhower a communist and that his actions in office had been treasonous caused many conservatives to break with Welch and the JBS. Both Goldwater and Buckley renounced the JBS, with Buckley considering Welch's claims as "paranoid and idiotic libels" (Buckley 2008). Buckley's biographer wrote that "Buckley was beginning to worry that with the John Birch Society growing so rapidly, the right-wing upsurge in the country would take an ugly, even Fascist turn rather than leading toward the kind of conservatism *National Review* had promoted" (Judis 1988).

In 1980, the JBS characterized Republican nominee Ronald Reagan as a "lackey" of communist conspirators. In September 1983, member of Congress Larry McDonald (D) from Georgia was a passenger on KAL 007, a Korean airliner, that was shot down by Soviet fighter planes when it strayed over Soviet airspace. McDonald had become the second president of JBS when Welch's health declined. The JBS considered McDonald's death to be part of the larger communist conspiracy that was then being waged against the United States.

Welch died in 1985. Since that time, "the line between the radical right and the conservative mainstream has been increasingly difficult to discern" (Terry 2013). As noted by one commentator, they (the JBS),

> have been marginalized by the leadership of the right because of their conspiracy theories. But a lot of the right wing of the Republican Party was and is highly influenced by the John Birch Society. Step one in understanding the Birchers is that they are not that much more far out, compared to other people on the right. (Terry 2013)

As Chip Berlet, longtime tracker of the conservative right notes,

> Some of the longtime Bircher ideas and themes that have slipped into the conservative mainstream and now sound like Republican talking points include the belief that big government leads to collectivism which leads to tyranny; that liberal elites are treacherous; that the U.S. has become a nation of producers versus parasites; that the U.S. is losing its sovereignty to global treaties; that the "New World Order" is an actual plan by secret elites promoting globalization; and that multiculturalism is a conspiracy of "cultural Marxism." (Terry 2013)

In 1989, the JBS moved its headquarters to the hometown of Senator Joseph McCarthy in Wisconsin. Today, adherents of the Tea Party, the conservative movement within the Republican Party, are the intellectual successors to the John Birch Society (Gopnik 2013). The JBS leadership aligns itself with the Tea Party and has become a sponsor of the Conservative Political Action Conference, the largest conservative conference in the United States (Mallon 2016). The JBS today still worries about threats to U.S. sovereignty and is adamantly opposed to free trade, illegal immigration, and the United Nations. Agenda 21, a nonbinding UN plan to promote sustainable development, is viewed by the JBS as a U.S. government effort to

> curtail your freedom to travel as you please, own a gas-powered car, live in suburbs or rural areas, and raise a family; the fight against ISIS "is a charade to help build the New World Order"; the most troubling aspect of "Our Nation's Expanding Refugee Program" appears to be "the UN's role" in it. (Mallon 2016)

Though the JBS still wields some intellectual credibility among conservatives, it has become more of a novel curiosity among extreme-right-wing conservatives who, while giving credit to the JBS for its ideas, nevertheless consider the organization a relic of the past.

See also: Tea Party Movement

Further Reading

Bennett, Stephen Earl. August 1971. "Modes of Resolution of a 'Belief Dilemma' in the Ideology of the John Birch Society." *The Journal of Politics* 33, 3, 735–772.

Bryant, John. July 5, 2000. "The John Birch Society—Exposed!" *The Birdman.org.* http://www.thebirdman.org/Index/NetLoss/NetLoss-Oliver.html (Accessed May 29, 2017).

Buckley, William F., Jr. March 1, 2008. "Goldwater, the John Birch Society, and Me." *Commentary Magazine.* https://www.commentarymagazine.com/articles/goldwater-the-john-birch-society-and-me/ (Accessed May 29, 2017).

Gopnik, Adam. October 11, 2013. "The John Bircher's Tea Party." *The New Yorker.* http://www.newyorker.com/news/daily-comment/the-john-birchers-tea-party (Accessed May 29, 2017).

John Birch Society. https://www.jbs.org/ (Accessed January 30, 2018).

Judis, John B. 1988. *William F. Buckley, Jr.—Patron Saint of the Conservatives.* Simon & Schuster.

Lefler, Dion. October 27, 2012. "Fluoride Fight Has Long Roots, Passionate Advocates." *The Wichita Eagle.* http://www.kansas.com/news/article1101667.html (Accessed May 29, 2017).

Mallon, Thomas. January 11, 2016. "A View from the Fringe: The John Birch Society and the Rise of the Radical Right." *The New Yorker*. http://www.newyorker.com /magazine/2016/01/11/a-view-from-the-fringe (Accessed May 29, 2017).

Obeidallah, Dean. September 20, 2014. "How Long Can the Republicans Hide the Crazy?" *Daily Beast*. http://www.thedailybeast.com/articles/2014/09/20/how-long-can-the-republicans-hide-the-crazy (Accessed May 29, 2017).

Perlstein, Rick. August 6, 2013. "Growing Up in the John Birch Society." *The Nation*. https://www.thenation.com/article/growing-john-birch-society/ (Accessed May 29, 2017).

Regnery, Alfred S. 2008. *Upstream: The Ascendance of American Conservatism*. Threshold Editions.

Terry, Don. March 1, 2013. "Bringing Back Birch." *Southern Poverty Law Center—Intelligence Report*. https://www.splcenter.org/fighting-hate/intelligence-report/2013/bringing-back -birch (Accessed May 27, 2017).

Welch, Robert Henry. 1963. *The Neutralizers*. John Birch Society.

JOHNSON, WILLIAM DANIEL

William Daniel Johnson (b. 1954) is a white nationalist and chairperson of the American Freedom Party (AFP), "a group that exists to represent the political interests of White Americans and aims to preserve the customs and heritage of the European American people" (Harkinson 2016). In 1985, "under the name of James O. Pace, Johnson wrote a book advocating a constitutional amendment (the 'Pace Amendment') that would repeal the 14th and 15th Amendments to the United States Constitution" (amendments dealing with citizenship and voting) (Southern Poverty Law Center, William Daniel Johnson). The Pace Amendment proposed to "deport almost all non-whites from the United States" while allowing indigenous Americans and Hawaiians to remain in the country on tribal reservations. According to Johnson (aka Pace), "whiteness" would be defined in the following manner:

> No person shall be a citizen of the United States unless he is a non-Hispanic white of the European race, in whom there is no ascertainable trace of Negro blood, nor more than one-eighth Mongolian, Asian, Asia Minor, Middle Eastern, Semitic, Near Eastern, American Indian, Malay or other non-European or non-white blood, provided that Hispanic whites, defined as anyone with an Hispanic ancestor, may be citizens if, in addition to meeting the aforesaid ascertainable trace and percentage tests, they are in appearance indistinguishable from Americans whose ancestral home is in the British Isles or Northwestern Europe. Only citizens shall have the right and privilege to reside permanently in the United States. (Pace 1985)

Johnson attended Brigham Young University, "where he majored in Japanese after having served as a Mormon missionary in Japan" (Keller 2010). After receiving a law degree from Columbia University in 1981, "Johnson worked for law firms in Japan and South Korea before returning to the United States to live in California" (Keller 2010). Johnson's 1985 book, *Amendment to the Constitution: Averting the Decline and Fall of America*, written under the name of James O. Pace, elucidated Johnson's belief that "racial mixing and diversity caused social and cultural degeneration in the United States" (Southern Poverty Law Center, American Freedom Party).

He wrote, "We lose our effectiveness as leaders when no one relies on us or can trust us because of our nonwhite and fractionalized nature. . . . Racial diversity has given us strife and conflict and is enormously counterproductive" (Pace 1985).

Johnson attempted to gain support for the so-called Pace Amendment "among members of Congress and promoted the Pace Amendment at the World Congress of the Aryan Nations, a neo-Nazi group" that was among the most powerful racist extremist groups in the United States during the 1980s and 1990s (Southern Poverty Law Center, William Daniel Johnson). Aryan Nations founder Richard Butler "wrote an endorsement of Johnson's book that was featured on the book's dust-cover" (Southern Poverty Law Center, William Daniel Johnson).

In 1989, Johnson ran in a Wyoming special election for the vacated House of Representatives seat of Dick Cheney, who had been nominated as George H. W. Bush's secretary of defense (Southern Poverty Law Center, William Daniel Johnson). Johnson's campaign manager "was a Klansman who told reporters that the Klan is basically a civil rights organization that stands up for the rights of white people" (Southern Poverty Law Center, William Daniel Johnson). After several failed political attempts over the next 20 years, Johnson established his own political party in 2009 known as the American Third Position (A3P). Johnson became the party's chairperson and leading spokesperson while Kevin MacDonald, a California State University at Long Beach professor who professes "that Jews are genetically driven to destroy Western societies," signed on as director of the new party (Keller 2010). The party was established to represent the views of white Americans and took a zero-immigration policy stance, advocating for "incentives for recent, legal immigrants to return to their respective lands" (Keller 2010).

In recruitment videos for A3P, Johnson "used coded words to recruit extremists to the party." In one video, Johnson says, "We of the Third Position look to the future and embrace principles that will secure the existence of our people and a future for our children." In another, he states: "We need you to help us to secure the existence of our people and the future for our children" (Southern Poverty Law Center, American Freedom Party). The phrasing of these appeals is "almost identical to the infamous Fourteen Words, the motto coined by white supremacist David Lane," who was sentenced to life in prison after being found guilty of the murder of Jewish talk show host Alan Berg in 1984 (Southern Poverty Law Center, American Freedom Party). Lane's phrase, "derived from a passage in Hitler's *Mein Kampf*," was, "We must secure the existence of our people and a future for white children" (Southern Poverty Law Center, American Freedom Party). In March 2010, "both Johnson and MacDonald attended an event sponsored by the Institute for Historical Review, a notorious Holocaust denial group" (Southern Poverty Law Center, American Freedom Party).

In early 2013, A3P changed its name to the "American Freedom Party (AFP), following what its website claimed was a surprisingly strong finish in the 2012 presidential election" (Southern Poverty Law Center, AFP). The AFP attempts to appeal to independents and libertarians by "expressing concern over crime, the economy, drone attacks, and government surveillance, as well as a financial mismanagement and a gutted industrial base and crumbling infrastructure" (Southern

Poverty Law Center, AFP). The party claims that it "represents the interests of White Americans and all Americans who support our interests" (Southern Poverty Law Center, AFP).

In 2016, the presidential campaign of Donald Trump, which had attracted the support of white nationalists, white supremacists, neo-Nazis, and other extremists with its anti-immigration, anti-Muslim, and "Make America Great Again" slogan, selected Johnson to be a California Republican state delegate for the presidential campaign in that state. Though Johnson's white nationalist views were well known, it wasn't until a media backlash occurred over Johnson's selection as a delegate that the Trump campaign stated that a "database error" had allowed Johnson to be selected (Harkinson 2016).

See also: American Freedom Party; Aryan Nations; Butler, Richard; Fourteen Words; Holocaust Denial; Institute for Historical Review; Lane, David; MacDonald, Kevin; Neo-Nazis; White Nationalism; White Supremacist Movement

Further Reading

American Freedom Party. "Leadership." http://theamericanfreedomparty.us/leadership/ (Accessed April 22, 2017).

Harkinson, Josh. July/August 2016. "Trump Selects a White Nationalist Leader as a Delegate in California." *Mother Jones.* http://www.motherjones.com/politics/2016/05/donald -trump-white-nationalist-afp-delegate-california (Accessed April 22, 2017).

Keller, Larry. May 30, 2010. "New White Supremacist Party Has Mass Electoral Ambitions." *Southern Poverty Law Center—Intelligence Report.* https://www.splcenter.org/fighting -hate/intelligence-report/2010/new-white-supremacist-party-has-mass-electoral -ambitions (Accessed April 22, 2017).

Pace, James O. (aka William Daniel Johnson). 1985. *Amendment to the Constitution: Averting the Decline and Fall of America.* Johnson, Pace, Simmons, and Fennell Publishers.

Southern Poverty Law Center. "American Freedom Party." https://www.splcenter.org/fighting -hate/extremist-files/group/american-freedom-party (Accessed April 22, 2017).

Southern Poverty Law Center. "William Daniel Johnson." https://www.splcenter.org/fighting -hate/extremist-files/individual/william-daniel-johnson (Accessed April 22, 2017).

JONES, ALEX

Alex Jones (b. 1974) is a right-wing American radio show host and conspiracy theorist. His radio show emanates from Austin, Texas, where Jones warns, without any evidence, "that everything from the Oklahoma City bombing, to 9/11," to the Boston Marathon bombings are "false flag" operations perpetrated by the U.S. government in support of "globalist" forces intent on taking over the world (Southern Poverty Law Center). His program attracts some 2 million listeners weekly. Jones has been called "the most paranoid man in America" by *Rolling Stone* and the "king of conspiracy" by CNN. He regularly rants on his radio program about the plots of the "New World Order" to impose world government, to inter dissenters in concentration camps, and to enforce a universal eugenics code. Jones calls upon "true patriots" to prepare themselves against the forces of the New World Order by stockpiling guns and food, building bunkers, and investing in precious metals (Southern Poverty Law Center). Jones revels in his agitator status, stating that he is "proud to be listed as a criminal against Big Brother" (Coscarelli 2013). Jones's website, *InfoWars.com*, "has been labeled a fake news website" by *U.S. News & World Report*, *The L.A. Times*, and *The Washington Times*.

Jones was born in Dallas, Texas. During his teenage years, he read *None Dare Call It Conspiracy*, "a book by a public relations representative of the John Birch Society" (Southern Poverty Law Center). Published in 1972, the book "laid out a scenario in which international bankers financed and orchestrated the Russian Revolution," and later determined to impose global government by centralizing monetary policy, imposing personal income taxes, and instituting social welfare programs (Southern Poverty Law Center). Near the end of Jones's teenage years, the Federal Bureau of Investigation attempted to end a 51-day siege on the Branch Davidian compound near Waco, Texas. The Branch Davidian's leader, David Koresh, and 75 others were burned to death along with the compound. Jones came to prominence in 1998 when he initiated an effort to rebuild the "Branch Davidian compound's church" in Waco (LA Times 1999). Jones claimed that David Koresh and his followers were American citizens who were murdered at the hands of the federal government, particularly Attorney General Janet Reno and members of the Clinton administration (Marcotte 2016).

Jones was fired in 1999 from his radio talk show in Austin, Texas, despite his high ratings and winning a poll in which he was chosen Austin's best radio talk show host. Later the same year, he set up his own independent program and quickly gathered viewers. After Jones claimed that 9/11 was an event perpetrated by the Bush administration, listeners left his program in droves. In 2013, a diatribe by Jones on CNN after the Sandy Hook Elementary School massacre elicited scorn from both the left and the right. In the interview, Jones shouted at the host, "1776 will commence again if you try to take our firearms! It doesn't matter how many lemmings you get out there on the street, begging to have their guns taken. We will not relinquish them! Do you understand?" (Southern Poverty Law Center).

As noted by the Southern Poverty Law Center,

> Such meltdowns do little to advance Jones' cause with a mainstream audience. But in his view, most of this audience consists of consumerist "sheeple" who don't think for themselves. He believes that he is speaking truth to power, galvanizing the "sheeple" into joining enlightened liberty-loving patriots (his audience) in opposing the growing tyranny. It's a classic come-on: I know something you don't. Jones manipulates the psychological fears of the vulnerable into complete acceptance of nearly anything he says—regardless of how loony it may be. Wrapping himself in the American flag (the people's flag, not the government's), he invokes Thomas Jefferson and George Washington as his icons.

Jones labels himself a libertarian and "aggressive constitutionalist" who is committed to "defending individual liberties, the Bill of Rights, property rights, and the security of U.S. borders against illegal immigration" (InfoWars, Who is Alex Jones). Jones was a severe critic of the presidential administration of Barack Obama, calling

Obama a "Wahhabist" and a sympathizer of al Qaeda. On several occasions, Jones has voiced his opposition to gay marriage. In early 2016, Jones intoned on his radio program that the occupiers of the Malheur National Wildlife Refuge were "government provocateurs" who were acting on behalf of the "Obama Administration and globalist elites whose ultimate goal is the institution of Martial Law and the total end to American sovereignty" (InfoWars 2016).

See also: John Birch Society

Further Reading

Coscarelli, Joe. November 17, 2013. "An Interview with Alex Jones, America's Leading (and Proudest) Conspiracy Theorist." *New York Magazine.* http://nymag.com/daily /intelligencer/2013/11/alex-jones-americas-top-conspiracy-theorist.html   (Accessed February 11, 2017).

InfoWars. "Who Is Alex Jones and What Is the InfoWar? . . . And Why Should You Care?" http://www.infowars.com/about-alex-jones/ (Accessed February 11, 2017).

InfoWars. January 3, 2016. "Feds Arrive in Oregon to 'Take Control of the Situation.'" http://www.infowars.com/feds-arrive-in-oregon-to-take-control-of-the-situation/ (Accessed February 11, 2017).

LA Times. September 20, 1999. "Branch Davidian Church to Be Rebuilt." http://articles.latimes .com/1999/sep/20/news/mn-12289 (Accessed July 31, 2017).

Marcotte, Amanda. September 19, 2016. "The Clinton BS Files: Conspiracy Theorists Paint the Branch Davidian Mass Suicide as Murder at the Hands of the Clinton Administration." *Salon.* http://www.salon.com/2016/09/19/the-clinton-bs-files-conspiracy-theorists -paint-the-branch-davidian-mass-suicide-as-murder-at-the-hands-of-the-clinton -administration/ (Accessed July 31, 2017).

Southern Poverty Law Center. "Alex Jones." https://www.splcenter.org/fighting-hate/extremist -files/individual/alex-jones (Accessed February 11, 2017).

K

KAHANE, MEIR DAVID

Meir David Kahane (1935–1990) was an Orthodox Jewish rabbi and ultranational-ist politician whose work in support of Israeli nationalism "laid the foundation for the rise of modern Jewish militantism and far right-wing political groups in Israel" (Council on Foreign Relations). Kahane was known as an extreme advocate for Jewish causes. He founded the Jewish Defense League in 1968 in New York City as a way "to protect Jews from local manifestations of anti-Semitism, particularly those perpetrated by African-Americans" (Jew Age). The JDL "promoted Jewish vigilantism and urged Jews to arm themselves under the slogan 'every Jew a .22'" (Council on Foreign Relations). Members of JDL "went on to target the offices and representatives of Soviet-bloc nations, the Palestine Liberation Organization, Arab states, and Jewish organizations it saw as either overly liberal or moderate" (Council on Foreign Relations). Kahane publicly referred to Arabs as "dogs," and liberal Israelis reviled him, picketed him, and pelted him with eggs (Kifner 1990). In 1971, Kahane emigrated to Israel and established the Kach ("Thus") Party. Kahane was elected to the Israeli Knesset (Parliament) in 1984, but he "refused to take the standard oath of office and insisted on adding a Biblical verse from Psalms, to indicate that when the national laws and Torah conflict, Torah (Biblical) law should have supremacy over the laws of the Knesset" (Jew Age). In 1988, the Kach Party was outlawed for its violent and racist views after the Knesset passed legislation banning parties with a racist platform. Kahane was assassinated in New York City in 1990 by an Arab disguised as an Orthodox Jew, who shot and killed Kahane after he had delivered an address to a "Zionist conference in a hotel in midtown Manhattan" (McQuiston 1990). Kahane's killer was later linked to the mastermind of the first World Trade Center bombing in 1993.

Kahane was born into an Orthodox Jewish family in Brooklyn, New York. In the 1950s, his strong anticommunist views garnered the attention of the Federal Bureau of Investigation, who hired Kahane as a consultant in order "to infiltrate the right-wing John Birch Society and report back to the FBI" (Jew Age). In 1968, Kahane founded the Jewish Defense League (JDL). He brooded over the num-ber of Jews fleeing inner-city neighborhoods, or emigrating to Israel, and orga-nized "self-defense groups" and patrols in "deteriorating Jewish neighborhoods" while demanding that the Soviet Union allow Jews to emigrate to Israel (Jew Age). Warning against a "second Holocaust" of Jews in the United States, Kahane and the JDL protested "against anti-Semitic teachers in the public school system, pro-vided escorts for elderly Jews and educated Jewish youth in the art of self-defense" (Jew Age). Kahane's campaign against the policies and politics of the Soviet Union transformed the JDL from a "vigilante club to a mass activist organization with membership of more than 15,000" (Jew Age).

When Kahane emigrated to Israel in 1971, the JDL dropped most of its activities. In Jerusalem, Kahane founded the Kach ("Thus") Party and became a vocal "exponent of the most extreme anti-Arab position in Israeli politics, advocating the expulsion of the Palestinian population from the occupied territories" (McQuiston 1990). Before cheering crowds, Kahane stated, "I don't want to kill Arabs, I just want them to live happily, elsewhere. Give me the strength to take care of them once and for all" (Kifner 1990).

Kahane was elected to the Knesset in 1984 when the Kach Party received enough votes in the national election to warrant representation. Most Israeli commentators "dismissed him as an American import" and a "racist lunatic," "but it soon became apparent that Kahane had tapped in to a populist anti-Arab sentiment" (McQuiston 1990). Kahane commented that he "touched a simple and honest nerve" in the Jewish people and that his appeal was "based on mounting fears Israelis had of Arabs and of a desire to end what they called the Arab problem once and for all" (Kifner 1990). On several occasions, Kahane joined with protestors marching hand in hand shouting, "Kill the Arabs." Commentators noted that Kahane's message appealed to young voters for several reasons: "nationalism had become increasingly acceptable; personal violence between Arabs and Jews had increased, and confidence in Israel's major parties had weakened" (Kifner 1990).

In November 1990, Kahane returned to the United States to deliver a speech before an audience of "mostly Orthodox Jews" in midtown Manhattan (Jew Age). After the speech, an Arab man, El Sayyid Nosair, who was dressed as a Sephardic Jew, fired two shots and killed Kahane. After fleeing the scene, Nosair was apprehended and charged with murder. Subsequently "acquitted of murder but convicted on gun possession charges," Nosair was recharged, convicted, and sentenced to life in prison "after the discovery of his membership in one of Sheik Omar Abd El-Rahman's terror cells connected to Al-Qaeda and responsible for the 1993 World Trade Center bombing" (Jew Age).

Both Kach and Kahane Chai, a violent offshoot of Kach, have been declared terror groups by the U.S. and Israeli governments. Supporters of these organizations continue to commit violent acts from time to time. Kahane's brand of nationalism, vilification of minority groups, and appeal to populism has been evident around the world in recent years and most recently was a hallmark of Donald Trump's election to the U.S. presidency in November 2016.

See also: Jewish Defense League; John Birch Society

Further Reading

Council on Foreign Relations. March 20, 2008. "Kach, Hahan Chai (Israel, Extremists)." https://www.cfr.org/backgrounder/kach-kahane-chai-israel-extremists (Accessed May 22, 2017).

Jew Age. "Martin David (Meir David) Kahane—Biography." http://www.jewage.org/wiki/ru/Article:Martin_David_(Meir_David)_Kahane_-_biography (Accessed May 22, 2017).

Kifner, John. November 6, 1990. "Obituary: Meir Kahane, 58, Israeli Militant and Founder of the Jewish Defense League." *The New York Times*. http://www.nytimes.com/1990/11/06 /obituaries/meir-kahane-58-israeli-militant-and-founder-of-the-jewish-defense-league .html?pagewanted=all (Accessed May 22, 2017).

McQuiston, John T. November 6, 1990. "Kahane Is Killed After Giving Talk in New York Hotel." *The New York Times*. http://www.nytimes.com/1990/11/06/nyregion/kahane-is -killed-after-giving-talk-in-new-york-hotel.html (Accessed May 22, 2017).

KAHL, GORDON

Gordon Kahl (1920–1983) was a member of the extremist group Posse Comitatus and an adherent of the sovereign citizens movement. Starting in the 1960s, Kahl "refused to file federal income taxes on the grounds that the American government was being operated under the ideals of the Communist Manifesto and, as such, violated his religious principles" (Reed). Kahl also held that the Internal Revenue Service (IRS) was illegitimate inasmuch as it was part of the executive branch of government. Thus, Kahl believed that the IRS's existence was in violation of Article I, Section 8, which placed taxation powers within the purview of the legislative branch (Congress) and not the executive branch. Kahl also believed that by paying taxes "he would be sent to hell" (Reed). Kahl was involved in a shootout with federal and state authorities near Medina, North Dakota, in which two U.S. marshals were killed and another was severely injured. After the shootout, Kahl fled North Dakota, eventually finding refuge in the home of a fellow Posse member. When federal authorities were tipped off to Kahl's presence, they surrounded the home and Kahl was killed in a shootout. Kahl became the first official "martyr" of the Posse cause, and his efforts, as well as others', established the philosophies of the Posse Comitatus, which appealed to antigovernment adherents (i.e., self-sufficiency, localism, and antitax revolt).

Kahl was born in North Dakota "and served in World War II as a turret gunner for the Army Air Corps" (Reed). Upon his discharge from the service, he married and eventually had six children. Kahl worked on and off as a mechanic, but it was the payment of federal taxes that caused him to despise the IRS, and by extension, the federal government (Richards 1984). In 1977, a federal judge in Midland, Texas, sentenced Kahl to a year in jail and "five years probation for his failure to pay income taxes in 1973 and 1974" (Reed). Kahl reportedly told the judge that he might as well serve the entire six years in jail because he would not pay his taxes. The judge, thinking Kahl to be mentally unstable, committed him to a federal psychiatric program in Springfield, Missouri. When Kahl refused to say anything to psychiatrists for three months, he was sent to the federal penitentiary in Leavenworth, Kansas, where he served an additional nine months. He was released on the condition that he report regularly to a probation officer. He did not (Richards 1984).

In March 1981, an arrest warrant was issued for Kahl for his failure to report to his probation officer in Bismarck, North Dakota. After several months, the federal government seized 80 acres of Kahl's farm and auctioned off the land to satisfy a lien of $7,074 in back taxes (Richards 1984). Kahl had stated that the next time that law enforcement came for him, he would not be taken alive.

By this time, Kahl had become a member of Posse Comitatus, an antigovernment survivalist group that does not recognize the authority of the federal or state government. The group, in fact, recognizes no legal or judicial authority above that of the county sheriff. On February 13, 1983, Kahl and 14 other tax protestors met in Medina, North Dakota. Kahl was accompanied by his wife, Joan, and his son, Yorivon. The county sheriff who usually attended the meetings was absent. He was with federal authorities at a roadblock outside town waiting for Kahl. Kahl suspected that federal authorities might be lying in wait for him.

As Kahl left the meeting, he was confronted by a roadblock just outside town. Both Kahl and his son Yori were armed with rifles. As U.S. marshals and local law enforcement attempted to arrest Kahl, he and his son fled their vehicle and took up positions. After a tense standoff, Yori Kahl reportedly fired and fatally wounded a U.S. marshal. Kahl would soon kill a second marshal. During the firefight, a third U.S. marshal was wounded, together with a Medina police officer. The day after the confrontation, 100 law enforcement officers surrounded Kahl's home but did not find him home. Kahl had fled south to Texas and then to Arkansas. In his home, however, were numerous weapons, ammunition, and white supremacist literature that had been published by Posse Comitatus groups.

Kahl found refuge in the home of fellow Posse member Leo Ginter and Arthur Russell, an individual who had expressed his distrust of the government on several occasions (Reed). In June 1983, Russell's daughter, realizing that her father was harboring a fugitive, alerted the Federal Bureau of Investigation (FBI). The FBI put Ginter and Russell under surveillance and looked for an opportunity to arrest Kahl. On June 3, "two SWAT teams and several Arkansas state troopers, as well as Lawrence County, Arkansas County Sheriff Gene Matthews" surrounded Ginter's home near Smithville, Arkansas (Reed). When Ginter tried to leave the house, he was stopped by law enforcement, who then moved in to Ginter's house. When Sheriff Matthews entered Ginter's home, he found Kahl emerging from behind the refrigerator door. Kahl and Matthews fired simultaneously. Kahl was "killed instantly by a shot to the head from Matthews' .41 caliber handgun" (Reed). Matthews was shot in the arm. When the FBI agents outside heard the gunfire, they shot several shotgun blasts into the kitchen through the window. Buckshot struck Sheriff Matthews, who later stumbled outside and collapsed. He would later die from his wounds. The SWAT team, unaware that Kahl was dead, fired thousands of rounds into the home, eventually setting it on fire. The next day, Kahl's burned remains were found.

Right-wing conspiracy groups contended that "Kahl had been brutally murdered" and that the fire had been set to cover up the actions of the government (Reed). James Wickstrom, a white supremacist known for his ties to Posse Comitatus, stated that Kahl's death would "stimulate" Posse growth. After the shootout in Medina, Wickstrom stated that the federal government had "planned the entire shootout from the beginning" (United Press International 1983). Wickstrom believed that the U.S. marshals had been sent to arrest Kahl in order to "shut his mouth because the tax-resistance movement across North Dakota is booming at this time" (United Press International 1983).

See also: Posse Comitatus; Sovereign Citizens Movement; Wickstrom, James

Further Reading
Balleck, Barry J. 2015. *Allegiance to Liberty: The Changing Face of Patriots, Militias, and Polit-ical Violence in America.* Praeger.
Reed, Bernard. January 2, 2010. "Gordon Kahl (Shooting of)." *Encyclopedia of Arkansas History & Culture.* http://www.encyclopediaofarkansas.net/encyclopedia/entry-detail .aspx?entryID=5483 (Accessed April 22, 2017).
Richards, Don L. April 1984. "Death and Taxes." *WebArchive.org.* https://web.archive.org /web/20091027113923/http://geocities.com/dangbob01/kahl.htm (Accessed April 22, 2017).
United Press International. February 15, 1983. "A Wisconsin Leader of the Militant Anti-Federalist Posse Comitatus . . . " http://www.upi.com/Archives/1983/02/15/A-Wisconsin -leader-of-the-militant-anti-federalist-Posse-Comitatus/5785414133200/ (Accessed April 22, 2017).
U.S. Marshals Service. February 13, 1983. "History—No Greater Tragedy." https://www .usmarshals.gov/history/muir-cheshire/kahl.html (Accessed April 22, 2017).

KREIS, AUGUST

August Kreis (b. 1954) is a Christian Identity minister and white supremacist who was convicted of child molestation in 2015 and is now serving a 50-year sentence for that crime. Kreis once headed a competing splinter faction of the Aryan Nations, Richard Butler's Idaho-based group that was once the most powerful neo-Nazi organization in the United States. Kreis has advocated "for the mass murder of Jews, non-whites, and 'race traitors' and has been an avid proponent of 'lone wolf' domestic terrorism" (Southern Poverty Law Center). Kreis had a long criminal history before his 2015 child molestation conviction (Southern Poverty Law Center).

Kreis served in the navy during the Vietnam War but drifted aimlessly after his discharge. In the late 1970s, he embraced white supremacism by joining a Ku Klux Klan (KKK) group in New Jersey. Sometime in the 1980s, he had an ideological shift where he no longer saw blacks as the primary enemy. As he told a New York newspaper, "In the beginning, I thought the blacks were the problem. I didn't understand there was an underlying cause. . . . The Jew is the enemy of all races on the planet" (Southern Poverty Law Center). During this time, Kreis became heavily involved with Christian Identity, which views Jews as the spawn of Satan, and was mentored by James Wickstrom, who had also conducted paramilitary training on behalf of the antigovernment and anti-Semitic group Posse Comitatus.

In February 1993, Kreis and his two daughters "appeared on the *Jerry Springer Show* where he called the Holocaust a 'myth'" and told the Jewish Springer, "I've got your grandmother in the trunk of my car. . . . She's a lampshade. She's soap" (Southern Poverty Law Center). In 1994, Kreis began a protest movement against an interdenominational, antiracist coalition of preachers in Pennsylvania, threatening them with violence from the KKK, neo-Nazis, and skinheads. Kreis once e-mailed the groups, stating, "We will be watching you. . . . You will pay the ultimate price. . . . You're doing Lucifer's work, and you will pay" (Southern Poverty Law Center).

Kreis joined Aryan Nations in 1999 and quickly moved up the ranks. Aryan Nations' leader Richard Butler "invited Kreis to deliver a keynote address at a three-day Aryan World Congress in 2000" (Morlin 2000). Butler appointed Kreis as the webmaster for Aryan Nations and later as the "Regional Ambassador for the Northeast, meaning that Kreis coordinated activities in seven states" (Southern Poverty Law Center). In 2002, Kreis's world came crashing down when the Southern Poverty Law Center won a $6.3 million judgment against Aryan Nations and Butler. The result was that Butler had to sell the Aryan Nations compound to satisfy the judgment. Less than two years later, Butler would die, leaving Aryan Nations in a state of disarray.

After Aryan Nations' demise, Kreis moved to South Carolina, where he equated the neo-Nazi movement with Islamic jihadists, calling both groups "freedom fighters." In 2011, "Kreis was charged with three felony counts for allegedly cheating the U.S. government" (Morlin 2011).

In February 2014, "Kreis was arrested on six counts of sexually abusing children in South Carolina" (Morlin 2014). After a three-day trial in 2015, he was convicted on three counts of child molestation, involving abuse of two young girls between the ages of 10 and 14, and was sentenced to 50 years in prison (Monk 2015). Moments before Kreis's sentencing in November 2015, he turned to the jury that had convicted him and said: "I will always hate the Jew. This government is run by an evil group of people, and please—vote for Trump" (Gillman 2015).

See also: Aryan Nations; Butler, Richard; Christian Identity; Neo-Nazis; Posse Comitatus; White Supremacist Movement; Wickstrom, James

Further Reading

Gillman, Ollie. November 6, 2015. "'Vote for Trump!' Neo Nazi Child Molester's Message to Jury Before He Was Jailed for 50 Years." *Daily Mail.* http://www.dailymail.co.uk/news/article-3307432/Vote-Trump-Neo-Nazi-child-molester-s-message-jury-jailed-50-years.html (Accessed April 1, 2017).

Monk, John. November 5, 2015. "Judge Gives Lexington County Neo-Nazi 50 Years for Child Molestation." *The State.* http://www.thestate.com/news/local/crime/article43249878.html (Accessed April 1, 2017).

Morlin, Bill. July 15, 2000. "Posse Leader Joins Aryan World Congress; Annual World Congress Expected to Draw Dozens to North Idaho." *The Spokesman-Review.* https://www.highbeam.com/doc/1P2-27291908.html (Accessed April 1, 2017).

Morlin, Bill. May 31, 2011. "Racist Leader, Refusing to Surrender Tomorrow, Faces Arrest for Fraud." *Southern Poverty Law Center—Hatewatch.* https://www.splcenter.org/hatewatch/2011/05/31/racist-leader-refusing-surrender-tomorrow-faces-arrest-fraud (Accessed April 1, 2017).

Morlin, Bill. February 20, 2014. "Racist Leader August Kreis Arrested for Sexual Abuse of Children." *Southern Poverty Law Center—Hatewatch.* https://www.splcenter.org/hatewatch/2014/02/20/racist-leader-august-kreis-arrested-sexual-abuse-children (Accessed April 1, 2017).

Southern Poverty Law Center. "August Kreis." https://www.splcenter.org/fighting-hate/extremist-files/individual/august-kreis (Accessed April 1, 2017).

KU KLUX KLAN

The Ku Klux Klan, also known as the KKK or the Klan, is the name ascribed to three distinct periods of extremist activity characterized by sentiments of "white supremacy, white nationalism, anti-immigration, and, in later iterations, anti-Catholicism, anti-Semitism, and Nordicism" (Anti-Defamation League). Historically, the KKK has resorted to terrorism against groups or individuals whom they opposed (O'Donnell and Jacobs 2006). The KKK's ultimate goal has been the "purification" of American society in order to secure a white, Anglo-Saxon, protestant nation. The KKK has traditionally been associated with right-wing extremism (Southern Poverty Law Center, 2011). Today's KKK is a shadow of the organization as it appeared at its zenith in the 1920s. With the advent of new and more sophisticated hate groups, the KKK and its tactics have been perceived as old and outdated (Anti-Defamation League Report). In addition, the KKK must now compete for membership with other types of white supremacist groups that are much more technology savvy and communicate a message that spans many issue areas, such as immigration, economics, citizens' rights, and the like. Where once the KKK could boast millions of adherents, today there are probably no more than a few thousand active in KKK organizations around the United States (U.S. History).

The original Ku Klux Klan "was organized by ex-Confederate elements to oppose Reconstruction policies" after the U.S. Civil War and maintain white supremacy by terrorizing freed slaves and their supporters (Anti-Defamation League). The Klan was first organized in Pulaski, Tennessee, in 1866 by former Confederate general Nathan Bedford Forrest. The first incarnation of the Klan sowed fear through "its strange disguises, its silent parades, its midnight rides, [and] its mysterious language and commands, all of which were found to be most effective in playing upon fears and superstitions" (Infoplease). The Klan covered their faces and wore white to portray themselves as the spirits of dead Confederates returning to exact vengeance. The Klan was focused on keeping newly enfranchised blacks away from the voting polls, but measures passed by the U.S. Congress to combat the Klan took a toll, and by the end of Reconstruction the Klan had largely disappeared.

The Klan enjoyed its most prolific presence in the United States during its second era that began during World War I. Following the release of D. W. Griffith's movie, *The Birth of a Nation*, in 1915, interest in Klan activity surged. The movie, which glorified the Confederacy and the Ku Klux Klan, won praise from President Woodrow Wilson, who lauded the film, commenting that it was "like writing history with lightning" (Janik 2015). In November 1915, William J. Simmons, a Georgia preacher, and several friends who had also been inspired by *The Birth of a Nation* climbed Stone Mountain outside of Atlanta and burned a cross, thereby birthing the second iteration of the Ku Klux Klan. The new Klan was not simply about white supremacy or denying blacks their civil rights. Rather, its appeal was in "its militant advocacy of white supremacy, anti-Catholicism, anti-Semitism, and immigration restriction, but the organization also attracted the support of many middle-class Americans by advocating improved law enforcement, honest government, better public schools, and traditional family life" (Lay 2005). At the peak of its power in the mid-1920s, the membership of the Ku Klux Klan numbered between

Members of the Ku Klux Klan (KKK) are initiated at a ceremony. The KKK was founded in the South after the Civil War for the purpose of harassing and intimidating freed slaves. Though the KKK's membership once numbered in the millions, the modern KKK is characterized by various offshoot groups claiming to carry on the white supremacist legacy of the original organization. (The Illustrated London News Picture Library)

4 to 5 million (Lay 2005). The state governments of "Alabama, Colorado, Georgia, Indiana, Louisiana, Oklahoma, Oregon, and Texas included officials who were Klan members, and those governments were profoundly influenced by the Klan during the 1920s" (Lay 2005). In many other parts of the country, "the organization won electoral victories in many municipal elections." By 1924, "the perceived power of the Klan was such that neither major political party was willing to denounce it formally" (Lay 2005).

At the pinnacle of its power, the second Klan era spiraled into a steep decline as it was racked with internal feuding, political scandals, and the fading image of the group as the sole protector of white rights. The Great Depression severely hampered membership as new recruits could not pay dues to finance Klan activities. By 1944, the second era of the Klan had come to an end when it officially disbanded (Lay 2005).

Samuel Green, an Atlanta physician, attempted to revive the Klan soon after its official demise, but his death in 1949 left the movement hopelessly fragmented. Most of the membership that remained was in small, fanatical groups in contrast to the large numbers that the Klan had enjoyed during its heyday in the 1920s.

The U.S. Supreme Court ruling of *Brown v. Board of Education* in 1954 reenergized the Klan for a time as Southern whites engaged in "massive resistance to federal mandates for desegregation, and the Klan emerged as a key player in this resistance" (Southern Poverty Law Center, 2011). In 1955, the Knights of the Ku Klux Klan (KKKK) was organized in Atlanta, Georgia. Like the organizers of the second era of the Klan, the founders of the new Klan movement rallied atop Atlanta's Stone Mountain. The rally drew 3,500 attendees determined to maintain racial segregation in the South (Lay 2005).

The third era of the Klan was particularly violent as attacks against blacks and civil rights workers occurred throughout the South during the early 1960s. On

September 15, 1963, in Birmingham, Alabama, a bomb shattered the Sunday-morning worship services of the 16th Street Baptist Church, a known gathering place for civil rights leaders (History.com). The bombing killed four young black girls and injured several more, precipitating violent clashes between protestors and police that drew national attention to the civil rights struggle. Alabama's governor, George Wallace, vocally opposed desegregation, and Birmingham had "one of the strongest and most violent chapters of the KKK." The Birmingham city police commissioner was known for his use of brutal tactics against demonstrators, particularly blacks (History.com). It wasn't until 1977 that the first prosecutions for those responsible for the bombing were conducted. In that year, a Klan member was tried and convicted for the Birmingham Baptist Church bombing. Other prosecutions would lead to convictions in 2001 and 2002 (History.com).

Another violent incident in which a third-era Klan group was involved was the murder of three civil rights workers, two white and one black, during the Freedom Summer voter registration drive that took place in Mississippi in the summer of 1964. On June 21, 1964, three volunteers of the Freedom Summer movement—James Cheney, Andrew Goodman, and Michael Schwerner—were murdered by Klansmen after having been pulled over and jailed in Neshoba County, Mississippi. When the three young men went missing, a massive search of the area was conducted by the Federal Bureau of Investigation (FBI). After three days, the burned-out car of the three civil rights workers was found in a swamp. However, it would be two months before the three men's bodies were discovered buried in an earthen dam (Joiner 2016). The FBI investigation revealed that members of the county sheriff's office, who had detained the civil rights workers, as well as members of the local Ku Klux Klan and members of the Philadelphia, Mississippi Police Department had been involved in the incident (PBS). In 1967, 18 men were tried and convicted on civil rights charges. An all-white jury convicted seven of the men for violating the civil rights of the Freedom Summer volunteers, but none of those convicted served more than six years in prison. In 2005, 41 years after the fact, Edgar Ray Killen, a Baptist preacher, was convicted of manslaughter and sentenced to 60 years in prison (Joiner 2016). However, no investigation ever revealed who definitively killed Cheney, Goodman, and Schwerner, and in 2016 the state of Mississippi officially closed the case (Joiner 2016).

After the Civil Rights Act was passed in 1964, blacks gained a political voice in the South. As a result, the Klan lost its power and became marginalized. Legal actions against the Klan in civil cases severely curtailed the scope and influence of local organizations, and several were forced to disband following legal judgments against them.

Near the middle of the 1970s, the Klan experienced a mini revival when David Duke reorganized the Knights of the Ku Klux Klan. Duke was a new leader who wanted to shed the image of the KKK as a bunch of vigilantes running around in robes. Instead, Duke wanted to replace the robes with suits and ties and get members into positions of prominence. For his part, Duke ran for various political offices for a number of years, being successful only once when he was elected as a state legislator to the Louisiana House of Representatives.

During the 1980s and 1990s, the growing militant racism and anti-Semitism of Klan members caused many to associate with more virulent white supremacist groups, such as Aryan Nations and the National Alliance, as well as other neo-Nazi factions. In 1981, the Southern Poverty Law Center (SPLC) took a Klan group led by Louis Beam to court after the Klan had harassed and intimidated Vietnamese shrimpers in and around Galveston Bay in Texas. The Klan had burned crosses near the shrimpers and in some cases had fired shots at them as well as burned their boats. After the SPLC brought suit against the claim, the Klan was "permanently enjoined against violence, threatening behavior, or any other harassment of the Vietnamese shrimpers" (Greenhaw 2011).

In 1985, the SPLC won a civil rights suit against members of the Carolina Knights of the Ku Klux Klan for harassment and terrorist threats against a black prison guard and members of his family. In January 1985, a federal judge issued an order against the Carolina Knights that prohibited the group's "grand dragon," Frazier Glenn Miller, and his followers from "holding parades in black neighborhoods, and from harassing, threatening or harming any black person or white persons who associated with black persons" (Southern Poverty Law Center, Person).

In 1987, the Southern Poverty Law Center sued the United Klans of America "for the lynching of Michael Donald, a black teenager in Mobile, Alabama" (LA Times 1987). The $7-million verdict against the organization forced the United Klans into bankruptcy. In July 1998, the SPLC won a $37.8-million verdict against two KKK chapters (Christian Knights of the Ku Klux Klan and Invisible Empire, Inc.) for the arson of a historic black church (Southern Poverty Law Center, Macedonia). Finally, the SPLC won a case against the Imperial Klans of America (IKA), then the nation's second-largest Klan organization, in November 2008. The plaintiff in the case, Jordan Gruver, was awarded $2.5 million by a jury that determined that he (Gruver) had been severely beaten by two members of the IKA. The award bankrupted IKA, and the organization eventually disbanded (AP 2008).

In 2016, the KKK burst back on to the American national scene when Republican presidential nominee Donald Trump was endorsed by one of the KKK's "official" newspapers, *The Crusader*. Under the banner "Make America Great Again," the entire front page of an issue of *The Crusader* before the November 2016 election featured an article in which the question was asked, "What made America great in the first place?" The article continued, "The short answer to that is simple. America was great not because of what our forefathers did—but because of who our forefathers were. America was founded as a White Christian Republic. And as a White Christian Republic it became great" (Holley 2016). Though the Trump campaign disavowed the endorsement, there was no doubt that Donald Trump's overtly nationalist, anti-immigration rhetoric attracted tens of thousands of racists, white nationalists, white supremacists, and neo-Nazis to his campaign banner (Osnos 2016). After Trump's stunning upset of rival Hillary Clinton, former KKK Grand Wizard David Duke commented, "Make no mistake about it, our people have played a HUGE role in electing Trump!" (Cancryn 2016). Though Duke was not clear as to who "our people" referred to, it was evident to most readers that Duke was referring to extremists, like himself, who wished to see curbs on immigration, aggressive actions against Muslims, and other nationalist items pushed by white voters.

Though the Trump victory did accord a measure of prominence to the Ku Klux Klan, there is no question that the Klan is a shell of the organization that made it one of the most powerful political forces in the United States during the 1920s. Today, the KKK is a "collection of mostly small, disjointed groups with no predominant leadership or stability" (Anti-Defamation League, Robes). While many Klan groups are

> adept at exploiting the media by staging political endorsements, leafleting, and occasional rallies, most organized Klan groups suffer from a lack of cohesion and paucity of members, key factors in its long-term trend of decline. Other factors in its decline include a perception that Klan groups are old or outdated, as well as the presence of other types of white supremacist groups that compete for membership with Klan groups. (Anti-Defamation League)

Many Klan groups today promote a traditional Klan ideology that would be recognized by Klan members of the past (i.e., white supremacy). However, many Klan groups "updated" their ideology by infusing it with varying degrees of neo-Nazi beliefs and affiliations. For some Klan groups, "neo-Nazi tenets have resulted in symbiotic relationships with neo-Nazi groups" (Anti-Defamation League). Klan groups today still use robes and other historic symbols of the organization to make their case (e.g., cross burnings), but they are much more likely to rally against illegal immigration, urban crime, economic dislocation, and same-sex marriage (Knickerbocker 2007). However, a more visible target of the KKK's vitriol in recent years has been Islam. Klan supporters in recent years have been quick to distribute anti-Muslim fliers urging readers to help the Klan in its fight to prevent the spread of radical Islam (Anti-Defamation League).

Most of the Klan's strength remains in the Deep South, though there are several Klan groups scattered about the country (Southern Poverty Law Center, Ku Klux Klan). While their rhetoric and their hate speech remain potent, the KKK has largely been replaced by more virulent white supremacists, such as neo-Nazis, and have had their message more expertly co-opted by other right-wing extremist groups that are more adept at using the new technologies associated with the distribution of hate across the Internet.

See also: Aryan Nations; Beam, Louis; Duke, David; Miller, Frazier Glenn; National Alliance; Neo-Nazis; Southern Poverty Law Center; White Nationalism; White Supremacist Movement

Further Reading

Anti-Defamation League. "The State of the Ku Klux Klan in the United States." https://www .adl.org/sites/default/files/documents/assets/pdf/combating-hate/tattered-robes-state -of-kkk-2016.pdf (Accessed June 8, 2017).

Anti-Defamation League Report. "KKK Declining in Stature and Significance." https://www .adl.org/news/press-releases/adl-report-kkk-declining-in-stature-and-significance (Accessed June 8, 2017).

AP. November 15, 2008. "Klan Group Ordered to Pay $2.5 Million." *NBC News*. http://www
.nbcnews.com/id/27728315/ns/us_news-crime_and_courts/t/klan-group-ordered-pay
-million/#.WTq5oNy1vRY (Accessed June 9, 2017).

Balleck, Barry J. 2015. *Allegiance to Liberty: The Changing Face of Patriots, Militias, and Political Violence in America*. Praeger.

Cancryn, Adam. November 9, 2016. "David Duke: 'Trump Win a Great Victory for Our
People.'" *Politico*. http://www.politico.com/story/2016/11/david-duke-trump-victory
-2016-election-231072 (Accessed June 9, 2017).

Encyclopedia Britannica. January 19, 2018. "Ku Klux Klan." https://www.britannica.com/topic
/Ku-Klux-Klan (Accessed June 8, 2017).

Friedersdorf, Conor. March 27, 2015. "The Audacity of Talking about Race with the Ku Klux
Klan." *The Atlantic*. https://www.theatlantic.com/politics/archive/2015/03/the-audacity
-of-talking-about-race-with-the-klu-klux-klan/388733/ (Accessed June 8, 2017).

Greenhaw, Wayne. 2011. *Fighting the Devil in Dixie: How Civil Rights Activists Took on the Ku
Klux Klan in Alabama*. Zephyr Press.

History.com. "Birmingham Church Bombing." http://www.history.com/topics/black-history
/birmingham-church-bombing (Accessed June 9, 2017).

Holley, Peter. November 2, 2016. "KKK's Official Newspaper Supports Donald Trump for
President." *The Washington Post*. https://www.washingtonpost.com/news/post-politics
/wp/2016/11/01/the-kkks-official-newspaper-has-endorsed-donald-trump-for
-president/?utm_term=.8d8ca7f1d383 (Accessed June 9, 2017).

Infoplease. "Ku Klux Klan: The First Ku Klux Klan." https://www.infoplease.com/encyclo
pedia/history/united-states-canada-and-greenland/us-history/ku-klux-klan/the-first
-ku-klux-klan (Accessed June 8, 2017).

Janik, Rachel. February 8, 2015. "'Writing History with Lightning:' *The Birth of a Nation* at 100."
Time. http://time.com/3699084/100-years-birth-of-a-nation/ (Accessed June 8, 2017).

Joiner, Lottie L. June 21, 2016. "Mississippi Close the Case on Freedom Summer Murders."
Daily Beast. http://www.thedailybeast.com/mississippi-closes-the-case-on-freedom-sum
mer-murders (Accessed June 9, 2017).

Knickerbocker, Brad. February 9, 2007. "Anti-Immigrant Sentiments Fuel Ku Klux Klan
Resurgence." *The Christian Science Monitor*. http://www.csmonitor.com/2007/0209/p02s02
-ussc.html (Accessed June 9, 2017).

LA Times. February 13, 1987. "The Nation Klan Must Pay $7 Million." http://pqasb.pqarchiver
.com/latimes/doc/292654927.html?FMT=ABS&FMTS=ABS:FT&type=current&date=Fe
b13,1987&author=&pub=LosAngelesTime(pre-1997Fulltext)&edition=&startpage=2&
desc=TheNationKlanMustPay$7Million (Accessed June 9, 2017).

Lay, Shawn. July 7, 2005. "Ku Klux Klan in the Twentieth Century." *Georgia Encyclopedia*.
http://www.georgiaencyclopedia.org/articles/history-archaeology/ku-klux-klan-twentieth
-century (Accessed June 8, 2017).

O'Donnell, Patrick and David Jacobs. 2006. *Ku Klux Klan: America's First Terrorists Exposed*.
Idea Men Productions.

Osnos, Evan. February 29, 2016. "Donald Trump and the Ku Klux Klan: A History." *The
New Yorker*. http://www.newyorker.com/news/news-desk/donald-trump-and-the-ku-klux
-klan-a-history (Accessed June 8, 2017).

PBS. "Murder in Mississippi." *PBS: American Experience*. http://www.pbs.org/wgbh/american
experience/features/freedomsummer-murder/ (Accessed June 9, 2017).

Southern Poverty Law Center. "Ku Klux Klan." https://www.splcenter.org/fighting-hate/extrem
ist-files/ideology/ku-klux-klan (Accessed June 8, 2017).

Southern Poverty Law Center. "Macedonia v. Christian Knights of the Ku Klux Klan—Case Number 96-14-217." https://web.archive.org/web/20070930152516/http://www.splcenter.org/legal/docket/files.jsp?cdrID=29 (Accessed June 9, 2017).

Southern Poverty Law Center. "Person v. Carolina Knights of the Ku Klux Klan—Case Number 84-534." https://www.splcenter.org/seeking-justice/case-docket/person-v-carolina-knights-ku-klux-klan (Accessed June 9, 2017).

Southern Poverty Law Center. February 28, 2011. "Ku Klux Klan: A History of Racism." https://www.splcenter.org/20110301/ku-klux-klan-history-racism (Accessed June 8, 2017).

U.S. History. "The Modern Ku Klux Klan." http://www.u-s-history.com/pages/h1657.html (Accessed June 8, 2017).

LAND SEIZURE MOVEMENT

Many "patriots" and right-wing extremists believe that the federal government has no right to own land in the United States under the terms of the Constitution. Currently, the federal government owns roughly 640 million acres of land, or about 28 percent of the 2.27 billion acres of land in the United States (Congressional Research Service 2014). More extreme views state that not even states have the right to own land and that the only judicial authority that should be recognized in the United States is that of the county sheriff. Most of the land owned by the federal government is found in the western part of the United States, and farmers and ranchers have been particularly vocal that land should not be held by the federal government. In 2014, Nevada rancher Cliven Bundy engaged in a standoff with federal authorities when they moved in to seize his cattle for nonpayment of grazing fees. In early 2016, Bundy's son, Ammon, and several others occupied the Malheur National Wildlife Refuge in Oregon, demanding the return of Refuge land, and all other federal properties, to their respective states and localities. The Bundys, as well as others, contend that grazing livestock on federal lands conveys property rights to those lands. The same contention is made in the case of state-based water claims that ranchers believe give them de facto ownership of all federal lands that surround their private property. Many extremists today continue to push for the return of federal lands to state and local control, though there is some indication that the movement's influence is beginning to wane (Rowland 2016).

The idea of federal ownership has long been contentious but has consistently been upheld by the actions of the U.S. Supreme Court. In the 1970s and 1980s, a movement known as the Sagebrush Rebellion arose in the western United States, where individuals and states attempted to gain more state and local control over federal lands, with some calls for outright transfer of the lands to the states. The sentiment waned toward the end of the 20th century, but it has been revived by individual citizens, politicians, and organized groups in the 21st century, particularly by those with interests in the grazing of livestock, mineral extraction, and other economic development that supporters believe could be realized with greater local control.

Many supporters of the seizure of federal lands today are individuals and government officials who are either antifederal government or subscribe to a belief that the federal government has taken on responsibilities not intended by the Constitution. In Utah, that state's conservative politicians have for years been advocating the seizure of federal lands in order that these lands be returned to the state. In 2016, the Utah legislature and governor pushed the attorney general to sue the federal government for the return of over 30 million acres of federal land within the state. The lawsuit to date has cost the state more than $2 million, though it has yet to be filed in federal court (Clarke 2016). In February 2017, a federal court in Nevada handed down a ruling against rancher Wayne Hage, who, like Cliven Bundy, owed hundreds of thousands of dollars in penalties for grazing his cattle on federal lands without paying appropriate grazing fees (Molvar 2017). These setbacks are unlikely to assuage the sentiments of advocates of federal land devolution who, for decades, have asserted their own understanding of the Constitution and the "traditions" of Western history to justify their calls for the return of federal lands.

In October 2016, Ammon Bundy and five others were found not guilty in a 41-day armed takeover of the Malheur National Wildlife Refuge in Harney County, Oregon. Despite their acquittal, Bundy and his group seem to be losing ground in their quest to gain more control over federal lands. In September 2016, the Western Conference of Attorneys General issued a legal analysis that put a lawsuit proposed by Utah on shaky ground as precedents from the Supreme Court and other federal courts cast significant doubt on the state's probability of success (Price 2016). Another sign of trouble is that the American Lands Council, a group that has advocated for the seizure of public lands, has seen its membership decline by 45 percent (Saeger 2016). Additionally, as noted by columnist Jenny Rowland (2016),

> state and national bills to seize public lands have failed across the country, counties across the west are passing resolutions reaffirming the value of public lands, neither major presidential candidates have backed the idea, and poll after poll show this is a losing issue among voters in the West.

Despite the dip in support for the seizure of federal lands, the sentiment for the return of lands among those that distrust, and outright hate, the federal government will not dissipate any time soon. Those who see the government as intrusive, obstructive, and overreaching the powers granted to it by the U.S. Constitution will continue to agitate in sometimes violent ways, believing that it is their patriotic duty to hold their government to account for abuses. Particularly in the western portions of the United States, where anywhere between 20 and 85 percent of state land is federally owned (Congressional Research Service 2014), extremists will continue to push the boundaries of the federal government in their quest to lessen its power and influence.

See also: Bundy Ranch Standoff; Malheur National Wildlife Refuge Standoff; Sagebrush Rebellion

Further Reading

Clarke, Chris. October 5, 2016. "Terror and Prejudice in the Public Land Seizure Movement." *KCET*. https://www.kcet.org/redefine/terror-and-prejudice-in-the-public-land-seizure-movement (Accessed April 24, 2017).

Congressional Research Service. December 29, 2014. "Federal Land Ownership: Overview and Data." https://fas.org/sgp/crs/misc/R42346.pdf (Accessed April 24, 2017).

Molvar, Erik. March 14, 2017. "Federal Court Smacks Down Bundy Land-Seizure Theories." *The Wildlife News*. http://www.thewildlifenews.com/2017/03/14/federal-court-smacks-down-bundy-land-seizure-theories/ (Accessed April 24, 2017).

Ochenski, George. October 17, 2016. "George Ochenski: Federal Land Transfer Movement Running Out of Options." *Missoulian*. http://missoulian.com/news/opinion/columnists/george-ochenski-federal-land-transfer-movement-running-out-of-options/article_a1e2d5c4-04d9-56c5-bffa-60c1f617345a.html (Accessed April 24, 2017).

Price, Michelle L. September 30, 2016. "Attorneys General Cast Doubt on Utah Land Push." *AP News*. https://apnews.com/e8a2cd9143e14b3397c5ba8d2bfde9c0 (Accessed April 24, 2017).

Rowland, Jenny. October 28, 2016. "Public Land Seizure Is a Dying Movement, Despite Bundy Verdict." *ThinkProgress*. https://thinkprogress.org/public-land-seizure-is-a-dying-movement-despite-bundy-verdict-fcb064a8859e (Accessed April 24, 2017).

Saeger, Chris. October 19, 2016. "Secretive American Land Council Sees Membership Drop 45%." *Western Values Project*. http://westernvaluesproject.org/secretive-american-lands-council-sees-memberships-drop-45/ (Accessed April 24, 2017).

LANE, DAVID

David Lane (1938–2007) was a member of the infamous domestic terror group The Order as well as the author of the so-called 14 Words ("We must secure the existence of our people and a future for white children"), "the best-known slogan of the U.S. white supremacist movement" (Southern Poverty Law Center). Lane was an accomplice in the assassination in 1984 of Jewish radio talk show host Alan Berg in Denver, Colorado, as well as the "robbery of $3.6 million from an armored car in Ukiah, California" (Southern Poverty Law Center). In March 1985, Lane was arrested on charges of "conspiracy and racketeering, along with 22 other members of The Order" and eventually sentenced to 40 years in prison. In 1987, "Lane was additionally accused of violating Alan Berg's civil rights by helping to assassinate him" (Southern Poverty Law Center). Lane was sentenced to an additional 150 years in prison "to be served consecutively with his earlier 40-year sentence" (Southern Poverty Law Center). While in prison, Lane became a prolific author of white nationalist and white supremacist propaganda. He and his wife, "whom he had married in prison in 1994, established 14 Word Press in 1995, dedicated to Lane's racist ideology and religion, which Lane called Wotanism" (the Germanic word for Odinism). Lane "also described Wotanism as an acronym for 'Will Of The Aryan Nation'" (Southern Poverty Law Center). Lane died in prison in 1987 from complications of epilepsy. However, he "remains one of the most important and influential ideologues in the contemporary white supremacist movement" (Southern Poverty Law Center).

Lane was born in Iowa as the third of four siblings. According to Lane, his father "was an alcoholic migrant worker who was physically abusive" toward the family. Lane's father died in 1942, and Lane and his siblings were shuffled into foster care. He was eventually adopted by a young Lutheran minister and his wife, who subjected him to "endless hours of services, of devotions, of vespers and matins, of prayers and bible studies, all of which I [Lane] despised from the first moment"

(Lane). Lane claimed that he became "bored" with Christianity and fascinated with Adolf Hitler and the cause of national socialism.

After graduating high school, Lane became a real estate broker, but he lost his job when he refused to sell homes to black customers in white neighborhoods. In the 1960s, Lane joined the John Birch Society, the rabidly anticommunist organization that claimed that the U.S. government had been infiltrated at every level by communist influence. Lane soon left the group because he "felt the single-minded purpose of the Society was misguided" (Southern Poverty Law Center). Moreover, Lane believed that Jews and not communists were the real enemy, a position that the John Birch Society explicitly rejected. As Lane would write, "By 1978 my research was essentially complete and the real problem was sharp in my mind. The Western nations were ruled by a Zionist conspiracy" (Lane).

Lane wrote a pamphlet entitled "The Death of the White Race" and organized a chapter of the Knights of the Ku Klux Klan in Denver, Colorado. Between 1979 and 1983, Lane was associated with the Aryan Nations, a group that revered Adolf Hitler and preached a particularly virulent form of anti-Semitism known as Christian Identity, which taught that Jews are the offspring of Eve and Satan. Lane would later reject Christian Identity "in favor of a racist version of the pre-Christian pagan religion commonly known as Odinism" (Southern Poverty Law Center).

In 1983, Lane met neo-Nazi and National Alliance member Bob Mathews. Mathews would soon form his own terror group, The Order, whose name he took from a prominent group mentioned in *The Turner Diaries* (1978), an apocalyptic fantasy novel written by National Alliance founder William Pierce. In the book, The Order hunts down "Jews, race mixers," government agents, and other "enemies of the people in a quest to ignite a nationwide race war" (Southern Poverty Law Center). Though the activities of Mathews's group were at first rhetorical and symbolic, the group soon turned to "counterfeiting and bank robbery. On June 19, 1984, 12 members of The Order robbed a Brinks armored car of $3.6 million in Ukiah, California" (Southern Poverty Law Center). Other armored car robberies followed. In all, the group made off with more than $4.1 million, while "killing three people, detonating bombs, counterfeiting money, organizing paramilitary training operations, and carrying out other crimes with the ultimate goal of overthrowing the 'Zionist Occupation Government (ZOG)'" (New York Times 1987).

The day before the Brinks robbery, June 18, 1984, four members of The Order traveled to Denver, Colorado, and killed Jewish radio talk show host Alan Berg in the driveway of his home. Lane was the getaway driver for the group. Berg had become a target of The Order because of his particularly pointed attacks on white supremacists and their ideas and his defense of liberal ideals. Berg was shot 12 times with a semiautomatic weapon that had been converted to an automatic weapon, a violation of federal law (Reid 1984).

By this time, the Federal Bureau of Investigation (FBI) had begun Operation Clean Sweep in a quest to destroy The Order. A former member of the group, Tom Martinez, who had been arrested on counterfeiting charges, became an informant for the FBI as part of a plea bargain. Martinez led the FBI to the group's leader, Bob Mathews, who died in a fiery shootout with FBI in December 1984. In March

1985, Lane and 22 other Order members were arrested under the terms of the Racketeer Influenced and Corrupt Organizations Act. Lane eventually received a 40-year sentence for his activities related to the criminal acts of The Order. Two years later, in October 1987, Lane and three other Order members were charged with violating Alan Berg's civil rights. Lane was convicted and sentenced to an additional 150 years of prison time.

In prison, Lane "produced articles for extremist journals, primarily focusing on the theme of racial survival" (Southern Poverty Law Center). It was in prison that Lane authored the infamous 14 Words: "We must secure the existence of our people and a future for white children." According to the Anti-Defamation League, "The term reflects the primary white supremacist worldview in the late 20th and early 21st centuries: that unless immediate action is taken, the white race is doomed to extinction by an alleged 'rising tide of color' purportedly controlled and manipulated by Jews." During this time, Lane also pronounced the "88 Precepts," a treatise intended to provide guidelines for securing, protecting, preserving, and establishing white territorial enclaves in North America and Europe. The number 88 was symbolic to both Lane and white nationalists as it represented "Heil Hitler," inasmuch as "H" is the eighth letter in the alphabet.

In 1995, Lane established 14 Word Press with his wife, Katja Lane, "whom he had married in prison the year before" (Southern Poverty Law Center). The press was devoted to Lane's racist ideologies and was used to describe the theology of his religion, which he called Wotanism, incorporating the "worship of Thor, Odin and other Norse-Germanic gods into an ideology promoting the survival of the Germanic culture and the Aryan race" (Southern Poverty Law Center). Wotanism served as a point of departure from most other white supremacist groups, but most members of The Order became adherents. Fourteen Word Press went defunct in 2001.

David Lane died on May 28, 2007, from complications of an epileptic seizure. His death touched off memorials and remembrances by white nationalists around the world. April Gaede, a neo-Nazi activist who had become an admirer of Lane, "was given custody of his body and [it was] announced that 'the gal from WAU (Women for Aryan Unity)' had established a fund to cover the expense of interring Lane's remains" (Southern Poverty Law Center). Gaede later stated that Lane had expressed his wish "to be cremated and placed in the capstone of a pyramid monument in a white homeland" (Southern Poverty Law Center). When this was not possible, Gaede wrote online, "Since we are not in a situation to build a monument in a White homeland, she [Gaede] was arranging instead to distribute Lane's ashes among 14 smaller, portable pyramids, which would then be enshrined in the homes of 14 white nationalist women. (The number of pyramids is a direct reference to the 14 words.) Lane's body reportedly was cremated in June 2007" (Southern Poverty Law Center).

Today, "the doctrines and influence of David Lane lives on in many white nationalist and white supremacist groups" (Southern Poverty Law Center). These groups regularly flash the hate symbol "14-88," which references the 14 Words and 88 Precepts.

See also: Aryan Nations; Christian Identity; Fourteen Words; Gaede, April; John Birch Society; Mathews, Bob; National Alliance; Neo-Nazis; Order, The; Pierce, William; *Turner Diaries, The*; White Nationalism; White Supremacist Movement

Further Reading

Anti-Defamation League. "14 Words." https://www.adl.org/education/references/hate-symbols/14-words (Accessed April 24, 2017).

Lane, David. "Autobiography of David Lane." *Fliphtml5.* http://online.fliphtml5.com/iiyi/dkfl/#p=2 (Accessed April 24, 2017).

Milton, Kleg. 1993. *Hate Prejudice and Racism.* State University of New York Press.

New York Times. November 8, 1987. "Jury Told of Plan to Kill Radio Host." http://www.nytimes.com/1987/11/08/us/jury-told-of-plan-to-kill-radio-host.html (Accessed April 24, 2017).

Reid, T. R. December 15, 1984. "Gun in Killing of Radio Host Reported Found." *The Washington Post.* https://www.washingtonpost.com/archive/politics/1984/12/15/gun-in-killing-of-radio-host-reported-found/c0158606-2645-4eab-b1c2-4d61796d0bdb/?utm_term=.8ece4d62eba9 (Accessed April 24, 2017).

Southern Poverty Law Center. "David Lane." https://www.splcenter.org/fighting-hate/extremist-files/individual/david-lane (Accessed April 24, 2017).

LAUCK, GARY "GERHARD"

Gary "Gerhard" Lauck (b. 1953) is an American neo-Nazi who has been "nicknamed the 'Farm Belt Fuhrer' because of his rural origins" (Southern Poverty Law Center). At age 11, he moved with his family to Lincoln, Nebraska, where his father was a professor of engineering at the University of Nebraska (Atkins 2011). From his Nebraska home, he founded the "NSDAP/AO, the German language acronym for the National Socialist German Worker's Party/Overseas Organization, the translated name of the original Nazi party's overseas unit" (Southern Poverty Law Center). Lauck reportedly "exported or smuggled millions of pieces of neo-Nazi propaganda into at least 30 countries from the 1980s to the 1990s" (Southern Poverty Law Center). In 1995, he was arrested in Denmark and was extradited to Germany for violating German law regarding the distribution of neo-Nazi propaganda (Lee 1999). He was tried and found guilty and sentenced to four years in prison. Lauck was released in 1999 and extradited back to the United States. However, by this time the advent of the Internet had passed by Lauck and his printed material propaganda. Today, he disseminates his neo-Nazi material via his Web site, NSDAP.info.

Lauck began demonstrating his affinity for all things Nazi by age 11. In school, his German accent made him the target of teasing by fellow classmates who believed he had a speech impediment. It was at this point, Lauck has stated, that he became a fanatic of Germany and national socialism, not only in his heart but in his mind. At 19, Lauck officially "changed his name to Gerhard to solidify his Nazi persona" (Southern Poverty Law Center).

In his early years, Lauck joined the National Socialist White People's Party (the successor to George Lincoln Rockwell's American Nazi Party), a neo-Nazi group, and the National Socialist Party of America, which later imploded because of the revelation that its leader was of Jewish descent and was also a child molester (Southern Poverty Law Center). In 1974, Lauck founded the NSDAP/AO with the intent to promote "a worldwide National Socialist-led White Revolution for the restoration of White Power in all White nations" (NSDAP.info). He gained the moniker the "Farm Belt Fuhrer" because of the "Hitlerite" moustache he sported as well as his put-on German accent. Lauck would sometimes "walk through the streets of Lincoln, Nebraska in Nazi uniforms," but he largely assumed a low profile in his community (Southern Poverty Law Center).

Lauck's greatest successes were overseas, where he was able to disseminate Nazi paraphernalia and propaganda at a time when several European countries maintained strict bans on the publication or distribution of such material. During the 1980s and 1990s, "Lauck produced, translated, and helped smuggle enormous amounts of German-language propaganda into Europe, as much as eight million pieces per year" (Southern Poverty Law Center). Overall, Lauck was able to place hate material in as many as 30 countries in 10 different languages. A once-prominent neo-Nazi leader, who eventually renounced his racist ways, wrote that Lauck "was the publisher and distributor of the bulk of neo-Nazi propaganda pasted up on the walls and windows from Berlin to Sao Paulo [Brazil], and was also the center of a worldwide umbrella organization with which practically every neo-Nazi had contact" (Southern Poverty Law Center).

After several run-ins and arrests during the 1970s for his public Nazi glorification activities, Lauck was arrested in Denmark in 1995 on international warrants stemming from his importation of illegal propaganda into Germany. He was extradited to Germany and "served four years in prison for his activities." By the time of his release from prison in 1999, "internet-based hate literature" had supplanted Lauck and rendered moot the illegal smuggling of neo-Nazi literature into Europe (Southern Poverty Law Center).

After his release from prison, Lauck "built his own website and wrote primarily in German" (Southern Poverty Law Center). In 2001, he set up a Web-hosting company where he encouraged European clients to move their Web sites to the United States to prevent the political repression that Lauck contended was sweeping across Europe. Today, Lauck's Web site NSDAP.info claims to be the "largest supplier of National Socialist propaganda material in the world" (NSDAP.info). The Web site is published in nearly 30 languages.

See also: American Nazi Party; Neo-Nazis; Rockwell, George Lincoln

Further Reading

Atkins, Stephen E. 2011. *Encyclopedia of Right-Wing Extremism in Modern American History.* ABC-CLIO.

Lee, Martin A. 1999. *The Beast Reawakens: Fascism's Resurgence from Hitler's Spymasters to Today's Neo-Nazi Groups and Right-Wing Extremists.* Routledge.

NSDAP.info. http://www.nsdap.info/ (Accessed April 24, 2017).

Southern Poverty Law Center. "Garry 'Gerhard' Lauck." https://www.splcenter.org/fighting-hate/extremist-files/individual/gary-gerhard-lauck (Accessed April 24, 2017).

LEAGUE OF THE SOUTH

The League of the South (LOS) is a racist organization that publicly advocates for positions of white supremacy and white nationalism while espousing neo-Confederate ideals. The LOS envisions a southern region of the United States that would be "a Christian theocratic state run by 'Anglo-Celtic' (i.e., white) people" that would politically and socially dominate blacks and other minorities (Southern Poverty Law Center). The LOS advocates for the secession of the states of the "old confederacy" and denounces the federal government and most states in the northeast (the old Union) as part of an "empire" that is overly materialistic and antireligious in nature. The group was founded by a group of Southern intellectuals, mostly university professors, but much of the original membership left the organization as it became more overtly racist. In recent years, the LOS has railed against multiculturalism, unchecked immigration, gay marriage, and other issues that it believes are leading to the ruination of the United States. Apart from secession of states from the United States, the LOS also encourages

> individuals and families to personally secede from the corrupt and corrupting influence of post-Christian culture in America. We call this "abjuring the realm," and it's a real and dramatic first step all of us can take by simply withdrawing our support of and allegiance to a regime that has imperiled our future. . . . Once our Southern culture is re-established, then the political issues will begin to take care of themselves. Good leaders flow naturally out of a healthy culture; however, power-hungry, self-seeking politicians are all we can expect from the debased cultural climate we have today. (League of the South, Core Beliefs)

The LOS was founded in 1994 by Michael Hill, a "history professor and specialist in Celtic history at Stillman College," and other Southern intellectuals (Southern Poverty Law Center). LOS began as "a religious and social movement that advocated a return to a more traditional and conservative, Christian-oriented culture" as epitomized by the gentility of the Old South (League of the South, About). LOS calls for a "natural societal order of superiors and subordinates," using as an example, "Christ [as] the head of His Church; husbands are the heads of their families; parents are placed over their children; employers rank above their employees; the teacher is superior to his students, etc." (League of the South, Core Beliefs).

In 1996, the LOS burst on to the political scene when it orchestrated a "Dump Beasley" campaign in South Carolina. David Beasley, then governor of South Carolina and "a moderate Republican, supported the removal of the Confederate Battle Flag from atop the state Capitol dome in Columbia" (Southern Poverty Law Center). The racist bent of LOS quickly emerged as Jack Kershaw, one of the group's founding members, told a reporter in 1998, "Somebody needs to say a good word [about] slavery. Where in the world are the Negroes better off today than in America?" (Southern Poverty Law Center).

By 2013, after seeing its membership dramatically rise and fall, LOS took cues from the white nationalist organization Council of Conservative Citizens and began to employ a strategy of small street demonstrations with no more than 30 members who stuck to strictly scripted messages. The LOS jettisoned "the use of the Confederate battle flag at its demonstrations in favor of a more innocuous 'Southern national flag,' a black St. Andrews cross over a white background" (Southern Poverty Law Center). In 2014, LOS began erecting billboards throughout the Southeast reading #SECEDE. In the fall of 2014, the group announced the "formation of a paramilitary unit called the 'Indomitables' to advance the cause of secession," though the group quickly fizzled (Southern Poverty Law Center).

In February 2017, Michael Hill, president of LOS, announced "Directive 02022017," a vigilante "defense force to combat the leftist menace to our historic Christian civilization" (Hatewatch Staff). As announced, the group was meant to "plan for contingencies—natural or man-made—that might affect the Southern people." The original announcement read,

> The League of the South is calling for all able-bodied, traditionalist Southern men to join our organization's Southern Defense Force for the purpose of helping our State and local magistrates across Dixie combat this growing leftist menace to our historic Christian civilization. As private citizens in a private organization, we will stand ready to protect our own families and friends, our property, and our liberty from leftist chaos. Moreover, we will be ready to assist our local and State authorities in keeping the peace should they find it necessary to "deputize" private citizens for that purpose. (Hatewatch Staff)

Some observers believe that Hill's announcement was prompted by President Donald Trump's promises to crack down on immigration and take a harder line against Islamic extremism. As Hill has previously stated, "People other than white Christians would be allowed to live in his South, but only if they bowed to 'the cultural dominance of the Anglo-Celtic people and their institutions'" (Southern Poverty Law Center).

See also: Council of Conservative Citizens; Hill, Michael; Neo-Confederates; White Nationalism; White Supremacist Movement

Further Reading

Hatewatch Staff. February 6, 2017. "League of the South Announces Formation of 'Southern Defense Force.'" *Southern Poverty Law Center—Hatewatch.* https://www.splcenter.org/hatewatch/2017/02/06/league-south-announces-formation-'southern-defense-force' (Accessed March 16, 2017).

League of the South. http://leagueofthesouth.com/ (Accessed March 16, 2017).

League of the South. "League of the South Core Beliefs Statement." https://web.archive.org/web/20080615205851/http://dixienet.org/NewSite/corebeliefs.shtml (Accessed March 16, 2017).

Smith, Janet and Ryan Lenz. November 15, 2011. "League of the South Rhetoric Turns to Arms." *Southern Poverty Law Center—Intelligence Report.* https://www.splcenter.org/fighting-hate/intelligence-report/2011/league-south-rhetoric-turns-arms (Accessed March 16, 2017).

Southern Poverty Law Center. "League of the South." https://www.splcenter.org/fighting-hate/extremist-files/group/league-south (Accessed March 16, 2017).

LIBERTY COUNSEL

Liberty Counsel is an organization that instigates litigation in support of Christian values. It was founded in 1989 by husband and wife Mathew and Anita Staver, both of whom are attorneys. Liberty Counsel states that it stands in absolute solidarity with Israel and was in full support of the U.S. military's policy of "banning homosexual activity within the armed forces. Liberty Counsel defends employment discrimination against gay workers, and opposes the addition of sexual orientation, gender identity, or similar provisions to hate crimes legislation. Liberty Counsel also opposes same-sex marriage, civil unions, and adoption by gay people" (Liberty Counsel, About). The Southern Poverty Law Center (SPLC) has designated Liberty Counsel a hate group. Liberty Counsel "debunks" the designation, stating that

> the SPLC's false labeling of people or organizations would mean that every civilization and its people and every major religious denomination would be similarly labeled by the SPLC as a hater or hate group. It is SPLC that demonizes good people and organizations and spews false accusations against those with whom it disagrees. The SPLC is reckless and its false labels are dangerous. (Liberty Counsel 2015)

Liberty Counsel is staffed by some 10 attorneys and 300 more "volunteer" attorneys who defend Christians who believe that their rights are being trampled upon by a secular society. With the expansion of LGBT rights, Liberty Counsel has worked "to ensure that Christians can continue to engage in anti-LGBT discrimination in places of business under the guise of 'religious liberty'" (Southern Poverty Law Center, Liberty Counsel). Founder Matt Staver "has warned about homosexuality, abortion, and the consequences for Christians who oppose homosexuality and marriage equality," stating they "will be targeted for the views" (Southern Poverty Law Center, Liberty Counsel). Staver has cited the work of Paul Cameron, "a discredited psychologist who paints LGBT adults as threats to children." Staver has also cited discredited "science" that indicates that homosexuality is a lifestyle choice, stating, "There is no evidence that a person is born homosexual. And there is evidence that people can change" (Southern Poverty Law Center, Liberty Counsel). Staver has also said,

> We are facing the survival of western values, western civilization. . . . One of the most significant threats to our freedom is in the area of sexual anarchy with the agenda of the homosexual movement, the so-called LGBT movement. It does several things, first of all it undermines family and the very first building block of our society, but secondly, it's a zero sum game as well and it's a direct assault on our religious freedom and freedom of speech. (Southern Poverty Law Center, Liberty Counsel)

Staver has called for a new "revolutionary war" in the wake of marriage equality and has confirmed that he would personally advocate for civil disobedience in the light of "any U.S. Supreme Court ruling favoring marriage equality," stating that, "collectively, we cannot accept that [marriage equality] as the rule of law"

(Hooper 2014; Mantyla 2015). Staver "has also supported the criminalization of homosexuality in the United States" and has stated in an *amicus curiae* brief to the U.S. Supreme Court that antisodomy laws in the United States should be upheld and that "this Court again should decline to deprive states of the power to enact statutes that proscribe harmful and immoral conduct" (Southern Poverty Law Center 2017).

Staver supports conversion, or reparative, therapy for gays, stating that "given the health risks associated with homosexual behavior, our youth deserve to know that unwanted same-sex attractions can be overcome." Many of the most "reputable American medical, psychological, psychiatric, and counseling associations in the United States have rejected conversion therapy, noting that homosexual orientation is normal and not a disorder and thus requires no attempts to change it" (Schlatter and Steinback 2011).

In the aftermath of the U.S. Supreme Court's ruling in *Obergefell v. Hodges* (2015), which legalized gay marriage in all 50 U.S. states, Liberty Counsel took "a leading role in defending Kim Davis, the Rowan County, Kentucky clerk who refused to grant same-sex marriage licenses claiming that her religion would not allow her to sign such licenses" (Southern Poverty Law Center 2017). Southern nationalists, white nationalists, and neo-Confederates, as well as the antigovernment Oath Keepers, pledged that they would protect Davis from further arrest after the Supreme Court refused to hear her appeal (Niewert 2015). Legal experts on conservative *Fox News* slammed Liberty Counsel's Mat Staver, saying that his statement questioning whether the U.S. Supreme Court "had the Constitutional authority to issue the same-sex marriage was ridiculously stupid" (Edwards 2015).

In 2016, Liberty Counsel was thrown into the national spotlight when it became known that the organization would defend Sandra Merritt in the wake of her indictment in Texas for tampering with a government record, a felony punishable by up to 20 years in prison. Merritt and a fellow antiabortion activist, David Daleiden, had shot undercover video in a Planned Parenthood clinic in Houston, Texas, with the intention of demonstrating that Planned Parenthood was involved in the selling of body parts of aborted fetuses. The videos shot were deceptively edited and "spawned numerous calls from the right to defund Planned Parenthood and investigate its practices" (Hatewatch Staff 2016). Staver, who has called Planned Parenthood a "corrupt organization," implied a conflict of interest in the case, noting that a prosecutor in the Houston office was a board member of Planned Parenthood (Ertelt 2016). Though the prosecutor named by Staver was not involved in the Planned Parenthood case, the "conspiracy theory" suggested by Staver picked up steam in several right-wing news arenas (Hatewatch Staff 2016).

In March 2017, Liberty Counsel was again in the national news when a federal court ordered that a lawsuit against the group could proceed. The lawsuit, brought by Janet Jenkins, alleges that Liberty Counsel assisted Jenkins's lesbian partner, Lisa Miller, in kidnapping and relocating the couple's daughter. Miller, who had renounced her lesbianism, fled with the couple's child to Nicaragua. Jenkins, along with attorneys from the Southern Poverty Law Center (SPLC), were successful in convincing the federal court that Liberty Counsel, as well as Mat Staver, could be fully investigated for Liberty Counsel's part in assisting in the kidnapping of Isabella, Jenkins's and Miller's daughter. A spokesperson for the SPLC stated, "We are pleased the court recognized that our allegations suggested 'significant wrongdoing' by these lawyers, including Mat Staver, and we will move swiftly to learn more about their wrongdoing and to hold everyone involved in the kidnapping to account" (Southern Poverty Law Center).

See also: Cameron, Paul; Oath Keepers

Further Reading

Edwards, David. September 7, 2015. "Fox News Panel Concludes that Kim Davis' Lawyer Is 'Ridiculously Stupid.'" *RawStory.com.* http://www.rawstory.com/2015/09/fox-news -panel-concludes-that-kim-davis-lawyer-is-ridiculously-stupid/ (Accessed June 3, 2017).

Ertelt, Steven. January 26, 2016. "Planned Parenthood Board Member Works in Office of D.A. Who Indicted David Daleiden." *LifeNews.com.* http://www.lifenews.com/2016/01 /26/planned-parenthood-board-member-works-in-office-of-d-a-who-indicted-david -daleiden/ (Accessed June 3, 2017).

Hatewatch Staff. January 29, 2016. "Anti-LGBT Hate Group Liberty Counsel to Defend Indicted Anti-Abortion Activist." *Southern Poverty Law Center—Hatewatch.* https:// www.splcenter.org/hatewatch/2016/01/29/anti-lgbt-hate-group-liberty-counsel -defend-indicted-anti-abortion-activist (Accessed June 3, 2017).

Hooper, Jeremy. April 1, 2014. "Liberty Counsel Continues Penchant for Inciting 'Revolution.'" *GoodAsYou.org.* http://www.goodasyou.org/good_as_you/2014/04/liberty-counsel -continues-penchant-for-inciting-revolution.html (Accessed June 3, 2017).

Liberty Counsel. "About Liberty Counsel." https://www.lc.org/about (Accessed June 3, 2017).

Liberty Counsel. October 5, 2015. "Debunking the SPLC 'Hate Group' Myth." https://www .lc.org/newsroom/details/debunking-the-splc-hate-group-myth-1 (Accessed June 3, 2017).

Mantyla, Kyle. March 13, 2015. "Mat Staver Will Disobey SCOTUS Marriage Equality Ruling Just as He'd Refuse to Turn a Jew Over to the Nazis." *Right Wing Watch.* http://www .rightwingwatch.org/post/mat-staver-will-disobey-a-scotus-marriage-equality-ruling -just-as-hed-refuse-to-turn-a-jew-over-to-the-nazis/ (Accessed June 3, 2017).

Niewert, David. September 10, 2015. "Oath Keepers Head to Kentucky to Repeat Bundy Ranch Tactics in Kim Davis Dispute." *Southern Poverty Law Center—Hatewatch.* https:// www.splcenter.org/hatewatch/2015/09/10/oath-keepers-head-kentucky-repeat- bundy-ranch-tactics-kim-davis-dispute (Accessed June 3, 2017).

Schlatter, Evelyn and Robert Steinback. February 27, 2011. "10 Anti-Gay Myths Debunked." *Southern Poverty Law Center—Intelligence Report.* https://www.splcenter.org/fighting -hate/intelligence-report/2011/10-anti-gay-myths-debunked (Accessed June 3, 2017).

Southern Poverty Law Center. "Liberty Counsel." https://www.splcenter.org/fighting-hate /extremist-files/group/liberty-counsel (Accessed June 3, 2017).

Southern Poverty Law Center. March 20, 2017. "Federal Court Permits Vermont Lesbian to Sue Liberty Counsel, Mat Staver for Role in International Kidnapping." https://www .splcenter.org/news/2017/03/20/federal-court-permits-vermont-lesbian-sue-liberty -counsel-mat-staver-role-international (Accessed June 3, 2017).

LIBERTY LOBBY

The Liberty Lobby was a right-wing organization founded in 1955 by Willis Carto as a patriotic lobby group dedicated to the preservation of the U.S. Constitution and the advancement of conservative principles. It became known, however, for its advocacy of white supremacism and anti-Semitism (Southern Poverty Law Center, Carto). Carto was "known for his promotion of anti-Semitic conspiracy theories and Holocaust denial" (Southern Poverty Law Center, Carto). The Liberty Lobby went defunct in 2001 after Carto was sued for fraud and mismanagement over another one of his ventures, *The Institute of Historical Review* (IHR), a pseudoacademic journal that published pieces defending Nazism and the perpetuation of Holocaust denial. The publishing arm of the Liberty Lobby, *The Spotlight*, also folded in 2001. Today, however, a Web site still exists that uses both the Liberty Lobby and *The Spotlight* monikers, claiming their roots in Carto's original organization.

The Liberty Lobby was organized at a time when Americans feared communism and a threat to the American way of life. As such, its dedication to the Constitution and conservative principles attracted many high-powered adherents. During the 1960s, the Liberty Lobby's newsletter boasted a circulation greater than that of older and better-known conservative publications, such as the *National Review*. National politicians and "big name conservatives appeared and spoke at Liberty Lobby meetings, including Christian Right hardliner Phyllis Schlafly in 1965. Even some Hollywood types backed Carto including Gloria Swanson and Eddie Albert" (Beirich 2008). The association of mainstream conservatives with Liberty Lobby was troubling to the larger conservative establishment given that the Liberty Lobby's board was reportedly populated "with anti-Semites and racists," including individuals who had openly "opposed school desegregation in the South" (Beirich 2008).

By the 1970s, most of the Liberty Lobby's acceptable conservative advocates had fallen away. Carto, no longer feeling bound to placate the right, established the *Institute for Historical Review*, a journal known for publishing articles related to Holocaust denial and in support of racist and white supremacist causes. In 1988, ultraconservative judge Robert Bork, a one-time Supreme Court nominee and "then on the Court of Appeals for the District of Columbia," ruled in *Liberty Lobby, Inc. v. Dow Jones & Co.* (1988) that the Liberty Lobby was "anti-Semitic," "effectively certifying Carto from that moment on as an extremist" (Beirich 2008).

Liberty Lobby is perhaps most well known for the Supreme Court case known as *Anderson v. Liberty Lobby, Inc.* (477 U.S. 242 [1986]). In the case, Liberty Lobby claimed that Jack Anderson, a conservative columnist, had libeled the organization by publishing false and derogatory statements about its operations. A district court ruled in favor of Anderson, but an appellate court reversed the ruling and Anderson appealed to the U.S. Supreme Court, which reversed the appellate court decision, thereby articulating the standard to grant summary judgment—the standard that allows a judgment to be "entered by a court for one party against another party summarily; i.e., without a full trial." *Anderson v. Liberty Lobby, Inc.* is one of the most cited Supreme Court cases (Most Cited Cases).

In 1993, Mark Weber, a member of the board of the IHR, wrested control of the IHR from Carto. The entire board of IHR later sued Carto for fraud and mismanagement of money that was left in a bequest for IHR. After protracted legal battles, Carto was ordered to pay millions of dollars to IHR (Southern Poverty Law Center). As a result of the judgments, Liberty Lobby folded in 2001, as did the organization's publication, *The Spotlight*.

After the loss of the Liberty Lobby, Carto formed the *American Free Press*, which continued to publish anti-Semitic articles, secret New World Order conspiracy theories, racist rants against Jews and Israel, and Holocaust denial stories. Carto also included pieces on Christian Identity, a theology that claims that Jews are the biological descendants of Eve and Satan (Southern Poverty Law Center, Carto).

Carto died in 2015. The Liberty Lobby name continues today as a Web site that claims to have its origins in the founding of Carto's original organization.

See also: Carto, Willis; Holocaust Denial; Institute for Historical Review; White Supremacist Movement

Further Reading

Beirich, Heidi. November 30, 2008. "Willis Carto: The First Major Biography." *Southern Poverty Law Center—Intelligence Report*. https://www.splcenter.org/fighting-hate/intelligence-report/2008/willis-carto-first-major-biography (Accessed May 4, 2017).

Kaplan, Jeffrey, editor. 2000. *Encyclopedia of White Power: A Sourcebook on the Radical Racist Right*. Alta Mira Press.

Liberty Lobby. http://www.libertylobby.org/index.html (Accessed May 3, 2017).

Most Cited Cases. https://web.archive.org/web/20091121082359/http://listproc.ucdavis.edu/archives/law-lib/law-lib.log9909/0171.html (Accessed January 30, 2018).

Nizkor Project. "Liberty Lobby and *The Spotlight*." http://www.nizkor.org/hweb/orgs/american/adl/paranoia-as-patriotism/liberty-lobby.html/ (Accessed May 4, 2017).

Southern Poverty Law Center. "Willis Carto." https://www.splcenter.org/fighting-hate/extremist-files/individual/willis-carto (Accessed May 4, 2017).

Southern Poverty Law Center. August 29, 2001. "The Spotlight, Extinguished." *Southern Poverty Law Center—Intelligence Report*. https://www.splcenter.org/fighting-hate/intelligence-report/2001/spotlight-extinguished (Accessed May 4, 2017).

LINDER, ALEX

Alex Linder (b. 1966) is a one-time member of the National Alliance, which was once the "premier neo-Nazi organization in the United States" (Southern Poverty Law Center). In 2000, Linder founded the "Vanguard News Network (VNN), an anti-Jewish, white separatist, neo-Nazi, Holocaust denial, and white nationalist website" (Anti-Defamation League). Linder founded VNN after having worked on CNN's political program, *Evans & Novak*, as a researcher. However, at CNN Linder became disillusioned with his inability to put forth his "racist satire of Jews and minorities" within the mainstream American media. While VNN has found a following among many in neo-Nazi circles, Linder's crude humor has turned off many in the white supremacist community who have viewed his literary attempts as pointless and faithless to the white cause. Though Linder is admittedly anti-Jewish and racist, he also tends to denigrate women, which does not win him many adherents. VNN's header, "No Jews. Just Right" is a brand of humor lost on many in the white supremacist community who desire a more hard-hitting and less cerebral brand of racism.

In 2005, Linder reportedly "announced his intention to establish the White Freedom Party," stating that it would be "America's first political party advocating Aryan interests and specifically naming the Jew as the agent of white genocide and greatest obstacle to our people's self-preservation as a distinct and protected people" (Southern Poverty Law Center). Upon its establishment, the White Freedom Party threatened to "WAGE NONSTOP WAR [emphasis in original] on the Jews, coloreds, and mainstream sellouts" (Anti-Defamation League). Because Linder was unable to secure any stable financial backing, the White Freedom Party never came to fruition.

Today, Linder is mostly known for minor protests against activities that he perceives to be crimes against white people. In 2007, Linder was arrested for assaulting a police officer at a protest in Knoxville, Tennessee, where he and other protestors were "rallying against genocide" in a case where a white couple was killed by three black assailants. In 2008, Linder organized "a similar protest on behalf of a teenage shooting victim who was a 'pure-blooded' white" (Southern Poverty Law Center). In 2009, "when an 88-year-old anti-Semite shot and killed a security guard at the U.S. Holocaust Memorial Museum" in Washington, D.C., "Linder praised the shooter for sacrificing himself to show his people that the Holocaust is a Big Lie: a deliberately concocted atrocity myth being used by Jews and their running dogs at Fox News and CNN to browbeat whites into submission to the Jewish Tyranny known as the New World Order" (Southern Poverty Law Center).

See also: National Alliance; Neo-Nazis

Further Reading

Anti-Defamation League. "Alex Linder/Vanguard News Network (VNN)." http://archive.adl.org/learn/ext_us/alex_linder.html?LEARN_Cat=Extremism&LEARN_SubCat=Extremism_in_America&xpicked=2&item=linder (Accessed January 4, 2017).

Southern Poverty Law Center. "Alex Linder." https://www.splcenter.org/fighting-hate/extremist-files/individual/alex-linder (Accessed January 4, 2017).

Vanguard News Network. http://www.vanguardnewsnetwork.com/ (Accessed January 30, 2018).

M

MACDONALD, KEVIN

Kevin MacDonald (b. 1944) has been dubbed the "neo-Nazi movement's favorite academic" (Southern Poverty Law Center, Kevin MacDonald). MacDonald is best known for his psychological concept of evolutionary theory, which he has used "to analyze Judaism as a group evolutionary strategy" (MacDonald 2002). While a professor at California State University, Long Beach, MacDonald published a trilogy of books in which he asserted "that Jews are genetically driven to 'destroy' Western societies" (Southern Poverty Law Center, Kevin Mac Donald). After retiring in 2014, MacDonald became the editor of the *Occidental Observer*, a publication that promotes "original content touching on the themes of White identity, White interests, and the culture of the West" (Occidental Observer).

MacDonald was born in Wisconsin. Coming to maturity in the 1960s, he considered himself a "flower child," and he became an anti-Vietnam War activist. After abandoning his Catholic roots, MacDonald earned a PhD in the behavioral sciences in 1981 from the University of Connecticut. In 1985, he assumed a teaching position at the California State University, Long Beach (CSULB). While at CSULB, MacDonald realized that he was haunted by his antiwar activism and the influence that Jews had exercised over him:

> Noticing that many of his fellow activists in the 1960s were Jewish, MacDonald developed his first inkling that Jews are compelled to challenge traditional American and Western ideals. He came to the conclusion that Jews take over political and cultural movements and front them with unsuspecting, token gentiles—just the way MacDonald felt that he was treated while protesting the Vietnam War. (Southern Poverty Law Center, Kevin MacDonald)

Over the course of the 1990s, MacDonald would publish three books that would provide white supremacists, neo-Nazis, and other race haters with new justifications for their anti-Semitic views. Perhaps MacDonald's most controversial conclusion is that the anti-Semitism expressed toward Jews throughout the centuries has been a "rational" response by people who have felt threatened by Jewish intellectual and financial superiority. MacDonald's assertion is "that Jews engage in an evolutionary strategy" that enhances their ability to outcompete others for resources (Southern Poverty Law Center, Kevin Mac Donald). Thus, "like viruses, Jews destabilize their host societies to their own benefit" (Southern Poverty Law Center, Kevin Mac Donald). MacDonald has regularly argued that "Jews are a hostile elite in American society" that have sought to undermine the traditional European roots of American society by fostering measures that have led to increased nonwhite immigration into the United States. According to the Anti-Defamation League's interpretation of MacDonald's thesis, "Jews maintain their elite position by fostering non-white immigration into America to alter the country's racial hierarchy."

For his part, MacDonald has claimed that his work has been misinterpreted and that he has been the victim of a systematic campaign by various groups to discredit him. However, MacDonald's work has been praised by the likes of David Duke, former Grand Wizard of the Knights of the Ku Klux Klan, and Don Black, founder and editor of *Stormfront*, the most popular Web site for white supremacists, neo-Nazis, and other "race scientists." MacDonald also testified on behalf of David Irving, a British Holocaust denier, in a 2000 libel trial in London.

In 2008, the psychology department at California State University, Long Beach, as well as the academic senate, "voted to formally dissociate themselves from Mac-Donald's work." The academic senate statement was as follows: "While the academic senate defends Dr. Kevin MacDonald's academic freedom and freedom of speech, as it does for all faculty, it firmly and unequivocally disassociates itself from the anti-Semitic and white ethnocentric views he has expressed" (Rider 2008).

After his retirement in 2014, MacDonald came out in full-throated support of David Duke, taking issue with the media's characterization of Duke as an "ex-Klansman." MacDonald stated that this characterization was "nothing more than the usual guilt by association argument" (Southern Poverty Law CenterMacDonald Lauds David Duke).

See also: Black, Don; Duke, David; *Occidental Observer*; *Stormfront*; White Nationalism; White Supremacist Movement

Further Reading

Anti-Defamation League. "Kevin MacDonald." *Anti-Defamation League—Extremism in America.* http://archive.adl.org/learn/ext_us/kevin_macdonald/ (Accessed January 6, 2017).

MacDonald, Kevin. 2002. *A People That Shall Dwell Alone: Judaism as a Group Evolutionary Strategy, with Diaspora Peoples.* iUniverse.

Occidental Observer. www.theoccidentalobserver.net/ (Accessed January 30, 2018).

Rider, Tiffany. October 6, 2008. "Academic Senate Disassociates Itself from Professor Mac-donald." *Daily 49er.* http://www.daily49er.com/news/2008/10/06/academic-senate-dis associates-itself-from-professor-macdonald/ (Accessed January 6, 2017).

Southern Poverty Law Center. "In a Bizarre, Inexplicable Move, Kevin MacDonald Lauds and Defends David Duke." *Southern Poverty Law Center—Hatewatch.* https://www.splcenter .org/hatewatch/2016/07/07/bizarre-inexplicable-move-kevin-macdonald-lauds-and -defends-david-duke (Accessed January 6, 2017).

Southern Poverty Law Center. "Kevin MacDonald." https://www.splcenter.org/fighting-hate /extremist-files/individual/kevin-macdonald (Accessed January 6, 2017).

MALCOLM X

Malcolm X was born Malcolm Little in 1925 in Omaha, Nebraska. He became "a prominent black nationalist leader and a spokesman for the Nation of Islam," an African American political and religious movement founded in 1930 that meant to improve the "spiritual, mental, social, and economic condition of African Americans in the United States and all of humanity" (Nation of Islam). Due largely to Malcolm X's efforts, "the Nation of Islam grew from a mere 400 members in 1952 to more than 40,000 members by 1960" (Biography). Malcolm X "exhorted blacks to cast off the shackles of racism by which they had been bound for 300 years by any means necessary," including violence (Biography). As a black activist, Malcolm X criticized white society in the United States in the harshest terms "for its crimes against black Americans." Many of his detractors "accused him of reverse racism," claiming he used the same racial tropes to whip up his supporters against whites as whites were accused of

Malcolm X became a prominent black nationalist leader and spokesman for the Nation of Islam during the struggle for Civil Rights in the 1960s. In a break from the nonviolent tactics favored by Martin Luther King Jr., Malcolm X favored a more confrontational approach to further the cause of black civil rights. (Library of Congress)

using against blacks (Biography). Shortly before his death in 1965, Malcolm X broke with the Nation of Islam (NOI). In February 1965, he was assassinated by three members of the group in an apparent retaliatory act for his defection.

Malcolm X was orphaned at an early age. His father "was killed when Malcolm was six and his mother was placed in a mental hospital when he was 13" (Biography). Malcolm's father, Earl Little, had allegedly died in a streetcar accident while the family was living in Lansing, Michigan. But a white racist group, the Black Legion, had previously attacked and burned the Little family home. Therefore, after the death of his father, Malcolm X was forever haunted by what he believed was the death of his father at the hand of whites. In 1946, at age 20, Malcolm was convicted of larceny and breaking and entering and sentenced to 10 years in prison (Biography), where he joined the Nation of Islam, a group that, aside from its lofty goal of improving the position of blacks in American society, "promoted black supremacy, advocated the separation of black and white Americans, and rejected the civil rights movement for its emphasis on integration" (Southern Poverty Law Center). When Malcolm emerged from prison in 1952, "he abandoned the surname of 'Little,' which he considered a relic of slavery, in favor of the surname 'X' in tribute to the unknown name of his African ancestors" (Biography).

After his release from prison, Malcolm X worked with the Nation of Islam's leader, Elijah Muhammad, to grow the black nationalist movement. Because Malcolm was articulate, passionate, and a naturally gifted orator, he began to eclipse Elijah Muhammad as the leader of the NOI. These qualities also attracted the attention of the federal government, who began to closely monitor Malcolm X and the activities of the NOI. Agents of the Federal Bureau of Investigation (FBI) "infiltrated the organization and placed bugs, wiretaps, cameras, and other surveillance equipment to monitor NOI activity" (Malcolm X). After Malcolm X's death, it was learned that one of his bodyguards was actually an FBI agent who had infiltrated the organization.

In 1963, Malcolm X "discovered that his mentor, Elijah Muhammad, was secretly having affairs with as many as six women within the NOI" (Malcolm X). Some of the relationships had resulted in the birth of children. As a strict Muslim, Malcolm X had believed that Elijah Muhammad was a prophet and that as a leader of Islam Elijah Muhammad should have followed the teachings of Muhammad and abstained from extramarital affairs. Malcolm X began to "feel guilty about the masses that he had led to join the NOI." He felt that the NOI was "a fraudulent organization built on too many lies to ignore" (Malcolm X).

In March 1964, Malcolm X severed his association with the Nation of Islam and went on a pilgrimage to Mecca. When he returned,

> Malcolm said he had met "blonde-haired, blued-eyed men I could call my brothers." He returned to the United States with a new outlook on integration and a new hope for the future. This time when Malcolm spoke, instead of just preaching to African-Americans, he had a message for all races. (Malcolm X)

Malcolm X then renounced Elijah Muhammad and left NOI, prompting FBI sources to warn "government officials that he had been targeted for assassination" (Biography). On February 14, 1965, Malcolm X's house in East Elmhurst, New York, where he lived with his wife and four daughters, was firebombed. The family escaped with no injuries. One week later, three NOI members shot Malcolm X at a speaking engagement in Manhattan. He was shot 21 times by both a shotgun and semiautomatic weapons. Wounds were found in his "chest, left shoulder, arms, and legs, including ten buckshot wounds from the initial shotgun blast to his chest" (Marable 2011). The three NOI gunmen were convicted and all sentenced to lengthy prison terms.

As noted by one biographer,

> Perhaps Malcolm X's greatest contribution to society was underscoring the value of a truly free populace by demonstrating the great lengths to which human beings will go to secure their freedom. "Power in defense of freedom is greater than power in behalf of tyranny and oppression," he stated. "Because power, real power, comes from our conviction which produces action, uncompromising action." (Biography)

See also: Farrakhan, Louis; Nation of Islam

Further Reading

Biography. "Malcolm X Biography." http://www.biography.com/people/malcolm-x-9396195 (Accessed March 17, 2017).

Malcolm X. "Biography: An Abridged Biography of Malcolm X." http://malcolmx.com /biography/ (Accessed March 17, 2017).

Marable, Manning. 2011. *Malcolm X: A Life of Reinvention*. Penguin Books.

Nation of Islam. "Nation of Islam in America: A Nation of Beauty & Peace." https://www.noi.org/noi-history/ (Accessed March 17, 2017).

Southern Poverty Law Center. "Nation of Islam." https://www.splcenter.org/fighting-hate/extremist-files/group/nation-islam (Accessed March 17, 2017).

MALHEUR NATIONAL WILDLIFE REFUGE STANDOFF

On January 2, 2016, Ammon Bundy, son of Cliven Bundy, and other armed individuals occupied the Malheur National Wildlife Refuge in Harney County, Oregon. Claiming that their occupation was a protest, the militants sought to advance their claim that the federal government, and particularly the U.S. Bureau of Land Management, was illegally administering lands that rightfully belonged to the sovereign state of Oregon, thereby violating the Constitution of the United States. Bundy's claims were part of a long-simmering dispute with the federal government because of its administration of large swaths of federally owned and administered land, particularly in the western United States. Shortly after the occupation began, Bundy dubbed those with him, and all like-minded individuals, as "Citizens for Constitutional Freedom." The standoff would end after nearly six weeks with Bundy and several of his compatriots being indicted on charges of conspiracy, possession of firearms in a federal facility, depredation of government property, and theft of government property.

The standoff ostensibly began when Bundy and his followers announced that they were taking action in protest of the resentencing of Dwight and Steven Hammond. The Hammonds had been convicted of illegally setting fires on their ranch that spread to neighboring federal land. Prosecutors claimed that the fires had been intentionally set by the Hammonds in order to cover up poaching activities that were taking place on federal land. For their part, the Hammonds claimed that they had set back fires on their property to save their ranch when lightning started fires on the federal land located nearby. The flames from the back fires spread to federal land and burned nearly 140 acres (Cleary 2016). Initially, the Hammonds were given light sentences, but prosecutors appealed the sentences, which led to longer sentences being imposed by a federal judge. The resentencing angered Bundy and his followers, and they seized the Malheur Refuge, demanding the immediate release of the Hammonds. For Ammon Bundy, the stiffer sentences handed down to the Hammonds were further evidence of a systematic attempt by the federal government to intimidate ranchers and serve notice to them that the federal government intended to rein in their actions relative to federal land. Two years prior to the standoff, Bundy had been at his father, Cliven's, ranch in Nevada when members of the Bureau of Land Management had seized the elder Bundy's cattle for nonpayment of federal grazing fees.

Though the Hammonds would disavow the occupation of the Malheur Refuge, Bundy would use their imprisonment to rally support. Some two dozen armed supporters would join Bundy in the early-morning hours of January 2 as the

Members of the self-proclaimed group Citizens for Constitutional Freedom occupy the Malheur National Wildlife Refuge near Burns, Oregon, in January 2016. The protestors sought to advance their claims that the federal government, particularly the Bureau of Land Management, was illegally administering lands and that all federally-owned land should be returned to their respective states. (Rob Kerr/AFP/Getty Images)

group took up positions against possible government action. Bundy would tell *The Oregonian*,

> The best possible outcome is that the ranchers that have been kicked out of the area, then they will come back and reclaim their land, and the wildlife refuge will be shut down forever and the federal government will relinquish such control. What we're doing is not rebellious. What we're doing is in accordance with the Constitution, which is the supreme law of the land. (Zaitz 2016)

Bundy went on to warn the government that he and many of the men with him at the refuge were willing to "fight and die to protect the rights of states, counties and individuals to manage local lands" (Zaitz 2016).

On January 4, Bundy began calling his group Citizens for Constitutional Freedom and reiterated his call for the federal government to cede all land under its control to the various states. In line with his sovereign citizens beliefs and in accordance with Posse Comitatus philosophy, Bundy called on neighboring county sheriffs to support his cause (Njus 2016). A self-proclaimed "judge" of the sovereign citizens movement stated he would "hold a trial with the redress of grievance against county and other government officials" (Njus 2016). Members of the extremist group Oath Keepers stated on January 15 that the standoff between the protesting group and government officials would produce a "conflagration so great, [that] it cannot be stopped, leading to a bloody, brutal civil war" (Boggioni 2016).

As the standoff dragged on, state and federal authorities looked for ways to apprehend the leaders of the occupation. On January 26, members of the group headed to John Day, Oregon, where they intended to speak to supporters. As a group of several occupiers traveled from the Refuge, they were intercepted by members of the Federal Bureau of Investigation and Oregon State Police. Though several members of the group surrendered peacefully when stopped, including Ammon Bundy, the driver of one vehicle, Robert "LaVoy" Finicum sped away from law enforcement officials only to crash his pickup into a snowbank a short time later. As he exited his vehicle, Finicum was shot and killed by a member of the FBI Hostage Rescue Team as he apparently reached for a gun in his waistband. On February 10, the last four occupants at the Malheur National Wildlife Refuge surrendered and were taken into custody.

As he traveled to be with his sons, Ammon and Ryan, in Oregon, Cliven Bundy was arrested by federal authorities for his part in the Bundy Ranch Standoff two years earlier. In all, 27 militants were arrested in connection with the Malheur National Wildlife Refuge Standoff. On October 27, 2016, "Ammon Bundy and six other defendants were found not guilty of the indictments brought against them" (Lenz 2016). Though it was a stunning victory for Bundy and his supporters, Bundy, nevertheless remained in jail on charges related to the Bundy Ranch Standoff nearly two years earlier.

See also: Bundy Ranch Standoff; Finicum, Robert "LaVoy"; Posse Comitatus; Sagebrush Rebellion; Sovereign Citizens Movement

Further Reading

Boggioni, Tom. January 16, 2016. "Militia Head Warns Feds: Don't 'Waco' the Oregon Occupiers Unless You Want a 'Bloody, Brutal Civil War.'" *The Raw Story*. Raw Story Media.

Cleary, Tom. January 3, 2016. "Dwight & Steven Hammond: 5 Fast Facts You Need to Know." *Heavy.com*. http://heavy.com/news/2016/01/dwight-steven-hammond-oregon-ranchers-protest-prison-arson-fire-land-charges-sentences-age-bundy-armed-militia-judge-photos-family/ (Accessed November 22, 2016).

Lenz, Ryan. October 27, 2016. "Antigovernment Leaders Behind Malheur National Wildlife Refuge Occupation Acquitted." Southern Poverty Law Center. https://www.splcenter.org/hatewatch/2016/10/27/antigovernment-leaders-behind-malheur-national-wildlife-refuge-occupation-acquitted (Accessed November 22, 2016).

Njus, Elliot. February 22, 2016. "Armed Occupiers Promise Plan to Leave Refuge, but Signal Longer Stay." *The Oregonian/OregonLive.com*. Advance Publications.

Zaitz, Les. January 2, 2016. "Militia Takes Over Malheur National Wildlife Refuge Headquarters." *The Oregonian*. http://www.oregonlive.com/pacific-northwest-news/index.ssf/2016/01/drama_in_burns_ends_with_quiet.html (Accessed November 22, 2016).

MATHEWS, BOB

Robert Jay "Bob" Mathews (1953–1984) was an American white supremacist and neo-Nazi who formed the American white supremacist group The Order in 1983. The Order was once described by the Federal Bureau of Investigation (FBI) as the most "dangerous domestic terror group" in the United States (ABC News 2005).

Among the infamies of The Order were counterfeiting, bank robberies, armored car heists, and assassinations. Mathews was convinced that the white race in the United States was under threat from minorities and illegal immigration. He moved his family to the American Northwest, which was then a bastion for white nationalist, white supremacist, and neo-Nazi groups. Mathews believed that the Northwest should be a "whites-only" sanctuary. He died in a shootout with the FBI in December 1984.

Mathews was born in Texas. At age 11, he stunned his middle-class parents when he announced that he had joined the ultraconservative John Birch Society (ABC News 2005). When he entered high school, he joined the Mormon Church and formed what became known as the Sons of Liberty, an "anti-communist militia made up almost entirely of Mormon survivalists" (American USSR). After being arrested for tax fraud in the early 1970s (Mathews had claimed 10 dependents on his W-4 form) and serving probation, Bob Mathews moved with his family to Washington, where the family purchased land for a new home in 1974 (Balleck 2015).

From his own experiences and readings, Mathews believed that whites in the United States were on the verge of extinction from intermarrying and the challenges being placed upon the race by societal forces, all of which were being driven by the American government. Mathews made a concerted attempt to create a whites-only homeland in the Pacific Northwest—the White American Bastion. In 1983, Mathews made a speech before the National Alliance (NA)—a white nationalist, anti-Semitic, and white separatist group that had been founded by William L. Pierce in 1974—in which he called upon those assembled at the convention, particularly "the yeoman farmers and independent truckers" to rally to his "White American Bastion" notion and take back what was rightfully theirs. Reportedly, Mathews received the only standing ovation at the conference (Balleck 2015). Mathews became an avid reader and a proponent of NA founder William Pierce's fantasy novel, *The Turner Diaries*, written in 1978.

The Turner Diaries, written under Pierce's pseudonym Andrew MacDonald, depicts a time of violent revolution in the United States when the American government is overthrown and a race war ensues, "which leads to the extermination of all groups deemed by the author to be impure"—meaning Jews, homosexuals, and nonwhites (Anti-Defamation League). The book was called "explicitly racist and anti-Semitic by the *New York Times* and been labeled as the bible of the racist right by the Southern Poverty Law Center" (Harkavy 2000).

Bob Mathews's fealty to *The Turner Diaries* would become evident in his choice for a new name for his group, which he hoped would foment the global revolution envisioned by the book. In September 1983, Mathews gathered with eight associates on his property in Washington and founded the group known as The Order, after the group so named in *The Turner Diaries*. Mathews made each man assembled swear an oath of allegiance to their cause, which was the maintenance and protection of the white race, and vow to fight against all elements that stood in the way of their goals being accomplished—the U.S. government and all minority and other groups that fought against the white race (ABC News 2005). Mathews had the members swear their oath while the one-month-old daughter of one of those assembled lay in the middle of the circle they had created. This white child, Mathews reportedly told those assembled, was the future of the white race and the reason why they would initiate violence and rebellion, in order to protect her and all others like her (ABC News 2005).

Mathews would come to view The Order as a silent brotherhood, wherein each man was bound by an oath of silence to protect the others in the group, no matter what violence they had committed. Those assembled with Mathews on that day included members of Aryan Nations and the National Alliance. With what he believed to be a loyal cadre of supporters, Mathews began a series of violent acts to support the cause of white separatism. Many of the activities undertaken by the group mimicked those taken by The Order in *The Turner Diaries*. The group began by robbing an adult book store, but considering this too dangerous, they moved on to counterfeiting and robbing banks. Mathews acted alone in robbing a bank just north of Seattle and other burglaries of various kinds that netted monies for "the cause." Yet all together, the money that The Order had secured was less than $100,000 (Martinez and Guinther 1999). This changed in March 1984 when members of The Order "set a bomb in a Seattle theater to mislead police while other members of the group robbed an armored car of nearly $500,000" (Nizkor Project). This haul was greatly surpassed just a few weeks later when the group held up an armored car near Ukiah, California, which netted over $3.6 million in cash (Cashman 1999). At the time, this was the largest armored car heist in U.S. history. Much of the money that the group had stolen would end up in the coffers of like-minded white supremacist groups, such as Pierce's National Alliance and the White Patriot Party (Martin 2011). The group "also purchased parcels of land in Idaho and Missouri to be used as paramilitary training camps" (Martin 2011). With their penchant for violent actions, The Order very quickly rose to among the most wanted on the FBI's Most Wanted List.

In the midst of the robberies, Mathews and other members of the group orchestrated the assassination of Denver talk show host Alan Berg. Berg, a controversial Jewish talk-radio personality, had made his career goading "right-wing and white-supremacist extremists on his call-in radio program" (Nizkor Project). On June 18, 1984, Order member Bruce Pierce shot Alan Berg at least a dozen times, killing him as he stepped out of his car at his home (ABC News 2005). The killing was meant to send a message to all opponents of the group, but particularly to its number one nemesis—Southern Poverty Law Center founder, Morris Dees. After the killing of Berg, the FBI managed to exert pressure on one member of the group, Tom Martinez, who had been arrested on counterfeiting charges. With many of The Order members dead, in jail, or awaiting trials that promised long prison sentences, the group was rapidly disappearing from view. As the FBI was led to Mathews's hiding place, he escaped and began a one-man crusade against the FBI and the federal government. Prior to his final showdown with federal law enforcement authorities, Mathews composed a long letter that effectively stated his intention to declare war on the U.S. government. In this letter, "he describes threats made against his family by the FBI as well as a number of attempts on his life at the behest of government-led agencies" (Balleck 2015). Stating he "quit being hunted and [would instead] become the hunter," Mathews determined to go down fighting. He wrote,

> I am not going into hiding, rather I will press the FBI and let them know what it is like to become the hunted. Doing so it is only logical to assume that my days on this planet are rapidly drawing to a close. Even so, I have no fear. For the reality of my life is death, and the worst the enemy can do to me is shorten my tour of duty in this world. I will leave knowing that I have made the ultimate sacrifice to ensure the future of my children.
>
> White men killing white men, Saxon killing Dane; When will it end, the Aryan's bane?
>
> I knew last night that today would be my last day in this life. When I went to bed I saw all my loved ones so clearly, as if they were there with me. All my memories flashed through my mind. I knew then that my tour of duty was up.
>
> I have been a good soldier, a fearless warrior. I will die with honor and join my brothers in Valhalla.
>
> For blood, soil, and honor. For faith and for race. For the future of my children. For the green graves of my sires. (Mathews 1984)

On December 8, 1984, Mathews was surrounded by federal agents in a home on Whitley Island near Foreland, Washington. Though called upon to surrender, he refused, whereupon smoke grenades were used to force his surrender. Unbeknownst to the FBI, Mathews was in possession of a gas mask, which allowed him to keep firing at the agents. Several flares were then shot into the house, which ignited ammunition and other explosives that Mathews had stockpiled. As the house burned, Mathews continued to fire at the agents, but the shots suddenly stopped as the fire reached the second floor, where he had barricaded himself. When his body was found, his pistol was still in his hand.

After Mathews's death, most of The Order members were convicted on a variety of charges, including "racketeering, conspiracy, counterfeiting, transporting stolen money, armored car robbery, and violation of civil rights" (Balleck 2015). Some were tried, but acquitted, of sedition. For many in the white nationalist and white supremacist movements, Bob Mathews is considered a martyr who was mercilessly hunted by a government intent of stripping him of his rights to protect his home and family from the undesirable elements of modern society.

See also: Aryan Nations; John Birch Society; National Alliance; Neo-Nazis; Pierce, William; *Turner Diaries, The*; White Nationalism; White Supremacist Movement

Further Reading

ABC News. October 2005. "The Order." *ABC News Special Report.*

Anti-Defamation League. "The Turner Diaries." https://www.adl.org/education/resources /backgrounders/turner-diaries (Accessed March 25, 2017).

Balleck, Barry J. 2015. *Allegiance to Liberty: The Changing Face of Patriots, Militias, and Political Violence in America.* Praeger.

Cashman, John R. 1999. *Emergency Response to Chemical and Biological Agents*. CRC Press, p. 5.

Harkavy, Ward. November 14, 2000. "The Nazi on the Bestseller List." *The Village Voice*. http://www.villagevoice.com/news/the-nazi-on-the-bestseller-list-6417005 (Accessed March 25, 2017).

Jackson, Camille. October 14, 2004. "The Turner Diaries, Other Racist Novels, Inspire Extremist Violence." *Southern Poverty Law Center—Intelligence Report*. https://www.splcenter.org/fighting-hate/intelligence-report/2004/turner-diaries-other-racist-novels-inspire-extremist-violence (Accessed March 25, 2017).

Martin, Gus, editor. 2011. *The SAGE Encyclopedia of Terrorism*. 2nd ed. SAGE, p. 450.

Martinez, Thomas and John Guinther. 1999. *Brotherhood of Murder*. iUniverse.

Mathews, Robert J. 1984. "Robert Jay Mathews' Last Letter." *Mourning the Ancient*. http://www.mourningtheancient.com/mathews1.htm (Accessed March 25, 2017).

Nizkor Project. 1991. "Paranoia as Patriotism: Far Right Influences on the Militia Movement—The Order." http://www.nizkor.org/hweb/orgs/american/adl/paranoia-as-patriotism/the-order.html (Accessed March 25, 2017).

MCCARTHYISM

"McCarthyism" is a term that has "become a byname for defamation of character or reputation by means of widely publicized indiscriminate allegations, especially on the basis of unsubstantiated charges" (Encyclopedia Britannica). The term comes from a time in American history known as the Cold War in which communist infiltration of the American government was suspected because of a series of setbacks that the United States had suffered relative to the advance of communism around the world. McCarthyism takes its name from Wisconsin senator Joseph McCarthy, who conducted "a series of investigations and hearings during the 1950s in an effort to expose suspected communist influence and infiltration in various areas of the U.S. government, particularly the U.S. State Department" (Encyclopedia Britannica). McCarthyism largely ended in 1954 when McCarthy's efforts were discredited in the eyes of the public through a series of investigative reports and opinion pieces, many of them authored by journalist Edward R. Murrow. McCarthy died in 1957, but the legacy of McCarthyism lived on in the rise of extremist right-wing groups that perpetrated McCarthy's view that the government was riddled with communist sympathizers. Moreover, McCarthy laid the basis for conspiracy theorists as he intimated that the U.S. government was the perpetrator of clandestine acts against the American people and in league with the New World Order, elements that wished to subvert American sovereignty and bring about a one-world government.

Joseph McCarthy was born in 1908. He served in the Marine Corps during World War II as an intelligence briefing officer and attained the rank of major. After the war, McCarthy was elected in 1946 to the U.S. Senate, representing the state of Wisconsin. As the Cold War between the United States and the Soviet Union began to heat up, the specter of communist subversion of the American government began to show up in the popular press and even among government officials. On March 21, 1947, President Harry Truman issued Executive Order 9835,

> which required that all federal civil service employees be screened for "loyalty." The order specified that one criterion to be used in determining that "reasonable grounds

Senator Joseph McCarthy (R-Wis.), speaks with reporters in 1951. McCarthy's dogged efforts to seek out communist infiltration in the United States became infamous as McCarthy carried his attacks to the heart of the U.S. foreign policy apparatus, particularly the U.S. State Department. "McCarthyism" became synonymous with character defamation and unsubstantiated allegations. (Library of Congress)

exist for belief that the person involved is disloyal" would be a finding of "membership in, affiliation with or sympathetic association" with any organization determined by the attorney general to be "totalitarian, Fascist, Communist or subversive" or advocating or approving the forceful denial of constitutional rights to other persons or seeking "to alter the form of Government of the United States by unconstitutional means." (Goldstein 2006)

In the aftermath of Truman's order, "events at both home and abroad seemed to prove to many Americans" that the "Red menace" was real (History.com, McCarthy). In 1948, for example, former State Department official Alger Hiss was accused of being a communist by an admitted excommunist, Whittaker Chambers. Chamber accused Hiss of passing top-secret reports to communist agents. Hiss was convicted in 1950 of perjury "in regards to testimony about his alleged involvement in a Soviet spy ring before and during World War II" (History.com, Hiss).

In 1949, the Soviet Union detonated an atomic bomb. American officials had believed that the Soviets would be incapable of such an accomplishment for many years. The short time from the American acquisition of nuclear weapons to the Soviets acquiring them suggested to many that there were communist spies among the members of the Manhattan Project, who had developed the atomic bomb. Later that year, "communist forces claimed victory in the Chinese Civil War and established the People's Republic of China. In June 1950, North Korean communists, backed by the Soviet army, invaded pro-Western South Korea, with the United Nations eventually establishing a collective security action in defense of South Korea" (History.com, McCarthy).

As reelection loomed closer for McCarthy, his previous years of undistinguished service in the Senate began to appear as a liability for his reelection chances. Edmund Walsh, a Catholic and anticommunist like McCarthy, "suggested a crusade against so-called communist subversives. McCarthy enthusiastically agreed and took advantage of the nation's wave of fanatic terror against communism, and emerged on February 9, 1950, claiming he had a list of 205 people in the State Department who were known members of the American Communist Party" (Oh and Latham). Given the number of communist advances that the American people had witnessed in the previous years, the charge of communist infiltration was heartily embraced by the public. McCarthy relentlessly pushed his investigation, becoming chairperson of the Government Committee on Operations of the Senate and widening the scope of his investigation to "investigate all dissenters of American life, not just communists" (Oh and Latham). He continued "to investigate over a two year period, relentlessly questioning numerous individuals and officials within government departments—the resulting panic arising from the witch-hunts and fear of communism becoming known as McCarthyism" (Oh and Latham).

In the early 1950s, thousands of American who had worked "in government, served in the Army, worked in the movie industry, or came from various walks of life had to answer questions before McCarthy's panel," defending themselves against unsubstantiated accusations of their loyalty (USHistory). McCarthy rose to national prominence during this time as his investigations tried to "ferret out suspected communists from their prominent positions." But during the McCarthy investigations, the safeguards enshrined in the Constitution designed to protect individuals from such attacks were ignored, even trampled upon (USHistory).

In April 1954, McCarthy turned his attention to "exposing communist infiltration of the military" (History.com). Many people "had been willing to overlook the discomfort they felt with McCarthy's campaign against government employees they saw as 'elites'" (History.com). But McCarthy's popularity began to wane as hearings against the military were broadcast on national television:

> The American people watched as McCarthy intimidated witnesses and offered evasive responses when questioned. When he attacked a young Army lawyer, the Army's chief counsel [Joseph Welch] thundered, "Have you no sense of decency, sir?" The Army-McCarthy hearings struck many observers as a shameful moment in American politics. (History.com)

McCarthy's reputation was also tarnished as one of the United States' most respected journalists, Edward R. Murrow, began exposing the McCarthy hearings. Murrow's "most devastating editorial about McCarthy was carried out on his show, *See It Now*" (Encyclopedia Britannica). Through the televised hearings and Murrow's attack on McCarthy, "the nation grew to realize that McCarthy was 'evil and unmatched in malice'" (Oh and Latham). McCarthy was censured by the Senate and "lost his position as chairman of the Government Committee on Operation of the Senate. The media subsequently became disinterested in his communist allegations and McCarthy was virtually stripped of all his power" (Oh and Latham).

McCarthy died in 1957 at age 48, but the legacy of character defamation and baseless allegations would live on in the phenomenon that carries his name. McCarthy's relentless pursuit of communism would also live on in groups like the John Birch Society, which continued the drumbeat of communist subversion both within and outside the American government. Though McCarthy's actions had been condemned as "inexcusable," "reprehensible," "vulgar," and "insulting," his influence would inspire others who were convinced that nefarious forces were intent on destroying the foundations of American freedom and independence (History.com).

See also: John Birch Society

Further Reading

Encyclopedia Britannica. "McCarthyism." https://www.britannica.com/topic/McCarthyism (Accessed May 31, 2017).

Goldstein, Robert Justin. Fall 2006. "Prelude to McCarthyism: The Making of a Blacklist." *Prologue* 38, no. 3. https://www.archives.gov/publications/prologue/2006/fall/agloso.html (Accessed May 31, 2017).

History.com. "Alger Hiss Convicted of Perjury." http://www.history.com/this-day-in-history /alger-hiss-convicted-of-perjury (Accessed May 31, 2017).

History.com. "Joseph R. McCarthy." http://www.history.com/topics/cold-war/joseph-mccarthy (Accessed May 31, 2017).

Oh, Joyce and Amanda Latham. "Senator Joseph McCarthy, McCarthyism, and the Witch Hunt." The Cold War Museum. http://www.coldwar.org/articles/50s/senatorjosephmc carthy.asp (Accessed May 31, 2017).

USHistory. "53a. McCarthyism." http://www.ushistory.org/us/53a.asp (Accessed May 31, 2017).

METZGER, TOM

Tom Metzger (b. 1938) is a skinhead leader, white supremacist, and former member of the Ku Klux Klan. Metzger founded White Aryan Resistance (WAR), a neo-Nazi, white supremacist organization, in 1982. According to its Web site, WAR is "an educational repository on the benefits of racial separation, highlighting the dangers of multiculturalism and promoting racial identity and a territorial imperative" (WAR). Metzger "considers himself a champion of the Third Position," a movement that advocates "racism oriented toward attracting the white working class and is anti-capitalism in orientation" (Atkins 2011). Metzger describes himself as an "anti-corporate leftist, despite his neo-Nazi views, and has worked to indoctrinate workers and members of labor unions to his extremist views" (Southern Poverty Law Center). After WAR was bankrupted by a civil suit filed by Morris

Dees and the Southern Poverty Law Center, Metzger drifted in far-right circles, occasionally running for political office.

Metzger joined the U.S. Army as a young man. After he was discharged from the army in the early 1960s, his political interests drifted toward far-right causes, and he eventually joined the anticommunist John Birch Society. Metzger later "quit the organization because it did not share his anti-Semitic views," but he was also at odds with the society because of his opposition to the Vietnam War (Atkins 2011). After joining a variety of far-right and extremist organizations during the 1960s and early 1970s, Metzger formed an organization known as the White Brotherhood and joined the Knights of the Ku Klux Klan in 1975. The organization, headed by David Duke, was at the time one of the largest Ku Klux Klan groups in the United States. Metzger moved up quickly in the organization and was promoted by Duke to grand dragon, or state leader, of California (Southern Poverty Law Center).

In 1979, Metzger "and other armed Klansmen began patrolling the U.S.–Mexican border for illegal aliens" (Southern Poverty Law Center). Metzger called the organization the Border Watch, but the group did little in the way of preventing illegal immigration. They did, however, attract a lot of media attention. About this same time, "Metzger became an ordained minister in the Christian Identity movement" and ran for the U.S. Congress in California as a Democrat in 1980 (Southern Poverty Law Center). Metzger stunned the Democratic Party when he won the primary with 37 percent of the vote in a heavily conservative district. He was badly defeated in the general election by the Republican incumbent, but his showing made Metzger a "formidable figure on the racist right" (Southern Poverty Law Center). Metzger later ran for the U.S. Senate in 1982 but was again defeated.

In 1982, Metzger formed the White Aryan Resistance. His goal was to make WAR a mass political movement, and with the advent of cable television in the early 1980s, Metzger saw his chance. To distinguish himself from other racists, Metzger adopted the Third Position, a European philosophy that "repudiates both the capitalist West and the communist East" (Atkins 2011). He produced 45 half-hour programs known as *Race and Reason* and used local cable access stations to disseminate his message, and he soon gained many new followers, especially skinhead Nazis. Metzger also published a monthly newsletter that proclaimed itself "the most racist newspaper on earth," and he used "a telephone hotline to spread racist information and an electronic bulletin board so racist skinheads could more easily communicate with one another" (Southern Poverty Law Center). Before the advent of the Internet, Metzger used emerging technologies to great advantage in gathering recruits. He once said, "I was the first in the country to recognize skinheads and befriend them" (Southern Poverty Law Center).

Metzger also appreciated other racists. In 1985, he donated $100 to the Nation of Islam after hearing an anti-Semitic speech by the group's leader, Louis Farrakhan (Southern Poverty Law Center).

In 1988, "Metzger and his son organized the first-ever hate rock festival, Aryan Fest" (Southern Poverty Law Center). He was also featured on an episode of *The Geraldo Rivera Show* that ended in an on-stage fight and left Rivera with a broken nose. In the same year, Metzger sent Dave Mazella to organize a racist skinhead group in Portland, Oregon. Mazella carried a letter from Metzger to introduce him to the skinhead community in the city and arranged for skinheads to talk to Metzger by phone.

Three weeks after Mazella arrived in Portland, three skinheads beat "an Ethiopian graduate student to death in a street confrontation" (Southern Poverty Law Center). Upon hearing of the killing, Metzger commented that the killers had done their "civic duty." After the killers pled guilty to murder, the Southern Poverty Law Center and the Anti-Defamation League

> sued the Metzgers and WAR on behalf of the victim's family. Using the doctrine of vicarious liability, the plaintiff's attorneys argued that the Metzgers should be found liable for intentionally inciting the skinheads to engage in violent confrontations with minorities. A jury agreed, returning a record $12.5 million verdict against the Metzgers and WAR. Tom Metzger was personally responsible for $5.5 million of that sum. (Southern Poverty Law Center)

As a result of the verdict, Metzger lost his house "and was required to make monthly payments to the victim's estate for 20 years" (Southern Poverty Law Center). The verdict financially crippled both Metzger and WAR, but he continued to push his racist message, even traveling to Japan with t-shirts featuring a "nazified" Bart Simpson. Metzger was again sued for copyright infringement for unlawfully using the image of Bart Simpson from the Fox Broadcasting Company.

Since the 1990s, Metzger has continued to propagate his anti-Semitic messages, perpetuating the conspiracy theory that Jews and Israel have control of the American government. In February 2004, he told an audience at an Aryan Fest conference,

> Don't stockpile firearms! How many guns can you shoot at once, guys? Besides, I could brew up bigger weapons than guns in my kitchen. Don't operate like a battleship! Operate like a Nazi submarine! Use your periscope! We have to infiltrate! Infiltrate the military! Infiltrate your local government! Infiltrate the school board! Infiltrate law enforcement! (Atkins 2011)

Metzger now claims to be an atheist and claims that, "in addition to being pro-labor, he is pro-environment and anti-capitalist" (Southern Poverty Law Center). He encourages white supremacists to carry on their resistance by adopting a "lone wolf" or "leaderless resistance" strategy in order to insulate the movement and ensure that acts of violence are not detected by law enforcement.

See also: Christian Identity; Duke, David; John Birch Society; Neo-Nazis; Southern Poverty Law Center; White Supremacist Movement

Further Reading

Atkins, Stephen E. 2011. *Encyclopedia of Right-Wing Extremism in Modern American History*. ABC-CLIO, pp. 55–58.

Southern Poverty Law Center. "Tom Metzger." https://www.splcenter.org/fighting-hate/extrem ist-files/individual/tom-metzger (Accessed May 8, 2017).

White Aryan Resistance. "About." http://www.resist.com/ (Accessed May 8, 2017).

MICHIGAN MILITIA

The Michigan Militia, a paramilitary organization founded by Norman Olson and Ray Southwell in 1994, a time of increased antigovernment activity in the United States, was one of dozens of "loosely connected networks of extremist groups that opposed gun control and accused the Federal Government of conspiring to destroy individual liberty" (New York Times 1995). After Olson released an official statement blaming the Oklahoma City bombing on Japan as retaliation for the United States perpetrating a nerve gas attack on the Tokyo subway system, Olson and Southwell were forced from the militia's leadership. With the end of the presidency of liberal Bill Clinton in the United States in late 2000, and the election of a more "friendly" conservative in George W. Bush, patriot and militia activity waned in the United States. By the beginning of 2001, the Michigan Militia was nearly defunct (Bradsher 2001). However, in 2009, the Michigan Militia was reorganized and its numbers began to increase (MMCW).

After Olson left the Michigan Militia in 2005, he testified before a U.S. Senate Subcommittee on Terrorism. Olson's opening statement to that committee epitomized the belief among militia members that the federal government has vastly overreached the power granted to it in the U.S. Constitution and that such unchecked power was threatening the liberty of ordinary Americans:

> Not only does the Constitution specifically allow the formation of a Federal Army, it also recognizes the inherent right of the people to form militia. Further, it recognizes that the citizen and his personal armaments are the foundation of the militia. The arming of the militia is not left to the state but to the citizen. However, should the state choose to arm its citizen militia, it is free to do so (bearing in mind the Constitution is not a document limiting the citizen, but rather limiting the power of government). But should the state fail to arm its citizen militia, the right of the people to keep and bear arms becomes the source of the guarantee that the state will not be found defenseless in the presence of a threat to its security. It makes no sense whatsoever to look to the Constitution of the United States or that of any state for permission to form a citizen militia since logically, the power to permit is also the power to deny. If brought to its logical conclusion in this case, government may deny the citizen the right to form a militia. If this were to happen, the state would assert itself as the principle of the contract making the people the agents. Liberty then would depend on the state's grant of liberty. Such a concept is foreign to American thought. (Potowmack Institute)

Though the Michigan Militia claimed to have 12,000 members in its heyday in the mid-1990s, it probably can boast no more than a few hundred adherents today (Ridley 2015). Lee Miracle, a member of the Michigan Militia today, vilifies the Southern Poverty Law Center (SPLC)—"an organization that tracks extremist groups around the United States"—as "a discredited extremist left-wing group" in a YouTube video denouncing one of the SPLC's reports on militias (Makuch 2016).

Journalist Ben Makuch noted, after spending a weekend embedded with a Michigan Militia division, that

> whether the SPLC agrees or not, "militias are about as American as apple pie and handguns," and they appear throughout modern US history. For example, various militiamen of the Revolutionary War were the perfect embodiment of an armed citizenry rising up to defy the tyranny of the British Crown (think Mel Gibson in the jingoistic classic The Patriot), or Teddy Roosevelt and the "Rough Riders" fighting Spanish colonialism in Cuba before he became that overly macho president. (Makuch 2016)

With a resurgence of militia activity during the U.S. presidential administration of Barack Obama, incidents of antigovernment activity rose from 2009 to 2016. The almost universally held belief that Hillary Clinton, a liberal Democrat, would succeed Obama to the presidency in 2017 caused increases in militia memberships as well as in other extremist groups. As Makuch (2016) observed,

> Where this all goes in the next few years is anyone's guess. With the rise of Trump and other fringe right-wing movements around the world, it's fair to say militias may be symptomatic of the same larger political trends. Whether it was recession causing job loss, the election of another Democrat president bent on gun control, or the disenfranchisement of rural Americans from the urban yuppies running politics—many militiamen have a healthy distrust of the federal government. Some believe in staying vigilant against the prospect of Chinese communists dropping out of the sky Red Dawn–style, "shit hitting the fan," or total societal decay.

As noted by one Michigan Militia member, "I don't think the [U.S.] government need fear us at all. . . . Other than, if they stick their nose out just a little too far" (Makuch 2016).

See also: Militia Movement; Oklahoma City Bombing; Patriot Movement

Further Reading

Bradsher, Keith. April 30, 2001. "Citing Declining Membership, a Leader Disbands His Militia." *The New York Times.* http://www.outpost-of-freedom.com/mcveigh/tm02.htm (Accessed May 6, 2017).

Makuch, Ben. May 26, 2016. "What I Learned About Guns, Government, and Immigration from the Michigan Militia." *Vice.com.* https://www.vice.com/en_us/article/everything-we-learned-from-embedding-with-an-american-militia (Accessed May 6, 2017).

MMCW. http://mmcw.org/links.htm (Accessed May 6, 2017).

New York Times. April 30, 1995. "Terror in Oklahoma: Michigan Militia; Two Leaders of Paramilitary Group Resign." http://www.nytimes.com/1995/04/30/us/terror-in-oklahoma-michigan-militia-two-leaders-of-paramilitary-group-resign.html (Accessed May 6, 2017).

Potowmack Institute. June 15, 1995. "Testimony of Norman Olson of the Michigan Militia." https://web.archive.org/web/20080509165431/http://www.potowmack.org/emerappb.html (Accessed May 6, 2017).

Ridley, Gary. April 20, 2015. "Michigan Militia Still Active 20 Years After Oklahoma City Bombing." *Michigan Live.* http://www.mlive.com/news/flint/index.ssf/2015/04/militias_remains_active_20_yea.html (Accessed May 6, 2017).

MILITIA MOVEMENT

The militia movement in the United States has a long history associated with the notion of "well-regulated militias" as prescribed in the Second Amendment to the Constitution. Most militias include paramilitary elements, and members of these groups generally train, or claim proficiency in, the use of firearms. The militia movement today largely consists of disaffected, rural, white, right-wing extremists who mostly ascribe to Christian principles and believe the U.S. federal government has usurped power from localities and states, or has become irrelevant as the government no longer follows the plan of government as laid out in the U.S. Constitution. Members of the militia movement tend to be identified by their anti-government sentiments, their rabid defense of the right to keep and bear arms as prescribed in the Second Amendment, and their affinity for conspiracy theories that suggest that the federal government is secretly working to silence citizens who are critical of the government, or that the federal government has been co-opted by a cabal of conspirators that are intent on destroying American sovereignty and bringing the United States into the fold of a one-world government in order that the New World Order can be realized.

The militia experiences a great deal of cross-pollination with other extremist groups, including those who profess sentiments associated with white nationalism, white supremacy, anti-Semitism, sovereign citizenship, and the common-law court movement. In the post–World War II world, the militia movement has been characterized by activity in three distinct eras: (1) the 1970s and 1980s, in which militia sentiments were aroused by economic stagnation, the continuing influx of nonwhite immigration to the United States, and government mistrust; (2) the 1990s, in which militia groups exploded due to the heavy-handed treatment of American citizens as exhibited in incidents such as Ruby Ridge and the Waco standoff; and, (3) post-2008, when the United States' first African American president was elected and disaffected whites saw their historical control of the political system slipping away as exhibited by increases in illegal immigration, economic dislocation, and challenges to historical social, cultural, and political norms. Today, there are active militia groups in every state in the United States with membership in the thousands (Southern Poverty Law Center, Anti-Government Groups).

In the first era of the militia movement in the United States, groups such as the Minutemen of the 1960s and the Posse Comitatus in the 1970s came to the forefront in order to resist the long-expected communist invasion. Members of Posse Comitatus practiced survivalism and perpetrated conspiracy theories as well as an antigovernment and anti-Semitic message organized to protect themselves against what they believed was an attack on their social and political rights, particularly as these rights had been challenged by the changing social landscape associated with the civil rights movement. Posse members developed strong ties to Christian Identity, a movement that taught that whites were God's "chosen people" and that Jews were the result of a sexual liaison between Satan and Eve. Posse members believed that the American government had been taken over by a cabal of nefarious Jews who were intent on subjugating American citizens to a one-world government led by the Anti-Christ. These beliefs were stoked by "legitimate" groups, like the John Birch Society, that proclaimed that communists had already co-opted the American government and that the subtle subversion of American values and institutions was already under way.

The second and most prolific era of the militia movement in the United States occurred during the 1990s. In 1992, soon after the killing of Randy Weaver's wife and son at the hands of federal agents, militia-minded members gathered in Estes Park, Colorado. Though a large number of mainstream evangelical Christian groups were invited, only those on the extreme right showed up (Anti-Defamation League). Among those in attendance were Richard Butler, founder of Aryan Nations, Ku Klux Klan member Louis Beam, and Larry Pratt, founder of the Gun Owners of America and English First group, who had previously made calls for "citizen defense patrols" in defense of American values. The purpose of the gathering was to make sure that Ruby Ridge did not happen again. The solution as proposed at Estes Park: form citizen militias (Anti-Defamation League).

Following on the heels of the Ruby Ridge incident, the militia movement exploded in late 1992 after the election of Democrat Bill Clinton. A little more than one month after Clinton's inauguration, the second government–private citizen confrontation occurred—the standoff at Waco, Texas, between the religiously zealous Branch Davidians and federal agents, including members of the Bureau of Alcohol, Tobacco, Firearms, and Explosives and the Federal Bureau of Investigation (FBI). The standoff ended when the federal government initiated aggressive action to force the Branch Davidians out of their compound. The result was a devastating fire that resulted in the death of nearly 80 Branch Davidians, with nearly 20 of the fatalities being children (Balleck 2015). Two years after the Waco standoff, antigovernment advocate and suspected militia member Timothy McVeigh bombed the Alfred P. Murrah Federal Building in Oklahoma City, Oklahoma, believing that the U.S. government—the worst "bully" McVeigh had ever witnessed—deserved the wrath that he visited upon it and that would soon come to pass in the actions of others (Balleck 2015).

By the time of Oklahoma City, hundreds of militia groups were forming, convinced that the U.S. government was intent on silencing dissent in order to bring to pass a new world order, ostensibly fomented by the United Nations and controlled by secret organizations of Jews behind the scenes—the so-called Zionist Occupation Government. Militias organizing in the second era were also convinced that the long-feared seizure of private guns was at hand. The Brady Handgun Violence Prevention Act of 1993, "which required background checks of new gun purchases," and the Federal Assault Weapons Ban of 1994 motivated gun owners to join militias in droves, as such groups promised to directly confront the government in any mass roundup of weapons (Anti-Defamation League).

Militias such as the Militia of Montana, the Montana Freemen, and the Republic of Texas all made headlines during the 1990s with their antigovernment rhetoric and direct confrontation with federal officials. The Militia of Montana, for instance, insisted that the 14th Amendment to the U.S. Constitution was irrelevant as it did not apply to white Americans. So-called "sovereign citizens," a concept that had originated with the Posse Comitatus, claimed that "whites were a higher kind of citizen,"

> subject only to "common law," not the dictates of the government—while blacks are mere "14th Amendment citizens" who must obey their government masters. Although not all sovereigns subscribe to or even know about the theory's racist basis, most contend that they do not have to pay taxes, are not subject to most laws, and are not citizens of the United States. (Southern Poverty Law Center 2009)

In 1996, members of the Montana Freemen, a militia group that espoused the doctrine of individual sovereignty and rejected the authority of the federal government, engaged in an 81-day standoff with government authorities. The Montana Freemen called their land Justus Township and had engaged in paper terrorism, acts associated with the filing of false liens on the homes and property of government officials, and money order fraud. Members of the Montana Freemen were determined that the federal government would not proceed with foreclosure proceedings on Justus Township that had begun two years before. They refused to be evicted from the land and did not recognize the authority of either national or state authorities to compel them to leave. After tense negotiations, and with the memories of Ruby Ridge and Waco fresh in their minds, government law enforcement officials backed off until the Montana Freemen peacefully surrendered on June 14, 1996, after 81 days.

In 1997, the Republic of Texas militia group engaged in a seven-day standoff with government agents. The Republic of Texas recognized neither state nor federal authority and claimed that they were sovereign citizens of the Republic of Texas, which had been proclaimed as an independent republic in 1836 but had been illegally annexed by the United States in 1845. Claiming his home to be "sovereign territory" and akin to the extraterritorial nature of a foreign embassy, Republic of Texas founder Rick McLaren faced down Texas state troopers for seven days before finally surrendering in "military style." The Republic of Texas had earlier demanded that then governor George W. Bush resign his office. McLaren and his associates are currently serving lengthy prison sentences.

The militia movement began to lose members after the promised disruptions associated with Y2K failed to materialize. Those who had believed that economic and social upheaval would occur when the Y2K bug hit computer systems lost their affinity for the promises of the militia movement when life continued after Y2K came and went. The election of Republican George W. Bush in November 2000 further dampened enthusiasm for militias, as did the events of September 11, 2001. After 9/11, many antigovernment sentiments expressed by militia members turned to heartfelt expressions of patriotism and nationalism as the United States was perceived to be under attack. Radical fringe elements believed that the United States had orchestrated the attacks, but the vast majority rallied to the flag and supported the new U.S. government in its global war on terror (Anti-Defamation League).

The third and final era of the militia movement began in 2008. By this year, the growing radicalization of nativist sentiment, together with the weariness associated with the wars in Iraq and Afghanistan, began to motivate extremists to once again seek out the common affectations of the militia movement. Those on the right wing worried about the growing tide of illegal immigrants and the shrinking percentage of whites in the United States compared to the growing numbers of minority groups. The economic dislocation of the Great Recession of 2008 also caused many to fall back on well-known conspiracy theories that suggested that Jews were in control of the global financial system and that the economic upheaval being experienced was part of the master plan by Jews to bring down the global financial system in preparation for the New World Order. These fears were stoked by the prospects that a Democrat would return to office and would most likely press for new legislation that would severely curtail the rights of Americans to purchase weapons (Southern Poverty Law Center 2009).

Barack Obama's election to the U.S. presidency in November 2008 sent conspiratorial-minded citizens back into the ranks of the militia and patriot movements. Many of the far-right fears of conspiracy came "from the so-called 'birthers' who filed a series of lawsuits making the claim that Barack Obama was not a U.S. citizen" (Southern Poverty Law Center, Anti-Government Groups). A growing sense of foreboding that Obama was about to initiate a dictatorship permeated those on the right wing. For instance, in Pensacola, Florida, a retired FBI agent told a gathering of militia and "patriot" members

> that the federal government ha[d] set up 1,000 internment camps across the country and [was] storing 30,000 guillotines and a half-million caskets in Atlanta. They're there for the day the government finally declares martial law and moves in to round up or kill American dissenters, the former agent said. They're going to keep track of all of us, folks. (Southern Poverty Law Center 2009)

Intent on keeping Obama and the government at bay, new militia groups formed. The Oath Keepers, "a group of law enforcement officers, military men, and veterans" organized and pledged themselves to

> defend the Constitution against all enemies, foreign and domestic. That oath, mandated by Article VI of the Constitution itself, is to the Constitution, not to the politicians, and Oath Keepers declare that they will not obey unconstitutional orders, such as orders to disarm the American people, to conduct warrantless searches, or to detain Americans as "enemy combatants" in violation of their ancient right to jury trial. (Oath Keepers)

The Oath Keepers would eventually interject themselves into the Bundy ranch standoff in 2014 and the Malheur National Wildlife Refuge in 2016. In both cases, armed Oath Keepers positioned themselves alongside of individuals who refused the lawful orders of the federal government. In the case of Cliven Bundy, federal agents attempted to round up cattle that Bundy was illegally grazing on federal land. Bundy had refused to pay grazing fees to the federal government for years, claiming instead that the federal government had no right to own land in the western United States and the government's administration of such land was illegal, as was the order to pay grazing fees. The Oath Keepers again came to a Bundy's aid, this time Cliven Bundy's son, Ammon, in January 2016, when Ammon Bundy and a group of individuals took over the Malheur National Wildlife Refuge in Harney County, Oregon. As in the Bundy ranch standoff, Bundy demanded the return of federal land to state control. The Oath Keepers believed that the Bundys' cause in both instances was just, and they vowed to defend them against any government action.

Another militia organization to form since 2008 is the Constitutional Sheriff's and Peace Officers Association (CSPOA). The CSPOA is a concerted effort to recruit law enforcement officers into antigovernment activities. The men and women of the CSPOA "are being told by extremist leaders that they have the right to decide what laws they want to enforce and can keep federal law enforcement agents out of their counties. That is utterly untrue, the very opposite of constitutional, and it in fact encourages sheriffs and their deputies to defy the law of the land" (Southern Poverty Law Center 2016).

Both the Oath Keepers and the CSPOA hearken back to the sovereign citizens and common-law courts movements of the 1960s and 1970s. Increasingly, sovereign citizens, along with tax protestors and militia members, make up the largest portion of extreme right-wing individuals who express antigovernment sentiments and seek to blunt the power of the federal government. The resurgence of militia movements in the current era can trace its rise to real societal stress and strains, the seemingly unstoppable rise of multiculturalism, and the liberal administration of a black man. Thus, the current rise in militia groups is also associated with a strong race-based hatred (Southern Poverty Law Center 2009).

As in the two past eras, the three prominent elements that identify a thriving militia movement involve "shadowy conspiracies threatening American sovereignty, unwelcome demographic changes polluting American culture, and a potentially totalitarian government, driven by an illegitimate president, bent on seizing all firearms, trampling the Constitution and imposing a fascist-socialist system on a pathetically docile citizenry" (Southern Poverty Law Center 2009).

Many in the militia movement celebrated the election of Donald Trump in 2016. Said one group after Trump's victory, "Tonight we claim a victor, thank God, now the hard work begins, holding their feet to the fire to make sure that they do all in their power to help us restore our country back to what it should be a Constitutional Republic!" (Rathod 2016). Yet in the aftermath of Trump's election, the Oath Keepers believe that far-right extremists could become complacent and that militia activity will drop off as a result. Mark Pitcavage of the Anti-Defamation League agrees:

> The militia movement, more so than other right-wing extremist movements, is very focused on opposition to the federal government, in large part because of the conspiracies that govern the militia movement. The militia movement thrives the most when there is someone they can point to as an evil figure. If Trump's election spells the end of the latest surge in militia activity, this is one of the few areas where there might be a silver lining. (Rathod 2016)

See also: Aryan Nations; Beam, Louis; Bundy Ranch Standoff; Butler, Richard; Common-Law Court Movement; John Birch Society; Malheur National Wildlife Refuge Standoff; Militia of Montana; Montana Freemen; Oath Keepers; Paper Terrorism; Patriot Movement; Posse Comitatus; Ruby Ridge; Second Amendment; Sovereign Citizens Movement; Waco Standoff; Weaver, Randy; White Nationalism; White Supremacist Movement

Further Reading

Anti-Defamation League. "The Militia Movement." ttps://www.adl.org/education/resources/backgrounders/militia-movement (Accessed June 7, 2017).

Balleck, Barry J. 2015. *Allegiance to Liberty: The Changing Face of Patriots, Militias, and Political Violence in America.* Praeger.

Bauer, Shane. November/December 2016. "Undercover with a Border Militia." *Mother Jones.* http://www.motherjones.com/politics/2016/10/undercover-border-militia-immigration-bauer/ (Accessed June 7, 2017).

Hattem, Julian. January 7, 2016. "Militia Movement Growing at Rapid Rate." *The Hill.* http://thehill.com/policy/national-security/265062-militia-movement-growing-at-rapid-rate (Accessed June 7, 2017).

Jenkins, John Phillip. "Militia Movement." *Encyclopedia Britannica.* https://www.britannica.com/event/militia-movement (Accessed June 7, 2017).

Oath Keepers. "About Oath Keepers." https://www.oathkeepers.org/about/ (Accessed June 7, 2017).

Piven, Ben. January 6, 2016. "America's New Militia Movement: Patriot Groups Explode Over Obama." *Al-Jazeera America.* http://america.aljazeera.com/articles/2016/1/6/american-militia-movement-patriot-groups.html (Accessed June 7, 2017).

Rathod, Sara. November 10, 2016. "Militia Groups Are Basking in Trump's Victory." *Mother Jones.* http://www.motherjones.com/politics/2016/11/militia-reaction-trump-victory/ (Accessed June 7, 2017).

Southern Poverty Law Center. "Active Antigovernment Groups in the United States." https://www.splcenter.org/active-antigovernment-groups-united-states (Accessed June 7, 2017).

Southern Poverty Law Center. July 31, 2009. "The Second Wave: Return of the Militias." https://www.splcenter.org/20090801/second-wave-return-militias (Accessed June 7, 2017).

Southern Poverty Law Center. August 3, 2016. "Intelligence Report: 'Constitutional Sheriff's Movement Spreads, Promotes Defiance of Federal Laws." https://www.splcenter.org/news/2016/08/03/intelligence-report-constitutional-sheriffs-movement-spreads-promotes-defiance-federal-laws (Accessed June 7, 2017).

Zeskind, Leonard and Devin Burghart. September 9, 2013. "Is America's Militia Movement on the Rise?" *The Nation.* https://www.thenation.com/article/americas-militia-movement-rise/ (Accessed June 7, 2017).

MILITIA OF MONTANA

The Militia of Montana (MOM) was a paramilitary organization active in the United States from 1994 to 2001. MOM was founded by John and David Trochmann in January 1994, antigovernment activists who had both been members of Aryan Nations as well as sympathizers of the sovereign citizens movement. MOM was formed by the Trochmanns in the aftermath of the Ruby Ridge and Waco standoffs with the federal government. In both instances, federal agents had surrounded private land on the pretext that those on the land were in violation of federal gun laws. When both precipitated bloodshed, antigovernment activists around the country determined that they must arm themselves against potential government actions against them. In founding MOM, John Trochmann warned U.S. citizens that they needed to organize and arm themselves in order to prevent events such as Ruby Ridge and Waco. MOM is widely believed to be one of the first militia groups formed in the modern era of militia movements that began with the rise of antigovernment sentiments in the 1990s (Terrorism Research and Consortium Analysis).

Montanans' penchant for individualism, survivalism, and opposition to government interference provided a fertile ground for those who came to be associated with MOM. As noted by Ryan Lenz (2011) of the Southern Poverty Law Center, Montana

> is quintessentially Western, predominantly white, and home to a frontier ethos of militant individualism and support for the Second Amendment. Moreover, Montana's residents tend to distrust the federal government, which is seen as a distant meddler, and they are vigilantly protective of the privacy afforded by the state's remote location and rugged terrain.

MOM's ideology can be distilled into three essential points:

1. The best defense against the usurpation of fundamental freedoms by the tyranny of a run-away, out of control government is a well informed and well prepared Unorganized Militia of the Citizens of the State of Montana and of the other States of the Federal Union.
2. The Founders of our United States and the Framers of the Constitution were well aware of the dangers of the tyranny and treason of a run-away governmental bureaucracy and had a very primary reason for the inclusion of the Second Amendment to the Constitution.
3. There are conspirators that wish to form a socialist one world government under the United Nations are still at work treasonously subverting the Constitution in order to enslave the Citizens of the State of Montana, The United States of America and the World in a socialist union. (Militia of Montana)

As illustrated by the final point, the fealty to conspiracy theories demonstrated by MOM is a hallmark of extremist groups. On MOM's Web site, the admonition read,

> Join the army and serve the UN or
> Join the militia and serve America
> It's your choice = freedom or slavery
> Join or form your local militia today!!
> Be militant in your search for truth
> And in the defense of liberty!! (Militia of Montana)

Though MOM largely disappeared with the dawning of the 21st century, John Trochmann did not disappear as a spokesperson for the militia movement. In 2010, he told *USA Today* that domestic worries were leading to a resurgence of the militia movement to the point that new groups were even stronger than those that formed in the 1990s. Trochmann stated that "the financial crisis and related government bailout of the banking industry, together with President Obama's controversial health care legislation," have brought "new faces" into the militia movement. "Health care was one more straw in the camel's back," Trochmann said. "Perhaps it's the one that breaks it" (Johnson 2010). Though Trochmann emphasized that he did not advocate violence, "he believes that the U.S. government is now working against its own citizenry: People are going to have to unite to save their own lives. We believe the federal government has a great plan afoot to bring us to the standard of a Third World country" (Johnson 2010).

See also: Aryan Nations; Militia Movement; Patriot Movement; Ruby Ridge; Sovereign Citizens Movement; Trochmann, John and David; Waco Standoff; Weaver, Randy

Further Reading

Johnson, Kevin. April 16, 2010. "As Oklahoma City Date Nears, Militias Seen as Gaining Strength." *USA Today*. https://usatoday30.usatoday.com/news/nation/2010-04-16-militia-movement-on-the-rise_N.htm (Accessed May 25, 2017).

Lenz, Ryan. November 15, 2011. "A Gathering of Eagles: Extremists Look to Montana." *Southern Poverty Law Center—Intelligence Report*. https://www.splcenter.org/fighting-hate/intelligence-report/2011/gathering-eagles-extremists-look-montana (Accessed May 25, 2017).

Militia of Montana. http://www.barefootsworld.net/mom.html (Accessed May 25, 2017).

Miller, Wynn. April 26, 1995. "Right-Wing Militants Mix Political Fantasy, Violence." *Christian Science Monitor*. http://www.csmonitor.com/1995/0426/26191.html (Accessed May 25, 2017).

Nizkor Project. "Armed & Dangerous: Montana." http://www.nizkor.org/hweb/orgs/american/adl/armed-and-dangerous/montana.html (Accessed May 25, 2017).

Terrorism Research and Consortium Analysis. "Militia of Montana." https://www.trackingterrorism.org/group/militia-montana-mom (Accessed May 25, 2017).

Welch, Craig. April 30, 1995. "Out of the Shadows: Oklahoma Bombing Brings Scrutiny of Montana Militia's Pro-Gun, Anti-Feds Philosophy." *The Spokesman-Review*. http://www.spokesman.com/stories/1995/apr/30/out-of-the-shadows-oklahoma-bombing-brings/ (Accessed May 25, 2017).

MILLER, FRAZIER GLENN

Frazier Glenn Miller (b. 1940) is the virulently "racist founder of the Carolina Knights of the Ku Klux Klan and the White Patriot Party (WPP), an anti-Semitic white supremacist organization associated with Christian Identity and the Ku Klux Klan" (Southern Poverty Law Center). At a time of economic hardship in the 1980s, the WPP boasted a membership of nearly 3,000 as the group built its support on blaming the economic problems on Jewish bankers and the shadowy "Zionist Occupation Government," or ZOG, a popular anti-Semitic theory among white supremacists that Jews secretly control the economies and governments of certain countries and that the governments simply act as puppets of their Jewish overlords. The WPP supported apartheid and set up hotlines featuring recordings of a black man being lynched. Miller stated that the goal of WPP was "Southern independence" (Terrorist Research and Analysis Consortium). On April 6, 1987, WPP "declared war" on the federal government, which they maintained was a puppet of ZOG (Terrorism Knowledge Base). In April 2014, Miller was found guilty of shooting three people to death at a Jewish facility in Overland Park, Kansas. He was sentenced to death for his crime.

Miller joined the U.S. Army after quitting high school. In 1979, he retired "after 20 years of active duty, which included two tours in Vietnam and 13 years as a member of the elite Green Berets" (Southern Poverty Law Center). Miller states that within two minutes of reading a racist newspaper in the early 1970s, he knew he "had found a home within the American White Movement" (Southern Poverty Law Center). He joined the Nationalist Socialist Party of America and marched in a protest against the Communist Workers Party in Greensboro, North Carolina, in 1979, in which five members of the Communist Workers Party were killed. Though not directly involved, Miller's association with the event forced him out of the United States. As a result of death threats, his wife and children left him.

In 1980, Miller "formed the Carolina Knights of the Ku Klux Klan and began to amass weapons and conduct military training, much of it with the help of active-duty soldiers" (Southern Poverty Law Center). Miller's organization modeled itself after Hitler's Nazi Party and staged rallies and marches in an attempt to gain followers. Miller's group preferred fatigues over robes and continued their paramilitary training. Unbeknownst to most, Miller was receiving money from Bob Mathews, the notorious leader of The Order, the group responsible for the assassination of Jewish radio talk show host Alan Berg in Denver in 1984. In all, Miller received more than $200,000 in funds from Mathews, who had secured the money through a series of robberies and armored car heists (Southern Poverty Law Center). Foremost among those on The Order's hit list was Morris Dees, founder of the Southern Poverty Law Center (SPLC), who was at the time suing the Carolina Knights. In 1985, the SPLC caused the Carolina Knights to cease its paramilitary operations. In less than two years, however, Miller declared himself an Aryan warrior of The Order. After going underground, Miller was found and arrested by the Federal Bureau of Investigation. In a plea deal, he testified against 14 leading white supremacists, effectively making him a pariah in the white supremacist movement.

In the 2000s, Miller frequently posted on the anti-Semitic Web site *Vanguard News Network* (Southern Poverty Law Center). He also ran for governor in North Carolina and the state Senate, though he never mounted much of a challenge. In 2010, Miller ran for the U.S. Senate in Missouri, receiving only seven votes as a write-in candidate. Miller had promised to expose "the Jewish domination of the U.S. government, mass media, the federal reserve bank, and the decadent American culture" (Southern Poverty Law Center).

On April 13, 2014, Miller, who was convinced that he was dying of lung cancer, "murdered a 14-year-old boy, his grandfather, and a woman going to visit her mother at a Jewish assisted living" facility in Overland Park, Kansas (Southern Poverty Law Center). Miller perpetrated the attacks because he wanted to take as many Jews with him as he could before he died. The irony is that none of the three people he murdered were Jewish. During his arrest and trial, Miller continually shouted neo-Nazi slogans and anti-Semitic rants. In November 2015, "he was sentenced to death for his crimes," to which he shouted, "Heil Hitler!" (Southern Poverty Law Center).

Because of his betrayal of the white supremacy movement years before, the reaction to Miller's death sentence was mixed. The neo-Nazi *Vanguard News Network* praised Miller for "sticking to his guns," while the white supremacy site *Stormfront* wrote, "By every objective standard, Glenn Miller is an abject failure. His mission failed" (Beirich 2015).

See also: Christian Identity; Ku Klux Klan; Mathews, Bob; Neo-Nazis; Order, The; White Supremacist Movement

Further Reading

Beirich, Heidi. September 1, 2015. "White Supremacists React to Frazier Glenn Miller Guilty Verdict." *Southern Poverty Law Center—Hatewatch*. https://www.splcenter.org/hatewatch/2015/09/01/white-supremacists-react-frazier-glenn-miller-guilty-verdict (Accessed January 16, 2017).

Southern Poverty Law Center. "Frazier Glenn Miller." https://www.splcenter.org/fighting-hate/extremist-files/individual/frazier-glenn-miller (Accessed January 16, 2017).

Terrorism Knowledge Base. "White Patriot Party." http://web.archive.org/web/20070930013115/http://www.tkb.org/Group.jsp?groupID=127 (Accessed January 16, 2017).

Terrorist Research and Analysis Consortium. "White Patriot Party." https://www.trackingterrorism.org/group/white-patriot-party-wpp (Accessed January 16, 2017).

MONKEYWRENCHING

"Monkeywrenching" is a term used to denote an escalation from simple acts of civil disobedience to actions designed to disrupt or slow down the mechanisms of the institutions that activists wish to affect. The term came in to wide use "after the publication of author Edward Abbey's novel *The Monkey Wrench Gang* (1975), which described the activities of a group of 'environmental warriors' in Utah and Arizona" (Palmer). In the case of the Earth Liberation Front (ELF), monkeywrenching has been used against government-sanctioned activity, corporations, and individual business interests to sabotage such activities as clear cutting, environmental pollution, and recreational expansion on federal lands. In some instances of monkeywrenching, ELF members have spiked trees (to prevent their felling), poured sugar into the gas tanks of heavy equipment, and committed other acts of vandalism. Generally, monkeywrenching is not aimed at individuals. However, in the case of the common-law court movement, monkeywrenching has become very personal in that it targets individuals whom those of the sovereign citizens movement see as impediments to good governance.

So-called sovereign citizens have used monkeywrenching techniques to threaten thousands of people through pseudocourts known as common-law courts. These courts, which have no legal authority, have been used by sovereign citizens to "convict" citizens of crimes ranging from property theft to treason. In many instances, those "convicted" have been government officials or members of their families, particularly those who work for government oversight agencies, such as the Bureau of Land Management or the U.S. Forest Service. A more sinister form of monkeywrenching has occurred when sovereign citizens have filed lawsuits against such government officials in real courts, attesting to some wrongdoing, or filed false liens against their property, forcing the defendants to spend time and money to have such liens lifted. Over the past several years, hundreds of sovereign citizens and common-law court advocates have "gone to prison for such crimes as fraud, faking legal processes, impersonating, intimidating and threatening officials, even carrying out violent attacks" (Southern Poverty Law Center, 27 States). Increasingly, states are passing legislation making monkeywrenching activities illegal and imposing penalties ranging from heavy fines to prison terms.

See also: Common-Law Court Movement; Earth Liberation Front; Sovereign Citizens Movement

Further Reading

National Center for State Courts. 1999. "The Anti-Government Movement Guidebook." http://www.tulanelink.com/pdf/anti-gov_movement_guidebook.pdf (Accessed December 13, 2016).

Palmer, Eric. "Monkeywrenching." *Encyclopedia Britannica.* https://www.britannica.com/topic/monkeywrenching (Accessed August 4, 2017).

Southern Poverty Law Center. June 15, 1998. "27 States Act Against Antigovernment Movement's Common Law Courts." *Southern Poverty Law Center—Intelligence Report.* https://www.splcenter.org/fighting-hate/intelligence-report/1998/27-states-act-against-antigovernment-movement%E2%80%99s-common-law-courts (Accessed December 13, 2016).

Southern Poverty Law Center. June 15, 1998. "Common-Law Victims." *Southern Poverty Law Center—Intelligence Report.* https://www.splcenter.org/fighting-hate/intelligence-report/1998/common-law-victims (Accessed December 13, 2016).

MONTANA FREEMEN

The Montana Freemen (Freemen) were an antigovernment, Christian patriot movement that modeled its ideology after the Posse Comitatus groups of the 1970s. The Posse ideals, adopted by the Freemen, rejected the authority of any government beyond that of the county sheriff. At the heart of this ideology was the belief that most state governments, and every part of the federal government, had become illegitimate over time as these governments had strayed from the original intentions of the Founding Fathers. As such, Freemen felt that they owed no allegiance to any governmental unit that was corrupted and beyond redemption. Members of the Freemen considered themselves sovereign citizens in that they believed that there is no higher authority than the citizen and that citizens are agents unto themselves, being subjected to no higher authority than themselves. As such, sovereign citizens are endowed with all the power, which they "lend" to the government in order to provide peace, stability, and security. Going hand in hand with the sovereign citizen ideal is that of common-law courts. In Freemen thinking, if citizens are sovereign, then they can govern themselves. Inasmuch as the laws and powers of the federal government were rejected by the Freemen, they did not see themselves as being bound by the laws of the United States but only those laws that they, themselves, promulgated. Most Freemen did not pay any taxes, and most had had numerous run-ins with state and local authorities before joining the group.

In early 1995, the Montana Freemen was founded by LeRoy Schweitzer—"a dean in the antigovernment 'Patriot' movement"—and other anti-government individuals who were, in many cases, tax protestors (Morlin 2011). The Freemen set up their system of governance on a 960-acre parcel of land that they dubbed Justus Township. Many of those who were attracted to the Freemen were refugees from the 1980s farm crisis who had lost their land, or suffered greatly, due to the debt that they had incurred from securing federal loans. As one columnist noted, "The Freemen couldn't be dismissed as outsiders. Many of them were homegrown. They were relatives, neighbors and friends, salt-of-the-earth farmers and ranchers who one day started declaring themselves sovereign and not answerable to any laws but their own" (Thackeray 2006). Many had drifted into the Freemen cause because of the promise that their debt could be erased, a belief reinforced by sovereign citizen and common-law ideology that taught that because the federal government was illegitimate it had no power to tax, and therefore, no power to loan money to citizens. In this way of thinking, the loans that had saddled the Freemen with debt were not valid as they had been entered into with an agent (the federal government) that did not have the authority to engage in such lending practices. The Freemen surmised that as sovereign citizens, they could act as their own central bank, a practice that would lead to "fraud of epic proportions," involving 3,432 checks written by the Freemen totaling $15.5 billion, with actual losses totaling $1.8 billion (Southern Poverty Law Center).

Many Freemen were also adherents of Christian Identity, a theological belief that maintains that whites are God's chosen people and that Jews are the cursed offspring of Satan. According to Freemen beliefs, "Jews and their banking system were descended from Satan through Cain. Whites—noble, made in the image of God and able, unlike blacks, to blush—were the progeny of Adam and Eve" (Zeskind 1998). The belief that the Jews were at the heart of the economic distress that was experienced by the Freemen was a powerful motivational force as Freemen adherents were able to rationalize their illegal actions by convincing themselves that the illegitimacy of the government, at least in part, was the result of a global conspiracy by Jews to control the financial institutions of every major government in the world.

The Montana Freemen would be short-lived, for within 18 months of their founding, most of the group's leaders would be in jail on federal charges of fraud and conspiracy. The clash between the federal government and the Freemen started

A member of the Montana Freemen uses binoculars to keep track of members of the Federal Bureau of Investigation who had surrounded the Freemen compound in 1996 during an 81-day standoff. The Montana Freemen believed that the federal government had become illegitimate as it had strayed from the original intentions of the Founding Fathers. (John Ruthroff/AFP/ Getty Images)

on March 25, 1996, when LeRoy Schweitzer was arrested on federal warrants stemming from the Freemen's practice of writing bogus checks. As the Federal Bureau of Investigation (FBI) moved in to serve additional warrants to other Freemen at Justus Township, members of the group made it clear that they were armed and would not be taken peacefully. Given the warning, the FBI withdrew from around Justus Township in an effort not to repeat the bloodshed that had occurred with other antigovernment extremists at Ruby Ridge, Idaho, and Waco, Texas. After an 81-day standoff, during which several negotiators with extremist sympathies acted to bring about a peaceful settlement, the Freemen surrendered on June 13, 1996. Eventually, 16 Freemen would be sentenced to various prison terms, with Freemen founder LeRoy Schweitzer being given the longest sentence at 22 years.

Though the Freemen essentially ceased to exist after the standoff with the FBI, the group's ideas are alive and well in Montana and elsewhere in the country. As pointed out by Jim Lopach, a professor of constitutional law at the University of Montana,

Rural Montana has a broad streak of political individualism converging with a generally conservative nature and a strong distrust of government. . . . They [don't] see government as important in their lives. There [is] a pronounced fear of interlocal or inter-governmental cooperation. There [is] always a fear that it [will] lead to too much government and a loss of control. (Thackeray 2006)

The Southern Poverty Law Center, too, has noted that conditions for the rise of another group like the Montana Freemen is just below the surface:

> Law enforcement officers and courts have seen a surge of anti-government activity by "sovereign citizens," radicals who believe that most laws do not apply to them. Rooms at the Kalispell [Montana] Public Library host regular screenings of racist films. Christian Identity adherents are papering neighborhoods with their message that whites are the true chosen people of the Bible and Jews are directly descended from Satan. And, once again, so-called "Preparedness Expos" are being held so shoppers can get ready for the imminent collapse of government. (Lenz 2011)

To many observers, the conditions in the United States today seem to suggest the possibility of a "second act in a frightening drama" (Lenz 2011).

See also: Christian Identity; Common-Law Court Movement; Paper Terrorism; Posse Comitatus; Ruby Ridge; Schweitzer, LeRoy; Sovereign Citizens Movement; Waco Standoff

Further Reading

Anti-Defamation League. "Sovereign Citizen Movement." *Anti-Defamation League—Extremism, Terrorism & Bigotry.* https://www.adl.org/education/resources/backgrounders/sovereign -citizen-movement (Accessed March 14, 2017).

History Commons. "Profile: LeRoy Schweitzer." http://www.historycommons.org/entity.jsp ?entity=leroy_schweitzer_1 (Accessed March 14, 2017).

Lenz, Ryan. November 15, 2011. "A Gathering of Eagles: Extremists Look to Montana." *Southern Poverty Law Center—Intelligence Report.* https://www.splcenter.org/fighting-hate /intelligence-report/2011/gathering-eagles-extremists-look-montana (Accessed March 14, 2017).

Morlin, Bill. September 21, 2011. "Montana Freeman Leader Dies in Prison." *Southern Poverty Law Center—Hatewatch.* https://www.splcenter.org/hatewatch/2011/09/21/montana -freeman-leader-dies-prison (Accessed August 4, 2017).

Southern Poverty Law Center. "Four Montana Freemen Found Guilty." *Southern Poverty Law Center—Intelligence Report.* https://www.splcenter.org/fighting-hate/intelligence -report/1998/four-montana-freemen-found-guilty (Accessed March 14, 2017).

Thackeray, Lorna. March 25, 2006. "The Freemen Standoff." *Billings Gazette.* http://billings gazette.com/news/state-and-regional/montana/the-freemen-standoff/article_52ea8d8f -c28e-5170-8b65-8c5f71ea4fe9.html (Accessed March 14, 2017).

Zeskind, Leonard. June 15, 1998. "Montana Freemen Trial May Mark End of an Era." *Southern Poverty Law Center—Intelligence Report.* https://www.splcenter.org/fighting-hate /intelligence-report/1998/montana-freemen-trial-may-mark-end-era (Accessed March 14, 2017).

MURRAY, CHARLES

Charles Murray (b. 1943), along with Richard Herrnstein, is the author of the controversial 1994 book *The Bell Curve: Intelligence and Class Structure in American Life.* A decade before, Murray published *Losing Ground: American Social Policy*

1950–1980, "which argued that government programs designed to lift people out of poverty did exactly the opposite" by providing the poor with disincentives to work or form stable families (Southern Poverty Law Center). For this and many of his other works, Murray has become a poster child for far-right white nationalist and white supremacist causes who use Murray's conclusions to call for ethnic separation, sterilization programs for the poor, and anti-immigration policies to prevent the "dysgenesis" that such groups believe is taking place in American society. Murray has been an advocate for a "total elimination of the welfare state, affirmative action, and the Department of Education, arguing that public policy programs cannot overcome the innate deficiencies among some groups" that inherently lead to the social inequality observed in these groups (Southern Poverty Law Center).

Murray puts forth the thesis that "disadvantaged groups are disadvantaged because, on average, they cannot compete with white men who Murray believes are intellectually, psychologically, and morally superior to blacks, Latinos, the poor, and women"—even white women. As noted by his critics,

> In Murray's world, wealth and social power naturally accrue towards a "cognitive elite" made up of high-IQ individuals (who are overwhelmingly white, male, and from well-to-do families), while those on the lower end of the eponymous bell curve form an "underclass" whose misfortunes stem from their low intelligence. According to Murray, the relative differences between the white and black populations of the United States, as well as those between men and women, have nothing to do with discrimination or historical and structural disadvantages, but rather stem from genetic differences between the groups. (Southern Poverty Law Center)

Murray has rejected the criticisms of those who claim that his conclusions—that inequality is linked to genetic makeup and that those who are disadvantaged will never collectively gain equality with white males—are based on the discredited research of "explicitly racist scientists." Nevertheless, Murray cited several researchers in *The Bell Curve* who had received money from the Pioneer Fund, an organization devoted almost exclusively to the proposition that race and genetic factors account for a demonstrable difference in the IQ scores of different racial and ethnic groups. Among those cited was Richard Lynn, who asserts that blacks are genetically inferior to whites and East Asians. Yet Murray calls those he cites "some of the most respected psychologists of our time," though critics claim that these individuals are "Nazi sympathizers, eugenicists, and advocates of white racial superiority" (Southern Poverty Law Center).

Murray's claim that the United States is devolving into a dysgenic society, one where genetic deterioration will keep some in a perpetually underclass state, will eventually result in "a caste society, . . . with the underclass mired ever more firmly at the bottom and the cognitive elite ever more firmly anchored at the top" (Southern Poverty Law Center). Murray "argues that students with lower IQs are not as educable as smarter children and should be siphoned off to vocational programs instead of sent to college. He estimates that only 10 to 20 percent of young adults are capable of doing college-level work" (Weigel 2014).

Murray does not simply believe that blacks and Latinos are inferior to white men; he considers women as a whole, even white women, to be substantially inferior to men. For evidence, he points out that women possess only 2 percent of Nobel Prizes in the sciences and 10 percent in literature—numbers far less than their percentage of the population. Moreover, prizes in mathematics very rarely go to women, and even in philosophy, which is considered the most abstract field, "no woman has been a significant original thinker in any of the world's great philosophical traditions" (Southern Poverty Law Center).

See also: Pioneer Fund; White Nationalism; White Supremacist Movement

Further Reading

Herrnstein, Richard J. and Charles Murray. 1994. *The Bell Curve: Intelligence and Class Structure in American Life*. Free Press.

Southern Poverty Law Center. "Charles Murray." https://www.splcenter.org/fighting-hate/extremist-files/individual/charles-murray (Accessed February 13, 2017).

Sussman, Robert Wald. 2014. *The Myth of Race: The Troubling Persistence of an Unscientific Idea*. Harvard University Press.

Weigel, David. April 2, 2014. "Charles Murray, Public Menace." *Slate*. http://www.slate.com/blogs/weigel/2014/04/02/charles_murray_public_menace.html (Accessed February 13, 2017).

Zeiser, Bill. April 25, 2015. "We Are All Charles Murray." *Spectator.org*. https://spectator.org/58864_we-are-all-charles-murray/ (Accessed February 13, 2017).

NATION OF ISLAM

The Nation of Islam (NOI) was founded in 1930 as an organization to improve the "spiritual, mental, social, and economic condition of African Americans in the United States and all of humanity" (Nation of Islam, NOI History). During its first two decades, it gathered few members and was mostly known for its strange mix of doctrines and creeds that were not always consistent with the more traditional practice of Islam. NOI's growth exploded during the 1950s and 1960s, when the civil rights movement, and the violent reactions it provoked among whites, reinforced the notion of the "white devil" perpetrated by NOI doctrine. Between 1952 and 1964, membership in NOI grew from around 400 to between 100,000 and 300,000 (Southern Poverty Law Center). But NOI's bitter and abusive rhetoric "and its advocacy for self-defense and violence in place of nonviolence alienated it from the bulk of other civil rights groups of the day." Today, the NOI "has grown into one of the wealthiest and best-known organizations in black America. However, its theology of the superiority of blacks over whites is deeply racist. Moreover, NOI spews anti-Semitic and anti-gay rhetoric that has caused the Southern Poverty Law Center (SPLC) to designate the Nation of Islam as a hate group" (Southern Poverty Law Center).

The Nation of Islam was founded by Wallace D. Fard (Farad Muhammad) and "his messenger and successor, Elijah Muhammad" (Southern Poverty Law Center). As the civil rights movement accelerated in the 1950s, and produced a violent backlash from whites in the United States, thousands of African Americans flocked to NOI, swelling its ranks. Among the new adherents to the organization at this time were Malcolm X, who had joined NOI in prison, and Muhammad Ali (previously Cassius Clay), the heavyweight champion of professional boxing. Malcolm X, who became NOI's primary spokesperson, exhorted black Americans to throw off the "shackles of racism by any means necessary," including violence (Biography). By 1959, Martin Luther King Jr. "was warning of a hate group arising in our midst that would preach the doctrine of black supremacy" (Southern Poverty Law Center).

In 1964, Malcolm X split with NOI and denounced the "sickness and madness" of NOI's racist views. In 1965, he was assassinated by three members of NOI. His successor was Louis Farrakhan, who had joined NOI in 1955. Viewed as a charismatic speaker and a powerful organizer, Farrakhan filled the void left by Malcolm X's death and became the NOI's national spokesperson in 1967. When "Elijah Muhammad died in 1975, Farrakhan initially remained loyal to Elijah Muhammad's son, Wallace Deen Muhammad" (Southern Poverty Law Center). But when the younger Muhammad attempted to align NOI more with mainstream Islam,

Farrakhan broke from the group and proclaimed a "resurrected" Nation of Islam (Southern Poverty Law Center).

NOI's historical "characterization of whites as devils" was exacerbated under Farrakhan. Farrakhan, too, ramped up the anti-Semitic view espoused by NOI by continually denouncing Jewish influence in politics, business, and entertainment. During Jesse Jackson's 1984 presidential bid, Farrakhan made remarks "calling Adolf Hitler 'a very great man' and Judaism a 'dirty religion'" (Southern Poverty Law Center). NOI's anti-Semitism is a long-standing trope of the group. In 1962, American Nazi Party leader George Lincoln Rockwell had dubbed Elijah Muhammad the "Hitler of the Blacks." Similarly, "American neo-Nazi and White Aryan Resistance founder Tom Metzger has praised NOI's anti-Semitic rhetoric and has even donated a symbolic amount of money to the Nation" (Southern Poverty Law Center).

Farrakhan is also "well-known for bashing gays and lesbians, Catholics, and white devils" (white people), who Farrakhan refers to as "potential humans . . . [who] haven't evolved yet" (Southern Poverty Law Center). During the 1990s, Farrakhan attempted to moderate his message. But an attempt to reach out "to the Congressional Black Caucus failed after the Anti-Defamation League (ADL) published an article detailing a speech by a top NOI official in which he bashed Jews, Catholics, LGBT people, and whites" (Southern Poverty Law Center). The National Association for the Advancement of Colored People, though it "endorsed the Million Man March," the mass gathering of African American men in Washington, D.C., in 1995, where Farrakhan was a keynote speaker, "refused to participate in any other way" (Southern Poverty Law Center).

In 2010, Farrakhan publicly announced that NOI was embracing Dianetics, the "ideas and practices regarding the metaphysical relationship between mind and body developed by Church of Scientology founder L. Ron Hubbard." Farrakhan urged NOI members to participate in auditing sessions and to become trained as auditors (Gray 2012). Today, membership in the NOI is much less than at its height in the 1960s, but the organization still claims numbers upward of 50,000 (MacFarquhar 2007).

See also: Farrakhan, Louis; Malcolm X; Metzger, Tom; Rockwell, George Lincoln

Further Reading

Biography. "Malcolm X Biography." http://www.biography.com/people/malcolm-x-9396195 (Accessed March 17, 2017).

Gray, Eliza. October 5, 2012. "Thetans and Bowties: The Mothership of All Alliances: Scientology and the Nation of Islam." *New Republic.* https://newrepublic.com/article /108205/scientology-joins-forces-with-nation-of-islam (Accessed March 18, 2017).

MacFarquhar, Neil. February 26, 2007. "Nation of Islam at a Crossroad as Leader Exits." *The New York Times.* http://www.nytimes.com/2007/02/26/us/26farrakhan.html?page wanted=all (Accessed March 18, 2017).

Nation of Islam. https://www.noi.org/ (Accessed March 17, 2017).

Nation of Islam. 2017. "NOI History: Nation of Islam in America: A Nation of Beauty & Peace." https://www.noi.org/noi-history/ (Accessed March 17, 2017).

Southern Poverty Law Center. "Nation of Islam." https://www.splcenter.org/fighting-hate /extremist-files/group/nation-islam (Accessed March 18, 2017).

NATIONAL ALLIANCE

The National Alliance was "for over three decades the most dangerous and best organized neo-Nazi formation in the United States" (Southern Poverty Law Center, National Alliance). Its ideology was totally dedicated to the extermination of Jews and other nonwhite races, the execution of white sympathizers of such groups, and the establishment of an all-white homeland in the United States (Southern Poverty Law Center, National Alliance). The founder of the National Alliance, William Pierce, published a novel in 1975 entitled *The Turner Diaries*, which served as an inspiration for domestic terrorists and terrorist groups alike, including The Order and Timothy McVeigh, who, in 1995, killed nearly 170 people in the bombing of the Alfred P. Murrah Federal Building in Oklahoma City. Before the unexpected death of William Pierce in 2002, the U.S. Federal Bureau of Investigation "considered the National Alliance the best-financed and best-organized white nationalist organization of its kind in the country." In 2002, membership in the National Alliance was estimated at over 2,500 with an annual income of $1 million (Southern Poverty Law Center, National Alliance).

The National Alliance "developed out of the National Youth Alliance (NYA) which had been founded from the ashes of Youth for Wallace," an organization that had supported the prosegregationist presidential campaign of Alabama governor George Wallace in 1968 (Southern Poverty Law Center, William Pierce). When factional infighting tore the organization apart after Wallace's failed campaign, William Pierce gained control of the largest faction and renamed the group the National Alliance in 1974. From his hilltop compound near Mill Point, West Virginia, Pierce honed the message of the National Alliance to attract a disparate cross-section of anti-Semites, neo-Nazis, white supremacists, and antigovernment sympathizers from across the United States and the world. Though Pierce was relatively unknown to most of the country in the early 1970s, "he had been an associate of the leader of the American Nazi Party, George Lincoln Rockwell" (Southern Poverty Law Center, William Pierce).

At the time of Pierce's death in 2002, the National Alliance had forged relationships with neo-Nazis and white supremacist groups in both the United States and Europe. The group's annual income topped $1 million, mostly from the group's magazine, *Resistance*, as well as Resistance Records, "a racist white power music label started years before by skinheads that had been acquired by Pierce" (Southern Poverty Law Center, William Pierce).

Upon Pierce's death, a power struggle ensued among his successors that significantly weakened the organization. Several high-profile scandals that involved the leadership disillusioned the rank-and-file members, and the National Alliance lost many of its leaders and key activists. Today, the National Alliance, once the most "ideological and criminal powerhouse of the American radical right," has become moribund and almost irrelevant (Southern Poverty Law Center, National Alliance).

See also: Mathews, Bob; Neo-Nazis; Order, The; Pierce, William; Rockwell, George Lincoln; *Turner Diaries, The*

Further Reading

MacDonald, Andrew (aka William Pierce). 1978. *The Turner Diaries: A Novel*. Barricade Books.

Southern Poverty Law Center. "National Alliance." https://www.splcenter.org/fighting-hate/extremist-files/group/national-alliance (Accessed January 4, 2017).

Southern Poverty Law Center. "William Pierce." https://www.splcenter.org/fighting-hate/extremist-files/individual/william-pierce (Accessed January 4, 2017).

NATIONAL POLICY INSTITUTE

The National Policy Institute (NPI) is "a white nationalist and white supremacist think tank based in Alexandria, Virginia" (Wines and Saul 2015). The NPI is "dedicated to the heritage, identity, and future of people of European descent in the United States, and around the world" (National Policy Institute). It was founded in 2005 by William Regnery and Samuel T. Francis in conjunction with Louis R. Andrews. The NPI claims to publish books, journals, essays, blogs, and electronic media (including Facebook and other social media sites) "all dedicated to the revival and flourishing of *our* people [emphasis added]" (National Policy Institute). Louis R. Andrews, who became the NPI's chairperson when the group was founded, stated that he had supported Barack Obama for the U.S. presidency in 2008 because "I want to see the Republican Party destroyed, so it can be reborn as a party representing the interests of white people, and not entrenched corporate elites" (Washington 2009).

After Andrews's death in 2010, the new chairperson and face of the NPI became Richard Bertrand Spencer. Spencer has honed the SPI's message, communicating that it aims "to elevate the consciousness of whites, ensure our biological and cultural continuity, and protect our civil rights. The institute . . . will study the consequences of the ongoing influx that non-Western populations pose to our national identity" (Southern Poverty Law Center, Spencer). The NPI's senior fellows include Wayne Lutton, an extreme-right writer; Jared Taylor, editor of *American Renaissance*, which promotes pseudoscientific studies and research that purports to show the inferiority of blacks to whites; and Kevin Lamb, a noted racist (Southern Poverty Law Center, Groups). The NPI burst on to the scene of American political consciousness when the organization, as well as the alt-right movement, became a talking point during Donald Trump's 2016 presidential campaign. Speaking for NPI, Spencer warned white Americans that they "are increasingly under siege in their own country" and are "doomed to be a hated minority as people of color grow ever more numerous and politically powerful" (Marans 2016). Spencer praised Trump's nationalistic fervor and his disdain for "political correctness." As Spencer noted, you must have a "starting point" when attempting to change attitudes and policies. For Spencer and the NPI, that "starting point" is Trump: "The starting point he [Trump] has in mind is getting white people to openly embrace their 'white' identity, and to organize as a group with common interests." Spencer and his peers "maintain that creating an intellectual community of white activists is an essential step toward making America white again" (Marans 2016).

NPI has stated that "the dispossession of White Americans will have catastrophic effects for the entire world, not just for our people" (National Policy Institute). NPI has been classified as a white supremacist organization by the Southern Poverty Law Center, and the Anti-Defamation League has stated that the group was "founded to be kind of a white supremacist think tank" (Anti-Defamation League). Though the NPI is characterized as a white supremacist organization, it does not fall into the category that many Americans may associate with robes, tattoos, or skinheads. Rather, NPI tries "to take a more highbrow approach" to white supremacism, "couching white nationalist arguments as academic commentary on black inferiority, the immigration threat to whites and other racial issues" (Wines and Saul 2015). NPI's approach to white supremacy recalls David Duke's admonition to the KKK to "get out of the cow pasture and into the hotel meeting room" (Ellis 2016).

The Southern Poverty Law Center has stated that NPI's brand of white supremacy is seen as an attempt to make racism "respectable." The steps to respectable racism are: (1) Get a likeable, accessible frontman; (2) Clad yourself in the trappings of academia; and, (3) Make the Web work for you (Ellis 2016). Richard Spencer satisfies the first requirement, as he is seen as "polite and square-jawed, with a neat high-and-tight haircut. He doesn't sneer or curse, and he pitches big ideas about the future—like NPI becoming the alt-right equivalent of the Heritage Foundation, a lynchpin of mainstream conservative thought" (Ellis 2016). NPI has been very effective at the second step, the trappings of academia. The group couches most of its most controversial ideas in "pseudo-academic arguments, using ornate, polysyllabic, racial-slur free language. It makes people more willing to hear it" (Ellis 2016). Finally, Spencer "is very internet savvy. He knows that most of his target audience isn't going to sit down with a tome on the 'biological reality of race.' That's why he has a Twitter account and runs sites like AlternativeRight.com to deliver his ideology in bite-sized chunks" (Ellis 2016).

Spencer has stated that "NPI isn't only for building a movement; it's for sustaining and legitimizing one that already exists. Having our own institutions is going to take us beyond just being trolls or Trump fans," he says. "We need to destroy traditional conservatism. We're going to displace them, and we are going to be the right" (Ellis 2016).

In March 2017, the Internal Revenue Service stripped NPI of its tax-exempt status for failing to file tax returns. Whether the NPI has tax-exempt status or not does not mute its message. The NPI realizes that whether it is due to "economic stagnation, a culture of xenophobia and fear, growing distrust for the government and traditional institutions, or a myriad of other causes, people's loyalties are up for grabs" (Ellis 2016). Spencer has reinforced this notion by stating, "America as it is currently constituted—and I don't just mean the government; I mean America as constituted spiritually and ideologically—is the fundamental problem. I don't support and agree with much of anything America is doing in the world" (Wines and Saul 2015).

See also: Alt-Right Movement; *American Renaissance*; Bannon, Steve; *Breitbart News*; Spencer, Richard Bertrand; Taylor, Jared

Further Reading

Anti-Defamation League. "Alt-Right: A Primer About the New White Supremacy." https://www.adl.org/education/resources/backgrounders/alt-right-a-primer-about-the-new-white-supremacy (Accessed June 6, 2017).

Ellis, Emma Grey. October 9, 2016. "How the Alt-Right Grew from an Obscure Racist Cabal." *Wired.* https://www.wired.com/2016/10/alt-right-grew-obscure-racist-cabal/ (Accessed June 6, 2017).

Link, Taylor. March 14, 2017. "Richard Spencer's Nonprofit, Pro-Hate National Policy Institute Lost Its Tax-Exempt Status." *Salon.* http://www.salon.com/2017/03/14/richard-spencers-nonprofit-pro-hate-national-policy-institute-lost-its-tax-exempt-status/ (Accessed June 6, 2017).

Marans, Daniel. March 7, 2016. "How Trump Is Inspiring a New Generation of White Nationalists." *Huffington Post.* http://www.huffingtonpost.com/entry/trump-white-nationalists_us_56dd99c2e4b0ffe6f8e9ee7c (Accessed June 6, 2017).

National Policy Institute. "Who Are We." http://www.npiamerica.org/ (Accessed June 6, 2017).

Southern Poverty Law Center. "Richard Bertrand Spencer." https://www.splcenter.org/fighting-hate/extremist-files/individual/richard-bertrand-spencer-0 (Accessed June 6, 2017).

Southern Poverty Law Center. "The Groups." *Southern Poverty Law Center—Intelligence Report.* https://www.splcenter.org/fighting-hate/intelligence-report/2015/groups (Accessed June 6, 2017).

Washington, Jesse. June 11, 2009. "Gunman May Reflect Growing Racial Turmoil." *NBC News.* http://www.nbcnews.com/id/31271698/ns/us_news-crime_and_courts/t/gunman-may-reflect-growing-racial-turmoil#.WTbMyty1vRY (Accessed June 6, 2017).

Wines, Michael and Stephanie Saul. July 5, 2015. "White Supremacists Extend Their Reach Through Websites." *The New York Times.* https://www.nytimes.com/2015/07/06/us/white-supremacists-extend-their-reach-through-websites.html?_r=1 (Accessed June 6, 2017).

NATIONAL PRAYER NETWORK

The National Prayer Network (also known as TruthTellers.org) is an Oregon-based Christian organization that disseminates New World Order conspiracy theories and is critical of Judaism and what it considers Jewish supremacism in American media and television programming. The group is led by Ted Pike, who bills himself as "the primary national opponent to federal hate crimes legislation" (National Prayer Network, Rev. Ted Pike). Pike is best known for "pushing out anti-Semitic propaganda and for warning that there is a tendency in the United States toward Jewish domination of society" (Right Wing Watch). Pike criticizes Jews for supporting liberal policies and claims "that liberalism has striven to substitute secular, immoral, globalist values that will eventually make America amenable to participation in a Zionist-controlled new world order" (Anti-Defamation League). Pike has also warned that "Jewish international bankers were behind the Bolshevik Revolution, and that the state of Israel was the first stage in Satan's plan to take this world from Christ and give it to the Antichrist" (Right Wing Watch). Pike singles out the Anti-Defamation League "for attacks" and alleges that the ADL has created programs and influenced legislation "that makes it illegal for Christians to criticize homosexuality" (Anti-Defamation League). Pike has described "secular Jews as the wreckers of our civilization" and "urges Christians to stop giving aid and comfort to them" (Anti-Defamation League).

Pike has decried the "moral erosion" in the United States, criticizing a CBS program that presented a fictional portrayal of wife-swapping couples, and he continues to blame what he dubs the "Jewish media." According to one source, Ted Pike "is a notorious anti-Semite who uses Christianity as his front to promote hatred and suspicion and polarize and divide people who MAY[emphasis in original] otherwise receive a true Biblical message" (Maugans).

The National Prayer Network under Pike's direction has accused critics of his group, such as the Southern Poverty Law Center and Anti-Defamation League, of being "Christian haters" and "Jewish supremacists" who "want to actually outlaw Christian political activity and evangelism. The ADL created hate crime laws that will particularly outlaw reproof of sodomy and evangelism of non-Christians, especially Jews" (Right Wing Watch).

As spokesperson of the National Prayer Network, Pike has lamented that "patriots" have not done enough to defeat the "homosexual lobby" and its drive to enact its agenda of wide-ranging hate crimes legislation in the United States. If true patriots do not act to stem the tide of moral degeneracy in the United States, Pike warns,

> Let me remind you how infinitely more wearying it will be to exist night and day, year after year, shivering and starving in the gulags of the New World Order. If we allow [hate crimes bills] to first take away our free speech, then all other freedoms are going down the drain. Once that happens, there will be nothing to restrain mass arrest, imprisonment, deportation, and murder of probably millions. (Scherr 2009)

The National Prayer Network has also intoned that hate crimes legislation will protect pedophiles because "especially within the homosexual community [they] are an increasingly powerful political force" (Scherr 2009). Pike continually blames the "Jewish supremacists" who are trying to "corrupt Christian nations so they can rule the world from Jerusalem" (Scherr 2009).

After the hate crimes bill passed, white supremacist groups spoke out and stated that passage of the legislation implied that "it's ok to rob, rape and murder as long as one declares the criminal act had nothing to do with race, etc." (Scherr 2009).

See also: Christian Identity; Patriot Movement; White Supremacist Movement

Further Reading

Anti-Defamation League. June 7, 2012. "'Christian News' Promotes Anti-Semitic Writers." https://www.adl.org/blog/christian-news-promotes-anti-semitic-writers (Accessed May 31, 2017).

Maugans, Randy. "Ted Pike & the National Prayer Network." *Christian Media Research.* http://www.christianmediaresearch.com/tedpike.html (Accessed May 31, 2017).

National Prayer Network. http://www.truthtellers.org/ (Accessed May 31, 2017).

National Prayer Network. "Rev. Ted Pike: Biography." *TruthTellers.* https://www.truthtellers .org/tedpikebiography.html (Accessed May 31, 2017).

Right Wing Watch. May 5, 2008. "The Nazi Thing." http://www.rightwingwatch.org/post
/the-nazi-thing/ (Accessed May 31, 2017).

Scherr, Sonia. July 17, 2009. "Religious Right Promotes Falsehoods in Last-Ditch Attempt
to Stall Federal Hate Crimes Bill." *Southern Poverty Law Center—Hatewatch*. https://
www.splcenter.org/hatewatch/2009/07/17/religious-right-promotes-falsehoods-last
-ditch-attempt-stall-federal-hate-crimes-bill (Accessed May 31, 2017).

NATIONAL SOCIALIST MOVEMENT

The National Socialist Movement (NSM) is currently the "largest neo-Nazi group
in the United States" (Anti-Defamation League). As noted by the Anti-Defamation
League, however, "This is due primarily to setbacks experienced by other major
neo-Nazi groups in the country between 2002 and 2007." The group has been led
by Jeff Schoep since 1994. Despite the stability provided by Schoep, the NSM has
not attracted the large numbers that its predecessors did in the late 1990s and early
2000s. Today its membership consists of only several hundred members (Anti-
Defamation League). The group is known for its virulent "anti-Jewish rhetoric, its
racist views, and its wearing of Nazi uniforms" (Southern Poverty Law Center). In
2007, however, NSM traded in its "brown shirts" for black "Battle Dress Uniforms"
(Southern Poverty Law Center). On its Web site, nsm88.org, NSM puts forth its "25
Points of American National Socialism" (National Socialist Movement). Among the
"25 Points" is the imperative that "all non-White immigration must be prevented.
We demand that all non-Whites currently residing in America be required to leave
the nation forthwith and return to their land of origin: peacefully or by force." The
NSM states, "The leaders of the movement promise to work ruthlessly—if need be
to sacrifice their very lives—to translate this program into action."

NSM "has its roots in the original American Nazi Party founded by George
Lincoln Rockwell in 1959" (Southern Poverty Law Center). After Rockwell was
assassinated in 1967, two of his followers formed the National Socialist American Workers Freedom Movement in St. Paul, Minnesota. In 1994, the leadership
passed to Jeff Schoep, who, at 21, sought to reinvigorate the ranks of the neo-Nazi
movement by attracting younger followers, many of whom had drifted away from
older Ku Klux Klan and skinhead groups. The biggest gains in NSM's membership came when a major power vacuum in neo-Nazi leadership emerged with
the deaths of William Pierce, leader of the National Alliance, and Richard Butler,
leader of the Aryan Nations, in 2002 and 2004, respectively. The neo-Nazi leadership ranks were further reduced in 2004 when Matt Hale, leader of the World
Church of the Creator (later renamed the Creativity Movement), "was sentenced to
40 years in prison for soliciting the murder of a federal judge" (Southern Poverty
Law Center).

NSM generally overshadowed other neo-Nazi groups of its era, including Kevin
Strom's National Vanguard, with its theatrical street tactics undertaken in traditional Nazi uniforms. NSM was also unique in that it allowed members to join its
ranks while still maintaining membership in other extremist groups. NSM mirrors
the ideology expressed by the original American Nazi Party in almost every way.
The group idolizes and reveres Adolf Hitler, referring to him as "Our Fuhrer, the

beloved Holy Father of our age . . . a visionary in every respect" (National Socialist Movement, FAQ). In addition, the group maintains that its core beliefs

> include defending the rights of white people everywhere, preservation of our European culture and heritage, strengthening family values, economic self-sufficiency, reform of illegal immigration policies, immediate withdrawal of our national military from an illegal Middle Eastern occupation, and promotion of white separation. (National Socialist Movement, About Us)

NSM is perhaps best known for instigating the 2005 Toledo riot. In December of that year, NSM made a public statement that it would march in Toledo, Ohio, through a predominantly black neighborhood to protest gang activity in the city. The march sparked rioting by counterprotestors and neighborhood residents, costing the city more than $336,000 in additional police expenses and prompting a citywide 48-hour curfew. NSM leader Jeff Schoep said of the destruction, "The Negro beasts have proved our point for us" (Southern Poverty Law Center). The group threatened a similar march in the aftermath of the shooting of Trayvon Martin, "an unarmed African-American teenager who was shot and killed by a neighborhood watchman" in Sanford, Florida, in February 2012 (Southern Poverty Law Center). However, the march never materialized.

In November 2016, following the election of Donald Trump, NSM changed its logo, replacing the swastika with "an Odai rune (a symbol from a pre-Roman alphabet that was also adopted by the Nazis) in an attempt to become more integrated and more mainstream" (Kovaleski et al. 2016).

See also: American Nazi Party; Aryan Nations; Butler, Richard; Creativity Movement; Hale, Matt; Ku Klux Klan; National Alliance; National Vanguard; Neo-Nazis; Pierce, William; Rockwell, George Lincoln; Schoep, Jeff; Strom, Kevin; White Supremacist Movement

Further Reading

Anti-Defamation League. "The National Socialist Movement." *Anti-Defamation League—Extremism, Terrorism&Bigotry.* https://www.adl.org/education/resources/profiles/national-socialist-movement (Accessed March 13, 2017).

Kovaleski, Serge F., Julie Turkewitz, Joseph Goldstein, and Dan Barry. December 10, 2016. "An Alt-Right Makeover Shrouds the Swastikas." *The New York Times.* https://www.nytimes.com/2016/12/10/us/alt-right-national-socialist-movement-white-supremacy.html?_r=0 (Accessed March 13, 2017).

National Socialist Movement. "25 Points of American National Socialism." http://www.nsm88.org/25points/25pointsengl.html (Accessed March 13, 2017).

National Socialist Movement. "About Us." http://www.nsm88.org/aboutus.html (Accessed March 13, 2017).

National Socialist Movement. "Frequently Asked Questions About National Socialism (Nazism) and the National Socialist Movement." http://www.nsm88.org/faqs/frequently asked questions about national socialism.pdf (Accessed March 13, 2017).

Southern Poverty Law Center. "National Socialist Movement." https://www.splcenter.org/fighting-hate/extremist-files/group/national-socialist-movement (Accessed March 13, 2017).

NATIONAL VANGUARD

National Vanguard is a white supremacist, white nationalist, and anti-Semitic organization based in Charlottesville, Virginia. It was founded in 2005 by Kevin Strom, a former protégé of National Alliance founder William Pierce. When Pierce died in 2002, Strom was slated to become the new leader of National Alliance (NA). Strom had created NA's weekly radio show, *American Dissident Voices*, had been editor of NA's publication, *National Vanguard*, and had "convinced Pierce to venture into the white power music business" (Southern Poverty Law Center, National Vanguard). However, after Pierce's death, a power struggle ensued in NA that led to the appointment of Erich Gliebe over Strom. Gliebe orchestrated the expulsion of Strom and other disgruntled NA members. In retaliation, Strom took hundreds of NA members with him and formed the National Vanguard; he was able to take the name of the NA's publication with him because he had transferred the rights to the name to his wife before the group split. In a few short months, the membership rolls of the National Vanguard soared, until Strom was arrested, and eventually convicted, on child pornography charges.

When Strom left the National Alliance in 2005, he gained the support of other prominent white supremacists, including David Duke and Don Black, founder of the neo-Nazi Internet forum *Stormfront*. Many members of NA, "angry over Gliebe's perceived failures as chairman of the organization," defected to National Vanguard, increasing Strom's influence within white supremacist circles (Southern Poverty Law Center, National Vanguard). Strom's foray into white power music also attracted the attention of April Gaede, a former high-profile member of the National Alliance who had been a strong supporter of William Pierce. For several years in the 2000s, Gaede's twin daughters, Lynx and Lamb, performed white supremacist music under the name Prussian Blue.

National Vanguard overshadowed the more famous National Alliance until early January 2007, when Strom was arrested near his home in Stanardsville, Virginia, "for possessing and receiving child pornography, as well as enticing a minor to perform sex acts" (Southern Poverty Law Center, Kevin Strom). Because of the backlash from his supporters as a result of the charges, Strom disbanded National Vanguard in March 2007. He subsequently faced two trials on charges of child pornography. In the first, he prevailed. However, in January 2008, "Strom faced a second trial on the charge of possessing child pornography." He struck a plea deal wherein "he pled guilty to possessing child pornography and prosecutors dropped several counts of receiving child pornography" (Southern Poverty Law Center, Strom). Strom was sentenced to 23 months in jail. With time served, he was released from prison in September 2008 (Southern Poverty Law Center, Strom).

Upon his release, Strom dabbled in movement politics and ran two racist Web sites. After Erich Gliebe resigned his position at the National Alliance in 2014, Strom was invited back to NA by its new leader, William Williams, to be the organization's communication director. However, white supremacists continued to view Strom with contempt because of his child pornography conviction.

National Vanguard does not currently exist as an organization, but Strom continues to use the National Vanguard name for a Web site in support of white supremacist causes. In an "About Us" section on the site, National Vanguard states,

> Without racial divergence, the evolution of life itself could never have taken place.
>
> But powerful forces are attempting to obliterate all racial, ethnic and cultural differences worldwide, with the goal of "uniting humanity" into one global, anonymous mass. Open borders, "outsourcing," and the growth of corporate and governmental globalism are all elements in the systematic destruction of human biological and cultural diversity.
>
> The European race is uniquely beautiful and creative. It is imperative that we survive and progress. (National Vanguard)

See also: Black, Don; Duke, David; Gaede, April; Gliebe, Erich; National Alliance; Neo-Nazis; Pierce, William; *Stormfront*; Strom, Kevin; White Nationalism; White Supremacist Movement

Further Reading

National Vanguard. "About Us." http://nationalvanguard.org/about/ (Accessed March 13, 2017).

Southern Poverty Law Center. "Kevin Strom." https://www.splcenter.org/fighting-hate/extremist -files/individual/kevin-strom (Accessed March 13, 2017).

Southern Poverty Law Center. "National Vanguard." https://www.splcenter.org/fighting-hate /extremist-files/group/national-vanguard (Accessed March 13, 2017).

NEO-CONFEDERATES

"Neo-Confederates" and "neo-Confederacy" are terms "used to describe 20th and 21st century revivals of pro-Confederate sentiment in the United States." Neo-Confederates "are strongly nativist and support measures to end immigration that they claim have turned the United States into a multicultural empire that fundamentally contradicts the meaning of America" (Southern Poverty Law Center). Neo-Confederates claim that Christianity and white heritage are cultural values that have been abandoned in the modern United States. Neo-Confederates also advocate traditional gender roles, strongly oppose homosexuality, and exhibit an "understanding of race that favors segregation and suggests white supremacy" (Hague 2010). In many cases, "neo-Confederates are openly secessionist and look to the antebellum South and the Confederate States of America (CSA)" for "lessons on leadership, values, morality and behavior" (Hague 2010). Neo-Confederate ideas can be found in modern incarnations in organizations such as the League of the South and the Council of Conservative Citizens. According to the Southern Poverty Law Center, neo-Confederatism is "a reactionary conservative ideology that has made inroads into the Republican Party from the political right, and overlaps with the views of white nationalists and other more radical extremist groups."

Neo-Confederates are accused of historical revisionism and "are openly critical of the presidency of Abraham Lincoln and the history of Reconstruction" (Southern

Poverty Law Center). Neo-Confederates view the U.S. Civil War, "often termed the war of Northern Aggression," as an "unconstitutional invasion of the Southern states by the Union forces that were perceived as the aggressor in the conflict" (Southern Poverty Law Center). Most neo-Confederates view President Lincoln as a war criminal, and neo-Confederates generally believe that key amendments to the U.S. Constitution—particularly the so-called "Civil War Amendments: the 13th, 14th, and 15th amendments—"are illegal and their implementation is therefore illegitimate" (Hague 2010).

As a result of these 19th-century actions, neo-Confederates today believe that the current federal government is illegitimate and has abandoned the principles set forth by the Founding Fathers. Most importantly, the United States has strayed from social, cultural, and political foundations upon which American society was built. Federal authority

> is asserted to be an unconstitutional infringement on states' rights and U.S. culture is considered to be "profane" and incompatible with traditional American society, given its promotion of equal rights for women, ethnic minorities, homosexuals, and non-Christian religions. Because the U.S. has become a "multicultural empire," neo-Confederate ideologues argue that it is doomed to dissolution into smaller, self-governing nation-states. This is because, in neo-Confederate belief, the idea that a state can be multi-ethnic is a contradiction in terms. Often drawing on eighteenth and nineteenth century political philosophers for justification, neo-Confederates contend that the ideal unit for governance is a small, ethnically homogeneous republic. Some advocates have gone so far as to propose a return to independent city-states and local fiefdoms. Thus, neo-Confederacy is closely intertwined with nationalist and secessionist sentiment. (Hague 2010)

Neo-Confederates are unabashedly Christian. They support public displays of Christianity, such as the 10 Commandments, and displays of the Christian cross (Religious Tolerance). Neo-Confederates are highly distrustful of the actions of the U.S. federal government and are ardent supporters of the Second Amendment's provision of the right accorded to Americans to keep and bear arms. Many neo-Confederates see a conflict between the Christian South in the United States and secular North (Sebesta and Hague 2002), and they identify with an Anglo-Celtic and Christian Identity view, believing that whites are God's "chosen race." Many neo-Confederates identify themselves as "Southern nationalists" (League of the South).

Consistent with their views that the South was an aggrieved party during the U.S. Civil War, and that the war was a war for "Southern independence," the Confederate battle flag ("Stars and Bars") is viewed with great pride and reverence among neo-Confederates. Neo-Confederates believe that the flag is not a symbol of hate but of resistance against tyranny and Southern independence. In 2015, Dylann Roof's prominent display of the Confederate flag in the aftermath of his "murder of nine black parishioners at Charleston's (South Carolina) Mother Emmanuel AME church" thrust the Confederate battle flag back into the national spotlight (Hatewatch Staff). After the Charleston Church shooting, a spike in neo-Confederate rallies and "flaggings" (prominent displays of the Confederate flag) were conducted in order to show "rebel pride" and a fealty to "Southern heritage." In one such public display, a convoy of pickup trucks driven by neo-Confederates "drove by a young African American child's birthday party hurling racial epithets and pointing firearms." On February 27, 2017, several "flaggers" who participated in the event "were sentenced to lengthy prison terms for aggravated assault, making terroristic threats, and violating the state of Georgia's gang act" (Bruner 2017).

Violence perpetrated by groups that espouse neo-Confederate views, such as the League of the South and the Council of Conservative Citizens, often elicits in the minds of the public the idea that neo-Confederatism is a movement with historically racist overtones. For their part, neo-Confederates reject this association, instead preferring to identify themselves simply as individuals who are proud of their Confederate heritage (Confederate American Pride).

Nevertheless, there are those who believe that neo-Confederates advance an ideology that justifies positions that are "anti-democratic, racist, sexist, elitist, religiously intolerant, and homophobic." According to one commentator, "It is considerably more than just support for the Confederate battle flag or nostalgia for the Old South. Neo-Confederacy is an active and ongoing attempt to reshape the United States in the Old South's image" (Hague 2010).

See also: Charleston Church Shooting (in Roof, Dylann Storm entry); Council of Conservative Citizens; League of the South; Roof, Dylann Storm; Second Amendment; White Nationalism; White Supremacist Movement

Further Reading

Bruner, Portia. February 27, 2017. "Judge Sentences 2 People Convicted in Confederate Flag Confrontation." *Fox 5 News.* http://www.fox5atlanta.com/news/238410026-story (Accessed June 5, 2017).

Confederate American Pride. http://www.confederateamericanpride.com/ (Accessed January 30, 2018).

Gallagher, Gary W. 1999. *The Confederate War.* Harvard University Press.

Hague, Euan. January 25, 2010. "The Neo-Confederate Movement." *Southern Poverty Law Center—Hatewatch.* https://www.splcenter.org/hatewatch/2010/01/26/neo-confederate -movement (Accessed June 5, 2017).

Hatewatch Staff. March 2, 2017. "Racial Divisions Along the Neo-Confederate Spectrum." *Southern Poverty Law Center—Hatewatch.* https://www.splcenter.org/hatewatch/2017/03 /02/racial-division-along-neo-confederate-spectrum (Accessed June 5, 2017).

League of the South. http://www.dixienet.org/ (Accessed January 30, 2018).

Religious Tolerance. "The Ten Commandments." http://www.religioustolerance.org/chr _10cc.htm (Accessed June 5, 2017).

Sebesta, Edward H. and Euan Hague. 2002. "The US Civil War as a Theological War: Confederate Christian Nationalism and the League of the South." *Canadian Review of American Studies* 32, no. 3. http://www.theocracywatch.org/civil_war_canadian _review.htm (Accessed June 5, 2017).

Southern Poverty Law Center. "Neo-Confederate." https://www.splcenter.org/fighting-hate /extremist-files/ideology/neo-confederate (Accessed June 5, 2017).

NEO-NAZIS

Neo-Nazism is a general term related to organizations that profess "fascist, white nationalist, white supremacist, or anti-Semitic beliefs" (Southern Poverty Law Center, Neo-Nazi). The political tendencies of such groups are the restoration of a Nazi order that will establish a new social and political system based on the doctrines similar to those of Nazi Germany. Neo-Nazis are most prominently characterized by a belief in white racial superiority, in their shared hatred of Jews, and in their love of Adolf Hitler. While they "may hate other minorities, gays and lesbians, and even sometimes Christians," neo-Nazis perceive "the Jew as their cardinal enemy, and trace social problems to a Jewish conspiracy that supposedly controls governments, financial institutions and the media" (Southern Poverty Law Center, Neo Nazi). In the United States, the neo-Nazi movement ostensibly began with George Lincoln Rockwell, who founded the American Nazi Party in 1959. Rockwell "instructed his members to dress in imitation of SA-style brown shirts" (SA was the original paramilitary wing of the Nazi Party) while flying the swastika of the Third Reich (Southern Poverty Law Center, Neo-Nazi). Later leaders of American neo-Nazism would include David Duke and William Luther Pierce, the founder of the National Alliance—"the one-time largest and most influential neo-Nazi organization in the United States" (Southern Poverty Law Center, William Pierce). Today, neo-Nazis may manifest themselves in suits and ties, as racist skinheads, or as aggressively tattooed individuals who spout anti-immigrant rhetoric while perpetuating myths of worldwide Jewish conspiracies to control the world. Members of the new alt-right movement, "a mixed group of racists, nationalists, anti-Semites, and misogynists," understand the underlying tensions in the United States today and aggressively exploit citizens' fears about the future of the United States (Beckett 2017). These new neo-Nazis believe that they have found a safe haven in the administration of Donald Trump (Beckett 2017).

Neo-Nazis are extremists on the far right. Some of the major factors that have accompanied a surge in neo-Nazism are the unstable economic, political, cultural, and social conditions that individuals have experienced in the post–World War II world, including

> the simultaneous inflation and recession caused in great part by dependence on Arab oil; the disruptions of globalization and the collapse of the Soviet empire; waves of nonwhite immigration into Europe (from places formerly ruled or dominated by Europeans) and the United States; the constant threat of war, especially in the Middle East and the Persian Gulf; and the continued sense among white men that they were losing power and prestige in areas ranging from world affairs to their living rooms to their relations with women. In the United States, racial issues, not resolved in the 1960s, took the form of conflict over school desegregation, affirmative action, social welfare provision, and government social spending in general. Moreover, the failure of the Vietnam War, based on untenable Cold War premises, produced an atmosphere of political and cultural resentment on the right that became increasingly strong over time. (Jewish Virtual Library)

Neo-Nazis were among the first to understand the impact of emerging technologies and the use of the Internet to indoctrinate members. And while most "neo-Nazi

Adherents of neo-Nazism rally near the Capitol Building in Washington, D.C. Neo-Nazis generally profess fascist, white nationalist, white supremacist, or anti-Semitic beliefs. (Rrodrickbeiler/Dreamstime)

frames and narratives are based on myths, demonization, and scapegoating, this does not make them less effective in building a functional identity for individuals" (Jewish Virtual Library). Neo-Nazis were among the first to perpetrate the Zionist Occupation Government conspiracy theory, which purports that a secret cabal of Jews controls the governments of most Western countries and is working behind the scenes to establish a one-world government through their use and manipulation of political leaders as well as the global economic system.

Neo-Nazis, including such traditional racist groups as the Ku Klux Klan and the Council of Conservative Citizens, have a strongly Christian character to them. A particularly virulent form of Christianity known as Christian Identity preaches that the white race are God's "chosen people" and that Jews are the spawn of Satan and Eve. Some neo-Nazis, however, reject Christianity (as it is "Jew based") and embrace various forms of mysticism and neopaganism. "Wotanism" ("Will Of The Aryan Nation") is a neo-Nazi, white separatist movement begun by David Lane, a member of the infamous neo-Nazi group The Order, that preaches that the Norse gods are the true representatives of the white race and should be accorded the honor of worship as opposed to Christ, who was a Jew (Southern Poverty Law Center, Lane).

Holocaust denial is another facet of neo-Nazism as many neo-Nazis "attempt to prove that the Holocaust was fiction and that the Nazis never engaged in a systematic campaign to exterminate the Jews" (Southern Poverty Law Center, Neo-Nazi). The Institute for Historical Review (IHR) was among the first to serve as the "international clearinghhouse" of Holocaust denial, or as advocates like to fancy themselves, Holocaust revisionists (Jewish Virtual Library). The IHR was founded in 1979 by Willis Carto, who founded the Liberty Lobby as a political lobby group to "promote patriotism." Carto was noted for his projects associated with extreme-right causes and neo-Nazi themes, an admiration for Adolf Hitler, and perpetuation of anti-Semitic conspiracy theories (Jewish Virtual Library).

Postwar neo-Nazism began in the United States in 1959 when George Lincoln Rockwell organized the American Nazi Party. The organization gained a great deal of publicity due to its advocacy of neo-Nazi principles and its prominent display of Nazi symbols, including the swastika. But the organization never gathered many members. After Rockwell's assassination by a disgruntled member in 1967, the neo-Nazi movement drifted aimlessly for a time, though many of the anti-Semitic themes of neo-Nazism were expressed by the antigovernment movement known as Posse Comitatus.

During the 1970s, David Duke was a rising star in the neo-Nazi ranks. He professed his neo-Nazi sentiments at an early age (Southern Poverty Law Center, Duke). While at Louisiana State University, Duke would build an "international reputation as the American face of white nationalism and pseudo-academic anti-Semitism" (Southern Poverty Law Center, Duke). Duke would run several times, unsuccessfully, for political office, though he would be elected for a brief stint to the Louisiana State Legislature in the early 1990s.

In the late 1970s, Richard Butler founded Aryan Nations and preached his particular brand of Christian Identity from his compound in Hayden Lake, Idaho. Aryan Nations preached the purity of the white race and that other races were "mud people." Many former Ku Klux Klan members joined Aryan Nations as they believed the group was the future of white supremacy. One of Butler's acolytes, Bob Mathews, wanted more direct action, as opposed to the speeches and demonstrations for which Aryan Nations became infamous (Balleck 2015). In 1983, Mathews formed The Order, perhaps the most terrorist minded of all neo-Nazi organizations. Under Mathews's direction, The Order perpetrated robberies, murder, and other crimes that landed The Order and its members on the FBI's Ten Most Wanted List (Balleck 2015). Aside from pulling off the most lucrative armored car heist in U.S. history ($3.6 million), The Order was responsible for the assassination of Jewish talk show host Alan Berg in Denver, Colorado, in 1984. David Lane, a prominent member of The Order, was the author of the famous 14 Words—"We must secure the existence of our people and a future for white children"—and the promoter of Wotanism, the religious belief held by many neo-Nazis (Southern Poverty Law Center, Lane). The 14 Words have become the unofficial motto of the neo-Nazi and white supremacist movements.

Also during the 1970s, William Luther Pierce founded the National Alliance (NA). NA would become "the largest and most active neo-Nazi organization in the United States for more than two decades" (Southern Poverty Law Center, Pierce). NA tapped into the emerging racist skinhead movement and hate rock music that emerged in the 1990s to bolster its numbers and increase its influence. In 1999, NA purchased Resistance Records, a struggling hate-rock business, which Pierce and his minions turned into a profitable business (Balleck 2015). Aside from his persona as the face of neo-Nazism, Pierce was the author (under the pseudonym Andrew MacDonald) of the infamous dystopian novel *The Turner Diaries*. Bob Mathews's group, The Order, was named after the antigovernment organization in the novel that waged war against a corrupt and Jewish-laden American government. In the novel, The Order kills all Jews and "race traitors" and establishes a pure white state in the United States, inasmuch as all other races have been exterminated. *The Turner Diaries* was also the inspiration for Timothy McVeigh's bombing of the Alfred P. Murrah Federal Building in Oklahoma City, Oklahoma, in April 1995, in which 168 people, including 20 children, were killed (Balleck 2015). As in the novel, McVeigh drove a rented truck full of fuel oil and ammonium nitrate fertilizer and detonated it in front of a federal building at just after 9:00 a.m. McVeigh was convinced that Jews controlled the U.S. government and that the government had become illegitimate by its actions at Ruby Ridge and Waco (Balleck 2015).

From the 1990s onward, a number of neo-Nazi elements have aligned themselves with the causes of extreme-right-wing groups like those associated with the patriot and militia movements. The rise of these groups "prompted neo-Nazi leader Louis Beam to call for 'leaderless resistance' against the government" (Jewish Virtual Library). With the demise of many mainstream neo-Nazi groups, such as Aryan Nations and the National Alliance, many displaced neo-Nazis have found their way into patriot and militia groups, where their white supremacist and anti-Semitic attitudes find an audience among those who believe that the government is under Jewish control and that the United Nations in conspiring to bring the United States under a one-world government wherein its sovereignty will be destroyed and all citizen malcontents, especially those who own guns, will be interred in special camps (Cobb 2013).

The Council of Conservative Citizens (CCC), founded in 1988 in Atlanta, Georgia, is the successor to the segregationist Citizen's Councils of America that was prominent in the United States during the 1950s and 1960s. The CCC is a far-right extremist organization that pushes causes that promote white nationalism and white separatism. Much of the CCC's message is anti-Semitic and anti-black, but the group also embraces the tropes of neo-Nazism. In 2015, Dylann Roof—who murdered nine black parishioners in a Charleston, South Carolina, church—drew much of his inspiration from what he read on the CCC's Web site (Conservative Headlines). After the massacre, Roof's penchant for white supremacism and neo-Nazi symbols became national news.

In 2017, a new dapper, buttoned-down crowd of neo-Nazis has arisen in the form of the alt-right movement. Alt-right "has been described as having a bent toward white nationalism, racism, and neo-Nazism, as well as anti-Semitism, nativism, Islamophobia, anti-feminism, and homophobia" (Krieg 2016). Alt-right's leader, Richard Spencer, is a white supremacist who advocates for an Aryan homeland in North America, necessitating a "peaceful ethnic cleansing" to halt the "deconstruction" of European culture that has been the hallmark of American life for more than 300 years (Lambroso and Appelbaum 2016). Spencer runs the National Policy Institute, a "white supremacist think tank in Alexandria, Virginia"

(Gray 2015). After Donald Trump's surprise victory in the 2016 U.S. presidential election, Spencer was caught on tape shouting, "Hail Trump, hail our people, hail victory, and the audience responded with Nazi salutes" (Buncombe 2017). Though Spencer protests the label of "neo-Nazi," his rhetoric and actions inescapably lead to this conclusion (Krieg 2016).

With the election of Donald Trump to the U.S. presidency, neo-Nazis feel as though they have found a kindred spirit. According to one observer, Trump's rise to power

> has encouraged the extremists to try to bridge their divides. Neo-Nazis and Ku Klux Klan leaders were jubilant over an openly xenophobic, politically incorrect presidential candidate who promised to stop illegal immigration and enact a Muslim ban— and they have pursued news coverage, attracting headlines and staging dramatic photos. (Beckett 2017)

It appears as though neo-Nazis and neo-Nazism is now a permanent fixture on the global scene. Despite national laws in many European countries that punish Nazi speech or displays, neo-Nazism has been emboldened by the xenophobic nationalism that has arisen in the last few years due to conflict in the Middle East and the continuing threat of Islamic fundamentalism. It is possible "that if militant religious fundamentalism, especially within Islam, continues to expand, there will be more intersections with fascist and Nazi ideas, a process that is already producing lethal threats to societies around the world" (Jewish Virtual Library).

See also: Alt-Right Movement; American Nazi Party; Aryan Nations; Beam, Louis; Butler, Richard; Carto, Willis; Christian Identity; Council of Conservative Citizens; Creativity Movement; Duke, David; Fourteen Words; Hale, Matt; Holocaust Denial; Institute for Historical Review; Irving, David; Ku Klux Klan; Lane, David; Mathews, Bob; National Alliance; Order, The; Pierce, William; Posse Comitatus; Racist Skinheads; Rockwell, George Lincoln; Roof, Dylann Storm; Spencer, Richard Bertrand; *Turner Diaries, The*

Further Reading

Anti-Defamation League. "Neo-Nazis." https://www.adl.org/education/resources/glossary -terms/neo-nazis (Accessed June 8, 2017).

Anti-Defamation League. December 20, 2016. "Richard Spencer Is Making Common Cause with Neo-Nazis." https://www.adl.org/blog/richard-spencer-is-making-common-cause -with-neo-nazis (Accessed June 8, 2017).

Balleck, Barry J. 2015. *Allegiance to Liberty: The Changing Face of Patriots, Militias, and Political Violence in America.* Praeger.

Beckett, Lois. June 4, 2017. "Is There a Neo-Nazi Storm Brewing in Trump Country?" *The Guardian.* https://www.theguardian.com/world/2017/jun/04/national-socialism-neo -nazis-america-donald-trump (Accessed June 8, 2017).

Buncombe, Andrew. May 22, 2017. "Richard Spencer Has Gym Membership Revoked After Woman Confronts Him for Being 'Neo-Nazi.'" *Independent.* http://www.independent .co.uk/news/world/americas/richard-spencer-neo-nazi-alt-right-christine-fair-a7750186 .html (Accessed June 8, 2017).

Cobb, Don. February 19, 2013. "The New America: Agenda 21 and the U.N. One World Government Plan." *RenewAmerica*. http://www.renewamerica.com/columns/cobb/130219 (Accessed June 8, 2017).

Conservative Headlines. http://conservative-headlines.com/ (Accessed June 8, 2017).

Gray, Rosie. December 27, 2015. "How 2015 Fueled the Rise of the Freewheeling, White Nationalist Alt Right Movement." *BuzzFeed News*. https://www.buzzfeed.com/rosiegray /how-2015-fueled-the-rise-of-the-freewheeling-white-nationali?utm_term=.suNMbXJ2l# .qtJ0x56aW (Accessed June 8, 2017).

Jewish Virtual Library. "Anti-Semitism: Neo-Nazism." http://www.jewishvirtuallibrary.org /neo-nazism-2 (Accessed June 8, 2017).

Krieg, Gregory. August 25, 2016. "Clinton Is Attacking the 'Alt-Right'—What Is It?" *CNN*. http://www.cnn.com/2016/08/25/politics/alt-right-explained-hillary-clinton-donald -trump/ (Accessed June 8, 2017).

Lambroso, Daniel and Yoni Appelbaum. November 21, 2016. "'Hail Trump!': White Nationalists Salute the President-Elect." *The Atlantic*. http://www.theatlantic.com/politics /archive/2016/11/richard-spencer-speech-npi/508379/ (Accessed June 8, 2017).

Southern Poverty Law Center. "David Duke." https://www.splcenter.org/fighting-hate/extremist -files/individual/david-duke (Accessed June 8, 2017).

Southern Poverty Law Center. "David Lane." https://www.splcenter.org/fighting-hate/extremist -files/individual/david-lane (Accessed June 8, 2017).

Southern Poverty Law Center. "Neo-Nazi." https://www.splcenter.org/fighting-hate/extremist -files/ideology/neo-nazi (Accessed June 8, 2017).

NEW BLACK PANTHER PARTY

The New Black Panther Party (NBPP) is a U.S. black separatist and black nationalist organization founded in Dallas, Texas, in 1989. Despite its name, it has no official affiliation with the original Black Panther Party, which was active in the United States in the 1960s and 1970s. In fact, "former members of the original Black Panthers have insisted that the NBPP is illegitimate and have firmly declared, 'There is no new Black Panther Party'" (Huey P. Newton Foundation). Former Black Panther Party member Bobby Seale has labeled the NBPP, "a black racist hate group" (Southern Poverty Law Center). The NBPP "portrays itself as a modern-day expression of the black power movement," complete with militantism, but it makes no apologies for its virulently racist attitudes and hatred of whites, Jews, and law enforcement officers (Southern Poverty Law Center).

As a black separatist group, the NBPP "believes that black Americans should have their own nation." NBPP's "10 Point Platform," which is a variation of the original Black Panther Party's 10-point platform, "demands that blacks be given a country, or state, of their own within which they can make their own laws." The NBPP demands that "all black prisoners in the United States" be released to "lawful authorities of the Black Nation," and "they claim that the blacks are entitled to reparations from slavery from the United States, all European countries, and the Jews" (New Black Panther Party, Freedom or Death).

The NBPP "is notable for its anti-white and anti-Semitic hatred." Its leaders have blamed the Jews for 9/11 and for the slave trade that shipped hundreds of thousands of Africans to the United States. The former party chairperson of NBPP,

Khalid Abdul Muhammad, has said, "There are no good crackers, and if you find one, kill him before he changes" (Southern Poverty Law Center). NBPP members "hold black supremacist beliefs, thinking that blacks are God's chosen people" and that blacks are morally superior to all other races (Southern Poverty Law Center). This ideology is remarkably similar to Christian Identity, a quasireligious philosophy that teaches that whites, not Jews, are God's chosen people and that the white race is morally and intellectually superior to all other races.

NBPP has co-opted virtually every symbol of the original Black Panther Party, including their name, their logo, their 10-point program, and their style of dress. Like the Panthers of the 1960s and 1970s, NBPP members "often wear coordinated, military-style uniforms when they march—black boots, black pants, black shirts with NBPP patches, and black berets" (Southern Poverty Law Center). In 1997, two original Black Panthers "won an injunction against the NBPP disallowing them from the using either the Panther name or its logo. However, the injunction was never enforced and the NBPP continues to use the Panther name and logo today" (Southern Poverty Law Center).

In 1994, Khalid Abdul Muhammed, a former personal assistant to Nation of Islam (NOI) leader Louis Farrakhan, joined the NBPP. He accused Jews of "being responsible for the slave trade" and called them "bloodsuckers." Styled after the Million Man March that NOI had organized two years earlier, Muhammad organized the Million Youth March in 1998 in New York City. At the event, Muhammad encouraged those assembled "to attack police officers with chairs and bottles and even take the officers' guns if attacked" (Southern Poverty Law Center). Soon after the event, Muhammad assumed control of the NBPP and became the group's national chairperson.

Muhammad died in February 2001 and was replaced by Malik Zulu Shabazz, a Washington, D.C., attorney, who had previously run unsuccessfully for D.C.'s city council. In a conference held on October 31, 2001, Shabazz would say, "Zionism is racism, Zionism is terrorism, Zionism is colonialism, Zionism is imperialism, and support for Zionism is the root of why so many were killed on September 11" (Southern Poverty Law Center). During his time as national chairperson, Shabazz worked to improve relations with the NOI, where many NBPP members had their roots. Shabazz stepped down from the NBPP in 2013 to become the president of the Black Lawyers for Justice association.

Local chapters of NBPP have made headlines for their menacing remarks and behaviors. In November 2008, "two NBPP members showed up wearing military-style fatigues and berets, at a Philadelphia, Pennsylvania polling station ostensibly to protect black voters from having their voting rights violated" (Southern Poverty Law Center). The Justice Department filed civil charges of voter intimidation against the two, plus NBPP leader Malik Zulu Shabazz, and won the case when the defendants failed to appear in court. The Obama administration dropped the charges. In 2012, an NBPP member in Sanford, Florida, offered a $10,000 "bounty" on the "Hispanic man who shot an unarmed black teen as he was walking through a gated community" (Southern Poverty Law Center). When asked whether he was inciting violence, the NBPP members replied, "An eye for an eye, a tooth for a tooth"

(Southern Poverty Law Center). In July 2016, an army Afghan war veteran, Micah Xavier Johnson, shot and killed five white police officers at a protest in Dallas, Texas. Johnson had expressed sympathies for NBPP and the black separatist cause.

See also: Black Nationalism; Black Panther Party; Christian Identity; Farrakhan, Louis; Nation of Islam; Seale, Bobby; Shabazz, Malik Zulu

Further Reading

Huey P. Newton Foundation. "There Is No New Black Panther Party: An Open Letter from the Huey P. Newton Foundation." http://web.archive.org/web/20140907064728/http://www.blackpanther.org/newsalert.htm (Accessed March 18, 2017).

New Black Panther Party. http://www.nbpp.org/home.html (Accessed March 18, 2017).

New Black Panther Party. "New Black Panther Party for Self Defense: Freedom or Death." http://www.nbpp.org/10-point-platform.html (Accessed March 18, 2017).

Southern Poverty Law Center. "New Black Panther Party." https://www.splcenter.org/fighting-hate/extremist-files/group/new-black-panther-party (Accessed March 18, 2017).

NEW CENTURY FOUNDATION

The New Century Foundation (NCF) was founded in 1990 by Jared Taylor, an American white nationalist, and is the parent organization for *American Renaissance*, a white supremacist publication. NCF, under the direction of Taylor, advocates for racial separation, intoning that such views are a natural expression of racial solidarity as opposed to white supremacism. Taylor believes that racial homogeneity is a natural human expression of individuals' innate desire to be with their own kind and believes that homogeneity is the key to peaceful coexistence between races. Taylor holds up Japan as "an exemplar of a racially homogenous society, and views Asians generally as genetically superior in intelligence to whites. He also view whites as genetically superior in intelligence to blacks" (Anti-Defamation League). The Anti-Defamation League notes that "Taylor eschews anti-Semitism, seeing Jews as white, greatly influential, and the 'conscience of society.'" The Southern Poverty Law Center has stated that NCF is a "self-styled think tank that promotes pseudo-scientific studies and research that purport to show the inferiority of blacks to whites—although in hifalutin language that avoids open racial slurs and attempts to portray itself as serious scholarship."

The main vehicle for the ideas advocated by the New Century Foundation is *American Renaissance*, the publication edited by Taylor that presents itself as a "forum for open-minded thinkers not afraid to take on the racial taboos of the time without stooping to racial epithets and the like" (Southern Poverty Law Center). NCF is the parent organization to *American Renaissance*, which serves as the front porch for the racist views of Taylor and the New Century Foundation. NCF's mission statement veils its racism by suggesting that it represents the views of the "majority" whose interests are being ignored in the current political environment:

NCF's purpose is to encourage sensible public policy on race and immigration. We believe accurate knowledge and the willingness to face potentially unpleasant truths—both of which are conspicuously absent in the public arena—are essential to this task. We also believe the European-American majority has legitimate group interests now being ignored. (New Century Foundation)

NCF conferences have included members of the Council of Conservative Citizens (a white nationalist and white supremacist organization that condemns "racial mixing," decries the evil "of illegal immigration, and laments the decline of American civilization"), Don Black (the white supremacist operator of *Stormfront*, a white nationalist and neo-Nazi Internet forum), and National Alliance leader Kevin Strom (Southern Poverty Law Center).

Like many organizations on the extreme right, NCF bemoans the loss of power of the white majority in the United States. With increasing multiculturalism and the perceived loss of American exceptionalism, NCF attracts members and adherents who wish to return the United States to an idealized time in the past where everyone in society knew their place. NCF's focus on "race and immigration" is simply a smokescreen to conceal a racist agenda. The pseudoscientific nature of *American Renaissance* also attempts to make NCF's racist agenda more palatable by publishing articles from "race scientists" who can, they claim, lay bare the demonstrable differences between the races.

See also: American Renaissance; Black, Don; Council of Conservative Citizens; National Alliance; Neo-Nazis; *Stormfront*; Strom, Kevin; Taylor, Jared; White Nationalism; White Supremacist Movement

Further Reading

Anti-Defamation League. "Jared Taylor/American Renaissance." https://www.adl.org/sites/default/files/documents/assets/pdf/combating-hate/jared-taylor-extremism-in-america.pdf (Accessed May 9, 2017).

New Century Foundation. "Mission Statement." https://www.guidestar.org/profile/61-6212159 (Accessed May 9, 2017).

Southern Poverty Law Center. "American Renaissance." https://www.splcenter.org/fighting-hate/extremist-files/group/american-renaissance (Accessed May 9, 2017).

NEWTON, HUEY P.

Huey P. Newton (1942–1989), along with Bobby Seale, founded the Black Panther Party (BPP) in 1966. The BPP became a central player in the black power movement of the 1960s and 1970s. The BPP's militaristic style and controversial rhetoric was a hallmark of the far-left-wing political activism that punctuated an era of protests over the Vietnam War and the social and political atmosphere that surrounded the civil rights movement. Though Newton was illiterate when he graduated high school, he would eventually earn a PhD in social philosophy (Gates 2002). In 1989, Newton was killed in Oakland, California.

Newton was born in Louisiana. He was named for former Louisiana governor Huey P. Long, who was known for his populist stances and his support of the poor. In 1945, Newton's family moved to Oakland, California. As a teenager, he was constantly in trouble with the law "for offenses such as gun possession and vandalism" (Jones 2009). While a student at Merritt College, Newton became involved in politics. He joined the Afro-American Association and read the works of several prominent revolutionaries during this time. It was at Merritt College that Newton met Bobby Seale, and the two founded the Black Panther Party in October 1966. Many of the party's beliefs were based on the militant rhetoric of Malcolm X, the former national director for the Nation of Islam. The Black Panther Party "advocated the right of self-defense for blacks and the Party became known for its deep involvement in the Black Power movement" and its enunciation of the 10-Point Program, a document that called for "better housing, jobs and education for African Americans, [as well as] an end to economic exploitation of black communities along with [a] military exemption" (Biography 2016).

Newton "believed that violence—or the threat of violence—might be needed to bring about social change" (Biography 2016). The Black Panthers often dressed in military fatigues and openly carried guns. In 1967, members of the Black Panthers entered the California legislative assembly carrying guns in order to protest a gun bill. The action "was a shocking one that made news across the country, and Newton emerged as a leading figure in the black militant movement" (Biography 2016).

The Black Panthers aimed to improve the lives of blacks and improve conditions in black communities. They therefore took a stance against police brutality and often clashed with police, particularly white cops. In October 1967, "Newton was arrested for the murder of an Oakland police officer that had pulled over Newton and another Black Panther in a traffic stop" (Biography 2016). A confrontation ensued, and the police officer was shot four times and died. Newton was convicted in September 1968 "of voluntary manslaughter and sentenced to 2 to 15 years in prison." Questions surrounding the shooting led to a "Free Huey" campaign in the public. In 1970, Newton was freed after the California Appellate Court ordered a new trial due to incorrect deliberation procedures at the initial trial (Biography 2016). After two trials ended in hung juries, charges against Newton were dropped when prosecutors decided not to retry the case a third time.

After Newton's release, he sought to change the public image of the Black Panthers as a confrontational, militant organization. Newton began to focus on community programs and outreach efforts in order to better inner-city black neighborhoods. These programs met with controversy, however, when it was discovered that several of the party's programs were founded from money from drug dealers and prostitution rings (Jones 2009). Newton's problems with the law continued as he was charged "in the murder of a 17-year-old Oakland prostitute and an assault on his tailor, allegedly pistol whipping him" (Biography 2016). Newton "fled to Cuba for three years but returned to the United States in 1977 and was tried on the charges against him." After two deadlocked trials, the prosecution decided not to retry the cases (Jones 2009).

After his legal troubles ended, Newton returned to school and studied social philosophy at the University of California, Santa Cruz, where he earned a PhD in social philosophy in 1980. In his final years, however, "he suffered from major drug/alcohol problems and faced more prison time for weapons possession, financial misappropriations and parole violations" (Biography 2016). On August 22, 1989, Newton was killed "in a West Oakland neighborhood plagued by violence and crack cocaine." He had been shot three times in the head (Stein and Basheda 1989). Though a suspect was later charged and convicted, speculation surrounding the murder was that Newton was killed in a drug deal that had gone bad (Jones 2009).

See also: Black Panther Party; Malcolm X; Nation of Islam; Seale, Bobby

Further Reading

Biography. February 25, 2016. "Huey P. Newton." http://www.biography.com/people/huey -p-newton-37369 (Accessed March 20, 2017).

Gates, Anita. February 13, 2002. "An American Panther, in His Own Words." *The New York Times.* http://www.nytimes.com/2002/02/13/arts/television-review-an-american -panther-in-his-own-words.html (Accessed March 20, 2017).

Jones, Jackie. February 17, 2009. "Black History Month Faces and Places: Huey P. Newton." *BlackAmericaWeb.* https://web.archive.org/web/20090313040704/http://www.blackameri caweb.com/?q=articles/life_style/home_family_life_style/6917 (Accessed March 20, 2017).

Stein, Mark A. and Valarie Basheda. August 22, 1989. "Huey New Found Shot to Death on Oakland Street: Black Panthers Founder Killed in High Drug Area." *Los Angeles Times.* http://articles.latimes.com/1989-08-22/news/mn-1089_1_newton-oakland-panthers (Accessed March 20, 2017).

Time. November 13, 1978. "Nation: The Odyssey of Huey Newton." content.time.com /time/magazine/article/0,9171,946144,00.html (Accessed March 20, 2017).

OATH KEEPERS

Founded in 2009 by Elmer Stewart Rhodes, Oath Keepers is an association of "former members of the American military, police, and first responders who have pledged to fulfill the oaths that they took to defend the Constitution against all enemies, foreign and domestic" (Oath Keepers, About). The Oath Keepers are viewed as a right-wing, antigovernment organization that is associated with the patriot and militia movements in the United States (Southern Poverty Law Center). The Oath Keepers are highly suspicious of the government, perpetuating and postulating imagined threats that the U.S. government intends to enslave the population and force the country into a one-world socialist government, akin to the "New World Order" (Southern Poverty Law Center).

Since its founding, members of the Oath Keepers have been involved in several high-profile antigovernment events, such as the Bundy ranch standoff, the Sugar Pine Mine incident, and the Malheur National Wildlife Refuge standoff. Oath Keepers have also provided "protection" in the case of the Ferguson, Missouri, riots and were present in Rowan County, Kentucky, when county clerk Kim Davis was put in jail after refusing to issue marriage licenses to gay couples. After the election of Donald Trump in 2016, members of the Oath Keepers issued a national pledge via Twitter that they would "protect electors from terrorist death threats" (Oath Keepers on Twitter).

The Oath Keepers is one of many right-wing, antigovernment organizations that was organized, or found new life, with the election in the United States of Barack Obama, the country's first African American president. During Obama's eight years in office, the number of such organizations increased dramatically, fueled by racism and hatred but also the belief that Obama would use executive powers to dramatically decrease the freedoms of the American people. As one Oath Keeper stated during President Obama's first term, "It might not be long . . . before President Obama finds some pretext—a pandemic, a natural disaster, a terror attack—to impose martial law, ban interstate travel, and begin to detain citizens en masse" (Sharrock 2010).

In 2016, the Oath Keepers claimed more than 30,000 members who were sworn to defend the Constitution but who had also taken oaths to *not* obey orders they deemed unconstitutional, including any orders "to disarm the American people, orders to conduct warrantless searches of the American people, or orders to detain American citizens as 'unlawful enemy combatants,' or to subject them to military tribunals" (Oath Keepers, About).

See also: Bundy Ranch Standoff; Malheur National Wildlife Refuge Standoff; Rhodes, Elmer Stewart

Further Reading

Oath Keepers. "About Oath Keepers." https://www.oathkeepers.org/about/ (Accessed November 22, 2016).

Oath Keepers. "Official Twitter of Oath Keepers." https://twitter.com/Oathkeepers (Accessed November 22, 2016).

Sharrock, Justine. March/April 2010. "Oath Keepers and the Age of Treason." *Mother Jones*. http://www.motherjones.com/politics/2010/03/oath-keepers (Accessed November 22, 2016).

Southern Poverty Law Center. "Oath Keepers." https://www.splcenter.org/fighting-hate/extremist-files/group/oath-keepers (Accessed November 22, 2016).

OCCIDENTAL OBSERVER

The *Occidental Observer* is a far-right-wing online magazine that presents news and politics from an anti-Semitic and white nationalist perspective. Its mission statement, as articulated by its founder and editor, Kevin MacDonald, is to "present original content touching on the themes of white identity, white interests, and the culture of the West" (MacDonald, Mission Statement). MacDonald started the *Occidental Observer* in 2009 as an online companion to the *Occidental Quarterly*, a quarterly print journal that was founded in 2001 as a racist journal "devoted to the idea that as whites become a minority the civilization and free governments that whites have created will be jeopardized" (Southern Poverty Law Center). The *Occidental Quarterly* is described by the Anti-Defamation League as "the primary voice for anti-Semitism from far-right intellectuals." The "*Occidental Observer* seeks to distinguish itself from the *Occidental Quarterly* by printing shorter and more obviously opinionated articles." Both publications feature a "wide array of writers who demonize Jews and non-whites for a variety of social ills" (Anti-Defamation League 2013). As of 2017, MacDonald retains editorship of both the *Occidental Observer* and the *Occidental Quarterly* (Occidental Quarterly).

MacDonald is best known for "his premise that Jews engage in an evolutionary strategy that enhances their ability to out-compete others for resources" (Southern Poverty Law Center). According to MacDonald, "like viruses," Jews "destabilize their host societies to their own benefit." MacDonald has regularly argued that Jews are a "hostile elite in American society" who have sought to undermine the traditional European roots of American society by fostering measures that have led to increased nonwhite immigration into the United States. According to the Anti-Defamation League's interpretation of MacDonald's thesis, "Jews maintain their elite position by fostering non-white immigration into America to alter the country's racial hierarchy" (Anti-Defamation League, Kevin MacDonald).

In a July 2015 *New York Times* article, the authors pointed out that publications like the *Occidental Observer* "try to take a more highbrow approach, couching white nationalist arguments as academic commentary on black inferiority, the immigration threat to whites and other racial issues" (Wines and Saul 2015). MacDonald replied to the *Times* article by quoting a portion of the mission statement he had articulated some years earlier in the *Occidental Observer*:

We reject labels such as "white supremacist" or "racist" that are routinely bestowed on assertions of white identity and interests as a means of muzzling their expression. All peoples have ethnic interests and all peoples have a legitimate right to assert their interests, to construct societies that reflect their culture, and to define the borders of their kinship group. (MacDonald, Mission Statement)

In March 2017, MacDonald vocally supported Representative Steve King (R-Iowa), who had tweeted positively about anti-Islamic and far-right-wing Dutch politician Geert Wilders and had repeated Wilders's comment, "We can't restore civilization with somebody else's babies" (MacDonald 2017). In his defense of King, MacDonald stated,

He [King] is opposed to allowing people into the US (or Europe) who hate Western civilization, and he complains that the left is out to destroy Western civilization and "replace it with something entirely different." He is unabashedly pro-Western civilization ("Western civilization is a superior civilization and we want to share it with everybody"), noting that the spread of Western civilization via the English language has been associated with increased personal freedom and higher standards of living. (MacDonald 2017)

See also: MacDonald, Kevin; Neo-Nazis; White Nationalism; White Supremacist Movement

Further Reading

Anti-Defamation League. "Kevin MacDonald." *Anti-Defamation League—Extremism in America.* http://archive.adl.org/learn/ext_us/kevin_macdonald/ (Accessed January 6, 2017).
Anti-Defamation League. November 2013. "Kevin MacDonald." https://www.adl.org/sites/default/files/documents/assets/pdf/combating-hate/kevin-macdonald-backgrounder-november-2013rev.pdf (Accessed March 15, 2017).
MacDonald, Kevin. "Mission Statement: The Occidental Observer." *Occidental Observer.* http://www.theoccidentalobserver.net/mission/ (Accessed March 15, 2017).
MacDonald, Kevin. March 14, 2017. "Rep. Steve King Gets Shamelessly Racist—Or Not." *Occidental Observer.* http://www.theoccidentalobserver.net/ (Accessed March 15, 2017).
Occidental Quarterly. "About TOQ." http://www.toqonline.com/about/ (Accessed March 15, 2017).
Southern Poverty Law Center. "Occidental Quarterly." https://www.splcenter.org/fighting-hate/extremist-files/group/occidental-quarterly (Accessed March 15, 2017).
Wines, Michael and Stephanie Saul. July 15, 2015. "White Supremacists Extend Their Reach Through Websites." *The New York Times.* https://www.nytimes.com/2015/07/06/us/white-supremacists-extend-their-reach-through-websites.html (Accessed March 15, 2017).

OKLAHOMA CITY BOMBING

The Oklahoma City bombing was an act of domestic terrorism in the United States perpetrated upon the Alfred P. Murrah Federal Building in Oklahoma City, Oklahoma, on April 19, 1995. The bombing "is considered the worst act of domestic terrorism in U.S. history, and the second most deadly terrorist act on U.S. soil apart from the attacks of September 11, 2001" (Federal Bureau of Investigation). The bombing "killed 168 people (including 20 children), injured more than 680 others, destroyed one-third of the Murrah Building, damaged or destroyed 324 other buildings, and destroyed or burned 86 cars causing an estimated $652 million in damage" (Balleck 2015).

The primary bomber, Timothy McVeigh, was assisted in the deadly act by Terry Nichols. The two met while in the U.S. Army and after their military stint, the pair became virulent antigovernment activists enraged at U.S. federal government actions during the incident at Ruby Ridge and the Waco standoff. The Oklahoma City bombing spawned the modern patriot and militia movements and was the inspiration and prelude to dozens of antigovernment plots planned or carried out by far-right-wing extremists. McVeigh was tried and convicted for his part in the Oklahoma City bombing and was executed in June 2001. His accomplice, Terry Nichols, is serving 161 sentences of life imprisonment without the possibility of parole.

The chief conspirators in the Oklahoma City bombing were Timothy McVeigh and Terry Nichols. Other conspirators, including Nichols's brother James and McVeigh's friend Michael Fortier served jail terms for their parts in the bombing. McVeigh and Nichols met in 1988 while in basic training for the U.S. Army at Fort Benning, Georgia (Balleck 2015). Both McVeigh and Nichols had joined the army as they had been unable to find steady employment and were disenchanted with the social and economic conditions that they found in the United States. McVeigh had developed an interest in guns and survivalism in high school and often read issues of *Soldier of Fortune* magazine. Having grown up in rural Michigan, Nichols, too, was familiar with guns and had an interest in survivalism. Both McVeigh and Nichols had been affected by the economic recession of the 1980s in the United States, and the military seemed to be a place to give them both structure and a steady paycheck (Balleck 2015).

McVeigh served in Operation Desert Storm in Iraq, and it was here that he determined that the U.S. government was the "biggest bully" in the world (Aitken 2001). After leaving the army, McVeigh drifted around the country, attending gun shows and reading antigovernment extremist literature. McVeigh read *The Turner Diaries*, a dystopian novel by National Alliance founder William Pierce, which described a future United States in which "patriots" institute a revolution against a corrupt government, eventually exterminating all Jews, gays, nonwhites, and "race traitors." In the novel, a "patriot" fills a rented truck with cases of dynamite and sacks containing a mixture of ammonium nitrate and heating oil and detonates the bomb in front of a federal building at just after 9:00 a.m. in the morning, killing hundreds of people. *The Turner Diaries* would provide the blueprint for McVeigh's bombing, and the message of the book—that government had become unresponsive to the people and filled with race traitors and others who did not represent the will of the people—resonated in the events that McVeigh witnessed around him.

As McVeigh drifted west from his native home near Buffalo, New York, he commented that antigovernment sentiment became more apparent the farther west he traveled (Balleck 2015). In August 1992, McVeigh became incensed by the actions of the federal government against Randy Weaver, a white supremacist and survivalist, and his family. At the Weavers' home at Ruby Ridge, Idaho, federal authorities, who sought Weaver on federal gun charges, laid siege to his compound in the mountains. Eventually, Weaver's 14-year-old son and wife were killed in confrontations with government agents. McVeigh's rage at what he considered an abuse of government power reinforced his belief "that the U.S. government was a bully" (Aitken 2001). According to McVeigh, he had been shocked by the brutality of U.S. actions in Iraq, particularly when he "was ordered to execute surrendering prisoners and to see the carnage left in the wake of the U.S. rout of the Iraqi Army" (Balleck 2015). McVeigh's antigovernment sentiments turned into rage as he and Nichols watched the unfolding 51-day government standoff between Branch David-

Remains of the Alfred P. Murrah Federal Building in Oklahoma City. On April 19, 1995, homegrown terrorist Timothy McVeigh detonated a truck bomb outside the building killing 168 people, and injuring nearly 700. (Federal Emergency Management Agency)

ians and federal agents in Waco, Texas, from February to April 1993. After government agents attempted to end the standoff, which resulted in a conflagration that consumed the Branch Davidian compound and killed nearly 80 people, including children, both McVeigh and Nichols determined that they would strike back against the government.

Over the course of several months, McVeigh and Nichols, sometimes with the assistance of Michael Fortier and Nichols's brother James, prepared for the attack by purchasing ammonium nitrate fertilizer, stealing weapons to finance their plans, and choosing their target (Balleck 2015). McVeigh planned an attack on the Alfred P. Murrah Federal Building in Oklahoma City because "it housed regional offices of such federal agencies as the Drug Enforcement Agency, the Secret Service, the Bureau of Alcohol, Tobacco, Firearms, and Explosives (ATF), and the Federal Bureau of Investigation" (Federal Bureau of Investigation). Both the ATF and FBI had been involved in the standoff in Waco (History.com).

On the morning of April 19, 1995, exactly two years to the day after the FBI had pumped tear gas into the Branch Davidian compound in Waco, burning the compound to the ground and killing all the Branch Davidians in the resultant fire,

"McVeigh parked a rented Ryder truck in front of the Murrah Building in downtown Oklahoma City." Inside the vehicle "was a powerful bomb made out of a deadly cocktail of agricultural fertilizer, diesel fuel, and other chemicals. McVeigh got out, locked the door, and headed towards his getaway car. He [had] ignited one timed fuse, then another" (Federal Bureau of Investigation). At precisely 9:02 a.m., just as in *The Turner Diaries*, the bomb exploded and 168 people, including 20 children, lost their lives.

Coming "on the heels of the World Trade Center bombing two years earlier, the immediate belief was that the bombing was the work of Middle Eastern terrorists" (Potok 2015). The FBI soon discovered the rear axle of the rented Ryder truck and were able to find the vehicle identification number, indicating that the truck had been rented in Kansas. After a dizzying investigation in which a composite sketch of McVeigh was circulated nationwide, the FBI discovered that McVeigh was actually in police custody, having been arrested the same day as the bombing "for driving a vehicle without a license plate" (CNN 2017). Traces of the chemicals "used in the explosives were found on McVeigh's clothes and other incriminating evidence that confirmed McVeigh's guilt was found" (Federal Bureau of Investigation). Terry Nichols, learning that he was wanted in connection with the bombing, turned himself in on April 21, 1995. Both Michael Fortier and James Nichols would later be charged as accessories to the crime, with Fortier having known about the plot and James Nichols having stored the ammonium nitrate fertilizer at his farm in upstate Michigan.

At his trial, McVeigh "instructed his lawyers to use a necessity defense," meaning that the bombing took place in defense of an imminent danger that McVeigh perceived emanated from the U.S. government. Though the lawyers balked at such a defense, McVeigh made the point that "imminent danger" did not have to equate with "immediate danger." In other words, the "illegitimate" actions of the U.S. government, while not posing an "immediate" threat to McVeigh, nevertheless posed an "imminent" threat inasmuch as the continuation of policies being conducted by the government would certainly bring about the "imminent" destruction of freedom and liberty in the United States. McVeigh's lawyers cited "the bombing of the Murrah Federal Building was a justifiable response to what McVeigh believed were the crimes committed by the U.S. Government at both Ruby Ridge, Idaho and Waco, Texas" (Balleck 2015).

McVeigh was eventually convicted in federal court on "11 counts of murder, conspiracy, and using a weapon of mass destruction" (CNN 2017). He was only charged for the 11 federal agents that died in the blast. He "was later sentenced to death and was executed by lethal injection on June 11, 2001" (Balleck 2015). Nichols was later found guilty of the deaths of federal agents as well as 161 counts of murder. "He was sentenced to life in prison without the possibility of parole." Both Fortier and James Nichols served prison terms of between 8 and 11 years (Balleck 2015).

As McVeigh was awaiting execution, his callous attitude regarding his actions stunned the country. An individual who had once served his country and government with distinction was now a cold-blooded mass murderer. Even though McVeigh's actions had caused the death of innocent people, including children,

Terry Nichols contended that McVeigh simply didn't care. As McVeigh would proclaim,

> To these people in Oklahoma who have lost a loved one, I'm sorry but it happens every day. You're not the first mother to lose a kid, or the first grandparent to lose a grandson or a granddaughter. It happens every day, somewhere in the world. I'm not going to go into that courtroom, curl into a fetal ball and cry just because the victims want me to do that. (Anonymous)

Upon his arrest, "McVeigh was wearing a t-shirt with a picture of Abraham Lincoln and the motto, *sic semper tyrannis* ('thus always to tyrants') printed on the front. On the back of the shirt was the picture of a tree with three droplets of blood dripping from it, and a quote by Thomas Jefferson: 'The tree of liberty must be refreshed from time to time with the blood of patriots and tyrants'" (Balleck 2015). Prior to and after his execution, there were those who hailed McVeigh's actions as those of a "patriot" fighting against an oppressive government. Gore Vidal, an American writer whose primary literary subject was the history of the United States and the devolution of American society that turned the country into a militaristic and decadent empire, dubbed McVeigh a "hero" and considered McVeigh's actions in the Oklahoma City bombing as a legitimate act of war against an illegitimate power. In comments after McVeigh's execution, Vidal praised McVeigh, likening him to Paul Revere and John Brown, "the anti-slavery campaigner who was executed after leading a raid into the south which sparked the American civil war" (Gibbons 2001). In May 2017, Jeremy Joseph Christian, a known antigovernment agitator and white supremacist, stabbed and killed two good Samaritans as they tried to prevent Christian from harassing a young hijab-wearing Muslim woman. A month earlier, on the anniversary of the Oklahoma City bombing, April 19, Christian had posted a status update on his Facebook page in which he stated, "May all the Gods Bless Timothy McVeigh a TRUE PATRIOT!!!" (Wang 2017).

In the aftermath of the Oklahoma City bombing, the antigovernment "patriot" and militia movements ramped up their membership and public presence as they railed against government tyrannies and overreach and questioned whether or not the federal government was still a legitimate representative of the American people (Southern Poverty Law Center, Key Events. The bombing reinforced the beliefs and fears of those "steeped in the conspiracy theories and white-hot fury of the American radical right," and "marked the beginning of a new kind of domestic political extremism"—

> a revolutionary ideology whose practitioners do not hesitate to carry out attacks directed at entirely innocent victims, people selected essentially at random to make a political point. After Oklahoma, it was no longer sufficient for many American right-wing terrorists to strike at a target of political significance—instead, they reached for higher and higher body counts, reasoning that they had to eclipse McVeigh's attack to win attention. (Southern Poverty Law Center 2015)

The patriot and militia movements live on today and have been bolstered by other antigovernment extremists, such as sovereign citizens and common-law courts advocates. Individual adherents of these groups continue to believe in "baseless conspiracy theories that involve global elites instituting a totalitarian government that will enslave Americans and send political dissidents to concentration camps being built by the Federal Emergency Management Administration" (Southern Poverty Law Center). Though such notions may seem ludicrous to the average observer, the zealousness with which antigovernment extremists expect an eventual showdown with the federal government cannot be understated. The Oklahoma City bombing is the quintessential example of this antigovernment zeal.

See also: Common-Law Court Movement; Militia Movement; National Alliance; Patriot Movement; Ruby Ridge; Sovereign Citizens Movement; *Turner Diaries, The*; Waco Standoff; Weaver, Randy

Further Reading

Aitken, Robin. June 11, 2001. "Inside McVeigh's Mind." *BBC News.* http://news.bbc.co.uk/2/hi/americas/1382540.stm (Accessed June 3, 2017).

Anonymous. March 29, 2001. "McVeigh Holds No Regrets for Carnage." *Lubbock Avalanche-Journal.* http://lubbockonline.com/stories/032901/nat_032901055.shtml#.WSnD9dy1vRY (Accessed June 23, 2017).

Balleck, Barry J. 2015. *Allegiance to Liberty: The Changing Face of Patriots, Militias, and Political Violence in America.* Praeger.

CNN. March 29, 2017. "Oklahoma City Bombing Fast Facts." http://www.cnn.com/2013/09/18/us/oklahoma-city-bombing-fast-facts/ (Accessed June 3, 2017).

Federal Bureau of Investigation. "Oklahoma City Bombing." https://www.fbi.gov/history/famous-cases/oklahoma-city-bombing (Accessed June 3, 2017).

Gibbons, Fiachra. August 16, 2001. "Vidal Praises Oklahoma Bomber for Heroic Aims." *The Guardian.* https://www.theguardian.com/world/2001/aug/17/edinburghbookfestival2001.mcveigh (Accessed June 3, 2017).

History.com. "Oklahoma City Bombing." http://www.history.com/topics/oklahoma-city-bombing (Accessed June 3, 2017).

Potok, Mark. June 10, 2015. "Remembering Oklahoma." *Southern Poverty Law Center—Intelligence Report.* https://www.splcenter.org/fighting-hate/intelligence-eport/2015/remembering-oklahoma (Accessed June 3, 2017).

Southern Poverty Law Center. April 15, 2015. "Oklahoma City Bombing: Key Events and Crimes of the Patriot Movement." *Southern Poverty Law Center—Hatewatch.* https://www.splcenter.org/hatewatch/2015/04/16/key-events-and-crimes-patriot-movement (Accessed June 3, 2017).

Southern Poverty Law Center. November 1, 2015. "Terror from the Right." https://www.splcenter.org/20100126/terror-right (Accessed June 3, 2017).

Wang, Amy B. May 28, 2017. "'Brave and Selfless' Oregon Stabbing Victims Hailed as Heroes for Standing Up to Racist Rants." *The Washington Post.* https://www.washingtonpost.com/news/post-nation/wp/2017/05/28/brave-and-selfless-oregon-stabbing-victims-hailed-as-heroes/?utm_term=.efa72c4b3b78 (Accessed June 3, 2017).

OPERATION RESCUE

Operation Rescue (OR) is an American antiabortion direct action organization. It describes itself on its Web site as "one of the leading pro-life Christian activist organizations in the nation" (OR-History). The Southern Poverty Law Center describes the organization as a "hard-line anti-abortion group" that has demanded criminal prosecution of Planned Parenthood officials (Potok 2015). Operation Rescue claims to engage in activities that are "on the cutting edge of the abortion issue, taking direct action to restore legal personhood to the pre-born and stop abortion in obedience to biblical mandates" (OR-History). Operation Rescue's tactics involves sit-in demonstrations to block the doors at abortion clinics and organizing and promoting large demonstrations at national events that will garner significant media attention. At the 1988 Democratic National Convention in Atlanta, Georgia, for example, over 1,200 OR members and supporters were arrested for disorderly conduct. Operation Rescue "also offers a $25,000 reward for reports of any criminal activity at abortion clinics that leads to a criminal conviction" (Operation Rescue 2010). Recently, Operation Rescue has been linked to the Center for Medical Progress (CMP), a group that has accused "Planned Parenthood of illegally selling body parts from aborted fetuses," allegations that were subsequently blamed for a spike in abortion clinic violence (Morlin 2017).

Operation Rescue was founded by Jeff White, but he stepped aside in 1999 after the organization was assessed an $880,000 judgment "for harassment and intimidation of Planned Parenthood doctors and staff. White turned the organization over to Troy Newman who moved the group's headquarters from California to Kansas in 2002, ostensibly to focus on a number of allegedly 'botched abortions' performed at Tiller's Women's Health Care Services, the practice of Dr. George Tiller," in Wichita, Kansas (Anonymous). Dr. Tiller was one of the few doctors in the United States at the time who performed late-term abortions. Over the course of several years, Operation Rescue harassed Dr. Tiller and his practice, even mobilizing support in the Kansas State Legislature to order the state's attorney general to reinstate misdemeanor charges that had been dismissed against Dr. Tiller. In September 2006, Operation Rescue had its tax-exempt status "revoked by the Internal Revenue Service (IRS) following charges of improper contributions, and illegal endorsements of political candidates" (Internal Revenue Service).

On May 31, 2009, Dr. Tiller was murdered by Scott Roeder while Dr. Tiller served as an usher at his church, the Reformation Lutheran Church of Wichita, Kansas (Stumpe and Davey 2009). Roeder had been associated with the Montana Freemen, an antigovernment group that opposed the overreach of the federal government. Roeder had been stopped in Topeka, Kansas, in 1996 for displaying a "Sovereign Citizen" plate "in lieu of a state-issued license plate" (AP 1996). He had no driver's license, proof of insurance, or vehicle registration. While searching his car, police "found explosive charges, a fuse cord, a pound of gunpowder and nine-volt batteries in his trunk" (AP 1996). Roeder was sentenced to probation, "but his probation was revoked a year later for failure to pay taxes and provide a social security number to his employer. It was later determined that Roeder was a member of the Sovereign Citizens Movement" (Anti-Defamation League).

Operation Rescue denounced Tiller's murder as "cowardly" and "antithetical to what we believe" (Stumpe and Davey 2009). OR's president, Troy Newman, categorically stated that Roeder had "never been a member, contributor, or volunteer with Operation Rescue" (Operation Rescue 2009). Roeder responded to Newman's claim by stating, "Well, my gosh. I've got probably a thousand dollars worth of receipts, at least, from the money I've donated to him" (Thomas 2009). Roeder also reportedly wrote a letter to Newman in which he said, "You better get your story straight, because my lawyer said it'd be good for me to show that I was supporting a pro-life organization" (Thomas 2009). Roeder was convicted in January 2010 of premeditated first-degree murder and sentenced to 50 years in prison. This sentence was later reduced to 25 years (AP 2016).

In 2015, the Center for Medical Progress, "which describes itself as a group of citizen journalists," produced videos in which it "accused Planned Parenthood of illegally selling body parts from aborted fetuses" (Potok 2015). The videos were criticized for deceptive editing, and the individuals associated with the production of the videos were charged with felony counts of eavesdropping and secretly recording conversations with Planned Parenthood representatives and other abortion providers (Morlin 2017). CMP has ties "to some of the hardest-line abortion extremists and groups associated with abortion clinic and provider violence" (Morlin 2017). Troy Newman, president of Operation Rescue, is a CMP board member. A whole array of fact-checking organizations could find "no evidence that Planned Parenthood had done anything wrong" (Potok 2015). Rather, CMP had "created a fake biomedical company for the sole purpose of trying to trap Planned Parenthood officials into selling body parts for profit, [and] had taken hours of undercover video and edited it down to eight- and nine-minute videos" (Potok 2015). As David S. Cohen, a law professor at Drexel University Thomas R. Kline School of Law, noted, "There's a direct connection between [Operation Rescue], the Center for Medical Progress and some of the worst characters in the anti-abortion extremist movement" (Potok 2015).

See also: Montana Freemen; Southern Poverty Law Center; Sovereign Citizens Movement

Further Reading

Anonymous. 2005. "Christin Alysabeth Gilbert Died from a Third-Trimester Abortion." *Justice for Christin.* http://www.justiceforchristin.com/ (Accessed May 26, 2017).

Anti-Defamation League. September 4, 2012. "Anti-Abortion Violence: America's Forgotten Terrorism." https://www.adl.org/news/article/anti-abortion-violence-americas-forgotten -terrorism (Accessed May 26, 2017).

AP. April 17, 1996. "Suspected Freeman Arrested with Bomb Fuse." *The Seattle Times.* http:// community.seattletimes.nwsource.com/archive/?date=19960417&slug=2324642 (Accessed May 26, 2017).

AP. November 23, 2016. "The Man Who Killed a Kansas Abortion Provider Has His Sentence Reduced." *Los Angeles Times.* http://www.latimes.com/nation/nationnow/la-na -kansas-trial-20161123-story.html (Accessed May 26, 2017).

Clarkson, Frederick. September 15, 1998. "Anti-Abortion Bombings Related." *Southern Poverty Law Center—Intelligence Report.* https://www.splcenter.org/fighting-hate/intel ligence-report/1998/anti-abortion-bombings-related (Accessed May 26, 2017).

Internal Revenue Service. "Recent Revocations of 501(c)(3) Determinations." https://web .archive.org/web/20070519024628/http://www.irs.gov/charities/charitable/article/0 ,,id=141466,00.html (Accessed May 26, 2017).

Morlin, Bill. April 3, 2017. "New Criminal Charges Filed Against Anti-Abortion Activists." *Southern Poverty Law Center—Hatewatch*. https://www.splcenter.org/hatewatch/2017 /04/03/new-criminal-charges-filed-against-anti-abortion-activists (Accessed May 26, 2017).

Operation Rescue. January 14, 2010. "Abortion Whistleblowers—Earn a $25,000 Reward." http://www.operationrescue.org/archives/abortion-whistleblowers-earn-a-10000-reward/ (Accessed May 26, 2017).

Operation Rescue. June 1, 2009. "Operation Rescue Statement Regarding Suspect in Tiller Killing." http://www.operationrescue.org/archives/operation-rescue-statement-regarding -suspect-in-tiller-killing/ (Accessed May 26, 2017).

Operation Rescue. http://www.operationrescue.org/ (Accessed May 26, 2017).

OR-History. "Who We Are." *Operation Rescue*. http://www.operationrescue.org/about-us/who -we-are/ (Accessed May 26, 2017).

Potok, Mark. August 31, 2015. "Group Attacking Planned Parenthood Linked to Extremists." *Southern Poverty Law Center—Hatewatch*. https://www.splcenter.org/hatewatch/2015 /08/31/group-attacking-planned-parenthood-linked-extremists (Accessed May 26, 2017).

Stumpe, Joe and Monica Davey. May 31, 2009. "Abortion Doctor Shot to Death in Kansas Church." *The New York Times*. http://www.nytimes.com/2009/06/01/us/01tiller.html ?_r=1&pagewanted=all& (Accessed May 26, 2017).

Thomas, Judy L. July 26, 2009. "Roeder Upset at Operation Rescue." *The Wichita Eagle*. http://www.kansas.com/news/special-reports/article1009125.html (Accessed May 26, 2017).

THE ORDER

The Order, also known as Bruder Schweigen (German for "brothers keep silent") or the Silent Brotherhood, was "one the most violent and notorious domestic terror groups in the United States during 1983 and 1984" (Balleck 2015). The group took its name from the infamous neo-Nazi novel *The Turner Diaries*, written by William Luther Pierce, founder of the United States' then-largest neo-Nazi organization, the National Alliance. The Order's founder, Robert (Bob) Jay Mathews, was a tax protestor in the 1970s who cultivated his white supremacist ties through his associations in Aryan Nations and the National Alliance. In late September 1983, "Mathews and eight other men—some neo-Nazis and others participants in the racist Christian Identity movement—took an oath to protect the white race and work toward an all-white homeland in the Pacific Northwest of the United States" (Egan). Over the course of 15 months, from October 1983 to December 1984, The Order engaged in counterfeiting, bank robbery, and armored car heists, netting the group some $4 million. The Order is most infamous for the assassination of Jewish radio talk show host Alan Berg, who was brutally gunned down by members of the group in his driveway in Denver, Colorado, in June 1984 (Egan). The Order would effectively disappear after a member of the organization was arrested for counterfeiting and turned informant for the Federal Bureau of Investigation (FBI). This led to a confrontation with several members of the group and the eventual death in December 1984 of founder Bob Mathews when he confronted FBI agents in a standoff on Whidbey Island in Washington state. A year after Mathews's death, "nine men and one woman—all members of the group—were convicted of rack-eteering and other charges" and "sentenced to terms of 40–100 years in prison" (Nizkor Project). The group continues to inspire right-wing and antigovernment extremists, and the racist, whites-only message of The Order lives on in many contemporary extremist groups.

In late September 1983, Bob Mathews and eight other men met at Mathews's home in Metaline Falls, Washington, and swore an oath to each other to wage war against the American government. To demonstrate the solemnity of the oath, they placed one of the men's six-week-old baby in the middle of a circle that they formed as a symbol of what was at stake (i.e., the white race). The assembled individuals took their name, The Order, from William Pierce's dystopian novel *The Turner Diaries*, in which a group known as "The Order determines to use violence and crime in order to destabilize the U.S. government and establish a whites-only society" (History Commons). The Order was determined to bring about the downfall of the government as it believed that it had fallen under the control of a cabal of prominent Jews and that this organization controlled the political and economic workings of the country as well as all media. Referred to by Order members as the Zionist Occupation Government (ZOG), members of The Order swore to use crime and violence to destabilize the government, to assassinate race traitors, and to wage a guerilla war of sabotage against the government until their goal of a whites-only homeland could be realized. Much of what Mathews envisioned for the group had already been suggested in *The Turner Diaries*.

To finance the group, "members of The Order turned to crime. They initially targeted pimps, drug dealers, and anybody else that they judged had no morals" (Egan). Although they made off with tens of thousands of dollars, it was insufficient to bankroll the revolution they envisioned. The group later turned to counterfeiting, but they also experienced limited success in this area.

Frustrated that the group seemed to not be making any progress, Mathews robbed a bank north of Seattle, Washington, in December 1983 and made off with over $26,000 (History Commons). In March 1984, the group perpetrated a robbery on an armored car, which netted them $43,000. A month later, The Order hijacked another armored car, this time securing $536,000, though $500,000 of the money was in checks and useless to the group (History Commons).

On May 27, 1984, members of The Order, on the directive of Bob Mathews, murdered Aryan Nations member Walter West after Mathews learned that a drunken West had been bragging about The Order's exploits "in and around Hayden Lake, Idaho, the location of Aryan Nations' compound" (History Commons). Less than a month later, The Order would commit their most notorious murder when members of the group machine-gunned Jewish talk show host Alan Berg to death in the driveway of his Denver, Colorado, home. Berg was targeted by the group because of his style of confronting anti-Semites and right-wing extremists who frequently called in to his radio show to verbally spar with Berg. Berg's Jewish heritage, and his vitriol toward white supremacists and extremism, earned him a spot on The Order's "hit list," a list that also included Southern Poverty Law Center founder Morris Dees, television producer Norman Lear, and a Kansas federal judge (Balleck

2015). Berg was killed on the evening of June 14, 1984, as he exited his car in his driveway. Order member Bruce Pierce pumped 12 or 13 shots into Berg's face and body from his .45 caliber MAC-10 submachine gun before jumping into a getaway car and speeding away with three other accomplices.

The next day, June 19, 1984, other members of The Order committed another armed car robbery near Ukiah, California. The group stopped the armored car and took over $3.6 million in the heist. In the confusion of the robbery, however, Mathews dropped a registered gun that quickly led the FBI to determine who they were looking for. Within a week, a member of The Order, Tom Martinez, was arrested in Pennsylvania for passing counterfeit bills printed by the group. Upon questioning by federal authorities, Martinez cut a deal to inform on the group in exchange for a more lenient sentence. As the federal government built its case against Mathews and other members of The Order, three FBI agents engaged Order member Gary Yarborough outside of his home on his wooded Idaho property. Yarborough escaped, but the agents found in Yarborough's home a large collection of material related to The Order's crimes, including a cache of weapons that included the MAC-10 used to kill Denver radio host Alan Berg (History Commons).

FBI informant Tom Martinez agreed to draw Mathews out, and he met with Mathews and other members of The Order in a motel room near Portland, Oregon, in November 1984. Mathews, sensing a trap, engaged in a gun battle with the FBI but escaped. Gary Yarborough, who had been with Mathews, was captured. Mathews fled to a home he had on Whidbey Island in Oregon. There he penned a four-page "Declaration of War" against the United States, which read in part,

> Throughout this land our children are being coerced into accepting nonwhites for their idols, their companions, and worst of all for their mates. A course which has taken us straight to oblivion. Yet our people do not see. Not by accident but by design these terrible things have come to pass. It is self-evident to all who have eyes to see that an evil shadow has fallen across our once fair land. Evidence abounds that a certain, vile, alien people have taken control of our country. How is it that a parasite has gained dominion over its host? Instead of being vigilant our fathers have slept.
>
> ...
>
> We now close this Declaration with an open letter to congress and our signatures confirming our intent to do battle. Let friend and foe alike be made aware: This Is War! We the following of sound body and mind under no duress, do hereby sign this document of our own free will, stating forthrightfully and without fear that we declare ourselves to be in a full and unrelenting state of war with those forces seeking and consciously promoting the destruction of our Faith and our Race. Therefore, for Blood, Soil and Honor, and for the future of our children, we commit ourselves to battle. Amen. (The Order)

On December 7, 1984, FBI agents cornered Mathews in his home on Whidbey Island. Mathews, who was heavily armed, barricaded himself inside his home and engaged in sporadic gunfire with the 150 agents who had him surrounded. After 35 hours of fruitless negotiation, the FBI fired "three M-79 Starburst illumination flares into the home, hoping that the house will catch fire and drive Mathews out. Instead, Mathews either chooses to remain inside the house, or is unable to leave. He dies in the flames" (History Commons). A year later, most of the members of The Order were in jail or awaiting trial.

The Order's brief but destructive reign of terror galvanized an emerging antigovernment movement, and the group's belief in ZOG and its rhetoric encouraging whites to purge the United States of immigrants and nonwhite peoples was taken up with renewed zeal by groups such as Aryan Nations and the National Alliance. Order member David Lane would articulate the essence of The Order's racist mantra by pronouncing the 14 Words, the motto of the racist, extremist right: "We must secure the existence of our people and a future for white children" (Southern Poverty Law Center). Lane would die in prison after being sentenced to 190 years for the crimes he committed while a member of The Order. But Lane's influence, and that of The Order, would be felt for years to come in the world of antigovernment extremists, inspiring the likes of Timothy McVeigh, the Oklahoma City bomber (Anti-Defamation League).

See also: Aryan Nations; Christian Identity; Fourteen Words; Lane, David; Mathews, Bob; National Alliance; Neo-Nazis; Pierce, William; *Turner Diaries, The*; White Nationalism; White Supremacist Movement

Further Reading

Anti-Defamation League. "The Order." https://www.adl.org/education/references/hate-symbols/the-order (Accessed June 6, 2017).

Balleck, Barry J. 2015. *Allegiance to Liberty: The Changing Face of Patriots, Militias, and Political Violence in America*. Praeger.

Egan, Nancy. "The Order: American White Supremacist Group." *Encyclopedia Britannica*. https://www.britannica.com/topic/The-Order (Accessed June 6, 2017).

History Commons. "U.S. Domestic Terrorism: The Order." http://www.historycommons.org/timeline.jsp?timeline=us_domestic_terrorism_tmln&haitian_elite_2021_organizations=us_domestic_terrorism_tmln_the_order (Accessed June 6, 2017).

Nizkor Project. "Paranoia as Patriotism: Far Right Influences on the Militia Movement." http://www.nizkor.org/hweb/orgs/american/adl/paranoia-as-patriotism/the-order.html (Accessed June 6, 2017).

The Order. "Declaration of War." *Mourning the Ancient*. http://www.mourningtheancient.com/mathews2.htm (Accessed June 6, 2017).

Southern Poverty Law Center. "David Lane." https://www.splcenter.org/fighting-hate/extremist-files/individual/david-lane (Accessed June 6, 2017).

ORLANDO NIGHTCLUB SHOOTING

The Orlando nightclub shooting occurred at Pulse, a gay nightclub in Orlando, Florida, on June 12, 2016. Omar Mateen, a 29-year-old American-born Muslim, perpetrated the attacks, killing 49 people and wounding 53 others. At the time, the shooting "was the deadliest mass shooting in U.S. history by a single shooter and also the deadliest incident of violence against LGBT people in United States history" (Shapiro and Frizell 2016). During the shootings, and in the three-hour standoff that followed between Mateen and local and federal law enforcement, Mateen "made a 911 call in which he pledged allegiance to the Islamic States of Iraq and Syria (ISIS) and called the Boston Marathon Bombers his 'home boys'" (Visser and Cowels 2016). Mateen claimed that he had initiated the shootings because of U.S. bombing campaigns in the Middle East, but acquaintances of Mateen's stated that he had talked about killing people and that he had used racial slurs and "had a lot of hatred for people. Black people, women, he did not like Jews, he did not like Hispanics, nor did he like gay or lesbian people" (Times of Israel 2016). Though Mateen had been investigated by the Federal Bureau of Investigation (FBI) for possible ties to other domestic terrorists, such as Nidal Hasan, the 2009 Fort Hood shooter, or the Tsarnaev brothers, the perpetrators of the Boston Marathon bombing, the FBI found no credible connections to either of these domestic terror events. FBI director James Comey believed that Mateen was a "lone wolf" who had been radicalized through the Internet as there "was no indication that this was a plot directed from outside the United States and we see no indication that he was part of any kind of network" (Shabad 2016). The shooting was viewed as "both an act of domestic terrorism and a hate crime" because it targeted the LGBT community. The shooting also reignited the ongoing debate about gun control in the United States. On June 15, 2016, just three days after the shootings, Senator Chris Murphy (D-CT) launched a nearly 15-hour filibuster in the U.S. Senate, promising to hold the Senate floor "for as long as I can" or "until Congress acts on gun control legislation" (Walsh and LoBianco 2016).

On the evening of June 11, 2016, the Pulse nightclub was hosting Latin Night, an event that drew mostly Hispanics to the club. About 320 people were in the nightclub when Mateen entered the club after "last call" drinks were being served at about 2:00 a.m. Mateen was armed with a semiautomatic rifle and "a 9mm Glock semi-automatic pistol" (Jansen 2016). During the shooting, many people contacted the outside world via text or telephone calls. Within 45 minutes of the commencement of the shootings, more than 100 law enforcement officers were outside the nightclub. About 15 to 20 minutes into the shooting, Mateen "went from an active shooter to a barricaded gunman" and had hostages (Barry 2016). At 2:45 a.m., "Mateen called *News 13* of Orlando and said, 'I'm the shooter. It's me. I am the shooter.' He then said he was carrying out the shooting on behalf of ISIS and began speaking rapidly in Arabic" (Miller 2016).

As Mateen remained holed up in the club, a crisis negotiator was called in to speak with him. The negotiator spoke with Mateen three times during the standoff, and Mateen claimed that he had bombs strapped to him and also that his "vehicle in the parking lot had enough explosives to take out a city block" (Hayes et al. 2017). At 5:07 a.m., SWAT officers stormed the building and confronted Mateen, using flashbangs to distract him. Mateen was shot eight times by "eleven officers who fired a total of about 150 bullets" (Doornbos 2016). By 5:53 a.m., Orlando declared that the scene was secure and the shooter was dead (Stapleton 2016).

Memorial for shooting victims outside of the Pulse nightclub in Orlando, Florida. On June 12, 2016, Omar Mateen, claiming allegiance to the Islamic State of Iraq and Syria (ISIS), attacked the Pulse nightclub, killing 49 people and wounding more than 50. (JCPJR Photography/ Dreamstime)

Fifty people, including Mateen, died in the shootings, and another 53 were injured, some critically (Barry 2016). In the aftermath of the shooting, the usual condemnations were expressed by various groups, including civic and community groups; local, state, and national politicians; and even international organizations, such as the United Nations Security Council, "which issued a statement condemning the shooting for targeting persons as a result of their sexual orientation." The statement "was even supported by some countries that suppress homosexual behavior and discussion, such as Egypt and Russia" (Sengupta 2016).

After Orlando, a study by *The Washington Post* noted that while gun ownership is declining overall in the United States, mass killings have increased in recent years "with half of the 12 deadliest shootings in the United States happening after 2007" (Ehrenfreund 2016). Other findings indicated that even with the increase in shootings, support for gun rights remains steadfast in the United States. The study indicated that the United States is a clear outlier in the number of gun deaths experienced per year, with deaths in the United States "nearly twice that of any other OECD (Organization of Economic Cooperation and Development) country." In the United States, "the South is the most violent region with gun deaths above that of any other region of the country" (Ehrenfreund 2016). Though Orlando was one of several high-profile mass shootings from 2012–2016, "less than half of Americans, 47%, say they favor stricter laws covering the sale of firearms" (Ehrenfreund 2016). Much of this can be attributed to the affinity that Americans have toward gun ownership rights, believing it to be a sacrosanct right of Americans enshrined by the Second Amendment to the Constitution.

See also: Boston Marathon Bombing; Fort Hood Shooting; Second Amendment

Further Reading
Barry, Dan. June 20, 2016. "Realizing It's a Small, Terrifying World After All." *The New York Times*. https://www.nytimes.com/2016/06/21/us/orlando-shooting-america.html?rref=collection%2Fnewseventcollection%2F2016-orlando-shooting&action=click&contentCollection=us&region=rank&module=package&version=highlights&contentPlacement=1&pgtype=collection&_r=0 (Accessed June 3, 2017).

BBC. June 15, 2016. "Orlando Nightclub Shooting: How the Attack Unfolded." *BBC News*. http://www.bbc.com/news/world-us-canada-36511778 (Accessed June 3, 2017).

Doornbos, Caitlin. August 5, 2016. "Autopsy: Pulse Shooter Omar Mateen Shot Eight Times." *Orlando Sentinel*. http://www.orlandosentinel.com/news/pulse-orlando-nightclub-shooting/omar-mateen/os-pulse-shooting-mateen-autopsy-20160805-story.html (Accessed June 13, 2017).

Ehrenfreund, Max. June 12, 2016. "Orlando Shooting: The Key Things to Know About Guns and Mass Shootings in America." *The Washington Post*. https://www.washingtonpost.com/news/wonk/wp/2016/06/12/orlando-shooting-the-key-things-to-know-about-about-guns-and-mass-shootings-in-america/?utm_term=.6daafdff3973 (Accessed June 3, 2017).

Ellis, Ralph, Ashley Fantz, Faith Karimi, and Eliott C. McLaughlin. June 13, 2016. "Orlando Shooting: 49 Killed, Shooter Pledged ISIS Allegiance." *CNN*. http://www.cnn.com/2016/06/12/us/orlando-nightclub-shooting/ (Accessed June 3, 2017).

Hayes, Christal, David Harris, Gal Tziperman Lotan, and Caitlin Doornbos. April 13, 2017. "New Pulse Review from Orlando Police Reveals Details, Lessons Learned." *Orlando Sentinel*. http://www.orlandosentinel.com/news/pulse-orlando-nightclub-shooting/os-pulse-presentation-orlando-police-20170412-story.html (Accessed June 3, 2017).

Jansen, Bart. June 15, 2016. "Weapons Gunman Used in Orlando Shooting Are High Capacity, Common." *USA Today*. https://www.usatoday.com/story/news/2016/06/14/guns-used-kill-49-orlando-high-capacity-common-weapons/85887260/ (Accessed January 30, 2018).

Miller, Michael E. June 15, 2016. "'I'm the Shooter. It's Me:' Gunman Called Local TV Station During Attack, Station Says." *The Washington Post*. https://www.washingtonpost.com/news/morning-mix/wp/2016/06/15/im-the-shooter-its-me-gunman-called-local-tv-station-during-attack-station-says/?utm_term=.ba40ee30bfba (Accessed June 3, 2017).

Sengupta, Somini. June 14, 2016. "After Orlando, Gay Rights Moves Off Diplomatic Back Burner." *The New York Times*. https://www.nytimes.com/2016/06/15/world/united-nations-gay-rights-diplomacy.html (Accessed June 3, 2017).

Shabad, Rebecca. June 13, 2016. "FBI Director Comey: 'Highly Confident' Orlando Shooter Radicalized Through Internet." *CBS News*. http://www.cbsnews.com/news/fbi-director-comey-highly-confident-orlando-shooter-radicalized-through-internet/ (Accessed June 3, 2017).

Shapiro, Julie and Sam Frizell. June 12, 2016. "Orlando Nightclub Attack Was Deadliest Mass Shooting in U.S. History." *Time*. http://time.com/4365325/orlando-shooting-pulse-nightclub-deadliest-history/ (Accessed August 5, 2017).

Stapleton, AnneClaire. July 17, 2016. "Timeline of Orlando Nightclub Shooting." *CNN*. http://www.cnn.com/2016/06/12/us/orlando-shooting-timeline/ (Accessed June 3, 2017).

Times of Israel. June 13, 2016. "Ex-Coworker: Orlando Shooter an 'Unhinged Racist Misogynist.'" http://www.timesofisrael.com/ex-coworker-orlando-shooter-an-unhinged-racist-misogynist/ (Accessed June 3, 2017).

Visser, Steve and John Couwels. September 24, 2016. "Orlando Killer Repeatedly Referenced ISIS, Transcript Shows." *CNN*. http://www.cnn.com/2016/09/23/us/orlando-shooter-hostage-negotiator-call/index.html (Accessed June 3, 2017).

Walsh, Deirdre and Tom LoBianco. June 16, 2016. "Nearly 15 Hours Later, Democratic Senator Ends Filibuster Over Guns." *CNN*. http://edition.cnn.com/2016/06/15/politics/gun-filibuster-senate-democrat/ (Accessed June 3, 2017).

PAPER TERRORISM

"Paper terrorism" is a term used to describe tactics employed by members of the sovereign citizens movement against those they dislike, most often government officials. In such cases, "sovereign citizens" use "laws" as weapons by filing false tax liens against their victims, false tax documents, or frivolous lawsuits. The irony of such filings is that sovereigns themselves generally believe that the judicial system is illegitimate and the federal government is a "usurper" that has taken over the lives of average Americans (Laird 2014). Sovereign citizens are likely to believe in "common-law courts," and therefore do not recognize their obligation to pay federal taxes, obtain driver's licences, pull over their cars for police, or "obey any other law they don't like" (Laird 2014). Paper terrorism has become so prevalent in some states that the Federal Bureau of Investigation (FBI) has labeled the activities of the sovereign citizen movement as domestic terrorism and have begun devoting more resources to fighting back against such groups (Southern Poverty Law Center).

Sovereign citizens generally do not recognize any government authority beyond the local level. While some sovereign citizens have resorted to violence, many use paper terrorism to make life miserable for their targets while at the same time clogging up the court system, which sovereigns generally despise. As noted by the American Bar Association,

> When involved in any legal matter, from pet licensing to serious criminal charges, sovereigns are known for filing legal-sounding gibberish, usually pro se, learned from other sovereigns who sell lessons in "law" online. Frequently, they cite the Uniform Commercial Code, maritime law and the Bible.
>
> They're also known for the sheer volume of their filings, which can double the size of a normal docket. This can frustrate and delay courts as they consider the defendant's competence and otherwise try to minimize disruptions. With many court systems fighting heavy caseloads and budget cuts, these extra headaches are unwelcome. (Laird 2014)

In addition to using government courts, some sovereigns use "their own common law courts where public officials may be tried in absentia" (Pitcavage 1998). The crimes of which public officials are accused in these courts are generally related to some vague notion of "treason" against the U.S. Constitution and the people of the United States. However, when sentences of death are publicly announced by such courts, they constitute a very real threat to the government officials who have been targeted.

Though the raft of court filings that constitute paper terrorism are bogus, states must sort through what is legitimate and illegitimate in each case. This can take months, cost hundreds of thousands if not millions of dollars, and further slow down an already overcrowded judicial docket. States are now fighting back by passing laws enacting tougher penalties against such filings that will "serve as a deterrent." In New York, for example, "a bill would 'ensure that appropriate punishments and deterrents exist in relation to the malicious filing of false or fictitious liens against . . . police officers and elected officials,' by making filing them a felony." The "punishment would be a fine of $10,000 per filing and up to a year in prison" (Rayfield 2013). Georgia, too, passed a law that "made it a crime to file false liens," imposing fines up to $10,000 and prison sentences of 1 to 10 years (Southern Poverty Law Center).

Those who have engaged in paper terrorism have learned the techniques through "sovereign citizen gurus who offer online instructions or paid seminars around the country" (Southern Poverty Law Center). One couple, later convicted of using paper terrorism tactics, claimed that they had received coaching from a learned sovereign citizen who taught them what was called "death by a thousand paper cuts" (Goode 2013). According to the couple, they acted out of frustration as they attempted to "fight back against corrupt banks that had handed off the couple's mortgage time after time and whose top executives never faced consequences for their actions" (Goode 2013). Frustration is frequently the mind-set of sovereign citizens, who wish to reclaim a sense of control that they believe has slipped away from them because of governmental action, or, in some cases, inaction.

See also: Common-Law Court Movement; Monkeywrenching; Posse Comitatus; Sovereign Citizens Movement

Further Reading

Chamberlain, Robert and Donald P. Haider-Markel. September 2005. "Lien on Me: State Policy Innovation in Response to Paper Terrorism." *Political Research Quarterly* 58, no. 3, 449–460.

Goode, Erica. August 23, 2013. "In Paper War, Flood of Liens Is the Weapon." *The New York Times.* http://www.nytimes.com/2013/08/24/us/citizens-without-a-country-wage -battle-with-liens.html (Accessed December 13, 2016).

Laird, Lorelei. May 2, 2014. "'Sovereign Citizens' Plaster Courts with Bogus Legal Filings—and Some Turn to Violence." *ABA Journal.* http://www.abajournal.com/magazine/article/sover eign_citizens_plaster_courts_with_bogus_legal_filings/ (Accessed December 13, 2016).

Pitcavage, Mark. June 29, 1998. "Paper Terrorism's Forgotten Victims: The Use of Bogus Liens Against Private Individuals and Businesses." *Anti-Defamation League.*

Rayfield, Jillian. May 19, 2013. "Growing, Lurking Threat: 'Paper Terrorism.'" *Salon.* http:// www.salon.com/2013/05/19/why_you_should_fear_paper_terrorism/ (Accessed December 13, 2016).

Southern Poverty Law Center. May 25, 2012. "Georgia Bill Attacks 'Paper Terrorism' as FBI Takes Aim at 'Sovereigns.'" *Southern Poverty Law Center—Intelligence Report.* https://www.splcenter.org/fighting-hate/intelligence-report/2012/georgia-bill-attacks -%E2%80%98paper-terrorism%E2%80%99-fbi-takes-aim-%E2%80%98sovereigns %E2%80%99 (Accessed December 13, 2016).

PATRIOT MOVEMENT

The patriot movement is an eclectic collection of groups and individuals who tend to be politically conservative, rural, small-government advocates who agitate to curb what they believe is the pernicious overreach of federal power that has existed since at least the 1950s (Balleck 2015). The patriot movement today includes militia members, tax protestors, sovereign citizens, "quasi-Christian apocalyptic/survivalists," and several combinations of these groups (Abanes 1996). Adherents of the patriot movement believe that individual liberties and fealty to constitutional processes are under assault by a federal government that is increasingly extending its power, despite protestations by the people, and is out of touch with the will of Americans. Patriots often view government officials, bureaucrats, and special interests as accumulating power in contravention to the founding documents of the American republic and intentions of the Founding Fathers. In many cases, however, "patriots" overlay their own interpretations and prejudices onto the actions of the federal government, supposing that such actions are contrary to the intentions of the Constitution and those of the founders. Assuming that they are the keepers of the "true" interpretation of the limits of power established by the Constitution, patriots ascribe actions they view as contrary to this interpretation to evil or malicious intention. A hallmark of the patriot movement is a predilection for conspiracy theories and a dogged insistence that the government intends to subvert the liberties of the people and bring them into submission (Balleck 2015). Adherents of the patriot movement are often associated with right-wing militia groups, antigovernment activities, or other sentiments that put them at odds with the current social and political climate. Law enforcement officials have come to view many in the patriot movement as "dangerous, delusional and sometimes violent" (Sullivan 2016).

The modern patriot movement has its roots in changing social and political forces of the 1950s and 1960s. The rise of the United Nations, the anticommunism fervor fueled by the John Birch Society, and the civil rights movement all led to an upheaval among American citizens who longed for an idealized conception of the past. The rapid social changes that occurred during the 1960s caused many conservatives to believe that American values were under assault. Traditional interpretations of what was "American" were challenged during this time, and the rapid rise of modernity (the ever-changing nature of the social, economic, and political climate) in which citizens found themselves necessitated either a radical adaptation or a radical reinterpretation of events. In the case of the patriot, reinterpretation prevailed over adaptation, and "theories" of various kinds were constructed or reimagined to resolve the dissonance.

One such conspiracy theory was that of the New World Order. On September 11, 1990, President George H. W. Bush used the term "new world order" in describing the post–Cold War world. Many "patriots" saw this as a "slip of the tongue revealing secret plans to create a one-world government" under the guise of the United Nations (Southern Poverty Law Center, Timeline). The United Nations was a focal point for patriots and antigovernment conspiracists who believed that the New World Order was embodied in a plan called "Agenda 21," a secret plan to take away citizens' property rights. In fact, Agenda 21 was a UN program meant to develop sustainable communities around the world (Southern Poverty Law Center).

Other notable conspiracies found in the patriot movement and among anti-government adherents included the "idea that the U.S. government was secretly planning to round up citizens and place them in concentration camps" run by the Federal Emergency Management Agency (Southern Poverty Law Center, Anti-Government Movement). Another theory stated "that the North American Free Trade Agreement, or NAFTA, was a prelude to merging the United States, Canada, and Mexico into one country" (Southern Poverty Law Center, Anti-Government Movement). Fears that a strengthened federal government would push gun control legislation and even engage in weapons confiscation also drove the patriot movement.

For patriots, a world that had once been clearly defined by an us-versus-them mentality (i.e., United States versus Soviet Union and democracy versus communism) was suddenly upended with the end of the Cold War. Patriots feared what an unchecked federal government might do to curb the liberties and freedoms of American citizens. Subsequent events validated some of these fears. In August 1992, white supremacist and antigovernment agitator Randy Weaver engaged in an 11-day standoff at his cabin in Ruby Ridge, Idaho. The standoff ended after Weaver's wife and son, as well as a U.S. marshal, were killed. Weaver had evaded federal authorities on weapons charges and had holed up in his heavily armed compound at Ruby Ridge. Just six months later, four agents of the Bureau of Alcohol, Tobacco, and Firearms (ATF) were killed when the group raided the Branch Davidian compound in Waco, Texas. Many Branch Davidians were killed as well. The ATF had gone to the compound to serve warrants on the belief that the Branch Davidians, and their leader David Koresh, were stockpiling weapons in preparation for the apocalypse or a showdown with the federal government. After a 51-day standoff, nearly 80 Branch Davidians died when the Federal Bureau of Investigation tried "to end the standoff by injecting tear gas into the building" where the Branch Davidians were hunkered down. The building burst into flames, and all who remained in the building perished.

Both Ruby Ridge and Waco galvanized the patriot and militia movements. Terry Nichols, who would later "be convicted of conspiracy in the Oklahoma City bombing, renounced his U.S. citizenship and announced that he would only adhere to 'common law,'" while the actual bomber of Oklahoma City, Timothy McVeigh, would state that the Waco standoff was a primary motivation in his retaliation against a federal government that had run amok and was no longer responsive to the will of the American people (Southern Poverty Law Center 2010). McVeigh's "bombing of the Alfred P. Murrah Federal Building in Oklahoma City, Oklahoma on April 19, 1995 killed 168 people, including 19 children" (Balleck 2015). McVeigh's attack on the Oklahoma City federal building was inspired by *The Turner Diaries*, an antigovernment fantasy novel in which government officials and other "enemies of the people" are rounded up and executed. McVeigh's actions closely resemble similar actions by antigovernment "patriots" in *The Turner Diaries* (Southern Poverty Law Center, Timeline).

Patriots' fear that an unchecked government would impose gun control was partially realized when the Brady Bill, which imposed a waiting period for handgun purchases, was signed into law by President Bill Clinton in November 1993. On January 1, 1994, "the first modern militia, the Militia of Montana, was founded by John Trochmann, a supporter of Randy Weaver" (Southern Poverty Law Center, Timeline). Over the next several years, dozens of patriot, militia, and other antigovernment groups would form in response to the perception that the federal government was intent on destroying individual freedoms and liberties.

The patriot movement, and other antigovernment groups associated with it, reached a zenith in 1996 when the Southern Poverty Law Center identified 858 antigovernment "patriot" groups. This number would drop to 194 groups by the end of Bill Clinton's presidency and would never rise above 171 during the presidential administration of George W. Bush, whose policies were viewed more favorably by those on the conservative right (Southern Poverty Law Center).

The antigovernment and patriot movements would experience a resurgence with the election of Barack Obama in 2008. As the first African American elected to the U.S. presidency, Obama faced opposition from traditional white supremacist and other racist groups that resented a black man in the country's highest office. Coupled with several other factors, including the rise of social media, "anger over major political, demographic and economic changes in America, as well as the popularization of radical ideas and conspiracy theories" perpetrated in the political and media mainstream, the patriot movement experienced an astonishing comeback during Obama's two terms in office (Southern Poverty Law Center, Timeline). Indeed, at the beginning of Obama's first term in early 2009, there were 149 "patriot" groups identified by the Southern Poverty Law Center. By 2012, near the end of his first term, there were 1,360 (Southern Poverty Law Center, Timeline). The reasons for this phenomenal increase were traced to fears of a collapse of the American economy as a result of the Great Recession of 2008, the stress of globalization on the traditional sense of the American self, the perceived loss of individual rights and economic opportunities, the animus toward Obama, the fear and distrust of a runaway government, and, perhaps most significantly, racial prejudice (Jansen 2012).

The perception that Barack Obama was not born a citizen of the United States, a conspiracy theory whose flame was fanned by conservative media outlets, social media, and right-wing pundits who hated Obama's policies, reinforced many patriots' distrust of Obama. During Obama's second term, the number of "patriot" groups subsided, reaching 623 in 2016 (Southern Poverty Law Center, Timeline). The number continues to fall as Obama's successor, Donald Trump, is seen as being far more amenable to patriot concerns.

The prevailing sense among patriots today is that the federal government ignores the Constitution and engages in the "systematic abuse of land rights, gun rights, freedom of speech, and other liberties," and this galvanizes the movement and infuses it with new recruits (Sullivan 2016). Many patriots feel that they must prepare themselves for the inevitable confrontation between law-abiding American citizens (themselves) intent on preserving their inherent rights and freedoms and an unresponsive, tyrannical government that has lost its way.

See also: John Birch Society; Militia of Montana; Ruby Ridge; Southern Poverty Law Center; *Turner Diaries, The*; Waco Standoff; Weaver, Randy

Further Reading

Abanes, Richard. 1996. *American Militias: Rebellion, Racism & Religion*. Inter Varsity Press.

Balleck, Barry J. 2015. *Allegiance to Liberty: The Changing Face of Patriots, Militias, and Political Violence in America*. Praeger.

Jansen, Patrick. March 8, 2012. "Right-Wing 'Patriot' Groups Girding for Actual Class Warfare, Report Says." *The Christian Science Monitor*. http://www.csmonitor.com/USA /2012/0308/Right-wing-patriot-groups-girding-for-actual-class-warfare-report-says (Accessed May 16, 2017).

Southern Poverty Law Center. "Antigovernment Movement." https://www.splcenter.org/fight ing-hate/extremist-files/ideology/antigovernment (Accessed May 16, 2017).

Southern Poverty Law Center. "The 'Patriot' Movement Timeline." *Southern Poverty Law Center—Intelligence Report*. https://www.splcenter.org/fighting-hate/intelligence-report /2015/patriot-movement-timeline (Accessed May 16, 2017).

Southern Poverty Law Center. May 20, 2010. "Meet the Patriots." *Southern Poverty Law Center—Intelligence Report*. https://www.splcenter.org/fighting-hate/intelligence-report /2010/meet-patriots (Accessed May 16, 2017).

Sullivan, Kevin. May 21, 2016. "Primed to Fight the Government: A Fast-Growing U.S. Movement Armed with Guns and the Constitution Sees a Dire Threat to Liberty." *The Washington Post*. http://www.washingtonpost.com/sf/national/2016/05/21/armed-with -guns-and-constitutions-the-patriot-movement-sees-america-under-threat/?utm_term =.fe981574ff72 (Accessed May 16, 2017).

Wilson, Jason. May 10, 2016. "The Rise of Militias: Patriot Candidates Are Now Getting Elected in Oregon." *The Guardian*. https://www.theguardian.com/us-news/2016 /may/10/patriot-movement-oregon-militias-donald-trump-election-2016 (Accessed May 16, 2017).

PEARSON, ROGER

Roger Pearson (b. 1927) is a retired British anthropologist who throughout his career has been a fierce advocate of "Aryan" racial superiority. He is the editor of *Mankind Quarterly*, which regularly publishes articles that purport to demonstrate the link between race and intelligence. Pearson believes in racial isolation, meaning that "interbreeding" between "higher" and "lower" races will result in the "devolution" of the more "highly evolved" race (Southern Poverty Law Center). Pearson stated in 1957 in *Northern World* magazine, a publication dedicated to Pan-Nordic solidarity and racial segregation: "If a nation with a more advanced, more specialized, or in any way superior set of genes mingles with, instead of exterminating, an inferior tribe, then it commits racial suicide, and destroys the work of thousands of years of biological isolation and natural selection" (Pearson 1996). Pearson has maintained ties to various Nazi and neo-Nazi groups and individuals and has been a major recipient of grants from the Pioneer Fund, an organization devoted to supporting the research of individuals purporting to find scientific "proof" that racial differences account for differences in intelligence (Southern Poverty Law Center).

Pearson believes that those of Nordic descent stand on top of the evolutionary scale. As such, he argues against miscegenation—the interbreeding of people of different races. As Pearson contends, "Those who are unfit can improve their prospects only by intermarriage with those who are fit. Those who are fit can suitably destroy their own prospects by marriage with those who are unfit" (Pearson 1966).

In 1958, Pearson founded the Northern League for Northern European Friendship, a "Pan-Nordic cultural organization dedicated to convincing Northern Europeans to recognize 'their common problems and their common destiny,' and to come to an appreciation . . . of the threat of biological extinction with which we [Nordics] are threatened" (Southern Poverty Law Center). From 1966 to 1967, Pearson teamed up with well-known anti-Semite Willis Carto to "explore every aspect of the Jewish Question" (Southern Poverty Law Center). Writing in the short-lived publication known as the *New Patriot*, and under the pseudonym "Stephan Langton," Pearson published such articles as "Zionists and the Plot Against South Africa," "Early Jews and the Rise of Jewish Money Power," and "Swindlers of the Crematoria" (Michael 2008). In 1978, Pearson took over the editorship of the journal *Mankind Quarterly*, which has been described as the "journal of scientific racism" (Leech 2005). In the same year, Pearson was elected "World Chairman of the World Anti-Communist League (WACL), an organization filled with European Nazis—ex officials of the Third Reich and Nazi collaborators" (Tucker 2002). In an exposé published by *The Washington Post*, journalist Paul Valentine (1974) called out the WACL for its efforts to marshal the "forces of authoritarianism, neo-fascism, racial hierarchy, and anti-Semitism." As a result of the article, Pearson lost his position as head of the WACL as well as his position on the editorial board of the "Heritage Foundation, a conservative think tank based in Washington, D.C." (Southern Poverty Law Center).

Pearson is the founder of the Institute for the Study of Man, an organization dedicated to studying "the origins and nature of man in order that contemporary Western society and its pressing problems might be more closely perceived" (Southern Poverty Law Center). The institute was funded with grants from the Pioneer Fund, the organization largely responsible for funding most studies related to the "science" of race and intelligence. In recent years, Pearson published a series of pieces meant to "rescue" the reputations of other academics noted for their overt racist research agendas: Arthur Jensen, William Shockley, and J. Philippe Rushton.

See also: Carto, Willis; Jensen, Arthur; Neo-Nazis; Pioneer Fund; Rushton, Jean-Philippe; White Supremacist Movement

Further Reading

Leech, Kenneth. 2005. *Race*. Church Publishing.

Mankind Quarterly. "Mankindquarterly.org." http://www.mankindquarterly.org/ (Accessed February 11, 2017).

Michael, George. 2008. *Willis Carto and the American Far Right*. University Press of Florida.

Pearson, Roger. 1966. *Eugenics and Race*. 2nd ed. Clair Press.

Pearson, Roger. 1996. *Heredity and Humanity: Race, Eugenics and Modern Science*. Scott Townsend Publishers.

Southern Poverty Law Center. "Roger Pearson." https://www.splcenter.org/fighting-hate /extremist-files/individual/roger-pearson (Accessed February 11, 2017).

Tucker, William. 2002. *The Funding of Scientific Racism: Wickliffe Draper and the Pioneer Fund*. University of Illinois Press.

Valentine, Paul. May 28, 1978. "The Fascist Specter Behind the World Anti-Red League." *Washington Post*. Referred to in Berlet, Chip. May 25, 2011. "McCain Advised Ultra-Right Group Tied to Death Squads." *Huffington Post*. https://www.huffingtonpost.com/chip -berlet/mccain-advised-ultra-righ_b_132612.html (Accessed January 22, 2018).

PHELPS, FRED

Fred Phelps (1929–2014) was the founder of Westboro Baptist Church (WBC), the organization that has become notorious for its vehement homophobic rhetoric and its teachings that God has abandoned the United States because of its tolerance of homosexuality and other "sins." Phelps founded WBC in 1955 in Topeka, Kansas. From its headquarters in Topeka, WBC, which consists almost exclusively of Phelps's family members and close friends, has launched its campaign of "ministry picketing" that targets any event that is believed to be associated with homosexuality. These events have included the funerals of LGBT people, military veterans, and disaster victims, as well as sporting events, movie premieres, Hollywood events (e.g., the Academy Awards), political events, university commencement exercises, and functions sponsored by mainstream Christian organizations that WBC considers corrupt. Phelps enshrined in the "theology" of WBC a nearly universal hate and contempt for any other religious group and the general American public. Over the course of more than five decades, Phelps honed WBC's message of hate by stating that "God Hates Fags," "God Hates Jews," "Thank God for Dead Soldiers," and "Thank God for AIDS" (Southern Poverty Law Center, Westboro Baptist Church). During most of his life, Phelps taught that the United States was doomed because of its acceptance of homosexuality and that God would destroy the country just as he had destroyed Sodom and Gomorrah.

Phelps was born in Mississippi and later attended the U.S. Military Academy at West Point. However, he turned the appointment down after attending a tent revival meeting and opting for a religious calling. In 1952, Phelps married his wife, and in 1954 they moved to Topeka, Kansas, where Phelps would establish WBC a year later. Although Phelps established WBC as nondenominational, he preached a doctrine similar to other Primitive Baptist organizations, teaching a literal interpretation of the Bible and a belief in the predestination of human beings (i.e., that only a certain number of "chosen" people would be saved on Judgment Day). Phelps's vitriolic message alienated most of his original parishioners, leaving only immediate members of his family and a few close friends. Of Phelps's 13 children, four would be estranged from their father at the end of his life because of their disagreement with his political and social views.

In 1991, WBC began its "ministry protests" to warn the country of impending disaster for its support of homosexuality and other "sins." Phelps and the WBC attributed the tragic and accidental deaths of individuals, as well as major terrorist events such as 9/11, to God's anger at the United States over its acceptance of homosexuality. Originally trained as a lawyer, Phelps was "disbarred from practicing law in Kansas in 1977 and in federal Courts in 1985" (Biles 2014). But his knowledge of the law allowed WBC to exploit First Amendment privileges at various events that Phelps and the church considered "sinful." As a result of the WBC's protests at the funerals of LGBT people and U.S. service personnel, the U.S. Congress and several states passed laws that forbade protesting within 300 feet of many cemeteries and within certain hours of when a funeral was to be held.

In August 2013, Fred Phelps was reportedly excommunicated from his own church for "rank blasphemy" when he spoke in support of members of Equality House, an LGBT organization that had been established across the street from Westboro Baptist Church in Topeka (Sleczkowski 2014). Phelps died of natural causes at age 84 on March 19, 2014.

See also: Anti-LGBT Movement

Further Reading

Biles, Jan. March 20, 2014. "Phelps' Life Turned from Brilliance to Hatred." *CJonline*. http://cjonline.com/local/2014-03-20/phelps-life-turned-brilliance-hatred (Accessed August 5, 2017).

Burke, Daniel. March 25, 2014. "Westboro Church Founder Fred Phelps Dies." *CNN*. http://www.cnn.com/2014/03/20/us/westboro-church-founder-dead/ (Accessed January 5, 2017).

Sleczkowski, Cavan. May 23, 2014. "Fred Phelps May Have Had a Change of Heart Toward Gays, Relative Says." *Huffington Post*. http://www.huffingtonpost.com/2014/05/23/fred-phelps-equality_n_5378433.html (Accessed January 5, 2017).

Southern Poverty Law Center. "Fred Phelps." https://www.splcenter.org/fighting-hate/extremist-files/individual/fred-phelps (Accessed January 5, 2017).

Southern Poverty Law Center. "Westboro Baptist Church." https://www.splcenter.org/fighting-hate/extremist-files/group/westboro-baptist-church (Accessed January 5, 2017).

PIERCE, WILLIAM

William Pierce (1933–2002) was an American white nationalist and political ideologue. As founder of the National Alliance, at one time the most powerful and influential white nationalist group in the United States, Pierce disseminated his message of white pride and power by virtue of radio broadcasts, print media, and music. Pierce's business interests were centered on his message of white nationalism, as the National Alliance oversaw *National Vanguard* magazine, which covered issues from a white nationalist perspective, as well as Resistance Records, a music company that Pierce had purchased from skinheads and neo-Nazis that produced music related to the cause of white pride and racial separateness. Through his publishing company, National Vanguard Books, Pierce produced hundreds of books, tracts, pamphlets, and other material that he disseminated around the country and the world. Pierce's own book, *The Turner Diaries* (1978), became known as the "Bible of white extremism" and inspired terrorists and terror groups alike with its antigovernment, anti-Semitic, and racist message. When Pierce died in 2002, the National Alliance boasted more than 2,500 members and an annual income of more than $1 million. Pierce, as leader of the National Alliance, was the most well-known and high-profile white nationalist in the world. Within a few years of his death, however, the National Alliance would virtually disappear due to factional infighting.

William Pierce was born to a legacy that included relations to the aristocracy of the Old South. In 1962, he earned a doctorate in physics and became associated with the anticommunist John Birch Society. Pierce found the Birch Society too one-dimensional, however, and he gravitated to the American Nazi Party, which had been founded by George Lincoln Rockwell. When Rockwell was assassinated in 1967, Pierce began working for Youth for Wallace, an organization of young people dedicated to the prosegregationist presidential campaign of Alabama governor George Wallace. The organization later became the National Youth Alliance that Pierce reorganized into the National Alliance in 1974.

For most of its existence, the National Alliance owed its success to Pierce's marketing and media skills. His ability to disseminate his message of white power and white nationalism through radio, print, and music extended the influence of the National Alliance far beyond any other white nationalist group of the time. The National Alliance often referred to the "temporary unpleasantness" that would follow the accession of the white race to absolute power in the United States. Such power would come about as a result of "ethnic cleansing," as nonwhite peoples as well as "race traitors" would be purged in order to create an all-white nation. Pierce "once described how he hoped to 'lock Jews, race traitors' and other enemies of the 'Aryan' race into cattle cars and send them to the bottom of abandoned coal mines" (Southern Poverty Law Center, National Alliance).

Pierce rejected being labeled as a neo-Nazi, though there were things that he admired about Hitler and his ability to manage and organize the German government. However, according to the Southern Poverty Law Center (William Pierce),

> Pierce was explicitly Hitlerian in ideology, seeking to create a Nazi-like state in which the NA [National Alliance] would rule the nation. He was also, in effect, a Leninist, in the sense that he never believed that the white masses—people whom he regularly referred to as "lemmings"—could lead themselves. Instead, the NA would be the "vanguard party," much like the Bolsheviks in Russia, that would lead them in a racially based, authoritarian society that would be marked by Germanic music and "healthy" racial values. That ideology and Pierce's embrace of Hitler's "leadership principle" kept members of the group dependent on Pierce personally, a situation that would damage the Alliance later.

Perhaps Pierce's most notable contribution to the cause of white nationalism was his novel about an impending race war in the United States known as *The Turner Diaries*. In the book, which Pierce wrote under the pseudonym Andrew MacDonald, Pierce describes his antihero Earl Turner, "who fights against the System—an anti-white, anti-gun U.S. government that continually puts more restrictions on its citizens. By the novel's end, Turner works for an elite survivalist group known as the Order" (Southern Poverty Law Center, William Pierce). Eventually, all traces of racial impurity and racial treacherousness are eradicated from American society as the perfect white nation is established.

In later years, Pierce would attempt to distance himself from the violence committed by devotees of *The Turner Diaries*, though secretly Pierce hoped the book's message would inspire his long-predicted race war. In 1983, Bob Mathews, a Pierce follower and white nationalist, survivalist, and anti-Semite, founded one of the most notorious terrorist organizations in the history of the United States, The Order. From its base in the Pacific Northwest, where Mathews intended to establish a whites-only homeland, The Order carried out assassinations of its enemies, and robbed, bombed, and confronted the federal government in acts of violence and terrorism. Mathews would eventually be "martyred" in a shootout with federal authorities in late 1984.

Several years later, in 1995, Timothy McVeigh would be inspired by *The Turner Diaries* as he carried out an attack on a federal building in Oklahoma City strongly resembling an attack described in the book. The attack, "which killed 168 people, including 19 children," was McVeigh's attempt to strike back at an overly intrusive and overreaching federal government that he believed had lost the right to govern the people of the United States (Balleck 2015). In 1998, three white men who were convicted of killing a black man by dragging him to death behind their pickup truck, stated, "We're starting *The Turner Diaries* early" (Southern Poverty Law Center, William Pierce).

Though Pierce was a giant in the white nationalist movement, his death and the cult of personality that had developed alongside him doomed the influence of the National Alliance. When Pierce died in 2002, he was memorialized as "Our Eternal Chairman" and compared to the greatness of Adolf Hitler. But Pierce's own words doomed the organization as his harsh and condescending final speech "described other hate groups as filled with freaks and weaklings" (Southern Poverty Law Center, National Alliance). Within a few months of his death, infighting among his successors severely damaged the National Alliance with fractures occurring among the group's membership. By 2009, the "National Alliance had lost nearly all of its members" and its influence was practically nonexistent (Southern Poverty Law Center, National Alliance). Though he oversaw the rise of one of the most powerful white nationalist groups the United States has ever seen, William Pierce was also partly responsible for its eventual fall.

See also: John Birch Society; Mathews, Bob; National Alliance; Neo-Nazis; Rockwell, George Lincoln; *Turner Diaries, The*

Further Reading

Anti-Defamation League. "William Pierce." http://archive.adl.org/learn/ext_us/pierce.html (Accessed January 4, 2017).

Balleck, Barry J. 2015. *Allegiance to Liberty: The Changing Face of Patriots, Militias, and Political Violence in America.* Praeger.

Griffin, Robert S. 2001. *The Fame of a Dead Man's Deeds: An Up-Close Portrait of White Nationalist William Pierce*. 1st Book Library.

MacDonald, Andrew (aka William Pierce). 1978. *The Turner Diaries: A Novel*. Barricade Books.

Southern Poverty Law Center. "National Alliance." https://www.splcenter.org/fighting-hate /extremist-files/group/national-alliance (Accessed January 4, 2017).

Southern Poverty Law Center. "William Pierce." https://www.splcenter.org/fighting-hate /extremist-files/individual/william-pierce (Accessed January 4, 2017).

PIONEER FUND

The Pioneer Fund was established in 1937 by Wickliffe Draper, a Massachusetts-born descendant of a long line of prominent Americans. Draper was an ardent eugenicist and formed the Pioneer Fund "to support research into the issues of heredity and eugenics" (Southern Poverty Law Center). Draper provided "the Pioneer Fund's original mandate which was to pursue race betterment by promoting the genetic stock of those deemed to be descended predominantly from white persons who settled in the original thirteen states prior to the adoption of the Constitution" (Southern Poverty Law Center). Today, the Pioneer Fund provides grants that support "studies of race and intelligence, as well as eugenics" (Southern Poverty Law Center). The money provided by the Pioneer Fund largely goes to Anglo-American race scientists searching for clues to the breeding and betterment of "perfect human beings."

Many of the individuals involved with the Pioneer Fund in its early days had contacts with Nazi scientists who provided the basis and justifications for Hitler's drive to achieve racial purification. In the 1960s, many of the Pioneer Fund's supporters were active in their opposition to the American civil rights movement. A major recipient of Pioneer Fund grants was Arthur Jensen, the UC-Berkeley educational psychologist who stated that black children would never be helped by Project Head Start, the government program designed to provide children of low-income families with early educational intervention, because they (black children) were inherently less intelligent due to their race. As Jensen noted, "No amount of social engineering would improve the performance of black children, adding that only 'eugenic foresight' would provide a solution" (Southern Poverty Law Center).

Between 1975 and 1996, the Pioneer Fund provided more than $1 million to Roger Pearson, a British eugenics activist and director of the Institute for the Study of Man. Pearson, "who came to the United States in the mid-1960s, teamed up with Willis Carto," a promoter of anti-Semitic conspiracy theories and a Holocaust denier, to create a magazine known as *The New Patriot*, which published articles with such titles as "Zionists and the Plot Against South Africa," "Early Jews and the Rise of Jewish Money Power," and "Swindlers of the Crematoria" (Southern Poverty Law Center). In the mid-1990s, the Pioneer Fund began supporting the work of contributors to *The Bell Curve*, a 1994 book "that claimed that differences in intelligence among different racial groups" could be explained, at least in part, by genetic makeup (Southern Poverty Law Center).

The Pioneer Fund was led by psychology professor and Canadian researcher J. Philippe Rushton from 2002 until his death in October 2012. Rushton contended that the larger sexual characteristics of blacks (i.e., genitals, breasts, and buttocks) are inversely related to brain size and, thus, intelligence. During his time as the president of the Pioneer Fund, Rushton received nearly half a million dollars, and Jared Taylor, Rushton's friend and publisher of *American Renaissance*, a white supremacist publication, received large donations to perpetuate his contention that "blacks are incapable of sustaining any kind of civilization" (Southern Poverty Law Center).

In 2013, Richard Lynn became the president of the Pioneer Fund. Lynn is an English emeritus professor of psychology at the University of Ulster and an assistant editor of *Mankind Quarterly* (Southern Poverty Law Center). Lynn is known for his belief that racial differences account for differences in intelligence.

See also: American Renaissance; Carto, Willis; Jensen, Arthur; Pearson, Roger; Taylor, Jared; White Nationalism; White Supremacist Movement

Further Reading

Falk, Avner. 2008. *Anti-Semitism: A History and Psychoanalysis of Contemporary Hatred.* ABC-CLIO.

Southern Poverty Law Center. "Pioneer Fund." https://www.splcenter.org/fighting-hate/extremist-files/group/pioneer-fund (Accessed February 11, 2017).

Tucker, William. 2002. *The Funding of Scientific Racism: Wickliffe Draper and the Pioneer Fund.* University of Illinois Press.

POSSE COMITATUS

The rise of the modern patriot/militia movement undoubtedly began with the group known as the Posse Comitatus ("force [or power] of the county") (National Center for State Courts, 1999). Founded in 1967 in Oregon by Henry Lamont "Mike" Beach, the Posse Comitatus was a right-wing extremist organization that advocated resistance to the oversight of federal authority of almost every kind, ranging from the payment of taxes to the issuance of drivers licenses. A similar organization to Posse Comitatus, the United States Christian Posse Association, was founded in California by William Potter Gale at about the same time. These and other groups began to proliferate during the 1970s as "average" Americans began to protest what they perceived as the "heavy-handedness" of the U.S. government. The primary ideology of all these groups was "that there was no legitimate form of government above that of the county, and no higher law enforcement authority than that of the county sheriff" (Balleck 2015). The Posse Comitatus movement would eventually spin off into the common-law court movement and the sovereign citizens movement. Posse Comitatus is the intellectual forefather of most patriot and militia groups in the United States today.

Posse Comitatus began, in part, as an organization focused on a false belief that the federal government does not have the power to tax individuals. But tax protestation, as espoused by Posse Comitatus, was nothing new. There had been tax protestors even prior to the American Revolution. But the right-wing nature of tax protestation took off as a conservative reaction to the New Deal policies of President

Franklin D. Roosevelt. At this moment, the tax protest movement became laced with anti-Semitic overtones as conspiracies began to circulate that Jewish banking interests were manipulating the American economy (Southern Poverty Law Center 1998). By the 1970s, a growing disenchantment with liberal policies in the United States began to manifest in groups that were looking for scapegoats. Gale began espousing the ideas of Posse Comitatus alongside those of Christian Identity, a decades-old belief that held that Jews were the offspring of Eve and Satan.

From the beginning, Posse ideology attracted adherents of Christian Identity to the group and vice versa. Christian Identity, which was inherently anti-Semitic, looked to the Bible as a document inspired by God. Posse members, looking for the source of the "conspiracy" to hide the true history of the country, found justification in Christian Identity ideology, which pointed to "international bankers," most of whom were Jews, as the conspirators who had subverted the truth. This Posse/Identity link served both groups well "during the farm crisis of the 1980s":

> When inflation, falling land values, rising interest rates, and poor lending practices combined to create a financial crisis that threatened to overwhelm farmers of little or moderate means . . . the Posse offered a culprit—the international (Jewish) banking conspiracy which had destroyed the Constitutional/Biblical monetary system and replaced it with one based on credit designed to suck people dry. (National Center for State Courts, 1999)

By the 1980s, Posse Comitatus had galvanized its philosophies into calls for self-sufficiency, localism, and antitax revolt. Indeed, most Posse members "refused to pay taxes, obtain driver's licenses, or otherwise comply with any government regulation" (Balleck 2015). Posse Comitatus and similar groups did not believe in floating exchange rates for currency, instead believing that the only valid forms of currency are those that can be backed up dollar for dollar by gold. This, they insisted, was a requirement of the Constitution (Nizkor Project).

Justification for claims and actions of the Posse Comitatus were found in what was known as the "hidden history" of the United States. According to this theory, Posse members believe "that the true history of the United States, and thus the 'true laws' of the United States, have been hidden from the people by a massive, long-lasting conspiracy." The Posse believed that

> the rule for the Judiciary, both State and Federal, has been subtle subversion of the Constitution of these United States. The subversion and contempt for the Constitution by the Judiciary is joined by the Executive and Legislative branches of government. It is apparent that the Judiciary has attempted to alter our form of Government. By unlawful administrative acts and procedures, they have attempted to establish a Dictatorship of the Courts over the citizens of this Republic. The legal profession has, with few exceptions, conspired with the Judiciary for this purpose. (National Center for State Courts, 1999)

Posse leaders thus developed tales of conspiracy and cover-up designed to subvert liberty that had taken place since the founding. The "true laws of the United

States had been covered up" by a vast band of conspirators, which included legislators, judges, and lawyers. Posse adherents set about to "find" these laws "through searching through law books and legal codes, the writings of the founders and early legal scholars, the Uniform Commercial Code, the Bible, and other documents" (Balleck 2015).

Though Posse Comitatus would not survive the 1990s, its influence would be felt far beyond its brief existence. Indeed, given its various philosophies, a penchant for survivalism would come to epitomize those with Posse sympathies. The common-law court movement and "sovereign citizens" are legacies of the Posse Comitatus. The sovereign citizen movement "claims that a U.S. citizen can become a 'sovereign citizen' and thereby be subject only to common law" and/or "constitutional law, not to statutory law (including most taxes)" (Anti-Defamation League). This sovereign citizen movement "gave rise to the 'redemption movement' which claims that the U.S. government has enslaved its citizens by using them as collateral against foreign debt" (Southern Poverty Law Center 2002). Those who promote redemption schemes utilize the mechanisms of "false liens"—wherein liens that have no basis in fact are filed against government officials and judges—as a tool of harassment. "Paper terrorism" refers "to the use of false liens, frivolous lawsuits, bogus letters of credit, and other legal documents which have no basis in fact but are used to intimidate government officials" (Pitcavage 1998).

See also: Beach, Henry Lamont "Mike"; Butler, Richard; Christian Identity; Common-Law Court Movement; Gale, William Potter; Kahl, Gordon; Monkeywrenching; Paper Terrorism; Sovereign Citizens Movement

Further Reading

Anti-Defamation League. "What Is a Sovereign Citizen?, Message to Students." *Militia Watchdog Archives.* https://www.adl.org/education/resources/backgrounders/sovereign-citizen -movement (Accessed December 13, 2016).

Balleck, Barry J. 2015. *Allegiance to Liberty: The Changing Face of Patriots, Militias, and Political Violence in America.* Praeger.

National Center for State Courts. 1999. "Anti-Government Movement Guidebook." http:// www.tulanelink.com/pdf/anti-gov_movement_guidebook.pdf (Accessed December 13, 2016).

Nizkor Project. 1991. "Paranoia as Patriotism: Far Right Influences on the Militia Movement." http://www.nizkor.org/hweb/orgs/american/adl/paranoia-as-patriotism/posse-comitatus. html (Accessed December 13, 2016).

Pitcavage, Mark. June 29, 1998. "Paper Terrorism's Forgotten Victims: The Use of Bogus Liens Against Private Individuals and Businesses." *Anti-Defamation League.* Referenced in Southern Poverty Law Center. December 18, 2002. "Mark Pitcavage of the Anti-Defamation League Discusses Race-Based Gangs and other Extremists in Prison." https://www.splcen ter.org/fighting-hate/intelligence-report/2015/mark-pitcavage-anti-defamation-league -discusses-race-based-gangs-and-other-extremists (Accessed January 22, 2018).

Southern Poverty Law Center. June 15, 1998. "Hate Group Expert Daniel Levitas Discusses Posse Comitatus, Christian Identity Movement and More." *Southern Poverty Law Center— Intelligence Report.* https://www.splcenter.org/fighting-hate/intelligence-report/1998/hate

-group-expert-daniel-levitas-discusses-posse-comitatus-christian-identity-movement
-and-more (Accessed December 13, 2016).
Southern Poverty Law Center. Winter 2002. "New Multi-Million Dollar Scam Takes Off in
Antigovernment Circles." *Southern Poverty Law Center—Intelligence Report.* http://www
.splcenter.org/get-informed/intelligence-report/browse-all-issues/2002/winter/beyond
-redemption (Accessed December 13, 2016).

R

RACIST SKINHEADS

According to the Southern Poverty Law Center (2012), racist skinheads "are among the most dangerous radical-right threats facing law enforcement today." Generally "the products of a violent and criminal subculture," racist skinheads tend to be men and women who have been "imbued with neo-Nazi beliefs about Jews, blacks, LGBT people and others, while notoriously being difficult to track" due to their generally unorganized and unaffiliated status with mainstream extremist groups (Southern Poverty Law Center 2012). Organized "into small, mobile crews or acting individually, skinheads tend to move around frequently and often without warning, even as they network and organize across regions. For law enforcement, this poses a particular problem in responding to crimes and conspiracies crossing multiple jurisdictions" (Southern Poverty Law Center 2012).

Unlike the Ku Klux Klan, racist skinheads are not a native manifestation of the United States. The skinhead movement actually "was started in the 1960s by working class youths in England. Instead of opting for the flamboyant and 'fancy-dress' escapism of the 'long-hairs,' the skinheads embraced working-class fashion: cropped hair, meant-to-last shoes and boots, white T-shirts and worn Levis" (Abbots 1994). Racism among skinheads first appeared in the 1970s when poor economic conditions in England encouraged neo-Nazi groups to recruit skinheads into their ranks, "most of whom were in low paying jobs or on welfare" (Abbots 1994). "Playing on the traditional nationalistic ideas of the working class," the fascist groups "did their best to turn the skinheads against their immigrant neighbors" (Abbots 1994). The nonviolent skinhead movement experienced a revival in the early 1980s with the advent of the punk rock movement.

The nativist sentiments espoused by neo-Nazis in Europe spread quickly to the United States in the 1980s. At the time, the United States was experiencing its own economic downturn, and many citizens were out of work. Skinhead activity was first reported in Texas and in the Midwest. Skinheads became immediately recognizable for their trademark style—"shaved head, combat boots, bomber jacket, neo-Nazi and white power tattoos" (Southern Poverty Law Center 2012). A major force behind the national growth of racist skinheads in the United States "was Tom Metzger, a former Klansman and former leader of the neo-Nazi group White Aryan Resistance (WAR)" (Southern Poverty Law Center 2012). "Around 1986, Metzger founded an organized skinhead outreach campaign" (Southern Poverty Law Center 2012). Together with his son, John, Metzger "sought to ground the dispersed movement in ideology and direct its wild and chaotic youthful energy into building smart, well-trained, and obedient street cells around the country" (Southern Poverty Law Center 2012).

In 1988 in Oklahoma, Metzger held the first major hate rock festival for skinheads, known as "Aryan Fest." Later that year, racist skinheads burst onto the scene in the United States when two of Metzger's acolytes "attacked a group of Ethiopian immigrants in the middle of the street" in Portland, Oregon, killing one of the students (Southern Poverty Law Center, Racist Skinhead). The Southern Poverty Law Center and the Anti-Defamation League would bring a civil rights lawsuit against Metzger and WAR, and the resulting $12.5 million judgment bankrupted Metzger and effectively ended WAR as an organization.

Other racist skinhead attacks during the late 1980s and early 1990s resulted in the murders of blacks in Birmingham, Alabama, and Arlington, Texas. Those responsible for the murders were part of what became known as the "Confederate Hammerskins, a confederation of skinheads that had been founded in Dallas in 1987" (Southern Poverty Law Center, Racist Skinhead).

In 1994, the Hammerskin Nation (HN) was formed with the idea to "unite all of the regional Hammerskin groups into a national and even international force, with affiliated chapters in Europe" (Southern Poverty Law Center 2012). For a while, the plan worked as HN became "the most powerful skinhead organization in the country by the end of the 1990s." Throughout this period, the skinhead movement continued to grow and "was responsible for hundreds of racially motivated crimes around the country" (Southern Poverty Law Center, Racist Skinhead).

The end of the Cold War and the uncertainty that surrounded this time in American history helped spur the skinhead movement. Gone was the looming menace of the Soviet Union and communist takeover. What was left was surging immigration into the United States from countries in Eastern Europe, the Middle East, and Latin America. These immigrant movements challenged the accepted notion of white supremacy in the country, a phenomenon that racist skinheads and other extremists resented.

By the mid-2000s, the influence of the Hammerskins had been replaced by the Vinlanders. This group, which was "incredibly violent, full of swagger, and loathe to take orders from anyone," attempted to revitalize the racist skinhead movement. However, the Vinlanders' founder, Brien James, informed the extremist world in 2007 that the Vinlanders were separating "themselves from the racist movement. The announcement explained":

> We do not see anything positive being accomplished, for our nation or our people, by participating in the white racialist movement as it stands. We have attempted to change this movement from within and have not succeeded. It is our opinion that a large number of the people involved in the greater movement are paid informants, social outcasts, and general losers in life. (Southern Poverty Law Center 2012)

In addition to their social and cultural influence, racist skinheads shaped the music scene as the phenomenon of "hate rock" exploded alongside the punk rock movement, "spreading lyrics that were anti-immigrant, anti-black, and anti-Semitic" (Southern Poverty Law Center 2012). William Pierce, founder of the neo-Nazi

National Alliance, "understood the potential of hate rock music." He stated, "Music speaks to us at a deeper level than books or political rhetoric: music speaks directly to the soul" (Southern Poverty Law Center 2012). In 1999, Pierce purchased the hate-rock label Resistance Records and "built the company into a major force in the racist skinhead movement" (Southern Poverty Law Center 2012). By the early 2000s, "skinhead culture was defined by loud hate-rock, cases of cheap beer, bloody 'boot parties' directed against immigrants and others, and the flagrant display of neo-Nazi iconography and paraphernalia" (Southern Poverty Law Center 2012).

Today, the racist skinhead culture is still prominent in the United States. Racist skinheads "have been a regular element in American prisons and juvenile correction facilities. The U.S. military has also had to contend with racist skinheads in its rank" (Southern Poverty Law Center 2012). Hate rock "from racist skinheads has bled into the flow of rebellious teen music. And skinheads have taken their 'boot parties' from the street to the Internet, targeting young people for recruitment into their supposed movement" (Southern Poverty Law Center 2012).

Dylann Roof's massacre of nine black parishioners at a Charleston, South Carolina, church in June 2015 won him some "cred" among some racist skinheads when he declared before the shooting, "You [black people] are raping our women and taking over the country" (Ferranti 2015). Roof's crime is exactly the kind celebrated in U.S. prisons among white nationalists and white supremacists. A skinhead doing time in federal prison stated, "Dylann will be my next tattoo" (Ferranti 2015).

See also: Aryan Nations; Metzger, Tom; National Alliance; Neo-Nazis; Pierce, William; Roof, Dylann Storm; Southern Poverty Law Center; White Nationalism; White Supremacist Movement

Further Reading

Abbots, Jennifer. April 19, 1994. "True 'Skinheads' Are Not the Racist Thugs of Media Fame." *The New York Times*. http://www.nytimes.com/1994/04/19/opinion/l-true-skin heads-are-not-the-racist-thugs-of-media-fame-829412.html (Accessed June 5, 2017).

Ferranti, Seth. June 19, 2015. "What Racist Skinheads in Prison Think About Dylann Roof." *Vice*. https://www.vice.com/en_us/article/what-racist-skinhead-prisoners-think-about -dylann-roof-619 (Accessed June 5, 2017).

Pollard, John. 2016. "Skinhead Culture: The Ideologies, Mythologies, Religions, and Conspiracy Theories of Racist Skinheads." *Patterns of Prejudice* 50, no. 4–5.

Southern Poverty Law Center. "Racist Skinhead." Southern Poverty Law Center. https://www .splcenter.org/fighting-hate/extremist-files/ideology/racist-skinhead (Accessed June 5, 2017).

Southern Poverty Law Center. June 25, 2012. "Racist Skinheads: Understanding the Threat." https://www.splcenter.org/20100126/racist-skinheads-understanding-threat (Accessed June 5, 2017).

RHODES, ELMER STEWART

Elmer Stewart Rhodes (b. 1966) is the founder and national president of Oath Keepers, a right-wing, antigovernment group associated with the patriot and militia movements. Rhodes joined the U.S. Army after high school and became a paratrooper. However, a night parachuting accident caused a disabling injury, and Rhodes was honorably discharged from the service. In 2004, he graduated from Yale Law School, and in 2008, he was a volunteer in Ron Paul's presidential campaign. It was during this campaign that Rhodes began to rail against the "full-blown smear campaign" that was being leveled by the "political establishment" against Paul. Rhodes claimed an "epiphany" in 2008 that became the basis for the formation of the Oath Keepers (Southern Poverty Law Center).

Rhodes claims that a warning sounded by a retired army colonel prompted him to action. The colonel, "arguing that the U.S. Bill of Rights and U.S. Constitution were in peril, stated that soldiers, veterans, and law enforcement officers" would be the saviors of these cherished documents, if they could be saved at all (Southern Poverty Law Center). On April 19, 2009, in Lexington, Massachusetts, (Patriot's Day in Massachusetts) Rhodes set forth the "10 orders that Oath Keepers must not obey" and began to team with Tea Party groups around the country to spread his message. Within a year of the group's founding, Rhodes claimed there were Oath Keeper members in every state, and by 2014, he claimed that the Oath Keepers had more than 30,000 members on its rolls (Southern Poverty Law Center).

Rhodes moved to Montana in 2010 to join a growing movement of antigovernment patriot groups in that state who "envision a coming 'last stand' confrontation against globalist tyrants [that are] expected to steamroll across the U.S., crushing our freedoms" (Southern Poverty Law Center). Rhodes "continues to appear at patriot organizing rallies and has joined forces with other anti-government groups," most notably the Tenth Amendment Center (Southern Poverty Law Center). Though trained as a lawyer, Rhodes continues to insist, in the spirit of the sovereign citizen and nullification movement, "that states have the rights to disregard federal laws" if they so choose, and that all gun control laws are illegitimate and should "trigger resistance." After the Newton, Connecticut, massacre in December 2012, Rhodes held rallies at several statehouses across the country, warning lawmakers that "they would be held accountable" if they dishonored their constitutional oaths (Southern Poverty Law Center).

Since the group's founding, Oath Keepers have interjected themselves into several high-profile confrontations with the federal government, including the Bundy ranch standoff, the Sugar Pine Mine incident, and the Malheur National Wildlife Refuge standoff.

See also: Bundy Ranch Standoff; Malheur National Wildlife Refuge Standoff; Oath Keepers; Tenth Amendment Center

Further Reading

Acosta, Jim. November 18, 2009. "Who Are the Oathkeepers?" *CNN* (Accessed November 21, 2016).   http://www.aim.org/on-target-blog/jim-acosta-bias-from-cnn/.

Oath Keepers. "Oath Keepers Board of Directors." https://www.oathkeepers.org/board-of-directors/ (Accessed November 21, 2016).

Southern Poverty Law Center. "Elmer Stewart Rhodes." https://www.splcenter.org/fighting-hate/extremist-files/individual/elmer-stewart-rhodes-0 (Accessed November 21, 2016).

ROBB, THOMAS

Thomas Robb (b. 1946) is a Christian Identity pastor based in Arkansas who is also the "head of the Knights of the Ku Klux Klan (KKKK), a group he took over after the departure of David Duke" (Southern Poverty Law Center). The Knights Party, another name used by Robb to identify the KKKK, runs radio and TV programs through KKKradio.com and WhitePrideTV.com (Robb 2016). Robb publishes white pride and white supremacist material through his magazine *The Crusader*, which bills itself as "The Premier Voice of White Resistance" (Robb 2016). Robb espouses racist and anti-Semitic ideals as an adherent of Christian Identity, a pseudoreligious theology that teaches that Jews are the offspring of Eve and Satan. Robb's ministry is clear in its belief that whites are the chosen people. The mission statement of Robb's ministry reads:

> We believe that the Anglo-Saxon, Germanic, Scandinavian, and kindred people are THE [emphasis in original] people of the Bible—God's separated and anointed Israel. We do not hold that this implies the white race is especially holy or perfect, without fault or blame. However, it does mean that we have a great responsibility for imparting Christianity throughout the world, to assist in ushering in the Kingdom (government) of God (here on earth as it is in Heaven) and for following all of the Biblical guidelines in both the Old and New Testaments thereby providing an example to those not of our racial heritage to follow and enabling them to prosper.
>
> For the mission God has bestowed upon His chosen people, the white race, he requires their separation. They must honor their heritage—not despise it. Other races must honor their heritage as well. In a well ordered world—this is God's way. (Thomas Robb Ministries)

Robb attended college at the Soldiers of the Cross Training Institute in Colorado. While there, he earned a bachelor's degree and a doctorate degree in theology. His mentor was an individual who had previously been associated with George Lincoln Rockwell, the founder of the American Nazi Party. Robb took over the Knights of the Ku Klux Klan after David Duke left the organization in the 1980s. Like Duke, "Robb favored a more mainstream approach to portray the Klan as a civic organization as opposed to a hate group" (Southern Poverty Law Center). Robb has defended the Klan "as a harmless organization, claiming that his is gentle, upbeat, and friendly" (Ronson). In a PBS documentary, "Robb claimed that a Klan hood is like a businessman's tie, claiming that it's just tradition" (Maguire 2008).

Robb renamed the Knights of the Ku Klux Klan as "the Knights Party" in an attempt to gain more acceptance for the group. He has spoken at Aryan Nations events and has appeared at a variety of gatherings that have included prominent white nationalists, white supremacists, and neo-Nazis. Robb "has been a regular contributor to *Stormfront*, a white supremacist web forum run by long-time white supremacist Don Black" (Southern Poverty Law Center).

In the aftermath of Barack Obama's election in 2008, Robb predicated a "race war . . . between our people, who I see as the rightful owners and leaders of this great country, and their people, the blacks" (Southern Poverty Law Center). In the summer of 2013, Robb announced a "Klan Kamp" dedicated to "instilling the tools to become actively involved in the struggle for our racial redemption in both young and old campers" (Brantley 2013). The faculty of the "Kamp" included "white supremacist Paul Fromm and Billy Roper, the neo-Nazi former head of the White Revolution organization" (Brantley 2013).

In March 2016, Robb declared presidential candidate Donald Trump "the pick of the litter" and said he was attracted to Trump's hard-line position on immigration (Ramsey 2016). In November 2016, just before the election, Robb's publication, *The Crusader*, endorsed Trump's candidacy with the headline "Make America Great Again" (Sakuma 2016). The full-page spread in the magazine was very enthusiastic about Trump's campaign, though an official spokesperson for the campaign indicated that Trump did not embrace the endorsement.

See also: Black, Don; Duke, David; Fromm, Paul; Neo-Nazis; *Stormfront*; White Supremacist Movement

Further Reading

Brantley, Max. June 21, 2013. "'Klan Kamp': Thomas Robb's Training Program for White Supremacists in the Arkansas Ozarks." *Arkansas Times*. http://www.arktimes.com/Arkan sasBlog/archives/2013/06/21/klan-kamp-thomas-robbs-training-program-for-white -supremacists-in-the-arkansas-ozarks (Accessed April 1, 2017).

Maguire, Ellen. February 19, 2008. "PBS's 'Banished' Exposes the Tainted Past of Three White Enclaves." *The Washington Post*. http://www.washingtonpost.com/wp-dyn/content /article/2008/02/18/AR2008021802005.html (Accessed April 1, 2017).

Ramsey, David. March 4, 2016. "Current Leader of KKK: Donald Trump Is 'The Pick of the Litter.'" *Arkansas Times*. http://www.arktimes.com/ArkansasBlog/archives/2016/03/04 /current-leader-of-kkk-Donald-trump-is-the-pick-of-the-litter (Accessed April 1, 2017).

Robb, Thomas. Fall 2016 "Make American Great Again." *The Crusader: The Premier Voice of White Resistance*. http://www.scribd.com/document/329628320/KKK-Newspaper-Trump -Endorsement-Issue (Accessed April 1, 2017).

Ronson, Jon. 2001. "New Klan." *JonRonson.com*. https://web.archive.org/web/2008051511 2306/http://www.jonronson.com/klan.html (Accessed April 1, 2017).

Sakuma, Amanda. November 2, 2016. "KKK Paper 'The Crusader' Backs Trump; Campaign Rejects It.'" *NBC News*. http://www.nbcnews.com/storyline/2016-election-day /kkk-paper-crusader-backs-trump-campaign-rejects-backing-n676686 (Accessed April 1, 2017).

Southern Poverty Law Center. "Thomas Robb." http://www.splcenter.org/fighting-hate/extrem ist-files/individual/thomas-robb (Accessed April 1, 2017).

Thomas Robb Ministries. "Our Mission." http://www.christianidentitychurch.net/our_mission .htm (Accessed April 1, 2017).

ROCKWELL, GEORGE LINCOLN

George Lincoln Rockwell (1818–1967) was the founder of the American Nazi Party. During the era of McCarthyism, the rise of the John Birch Society, and rampant anticommunism throughout the United States, Rockwell became swept up in what he perceived as a devolution of American society and culture. Rockwell was troubled by the political push for racial integration as well as the belief that communists had infiltrated every level of American government. In this atmosphere, Rockwell became a supporter of the ideas of Adolf Hitler and Nazism. He read Hitler's national socialist treatise, *Mein Kampf* (My Struggle) as well as the *Protocols of the Elders of Zion*, an anti-Semitic text "purporting to outline a Jewish plan for world domination." In 1959, Rockwell published a poem entitled "The Fable of the Ducks and the Hens," an *Animal Farm* parody meant to highlight the influence of Jews in 20th-century United States.

Rockwell enrolled in Brown University in 1938. In his courses, he quickly came to reject the ideas of racial and individual equality, explicitly rejecting the idea that people were unequal due solely to their environment. After only a year, Rockwell left Brown and was commissioned into the U.S. Navy. He was recalled to active duty at the beginning of the Korean War as a lieutenant commander. He was stationed in San Diego, California, where he trained navy and marine corps pilots (Haley 1966). Eventually, after 19 years of service, Rockwell would obtain the rank of commander. He was honorably discharged in 1960, one year short of 20 years, ostensibly because he was "not deployable" due to his political views.

Prior to his separation from the navy, Rockwell had been associated with many individuals "on the farthest fringe of the right wing" (Goodrick-Clarke 2003). In 1958, Rockwell experienced his "personal political Rubicon, when he broke with other fringe groups, took up the swastika and created the American Nazi Party [in early 1959]" (Simonelli 1999). Rockwell's intention was to gain media attention. To this end, he held rallies at prominent locations, such as the National Mall in Washington, D.C., and Union Square in New York City. When asked by a reporter how many American Jews Rockwell believed were traitors, he replied "90 percent" (Schonfeld 2001).

During Rockwell's lifetime, the American Nazi Party never mustered more than 200 "stormtroopers" (Potok 2001). On August 25, 1967, Rockwell was shot and killed in Arlington, Virginia, by a former member of his group. Though his tenure as the "fuhrer" of American Nazism was short, it had a lasting impact. As noted by Mark Potok (2001) of the Southern Poverty Law Center, Rockwell left a lasting legacy that has greatly contributed to all neo-Nazi groups that followed him:

First, Rockwell established the concept of "White Power," expanding Hitler's vision of the master race to include Slavs, Greeks, Spaniards and others without Aryan roots. . . .

Second, he became "the first postwar American neo-Nazi to appreciate the strategic necessity of Holocaust denial," and, [popularized] the idea that Jews had pulled off a "monstrous and profitable fraud." . . .

Third, Rockwell married the generally atheistic ideology of orthodox Nazism to Christian Identity, [a theology] that describes Jews as biologically satanic and people of color as soulless.

Rockwell actually despised Christianity as a Jewish-inspired myth, but he was quite willing to use the Bible in an attempt to gain more popular support. . . .

Today, these legacies form part of the bedrock that underlies the American—and indeed, to some extent, the European—radical right.

See also: American Nazi Party; Aryan Nations; Carto, Willis; Christian Identity; Holocaust Denial; John Birch Society; National Alliance; National Socialist Movement; Neo-Nazis; White Nationalism; White Supremacist Movement

Further Reading

Goodrick-Clarke, Nicholas. 2003. *Black Sun: Aryan Cults, Esoteric Nazism, and the Politics of Identity.* New York University Press.

Haley, Alex. April 1966. "George Lincoln Rockwell: A Candid Conversation with the Fanatical Fuhrer of the American Nazi Party." *Playboy.* https://web.archive.org/web/2008 1202155045/http://www.playboy.com/arts-entertainment/features/george-lincoln -rockwell/george-lincoln-rockwell-01.html (Accessed March 13, 2017).

Potok, Mark. August 29, 2001. "The Nazi International." *Southern Poverty Law Center— Intelligence Report.* https://www.splcenter.org/fighting-hate/intelligence-report/2001/nazi -international (Accessed March 13, 2017).

Schaerffenberg, A. V. 2017. "Who Was George Lincoln Rockwell." American Nazi Party. http://www.anp14.com/rockwell/index.php (Accessed March 13, 2017).

Schonfeld, Reese. 2001. *Me and Ted Against the World: The Unauthorized Story of the Founding of CNN.* HarperCollins.

Simonelli, Frederick J. 1999. *American Fuehrer: George Lincoln Rockwell and the American Nazi Party.* University of Illinois Press.

ROGERS, KYLE

Kyle Rogers (b. 1977) heads the South Carolina chapter of the Council of Conservative Citizens (CCC), a group that grew directly out of the White Citizens Councils of the 1950s and 1960s. Rogers ran the CCC's national Web site until June 2015 and focused its content on sensationalized "black-on-white" crime stories. Rogers brought a "much more blatantly racist, anti-Semitic and anti-immigrant activism" tone to the site (Southern Poverty Law Center). Charleston shooter Dylann Roof credited CCC's Web site for "opening his eyes to the supposed epidemic of black on white crime before he went on to kill nine members of the Mother Emanuel A.M.E. church in Charleston in June 2014" (Southern Poverty Law Center). After Roof's manifesto was discovered, in which he credited CCC as his inspiration for his killing spree, Rogers relinquished control over the CCC Web site to a member of League of the South, a racist Southern nationalist organization. Rogers now runs an independent Web site in which he continues to post "news" intended to highlight the crimes that black Americans perpetrate, particularly against their fellow white citizens.

Rogers was born in 1977, and his association with white supremacism began in his twenties when he joined a chapter of the CCC in Columbus, Ohio. When Rogers moved to South Carolina in 2004, he reconnected with the CCC and began a vigorous defense in favor of public displays of the Confederate battle flag. Rogers, who was trained as a computer engineer, demonstrated a penchant for propaganda, and his posts on the CCC's national Web site attracted commentary and followers. For instance, in 2011, Rogers pushed for a boycott of the Marvel movie *Thor* because one of the Norse gods portrayed in the movie was played by a black man. Many contemporary white supremacists revere the ancient Norse gods, calling them the "progenitors of the Europeans" and the "whitest of gods" (Southern Poverty Law Center).

In Rogers's adopted state of South Carolina, the public display of the Confederate battle flag became a contentious political issue during the mid-2000s. Rogers claimed that the National Association for the Advancement of Colored People was "busing in welfare mothers" to demonstrate against the flag. Rogers was able to turn his defense of the Confederate flag into a profitable business as he opened an online company known as Patriotic Flags that marketed white nationalist and racist flags and apparel (Southern Poverty Law Center).

In 2012, Rogers railed against media bias in the Trayvon Martin case, alleging that the mainstream media was publishing false reports and whitewashing information about the black teenager after he was shot by a white neighborhood watch volunteer in Florida. Because of Rogers's racist rants on the CCC Web site, in February 2012 "the CCC website registered 170,000 unique visits in a single day" (Hatewatch Staff, June 19). Rogers used similar rhetoric "following the death of Michael Brown in Ferguson, Missouri in 2014" (Hatewatch Staff, June 19).

Rogers's racist views have sometimes caused embarrassment for his political allies. Rogers "served as a delegate to the Charleston County Republican convention in 2007," and in 2013 it was revealed that Rogers "was a member of the county's Republican Executive Committee. Republican officials claimed to be ignorant of Rogers' ties to the organization and asked him to resign, saying that they were unable to legally eject him" (Hatewatch Staff, June 20).

Rogers has also posted to the racist forum *Stormfront* under a pseudonym, railing against Jews and the alleged Jewish domination of the media. In 2012, CCC founder and CEO Gordon Lee Baum said Rogers was a natural writer with a unique grasp of history, "one of the smartest guys we've got" (Southern Poverty Law Center). Baum regarded Rogers as one of the brightest stars in the white nationalist movement.

Rogers's star was considerably tarnished in the aftermath of Dylann Roof's shooting rampage at a historically black church in Charleston, South Carolina, in June 2015. A manifesto penned by Roof revealed "many of the motivations for his heinous crime. In it, Roof specifically notes that the CCC's website was his 'gateway' into the radical right" (Hatewatch Staff, June 19). Roof's manifesto read,

> The event that truly awakened me was the Trayvon Martin case. I kept hearing and seeing his name, and eventually I decided to look him up. I read the Wikipedia article and right away I was unable to understand what the big deal was. It was obvious that Zimmerman was in the right. But more importantly this prompted me to type in the words "black on White crime" into Google, and I have never been the same since that day. The first website I came to was the Council of Conservative Citizens. There were pages upon pages of these brutal black on White murders. I was in disbelief. At this moment I realized that something was very wrong. How could the news be blowing up the Trayvon Martin case while hundreds of these black on White murders got ignored? (Hatewatch Staff, June 19)

Soon after Roof's revelation, Rogers left his post as the CCC webmaster as he was unable to accept his role in the brutal mass murder. Since the murders, Rogers has focused on peddling Confederate battle flags on his Web site, though his words on the CCC Web site were a reason why "the Confederate battle flag no longer flies on the grounds of the South Carolina capitol in Columbia" (Southern Poverty Law Center). Rogers continues to make posts to racist sites, though they appear to be much less sensational than in the past. In 2015, Rogers sold Donald Trump T-shirts from his Twitter account and his Patriot Flags' eBay account (Southern Poverty Law Center).

See also: Baum, Gordon; Council of Conservative Citizens; Roof, Dylann Storm; *Stormfront*; White Nationalism; White Supremacist Movement

Further Reading

Hatewatch Staff. June 19, 2015. "Charleston Shooter's Alleged Manifesto Reveals Hate Group Helped to Radicalize Him Online." *Southern Poverty Law Center—Hatewatch.* https://www.splcenter.org/hatewatch/2015/06/20/charleston-shooters-alleged-mani festo-reveals-hate-group-helped-radicalize-him-online (Accessed May 11, 2017).

Hatewatch Staff. June 20, 2015. "The Council of Conservative Citizens: Dylann Roof's Gateway into the World of White Nationalism." *Southern Poverty Law Center—Hatewatch.* https://www.splcenter.org/hatewatch/2015/06/21/council-conservative-citizens-dylann -roofs-gateway-world-white-nationalism (Accessed May 11, 2017).

Lenz, Ryan. July 6, 2012. "The CCC's Kyle Rogers Makes Himself Known on Storm-front." *Southern Poverty Law Center—Hatewatch.* https://www.splcenter.org/hatewatch /2012/07/06/cccs-kyle-rogers-makes-himself-known-stormfront (Accessed May 11, 2017).

Southern Poverty Law Center. "Kyle Rogers." https://www.splcenter.org/fighting-hate/extremist -files/individual/kyle-rogers (Accessed May 11, 2017).

ROOF, DYLANN STORM

Dylann Storm Roof (b. 1994) is the American mass murderer responsible for the Charleston, South Carolina, church shooting in June 2015. Roof claimed to be a white supremacist and justified his acts based on information he found on the Internet regarding "black-on-white" crime. Roof wanted to ignite a race war to purge blacks from American soil. Thus, on June 17, 2015, he entered the prayer service of the Emanuel African Methodist Episcopal Church, one of the oldest and most historically significant churches in the South. There, Roof killed nine parishioners, including senior pastor and South Carolina state senator Clementa C. Pinckney. Following a nationwide manhunt after security footage showed Roof entering the church, Roof was captured the following day in North Carolina. Three days "after the shooting, a Web site entitled The Last Rhodesian was found and confirmed to be owned by Roof. The site was "plastered with photos of Roof wearing, or posing with, symbols of white supremacy and neo-Naziism" (Hatewatch Staff 2015). Roof's Web site outlined his views on blacks, which he admits were largely shaped by what he learned on the Internet after googling "black on white crime." The first site he went to was that "of the Council of Conservative Citizens (CCC), a white supremacist group that is the successor to the White Nationalist Councils that used to dominate southern political and social life" (Hatewatch Staff 2015). On the site, "Roof read about the 2012 shooting of Florida teen Trayvon Martin, and was presented with the distorted view that was presented by the CCC. In December 2016, Roof was convicted in federal court of all 33 federal hate crime charges against him" and was sentenced to death (Vann Digital 2017). Roof later "plead guilty in South Carolina state court to nine charges of murder and three counts of attempted murder" (AP 2017).

Roof was born in South Carolina. As a teenager, he was socially withdrawn with few friends. His maternal uncle commented that at 19 years old, Roof "still didn't have a job, a driver's license or anything like that and he just stayed in his room a lot of the time" (Flitter and Allen 2015). In his isolation, Roof watched the news and became particularly fascinated "by the case of Trayvon Martin, the Florida black teenager who was killed by a white neighborhood watch member, George Zimmerman" (NPR 2017). Roof's later-discovered "manifesto" detailed the effect that the case had on him:

> The event that truly awakened me was the Trayvon Martin case. I kept hearing and seeing his name, and eventually I decided to look him up. I read the Wikipedia article and right away I was unable to understand what the big deal was. It was obvious that Zimmerman was in the right. But more importantly this prompted me to type in the words "black on White crime" into Google, and I have never been the same since that day. The first website I came to was the Council of Conservative Citizens. There were pages upon pages of these brutal black on White murders. I was in disbelief. At this moment I realized that something was very wrong. How could the news be blowing up the Trayvon Martin case while hundreds of these black on White murders got ignored? (NPR 2017)

Roof became obsessed with the Trayvon Martin case and began ranting that "blacks were taking over the world" (Silverstein 2017). Though Roof "reportedly told friends and neighbors that he planned to kill people, including perpetrating attacks on the College of Charleston, none of his threats were taken seriously" (Fox News 2015). It was later revealed that Roof's social seclusion was the result of autism as well as obsessive compulsive disorder and bouts of anxiety and depression (Hawes 2017). Even those who knew him best described Roof as "odd and withdrawn, socially clueless and devoid of emotion—not cruel or rude but simply blank. Once, when asked if he was afraid of anything, Roof replied: people" (Hawes 2017).

On the evening of June 17, 2015, Roof entered Emanuel African Methodist Episcopal Church in Charleston, South Carolina, during its evening prayer service. Roof "sat among the parishioners for nearly an hour" before he pulled out a .45 caliber Glock handgun that he had purchased with money that his parents had given him for his 21st birthday (Morlin 2016). Roof had hoped to kill as many parishioners as possible with the 88 hollow-point bullets he had brought with him—88 symbolizing "Heil Hitler" as "H" is the eighth letter in the alphabet. Roof expected to encounter police and intended to save at least one bullet for himself to commit suicide like other mass killers who had gone before him (Morlin). According to his

On June 17, 2015, Dylann Storm Roof entered the prayer service of the Emanuel African Methodist Episcopal Church in Charleston, South Carolina, and murdered nine parishioners. Roof claimed he was influenced by white supremacist writings found commonly on many right-wing websites. (Grace Beahm-Pool/Getty Images)

roommate, "Roof had expressed support of racial separation in the United States and intended to start a racial war" (Shapiro 2015). However, an African American friend of Roof's stated that he had never witnessed Roof expressing racial prejudice, while others believe that he intended to attack the College of Charleston but was dissuaded because of security. He then chose the church (Krol 2015).

After Roof was identified on video surveillance footage entering the church, a nationwide manhunt ensued. Roof was arrested the morning after the murders near Shelby, North Carolina. Subsequent interrogations suggested that Roof had been planning some sort of attack for about six months.

On June 20, 2015, a Web site registered to Dylann Roof entitled The Last Rhodesian was discovered. The site contained "photos of Roof posing with a handgun and a Confederate battle flag, as well as with other neo-Nazi and white supremacist symbols and codes" (Hatewatch Staff 2015). Roof was also seen "spitting on the American flag, as well as burning it." The "website contained an unsigned 2,444 word manifesto published by Roof." In it, Roof outlined his opinions and broke the text into sections with titles, "Blacks," "Jews," "Hispanics," "East Asians," "Patriotism," and "An Explanation" (Lewis, Holpuch, and Glenza 2015). Roof explained:

I have no choice. I am not in the position to, alone, go into the ghetto and fight. I chose Charleston because it is most historic city in my state, and at one time had the highest ratio of blacks to Whites in the country. We have no skinheads, no real KKK, no one doing anything but talking on the internet. Well someone has to have the bravery to take it to the real world, and I guess that has to be me. (Lewis, Holpuch, and Glenza 2015)

The interesting aspect of Roof's radicalization is that

> he wasn't radicalized by shaving his head bald and joining a neo-Nazi skinhead gang. He didn't attend Ku Klux Klan rallies to soak up hatred around burning crosses. Nor did he attend Aryan Nations churches where the racist religion of Christian Identity is preached. Dylann Storm Roof learned to hate online. Roof used a computer to research racial crimes committed on white victims. He walked away with the convoluted notion that a race war going to be his answer. (Morlin)

On December 7, 2016, Roof was convicted on all 33 counts on which he had been indicted. During the trial, Roof had fought with his defense team, who had wished to use psychiatric evidence that demonstrated that Roof was mentally unbalanced when he had committed the crimes. Roof, however, objected to this line of defense because he believed that white nationalist groups would view him as "defective" instead of as a "perfect specimen" (Cullen 2017). "His feelings about keeping any mental illness or weakness secret seemed related to his white nationalist feelings about sterilization and eliminating non-perfect, non-white people (like the Nazis did)," Roof's lawyers noted (Cullen 2017). Roof was sentenced to death by lethal injection on January 11, 2017. On April 10, 2017, he "was sentenced to nine life sentences after pleading guilty to state murder charges" (AP 2017).

After Roof's manifesto appeared on the national news and he pointed out that he had been influenced by racist and extremist Web sites, particularly information he found on the Council of Conservative Citizens (CCC) Web site, the CCC took their site down and claimed that they were "not responsible for Roof's actions." However, the organization issued a statement in which they said that Roof had some "legitimate grievances" against black people and that the group's Web site "accurately and honestly report[s] black-on-white violent crime" (Thompson 2015). Another white supremacist called Roof's actions "a preview of coming attractions" (Thielman 2015).

Since his incarceration, Roof has been assaulted in prison, though he was not seriously injured. On May 10, 2017, Roof's request for a new trial was denied. Though diagnosed as autistic, Roof denies that he has autism and has stated "that he would rather die than rely on an autism defense, stating 'it would ruin me' and 'everybody would think I am a weirdo'" (Jarvie 2017).

See also: Council of Conservative Citizens; Neo-Nazis; Rogers, Kyle; White Nationalism; White Supremacist Movement

Further Reading

AP. April 10, 2017. "Dylann Roof: Charleston Church Shooter Gets Nine Life Sentences in State Case." *NBC News*. http://www.nbcnews.com/news/us-news/dylann-roof-charleston-church-shooter-pleads-guilty-state-charges-n744746 (Accessed May 13, 2017).

Cullen, Terence. May 11, 2017. "Dylann Roof Didn't Want Other Racists to Think He Was 'Defective' for Mental Illness Legal Defense." *New York Daily News*. http://www

.nydailynews.com/news/national/dylann-roof-didn-racists-defective-article-1.3156566 (Accessed May 13, 2017).

Flitter, Emily and Jonathan Allen. June 19, 2015. "South Carolina Massacre Suspect Dylann Roof Had Apparent Interest in White Supremacy." *The Sydney Morning Herald*. http://www.smh.com.au/world/south-carolina-massacre-suspect-dylann-roof-had-apparent-interest-in-white-supremacy-20150618-ghrtrg.html (Accessed May 13, 2017).

Fox News. June 20, 2015. "Friend of Dylann Roof Says Suspect Planned Attack on College of Charleston." http://www.foxnews.com/us/2015/06/20/friend-dylann-roof-says-suspect-planned-attack-on-college-charleston.html (Accessed May 13, 2017).

Hatewatch Staff. June 19, 2015. "Charleston Shooter's Alleged Manifesto Reveals Hate Group Helped to Radicalize Him Online." *Southern Poverty Law Center—Hatewatch*. https://www.splcenter.org/hatewatch/2015/06/20/charleston-shooters-alleged-manifesto-reveals-hate-group-helped-radicalize-him-online (Accessed May 13, 2017).

Hawes, Jennifer Berry. May 12, 2017. "Defense Experts Portray Dylann Roof as Obsessive, Delusional Loner." *The Post and Courier*. http://www.postandcourier.com/church_shooting/defense-experts-portray-dylann-roof-as-obsessive-delusional-loner/article_7b82038a-3687-11e7-8fc8-7b9f2fb39774.html (Accessed May 13, 2017).

Jarvie, Jenny. May 11, 2017. "Dylann Roof Told Judge He Would Rather Die Than Be Labeled Autistic or Mentally Ill." *Los Angeles Times*. http://www.latimes.com/nation/la-na-south-carolina-dylan-roof-201711-story.html (Accessed May 13, 2017).

Krol, Charlotte. June 20, 2015. "Dylann Roof's Friend: Charleston Church 'Wasn't Primary Target.'" *The Telegraph*. http://www.telegraph.co.uk/news/worldnews/northamerica/usa/11688181/Dylann-Roofs-friend-Charleston-church-wasnt-primary-target.html (Accessed May 13, 2017).

Lewis, Paul, Amanda Holpuch, and Jessica Glenza. June 21, 2015. "Dylann Roof: FBI Probes Website and Manifesto Linked to Charleston Suspect." *The Guardian*. https://www.theguardian.com/us-news/2015/jun/20/dylann-roof-fbi-website-manifesto-charleston-shooting (Accessed May 13, 2017).

Morlin, Bill. December 19, 2016. "Unrepentant and Radicalized Online: A Look at the Trial of Dylann Roof." https://www.splcenter.org/hatewatch/2016/12/19/unrepentant-and-radicalized-online-look-trial-dylann-roof (Accessed January 22, 2018).

NPR. January 10, 2017. "What Happened When Dylann Roof Asked Google for Information About Race?" http://www.npr.org/sections/thetwo-way/2017/01/10/508363607/what-happened-when-dylann-roof-asked-google-for-information-about-race (Accessed May 13, 2017).

Shapiro, Emily. June 18, 2015. "Charleston Shooting: A Closer Look at Alleged Gunman Dylann Roof." *Yahoo News*. https://www.yahoo.com/gma/charleston-shooting-closer-look-alleged-gunman-dylann-roof-203816813--abc-news-topstories.html (Accessed May 13, 2017).

Silverstein, Jason. June 20, 2017. "Dylann Roof Was Obsessed with Trayvon Martin, Wanted to Save the 'White Race': Friend." *New York Daily News*. http://www.nydailynews.com/news/national/dylann-roof-obsessed-trayvon-martin-white-race-article-1.2263647 (Accessed May 13, 2017).

Thielman, Sam. June 28, 2015. "White Supremacist Calls Charleston 'A Preview of Coming Attractions.'" *The Guardian*. https://www.theguardian.com/us-news/2015/jun/28/harold-covington-northwest-front-dylann-roof-manifesto-charleston-shooting (Accessed May 13, 2017).

Thompson, Catherine. June 22, 2015. "Group That May Have Influenced Charleston Killer: He Had Some 'Legitimate Grievances.'" *TPM Livewire*. http://talkingpointsmemo.com /livewire/ccc-dylann-roof-legitimate-grievances (Accessed May 13, 2017).

Vann Digital. January 10, 2017. "Dylann Roof Gets Death Penalty for Racially Motivated Charleston Church Shooting." http://www.vanndigital.com/dylann-roof-gets-death-pen alty-racially-motivated-charleston-church-shooting/ (Accessed May 13, 2017).

RUBY RIDGE

Together with the Waco siege, the siege at Ruby Ridge, Idaho, in 1992 did more to galvanize antigovernment extremism than any other event in modern U.S. history. In this fateful moment, the collective fear held by many citizens that the U.S. government had become tyrannical, unresponsive, and abusive was confirmed. The government's actions at Ruby Ridge, coupled with Waco less than a year later, would create antigovernment extremists such as Timothy McVeigh and Terry Nichols, who would perpetrate the largest single incident of domestic terrorism in U.S. history—the bombing of the Alfred P. Murrah Federal Building in April 1995.

Ruby Ridge, Idaho, was the home of Randy and Vicki Weaver, individuals who believed that the world had become irretrievably corrupted and that an apocalyptic conflict was inevitable. The Weavers had moved their family to the mountainous terrain of Idaho, believing that in the seclusion and solitude they could withstand the coming onslaught. The Weavers home-schooled their children, believing public schools to be filled with false teachings and the vanities of the world. Like many who fled to the northwestern United States in the 1980s and 1990s, the Weavers believed that their rugged individualism could help them survive a conflict that, in one way or another, would involve the U.S. government.

The events at Ruby Ridge were the culmination of attempts by federal investigators to link Randy Weaver with extremist activities associated either with Aryan Nations or the Covenant, Sword, and Arm of the Lord (Reality Productions 2000). For several years prior to the siege, Randy Weaver had been in a legal dispute with a neighbor. The neighbor had lost the dispute but proceeded to write letters to the Federal Bureau of Investigation (FBI) and the Secret Service contending that Weaver had threatened to kill prominent government officials, including the president of the United States (Balleck 2015). Subsequent investigations by these agencies established no wrongdoing on Weaver's part. Nevertheless, Weaver's casual association with extremist groups, such as Aryan Nations, warranted continued attention from the federal government. Eventually, an informant from the Bureau of Alcohol, Tobacco, and Firearms (ATF) would accuse Weaver of attempting to sell sawed-off shotguns with a length less than the limit allowed by federal law. In early 1991, both Randy and Vicki Weaver were arrested when ATF agents posed as stranded motorists and the Weavers stopped to help them.

An erroneous communication between the federal court overseeing Weaver's case and Weaver himself led to "a bench warrant being issued for Weaver's arrest" (Balleck 2015). Weaver had been informed by his probation officer that his trial was to begin March 20, 1991. In fact, "the trial was scheduled for February 20, 1991" (Balleck 2015). When Weaver failed to appear, the judge overseeing the case issued his warrant. With the failure-to-appear warrant, the case passed from the ATF to the U.S. Marshall's Service (USMS). Realizing the mix-up in dates, the USMS determined that it would wait for March 20 to determine if Weaver would appear. Before this date passed, however, the U.S. Attorney's Office empaneled a grand jury that eventually issued an indictment for failure to appear, though the grand jury was never made aware of the date mix-up. With the grand jury's indictment, Randy Weaver was now considered a fugitive. He had not fled; he was simply holed up in his house on Ruby Ridge, where he made it clear that he would resist any attempt by federal officials to take him by force (New York Times 1992). Over the next several months, federal officials attempted to negotiate with Weaver for his surrender, but he refused to leave the safety of his property at Ruby Ridge.

By this time, Randy Weaver's antigovernment sentiments were well known. He distrusted the government and most federal officials. This distrust was only exacerbated by the mix-up in trial dates that had led to Weaver's being labeled a fugitive. He became convinced that he could not receive a fair trial and that his only recourse was to wait out the government. Weaver's intransigence was strengthened by other suspicious circumstances. When a deputy U.S. marshal asked Bill Grider, an acquaintance of Weaver's, what he believed Weaver's intentions were, Grider responded, "Let me put it to you this way. If I was sitting on my property and somebody with a gun comes to do me harm, then I'll probably shoot him" (Walter 2002).

For more than a year, U.S. federal officials monitored Randy Weaver at his Ruby Ridge compound and looked for opportunities where Weaver could be removed from Ruby Ridge and arrested. On August 21, 1992, six U.S. marshals were sent to the area to bring Weaver into custody. As they approached the Weaver cabin, the family's dogs began barking, alerting Randy Weaver and others in the cabin of the marshals' presence. Weaver's friend, Kevin Harris, "and Weaver's 14-year-old Samuel ('Sammy') emerged from the cabin to determine why the dogs were barking" (Balleck 2015). At this point, the marshals retreated back on the path from where they had come. Randy Weaver had taken a different trail from the cabin and came upon the marshals, who ordered Weaver to stop and/or surrender. Reportedly, he cursed at them and retreated on the trail toward the cabin. Kevin Harris and Sammy Weaver then came upon the marshals. There is some question around who fired first. Reportedly, Deputy U.S. Marshal (DUSM) Art Roderick shot and killed one of the Weavers' dogs that had accompanied Harris and Sammy Weaver, after which Sammy returned fire at Roderick (USMS Section B). As the marshals began firing at Harris and Weaver, Sammy retreated up the path toward the cabin. He was shot dead by one of the marshals, at which point "DUSM Bill Degan was shot and killed by Kevin Harris" (Balleck 2015).

With the death of a U.S. marshal, the FBI mobilized the Hostage Rescue Team (HRT) from Quantico, Virginia. The HRT set up sniper/observer positions around the Ruby Ridge property and were briefed on rules of engagement (ROE) that the snipers interpreted as giving them the "green light" to "shoot on sight" (Department of Justice 1992). The military nature of the ROE varied from standard FBI practice of agents only using deadly force in "self-defense or the defense of another," and that "verbal warning should, whenever possible, be given before the application of deadly force" (Walter 1995). Yet the ROE given in the case of Ruby Ridge were as follows:

1. If any adult male is observed with a weapon prior to the announcement, deadly force can and should be employed, if the shot can be taken without endangering any children.
2. If any adult in the compound is observed with a weapon after the surrender announcement is made, and is not attempting to surrender, deadly force can and should be employed to neutralize the individual.
3. If compromised by any animal, particularly the dogs, that animal should be eliminated.
4. Any subjects other than Randall Weaver, Vicki Weaver, Kevin Harris, presenting threats of death or grievous bodily harm, the FBI rules of deadly force are in effect. Deadly force can be utilized to prevent the death or grievous bodily injury to oneself or that of another. (Department of Justice 1992)

On August 22, 1992, the day after the death of Sammy Weaver and USMS Bill Degan, Lon Horiuchi, an HRT sniper, "shot and wounded Randy Weaver from a position of more than 200 yards as Weaver lifted the latch on a shed to visit the body of his dead son" (Witkin 1995). As "Weaver, his daughter, and Kevin Harris retreated toward the cabin," Horiuchi fired a second shot that "struck and killed Vicki Weaver, who was standing in the doorway of the cabin holding her 10-month-old daughter" (Balleck 2015). A U.S. Department of Justice report would find that Horiuchi's "lack of a call for surrender was inexcusable given that the Weavers and Harris were running for cover toward the cabin" (Balleck 2015). As a result of Horiuchi's actions, the ROE were revoked. The Department of Justice report also found that Horiuchi's actions did not "satisfy constitutional standards for legal use of deadly force" (qtd. in Balleck 2015). On August 24, 1992, the assistant director of the FBI wrote a memo in which he assailed the government's actions at Ruby Ridge and suggested that Weaver was in a fairly strong legal position given the assault that occurred on his private property (qtd. in Balleck 2015).

The siege at Ruby Ridge was ultimately resolved when federal negotiators, including Bo Gritz, a self-proclaimed antigovernment survivalist, made it known to Weaver that if he did not surrender, the situation would have to be resolved through the use of tactical force (Bock and Koontz 1995). On August 31, 1992, Weaver and his daughters surrendered. Weaver and Kevin Harris were arrested, though only Weaver served any time (four months) due to the original violation-of-probation charge. Harris was acquitted on charges of first-degree murder while HRT sniper Lon Horiuchi was indicted on manslaughter charges, only to have the charges later dismissed. Both Weaver and Harris were later awarded large settlements in response to lawsuits that charged that the U.S. government had denied them their rights during the events surrounding the siege at Ruby Ridge.

See also: Militia Movement; Patriot Movement; Waco Standoff

Further Reading

Balleck, Barry J. 2015. *Allegiance to Liberty: The Changing Face of Patriots, Militias, and Political Violence in America*. Praeger.

Bock, Alan W. and Dean Koontz. 1995. *Ambush at Ruby Ridge: How Government Agents Set Randy Weaver Up and Took His Family Down*. Dickens Press.

Department of Justice, OPR Ruby Ridge Task Force Report. June 10, 1994. Section IV. Specific Issues Investigated, F. "FBI's Rules of Engagement" and "Operations" on August 21 and 22, 1992.

New York Times. March 13, 1992. "Marshals Know He's There But Leave Fugitive Alone." *The New York Times*, A14.

Reality Productions. 2000. *Randy Weaver Interview at Ruby Ridge*.

United States Marshals Service. August 21, 1992. "Ruby Ridge: Report of the Subcommittee on Terrorism, Technology, and Government Information." "Firefight" (Section B).

Walter, Jess. 1995. *Every Knee Shall Bow: The Truth and Tragedy of Ruby Ridge & the Randy Weaver Family*. HarperCollins.

Walter, Jess. 2002. *Ruby Ridge: The Truth and Tragedy of the Randy Weaver Family*. Harper Perennial.

Witkin, Gordon. September 11, 1995. "The Nightmare of Idaho's Ruby Ridge." *U.S. News & World Report*.

RUDOLPH, ERIC ROBERT

Eric Robert Rudolph (b. 1966) is an antiabortion extremist and bomber of the 1996 Olympic Games in Atlanta, Georgia. Because of the high-profile nature of his crimes, Rudolph may be one of the most infamous perpetrators of American domestic terrorism. Rudolph is best known for bombing Centennial Olympic Park in Atlanta, Georgia, during the course of the XXVI Olympiad. During Rudolph's bombing spree, two people were killed and more than 120 were injured (Department of Justice 1998). Rudolph spent five years on the FBI's 10 Most Wanted Fugitives list until he was captured in May 2003. Upon his capture, Rudolph revealed that his motive for the Centennial Olympic Park bombing was an attempt to shut down the Olympic Games, thereby embarrassing the U.S. government (AP 2005). In addition, Rudolph revealed that his attacks were meant to kill or injure government officials in as much as any government that condones abortion "deserves death" (AP 2005). Rudolph struck a plea bargain and avoided a possible death sentence. He was sentenced to four life sentences plus 120 years for his crimes and resides at the ADX Supermax prison in Florence, Colorado.

Rudolph was born in Merritt Island, Florida (History.com). When he was young, Rudolph's mother took her son with her as she attended meetings of the Church of Jesus Christ Christian, a Christian Identity church (CNN 2005). Christian Identity is a white supremacist and anti-Semitic belief that holds that the white race are God's "chosen people," and that all other races are "mud people," particularly Jews, who are considered the offspring of Eve and Satan. Rudolph claims that his antigovernment views were not the result of Christian Identity teachings but rather his Roman Catholic beliefs that taught that abortion is murder (AP 2005). After Rudolph received his GED, he joined the army and took basic training at Fort Benning, Georgia. While in the military, Rudolph gained some experience in explosives. He was discharged from the military in January 1989 due to marijuana use (Gettleman 2003).

On July 27, 1996, Rudolph "placed a 40-pound pipe bomb loaded with three-inch masonry nails at the Centennial Olympic Park in Atlanta, Georgia during the XXVI Olympiad" (History.com). He anonymously called police, warning them that the device had been placed, but it detonated far earlier than he indicated. The detonation injured dozens and killed a middle-aged woman. A Turkish cameraperson died while rushing to the scene. A part-time security guard who discovered the bomb, Richard Jewell, was initially suspected in the bombing, but after three months he was cleared and federal law enforcement were left with few suspects.

On January 16, 1997, "two bombs went off at an Atlanta-area medical clinic that performed abortions, injuring seven people" (History.com). After the initial bombing, which just damaged the building, a second explosion occurred as police and emergency service personnel were on the scene. The obvious intent to kill or injure emergency personnel appeared similar to the motivation of the earlier bombing at Centennial Olympic Park, which was meant to draw law enforcement personnel to the scene (because of the called-in bomb threat) and cause their death or injury. Moreover, the construction of the bombs at both the Atlanta abortion clinic and Centennial Olympic Park were very similar. A few days after the abortion clinic bombing, another bomb exploded at a gay and lesbian nightclub in Atlanta, injuring four people (History.com).

On January 29, 1998, "a bomb similar to those used in the attacks in Atlanta exploded at a women's health clinic in Birmingham, Alabama, killing an off-duty security guard and critically injuring a nurse" (History.com). Rudolph became a suspect after witnesses reported spotting a truck, which later turned out to be Rudolph's, near the scene. Authorities "launched a massive manhunt for Rudolph in North Carolina after it was reported that he had been spotted stockpiling supplies" (History.com).

In 1998, Rudolph was officially charged in connection with the bombings in Georgia and Alabama (Federal Bureau of Investigation). Now a fugitive, Rudolph "landed on the FBI's Top Ten Most Wanted Fugitives list and a $1 million reward was offered for his capture" (History.com). On May 31, 2003, "Rudolph was arrested by a rookie police officer who found him digging through a grocery store dumpster in Murphy, North Carolina" (History.com). While incarcerated, Rudolph issued an 11-page rambling manifesto in which he railed against abortion, likening it to the "holocaust" and to "murder," while calling homosexuality "aberrant sexual behavior" (CNN 2005). Rudolph also stated that the Centennial Olympic Park bombing was meant to "shame the United States for its legalization of abortion. He said his goal was to knock out Atlanta's power grid and shut down the Olympics" (CNN 2005). Rudolph also stated that any government that supported abortion was "an enemy that deserves death" (AP 2005).

Though it was supposed that Rudolph's antigovernment sentiments had won him supporters who helped to hide his presence from federal authorities for five years, the FBI played down this notion, stating that

Rudolph is such a loner that we strongly believed he simply wouldn't have trusted anybody. He had access to news; he had newspaper articles in his camp. He knew he was being pursued. I don't think he would have made himself vulnerable to being compromised or betrayed by letting anyone know where he was. (Federal Bureau of Investigation)

After Rudolph published his manifesto, white nationalists and antigovernment activists considered him a hero (Anti-Defamation League).

In 2005, Rudolph accepted a plea deal in which he revealed the presence of hidden explosives he had stored in the North Carolina mountains in exchange for a life sentence. Rudolph was "sentenced to serve a total of four consecutive life sentences in prison, plus 120 years for his crimes" (CNN 2016). He was sentenced to the federal Supermax facility in Florence, Colorado, which houses inmates who are considered the most dangerous to society.

In February 2013, Rudolph, "with help from his brother, published his auto-biography, *Between the Lines of Drift: The Memoirs of a Militant.*" In March 2013, the U.S. Attorney's Office in Birmingham, Alabama, "seized the royalties from Rudolph's book sales, totaling $200, to pay back the $1 million Rudolph has been ordered to pay in restitution" (CNN 2016).

See also: Christian Identity; White Nationalism

Further Reading

Anti-Defamation League. "A Dark & Constant Rage." https://www.adl.org/sites/default/files /documents/CR_5154_25YRS RightWing Terrorism_V5.pdf (Accessed May 24, 2017).

AP. April 14, 2005. "Eric Rudolph Lays Out the Arguments That Fueled Bomb Attacks." http://accesswdun.com/article/2005/4/147618 (Accessed May 24, 2017).

CNN. April 19, 2005. "Rudolph Reveals Motives." http://www.cnn.com/2005/LAW/04/13 /eric.rudolph/ (Accessed May 24, 2017).

CNN. August 22, 2005. "Rudolph's Mother: Son Not a 'Monster.'" https://web.archive.org /web/20140715230302/http://www.cnn.com/2005/LAW/08/22/rudolph.mother/index .html?_s=PM:LAW (Accessed May 24, 2017).

CNN. September 10, 2016. "Eric Robert Rudolph Fast Facts." http://www.cnn.com/2012 /12/06/us/eric-robert-rudolph---fast-facts/ (Accessed May 24, 2017).

Department of Justice. October 14, 1998. "Eric Rudolph Charge in Centennial Olympic Park Bombing." https://www.justice.gov/archive/opa/pr/1998/October/477crm.htm (Accessed May 24, 2017).

Federal Bureau of Investigation. "Eric Rudolph." https://www.fbi.gov/history/famous-cases /eric-rudolph (Accessed May 24, 2017).

Gettleman, Jeffrey (with David M. Halbfinger). June 1, 2003. "Suspect in '96 Olympic Bombing and 3 Other Attacks Is Caught." *The New York Times.* http://www.nytimes.com /2003/06/01/us/suspect-in-96-olympic-bombing-and-3-other-attacks-is-caught.html (Accessed May 24, 2017).

RUSHTON, JEAN-PHILIPPE

Jean-Philippe Rushton (1943–2012) was a professor of psychology at the University of Western Ontario who became known for his research on race and intelligence. His most infamous conclusion was the assertion that blacks have larger genitals, breasts, and buttocks than whites, a relationship inversely proportional to brain size, making whites inherently more intelligent than blacks. But Rushton did not believe that whites were the most intelligent race. This distinction was reserved for East Asians and their descendants, who Rushton argued "average a larger brain size, greater intelligence, more sexual restraint, slower rates of maturation, and greater law abidingness and social organization than do Europeans and their descendants" (Rushton 1995). In 2002, Rushton assumed control of the Pioneer Fund, an organization dedicated to advocates of eugenics, race superiority, and the notion that genetic superiority makes some races (i.e., whites and East Asians) inherently more intelligent than others (i.e., blacks). In 2000, the Charles Darwin Research Institute, founded by Rushton, received nearly $500,000 in grants from the Pioneer Fund, "or nearly 73 percent of the fund's total grants that year" (Southern Poverty Law Center, Intelligence Report). Rushton is known to have "spoken on the alleged IQ deficiencies of minorities at conferences sponsored by *American Renaissance* magazine," an extreme-right-wing publication that promotes white nationalism, white supremacism, and neo-Nazi ideologies (Southern Poverty Law Center, Rushton). Rushton's work has also appeared on VDARE.com, an extreme-right anti-immigrant hate site.

Rushton was born in England and "received a Ph.D. in social psychology from the London School of Economics and Political Science" (Southern Poverty Law Center, Rushton). He began teaching at the University of Western Ontario in 1977, where he became a tenured full professor in 1985. While at Western Ontario, Rushton "was twice reprimanded for conducting research on human subjects without prior approval" (Southern Poverty Law Center, Rushton). In 1989, "Rushton set up the Charles Darwin Research Institute in Port Huron, Michigan, just across the border from London, Ontario, possibly to avoid breaking Canadian laws on hate speech" (Southern Poverty Law Center, Rushton).

Though Rushton never considered himself racist, his leadership of the Pioneer Fund beginning in 2002 associated him with an institution that was founded to "improve the character of the American people through eugenics and procreation by people of white colonial stock" (Southern Poverty Law Center, Rushton). Upon taking the reins of the Pioneer Fund, Rushton populated the governing board with other race scientists, including Richard Lynn, who argued that East Asians and whites are genetically superior to blacks.

In 2005, Rushton published an article in *Psychology, Public Policy and Law*, a journal of the American Psychological Association. In the article, Rushton again made the claim "that Asians are smarter than whites, who are, in turn, smarter than blacks. The journal editors, apparently aware of Rushton's racist background, allowed three rebuttals to be published alongside of Rushton's article" (Southern Poverty Law Center, Rushton). In 2006, Rushton published a study that purported "that men were, on average, smarter than women" (Southern Poverty Law Center 2006). Through his work, Rushton became known as a "race realist" in white supremacist circles, publishing research that others considered politically incorrect or socially dangerous.

Rushton died in 2012 from cancer at the age of 68.

See also: American Renaissance; Pioneer Fund; Taylor, Jared; VDARE; White Nationalism; White Supremacist Movement

Further Reading

Rushton, Jean Philippe. 1995. *Race, Evolution, and Behavior: A Life History Perspective.* Charles Darwin Research Institute.

Southern Poverty Law Center. "Jean-Philippe Rushton." https://www.splcenter.org/fighting -hate/extremist-files/individual/jean-philippe-rushton (Accessed February 13, 2017).

Southern Poverty Law Center. January 31, 2006. "Academic Racists' Work Inching Toward Legitimacy." *Southern Poverty Law Center—Intelligence Report.* https://www.splcenter .org/fighting-hate/intelligence-report/2006/academic-racists-work-inching-toward -legitimacy (Accessed January 22, 2018).

Sussman, Robert Wald. 2014. *The Myth of Race: The Troubling Persistence of an Unscientific Idea.* Harvard University Press.

Tucker, William. 2002. *The Funding of Scientific Racism: Wickliffe Draper and the Pioneer Fund.* University of Illinois Press.

SAGEBRUSH REBELLION

The Sagebrush Rebellion was a movement during the 1970s and 1980s of ranchers, miners, outdoor enthusiasts, politicians, and ordinary citizens who protested the policies of the federal government in regards to federal land control. The rebellion sought to change federal policy on the grazing of livestock on federally owned land, the limits placed on mineral extraction, and other policies that, in the views of most rebels, restricted economic development of federal lands. Though the goals of the rebellion often conflicted depending on which group was making the claim, most rebels appeared to want a transfer of federal land to state and local jurisdictions or the privatization of the land back into the hands of citizens. Though there was a slowdown during the Reagan administration of the designation of new federal lands, the movement was never able to accomplish the rollback of any significant portions of federal land to state or local control. In fact, federal ownership of land in 2016 ranged between 20 and 85 percent in 13 western states (Congressional Research Service).

There has always been tension between advocates of local/state and federal control in the American experience; the Sagebrush Rebellion was the palpable expression of this tension. The settlement of western lands was encouraged by the Homestead Acts of 1862, but much of the land set aside for homesteaders in the west was mountainous terrain, contained poor soil, or lacked suitable water resources to make the growing of crops viable. By the early 20th century, the vast tracts of land unclaimed by homesteaders were controlled by the federal government. At the outset of the Great Depression, the federal government proposed to deed the surface rights of these lands to the states, but the states complained that the land had been overgrazed and would impose undue economic burdens on state budgets that were already strained by the conditions of the Depression (Peffer 1951). The Bureau of Land Management (BLM) was created in 1946 to manage the land that was now under the control of the federal government.

In 1976, the Federal Land Policy and Management Act was enacted and officially ended homesteading. With the passage of the act, all lands that had been under federal control were retained by the federal government, including the grazing, mining, and resource rights that attended these lands. Ranchers, miners, outdoor enthusiasts, and others began to complain about the heavy-handed procedures imposed upon them in utilizing federal lands. Groups like Posse Comitatus gained momentum during this time and foreshadowed the rise of the sovereign citizen movement as citizens began to be wary of the growing control being wielded by the federal government. By the late 1970s, governors, boards of county commissioners, state and federal legislators, and private citizens all began to lobby Congress for the transfer of federal land to the control of the states. A group of western senators created the League for the Advancement of States Equal Rights to press for the return of federal lands. Though various reversion bills were proposed, none ever passed Congress as many legislators were suspicious that the activities of many "rebellion" groups were being funded by the extractive mineral industries of the time (Thompson 2016).

In 1980, while campaigning in Utah, Ronald Reagan declared himself a sagebrush "rebel." With his election later that year, there was hope among many western interests that a significant portion of federal land would be returned to the control of the states. The appointment of James Watt, "a property-rights advocate, as Secretary of the Interior defused much of the sentiment" surrounding the rebellion. Though there was not a wholesale return of federal lands to the states, Watt and the Reagan administration "rolled back regulations and pledged to incorporate more local say into federal land management" (Thompson 2016).

The Sagebrush Rebellion died down during most of the 1980s as the primary opponents of federal control of state lands began to realize the costs that might be incurred with the transfer of such lands to state control. In 1982, Governor Richard Lamm of Colorado wrote in his book, *The Angry West*, that

> by asserting, even flaunting, a regional independence that never existed, the proud West becomes the foolish West. Worse, by continuing to act today as though it still has no need for the federal government, even as it continues to profit from federal largesse, it compounds its hypocrisy and undermines its credibility.

The issues that underpinned the Sagebrush Rebellion flared up again in the 1990s as citizens continued to chafe against the exercise of federal power. The incidents at Ruby Ridge and Waco were to many opponents of "runaway government" a reminder that federal power was no longer checked by the mechanisms designed to prevent abuse. Furthermore, ranchers in the west continued to taunt the federal government with acts of defiance against the BLM and other federal agencies. Renewed legislative efforts to restore federal lands to state control were revived during this time, though none were enacted into law.

With the election of Barack Obama in 2008, rebellion efforts once again gained momentum with the ascendancy of new patriot and antigovernment groups. In 2009, the Oath Keepers were founded with the express intent that government officials would uphold the Constitution. In 2012, "Utah Governor Gary Herbert signed a bill demanding that the federal government return control of millions of acres of public land to the state," foreshadowing similar measures that would be debated in Arizona, Colorado, Idaho, Montana, Nevada, New Mexico, Oregon, Washington, and Wyoming (McQuillan 2015). In April 2014, dozens of new rebels clashed with BLM officials over the agency's roundup of cattle rancher Cliven Bundy's cattle, claiming Bundy owed hundreds of thousands of dollars in grazing fees to the federal government. In January 2016, Ammon Bundy, Cliven

Bundy's son, together with several sympathizers, occupied the Malheur National Wildlife Refuge in Oregon, demanding the return of the land to the control of the state of Oregon. Both Cliven and Ammon Bundy later faced federal charges for their acts.

Though acts of rebellion in western states continue to wax and wane, it is likely that there will continue to be a variety of acts against the federal government as citizens exercise their rights of protest against what they consider the intrusive and unchecked power of the federal government.

See also: Bundy Ranch Standoff; Malheur National Wildlife Refuge Standoff; Oath Keepers; Posse Comitatus; Ruby Ridge

Further Reading

Congressional Research Service. March 3, 2017. "Federal Land Ownership: Overview and Data." https://www.fas.org/sgp/crs/misc/R42346.pdf (Accessed November 8, 2016).

Lamm, Richard. 1982. *The Angry West: A Vulnerable Land and Its Future.* Houghton-Mifflin.

McQuillan, Kindra. April 30, 2015. "State Bills to Study Federal-to-State Land Transfers." *High Country News.* http://www.hcn.org/articles/state-bills-to-study-federal-to-state-land-transfers (Accessed November 21, 2016).

Peffer, E. Louise. 1951. "Chapter 11: The Hoover Proposal." *The Closing of the Public Domain: Disposal and Reservation Policies, 1901–50*, Issue 10. Stanford University Press.

Swearingen, Marshall and Kate Schimel. February 4, 2016. "Timeline: A Brief History of the Sagebrush Rebellion." *High Country News.* http://www.hcn.org/articles/a-history-of-the-sagebrush-rebellion (Accessed November 21, 2016).

Thompson, Jonathan. January 14, 2016. "The First Sagebrush Rebellion: What Sparked It and How It Ended." *High Country News.* http://www.hcn.org/articles/a-look-back-at-the-first-sagebrush-rebellion (Accessed November 21, 2016).

SAN BERNARDINO SHOOTING

On December 2, 2015, a Muslim married couple from Redlands, California, Syed Rizwan Farook and Tashfeen Malik, perpetrated a mass shooting at the Inland Regional Center in San Bernardino, California. The shootings left 14 people dead and 22 others seriously wounded. According to the Federal Bureau of Investigation (FBI) investigation conducted in the aftermath of the shooting, both Farook and Malik were "homegrown violent extremists who had been inspired by foreign terrorist groups and radicalized by way of the internet over a period of several years prior to the attack" (Blankstein et al. 2015). Both Farook and Malik "expressed a commitment to jihadism and martyrdom in private messages to each other. Before the attack, the couple had amassed a stockpile of weapons, ammunition, and bomb-making equipment at their home" (LA Times). After the couple fled the scene of the shooting, they were pursued by police, who later killed them in a shootout (Ortiz). A friend of the shooters, Enrique Marquez Jr., was arrested in connection with the shooting for conspiracy to provide material support to terrorism. Both Farook and Marquez had discussed Islamic radicalism and had amassed weapons in preparation for perpetrating a variety of terrorist attacks in and around the Los Angeles area.

Marquez was eventually charged with conspiracy and for the illegal purchase of two assault rifles that were used by Farook and Malik. Because of the involvement of Muslims in the attack, in the aftermath of the shooting the "Council on American-Islamic Relations (CAIR) reported an escalation of anti-Muslim hate crimes" (Dorell). Donald Trump, who less than a year later would be elected president of the United States, called for a "total and complete ban on Muslims entering the United States 'until our country's representatives can figure out what is going on'" (Holland and Stephenson). The shootings also renewed the call for "common sense" gun control measures and increased background safety checks (ABC News).

Farook and Malik "used five firearms during the attack, and left behind three pipe bombs wired to a remote control. The pipe bombs did not detonate" (LA Times 2015). The weapons used were a M&P 15 semiautomatic rifle, two 9mm handguns, a .22 caliber rifle, and a DPMS Model A-15 semiautomatic weapon (LA Times 2015). Shortly before 11:00 a.m. on December 2, 2015, Farook and Malik fired five shots, killing two people outside the Inland Regional Center where a Christmas party was taking place. Farook had been at the event earlier in the morning but had left and then returned to perpetrate the attacks. After the initial killings, Farook entered the building and began firing at those in attendance. Both Farook and Malik "wore ski masks and black tactical gear (including load-bearing vests holding magazines and ammunition), but not ballistic or bulletproof vests" (Domonoske 2015). The entire shooting "took two to three minutes, during which the shooters fired more than 100 bullets" (LA Times 2015).

Even though Farook's face had been covered, those at the scene recognized his build and voice and were able to give a description to law enforcement. After finding evidence at Farook and Malik's home, and getting a description of their getaway vehicle, law enforcement located Farook and Malik four hours after the shooting, and a firefight ensued. Nearly two dozen officers "fired some 380 rounds at the killers while they returned with 76 rounds." After about five minutes, both Farook and Malik were killed (Ortiz 2015). In the aftermath of their deaths, it was revealed that "Farook and Malik had a six-month-old daughter that they had left with Farook's mother at their Redlands home the morning of the attack, stating they were going to a doctor's appointment" (Nagourney et al. 2015).

During the ensuing investigation, it became evident that both Farook and Malik had been inspired by Islamic and other terrorist organizations (Mozingo 2016). However, the case was considered as domestic terrorism as Farook was "a U.S. citizen of Pakistani descent and Malik was a Pakistani-born lawful permanent resident of the United States" (Mozingo 2016). FBI director James Comey indicated that the investigation revealed that the couple had been "talking about martyrdom and jihad" and had been planning the attack for at least a year, "including taking target practice and making plans to have their daughter cared for by her grandmother" (Blankstein et al. 2015). Comey stated that although the couple had been "radicalized by foreign terrorist organizations," there was no indication that they were part of any larger cell or terrorist network. This reinforced the idea that the couple were "lone wolves" who were carrying out jihad after largely being radicalized online (Stanglin and Johnson 2015).

San Bernardino County sheriff John McMahon speaks during a press conference after a mass shooting on December 2, 2015, in San Bernardino, California. Husband and wife couple Syed Rizwan Farook and Tashfeen Malik, who had been radicalized online, murdered 14 people and seriously wounded 22 others. (Gina Ferazzi/Los Angeles Times via Getty Images)

After the attacks, Enrique Marquez Jr. was arrested in connection with the case. Marquez was longtime friends with Farook, and the two had planned terror attacks for several years prior to the San Bernardino shooting. Marquez had apparently "spent time in Farook's home listening to, watching, and reading radical Islamic propaganda" (Blankstein et al. 2015). Marquez was charged with "three federal criminal counts: conspiracy to provide material support to terrorism, making a false statement regarding his acquisition of firearms used in the shootings, and immigration fraud" (Marquez had been involved in an immigration fraud sham marriage) (Queally, Winton, and Esquivel 2016). Marquez eventually pleaded guilty to charges of purchasing the weapons used in the attack and is scheduled to be sentenced in February 2018 (Rokos 2017).

The San Bernardino shootings reignited many Americans' fear that Islamic radicals were in their midst. Barely seven months later, this fear would be realized when another domestic radicalized Islamic terrorist perpetrated the worst mass killing in U.S. history at a gay nightclub in Orlando, Florida. Like the Colorado theater shooting and the Newtown Elementary School shooting before it, the San Bernardino shooting reignited the debate over gun control, background checks, and Second Amendment rights. Though President Obama suggested that the shooting provided an opportunity to make some "common sense gun safety laws and strengthen background checks" in the aftermath of the shooting, these proposals were opposed by Second Amendment activists. President Obama also "called for legislation to block people on the anti-terrorism No Fly List from purchasing weapons," though U.S. "Speaker of the House Paul Ryan opposed this saying that denying a person on the list the right to bear arms would violate their due process rights" (Slack, Singer, and Kelly 2015).

Donald Trump, who at the time was a front-runner for the Republican Party's nomination as president of the United States, created a controversy in the aftermath of the shooting when he suggested that all Muslim immigration into the United States should be banned for a time. Though Trump's proposal met with widespread condemnation, he "cited the internment of Japanese Americans, German Americans, and Italian Americans during World War II as precedent for his proposal" (Blefsky 2015; Keneally 2015). Trump's hard-line rhetoric appealed to right-wing extremists at the time, and his promise to make Americans safe again appealed to those who were fearful of a growing tide of radical Islamic extremists in the United States.

See also: Colorado Theater Shooting; Orlando Nightclub Shooting; Second Amendment

Further Reading

ABC News. December 2, 2015. "President Obama Responds to San Bernardino Shootings." http://abc7.com/news/president-obama-responds-to-san-bernardino-shootings/1107280/ (Accessed June 1, 2017).

Blankstein, Andrew, Robert Windrem, Pete Williams, Richard Esposito, and Hannah Rappleye. December 8, 2015. "San Bernardino Shooters Practiced for Attack a Year in Advance." *NBC News.* http://www.nbcnews.com/storyline/san-bernardino-shooting/san-bernardino-shooters-planned-attack-least-year-advance-n476521 (Accessed June 1, 2017).

Blefsky, Dan. December 8, 2015. "Trump's Plan to Bar Muslims' Is Widely Condemned Abroad." *The New York Times.* https://www.nytimes.com/2015/12/09/world/europe/donald-trumps-call-to-bar-muslims-reverberates-abroad.html (Accessed June 1, 2017).

Domonoske, Camila. December 3, 2015. "San Bernardino Shootings: What We Know, One Day After." *NPR.* http://www.npr.org/sections/thetwo-way/2015/12/03/458277103/san-bernardino-shootings-what-we-know-one-day-after (Accessed June 1, 2017).

Dorell, Oren. December 8, 2015. "Muslims Report More Bias Cases Across USA." *USA Today.* https://www.usatoday.com/story/news/2015/12/08/us-muslims-report-more-bias-cases-across-nation/76982412/ (Accessed June 1, 2017).

Holland, Steve and Emily Stephenson. December 7, 2015. "Donald Trump Urges Ban on Muslims Entering U.S." *Reuters.* http://www.reuters.com/article/us-usa-election-trump-idUSKBN0TQ2N320151207 (Accessed June 1, 2017).

Keneally, Meghan. December 8, 2015. "Donald Trump Cites These FDR Policies to Defend Muslim Ban." *Good Morning America.* https://www.yahoo.com/gma/donald-trump-cites-fdr-policies-defend-muslim-ban-180436247--abc-news-topstories.html (Accessed June 1, 2017).

LA Times. December 14, 2015. "Everything We Know About the San Bernardino Terror Attack Investigation So Far." *Los Angeles Times.* http://www.latimes.com/local/california/la-me-san-bernardino-shooting-terror-investigation-htmlstory.html (Accessed June 1, 2017).

Mozingo, Joe. September 9, 2016. "'The Worst Thing Imaginable:' Bodies and Blood Every-where After San Bernardino Terrorist Attack, DOJ Report Shows." *Los Angeles Times*. http://www.latimes.com/local/lanow/la-me-san-bernardino-terror--20160909-snap -story.html (Accessed June 1, 2017).

Nagourney, Adam, Ian Lovett, Julie Turkewitz, and Benjamin Mueller. December 3, 2015. "Couple Kept Tight Lid on Plans for San Bernardino Shooting." *The New York Times*. https://www.nytimes.com/2015/12/04/us/san-bernardino-shooting-syed-rizwan -farook.html?_r=0 (Accessed June 1, 2017).

Ortiz, Erik. December 3, 2015. "San Bernardino Shooting: Timeline of How the Rampage Unfolded." *NBC News*. http://www.nbcnews.com/storyline/san-bernardino-shooting /san-bernardino-shooting-timeline-how-rampage-unfolded-n473501 (Accessed June 1, 2017).

Queally, James, Richard Winton, and Paloma Esquivel. April 28, 2016. "FBI Arrests Brother of San Bernardino Terrorist and 2 Others on Marriage Fraud Charges." *Los Angeles Times*. http://www.latimes.com/local/lanow/la-me-ln-fbi-serves-san-bernardino-warrants -20160428-story.html (Accessed June 1, 2017).

Rokos, Brian. November 2, 2017. "Sentencing for Riverside Man Who Aided San Ber-nardino Shooter is Postponed." *The Sun*. https://www.sbsun.com/2017/11/02/sentenc ing-for-riverside-man-who-aided-san-bernardino-shooter-is-postponed/   (Accessed January 22, 2018).

Serrano, Richard A., Paloma Esquivel, and Corina Knoll. December 17, 2015. "Marquez and Farook Plotted Campus and Freeway Attacks, Prosecutors Allege." *Los Angeles Times*. http://www.latimes.com/local/lanow/la-me-ln-san-bernardino-marquez-20151217 -story.html (Accessed June 1, 2017).

Slack, Donovan, Paul Singer, and Erin Kelly. December 3, 2015. "Republicans Say No to New Gun Control Legislation After San Bernardino." *USA Today*. https://www.usatoday .com/story/news/politics/2015/12/03/ryan-urges-caution-on-gun-legislation/76714608/ (Accessed June 1, 2017).

Stanglin, Doug and Kevin Johnson. December 4, 2015. "FBI: No Evidence San Bernardino Killers Were Part of a Cell." *USA Today*. https://www.usatoday.com/story/news/nation /2015/12/04/suspects-family-shocked-killings/76773382/ (Accessed June 1, 2017).

SANDY HOOK ELEMENTARY SCHOOL SHOOTING

On December 14, 2012, 20-year-old Adam Lanza shot and killed 26 people, including 20 children, at Sandy Hook Elementary School in Newtown, Connecti-cut. Before perpetrating the massacre at the elementary school, Lanza had killed his mother in the home that he shared with her. When police arrived at the scene of the shootings, Lanza committed suicide. The shooting was the most deadly mass shooting in the history of the United States, following the 2017 Las Vegas musical festival shooting, the 2016 Orlando nightclub shooting, and the 2007 Virginia Tech shooting. The shooting, occurring only a few weeks after the reelec-tion of President Barack Obama, sparked a massive surge in gun sales and pro-posed new laws to enact more stringent gun control regulations. These proposals included expanding background checks and banning the sale and manufacture of certain types of semi-automatic weapons with magazine capacities greater than

10 rounds (Plumer 2012). Gun rights activists, many of whom viewed the massacre as an excuse orchestrated by the government to enact stringent new gun laws, organized to block any such proposals from coming to fruition. Ordinary citizens, too, fearing that certain guns would be outlawed in the aftermath of the shooting, purchased weapons in record numbers in anticipation of stricter gun laws. The shooting mobilized gun rights activists and opponents alike and once again brought issues pertaining to the Second Amendment to the forefront of the political landscape. It also spawned conspiracy theories by extremists who believed that the shooting was either orchestrated or faked by the U.S. government in order to take away the liberties of American citizens (Wiedeman 2016).

Killer Adam Lanza entered Sandy Hook Elementary shortly after 9:35 a.m., carrying a Bushmaster XM-15 rifle, a line of AR-15 pattern semiautomatic rifles. The rifle was capable of firing 45 rounds per minute (Bushmaster). Police arrived on the scene at 9:39 a.m. "and heard the last shot fired at 9:40.03 a.m., believing it to be Lanza shooting himself in the head with a Glock 20SF" (State of Connecticut 2015). Lanza had used multiple magazines during the shootings and "shot all but two of his victims multiple times" (Department of Emergency Services and Public Protection). After the shootings, police recovered a large quantity of unused ammunition along with three semiautomatic firearms and a shotgun that was found in Lanza's car (State of Connecticut 2015). In less than five minutes, Lanza had fired 156 shots from the XM-15 rifle and Glock handgun (State of Connecticut 2015).

The Sandy Hook Elementary School shooting mobilized both gun rights and control activists. On the gun rights side, the tragedy broke decades-old fundraising records. In 2013, the National Rifle Association (NRA) raised millions of dollars more than it had raised the year before. In addition, NRA membership soared, surpassing 5 million (Shen 2013). As the NRA's propaganda machine kicked into high gear, spreading rumors that new background check proposals were being used as an excuse to seize weapons, guns flew off the shelves. Bushmaster, the manufacturer of the assault rifle used by Lanza, enjoyed profits of $94 million in guns and ammunition sales through the end of September 2013, far surpassing the $500,000 in profits they had made the year before (Shen 2013). Sandy Hook also mobilized schools around the United States to arm themselves. After NRA president Wayne LaPierre argued that the massacre could have been prevented had teachers been allowed to carry weapons, 20 states passed laws to put more guns in schools, with some school districts training and arming teachers (Shen 2013). Finally, the NRA moved to punish lawmakers who voted for more stringent gun control regulations. In Colorado, the NRA poured more than $360,000 into a campaign to recall two state lawmakers after they backed stricter gun laws in the state. The two Democratic senators were successfully pushed out of office and a third senator resigned amid growing pressure against her (Shen 2013).

Though gun control was thrust to the forefront of the national political conversation after the Sandy Hook shooting, gun laws did not significantly change at the national level and changed only marginally in certain states (Goss 2014).

For extremists, conspiracy theories began to circulate immediately after the massacre. Some theories "alleged that the shooting was a hoax, or was a false flag operation staged by the United States government" (Vancouver Sun 2013; Sommerfeldt 2016). Others claimed that the attack was orchestrated by President Obama and gun control advocates to seize weapons from American citizens and curb the patriot and militia movements in the United States (Celock 2012; Bennett 2012). Days after the massacre, "a man walked around Newtown filming a video in which he declared that the massacre had been staged by 'some sort of New World Order global elitists' intent on taking away our guns and our liberty" (Wiedeman 2016). A week later, a Florida Atlantic professor wrote a blog post expressing doubt that the massacre had occurred (Wiedeman 2016).

Lenny Pozner, the father of one of the victims of the Sandy Hook shootings, understood these sentiments, as he had once been a serious conspiracy theorist himself. As one article stated,

> "I [Pozner] probably listened to an Alex Jones podcast after I dropped the kids off at school that morning," Pozner said, referencing the fearmongering proprietor of InfoWars. Pozner had entertained everything from specific cover-ups (the moon landing was faked) to geopolitical intrigue (the "real" reasons why the price of gold sometimes shifted so dramatically) and saw value in skepticism. But for him, the appeal of conspiracy theories was the same as watching a good science-fiction movie. "I have an imaginative mind," he said. (Wiedeman 2016)

Though conspiracy theorists questioned whether Sandy Hook had, in fact, occurred, in the end there was no doubt that 26 people, including 20 children, had been brutally murdered. The conspiracy theories that surrounded the Sandy Hook shooting were an attempt by right-wing extremists to relieve the dissonance that had been caused by their unabashed support of absolute gun rights. In the end, their campaigns of disinformation and misdirection succeeded as no meaningful gun control measures resulted from the Sandy Hook Elementary School shooting.

See also: Orlando Nightclub Shooting; Second Amendment

Further Reading

Bennett, Dashiell. December 18, 2012. "Newtown Conspiracy Theories, Debunked." *The Atlantic.* https://www.theatlantic.com/national/archive/2012/12/newtown-shooting-conspiracy-theories/320360/ (Accessed May 19, 2017).

Bushmaster. "Operating and Safety Instruction Manual." http://stevespages.com/pdf/bushmaster_xm15.pdf (Accessed May 19, 2017).

Celock, John. December 18, 2012. "Orly Taitz Blames Sandy Hook Massacre on Obama." *Huffington Post.* http://www.huffingtonpost.com/2012/12/18/orly-taitz-sandy-hook-obama_n_2325671.html (Accessed May 19, 2017).

Department of Emergency Services and Public Protection. 2013. "Sandy Hook Elementary School Shooting Reports." http://cspsandyhookreport.ct.gov/ (Accessed May 19, 2017).

Goss, Kristin. December 16, 2014. "Two Years After Sandy Hook, the Gun Control Movement Has New Energy." *The Washington Post.* https://www.washingtonpost.com/news/monkey-cage/wp/2014/12/16/two-years-after-sandy-hook-the-gun-control-movement-has-new-energy/?utm_term=.c5a471b1cdcf (Accessed May 19, 2017).

Plumer, Brad. December 17, 2012. "Everything You Need To Know About the Assault Weapons Ban, In One Post. *Washington Post.* https://www.washingtonpost.com/news/wonk/wp/2012/12/17/everything-you-need-to-know-about-banning-assault-weapons-in-one-post/?utm_term=.ae5d17fef3b8 (Accessed January 22, 2018).

Shen, Aviva. December 14, 2013. "How Newtown Transformed Gun Activism." Think-Progress. https://thinkprogress.org/how-newtown-transformed-gun-activism-88b1c12c387d (Accessed May 19, 2017).

Sommerfeldt, Chris. November 18, 2016. "Right-Wing Conspiracy Theorist Alex Jones Doubles Down on 'Completely Fake' Sandy Hook Massacre Claims." *New York Daily News.* http://www.nydailynews.com/news/politics/alex-jones-doubles-completely-fake-sandy-hook-claims-article-1.2878305 (Accessed May 19, 2017).

State of Connecticut. March 6, 2015. "Final Report of the Sandy Hook Advisory Commission." http://www.shac.ct.gov/SHAC_Final_Report_3-6-2015.pdf (Accessed May 19, 2017).

Vancouver Sun. January 16, 2013. "Conspiracy Theorists Claim Sandy Hook Tragedy Is Elaborate Government Hoax." http://www.vancouversun.com/news/Conspiracy+theorists+claim+Sandy+Hook+tragedy+elaborate+government/7822502/story.html (Accessed May 19, 2017).

Wiedeman, Reeves. September 5, 2016. "The Sandy Hook Hoax." *New York Magazine.* http://nymag.com/daily/intelligencer/2016/09/the-sandy-hook-hoax.html (Accessed May 19, 2017).

SCHOEP, JEFF

Jeff Schoep (b. 1973) is the commander of the National Socialist Movement, the largest national socialist organization in the United States. Schoep claims that he became a Nazi in the fourth grade after reading Adolf Hitler's *Mein Kampf* (My Struggle). At 19, Schoep joined a minor neo-Nazi group, the National Socialist American Workers Freedom Movement (NSAWFM), in St. Paul, Minnesota, and attempted to reinvigorate the group "by distributing literature, organizing rallies, and recruiting younger members—including unaffiliated skinheads—in order to bring a new face to the cause of racism" (Southern Poverty Law Center 2012). Schoep's efforts brought in dozens of new recruits, and he became a rising star in the neo-Nazi movement. In 1994, Schoep renamed the struggling NSAWFM the National Socialist Movement (NSM) and reached out to other racist groups, including members of the Ku Klux Klan and various skinhead groups, offering memberships in NSM for just $35 (Southern Poverty Law Center). Today, the NSM claims to be the "largest and most active" national socialist group in the United States and brands itself a "white civil rights organization," rejecting labels such as "racist" and "neo-Nazi" (National Socialist Movement). NSM has been associated with several instances of racial violence but is perhaps best known for its involvement in the 2005 Toledo riot in which the group's plan to protest gang activity by African Americans in Toledo, Ohio, sparked counterdemonstrations that led to a four-hour riot and the implementation of a citywide curfew.

Though only 21 when he assumed control of NSM, through Schoep's leadership the group became "one of the largest and most active neo-Nazi groups in the United States during the mid- to late 1990s" (Southern Poverty Law Center). The group was frequently criticized by more elitist white supremacist organizations, however, "for the crudeness of its propaganda and its members' fetishistic predilection for brown shirts, swastika armbands and shiny boots" (Southern Poverty Law Center). NSM's membership was bolstered by the near breakup of the National Alliance and the Aryan Nations in the early 2000s as well as the sentencing of the Creativity Movement's leader, Matt Hale, "to 40 years in prison for soliciting the murder of a federal judge" (Southern Poverty Law Center).

In 1998, Schoep assisted the mother of his daughter in stealing $4,000 worth of computer equipment and was subsequently arrested on felony burglary charges (Southern Poverty Law Center). Schoep pled guilty and was sentenced to probation but was blasted by the sentencing judge who pointed out Schoep's "blatant hypocrisy in fathering a child out of wedlock and engaging in theft—behaviors that neo-Nazis regularly ascribe to non-whites" (Southern Poverty Law Center).

Schoep became known for his effectiveness in recruiting young members to the ranks of NSM, targeting those between the ages of 14 and 17, although this strategy may have backfired, as revealed by leaked e-mails. In 2009, wikileaks.org revealed memos written by Schoep which read,

> When Col. Bishop and I have to play babysitter, and talk to people about drama, it makes us, all of you, and our Party look foolish. America is being overrun with Mexicans and other invaders, instead of expelling certain people, these members and the Party are better served if the drama is saved for the playground, and we all get back to work. (Scherr 2009)

In 2012, Schoep's ex-wife Joanna (whom he had married in 2008) revealed that Schoep had been accepting of her nonwhite ancestry and that of her 17-year-old daughter, who was part African American. This information, "anathema to neo-Nazis," was kept secret from the NSM membership (Hess 2012). Joanna Schoep stated that Schoep was not overtly racist, but he was a "raging anti-Semite who blamed the Jews for everything." According to Joanna Schoep, her ex-husband's "involvement in neo-Nazism was to boost his ego, gain a Jim Jones type of following and make some money" (Southern Poverty Law Center).

See also: Aryan Nations; Creativity Movement; Ku Klux Klan; National Alliance; National Socialist Movement; Neo-Nazis; White Supremacist Movement

Further Reading

Hess, Axl. March 16, 2012. "NSM 'Leader' Jeff Schoep Exposed as a Race-Mixer and Adulterer." *White Honor.* http://whitehonor.com/white-power/nsm-leader-jeff-schoep-exposed-as-a-race-mixer-and-adulterer/ (Accessed March 13, 2017).

National Socialist Movement. "About Us." http://www.nsm88.org/aboutus.html (Accessed March 13, 2017).

Scherr, Sonia. August 28, 2009. "Neo-Nazi Group's Dirty Linen Aired in Leaked E-Mails." *Southern Poverty Law Center—Hatewatch*. https://www.splcenter.org/hatewatch/2009 /08/28/neo-nazi-groups-dirty-linen-aired-leaked-e-mails (Accessed March 13, 2017).

Southern Poverty Law Center. "Jeff Schoep." https://www.splcenter.org/fighting-hate /extremist-files/individual/jeff-schoep (Accessed March 13, 2017).

Southern Poverty Law Center. May 25, 2012. "National Socialist Movement Leader Jeff Schoep's Ex-Wife Discusses Life With A Leading Neo-Nazi." https://www.splcenter .org/fighting-hate/intelligence-report/2012/national-socialist-movement-leader-jeff -schoeps-ex-wife-discusses-life-leading-neo-nazi (Accessed January 22, 2018).

SCHWEITZER, LEROY

LeRoy Schweitzer (1938–2011) was the leader of the Montana Freemen (Freemen), an antigovernment, Christian patriot movement based outside of Jordan, Montana. The Montana Freemen rejected federal authority and declared themselves to be sovereign citizens, subject only to local and (sometimes) state laws. They called the land on which they lived Justus Township and considered it a sovereign municipality with its own laws, courts, and judgments. Because they did not believe in the legitimacy of the U.S. government, Schweitzer's Freemen attempted to undermine the banking industry of the United States by writing billions of dollars' worth of bogus checks that came to be known as "Schweitzer checks" (Malay 2011). Before his arrest, Schweitzer had instructed some 800 of his followers, for a $100 fee, in how to defraud the government and others. In March 1996, Schweitzer and his followers were involved in a standoff with the Federal Bureau of Investigation (FBI) because of the group's criminal activities. The Freemen were well armed and had "enough food and fuel for months of survival [and] seemed poised to turn routine arrests for fraud and conspiracy into a Waco-style disaster" (Zeskind 1998). Because the FBI wanted to avoid confrontations with armed individuals such as those at Ruby Ridge, Idaho, in 1992 and Waco, Texas, in 1993, they withdrew a safe distance from Justus Township determined to wait out the Freemen. After an 81-day standoff, the Freemen surrendered to authorities in June 1996. In a subsequent trial on dozens of federal charges, Schweitzer was convicted and sentenced to 22 years in federal prison. He died of natural causes in the Colorado Supermax facility in 2011 at age 73.

LeRoy Schweitzer made his living as a crop duster in Montana. Throughout the 1980s, he became increasingly frustrated with government regulations. During this time, he became fascinated with the ideology of the Posse Comitatus, the antigovernment group that recognized no legal authority above the county sheriff, and even attended numerous Posse meetings. He also had contacts with The Order, the infamous antigovernment group that became known as the most dangerous domestic terror group in the United States (History Commons). By the mid-1980s, Schweitzer was a tax resister. By 1992, Schweitzer owed more than $389,000 in back taxes. As a result, the Internal Revenue Service seized his property and sold it at auction (History Commons).

Thoroughly radicalized by this time, Schweitzer sought out like-minded individuals, and they formed the Montana Freemen in early 1995. Their headquarters became Justus Township outside of Jordan, Montana. On the edge of the property, the Freemen posted a sign that read, "Do Not Enter. Private Land of the Sovereign. . . . The right of Personal Liberty is one of the fundamental rights guaranteed to every citizen, and any unlawful interference with it may be resisted" (History Commons). In order to support themselves and disrupt the government, Schweitzer and the Freemen engaged in what prosecutors called a conspiracy of "fraud of epic proportions, involving 3,432 checks totaling $15.5 billion. Of that amount, they said there were actual losses of $1.8 billion" (Southern Poverty Law Center).

The FBI investigated the Freemen, and arrest warrants were issued for Schweitzer and seven other individuals. When Schweitzer was arrested on March 25, 1996, "his arrest prompted 16 other members of the Freemen to barricade themselves" on the 960-acre ranch compound that was Justus Township (Southern Poverty Law Center). After an 81-day standoff, the Freemen surrendered without firing a shot. Schweitzer was later convicted "on 25 counts, including conspiracy, bank and wire fraud, failure to file federal income tax returns, fugitive possession of a firearm and threatening a federal judge" (Morlin 2011). Schweitzer, "who called himself the 'chief justice' of Justus Township, was also charged with armed robbery" after they confiscated the equipment of an ABC-TV news crew outside of the compound (Morlin 2011). At his sentencing, Schweitzer "stood gagged, chained, and handcuffed before the judge. When his gag was briefly removed, Schweitzer shouted that he was a citizen of the country of Montana, not of the United States" (Morlin 2011).

Schweitzer was sentenced to 22 years in federal prison and was required to serve his time at the Florence, Colorado, Supermax facility that housed such infamous inmates as Unabomber Ted Kaczynski, Oklahoma City bombing convicts Timothy McVeigh and Terry Nichols, and Atlanta Olympic bombing convict Eric Rudolph. Schweitzer died of natural causes in the Supermax prison on September 20, 2011.

See also: Justus Township (in Montana Freemen entry); Montana Freemen; Order, The; Paper Terrorism; Patriot Movement; Posse Comitatus; Ruby Ridge; Sovereign Citizens Movement; Waco Standoff

Further Reading

History Commons. "Profile: LeRoy Schweitzer." http://www.historycommons.org/entity.jsp?entity=leroy_schweitzer_1 (Accessed March 14, 2017).

Malay, Andy. September 23, 2011. "Freemen Leader LeRoy Schweitzer Dies in Prison." *Belgrade News.* http://www.belgrade-news.com/news/article_7038fb68-e611-11e0-b1d4-001cc4c03286.html (Accessed March 14, 2017).

Morlin, Bill. September 21, 2011. "Montana Freemen Leader Dies in Prison." *Southern Poverty Law Center—Hatewatch.* https://www.splcenter.org/hatewatch/2011/09/21/montana-freeman-leader-dies-prison (Accessed March 14, 2017).

Southern Poverty Law Center. "Four Montana Freemen Found Guilty." *Southern Poverty Law Center—Intelligence Report.* https://www.splcenter.org/fighting-hate/intelligence-report/1998/four-montana-freemen-found-guilty (Accessed March 14, 2017).

Zeskind, Leonard. June 15, 1998. "Montana Freemen Trial May Mark End of an Era." *Southern Poverty Law Center—Intelligence Report.* https://www.splcenter.org/fighting -hate/intelligence-report/1998/montana-freemen-trial-may-mark-end-era   (Accessed March 14, 2017).

SEALE, BOBBY

Bobby Seale (b. 1936) was a prominent political activist of the radical left in the 1960s and 1970s. Together with Huey P. Newton, Seale founded the Black Panther Party (BPP) in 1966 to organize and galvanize the black community and spur it to action. The goal of the organization was to express the needs and desires of blacks as they attempted to resist racist elements, then pervasive in the American political and cultural system, as well as the classism that was perpetuated by the system. Seale and Newton wrote the doctrines that would become the guiding ideology of the Black Panther movement. Entitled "What We Want Now!" and "What We Believe," these treatises "outlined the philosophical principles espoused by the Black Panther Party and were meant to educate both blacks and whites about the specifics of the party's platform" (Seale 1970). Both Seale and Newton had been great admirers of Malcolm X, a black activist and Nation of Islam minister who had been assassinated in 1965. The Black Panthers and its manifestos were meant to reflect Malcolm X's slogan to obtain "freedom by any means necessary"(Seale 1970).

Seale was one of the original eight individuals indicted for conspiracy to incite riots during the Democratic National Convention in Chicago, Illinois, in 1968. When the Chicago Eight, as they were known, went on trial in 1969, Seale's numerous protests and outbursts in court caused the judge in his case, Julius Hoffman, to order Seale bound and gagged for nearly a week during the course of the proceedings. Hoffman would eventually charge Seale with contempt and sentence him to four years in prison (Federal Judicial Center). This effectively severed Seale from the Chicago Eight trial, whereafter the remaining defendants became known as the Chicago Seven.

While serving his four-year sentence for contempt in the Chicago case, Seale was put on trial again in 1970 for what was alleged to be a criminal conspiracy to murder wayward Black Panther Party members. Known as the New Haven Black Panther trials, the charges stemmed from the murder of 19-year-old Black Panther Party member Alex Rackley, who was found dead in May 1969. Upon learning that Rackley was a police informant, several members of the BPP had carried out the murder. The BPP leader of the murder plan later turned state's evidence and cut a deal with the prosecution, implicating Seale as having ordered the murder. During Seale's trial, the jury was deadlocked, and the charges against him were dropped. The New Haven trials produced a backlash against the Black Panther Party, particularly from the generally sympathetic left, and lessened support in the black community for the party's tendency for violent retribution of defectors or those considered traitors. By the mid-1970s, the Black Panther Party would largely disappear from public view.

While Seale was still in prison, "his wife became pregnant, allegedly by a fellow Black Panther, Fred Bennett." When Bennett's body was found in a Black

Panther hideout, Seale was suspected of having ordered the murder (Lazerow and Williams 2006). Seale later wrote an article entitled "One Less Oppressor" in which he expressed appreciation for the murder of Bennett and stated, "The people have now come to realize that the only way to deal with the oppressor is to deal on our own terms and this was done" (Heath 1976).

After his release from prison in 1972, Seale ran for mayor of Oakland, California, in 1973. Though he received "the second highest number of votes in a nine-way field," he ultimately lost in a runoff to the incumbent mayor (Seale 1978). In 1974, "Seale and Huey Newton argued over a proposed movie about the Black Panther Party" (Randall 1996). According to several accounts, Newton and his bodyguards beat Seale "so badly that he required extensive medical treatment for his injuries." Seale went into hiding after the event and "ended his affiliation with the Black Panther Party in 1974. Seale later denied that any physical altercation" between him and Newton had taken place and dismissed rumors that he and Newton had ever been anything less than friends (Randall 1996).

See also: Black Panther Party; Malcolm X; Newton, Huey P.

Further Reading

Federal Judicial Center. "The Chicago Seven Conspiracy Trial: Bobby Seale." http://www.fjc.gov/history/home.nsf/page/tu_chicago7_bio_seale.html (Accessed March 17, 2017).

Heath, G. Louis. 1976. *The Black Panther Leaders Speak: Huey P. Newton, Bobby Seale, Eldridge Cleaver and Company Speak Out Through the Black Panther Party's Official Newspaper.* Scarecrow Press.

Lazerow, Jama and Yohuru R. Williams. 2006. *In Search of the Black Panther Party: New Perspectives on a Revolutionary Movement.* Duke University Press, p. 170.

Randall, Kahli. January 23, 1996. "Former Black Panther Draws Crowd of More Than 600." *The University Record.* http://www.ur.umich.edu/9596/Jan23_96/artcl20.htm (Accessed March 17, 2017).

Seale, Bobby. 1970. *The Story of the Black Panther Party and Huey P. Newton.* Black Classic Press.

Seale, Bobby. 1978. *A Lonely Rage: The Autobiography of Bobby Seale.* Times Books.

SECOND AMENDMENT

To many in the United States, the Second Amendment to the Constitution is a sacrosanct principle, so unquestioned in its meaning and applicability that perceived threats to this cherished ideal elicit impassioned defenses and equally passionate rebukes of would-be challengers. The Second Amendment consists of one line: "A well-regulated militia, being necessary for the security of a free state, the right of the people to keep and bear arms, shall not be infringed." Today, the Second Amendment is at the heart of the patriot and militia movements in the United States, but it has also become a hot-button issue for many on both the political left and right. The right to keep and bear arms is also frequently referred to by other extremist groups, such as white supremacists, white nationalists, and neo-Nazis, but the exact meaning of the Second Amendment has not been interpreted as broadly in the past as it is today. In fact, the dictum today is that every man, woman, and child in the United States has the right to own a gun and to wield that gun in their defense or in defense of their families, their property, or others. But this has not always been the accepted view of the Second Amendment. Indeed, as one author noted, "in the grand sweep of American history, this sentence [the Second Amendment] has never been among the most prominent constitutional provisions. In fact, for two centuries it was largely ignored" (Waldman 2014).

For most of its history, advocates of the Second Amendment linked it with the need for state militias at a time when the federal government maintained a very small standing army. Threats to states, be they internal or external, necessitated a "well-regulated militia" in order to protect citizens. Yet as the United States grew and federal power became more stable, the need for state militias waned. The need to "bear arms" subsided, but the right to own a weapon did not. As the Tennessee Supreme Court pointed out in 1840,

> A man in the pursuit of deer, elk, and buffaloes might carry his rifle every day for forty years, and yet it would never be said of him that he had borne arms; much less could it be said that a private citizen bears arms because he has a dirk or pistol concealed under his clothes, or a spear in a cane. (Waldman 2014)

Four times between 1976 and 1939, "the U.S. Supreme Court declined to rule that the Second Amendment gave individuals exclusive rights to own guns outside of the provision of a 'well-regulated militia'" (Waldman 2014). Even the National Rifle Association (NRA), the most powerful and politically impactful organization in support of gun rights, did not begin as an organization to defend to the death the right to keep and bear arms. Rather, the NRA began in the aftermath of the Civil War when "former Union general Ambrose Burnside, believing that too many Union soldiers couldn't shoot straight, founded the organization to promote rifle practice and improve marksmanship" (Achenbach, Higham, and Horwitz 2013). Over the years, the NRA lobbied quietly against extremely stringent gun control regulations, but "its principal focus was hunting and sportsmanship: bagging deer, not blocking laws." As late as the 1950s, the NRA's national headquarters bore an inscription of its purpose: "firearms safety education, marksmanship training, shooting for recreation" (Waldman 2014).

This changed in 1977. In what became known as the "Revolt in Cincinnati," extremist dissenters who were angry that the NRA intended to "retreat from politics" showed up at the organization's annual meeting and "voted out the organization's leadership." In its place, "activists from the Second Amendment Foundation and the Citizens Committee for the Right to Keep and Bear Arms found their way into the upper echelons of NRA leadership" (Waldman 2014). The NRA's new leadership was "dramatic, dogmatic and overtly ideological. For the first time, the organization formally embraced the idea that the sacred Second Amendment was at the heart of its concerns" (Waldman 2014).

Though the 1972 Republican platform had supported gun control, by 1980, the GOP had embraced a platform that proclaimed, "We believe the right of citizens to keep and bear arms must be preserved. Accordingly, we oppose federal registration of firearms." The GOP's nominee in 1980, Ronald Reagan, received the NRA's first-ever presidential endorsement (Waldman 2014).

From 1980 onward, the NRA engaged attorneys, professors, and activists to churn out articles, op-ed pieces, and law review submissions defending an interpretation of the Second Amendment that the right of a citizen to own guns could not be impeded. Notwithstanding the fact that from 1888 to 1959, "every single law review article on the Second Amendment concluded that the Amendment did not guarantee an individual right to a gun" (Waldman 2014). Yet the NRA sponsored essay contests, offered grants for book reviews, and created a cottage industry of academics whose responsibility was to defend the Second Amendment. In 2003, the NRA Foundation endowed the Patrick Henry professorship in constitutional law and the Second Amendment by providing $1 million to George Mason University Law School. Finally, in 2008, "the U.S. Supreme Court in the case of *District of Columbia v. Heller* ruled that the Second Amendment guarantees a right to own a weapon 'in common use' to protect 'hearth and home'" (Waldman 2014).

Today, the Second Amendment may be the most well known of the first 10 amendments to the U.S. Constitution that collectively make up the Bill of Rights, save perhaps the First Amendment. The power of those who lobby on behalf of the Second Amendment today is such that "congressmen and presidents bow to them" (Tezcan 2016). Moreover, the NRA and other gun lobbyists have promoted the "myth that the Second Amendment was enacted to facilitate armed rebellion against our own government, should it become tyrannical" (Guest 2013).

This myth is nowhere more evident than in the 2016 presidential campaign of Republican nominee, and eventual president, Donald Trump. After Trump complained for months about the possibility that he would lose the election due to it being "rigged," he declared that if Hillary Clinton "gets to pick her judges, nothing you can do, folks. Although the Second Amendment people—maybe there is. I don't know" (Sunshine 2016). As noted by one writer,

> While Trump claimed he was merely suggesting an electoral remedy, where gun rights advocates become a pivotal voting block, the more obvious interpretation—the one understood by many listeners—was that Trump was seeding the idea in followers' minds of an armed revolutionary struggle, or an assassination, to overthrow a democratically elected president. It's likely that at least one constituency is already thinking the same way. When it comes to Trump's so-called "Second Amendment people," the prime candidates for the role are the members of the heavily armed, Hard Right "Patriot movement." (Sunshine 2016)

As noted, protection of the Second Amendment, particularly as a cherished virtue handed down by the Founding Fathers, remains a central organizing component of the patriot and militia movements. Because of the power of various gun lobbies, particularly the NRA, and heavily armed supporters, there is no reason to believe that meaningful gun control measures will be enacted anytime in the near future.

See also: Militia Movement; Patriot Movement

Further Reading

Achenbach, Joel, Scott Higham, and Sari Horwitz. January 12, 2013. "How NRA's True Believers Converted a Marksmanship Group into a Mighty Gun Lobby." *The Washington Post*. https://www.washingtonpost.com/politics/how-nras-true-believers-converted-a -marksmanship-group-into-a-mighty-gun-lobby/2013/01/12/51c62288-59b9-11e2 -88d0-c4cf65c3ad15_story.html?utm_term=.921d9f443e38 (Accessed May 10, 2017).

Guest. January 24, 2013. "Second Amendment Vigilantes." *Southern Poverty Law Center— Hatewatch*. https://www.splcenter.org/hatewatch/2013/01/24/second-amendment -vigilantes (Accessed May 10, 2017).

Sunshine, Spencer. October 31, 2016. "Trump's 'Second Amendment People?': The U.S. Patriot Movement Today." Political Research Associates. http://www.politicalresearch .org/2016/10/31/trumps-second-amendment-people-the-u-s-patriot-movement -today/#sthash.9n7elgLx.dpbs (Accessed May 10, 2017).

Tezcan, Danielle. June 16, 2016. "The Second Amendment, Once Again." *Watching America*. http://watchingamerica.com/WA/2016/06/16/the-second-amendment-once-again/ (Accessed May 10, 2017).

Waldman, Michael. May 19, 2014. "How the NRA Rewrote the Second Amendment." *Politico*. http://www.politico.com/magazine/story/2014/05/nra-guns-second-amendment -106856?o=0 (Accessed May 10, 2017).

SHABAZZ, MALIK ZULU

Malik Zulu Shabazz (b. 1966) is a "racist black nationalist and black separatist advocate" who consistently rails about the inherently evil nature of white people and perpetuates the myth of Jewish conspiracies in all aspects of political, social, and moral life in the United States (Southern Poverty Law Center, Shabazz). Once a member of the Nation of Islam (NOI), Shabazz was ousted from the organization after he gave a particularly vitriolic speech that was considered highly anti-Semitic, anti-Catholic, and homophobic (Southern Poverty Law Center, Shabazz). Shabazz joined the New Black Panther Party (NBPP) in 1997 and assumed leadership of the group after its leader, Khalid Abdul Muhammad, died in 2001. As leader of the NBPP, Shabazz has pushed an agenda of black power, black nationalism, support for reparations for slavery, conspiracy theories involving Jews, allegations that Jews dominated the Atlantic slave trade, and virulent rants against the Jewish state of Israel (New Black Panther Party).

Shabazz was born Paris Lewis and raised in Los Angeles, California. His father was a Muslim who was killed when Shabazz was a child. Shabazz's grandfather, a member of the Nation of Islam, was a strong influence in his life. Shabazz graduated from Howard University and Howard University School of Law. In 1994, he invited NBPP leader Khalid Abdul Muhammad to speak before a Howard University crowd. As he introduced Khalid Muhammad, "Shabazz led the crowd in an anti-Semitic call and response" (Southern Poverty Law Center, Shabazz). Because of his actions, Shabazz was fired from his job. His then boss, Washington, D.C., mayor Marion Berry, stated that Shabazz's public statements "regarding other people's cultural history, religion and race . . . do not reflect the spirit of my campaign, my personal views or my spirituality" (Southern Poverty Law Center, Shabazz).

Shabazz and Muhammad became close colleagues after the event. In 1995, in connection with the Million Man March on Washington, D.C., Shabazz and Muhammad organized the African Black Holocaust and Nationhood Conference. At the conference, "speakers discussed Jewish involvement in the 'African holocaust' and disparaged any reference to the 'Holocaust of the Jews'" (Southern Poverty Law Center, Shabazz). Shabazz introduced Muhammed at the event as "a man who gives the white man nightmares . . . [and] a man who makes the Jews pee in their pants at night" (Southern Poverty Law Center, Shabazz). Muhammad became a strong mentor to Shabazz and encouraged Shabazz's path away from NOI and toward NBPP.

In 1998, Muhammad became the leader of NBPP. In support of the NBPP message, Shabazz appeared frequently in the media, advancing "vast conspiracy theories about the role of Jews in black oppression and insisted that world problems are caused by 'the very nature of white people'" (Southern Poverty Law Center, New Black Panther Party). Shabazz has also reinforced the black nationalist claim "that blacks, not Jews, are the original Hebrews of Israel" (Southern Poverty Law Center, New Black Panther Party).

Shabazz became the leader of the NBPP in early 2001 after Muhammad's sudden death from a brain aneurism. After the events of 9/11, Shabazz alleged "a Jewish conspiracy was behind the 9/11 terror attacks" (Southern Poverty Law Center, New Black Panther Party). For over 10 years, Shabazz led NBPP members in various protests and demonstrations "to protect black victims of hate crimes, often angrily denouncing white police officers and white residents" whom he claimed were complicit in the abuses of black people (Southern Poverty Law Center, New Black Panther Party). In 2011, Shabazz launched a blistering tirade against President Barack Obama for his support of the ouster of Libyan leader Muammar Qaddafi. Shabazz said of Obama's actions, "He [President Obama] represents the ideology of the white man, he represents the CIA set up, sabotage, lie on a African leader and bomb that man like he George Bush. He represents the white man" (Southern Poverty Law Center, Shabazz).

In October 2013, Shabazz left the NBPP to lead the Black Lawyers for Justice organization that he helped to cofound (Segal 2013). Shabazz has maintained his relationship with NBPP, however, protesting the death of a black man who died in police custody in Baltimore, Maryland, in April 2015. Later the same year, he spoke in Charleston, South Carolina, following the shooting of nine parishioners by a white supremacist at the Emanuel A. M. E. Church. Shabazz continues to preach a message of militancy against whites, Jews, and race traitors as he advances the goals of black separatism.

See also: Black Nationalism; Nation of Islam; New Black Panther Party

Further Reading

New Black Panther Party. "New Black Panther Party for Self Defense: Freedom or Death." http://www.nbpp.org/10-point-platform.html (Accessed March 18, 2017).

Segal, Oren. October 17, 2013. "New Black Panther Party Announces New Chairman, Same Hateful Message." Anti-Defamation League. https://www.adl.org/blog/new-black

-panther-party-announces-new-chairman-same-hateful-message (Accessed March 18, 2017).

Southern Poverty Law Center. "Malik Zulu Shabazz." https://www.splcenter.org/fighting -hate/extremist-files/individual/malik-zulu-shabazz (Accessed March 18, 2017).

Southern Poverty Law Center. "New Black Panther Party." https://www.splcenter.org/fight ing-hate/extremist-files/group/new-black-panther-party (Accessed March 18, 2017).

SOUTHERN POVERTY LAW CENTER

The Southern Poverty Law Center (SPLC) is a nonprofit legal advocacy organization that specializes in civil rights and public interest litigation. SPLC was founded in 1971 by Morris Dees and Joseph L. Levin Jr. as a civil rights law firm and is based in Birmingham, Alabama. SPLC is noted for its publication of material "that identifies and tracks anti-government extremist groups, hate groups, anti-Muslim groups, anti-Semitic groups, and anti-immigration groups" (Southern Poverty Law Center, What We Do). Through Dees's efforts, SPLC has won several high-profile cases against white supremacist and anti-Semitic groups, such as Aryan Nations, White Aryan Resistance, and the United Klans of America. SPLC employs a litigation strategy of filing civil suits against extremist organizations on behalf of victims, and targeting organizations' land holdings, publication houses, trademarking, and other assets. The SPLC maintains extensive educational programs that promote tolerance (SLU 2006). According to the organization's Web site, SPLC "is dedicated to fighting hate and bigotry and to seeking justice for the most vulnerable members of our society. Using litigation, education, and other forms of advocacy, the SPLC works toward the day when the ideals of equal justice and equal opportunity will be a reality" (Southern Poverty Law Center, What We Do). The SPLC has been criticized in some circles, with one critic stating that the SPLC "began with an admirable purpose but long ago transformed into a machine for raising money and launching left-wing political attacks. Lately it's become more of a threat to free speech and civil debate than a defender of the weak or a foe of violent extremism" (Simpson 2012).

The SPLC was originally founded to fight issues related to poverty, racial discrimination, and the death penalty. In 1979, Dees and the SPLC began filing lawsuits against chapters of the Ku Klux Klan (KKK) and other extremist organizations for damages caused as a result of the activities of the organization (e.g., murder). The favorable verdicts realized by SPLC encouraged the organization to begin tracking the existence of extremist organizations as well as the emergence of new ones. In 1981, the SPLC began its Klanwatch program, which eventually expanded into the *Hatewatch* blog, which tracks "seven different types of hate groups and other extremist organizations" (Southern Poverty Law Center, Family Research Council).

The headquarters of SPLC has been firebombed, and Dees has been the subject of several conspiratorial assassination plots (Klass 2007). The SPLC cooperates with law enforcement and offers law enforcement agencies training that focuses "on the history, background, leaders and activities of far-right extremists in the United States" (Southern Poverty Law Center, What We Do). The SPLC has initiated a number of civil rights cases against extremist groups "and has been credited with devising innovative ways to cripple hate groups through the seizure of their assets" (Sack 1996). However, the SPLC's activities have also "led to criticism from civil libertarians that the SPLC's tactics chill free speech and set legal precedents that could be applied against activist groups which are not hate groups" (Michael 2012).

There have even been claims that the SPLC's activities have inspired violent acts against those whom it has deemed violent. In 2012, for example, 28-year-old gunman Floyd Corkins stormed into the headquarters of the Family Research Council (FRC) in Washington, D.C., and opened fire. The Family Research Council "was designated a 'hate group' by the SPLC

Morris Dees, founder of the Southern Poverty Law Center (SPLC), poses next to a civil rights monument. The SPLC is a civil rights and public interest litigation organization that is the foremost tracker of hate and extremist groups in the United States. (Acey Harper/The LIFE Images Collection/Getty Images)

in 2010" for what SPLC considered the FRC's "false claims" against the LGBT community and its battles "against same-sex marriage, hate crime laws, anti-bullying programs and the repeal of the military's 'Don't Ask, Don't Tell' policy" (Southern Poverty Law Center, Family Research Council). FRC's president, Tony Perkins, blamed the SPLC for inciting the shooting:

> Let me be clear that Floyd Corkins was responsible for firing the shot yesterday. But Corkins was given a license to shoot an unarmed man by organizations like the Southern Poverty Law Center that have been reckless in labeling organizations hate groups because they disagree with them on public policy. (Ariosto 2012)

In February 2014, Lieutenant General (Ret.) William G. Boykin, executive vice president of the FRC, called the SPLC's association of the Family Research Council with virulent hate groups such as the KKK and Aryan Nations "completely unacceptable." In a letter penned by Boykin and signed

> by 14 other conservative and Christian leaders, the letter called SPLC a heavily politicized organization producing inaccurate and biased data on "hate groups" not "hate crimes." . . . Where once SPLC's hate list was reserved for groups like the Aryan Nation and the KKK, in 2010 SPLC started citing as hate groups those Christian groups that oppose same-sex marriage or believe homosexuality is not inborn, or are otherwise critical of homosexuality. (Ruse 2014)

Boykin's letter "concluded that it is completely inappropriate for the Department of Justice to recommend public reliance on the SPLC hate group lists and data and demanded that all ties between the FBI and the SPLC be severed" (Ruse 2014). In March 2014, the FBI removed the SPLC from its list of hate crime resources (Ruse 2014).

The SPLC's designation of hate groups has come under fire from those who say an overboard definition of "hate" "vilifies innocent people and stifles vigorous debate about issues critical to America's future" (Jonsson 2011). This criticism emerged again in October 2016 when the SPLC published "A Journalist's Manual: Field Guide to Anti-Muslim Extremists." In the guide were the usual anti-Muslim suspects, such as Pamela Geller and Frank Gaffney Jr., but also included was Maajid Nawaz, "a British activist who runs the Quilliam Foundation, which calls itself the world's first counter-extremism think tank" (Southern Poverty Law Center 2016). Nawaz is well respected in certain antiterror circles. A "self-described former extremist, Nawaz spent four years in an Egyptian prison and now argues for a pluralistic and peaceful vision of Islam. Nawaz stood for Parliament as a Liberal Democrat in 2015, and advised Prime Ministers Tony Blair, Gordon Brown, and David Cameron" (Graham 2016). But the SPLC listed Nawaz as anti-Muslim when "he tweeted out a cartoon in 2014 of Jesus and Muhammad . . . despite the fact that many Muslims see it as blasphemous to draw Muhammad." Nawaz claimed he wanted "to carve out a space to be heard without constantly fearing the blasphemy charge" (Southern Poverty Law Center 2016).

After being designated as anti-Muslim by the SPLC, Nawaz stated,

> They [the SPLC] put a target on my head. The kind of work that I do, if you tell the wrong kind of Muslims that I'm an extremist, then that means I'm a target. They don't have to deal with any of this. I don't have any protection. I don't have any state protection. These people are putting me on what I believe is a hit list. (Graham 2016)

Though Nawaz demanded that SPLC issue a correction, retraction, and apology of his designation as an anti-Muslim, the SPLC did not comply. Mark Potok, senior fellow at SPLC who wrote the guide, responded to Nawaz's criticism that the SPLC was engaging in McCarthyism:

> If criticizing any number of people is McCarthyism, then I guess the only answer is to never criticize anyone. One can disagree or agree with a particular listing that we've

made. . . . In some sense, to make a statement like that is to say that we shouldn't criticize. . . . Our point is not to make these people targets for violence. The point is to tamp down the really baseless targeting. (Graham 2016)

The SPLC today remains the foremost source on individual extremists and hate groups, compiling more information than any other single organization.

See also: Aryan Nations; Boykin, Lieutenant General William G. "Jerry" (Ret.); *Breitbart News*; Family Research Council; Gaffney, Frank, Jr.; Geller, Pamela; Ku Klux Klan; Militia Movement; Patriot Movement; Perkins, Tony; White Aryan Resistance; White Nationalism; White Supremacist Movement

Further Reading

Ariosto, David. August 17, 2012. "SPLC Draws Conservative Ire." *CNN*. http://www.cnn .com/2012/08/17/us/us-southern-poverty-law-center-profile/index.html   (Accessed May 26, 2017).

Finkleman, Paul, ed. 2006. *The Encyclopedia of American Civil Liberties*. 3 vols. Routledge.

Graham, David A. October 29, 2016. "How Did Maajid Nawaz End Up on a List of 'Anti-Muslim Extremists'?" *The Atlantic*. https://www.theatlantic.com/international/archive /2016/10/maajid-nawaz-splc-anti-muslim-extremist/505685/ (Accessed May 26, 2017).

Jonsson, Patrik. February 23, 2011. "Annual Report Cites Rise in Hate Groups, But Some Ask: What Is Hate?" *Christian Science Monitor*. http://www.csmonitor.com/USA /Society/2011/0223/Annual-report-cites-rise-in-hate-qgroups-but-some-ask-What-is -hate (Accessed May 26, 2017).

Klass, Kym. September 27, 2007. "Southern Poverty Law Center Beefs Up Security." *Montgomery Advertiser*. https://web.archive.org/web/20070927192930/http://www .montgomeryadvertiser.com/apps/pbcs.dll/article?AID=%2F20070814%2FNEWS%2 F708140328%2F1001 (Accessed May 26, 2017).

Michael, George. 2012. *Confronting Right Wing Extremism and Terrorism in the USA*. Routledge.

Ruse, Austin. March 26, 2014. "FBI Dumps Southern Poverty Law Center as Hate Crimes Resource." *Breitbart News*. http://www.breitbart.com/big-government/2014/03/26/fbi -dumps-southern-poverty-law-center/ (Accessed May 26, 2017).

Sack, Kevin. May 12, 1996. "Conversations/Morris Dees; A Son of Alabama Takes on Americans Who Live to Hate." *The New York Times*. http://www.nytimes.com/1996/05/12 /weekinreview/conversations-morris-dees-a-son-of-alabama-takes-on-americans -who-live-to-hate.html (Accessed May 26, 2017).

Simpson, James. October 7, 2012. "Southern Poverty Law Center: Wellspring of Manufactured Hate." *Capital Research Center*. https://capitalresearch.org/article/southern -poverty-law-center-wellspring-of-manufactured-hate/ (Accessed May 26, 2017).

SLU. November 5, 2006. "With Justice for All." *The Times-Picayune*. https://web.archive .org/web/20080417164536/http://www.nola.com/picayunes/t-p/covingtonpicayune /index.ssf?FbaseFnews-F1162622544266020.xml&coll=1 (Accessed May 26, 2017).

Southern Poverty Law Center. https://www.splcenter.org/ (Accessed May 26, 2017).

Southern Poverty Law Center. "Family Research Council." https://www.splcenter.org/fighting -hate/extremist-files/group/family-research-council (Accessed May 26, 2017).

Southern Poverty Law Center. "What We Do." https://www.splcenter.org/what-we-do (Accessed May 26, 2017).

Southern Poverty Law Center. October 25, 2016. "A Journalist's Manual: Field Guide to Anti-Muslim Extremists." https://www.splcenter.org/20161025/journalists-manual -field-guide-anti-muslim-extremists (Accessed May 26, 2017).

SOVEREIGN CITIZENS MOVEMENT

The formation of Posse Comitatus in the late 1960s promoted an ideology that there was no government authority higher than that of the county sheriff. Eventually, this notion spawned a movement of "sovereign citizens"—individuals who believe themselves to be subject only to the code of "common law" established by the U.S. Constitution. The sovereign citizens movement espouses the idea that individuals are not subject to any higher authority. That is, they owe no allegiance to any government, law, or code of justice prescribed by any authority. In effect, they are sovereign entities unto themselves. Sovereign citizens generally do not believe in paying taxes, possessing drivers licenses, obeying speeding laws, and a whole host of other government-imposed regulations.

Sovereign citizens hold that there are two types of citizens:

> There are "Fourteenth Amendment citizens," who are subject to the laws and taxes of the federal and state governments; and "sovereign citizens," who are subject only to "the common law." Sovereign citizens claim that they have absolute mastery over all their property (including freedom from taxes, regulations, ordinances or zoning restrictions), that they essentially do not have to pay taxes (aside from tariffs and a few other insignificant taxes); that they are not citizens of the United States but are "non-resident aliens" with respect to that "illegal corporation;" that the only court which has jurisdiction to try them for any matter is a "common law court;" that they can never be arrested or tried for a crime or matter in which there is no complaining victim; as well as various other notions. (Anti-Defamation League)

The basis of the sovereign citizens movement "is rooted in racism and Anti-Semitism" (Southern Poverty Law Center). In the early 1980s, "the philosophy attracted many white supremacists and anti-Semites" who believed that the U.S. government had been subverted by Jewish financial interests and had buckled to social pressure to enact civil rights legislation. In the beginning of the movement, "being white was nearly a prerequisite to calling oneself a sovereign citizen" (Southern Poverty Law Center). These individuals "argued that the 14th Amendment to the Constitution, which guaranteed citizenship to African-Americans and everyone else born on U.S. soil, also made black Americans permanently subject to federal and state governments, unlike themselves" (Southern Poverty Law Center). However, many adherents of the sovereign citizens movement today are African Americans who are either unaware of the movement's beginnings or don't care. They are attracted by the sentiment that they are acting as sovereign agents, ignoring the legal constraints of a government that they feel is unresponsive to their needs.

The Federal Bureau of Investigation (FBI) has stated "that the Sovereign Citizens Movement might be dismissed as a nuisance," a collection of individuals who believe that all governments operate illegally (Federal Bureau of Investigation 2011).

But the death of several law enforcement officials over the years at the hands of sovereign citizens and the growing list of crimes committed by sovereign citizens—including financial scams, fraud, money laundering, counterfeiting, and impersonation of law enforcement officials—has compelled the FBI to label the sovereign citizens movement a "domestic terror movement" (Federal Bureau of Investigation 2011). According to the FBI,

> The sovereign-citizen threat likely will grow as the nationwide movement is fueled by the Internet, the economic downturn, and seminars held across the country that spread their ideology and show people how they can tap into funds and eliminate debt through fraudulent methods. As sovereign citizens' numbers grow, so do the chances of contact with law enforcement and, thus, the risks that incidents will end in violence.

Adherents of the sovereign citizens movement "sometimes refer to themselves as 'freemen' or 'constitutionalists'" (Pepke 1998). They believe themselves to be free from all government control and restraint. Terry Nichols, convicted of conspiracy in the bombing of the Alfred P. Murrah Federal Building in Oklahoma City in 1995, considered himself a sovereign citizen (Pepke 1998). Sovereign citizens "believe that the expansion of government over the decades" has caused it to stray from the original "limited" nature intended by the founders. Therefore, "because the government operates outside of its jurisdiction, and does not act in the best interest of its people," sovereign citizens feel free to ignore the laws that government promulgates (Anti-Defamation League). As sovereign citizens, answerable only to themselves, they are not bound by any law passed by the government.

See also: Common-Law Court Movement; Montana Freemen; Paper Terrorism; Posse Comitatus

Further Reading

Anti-Defamation League. "What Is a Sovereign Citizen." *Anti-Defamation League: The Militia Watchdog.* http://archive.adl.org/mwd/students.html#1 (Accessed December 14, 2016).

Federal Bureau of Investigation. September 11, 2011. "Sovereign Citizens: A Growing Domestic Threat to Law Enforcement." *FBI Law Enforcement Bulletin.* https://leb.fbi.gov /2011/september/sovereign-citizens-a-growing-domestic-threat-to-law-enforcement (Accessed December 14, 2016).

Pepke, David Ray. 1998. *Heretics in the Temple: Americans Who Reject the Nation's Legal Faith.* NYU Press.

Southern Poverty Law Center. "Sovereign Citizens Movement." https://www.splcenter.org /fighting-hate/extremist-files/ideology/sovereign-citizens-movement (Accessed December 14, 2016).

SPENCER, GLENN

Glenn Spencer (b. 1938) is an American anti-illegal immigration activist and the founder and president of American Border Patrol, an organization that acts as a "shadow border patrol by using citizen patrols and electronic surveillance equipment" to monitor illegal immigration on the United States' southern border (Southern Poverty Law Center, Glenn Spencer). Spencer is well known for his criticisms of Mexicans. According to the Southern Poverty Law Center (Glenn Spencer), Spencer "may have done more than anyone to spread the myth of a secret Mexican conspiracy to reconquer the [American] Southwest (an effort supposedly known as 'la reconquista.'"

Spencer was born and raised in California. Toward the end of the 1980s, he saw tremendous changes in California and Los Angeles and turned his attention to what he considered the burgeoning problem of illegal immigration. In 1992, he retired, and after 10 years of activism in California, he moved to Arizona, where he launched American Border Patrol in 2002.

According to Spencer, his anti-immigration activism was spurred on by what he saw as Mexican involvement in the L.A. riots that occurred as the result of the acquittal of four police officers who were accused of beating Rodney King. Because of this incident, Spencer joined the "Voice of Citizens Together, also known as American Patrol" (Southern Poverty Law Center, American Border Patrol). In 1994, Spencer was "a primary backer of Proposition 187, which aimed to bar children of undocumented immigrants from access to schools or the receipt of any public services" (Southern Poverty Law Center, American Border Patrol). Spencer became a hardened anti-immigrant ideologue, "calling for the immediate round up and deportation of all undocumented workers, demanding the banning of all foreign-language TV and radio broadcasts, and insisting that the military be deployed to safeguard the border" (Southern Poverty Law Center, American Border Patrol). About this same time, Spencer began to disseminate the so-called Aztlan conspiracy theory, "a plan that originated from a real document distributed in 1969 by the Chicano youth liberation movement." The plan "called on Chicanos (native-born Americans of Mexican ancestry) to reclaim the land of their birth and unite to fight oppression, exploitation and racism" (Southern Poverty Law Center, American Border Patrol). To Spencer and other anti-immigrant activists, "such as Barbara Coe of the hate group California Coalition for Immigration Reform, the plan was nothing less than an explicit blueprint." As Spencer proclaimed at a rally in July 2000:

> The dream of conquering Aztlan lies deep in the heart of the Mexican psyche. . . . This explains why some are willing to risk death. Their goal is more than jobs, it is conquest. They believe what they are doing is noble. They are defying the Gringo to take back what is rightfully Mexico's. (Southern Poverty Law Center, American Border Patrol)

By 2000, Spencer "had grown disillusioned with California and its growing Latino population" (Southern Poverty Law Center, Glenn Spencer). In 2002, he moved to Arizona, where he "created American Border Patrol—a private organization that was meant to be a 'shadow' for the U.S. Border Patrol" (Southern Poverty Law Center, Glenn Spencer). Spencer's organization utilized citizen volunteers with ATVs, as well as high-tech sensors and infrared video cameras, to "catch" illegal immigration in the act, thereby embarrassing the federal government into militarizing the southern border with Mexico. In 2004, Spencer claimed that two of his American Border Patrol agents crossed the border from Mexico into the United States with a backpack that contained a fake weapon of mass destruction, demonstrating the porousness of the border.

After the election of Barack Obama in 2008, Spencer stated that the new Obama administration "was prepared to make a full frontal assault on the sovereignty of the United States" (Southern Poverty Law Center, Glenn Spencer). Spencer went on to claim that "Barack Obama represents the greatest threat to the United States of America since the Civil War. Brainwashed Americans have just voted to commit national suicide" (Southern Poverty Law Center, Glenn Spencer).

Today, Spencer continues his border-monitoring activities, posting articles and photos on the American Border Patrol Web site. Before the election of Donald Trump in November 2016, Spencer believed himself to be the perfect consultant for Trump's plan to build a wall along the U.S. border with Mexico. Spencer stated, "I don't believe that any of his advisers knows as much or has read as much literature on the topic as I have" (Peinado 2016).

See also: American Border Patrol/American Patrol; Coe, Barbara

Further Reading

American Border Patrol. 2014. "What Does the Border Fence Really Look Like." http://americanborderpatrol.com/ (Accessed March 9, 2017).

Peinado, Fernando. October 14, 2016. "In Advance of Trump's Wall, Arizona Rancher Invents System for Detecting Migrants." *Univsion.* http://www.univision.com/univision-news/immigration/in-advance-of-trumps-wall-arizona-rancher-invents-system-for-detecting-migrants (Accessed March 9, 2017).

Southern Poverty Law Center. "American Border Patrol/American Patrol." https://www.splcenter.org/fighting-hate/extremist-files/group/american-border-patrolamerican-patrol (Accessed March 9, 2017).

Southern Poverty Law Center. "Glenn Spencer." https://www.splcenter.org/fighting-hate/extremist-files/individual/glenn-spencer (Accessed March 9, 2017).

SPENCER, RICHARD BERTRAND

Richard Spencer (b. 1978) is a white supremacist who advocates for an Aryan homeland in North America, necessitating a "peaceful ethnic cleansing" to "halt the deconstruction of European culture" that has been the hallmark of American life for more than 300 years (Lambroso and Appelbaum 2016). Spencer is the "president of the National Policy Institute (NPI), a white nationalist think tank" that is "dedicated to the heritage, identity, and future of people of European descent in the United States, and around the world" (National Policy Institute). Spencer has been credited as being the author of the term "alt-right," a phrase that has come to denote the white identity movement (Wallace-Wells 2016). *Breitbart News*, a far-right American news organization, "has described Spencer's website *AlternativeRight.com* as the center of alt-right thought" (Corn 2016). Spencer

Richard Bertrand Spencer is a white supremacist who advocates for an Aryan homeland in the United States. Spencer is credited as being the author of the term "alt-right," a phrase that has come to denote the renewed interest in white nationalism and white supremacism in the United States. (Evelyn Hockstein/For The Washington Post via Getty Images)

has "repeatedly quoted from Nazi propaganda and has denounced the influence of Jews in the media, government, and entertainment" (Stahl 2016). Spencer and the alt-right movement "drew considerable attention in the media in the weeks following the election of Donald Trump" when, at an NPI conference—in response to Spencer's cry "Hail Trump. Hail our People. Hail Victory!"—"a number of his supporters jumped to their feet and gave the Nazi salute" (Goldstein 2016). Spencer dismissed the salutes as merely "exuberance" being displayed by his supporters.

Spencer's mantra is that white people have been "dispossessed in the United States by a combination of rising minority birth rates, immigration from non-white and non-Christian countries, and government policies that he abhors" (Southern Poverty Law Center). After obtaining a bachelor's degree from the University of Virginia and a master's degree in humanities from the University of Chicago, "Spencer took a job at *American Conservative* magazine, though he was later fired from this position because of his radical views" (Southern Poverty Law Center). In 2010, "Spencer founded the website *AlternativeRight.com*, which he edited until 2012, and from which the term 'alt-right' was coined" (Goldstein 2016).

In 2014, Spencer was deported from Budapest, Hungary, after trying to convene an NPI conference for white nationalists in that country. Due to the Schengen Agreement, which abolishes internal border checks in the European Union, Spencer's deportation necessitated his ban from the other 26 countries of the European

Union for a period of three years. Also in 2014, residents in Montana, through an organization known as Love Lives Here, initiated a nondiscrimination resolution through the Whitefish, Montana, City Council to protest Spencer's residency in that community. Spencer splits his time between residences in Virginia and Montana, though many of his publishing and journalistic endeavors list their address as Whitefish, Montana (Sakariassen 2013).

During the American presidential campaign of 2016, Spencer was an ardent supporter of Donald Trump and called his victory "the victory of will," "echoing the title of the Nazi-era propaganda film *Triumph of the Will*" (Goldstein 2016). In November 2016, thousands of students, faculty, and staff at Texas A&M University signed a petition that asked university officials to prevent Spencer from speaking at the school in December (Mangan 2016). On January 15, 2017, (Martin Luther King Jr's birthday), "Spencer launched *AltRight.com*, another commentary website for alt-right members" (Viets 2017). According to the Southern Poverty Law Center, the new site has "an editorial staff handpicked from the most influential corners of the radical right" (Viets 2017). But what distinguishes *AltRight.com* from Spencer's previous endeavors is the noted anti-Semitism of the site, which previously had not been a hallmark of Spencer's thought. Spencer's attempt to bring alt-right thinkers together in one place is his "attempt to unify American and European ethnos-nationalists under one roof" (Viets 2017).

See also:; Alt-Right Movement; White Nationalism; White Supremacist Movement

Further Reading

AltRight.com. http://alternativeright.com/ (Accessed January 30, 2018).

Corn, David. November 14, 2016. "Here's Why It's Fair—and Necessary—to Call Trump's Chief Strategist a White Nationalist Champion." *Mother Jones*. http://www .motherjones.com/politics/2016/11/why-its-fair-and-necessary-call-trumps-chief -strategist-stephen-bannon-white-nationalist (Accessed March 15, 2017).

Goldstein, Joseph. November 20, 2016. "Alt-Right Gathering Exults in Trump Election with Nazi-Era Salute." *The New York Times*. http://www.nytimes.com/2016/11/21/us /alt-right-salutes-donald-trump.html?_r=0 (Accessed March 15, 2017).

Lambroso, Daniel and Yoni Appelbaum. November 21, 2016. "'Hail Trump!': White Nationalists Salute the President-Elect." *The Atlantic*. http://www.theatlantic.com/politics /archive/2016/11/richard-spencer-speech-npi/508379/ (Accessed March 15, 2017).

Mangan, Katherine. November 28, 2016. "Richard Spencer, White Supremacist, Describes Goals of His 'Danger Tour' to College Campuses." *The Chronicle of Higher Education*. http://www.chronicle.com/article/White-Supremacist-Describes/238515?key=yop9k7 -B1QiWD6aZpWTJr09nFIFTqhJZ9j__fsmc1XpXmwCLCoQujzMc16qtU3gjUW1u ZjZlWkRiRGI2M3QtREZBdTYzb1VYYUxjQ2FzdjhLeWtUYktBR3ltQQ (Accessed March 15, 2017).

National Policy Institute. "Who Are We?" http://www.npiamerica.org/ (Accessed March 15, 2017).

Sakariassen, Alex. May 13, 2013. "Rachel Maddow Calls Out White 'Nationalist' Nonprofit in Flathead." *Missoula Independent*. http://missoulanews.bigskypress.com/IndyBlog /archives/2013/05/13/rachel-maddow-calls-out-white-nationalist-nonprofit-in-flathead (Accessed March 15, 2017).

Southern Poverty Law Center. "Richard Bertrand Spencer." https://www.splcenter.org/fighting-hate/extremist-files/individual/richard-bertrand-spencer-0 (Accessed March 15, 2017).

Stahl, Jeremy. November 21, 2016. "Meet the Neo-Nazi Whom Steve Bannon's Site Describe as a Leading 'Intellectual.'" *Slate*. http://www.slate.com/blogs/the_slatest/2016/11/21/meet_the_neo_nazi_steve_bannon_s_site_described_as_a_leading_intellectual.html (Accessed March 15, 2017).

Viets, Sarah. January 17, 2017. "Richard Spencer Launches 'Alt-Right' Website on Martin Luther King, Jr.'s Birthday." *Southern Poverty Law Center—Hatewatch*. http://www.splcenter.org/hatewatch/2017/01/17/richard-spencer-launches-alt-right-website-martin-luther-king-jrs-birthday (Accessed March 15, 2017).

Wallace-Wells, Benjamin. May 5, 2016. "Is the Alt-Right for Real?" *The New Yorker*. http://www.newyorker.com/news/benjamin-wallace-wells/is-the-alt-right-for-real (Accessed March 15, 2017).

STEIN, DAN

Dan Stein (b. 1955) is the president and executive director of the Federation for American Immigration Reform (FAIR). FAIR advocates for major reforms in U.S. immigration policy that would significantly reduce the number of immigrants allowed into the country, particularly those from nonwhite countries. FAIR "has been designated as a hate group by the Southern Poverty Law Center (SPLC)" because of its official statements as well as those made by its founder, John Tanton, and other officials (Southern Poverty Law Center, FAIR). Stein has complained that immigrants in the United States today are engaged in a campaign of "competitive breeding where they intend to diminish the power of the white majority" by producing more children (Southern Poverty Law Center, Dan Stein). Stein also serves as an editorial advisor for *The Social Contract*, "a nativist hate journal published by John Tanton" (Southern Poverty Law Center, Dan Stein).

Stein graduated from Indiana University and Catholic University's Law School. Before his stint at FAIR, Stein was the "executive director of the Immigration Reform Law Institute (IRLI), a non-profit public interest law firm devoted to limiting immigration to levels consistent with the national interest of the United States" (Southern Poverty Law Center, Dan Stein). IRLI acts as the legal arm of FAIR.

In the past, Stein has praised John Tanton, the founder of FAIR and a self-described white nationalist, as a "Jeffersonian or Renaissance man of intellect" (Hsu 2009). In 1991, Stein sent a document to FAIR entitled "The Defenders of American Culture Rise to the Call of Arms." In the document, "Stein praised attacks on 'multiculturally and politically correct' school curricula, as well as attacks on 'the political agenda of those who openly attack the contributions of Western Civilization" (Southern Poverty Law Center, FAIR). Like most members of FAIR, Stein is committed to a repeal of the Immigration and Nationality Act of 1965, "a law that ended decades of racial quotas that favored immigration from northern Europeans" (Southern Poverty Law Center, Dan Stein). Stein has called the act a "retaliation" against Anglo-Saxon dominance and has said that it causes minority groups to become engaged in acts of "revengism" against whites.

In addition to his executive positions at FAIR and IRLI, Stein "serves as editorial advisor of *The Social Contract*, a hate journal published by FAIR founder John Tanton" (Southern Poverty Law Center, Dan Stein). Under Stein's editorship, the journal published a special issue entitled "Europhobia: The Hostility Toward European-Descended Americans." In the issue, the argument is put forth that multiculturalism in the United States is replacing the highly successful "Euro-American culture" with the "dysfunctional" cultures of Third World countries (Southern Poverty Law Center, FAIR).

In 1997, noted white nativist Garrett Hardin published an editorial in the *Wall Street Journal* in which he stated that only "intelligent people" should breed. When interviewed by Tucker Carlson of the *Wall Street Journal* about Hardin's comments, Stein commented, "Yea, so what? . . . What is your problem with that?" (Carlson 1997). Speaking in praise of the Minutemen border movement, wherein private individuals extrajudicially monitored and patrolled the border between the United States and Mexico, Stein remarked, "For many Americans, the Minutemen Project looks more like Lexington and Concord. It represents the escalation of action required to face down the arrogance and contempt of selfish greed. In my view, those who see it differently mistake the matter entirely" (Southern Poverty Law Center, FAIR).

See also: Federation for American Immigration Reform; Holocaust Denial; Tanton, John; White Nationalism

Further Reading

Carlson, Tucker. October 2, 1997. "The Intellectual Roots of Nativism." *Wall Street Journal*. https://www.wsj.com/articles/SB875739465952259500 (Accessed March 13, 2017).

Hsu, Spencer S. September 15, 2009. "Immigration, Health Debates Cross Paths." *Washington Post*. http://www.washingtonpost.com/wp-dyn/content/article/2009/09/14/AR2009091401498.html (Accessed March 13, 2017).

Southern Poverty Law Center. "Dan Stein." https://www.splcenter.org/fighting-hate/extremist-files/individual/dan-stein (Accessed March 13, 2017).

Southern Poverty Law Center. "Federation for American Immigration Reform." https://www.splcenter.org/fighting-hate/extremist-files/group/federation-american-immigration-reform (Accessed March 13, 2017).

STOCKHEIMER, THOMAS

Thomas Stockheimer (1932–2013) was a tax protestor and activist in the late 1960s who founded the Wisconsin chapter of the Posse Comitatus (Latin for "force of the county") in 1970. Stockheimer was considered a Christian zealot and a white supremacist who advocated a militant approach against the federal government, particularly in regard to the payment of federal taxes. Stockheimer is notorious for his orchestration of the brief abduction and assault of an Internal Revenue Service (IRS) agent in 1974. The incident became the inspiration for a book entitled *The Terrorist Next Door: The Militia Movement and the Radical Right* (2008) (Levitas 2002). Stockheimer was later "convicted of assault and after losing appeals became a fugitive. Stockheimer's anti-Semitism, racism, and anti-tax philosophy attracted James Wickstrom to Posse Comitatus" (History Commons). Wickstrom later joined Posse Comitatus and became active in the Christian Identity movement.

In the 1960s, Stockheimer started an organization called the Little People's Tax Advisory Committee. His vitriol toward the federal government and the payment of taxes was such that he and "some of his followers decided to lure an IRS agent to a farm in Abbotsford, Wisconsin" in 1974 (History Commons). By this time, Stockheimer was a devoted member of Posse Comitatus, an extremist organization that by the 1970s had become synonymous with antigovernment activity and antitax sentiments. The Posse did not recognize any governmental authority above the county level, and the IRS represented the federal overreach that members of the Posse detested.

On August 16, 1974, "Stockheimer and several of his compatriots lured IRS agent Fred Chicken to the farm of Alan Grewe" (History Commons). Chicken was coming to the Grewe farm to review Grewe's tax records. But Stockheimer and his friends were waiting for Chicken in Grewe's living room. A couple of years before, another right-wing activist had encouraged individuals to use "witnesses, tape recorders, cameras, and visible weapons" when dealing with federal agents (Pearl 2015). Stockheimer had all of these available for the well-planned ambush of Chicken.

When Chicken was confronted with the array of individuals against him, he attempted to leave. Stockheimer struck Chicken with his fist and shoved him across the room. Then Stockheimer introduced himself and pushed a copy of the Posse Comitatus articles of incorporation into Chicken's hand (Levitas 2002). After several hours, Stockheimer and the group released Chicken. A month later, "Stockheimer organized nearly 100 supporters and disrupted a hearing of the State Department of Natural Resources in Eau Claire, Wisconsin" (Southern Poverty Law Center). Stockheimer's Posse Comitatus comrades "carried out attacks and failed plots against other IRS agents as well, the most notorious of which was Posse leader Gordon Kahl's 1983 rampage in which two US Marshals—not IRS agents—were killed" (Pearl 2015).

Stockheimer would fade into obscurity after violating his parole for his assault of Chicken. His legacy, however, was recruiting James Wickstrom into the ranks of Posse Comitatus. Wickstrom met Stockheimer when he walked by Stockheimer's Little People's Tax Party office in Racine, Wisconsin. Stockheimer asked Wickstrom, "Do you really know who you are? Do you know that you're an Israelite?" (History Commons). Wickstrom was offended at first but became interested as he was told of William Potter Gale's belief that whites are the "true Israelite tribe and that Jews are the offspring of Satan" and are conspiring to destroy Western society while "blacks are subhuman, and no better than the beasts of the field" (History Commons). William Potter Gale, the founder of Christian Identity, and his ideas would resonate with Wickstrom, and he (Wickstrom) would go on to become one of the most virulent anti-Semites and white supremacists within the far-right extremist movements of the United States.

See also: Christian Identity; Gale, William Potter; Kahl, Gordon; Posse Comitatus; White Supremacist Movement; Wickstrom, James

Further Reading

Conner, Claire. 2014. *Wrapped in the Flag: What I Learned Growing Up in America's Radical Right, How I Escaped, and Why My Story Matters Today*. Beacon Press.

History Commons. "Profile: Thomas Stockheimer." http://www.historycommons.org/entity .jsp?entity=thomas_stockheimer_1 (Accessed May 1, 2017).

Levitas, Daniel. 2002. *The Terrorist Next Door: The Militia Movement and the Radical Right*. St. Martin's Press.

Pearl, Mike. April 15, 2015. "A Brief History of Violent Attacks Against the IRS." *Vice*. https://www.vice.com/en_us/article/a-brief-history-of-people-attacking-the-irs-992 (Accessed May 1, 2017).

Southern Poverty Law Center. June 15, 1998. "Hate Group Expert Daniel Levitas Discusses Posse Comitatus, Christian Identity Movement and More." *Southern Poverty Law Center—Intelligence Report*. https://www.splcenter.org/fighting-hate/intelligence -report/1998/hate-group-expert-daniel-levitas-discusses-posse-comitatus-christian -identity-movement-and (Accessed May 1, 2017).

STORMFRONT

Stormfront is the Web site founded by white supremacist Don Black in 1995. Black, a former Grand Wizard of the Knights of the Ku Klux Klan, established the site just one month before the Oklahoma City bombing in April 1995. Black had learned computer coding in prison while serving a three-year sentence for plotting to overthrow the Caribbean island government of Dominica in 1981. When he emerged from prison, Black realized the potential for the Internet to be a perfect conduit and purveyor of white supremacist thought and speech. Black believed that white supremacists, and other racist elements, needed a platform free from the mainstream media's "monopoly" on thought and speech, which filtered out the elements of hate sought by Black and other white supremacists. In March 2015, *Stormfront* celebrated its 20th year of existence and could count over 300,000 registered members in its ranks. As it was from the beginning, *Stormfront* remains one of the most popular sites on the Internet for white supremacists and other extremists to congregate and share their messages of hate.

From its founding, Don Black envisioned *Stormfront* to be a "safe place" where extremist thought could be expressed without the stigma that was attached to such sentiments by the mainstream media. Black believed it was important that those with racist beliefs be free to express themselves and draw hope and inspiration from others with similar feelings. In 1995, the Internet provided the perfect platform where people could express their vitriol from home, free from the backlash that might come if such sentiments were expressed through the general media or in public settings. At first, *Stormfront* attracted the vilest of individuals, who used every known racial epithet and stereotype to express themselves. However, Don Black, who was friends with and a protégé of David Duke, the former Grand Wizard of the Knights of the Ku Klux Klan, realized, as did Duke, that such speech very often turned off individuals who might harbor such thoughts but who believe that their public expression weakened their message. Like Duke, Black believed that white supremacist thought must "get out of the cow pasture and into hotel meeting rooms" (Southern Poverty Law Center, Don Black).

Stormfront has grown into one of the most popular "forum[s] for white nationalists and other racial extremists to post articles, engage in discussions, and share news of upcoming racist events" (Southern Poverty Law Center, Stormfront). Since 2008, it has censored explicitly hate-filled posts in an attempt to be more inclusive. It has generally tried to maintain "a relatively nonsectarian stance, making people from different sectors of the radical right feel welcome to join in" (Southern Poverty Law Center, Stormfront). With white nationalism and extremist thought on the rise, it seems certain that *Stormfront* will continue to gain in popularity as a place on the Internet where extreme racial sentiments will be expressed.

See also: Black, Don; Duke, David

Further Reading

Anti-Defamation League. "Don Black/Stormfront." *Anti-Defamation League—Extremism in America.* http://archive.adl.org/learn/ext_us/don-black/ (Accessed January 5, 2017).

Southern Poverty Law Center. "Don Black." https://www.splcenter.org/fighting-hate /extremist-files/individual/don-black (Accessed January 5, 2017).

Southern Poverty Law Center. "Stormfront." https://www.splcenter.org/fighting-hate /extremist-files/group/stormfront (Accessed January 5, 2017).

Southern Poverty Law Center. March 27, 2015. "Don Black's Stormfront Turns 20." *Southern Poverty Law Center—Hatewatch.* https://www.splcenter.org/hatewatch/2015/03/27 /don-blacks-stormfront-turns-20 (Accessed January 5, 2017).

STROM, KEVIN

Kevin Strom (b. 1956) is an avowed white nationalist, white separatist, neo-Nazi, and Holocaust denier. He is the founder of the National Vanguard, an organization formed by dissident members of the National Alliance, an anti-Semitic, white separatist, and white nationalist organization founded by William Pierce. Strom was introduced to far-right ideology when his high school history teacher provided him with material from the John Birch Society, the conservative advocacy group that is rabidly anticommunist and in favor of limited government. While in the John Birch Society, Strom met members of Pierce's National Alliance, after which Strom left the Birch Society, saying that the society was afraid of addressing the most pressing question in the United States—race. In 2007, Strom was arrested on "child pornography charges. In 2008, he was sentenced to 23 months of incarceration" with credit for time served and 15 years of supervised release (Southern Poverty Law Center, Kevin Strom). In 2013, Strom announced a new iteration of the National Alliance and once again began broadcasting the radio show *American Dissident Voices*.

Through his association with William Pierce, Strom quickly became indoctrinated into the virulently racist and anti-Semitic beliefs. In particular, Strom learned from Pierce firsthand the meaning of the Zionist Occupation Government, "the name given by the radical right to the federal government, the degeneracy of the civil rights movement, and the all-round superiority of the white race" (Southern Poverty Law Center, Kevin Strom). In 1985, under Pierce's tutelage, Strom created and hosted the National Alliance (NA) radio show, *American Dissident Voices*, and edited NA's publication, *National Vanguard*. Strom "became Pierce's favorite aide, and Pierce introduced Strom to the woman who would become Strom's wife" (Southern Poverty Law Center, Kevin Strom).

In 2002, William Pierce died unexpectedly, and it was widely expected that Strom would be his successor in the National Alliance. However, Strom was passed over for the post by another NA operative, Erich Gliebe. In 2005, Gliebe expelled Strom from the NA for attempting a coup against him. Having anticipated the expulsion, "Strom had secretly transferred the NA's website name—*National Vanguard*—to his second wife, having divorced his first wife a few years earlier" (Southern Poverty Law Center, National Vanguard). Much of the NA membership followed Strom, and he seemed poised to succeed Pierce as the new leader of the neo-Nazi, white supremacist groups that were then experiencing a resurgence in membership.

However, in January 2007, Strom was arrested by federal agents near his home in Virginia for possessing and receiving child pornography. The arrest sent major waves of dissent through the white supremacist world, and Strom disbanded *National Vanguard* in March 2007. In January 2008, "Strom pleaded guilty to possession of child pornography in exchange for having multiple counts of receiving child pornography dismissed" (Southern Poverty Law Center, National Vanguard). He was sentenced to 23 months in federal prison and was released in September 2008 after having already served more than a year in jail awaiting his trial.

In 2014, Erich Gliebe "resigned his position as chief of the National Alliance and appointed William Williams as his successor" (Southern Poverty Law Center, Kevin Strom). Williams subsequently brought Strom back into the NA fold, saying of Strom, "He's a fixture in the National Alliance. I can't imagine the Alliance without him. All this bunk about him being a child porn enthusiast is just so much hype. That's the movement. We get more trouble from these so-called movement people than we do from the Southern Poverty Law Center" (Southern Poverty Law Center, Kevin Strom). After Williams was barred from the National Alliance headquarters, Strom became the de facto head of the group, which at present has no more than a few dozen members. Strom, however, continues "to publish racist propaganda on the *National Vanguard* website" as well as host the radio program *American Dissident Voices* (Southern Poverty Law Center, National Vanguard).

See also: Gliebe, Erich; John Birch Society; National Alliance; National Vanguard; Pierce, William; White Nationalism; White Supremacist Movement

Further Reading

National Vanguard. "About Us." http://nationalvanguard.org/ (Accessed March 10, 2017).

Southern Poverty Law Center. "Kevin Strom." https://www.splcenter.org/fighting-hate /extremist-files/individual/kevin-strom (Accessed March 10, 2017).

Southern Poverty Law Center. "National Vanguard." https://www.splcenter.org/fighting -hate/extremist-files/group/national-vanguard (Accessed March 10, 2017).

STUDENTS FOR A DEMOCRATIC SOCIETY

Students for a Democratic Society (SDS) was a radical student organization of the 1960s. At its height, it was the largest and most influential organization of its kind. SDS was cofounded in Ann Arbor, Michigan, in 1960 by Alan Haber and Tom Hayden. Initially, the organization attracted a handful of members in chapters throughout the country. In 1962, the organization published the Port Huron Statement, which was the group's manifesto about the challenges facing the United States and the need for citizens to engage in "participatory democracy" in order to confront the dangers that threatened to destroy the country. The Port Huron Statement also articulated a vision for the attainment in American society of equality, economic justice, and peace. Though the membership of SDS remained small, the organization was always committed to the civil rights movement and the social and political changes that were accompanying it. With the escalation of the Vietnam War in 1965, "SDS grew rapidly as young people, in particular students, protested the activities of the U.S. government in connection with the war" (SDS Archives). The "polite protests" that had characterized the activities of SDS in its early years eventually "turned into stronger and more determined resistance as rage and frustration increased all across the country" (SDS Archives). By the late 1960s, internal frustration with the lack of tangible results created factional squabbling within the group. The group eventually split into several factions, with more radical and violent individuals joining the Weather Underground, an organization that used terror tactics to achieve results. By the mid-1970s, SDS as a political force had largely disappeared from the landscape.

In 1968, founding member Tom Hayden was among protestors at the Democratic National Convention that took place in August of that year. After a series of protests turned into violent riots and confrontations with Chicago police, Hayden and seven others were arrested and charged for conspiracy for incitement to riot. In what would become known as the Chicago Eight trial, Hayden and his fellow defendants would eventually be exonerated of the charges against them.

However, the lack of real social and political change frustrated many SDS members. In the summer of 1969, SDS convened its ninth annual conference in Chicago, Illinois, with more than 2,000 people in attendance. By this time, many factions had arisen in SDS. The largest was the essence of the "old" SDS—the Worker Student Alliance (WSA). The counter to the SDS-WSA was the SDS-Revolutionary Youth Movement (SDS-RYM) led by Bernardine Dohrn. As the various factions began to fight with one another, the conference fell into chaos as fighting and name calling ensued (Sale 1973). The SDS-RYM walked out of the conference, and by its end, there were effectively two SDS organizations—SDS-WSA, the core of the original SDS group, and the SDS-RYM, the radicalized faction intent on initiating more aggressive action to achieve the aims of SDS.

By the fall of 1969, SDS-RYM also split into several factions and disintegrated. The most militant faction, who began to call themselves the Weathermen or the Weather Underground, began to protest violently in the streets and then resorted to a series of bombing campaigns, particularly aimed at government offices and police stations. The Weathermen had taken their name "from a Bob Dylan song with lyrics, 'You don't need a weatherman to know which way the wind blows'" (Sale 1973).

SDS-WSA continued its activities, focusing on fighting racism and supporting workers' struggles and strikes. In 1972, SDS-WSA organized demonstrations against Democratic presidential nominee George McGovern, claiming that he had retreated from his original tough stance in opposition to the Vietnam War. Hundreds of SDS-WSA members staged a sit-in protest at the hotel at which McGovern and his staff were staying.

In 1973, SDS-WSA increasingly turned its attention to ending racism and circulated a petition among its members entitled "A Resolution Against Racism" (Revolvy). From this new emphasis, SDS formed the Committee Against Racism. In 1974, SDS-WSA was dissolved, and its members voted to create a separate organization within the International Committee Against Racism.

After its dissolution, a few SDS members went on to careers in Democratic Party politics, including Tom Hayden. On Martin Luther King Jr's birthday in 2006, a new version of SDS was created. The new SDS announced itself as "a radical multi-issue organization that leads campaigns to win change, and builds people power in our schools and communities!" (National Students for a Democratic Society).

See also: Weather Underground

Further Reading

Editors of Encyclopedia Britannica. July 20, 1998. "Students for a Democratic Society." *Encyclopedia Britannica.* https://www.britannica.com/topic/Students-for-a-Democratic-Society (Accessed March 17, 2017).

Revolvy. "Students for a Democratic Society." https://www.revolvy.com/main/index.php?s=StudentsforaDemocratic20Society&item_type=topic (Accessed March 17, 2017).

Sale, Kirkpatrick. 1973. *SDS: The Rise and Development of the Students for a Democratic Society.* Random House. http://www.sds-1960s.org/books/sds.pdf (Accessed March 17, 2017).

SDS Archives. "Students for a Democratic Society (SDS)." Links to Resources from Students for a Democratic Society. http://www.sds-1960s.org/ (Accessed March 17, 2017).

SUNIC, TOMISLAV

Tomislav (Tom) Sunic (b. 1953) is a Croatian American white nationalist author and a frequent speaker on the white nationalist speaker circuit. Sunic has written dozens of articles and several books, one of which—*Homo Americanus* (2007)—explores the foundations of Judeo-Christian thought and its social and political manifestations in the United States. In the introduction to the book, Kevin MacDonald, editor of the *Occidental Observer*, which covers "white identity, white interests, and the culture of the West" (MacDonald), wrote that Sunic's book "addresses the modern world of hyper-liberalism, globalist capitalism and the crisis of our inherited Indo-European civilization" (Sunic 2007). Sunic has frequently been published in *American Renaissance*, a monthly white supremacist journal, and has been an invited speaker to "gatherings of radical conservatives, white nationalists, and individuals and groups accused of promoting racist and anti-Semitic views" (Keller 2010). Sunic is the director of the American Freedom Party, formerly known as the Third Position Party, an American political party that explicitly promotes white nationalism in its party platform.

Sunic was born in Zagreb, Croatia, and immigrated to the United States in 1982. In 1985, he earned his master's degree from California State University at Sacramento and later received a doctorate in political science from the University of California at Santa Barbara in 1988. In 2015, he became a naturalized citizen of the United States. Sunic taught for a time in the California Higher Education System and later served in the Croatian diplomatic corps. In the early 2000s, Sunic criticized European restrictions on freedom of speech—particularly in regard to what was considered "hate speech"—and what he considered "liberal" policies regarding nonwhite immigration. During this time, he spoke before conferences organized and attended by historical revisionists, even lecturing beside an individual who would later be imprisoned in Germany for being a Holocaust denier.

Sunic has spoken at numerous meetings "sponsored by members of the Ku Klux Klan (KKK), neo-Nazis, and neo-Confederates" (Southern Poverty Law Center). He "has hosted a radio show on the white supremacist 'Voices of Reason Radio Network,' on which he has interviewed white supremacists and neo-Nazis," such as David Duke, Jamie Kelso, and Kevin MacDonald (Southern Poverty Law Center). In June 2008, "Sunic hosted the Pacifica Forum, an anti-Semitic group that promotes Holocaust denial. That same year, he spoke before the Council of Conservative Citizens," an American far-right organization that promotes white nationalism, white separatism, and white supremacy (Southern Poverty Law Center). In 2010, Sunic spoke before a KKK meeting in Harrison, Arkansas, in which he complained about the "massive influx of illegal immigration in America and Europe which is drastically changing the social, moral, and racial fabric of our White European countries" (Southern Poverty Law Center). While at the Arkansas event, Sunic "stayed at the home of a Christian Identity pastor, who was the leader of the Knights of the Ku Klux Klan, a group originally founded by David Duke" (Southern Poverty Law Center). In March 2010, Sunic took up his post at the American Freedom Party, "a group that has been designated as a hate group by the Southern Poverty Law Center" (Keller 2010).

See also: American Freedom Party; Christian Identity; Council of Conservative Citizens; Duke, David; Holocaust Denial; MacDonald, Kevin; Neo-Nazis; *Occidental Observer*; White Nationalism; White Supremacist Movement

Further Reading

Keller, Larry. March 24, 2010. "Croatian Extremist Joins White Hate Group Leadership." *Southern Poverty Law Center—Hatewatch*. https://www.splcenter.org/hate watch/2010/03/24/croatian-extremist-joins-white-hate-group-leadership (Accessed March 15, 2017).

MacDonald, Kevin. "Mission Statement: Introducing the Occidental Observer." *Occidental Observer*. http://www.theoccidentalobserver.net/mission/ (Accessed March 15, 2017).

Southern Poverty Law Center. "Tomislav Sunic." https://www.splcenter.org/fighting-hate /extremist-files/individual/tomislav-suni%C4%87 (Accessed March 15, 2017).

Sunic, Tomislav. 2007. *Homo Americanus: Child of the Postmodern Age*. BookSurge Publishing.

SYMBIONESE LIBERATION ARMY

The Symbionese Liberation Army (SLA) was a left-wing revolutionary organization active in the United States from 1973 until 1975. It is most famous for its kidnapping of newspaper heiress Patty Hearst in 1974. Though the SLA began to coalesce as a group in 1971, it wasn't until 1973 that the de-facto founder and leader of the SLA, Donald DeFreeze (a.k.a. General Field Marshal Cinque) gathered together a small band of exconvicts and UC-Berkeley students to form the organization (DiscoverTheNetworks). The group never numbered more than a couple dozen members. The name DeFreeze chose to begin his revolution, Cinque, was the name of the rebellion leader aboard the slave ship *Amistad* in 1839 (University of Missouri-Kansas City). The "symbionese" portion of the group's name came from the term "symbiosis," wherein different types of organisms come together to live in harmony and partnership for the good of the whole. For DeFreeze, "symbionese was in reference to different types of people—black and white, young and old, male and female—living in harmony" (DiscoverTheNetworks). After a shootout with federal authorities in May 1974 in which DeFreeze was killed, the remaining members of the SLA were eventually captured and imprisoned. The group effectively ceased to exist in 1975.

As did most leaders of left-wing groups of the time, upon founding the SLA, DeFreeze issued a manifesto and a declaration of war. Entitled "The Symbionese Federation & Symbionese Liberation Army Declaration of Revolutionary War & the Symbionese Program," the manifesto declared in part,

> The Symbionese Federation and The Symbionese Liberation Army is a united and federated grouping of members of different races and people and socialistic political parties of the oppressed people of The Fascist United States of America, who have under black and minority leadership formed and joined The Symbionese Federated Republic and have agreed to struggle together in behalf of all their people and races and political parties' interest in the gaining of Freedom and Self Determination and Independence for all their people and races. . . .
>
> We of the Symbionese Federation and The S.L.A. define ourselves by this name because it states that we are no longer willing to allow the enemy of all our people and children to murder, oppress and exploit us nor define us by color and thereby maintain division among us, but rather have joined together under black and minority leadership in behalf of all our different races and people to build a better and new

world for our children and people's future. We are a United Front and Federated Coalition of members from the Asian, Black, Brown, Indian, White, Women, Grey and Gay Liberation Movements. (DeFreeze 1973)

Members of the SLA murdered the superintendent of the Oakland School System, Marcus Foster, in 1973. Foster was targeted by the SLA for issuing identification cards for the Oakland School System, having been called a "fascist" by DeFreeze. In April 1975, "members of the SLA shot and killed a mother of four during a bank robbery." When later asked to reflect on the murder, "the trigger-woman, Emily Harris," said, "Oh, she's dead, but it doesn't really matter. She was a bourgeois pig anyway. Her husband is a doctor" (DiscoverTheNetworks).

The most infamous act of the SLA was the kidnaping of newspaper heiress Patricia Hearst in February 1974. Upon her abduction, the SLA demanded that

Hearst's father, *San Francisco Examiner* managing director Randolph Hearst, distribute food to the hungry of the San Francisco Bay area. Initially, the SLA demanded that $4 million worth of free food be distributed in return for Patty Hearst's return. This amount later grew to $400 million. Though some food was distributed, the program was discontinued when thousands of people showed up for the food giveaways (Welch 1974).

Thirteen days after her capture, "the SLA released an audio tape in which Patty Hearst was heard espousing SLA ideology. After this initial communique, Hearst announced that she had joined the SLA and had taken on the name of 'Tania'" (Brown 2002). A mere 10 weeks after her abduction, Patty Hearst "was filmed robbing the Hibernia bank in San Francisco." She later opened fire on a department store after a botched shoplifting attempt by SLA members and may have been the getaway driver in other robbery attempts (Brown 2002).

A surveillance photo shows kidnapped heiress Patty Hearst carrying a weapon during a robbery at a San Francisco bank in April 1974. The Symbionese Liberation Army, a left-wing revolutionary organization active in the United States from 1973 until 1975, had kidnapped Hearst to bring attention to the plight of the homeless in the San Francisco Bay Area. (Tony Korody/Sygma/Sygma via Getty Images)

On May 16, 1974, several members of the SLA, including Donald DeFreeze, were killed by Federal Bureau of Investigation agents in a shootout in Los Angeles. Remaining members of the SLA found their way back to the San Francisco Bay area, where they committed several more robberies. Finally, on September 18, 1975, Patty Hearst was captured. She was convicted of the Hibernia Bank robbery, though her defense team argued that she was the victim of Stockholm syndrome, "wherein a hostage exhibits loyalty to their abductor" (Welch 1974). Hearst was convicted, though she served only 21 months of a seven-year prison term after being pardoned by President Jimmy Carter.

The short and turbulent existence of the Symbionese Liberation Army demonstrates the depth and breadth of commitment that members of this organization had to their cause of bringing about a social revolution within the United States. Though it was determined to bring about political change in the United States through violent means, the SLA never attracted enough support to be a viable revolutionary force. In fact, had it not been for the kidnapping of Patty Hearst, it is quite possible that the SLA would be a mere footnote in the history of political violence in the United States (Balleck 2015).

See also: Weather Underground

Further Reading

Balleck, Barry J. 2015. *Allegiance to Liberty: The Changing Face of Patriots, Militias, and Political Violence in America.* Praeger.

Brown, Sarah. January 17, 2002. "America's Hippy Extremists." *BBC.* news.bbc.co.uk/2/hi /americas/1765993.stm (Accessed March 17, 2017).

DeFreeze, Donald (aka Cinque). August 21, 1973. "The Symbionese Federation and the Symbionese Liberation Army Declaration of Revolutionary War and the Symbionese Program." *Freedom Archives.* https://freedomarchives.org/Documents/Finder/DOC514 _scans/514.SLA.DeclarationofRevWar.8.21.1973.Communique.pdf (Accessed March 17, 2017).

DiscoverTheNetworks. "Symbionese Liberation Army." http://www.discoverthenetworks .org/printgroupProfile.asp?grpid=6466 (Accessed March 17, 2017).

University of Missouri-Kansas City. "Cinque." http://law2.umkc.edu/faculty/projects/ftrials /amistad/ami_bcin.htm (Accessed March 17, 2017).

Welch, Calvin. March 25, 1974. "The Legacy of the SLA." *Foundsf.* www.foundsf.org/index .php?title=The_Legacy_of_the_SLA (Accessed March 17, 2017).

T

TANTON, JOHN

John Tanton (b. 1934) has been dubbed by the Southern Poverty Law Center, John Tanton (SPLC) as the "racist architect of the modern anti-immigrant movement." Tanton is best known as the founder of the Federation for American Immigration Reform (FAIR), which has been called by former Reagan administration official Linda Chavez, "the most influential organization in the country on immigration" (Southern Poverty Law Center, John Tanton). The SPLC points out that the "organized anti-immigration movement is almost entirely the handiwork" of Tanton. Besides FAIR, Tanton has either funded or founded a dozen other groups devoted to anti-immigration policies (Southern Poverty Law Center, John Tanton's Network). Among these are the "American Immigration Control Foundation, the American Patrol/Voices of Citizens Together, the California Coalition for Immigration Reform, Californians for Population Stabilization, the Center for Immigration Studies, NumbersUSA, Population-Environment Balance, Pro English, ProjectUSA, The Social Contract Press, U.S. English, and U.S. Inc." (Southern Poverty Law Center, John Tanton's Network). Many of Tanton's organizations, including FAIR, have received funds from the Pioneer Fund, "a white supremacist organization dedicated to perpetuating race betterment through the support of quasi-scientific studies regarding race and eugenics" (Southern Poverty Law Center, John Tanton's Network). Tanton has also been linked to neo-Nazi causes and has stated that "for European-American society and culture to persist requires a European-American majority, and a clear one at that" (Beirich 2009).

Tanton's white nationalist views first came to light in 1988, "when a series of memos he wrote to FAIR were leaked to the press" (Southern Poverty Law Center, John Tanton). In these, Tanton complained of the "Latin onslaught" of American society. Tanton's group, U.S. English, was already active at this time and "opposed bilingualism in public schools and government agencies" (Southern Poverty Law Center, John Tanton). However, his writings also bring to light his associations "with Holocaust deniers, former Ku Klux Klan (KKK) lawyers, and leading members of the white nationalist movement" (Southern Poverty Law Center, John Tanton). Tanton is the founder and publisher of *The Social Contract Press*, an arm of his foundation, U.S. Inc. The *Press* has published several journal articles praising Euro-American culture and decrying the "unwarranted hatred and fear" of whites and white culture that Tanton blames on an emphasis on multiculturalism in the United States, particularly as it has been presented by immigrant groups.

In 1994, The Social Contract Press became infamous for its republication of the racist novel *The Camp of Saints* (1994) by author Jean Raspall, which describes

> "swarthy hordes" of Indian immigrants who take over France, send white women to "a whorehouse for Hindus" and engage in a grotesque orgy of men, women and children. The immigrants are described as "monsters," "grotesque little beggars from the streets of Calcutta" and worse. (Southern Poverty Law Center, John Tanton)

Despite its subject matter, Tanton claims that he was "honored" to publish such an important text. The novel has been likened to *The Turner Diaries*, a key polemic of the American white supremacist and white nationalist movements.

Tanton's anti-immigration stance, and that of FAIR, largely centers on attempts to repeal the 1965 Immigration and Nationality Act, a law that ended decades of racial quotas that favored immigration from northern Europe. Members of FAIR have frequently testified about immigration policy before Congress, but its agenda has been called into question with revelations that it (FAIR) has received donations from the Pioneer Fund, a racist foundation that promotes studies that examine the link between race and intelligence.

See also: Center for Immigration Studies; Federation for American Immigration Reform; Holocaust Denial; Neo-Nazis; Pioneer Fund; Stein, Dan; *Turner Diaries, The*; White Nationalism; White Supremacist Movement

Further Reading

Beirich, Heidi. November 30, 2008. "John Tanton's Private Papers Expose More Than 20 Years of Hate." *Southern Poverty Law Center—Intelligence Report*. https://www.splcenter.org/fighting-hate/intelligence-report/2008/john-tanton's-private-papers-expose-more-20-years-hate (Accessed March 13, 2017).

Beirich, Heidi. January 31, 2009. "The Nativist Lobby: Three Faces of Intolerance." Southern Poverty Law Center. https://www.splcenter.org/20090201/nativist-lobby-three-faces-intolerance (Accessed March 13, 2017).

Southern Poverty Law Center. "John Tanton." https://www.splcenter.org/fighting-hate/extremist-files/individual/john-tanton (Accessed March 13, 2017).

Southern Poverty Law Center. "John Tanton's Network." https://www.splcenter.org/fighting-hate/intelligence-report/2015/john-tantons-network (Accessed March 13, 2017).

TAYLOR, JARED

Jared Taylor (b. 1951) is the founder of the New Century Foundation and the editor of *American Renaissance*, a pseudoacademic journal that publishes the works of eugenics proponents as well as "anti-black and anti-Latino racists." *American Renaissance* has been described "as an outlet for white supremacist thought and is known as a publication that promotes white identity" (Southern Poverty Law Center). Taylor regularly attacks the diversity and multiculturalism of American society. He describes himself as a "race realist," advancing the idea that it is natural and a healthy self-expression of identity for people and groups to segregate themselves along racial lines (Anti-Defamation League). Though Taylor denies that he is a white supremacist, much of his rhetoric is focused on how blacks lag behind whites in academics due to the alleged scientifically proven differences between races. Taylor also promotes the racial stereotype that blacks and Hispanics are more likely to commit crimes than whites and that they carry more communicable diseases. Taylor rails against the multiculturalism of American society and believes that whites are losing their majority status in the United States, which will soon mean a loss of their predominant position in society.

Taylor was born in Japan to Christian missionary parents. In 1973, he graduated with a bachelor's degree in philosophy from Yale University. In 1990, he founded the New Century Foundation and *American Renaissance* to promote his ideas on race. In 1992, Taylor published a book that claimed that historical racism could not adequately explain the high rates of crime, poverty, and academic failure among blacks. Though Taylor has been described by the Southern Poverty Law Center as "a white nationalist and a white supremacist," he retorts that he is simply a believer in the "correlation between race and intelligence, believing that whites are more intelligent than blacks and East Asians are more intelligent than whites" (Southern Poverty Law Center). As Taylor once said in an interview,

> I think Asians are objectively superior to Whites by just about any measure that you can come up with in terms of what are the ingredients for a successful society. This doesn't mean that I want America to become Asian. I think every people has a right to be itself, and this becomes clear whether we're talking about Irian Jaya or Tibet, for that matter. (Swain and Nieli 2003)

Interestingly, Taylor does not seem to be an anti-Semite as many other white supremacists are wont to be. However, critics of this assertion note that there have been instances when he has failed to condemn overtly anti-Semitic rhetoric at rallies sponsored by the New Century Foundation (Southern Poverty Law Center).

Taylor suspended the publication of *American Renaissance* in 2012, but much of its content was transferred to his new Web site—Amren.com. In 2015, Taylor briefly reemerged into the media limelight after Dylann Roof—who killed nine black parishioners at a Charleston, South Carolina, church—cited as part of his "manifesto" propaganda material from the Council of Conservative Citizens (CCC), a far-right organization that propagates a variety of white nationalism and white supremacist arguments. As noted by the Southern Poverty Law Center, Taylor's support of the CCC was ironic in that he was speaking for a group that believed the problem to be black-on-white crime, and not vice versa, as was the case in Roof's killing of black churchgoers.

See also: Council of Conservative Citizens; New Century Foundation; Roof, Dylann Storm; White Nationalism; White Supremacist Movement

Further Reading

Anti-Defamation League. "Jared Taylor: American Racist." *Anti-Defamation League—Combating Hate: Domestic Extremism and Terrorism.* http://www.adl.org/combating-hate

/domestic-extremism-terrorism/c/jared-taylor-academic-racist.html#.WG_p2n1_OxU (Accessed January 6, 2017).

Southern Poverty Law Center. "Jared Taylor." https://www.splcenter.org/fighting-hate /extremist-files/individual/jared-taylor (Accessed January 6, 2017).

Swain, Carol M. and Russ Nieli. 2003. *Contemporary Voices of White Nationalism in America*. Cambridge University Press.

TEA PARTY MOVEMENT

The Tea Party movement is a conservative American political movement associated with the Republican Party. Members of the movement "have called for a reduction of the U.S. national debt and the federal budget deficit by reducing government spending and lowering taxes" (Montopoli 2012). The movement "opposed government-sponsored universal healthcare and vigorously imposed the passage of the Affordable Care Act (ACA), also known as Obamacare" (Montopoli 2012) and advocated for stronger immigration controls. The Tea Party movement has been described by political pundits "as a mixture of libertarian, populist, and conservative activism" (Connolly 2010). The Tea Party was best known for sponsoring multiple protests against the Obama administration while supporting various extremely conservative political candidates (Bowman and Marisco 2014). While common wisdom holds that the Tea Party propelled the candidacy, and eventual election, of Donald Trump to the U.S. presidency, others contend that Trump's ascendancy marks the end of the Tea Party as an effective force for political mobilization (Geraghty 2016; Jossey 2016).

The Tea Party movement arose in the aftermath of Barack Obama's election to the U.S. presidency in 2008. As Obama announced that his administration would give financial aid to bankrupt homeowners and financial institutions that had been affected by the global financial

A Tea Party supporter holds a sign demanding President Obama's birth certificate. The Tea Party is a conservative political movement that rose to prominence after the election of Barack Obama in 2008. The Tea Party calls for a reduction of the U.S. national debt and the federal budget deficit. (Cheryl Casey/ Dreamstime)

crisis of 2008, populist anger spilled over. On February 19, 2009, "Rich Santelli, a commentator on business news network CNBC, referenced the Boston Tea Party in his response to President Obama's mortgage relief plan." Standing on the floor of the Chicago Mercantile Exchange, Santelli "railed against government bail-outs for those he believed had made poor investments, saying such aid was 'promoting bad behaviour'" (Connolly 2010). Santelli also stated that the bailout of homeowners "would 'subsidize the losers' mortgages' and proposed a Chicago Tea Party to protest government intervention in the housing market" (Ray).

The five-minute clip of Santelli that was posted on the Internet became a viral sensation, and the "Tea Party rallying cry struck a chord for the millions of Americans who had already seen billions of dollars flow to sagging financial firms," which many blamed for initiating the crisis in the first place. Unlike previous populist movements that directed their ire at business and bankers, "the Tea Party movement focused its ire at the federal government and extolled the virtues of free market principles" (Ray).

Within weeks, the ranks of the nascent Tea Party swelled, drawing in disaffected Republicans. In addition, the antigovernment character of the movement drew in thousands from the patriot and militia movements along with conspiracy-minded individuals who believed that Barack Obama was not a citizen of the United States ("Birthers"), and, therefore, was ineligible to serve as president of the United States, "as well as those who considered that Obama was a socialist and those who believed that Obama, who frequently discussed his Christianity publicly, was secretly a Muslim" (Ray).

In 2010, dozens of Tea Party–affiliated candidates challenged mainstream Republicans for their seats. In several instances, Tea Party candidates won both the primary challenges and the general election. In circumstances where rank-and-file Republicans survived their primary challenges and were reelected, they were forced to support a growing groundswell of anti-Obama and antigovernment sentiment that severely hampered governance. After the 2010 midterm elections, Republicans gained 60 seats in the House to take "control of the body, and significantly reduced the Democratic majority in the Senate." Many observers credited the electoral swing to the Tea Party's appeal. Over the next two years, mainstream Republicans

> attempted to bring Tea Party advocates into the Party's fold to avoid the fratricidal competition that had cost them a number of races in 2010. One notable influence of the Tea Party in 2012 was the inclusion of language in the Republican Party platform that opposed Agenda 21, a United Nations (UN) resolution that promoted sustainable growth and that some Tea Party activists believed represented a UN plot to subvert American sovereignty. (Ray 2017)

In 2013, Tea Party–led Republicans forced a government shutdown in an attempt to scuttle the Affordable Care Act, which they had already "voted more than 40 times to repeal, defund, or delay the legislation." The shutdown lasted 17 days, "but no significant concessions were made to Tea Party demands" (Ray).

In 2014, Republicans made sizeable gains in the House of Representatives and won a majority in the U.S. Senate in addition to capturing numerous state governorships and winning or maintaining "control of many state legislatures. Establishment Republicans viewed the result as a return to mainstream conservative values whereas members of the Tea Party saw the electoral results as a maturation of the movement" (Jossey 2016).

At its height, Tea Party activists were predominantly white, religious, conservative, from the South, and generally voted Republican (Montopoli 2012). When polled about what they were most angry about,

> the top four answers among Tea Party members were: the health care reform bill [ACA] (16 percent), the government not representing the people (14 percent), government spending (11 percent) and unemployment and the economy (8 percent). More than nine in ten (92 percent) said America was on the wrong track while 80 percent disapproved of President Obama's job performance. (Montopoli 2012)

The anger expressed by the Tea Party was co-opted by Donald Trump's candidacy in 2016, and it was Trump's expression of many of the Tea Party's ideals that has brought about the virtual disappearance of the once-powerful political force. Though some contend that the Tea Party has waned because its leaders have moved on, or because the movement produced too many embarrassing candidates, or because "members of the Tea Party never really cared about governance," just attitude, there are a substantial number who claim that the Tea Party actually won, as demonstrated by the number of Tea Party politicians who are now considered "establishment" figures (Geraghty 2016).

Glenn Beck, "one of the few big-name tea partiers that has consistently opposed Donald Trump," suggested that "no real members of the movement supported Trump—and that any that did were, in fact, driven by the racism that critics carped about" (Geraghty 2016). "'I don't think these are Tea Party people who are following [Trump],' Beck said. 'Some of them may be, but I think these—I mean, you can't—if you were a Tea Party person, then you were lying. You were lying. It was about Barack Obama being black. It was about him being a Democrat, because this guy is offering you many of the same things, as shallow as the same way'" (Geraghty 2016).

See also: Militia Movement; Patriot Movement

Further Reading

Bowman, Karlyn and Jennifer Marisco. February 24, 2014. "As the Tea Party Turns Five, It Looks a Lot Like the Conservative Base." *Forbes.* https://www.forbes.com/forbes/welcome/?toURL=https://www.forbes.com/sites/realspin/2014/02/24/as-the-tea-party-turns-five-it-looks-a-lot-like-the-conservative-base/ (Accessed June 8, 2017).

Connolly, Katie. September 16, 2010. "What Exactly Is the Tea Party?" *BBC News.* http://www.bbc.com/news/world-us-canada-11317202 (Accessed June 8, 2017).

Geraghty, Jim. January 19, 2016. "The Death of the Tea Party." *National Review.* http://www.nationalreview.com/article/430028/tea-partys-end (Accessed June 8, 2017).

Jossey, Paul H. August 14, 2016. "How We Killed the Tea Party." *Politico*. http://www
.politico.com/magazine/story/2016/08/tea-party-pacs-ideas-death-214164 (Accessed
June 8, 2017).

Montopoli, Brian. December 14, 2012. "Tea Party Supporters: Who They Are and What
They Believe." *CBS News*. http://www.cbsnews.com/news/tea-party-supporters-who
-they-are-and-what-they-believe/ (Accessed June 8, 2017).

Nesbit, Jeff. April 5, 2016. "The Secret Origins of the Tea Party." *Time*. http://time.com
/secret-origins-of-the-tea-party/ (Accessed June 8, 2017).

Ray, Michael. Updated December 11, 2017. "Tea Party Movement." *Encyclopedia Britannica*.
https://www.britannica.com/topic/Tea-Party-movement (Accessed June 8, 2017).

Tea Party. https://www.teaparty.org/ (Accessed January 30, 2018).

TENTH AMENDMENT CENTER

Founded in 2006, the Tenth Amendment Center (TAC) is dedicated to the principle enshrined in the U.S. Constitution—that the power of the federal (national) government should be limited. The motto of the TAC is "The Constitution. Every Issue. Every Time. No Exceptions. No Excuses," and it claims to be the nation's "leading source for constitutional education and nullification activism" (Tenth Amendment Center, Tenth Amendment Center (not Facebook)).

Founded by Michael Boldin, who also serves as the organization's executive director, the TAC is dedicated to a broad interpretation of the 10th Amendment to the U.S. Constitution: "The powers not delegated to the United States by the Constitution, nor prohibited by it to the States, are reserved to the States respectively, or to the people." This sentiment is adhered to by those who have been dubbed "tenthers," who insist that the enumerated powers entrusted to the national government should be narrowly interpreted so as to make illegitimate much of what the national government does today. The TAC favors a strictly limited constitutional government, insisting that this was the intention of the Founding Fathers, who realized that government, over time, tends to take more power unto itself. This sentiment is found in the system of separation of powers, checks and balances, and, last but not least, federalism. This last principle, that the power of government is divided between state and national governments, is the basis of the Tenth Amendment Center and the "tenther" movement.

At the heart of the TAC's tenets is the doctrine of "nullification." Adherents believe that states, by virtue of a reading of the 10th Amendment, have the sovereign right to "nullify" national laws that conflict with state laws or that are viewed as inherently unconstitutional. The notion of nullification is not new, having been espoused as far back as the 1820s by then vice president of the United States, John C. Calhoun. Today, the TAC finds itself on the political right and finds its supporters among "hard-line libertarians and neo-Confederates who are still angry at the powers the federal government accumulated after the Civil War that allowed it, among other things, to act against segregation, discrimination and other social ills" (Southern Poverty Law Center).

The TAC gained in prominence during the administration of Barack Obama and severely criticized "the U.S. Supreme Court's decision in 2012 to uphold President

Obama's signature health care law," dubbed Obamacare, as "an assumption of undelegated powers." The TAC "urged tenthers to lobby state legislatures to nullify the legislation" (Southern Poverty Law Center).

See also: Land Seizure Movement; Patriot Movement

Further Reading

Southern Poverty Law Center. "Michael Boldin." https://www.splcenter.org/fighting-hate/extremist-files/individual/michael-boldin (Accessed November 21, 2016).
Tenth Amendment Center. http://tenthamendmentcenter.com/ (Accessed November 21, 2016).
Tenth Amendment Center. Facebook Page. https://www.facebook.com/tenthamendmentcenter/about/?ref=page_internal (Accessed November 21, 2016).

THREE PERCENTERS

The Three Percenters (also styled as 3 Percenters, 3%ers, III%ers, the Three Percenters Club, and the 3 Percenters Movement) is a patriot movement that was created after the election of Barack Obama as president of the United States in 2008. The Three Percenters believed that Obama's elections signaled an ominous shift in American politics that would lead to increasing government interference in individual affairs, and, more ominously, a greater push for stricter gun control legislation. The various groups associated with the "3 Percent" movement claim to take their designation from the 3 percent of the total population who took up arms against the British Empire during the American Revolution.

The official Web site of the Three Percenters claims that

the Three Percenter movement started shortly after the attack on the world trade centers. The movement has continued to gain momentum as our federal government grows more powerful. The states are losing control, federal judges are overruling the people, liberals and democrats are determined to disarm citizens, and the political climate is aggressive and leaning towards socialism. Our founding fathers warned us about this with their intentional laws written into the constitution and the bill of rights. Three Percenters are ex and current military, police, and trained civilians that will stand up and fight if our rights are infringed in any way. (threepercentersclub.org)

The Three Percenters are a loose coalition of individuals who identify with many elements of the patriot and militia movements. Their belief that the government continues to overreach its constitutional limits and that average citizens must take a stand against continued government abuses is a hallmark of this philosophy. As indicated by the Three Percenters, many of their members tend to be ex and current military members and police and other law enforcement personnel. In this way, many Three Percenters tend to also be members of the Oath Keepers and other antigovernment groups. The Three Percenters believe that the "solution" to the current problems in the United States can be found in standing up for and protecting the U.S. Constitution (threepercentersclub.org). If the government fails to represent the people, the Three Percenters vow to take action, though they are purposely vague about what such action might be (threepercentersclub.org).

See also: Oath Keepers

Further Reading

Sunshine, Spencer. January 5, 2016. "Profiles on the Right Three Percenters." *Political Research Associates.* http://www.politicalresearch.org/2016/01/05/profiles-on-the-right -three-percenters/#sthash.PNMawnEH.dpbs (Accessed December 13, 2016).

Threepercentersclub.org. "About Us." http://threepercentersclub.org/index.php/pages/about -us (Accessed December 13, 2016).

TROCHMANN, JOHN AND DAVID

John (b. 1943) and David (b. 1945) Trochmann are the cofounders of the Militia of Montana (MOM), often believed to be the first official militia group to form in the aftermath of the Ruby Ridge and Waco standoff incidents with the U.S. federal government. MOM was officially founded by the Trochmann brothers in January 1994 with assistance from John Trochmann's nephew, Randy Trochmann, and financier, Bob Fletcher (Welch 1995). John and David Trochmann "had been members of Aryan Nations, the Idaho-based neo-Nazi organization that promoted white supremacism, anti-Semitism, and agitated for a white racist state. John Trochmann had even been a featured speaker at an Aryan Nations Congress in 1990" (Nizkor Project). The Trochmanns were also adherents of the sovereign citizens movement, "believing that individuals are not subject to the authority of either state or federal government unless they formally chose to enter into a 'contract' with the government (e.g. having a Social Security Number)" (Loons 2014). The Trochmanns were involved in militia activity beginning in 1991 and were members of the Citizens for Justice cause late in 1992 in support of antigovernment activist and white supremacist Randy Weaver, who had been confronted by government agents at his home at Ruby Ridge, Idaho, in August 1992. After the events of the Waco standoff in April 1993, the Trochmanns became convinced that the federal government was intent on seizing all private guns and bringing "subversives" into submission while establishing the New World Order. The Militia of Montana was formed to counter this threat. Though still active today, MOM is a shadow of the organization that existed during the raucous antigovernment days of the 1990s.

John Trochmann was raised in Montana and was a maker of snowmobile parts. Beginning in the 1980s, he and his brother David became involved in antigovernment causes and became devotees of conspiracy theories, including theories "that unseen powers" were using the United Nations "to overturn the American Constitution and invoke martial law as they absorb the United States into an international totalitarian state" (Loons 2014). But it was the events at Ruby Ridge, Idaho, and the subsequent Waco standoff between Branch Davidians and the federal government that convinced the Trochmanns that they needed to take a more aggressive stance against the perceived abuses perpetrated by the federal government. John Trochmann's wife had "delivered food to the Weaver family during the several months that preceded the Ruby Ridge standoff between the Weaver family and federal agents" (Terrorism Research and Consortium Analysis). Trochmann's and Weaver's views on the government were compatible, and Trochmann's sympathies for Weaver grew after his wife and son were killed during the Ruby Ridge standoff.

After the conflagration that consumed the Branch Davidian compound in April 1993, John and David Trochmann decided to form the Militia of Montana in January 1994. MOM quickly grew in membership and notoriety, fueled by the antigovernment feelings engendered by Rudy Ridge and Waco. In June 1994, more than 800 people attended a gathering in Kalispell, Montana, at which John Trochmann spoke. Trochmann would later state that "gun control is people control" and that MOM had more than 12,000 members "trained in guerilla warfare, survivalist techniques, and other unconventional tactics in preparation for withstanding the perceived federal government onslaught to seize their weapons presaged by the Waco Siege" (Hoffman 1999).

On March 3, 1995, John Trochmann and three other armed men were arrested when they entered the Musselshell County (Montana) Courthouse to protest the seizure of a fellow MOM member's house by the Internal Revenue Service. Three confederates of the group waiting outside the courthouse were also arrested. Between them, the group "had semiautomatic handguns, six assault rifles, video gear, and $80,000 in cash, gold, and silver" (Miller 1995). Styling themselves as the "Garfield County Freemen," it was later revealed that Trochmann and his cohorts planned to "kidnap, try, and hang a judge, and videotape the proceedings, according to the Musselshell County Attorney" (Miller 1995).

The Trochmanns organized MOM followers against the Brady Handgun Bill, which attempted to impose waiting periods for the purchase of certain weapons. The bill was named after President Ronald Reagan's press secretary, James Brady, who was critically wounded in an assassination attempt on Reagan's life in 1981. MOM also protested the Federal Assault Weapons Ban, a U.S. federal law that "prohibited the manufacture for civilian use of certain semi-automatic firearms." After the Oklahoma City bombing in April 1995, MOM cofounder Robert Fletcher warned the press to "expect more bombs!" (Southern Poverty Law Center).

MOM's membership plummeted in the aftermath of the dawning of the 21st century, when fears and conspiracy theories about Y2K failed to materialize. The enthusiasm for military exercises and drilling declined as few in MOM wished to provoke a direct confrontation with the federal government. MOM continues to operate a Web site, but the Trochmanns have largely faded from the view of active antigovernment extremists.

See also: Aryan Nations; Militia Movement; Militia of Montana; Patriot Movement; Sovereign Citizens Movement; Weaver, Randy; White Nationalism; White Supremacist Movement

Further Reading

Hoffman, Bruce. 1999. *Inside Terrorism*. Columbia University Press.

Loons. November 26, 2014. "#1219: John Trochmann." *Encyclopedia of American Loons*. http://americanloons.blogspot.com/2014/11/1219-john-trochmann.html (Accessed May 25, 2017).

Militia of Montana. http://www.barefootsworld.net/mom.html (Accessed May 25, 2017).

Miller, Wynn. April 26, 1995. "Right-Wing Militants Mix Political Fantasy, Violence." *Christian Science Monitor*. http://www.csmonitor.com/1995/0426/26191.html (Accessed May 25, 2017).

Nizkor Project. "Armed & Dangerous: Montana." http://www.nizkor.org/hweb/orgs/american/adl/armed-and-dangerous/montana.html (Accessed May 25, 2017).

Southern Poverty Law Center. May 8, 2001. "False Patriots." *Southern Poverty Law Center—Intelligence Report*. https://www.splcenter.org/fighting-hate/intelligence-report/2001/false-patriots (Accessed May 25, 2017).

Terrorism Research and Consortium Analysis. "Militia of Montana." https://www.trackingterrorism.org/group/militia-montana-mom (Accessed May 25, 2017).

Welch, Craig. April 30, 1995. "Out of the Shadows: Oklahoma Bombing Brings Scrutiny of Montana Militia's Pro-Gun, Anti-Feds Philosophy." *The Spokesman-Review*. http://www.spokesman.com/stories/1995/apr/30/out-of-the-shadows-oklahoma-bombing-brings/ (Accessed May 25, 2017).

THE TURNER DIARIES

The Turner Diaries is a 1978 dystopian novel that is a favorite in far-right circles and among extremists because it discusses a revolution that overthrows the U.S. government and sets up a neo-Nazi regime. The book was written by William Luther Pierce, founder of the neo-Nazi group National Alliance, under the pseudonym Andrew MacDonald. The novel is particularly popular among white nationalists and white supremacists because of its racist message. The novel is about a dystopian future in which "non-white minorities have disarmed and oppressed white Americans, leading to an armed white nationalist revolution that eventually triumphs and embarks on a campaign of global genocide against non-whites" (Berger 2016). *The Turner Diaries* has inspired dozens of violent antigovernment acts and has been alternately called the "Bible of the Right" and "probably the most widely-read book among far-right extremists" in the United States (Anti-Defamation League). The novel has been directly linked to the domestic terror group The Order, which was founded in 1983 by Bob Mathews and preached a virulent anti-Semitic and whites-only message to its members. Mathews's inspiration for his organization, The Order, is taken directly from *The Turner Diaries*. Most famously, Timothy McVeigh's bombing of the Alfred P. Murrah Federal Building in Oklahoma City, Oklahoma, in 1995 was directly influenced by the novel. A fictional scenario in the novel, in which antigovernment extremists bomb the FBI building in Washington through the use of a rented truck packed with an ammonium nitrate fertilizer bomb, was the direct inspiration of McVeigh's act in Oklahoma City in which 168 people were killed. The racist message of *The Turner Diaries* inspired Order member David Lane to enunciate the 14 Words, the unofficial manifesto of white nationalism: "We must secure the existence of our people and a future for white children" (Berger 2016).

The Turner Diaries is the fictional diary of Earl Turner, a white nationalist who is confronted with

> a racist's vision of a nightmare world, in which "The System"—African American enforcers led by Jewish politicians—attempt to confiscate all guns in the United States. A secretive organization known as The Order rises up to take back the country for white supremacists, eventually winning an apocalyptic insurgency and nuclear war, first taking over the country and later the world. (Berger 2016)

After the passage of the "Cohen Act" in the novel, all private ownership of guns is outlawed. The U.S. Supreme Court also "legalizes rape with the argument that laws against rape are racist. For white nationalists, the obvious framing of the fictional diary is clear: Jews want to take your guns and blacks want to rape white women" (Anti-Defamation League). In the novel, "The Order rises up to take back the country for whites" and eventually succeeds in taking back the country and later the world (Berger 2016).

William Pierce, author of *The Turner Diaries*, imagined in his work a return to a United States where white nationalism was the norm, much as it was for much of the country's history. The idea of an all-white homeland is critical to the novel's message:

> In the wake of the Civil War, institutionalized white supremacy began to erode, a process that accelerated into the 20th Century. Against the backdrop of the civil rights movement, white nationalism began to develop complex ideologies, with a number of different strains emerging. (Berger 2016)

Among the strains that emerged in response to the perceived erosion of white supremacy were groups such as the Ku Klux Klan and philosophies such as neo-Nazism and Christian Identity, both virulent preachers of anti-Semitism. As one passage in the novel points out,

> If the White nations of the world had not allowed themselves to become subject to the Jew, to Jewish ideas, to the Jewish spirit, this war would not be necessary. We can hardly consider ourselves blameless. We can hardly say we had no choice, no chance to avoid the Jew's snare. We can hardly say we were not warned. . . .
>
> The people had finally had their fill of the Jews and their tricks. . . . If the Organization survives this contest, no Jew will—anywhere. We'll go to the Uttermost ends of the earth to hunt down the last of Satan's spawn. (MacDonald 1978)

As an antigovernment tract, *The Turner Diaries* epitomizes the fears of right-wing extremists who believe that the U.S. government has strayed from the constraints and purposes with which it was originally founded. The notion in the novel that the government is controlled by Jewish influences, and that laws protect minorities in their predatory nature upon the white population, reinforces what many white nationalists and white supremacists believe is the abject reality in the United States. For antigovernment activists, one passage of the novel is telling:

> Looking at it philosophically, one can't avoid the conclusion that it is corruption, not tyranny, which leads to the overthrow of governments. A strong and vigorous government, no matter how oppressive, usually need not fear revolution. But a corrupt, inefficient, decadent government—even a benevolent one—is always ripe for revolution. The system we are fighting is both corrupt and oppressive, and we should thank god for corruption. (MacDonald 1978)

Two portions of *The Turner Diaries* are particularly disturbing. Before the fictional hero, Earl Turner, sacrifices himself by flying a plane laden with explosives into the Pentagon, the Organization—the overarching revolutionary group that has initiated revolution against the U.S. government—"lynches tens of thousands of 'race traitors,' including liberal actors and politicians and white women who slept with black men, hanging them from utility poles with placards around their neck reading, 'I defiled my race.' From this moment—'The Day of the Rope'—the Revolution lurches into genocide" (Anti-Defamation League). In the epilogue to the novel in the year 2099, 100 years after the events of Turner's diary, the Organization has conquered the rest of the world and has eliminated all nonwhite races. The Organization has perpetrated genocide of all nonwhites throughout Africa, Puerto Ricans (described as a "repulsive mongrel race") have been exterminated, and Asia has been destroyed by a full-scale assault with nuclear, chemical, radiological, and biological weapons, leaving the continent uninhabitable. In the United States, any remaining nonwhite peoples in the country have been hunted down and killed. Thus "just 110 years after the birth of the 'Great One' [Adolf Hitler], the dream of a white world finally became a certainty . . . and that the Order would spread its wise and benevolent rule over the earth for all time to come" (Anti-Defamation League).

Though only a fantasy novel, racist right-wing extremists and antigovernment agitators have elevated *The Turner Diaries* to cultlike status, holding it up as the inspiration and blueprint by which white nationalists can retake all that they have lost. In some circles, *The Turner Diaries* is held up beside Hitler's *Mein Kampf* as the definitive tract about the Jewish and nonwhite threat to the modern United States. Bob Mathews's vision for his terror organization, The Order, mimicked what he read in the novel. Indeed, at the founding of The Order in 1983, members held a white infant in their arms as they gathered in a circle and pledged their lives to the protection of the white race (Balleck 2015). This act would later inspire David Lane's "White Genocide Manifesto," in which Lane echoed William Pierce's disdain for "complex ideological formulations," instead arguing that "racial integration is only a euphemism for genocide, and that the 'white race' is on the verge of extinction due to interbreeding with other races" (Berger 2016). Lane's "worldview would later be distilled into the one-sentence oath" that has come to epitomize white nationalism: "We must secure the existence of our people and a future for white children."

The inspiration that Timothy McVeigh drew from *The Turner Diaries* is perhaps the most infamous, and most tragic, legacy of the novel. In the novel, Turner packs a rental truck full of ammonium nitrate fertilizer, turning it into a lethal bomb whose target is the FBI headquarters in Washington, D.C. The bomb explodes just after 9:00 a.m., killing more than 700 people. McVeigh, who wished to exact revenge for the U.S. government's killing of nearly 80 Branch Davidians in the Waco standoff, as well as the deaths of Randy Weaver's son and wife at Ruby Ridge, aimed to bomb the federal building in Oklahoma City, where there was a field office of the FBI. McVeigh drove his rented Ryder truck packed full of fuel oil and ammonium nitrate fertilizer to the Alfred P. Murrah Federal Building in Oklahoma City on April 19, 1995—exactly two years after the deaths of the Branch Davidians at Waco. He parked the truck in front of the building, where a daycare center resided on the first floor, and set fuses to detonate the bomb at exactly 9:02 a.m., just as Earl Turner had done in the novel. McVeigh's actions took the lives of 168 innocent people, including 20 children. Before the bombing, McVeigh had mailed a letter to his sister in which he warned that "something big is going to happen, followed by a second envelope with clippings from *The Turner Diaries*. When she learned of her brother's arrest in connection with the Oklahoma City bombing, McVeigh's sister burned the clippings" (Anti-Defamation League).

After the bombing, FBI agents found "a passage from *The Turner Diaries* in McVeigh's getaway car" (Anti-Defamation League). It was Earl Turner's estimation of the effects of his act of terrorism on the United States. It read,

> The real value of our attacks today lies in the psychological impact, not in the immediate casualties. For one thing, our efforts against the System gained immeasurably in credibility. More important, though, is what we taught the politicians and the bureaucrats. They learned today that not one of them is beyond our reach. They can huddle behind barbed wire and tanks in the city, or they can hide behind the concrete walls and alarm systems of their country estates, but we can still find them and kill them. (MacDonald 1978)

As noted by journalist J. M. Berger (2016), "While *Turner* is rightly infamous for the violence it has inspired, most notably in Oklahoma City, its impact on the shape of white nationalism—and the movement's current resurgence—is an equal part of its dark legacy."

See also: Christian Identity; Fourteen Words; Lane, David; National Alliance; Neo-Nazis; Oklahoma City Bombing; Order, The; Pierce, William; White Nationalism; White Supremacist Movement

Further Reading

Anti-Defamation League. "The Turner Diaries." https://www.adl.org/education/resources/backgrounders/turner-diaries (Accessed June 5, 2017).

Balleck, Barry J. 2015. *Allegiance to Liberty: The Changing Face of Patriots, Militias, and Political Violence in America.* Praeger.

Berger, J. M. September 16, 2016. "How 'The Turner Diaries' Changed White National-ism." *The Atlantic*. https://www.theatlantic.com/politics/archive/2016/09/how-the-turner-diaries-changed-white-nationalism/500039/ (Accessed June 5, 2017).

CNN. April 28, 1997. "'Turner Diaries' Introduced in McVeigh Trial." http://www.cnn.com/US/9704/28/okc/ (Accessed June 5, 2017).

MacDonald, Andrew. 1978. *The Turner Diaries*. National Vanguard Books.

V

VANDERBOEGH, MICHAEL BRIAN

Michael Brian Vanderboegh (1953–2016) was an antigovernment militia group founder who advocated violent resistance to U.S. law. In the 1990s, at the height of the militia movement, Vanderboegh was associated with the Sons of Liberty, an organization dedicated to "self-defense against a tyrannical, Constitutional-flouting U.S. government determined to impose the Communist principles of gun control and universal health care" (Southern Poverty Law Center, Vanderboegh). In the mid-2000s, Vanderboegh assisted Stewart Rhodes in founding the Oath Keepers, an antigovernment organization closely associated with the patriot and militia movements in the United States. In 2008, Vanderboegh founded the Three Percenters, a movement focused on resistance to proposed gun control legislation and implementation. Vanderboegh took the name Three Percenters to pay homage to the "supposed percentage of American colonists that took up arms" against the British Empire in defense of their liberties (Southern Poverty Law Center, Vanderboegh). In his later years, Vanderboegh used inflammatory rhetoric to spread his message, often posting in patriot forums or on his own blog, the *Sipsey Street Irregulars*. In 2013 and 2014, Vanderboegh "emailed Connecticut State Police employees warning them of violent and bloody reprisals if they tried to enforce strict new state gun control legislation" passed in the aftermath of the Sandy Hook Elementary School shooting in December 2012 (Southern Poverty Law Center, Vanderboegh). Vanderboegh went so far as to publish "the home addresses and phone numbers of state senators that had voted for the legislation" (Southern Poverty Law Center). Vanderboegh's rhetoric often incited others to acts of violence, from breaking the windows of government officials to more widespread acts against those officials perceived to be oppressive.

Vanderboegh first appeared on the extremist scene after the federal siege of the Branch Davidian compound in Waco, Texas, in 1993. As a young man, Vanderboegh claimed sympathies with communist ideals, but he had a 180-degree conversion and became a vocal advocate of the U.S. Constitution, in particular the Second Amendment, which Vanderboegh believed entitled all Americans to the absolute right of unrestricted ownership of firearms (Morlin 2016). Vanderboegh saw himself as a moderate in the often-violent patriot and militia movements, and he joined other leaders in 1996 "by signing a document that distanced the movements from racist and neo-Nazis" who often publicly supported the goals of the movements (Southern Poverty Law Center, Vanderboegh).

In the mid-2000s, Vanderboegh "became associated with the anti-immigrant crusade" and took up border patrol activities along the Mexican border with a small group of Alabama militia members (Southern Poverty Law Center, Vanderboegh). The election of Barack Obama in 2008 prompted Vanderboegh to found the Three Percenters just one month after Obama's election in November. Vanderboegh and those who followed him believe that the Democratic Obama was determined to enact new, restrictive gun laws, perhaps even going so far as to seize lawfully held weapons from the possession of American citizens. Vanderboegh coined the "III Percent term, claiming that during the American Revolution the 'active forces in the field against the King's tyranny never amounted to more than 3% of the colonists'" (Morlin 2016). Vanderboegh never claimed that his group represented 3 percent of the American population, though he contended that the group represented at least 3 percent of the views of American gun owners. Vanderboegh said that he and the Three Percenters "are gun owners who will not disarm, will not compromise and will no longer back up at the passage of the next gun control act. Three Percenters say quite explicitly that we will not obey any further circumscription of our traditional liberties and will defend ourselves if attacked" (Morlin 2016).

Vanderboegh wrote a novel in 2008 entitled *Absolved*, which he stated was "a cautionary tale for the out-of-control gun cops of the ATF" and "a combination field manual, technical manual and call to arms for my beloved gunnies of the armed citizenry" (Southern Poverty Law Center, Vanderboegh). In the novel, militia fighters vehemently "denounce gay marriage and gun control laws, and there is a bloody shootout between law enforcement officials and a man who has stockpiled weapons with the intent of waging a campaign against government officials" (Southern Poverty Law Center, Vanderboegh).

U.S. federal law enforcement cite Vanderboegh's book "as inspiration for a 2011 plot in which militia members in Georgia conspired to attack cities with the biological agent ricin, blow up federal buildings, and assassinate law enforcement and other officials" (Southern Poverty Law Center, Vanderboegh). Previously, Vanderboegh's rhetoric has inspired his followers to vandalize the offices of 10 Democratic members of Congress who had voted for the Affordable Care Act, otherwise known as Obamacare. Vanderboegh was unapologetic about the incidents as he stated that the vandalism was "both good manners" and "a moral duty to warn the people" about the health care act (Southern Poverty Law Center, Vanderboegh).

On November 6, 2012, the date of the reelection of Barack Obama, Vanderboegh posted a blog entitled "Vote," encouraging people to go to the polls to vote against President Obama's reelection. At the end of the blog, he added the ominous warning, "At least later on you can say you tried everything else before you were forced to shoot people in righteous self-defense of life and liberty" (Editorial 2013).

In the wake of the Sandy Hook Elementary School shooting in Newton, Connecticut, in December 2012, Vanderboegh "sent e-mails to more than 1,000 employees of the Connecticut State Police warning them of imminent hostilities if they tried to enforce the state's tough new control laws" (Southern Poverty Law Center, Vanderboegh). In April 2014, Vanderboegh and other Three Percenters participated "in the standoff between anti-government extremists and federal government" officials at the Bundy ranch in Bunkerville, Nevada (Southern Poverty Law Center 2014). Though tensions were high and the possibility existed of a shootout between government officials and the heavily armed extremists, the government eventually withdrew. The patriot and militia groups claimed the retreat as a significant victory, and Vanderboegh wrote on his blog that "it is impossible to overstate the importance of the victory won in the desert today. The feds were routed—routed. There is no word that applies. Courage is contagious, defiance is contagious, victory is contagious. Yet the war is not over" (Southern Poverty Law Center 2014).

Though Vanderboegh's support of Bundy's cause was effusive in 2014, in 2016, he condemned Ammon Bundy, Cliven Bundy's son, when he and other antigovernment extremists "took over and occupied the Malheur National Wildlife Refuge in Oregon" (Southern Poverty Law Center, Vanderboegh).

Vanderboegh died on August 10, 2016. A good friend of his wrote of his passing,

True, the man had a strong (some would say "cantankerous" at times) personality. But underlying it was a calling—I don't know what else you'd call it—and fierce devotion for the truth. It was seeing others ignore that truth—particularly when doing so for gain at the expense and abuse of others—that brought his unyielding sense of justice to the fore. (Codrea 2016)

See also: Bundy Ranch Standoff; Malheur National Wildlife Refuge Standoff; Militia Movement; Oath Keepers; Patriot Movement; Rhodes, Elmer Stewart; Sandy Hook Elementary School Shooting; Three Percenters; Waco Standoff

Further Reading

Codrea, David. August 10, 2016. "Freedom Movement Loses Important Voice with Passing of Mike Vanderboegh." *Ammoland.* https://www.ammoland.com/2016/08/passing -mike-vanderboegh/#axzz4gcQB4IZN (Accessed May 9, 2017).

Editorial. April 21, 2013. "Gun Groups Lose 'Law-Abiding Citizen' Argument." *New Hampshire Register.* http://www.nhregister.com/article/NH/20130421/NEWS/304219972 (Accessed May 10, 2017).

Morlin, Bill. August 10, 2016. "Long-Time Militia Leader Mike Vanderboegh Has Died." *Southern Poverty Law Center—Hatewatch.* https://www.splcenter.org/hatewatch/2016 /08/10/long-time-militia-leader-mike-vanderboegh-has-died (Accessed May 9, 2017).

Southern Poverty Law Center. "Michael Brian Vanderboegh." https://www.splcenter.org /fighting-hate/extremist-files/individual/michael-brian-vanderboegh-0 (Accessed May 9, 2017).

Southern Poverty Law Center. July 9, 2014. "War in the West: The Bundy Ranch Standoff and the American Radical Right." https://www.splcenter.org/20140709/war-west -bundy-ranch-standoff-and-american-radical-right (Accessed May 10, 2017).

Sunshine, Spence. January 5, 2016. "Profiles on the Right: Three Percenters." *Political Research.* http://www.politicalresearch.org/tag/civil-liberties/#sthash.WJMirnXA.dpbs (Accessed August 7, 2017).

Vanderboegh, Michael Brian. June 29, 2014. "A Brief Three Percent Catechism—A Discipline Not for Faint-Hearted." *Sipsey Street Irregulars.* http://sipseystreetirregulars.blogspot .com/2014/06/a-brief-three-percent-catechism.html (Accessed May 10, 2017).

VANGUARD NEWS NETWORK

The *Vanguard News Network* (VNN) is an "anti-Semitic, white nationalist, white supremacist, and neo-Nazi website founded by neo-Nazi Alex Linder in 2000" (Terry 2014). A former member of the most active and important neo-Nazi organization in the United States, the National Alliance, Linder split with the group and spun off his own hate organization in the form of VNN. Linder had hopes that VNN would grow into a "White Viacom" composed of "an integrated global media and services company getting out the White message and serving the White market in a thousand forms" (Southern Poverty Law Center). VNN has proved relatively popular in neo-Nazi circles, but it never attained the market viability that Linder hoped. The Southern Poverty Law Center has called VNN "remarkably vulgar, offending even many of the most extreme racists and anti-Semites with Linder's potty humor, untrammeled misogyny (Linder says women 'should make everything happy and smooth running by providing offspring and sex and cookies and iced tea') and swaggering self-importance." In 2014, VNN was at the center of a national controversy when it became known that neo-Nazi gunman Frazier Glenn Miller—who perpetrated a shooting at two Kansas City, Missouri, Jewish community centers "that left three people dead, including a 14-year-old boy and his grandfather"—had posted to VNN more than 12,000 times over the years (Terry 2014).

VNN's motto is "No Jews, Just Right" (VNN). The site has been called a "swamp" by one white nationalist critic, who noted that multiple murderers have been linked to VNN. But perhaps the most infamous VNN-linked killer was Frazier Glenn Miller, who killed a 14-year-old boy and his grandfather outside of a Kansas City Jewish community center, believing them to be Jews when, in fact, they were not. Miller had swallowed Alex Linder's propaganda of a "principled solution to exterminating the Jews." In killing Jews, Miller believed "that he would win admiration of his peers at the VNN forum" (Terry 2014).

In 2007, white supremacists and neo-Nazis praised "former U.S. President Jimmy Carter's book, *Palestine: Peace Not Apartheid*, for its anti-Israel, conspiratorial and anti-Semitic propaganda value" (Anti-Defamation League 2007). For its part, "VNN praised Carter for standing up to the Zionist lobby and reaffirming" what VNN contributors firmly believed—that Jews are inherently evil (Anti-Defamation League 2007). After the publication of Carter's book, in addition to VNN, he received accolades from the neo-Nazi Web site *Stormfront* as well as from members of the Aryan Nations. The following are quotes praising Carter's book as posted on VNN:

> If anyone knows the truth about the Middle East, it's Carter. He was dealing with this same "peace process" BS 30 years ago. Israel is the problem and does not want any semblance of peace. The more wars, the better. Always has been the case, always will be.
>
> How about everything else the Jews have corrupted through their pernicious influence, like our government, our financial institutions, and the economic future of our children and grandchildren. Maybe Carter has thought this through and truly

believes the best way to bring down the power of the Jewish monopoly is through the exposing of the attrocities [*sic*] of the Nation of Israel itself. (VNN, 1/5/2007)

"Because of powerful political, economic, and religious forces in the United States, Israeli government decisions are rarely questioned or condemned," the former president writes. Translation: "The United States has a Zionist Occupied Government." Amen. (VNN, 10/20/2006)

VNN continues to be the destination of many "swamp" dwellers. A recent post to VNN included the headline: "Texas: Increasing the Fag Propaganda, or, the God of Equality Strikes Again." The post, by an individual calling themselves "Socrates," stated in part,

> Human equality: a sick idea that isn't even possible, since humans vary greatly, even within the same race and within the same family. Anyway, some high-schoolers are only 14 years old, for hell's sake (i.e., freshmen) and already they're getting "queered up"! The absolute worst thing a parent can do is send their children to a public school. Homeschool your kids. The queer lobby is going to push homosexuality until every person in America views faggotry as "normal" (instead of viewing it as the disease-ridden lifestyle that it is). (VNN, 5/29/2017)

Today, VNN is still a premier site for vitriolic speech. As one critic has noted, "Just remember, if VNN did not exist, White people would be forced to invent them because VNN is racism White supremacy with a 'face,' the only face that counts, a White person's face" (Wickett).

See also: Aryan Nations; Holocaust Denial; Linder, Alex; Miller, Frazier Glenn; National Alliance; Neo-Nazis; *Stormfront*; White Nationalism; White Supremacist Movement

Further Reading

Anti-Defamation League. January 12, 2007. "Anti-Semitic Reactions to Jimmy Carter's Book: White Supremacists." https://www.adl.org/news/article/anti-semitic-reactions-to-jimmy-carters-book-white-supremacists (Accessed June 1, 2017).

Southern Poverty Law Center. "Alex Linder." https://www.splcenter.org/fighting-hate/extremist-files/individual/alex-linder (Accessed June 1, 2017).

Terry, Don. April 14, 2014. "Vanguard News Network: A Track Record of Violence." *Southern Poverty Law Center—Hatewatch*. https://www.splcenter.org/hatewatch/2014/04/14/vanguard-news-network-track-record-violence (Accessed June 1, 2017).

Vanguard News Network. http://www.vanguardnewsnetwork.com/ (Accessed June 1, 2017).

Wickett, Josh. "VNN: Vanguard News Network." *Counter-Racism*. http://www.counter-racism.com/articles/internet/vnn.html (Accessed June 1, 2017).

VDARE

VDARE.com was a Web site established in 1999 by English immigrant Peter Brimelow, a former editor of *Forbes* magazine and a contributor to such conservative publications as the *Financial Post* and the *National Review*. VDARE is named for Virginia Dare, the first child born of English parents in the New World in 1587. Some of VDARE's most prominent contributors are race scientists, white nationalists, and anti-Semites. As such, the Southern Poverty Law Center and other groups have labeled VDARE a hate site, to which its founder retorts that it is guilty only through association (Brimelow 2006). VDARE is supported by the VDARE Foundation, also established by Brimelow. Also known as the Lexington Research Institute Limited, the VDARE Foundation is designated as a 501(c)3 charity.

VDARE has said it is "dedicated to preserving our historical unity as Americans into the 21st Century" (Southern Poverty Law Center, VDARE). The site is markedly anti-immigrant in tone, as is its founder, Peter Brimelow. Ironically, Brimelow himself is an immigrant to the United States from England. Yet Brimelow's and VDARE's message is that the greatest threat to the United States is not immigration per se but immigration from nonwhite countries. Brimelow has stated that the growing number of minorities in the United States threatens the very fabric of the country. In 2006, he wrote on the VDARE Web site,

> The mass immigration so thoughtlessly triggered in 1965 risks making America an alien nation—not merely in the sense that the numbers of aliens in the nation are rising to levels last seen in the 19th century; not merely in the sense that America will become a freak among the world's nations because of the unprecedented demographic mutation it is inflicting on itself; [and] not merely in the sense that Americans themselves will become alien to each other, requiring an increasingly strained government to arbitrate between them. (VDARE.com)

Though these words are strong, charges of racism and white nationalism among VDARE's contributors come from the likes of Kevin MacDonald and Jared Taylor. MacDonald, a California State University at Long Beach retired professor of psychology, has advanced a notion of evolutionary theory in which "group evolutionary strategy," such as that exhibited by Jews, has given that people notable advantages that allow Jews to outcompete non-Jews for resources. MacDonald has written on VDARE that

> Jewish activity collectively, throughout history, is best understood as an elaborate and highly successful group competitive strategy directed against neighboring peoples and host societies. The objective has been control of economic resources and political power. One example: overwhelming Jewish support for non-traditional immigration, which has the effect of weakening America's historic white majority. (VDARE.com, November 14, 2006)

In like manner, Jared Taylor, an avowed white nationalist, is the founder and editor of *American Renaissance*, a magazine noted for its decidedly white supremacist contributors. Taylor, and the organizations with which he associates, have been regularly described as promoting racist ideologies (Sussman 2014).

In 2017, VDARE.com announced the creation of a print journal featuring the "best" material from its webzine, entitled *VDARE Quarterly*. Donald Trump, the president-elect of the United States at that time, was featured on the cover.

See also: Brimelow, Peter; MacDonald, Kevin; Taylor, Jared; White Nationalism

Further Reading

Brimelow, Peter. July 24, 2006. "Is VDARE.COM 'White Nationalist.'" *VDARE*. http://www
.vdare.com/articles/is-vdarecom-white-nationalist (Accessed January 5, 2017).

Pareene, Alex. February 9, 2012. "CPAC Welcomes White Nationalists." *Salon*. http://
www.salon.com/2012/02/09/cpac_welcomes_white_nationalists/ (Accessed January
5, 2017).

Southern Poverty Law Center. "Peter Brimelow." https://www.splcenter.org/fighting-hate
/extremist-files/group/vdare (Accessed January 5, 2017).

Southern Poverty Law Center. "VDARE." https://www.splcenter.org/fighting-hate/extremist
-files/group/vdare (Accessed January 5, 2017).

Sussman, Robert W. 2014. *The Myth of Race: The Troubling Persistence of an Unscientific Idea*.
Harvard University Press.

VDARE.com. http://www.vdare.com/ (Accessed January 5, 2017).

VIRGINIA TECH SHOOTING

On April 16, 2007, South Korean national Seung-Hui Cho killed 32 people and injured 17 more on the campus of Virginia Polytechnic Institute and State University (Virginia Tech) in Blacksburg, Virginia. Cho used two semiautomatic pistols, and both his history of mental disorders and his access to lethal weaponry once again ignited debates over gun control and whether individuals with mental illnesses should be allowed to purchase weapons. Opposite of the gun control position, gun rights advocates argued that Virginia Tech's "gun-free safe zone policy" ensured that neither students nor faculty could be armed, the result being that Cho was able to inflict more casualties then he might have been able to otherwise. To date, the Virginia Tech shooting remains the deadliest school shooting in U.S. history.

As a child, "Cho was described as shy, frail, and wary of physical contact" (Smith 2007). He was diagnosed in middle school "with severe depression as well as selective mutism, an anxiety disorder" in which the sufferer is inhibited in the ability to initiate speech (Schulte and Craig 2007). Though Cho's mental problems had been recognized at virtually every school level, and "professors at Virginia Tech tried to get Cho to seek counseling, he chose not to" (Cullen 2007). On December 13, 2005, "Cho was ordered by a judge to seek outpatient care after making suicidal remarks to his roommates. He [was] evaluated at a mental health facility and released" (CNN 2017).

In February 2007, Cho picked up "a Walther P-22 pistol he purchased online from an out-of-state dealer at a local pawnshop in Blacksburg." The next month, "he purchased a 9mm Glock pistol and 50 rounds of ammunition" (CNN 2017). Beginning at 7:15 a.m. on the morning of April 16, 2007, Cho began his murderous rampage by killing two students outside of West Ambler Johnston Hall on the Virginia Tech campus. "About two hours after the initial shootings, and after Cho had mailed a package of writings and video recordings to *NBC News*, Cho entered Norris Hall which housed the Engineering Science and Mechanics Program, among others. Cho chained the three main doors of Norris Hall shut and left a note on the door saying that any attempt to open the door would detonate a bomb" (History.com). Cho then went from "room to room shooting people. Approximately 10 minutes after the shootings began, 30 people had been killed and another 17 had been wounded" (History.com). "In all, 27 students and five faculty members died as a result of Cho's actions. Cho, himself, committed suicide before law enforcement officials were able to confront him" (History.com).

Two days after the massacre, *NBC News* received Cho's package "indicating that it had been mailed between the first and second set of killings." Contained in the package "were photos of a gun-wielding Cho, along with a rambling video diatribe in which he ranted about wealthy 'brats,' among other topics" (History.com). A subsequent investigation determined that Cho had not specifically targeted any of his victims but had randomly shot them as he came across them (History.com).

The case immediately reignited the gun control debate in the United States with advocates of gun control arguing for tighter background investigations and limits to the sale of semiautomatic pistols like the type used by Cho. Proponents of gun rights blamed the massacre on Virginia Tech's "no-gun zones," stating that had students or faculty been able to carry weapons on campus, they may have been able to stop Cho before he killed so many (Schontzler 2007).

In the aftermath of the shooting, "the state of Virginia closed legal loopholes that had previously allowed individuals adjudicated as mentally unsound to purchase handguns without detection by the National Instant Criminal Background Check System (NICS)." The shootings "also led to the passage of the only major federal gun control law in the United States since 1994, the year in which the Brady Bill became effective" (History.com). The law, signed by President George W. Bush on January 5, 2008, strengthened the NICS by authorizing "up to $1.3 billion in federal grants so that states could improve their tracking of people who shouldn't be allowed to buy a gun" because they had been declared mentally ill by a court. The law had the support of the National Rifle Association (Cochran 2008).

In August 2007, a review panel, known as the "Massengill Report," after a retired Virginia State Police superintendent, delivered a report to Virginia governor Tim Kaine. The report was critical of Virginia Tech administrators for not having in place a warning system for active shooters that would have reduced the number of casualties. Moreover, the warnings sent to students during the shooting were considered vague and confusing (History.com). In 2014, "Virginia Tech was fined by the U.S. Department of Education for failing to issue a prompt campus-wide warning after the discovery of Cho's first two victims shortly after 7:15 a.m." (CNN 2017). The violation, which cited provisions of the Clery Act, stated that Virginia Tech had neglected to provide timely notification to students and faculty of a campus safety issue (CNN 2017). As a result of this action, colleges and universities strengthened their early warning systems in response to campus-wide emergencies.

See also: Colorado Theater Shooting; Columbine High School Shooting; Orlando Nightclub Shooting; Sandy Hook Elementary School Shooting

Further Reading

AP. April 16, 2017. "Virginia Tech Marks Decades Since Shooting That Killed 32." *CBS News*. http://www.cbsnews.com/news/virginia-tech-shooting-10-year-anniversary/ (Accessed June 6, 2017).

CNN. April 3, 2017. "Virginia Tech Shootings Fast Facts." http://www.cnn.com/2013/10/31 /us/virginia-tech-shootings-fast-facts/ (Accessed June 6, 2017).

Cochran, John. January 12, 2008. "New Gun Control Law Is Killer's Legacy." *ABC News*. http://abcnews.go.com/print?id=4126152 (Accessed June 6, 2017).

Cullen, Dave. April 20, 2007. "Pscychopath? Depressive? Schizophrenic? Was Cho Seung -Hui Like the Columbine Killers?" *Slate*. http://www.slate.com/articles/health_and _science/medical_examiner/2007/04/psychopath_depressive_schizophrenic.html (Accessed June 6, 2017).

History.com. "Massacre at Virginia Tech Leaves 32 Dead." http://www.history.com/this-day -in-history/massacre-at-virginia-tech-leaves-32-dead (Accessed June 6, 2017).

Jervis, Rick. April 14, 2017. "10 Years After Va. Tech Shooting: How Gun Laws Have Changed." *USA Today*. https://www.usatoday.com/story/news/nation/2017/04/14/va -tech-shooting-gun-laws-debate/100458024/ (Accessed June 6, 2017).

Schontzler, Gail. December 5, 2007. "MSU Sticks to Guns on Firearms Policy." *Bozeman Daily Chronicle*. http://www.bozemandailychronicle.com/news/article_efced713-ca66 -5c68-af5f-f8f38868ce56.html (Accessed June 6, 2017).

Schulte, Brigid and Tim Craig. August 27, 2007. "Unknown to Va. Tech, Cho Had a Disor- der." *The Washington Post*. http://www.washingtonpost.com/wp-dyn/content/article /2007/08/26/AR2007082601410_pf.html (Accessed June 6, 2017).

Smith, Vicki. August 30, 2007. "Cho's Problem's Date to Early Childhood." *ABC News*. https://web.archive.org/web/20080422011857/http://abcnews.go.com/US/wireStory? id=3540871 (Accessed June 6, 2017).

W

WACO STANDOFF

The Waco standoff was a siege conducted by the U.S. federal government on the compound of the Branch Davidians near Waco, Texas, between February 28 and April 19, 1993. The group was led by David Koresh, who had established the compound for the Branch Davidians, a sect that had separated from the Seventh-Day Adventists, at Mount Carmel, near Waco. In February 1993, Koresh was accused in a *Waco Tribune-Herald* exposé of being a "sinful messiah" and was allegedly guilty of statutory rape for taking multiple underage brides. Aside from allegations of sexual abuse and misconduct, Koresh was suspected by federal officials of stockpiling weapons and explosives in violation of federal law. Koresh and his followers believed in the end times and felt that the inevitable confrontation between good and evil would necessitate that the Branch Davidians defend themselves. When federal agents attempted to serve warrants on Koresh and his followers on February 28, 1993, a firefight erupted in which six Branch Davidians and four agents of the Bureau of Alcohol, Tobacco, Firearms, and Explosives (ATF) were killed. What followed was a 51-day siege that eventually resulted in federal agents lobbing tear gas into the Branch Davidian compound in an effort to end the standoff. Whether as a result of a fire caused by the tear gas canisters, or a fire deliberately set by the Branch Davidians themselves, the result was a conflagration that consumed the compound, killing 76 individuals, including 20 children (CNN 1997). Coming on the heels of the Ruby Ridge siege just six months before, the Waco standoff galvanized antigovernment sentiment and spurred the creation of patriot and militia groups intent on protecting themselves from federal overreach and intrusion. Oklahoma City bomber Timothy McVeigh stated that his motivation for destroying the Alfred P. Murrah Federal Building was, in part, in retaliation for the actions of the federal government in the Waco standoff (CNN 1997).

The Branch Davidians were formed in 1955 when a schism occurred in the Seventh Day Adventist Church following the death of Victor Houteff. Houteff had founded the Davidians on the belief that a biblically prophesied apocalypse was imminent and that God's people should gather to await the Second Coming of Jesus Christ (Smith 2013). The "gathering" took place on a "hilltop nine miles east of Waco, Texas which the Davidians named Mount Carmel, after a mountain in Israel which is mentioned in the Old Testament in Joshua 19:26" (Smith 2013). After Houteff's death, his widow, Florence Houteff, predicted that Armageddon was imminent, whereupon many Davidians built houses, sold their possessions, and squatted in tents, trucks, and buses (Balleck 2015).

The Branch Davidian compound explodes into flames, ending the standoff of David Koresh and his followers at this site near Waco, Texas, April 19, 1993. Elements of federal law enforcement had laid siege to the Branch Davidian compound for 51 days, following a confrontation in which federal agents, attempting to arrest Koresh on gun charges, had been killed. (Shelly Katz/Getty Images)

When the predicted apocalypse and Second Coming of Christ failed to materialize, control of Mount Carmel reverted to the group known as the "Branch Davidian Seventh-Day Adventist Association" (Branch Davidians). After several power struggles for control of the Branch Davidians, Vernon Howell eventually emerged as the undisputed leader of the group. On August 5, 1989, Howell proclaimed that "God had ordered him to procreate with the women of the Branch Davidians in order to establish a 'House of David'" (Balleck 2015). Howell explained that married couples would be separated and that husbands would be expected to become celibate while he had sexual relations with the wives (Fantz 2011). Howell also claimed "that God had commanded him to build an 'Army for God' to prepare for the end of days and ensure the salvation of his followers" (Balleck 2015). On May 15, 1990, Howell petitioned the Supreme Court of California to legally change his name "for publicity and business purposes" to David Koresh. His petition was granted on August 28, 1990 (Linedecker 1993).

In May 1992, officials of the McClennan County Sheriff's Department called the ATF to notify them of suspicions that the Branch Davidians were stockpiling weapons. The Sheriff's Department had been tipped off by a UPS driver who reported that a package delivered to the Branch Davidian compound had broken open during delivery, revealing firearms, grenade casings, and black powder (Balleck 2015). Additional reports of automatic gunfire at Mount Carmel prompted the ATF to begin surveillance of the property in the fall of 1992. At least one Branch Davidian who had left the Mount Carmel compound claimed that the group was stockpiling parts to convert AR-15s to machine guns, "violating the Hughes Amendment to the Firearm Owners Protection Act of 1986 which outlawed civilian ownership of any machine gun manufactured after the date of the promulgation of the Act" (Balleck 2015).

Using information gathered from informants and other sources, the ATF obtained search and arrest warrants for David Koresh and others based on the allegations that the Branch Davidians were in violation of federal law by converting semiautomatic to automatic weapons. The ATF also claimed that "Koresh was operating a methamphetamine lab" in "order to obtain military assets under legislation which allowed for such actions under the War on Drugs" (Sahagun 1993). The evidence to support this claim, however, was not based on any factual evidence but on information from disgruntled Branch Davidians who had left the compound six years earlier (Balleck 2015).

The search warrant requested by the ATF was authorized, and a search of the Mount Carmel compound was scheduled to occur on or before February 28, 1993, between 6:00 a.m. and 10:00 p.m. The day before the February 28 deadline, the *Waco Tribune-Herald* began publishing "The Sinful Messiah," a "series of articles that alleged that Koresh had physically abused children in the compound" and committed statutory rape on several underage girls by taking them as wives (England and McCormack 1993, Part I). The opening passage of the series began,

> If you are a Branch Davidian, Christ lives on a threadbare piece of land 10 miles east of here called Mount Carmel. He has dimples, claims a ninth-grade education, married his legal wife when she was 14, enjoys a beer now and then, plays a mean guitar, reportedly packs a 9mm Glock and keeps an arsenal of military assault rifles, and willingly admits that he is a sinner without equal. (England and McCormack 1993, Part I)

According to the paper, Koresh "was husband to over 140 wives and was entitled to any female in the group" that he desired. He was also reportedly "the father of at least a dozen children, some of these with mothers who had become Koresh's brides as early as 12- or 13-years-old" (England and McCormack 1993, Part I).

The ATF attempted to execute the search and arrest warrant on the Branch Davidian compound at Mount Carmel on Sunday morning, February 28, 1993. The raid had proceeded despite information that the ATF had received that indicated that the Branch Davidians knew the raid was imminent. Though the success of the raid depended on the Branch Davidians not being armed and engaging the agents as they served the warrants, the raid proceeded with agents hidden in cattle trailers pulled by pickups.

As the agents disembarked, shooting began in the compound. During the first few moments of shooting, David Koresh "was wounded in the wrist" (Balleck 2015). Within a minute, Branch Davidians were calling emergency services pleading for the shooting to stop. As the exchange of gunfire continued, ATF agents put two ladders up against the side of one of the buildings where the arms cache was believed to be located. As the agents crouched by an open window waiting to enter what was believed to be Koresh's room, one agent was struck and killed while another was wounded. Another agent was killed after shooting a shotgun at several Branch Davidians firing at him. Inside the arms room, "ATF agents killed a Branch Davidian gunman and discovered a large cache of weapons. However, coming under heavy fire two ATF agents were wounded and had to retreat" (Balleck 2015). An agent providing covering fire for the retreating agents was "shot by a Branch Davidian and killed instantly. Another agent was killed by gunfire as agents attempted to neutralize a Branch Davidian sniper" who was firing at the ATF teams from on top of a water tower (Balleck 2015). After 45 minutes of gunfire, six Branch Davidians were killed and several were wounded. Four ATF agents had been killed and another 16 wounded. A 1999 Federal Bureau of Investigation (FBI) report on the ATF raid on Mount Carmel later noted,

> The violent tendencies of dangerous cults can be classified into two general categories—defensive violence and offensive violence. Defensive violence is utilized by cults to defend a compound or enclave that was created specifically to eliminate most contact with the dominant culture. The 1993 clash in Waco, Texas at the Branch Davidian complex is an illustration of such defensive violence. History has shown that groups that seek to withdraw from the dominant culture seldom act on their beliefs that the endtime has come unless provoked. (Federal Bureau of Investigation)

After the death of four federal agents, the FBI took overall command at the Mount Carmel site. However, Koresh refused to surrender to authorities. Negotiators were able to secure the release of 19 children, ages five months to 12 years. However, 96 people remained on the compound. As the siege progressed, Koresh often negotiated with the FBI for more time as he stated that he needed to complete several religious documents before he could surrender. Koresh's stalling tactics alienated the federal negotiators who began to believe that the situation was deteriorating into a hostage crisis (Balleck 2015).

Koresh and most of his followers refused to give up. Koresh did order 11 people to leave the compound, though all the children who remained stayed with the rest of the Branch Davidians. FBI negotiators were not prepared for the religious zeal of Koresh and his followers. A number of experts on "apocalypticism in religious groups attempted to persuade the FBI that its siege tactics only reinforced the belief of those inside that the Branch Davidians were part of a Biblical end of times confrontation that had cosmic significance" (Stange 2001). The experts pointed out that while the Branch Davidians' beliefs may have seemed extreme, their behavior was consistent with their beliefs inasmuch as those inside the compound were likely to sacrifice themselves rather than submit (Stange 2001). The FBI voiced concern over this assessment, believing that Koresh might order the collective suicide of those in the compound, similar to the cult suicide committed by Jim Jones and the 900 members of the People's Temple in Jonestown, Guyana, in 1978. Koresh himself professed "that he embodied the Second Coming of Jesus

Christ and that he had been commanded by his father in heaven to remain in the compound" (Balleck 2015).

Because it was known that the Branch Davidians were heavily armed, the FBI's plan was to pump tear gas into the compound's buildings until the occupants were forced out. Loudspeakers were used "to inform the Branch Davidians in the buildings that no armed assault was taking place" but that they needed to surrender (Balleck 2015). The armored vehicles were fired upon as they approached the buildings, whereon the FBI ordered more tear gas to be pumped into the buildings.

On April 19, 1993—51 days after the standoff had begun—"three fires broke out almost simultaneously" in the buildings that composed the Mount Carmel compound (CNN 1997). Fanned by high winds, the fire spread quickly through the wooden structures, and within 45 minutes every building was burned to the ground. Only nine people of the 85 who had been in the compound survived the fire. Among the 76 Branch Davidians who died were 20 children under 18 years old (CNN 1997).

After the fire, the government maintained that they had not taken any action that would have caused the fire. Government officials made the claim that the Branch Davidians had set the fires deliberately (Department of Justice). At least 20 Branch Davidians died from gunshot wounds and not from the effects of the fire. Among these were five children under the age of 14. An "expert retained by the U.S. Office of the Special Counsel concluded that many of the gunshot wounds were mercy killings by the Branch Davidians," who performed them when there was no chance of escape from the fire (Danforth 2000). According to an FBI official, Koresh's top aide "shot and killed Koresh and then committed suicide with the same gun" (Danforth 2000).

Though surviving Branch Davidian members claimed that the activities of the government had started the fire that led to the deaths of Branch Davidians, U.S. attorney general Janet Reno "had specified that no pyrotechnic devices were to be used in the assault" (Klaidman 1999). Between 1993 and 1999, FBI spokespeople continually denied that any pyrotechnic devices had been used at Mount Carmel. Nevertheless, three pyrotechnic grenades were found in the rubble of the fire, which the FBI later admitted had been used to penetrate an outlying structure that was away from the main buildings (Klaidman 1999). However, these grenades were fired three hours before the fire erupted and could not have caused the blaze that engulfed the buildings on the compound. But when FBI documents "were turned over to Congress for an investigation in 1994, the page listing the possible use of any pyrotechnic devices was missing" (Klaidman 1999). Because of inconsistencies in FBI statements and reports, Attorney General Reno directed that an investigation be initiated. The investigation was complicated by the fact that Texas authorities had bulldozed the compound site less than a month after the fire (May 19). Nevertheless, it was finally revealed that "as many as 100 FBI agents had known" that pyrotechnics had been present at Mount Carmel, but none of them came forward until six years after the fire (Klaidman 1999).

By the time of the revelations in 1999, the public had begun to believe that there had been serious misconduct by the federal government at Waco. A *Time* magazine poll conducted on August 26, 1999, found "that 61 percent of the public believed that law enforcement officials had started the fire on the Branch Davidian compound" (Kopel 1999). Because of the lingering questions, Attorney General Janet Reno appointed former U.S. senator John Danforth to investigate the matter. A year-long investigation, in which the Office of the Special Counsel interviewed over 1,000 witnesses and sifted through 2.3 million pages of documents, yielded no conclusive physical evidence that the fire that consumed the Branch Davidian compound had been started by the actions of the government. The Danforth Report, issued on November 8, 2000, thus concluded that all allegations that the government had started the fire at Mount Carmel were meritless. David Koresh's attorney "called the Danforth Report a 'whitewash,' whereas former U.S. Attorney General Ramsey Clark—who had represented several Branch Davidians in their lawsuits against the government—said that the report 'failed to address the obvious'" (Balleck 2015). Clark stated, "History will clearly record, I believe, that these assaults on the Mt. Carmel church center remain the greatest domestic law enforcement tragedy in the history of the United States" (United Press International 2000).

Though the government had been held blameless by the Danforth Report, the reaction within extremist elements of the public was swift. As reported by the Anti-Defamation League,

> More than any other issue, though, the deadly standoffs at Ruby Ridge, Idaho, in 1992 and Waco, Texas, in 1993 ignited widespread passion. To most Americans, these events were tragedies, but to the extreme right, they were examples of a government willing to stop at nothing to stamp out people who refused to conform. Right-wing folk singers like Carl Klang memorialized the children who died at Waco with songs like "Seventeen Little Children." These events provided new life to a number of extremist movements, from Christian Identity activists to sovereign citizens, but they also propelled the creation of an entirely new movement consisting of armed militia groups formed to prevent another Ruby Ridge or Waco.

The fact that "Ruby Ridge and Waco both involved government action in response to what were deemed 'illegal firearms' added fuel to the fire that prompted the formation of the militia groups" (Balleck 2015). Most patriot and militia leaders of this time were radical gun rights advocates who believed that the Second Amendment meant that there was no such thing as an illegal firearm. Ruby Ridge and Waco intensified the fear and suspicion among these groups that the imminent confiscation of all guns by the government was just around the corner. The ranks of militia groups swelled during this time as many in the public felt that such groups were needed to protect their inherent right to keep and bear arms.

As noted by the Anti-Defamation League,

> The combination of anger at the government, fear of gun confiscation and susceptibility to elaborate conspiracy theories is what formed the core of the militia movement's ideology. Although there were white supremacists in the movement, and although groups and individuals within the movement often made common cause with or at least tolerated hate groups, the orientation of the militia movement remained

primarily anti-government and conspiratorial. The militia movement appealed to many radical libertarians just as it appealed to traditional proponents of extreme right-wing causes.

See also: Oklahoma City Bombing

Further Reading

Anti-Defamation League. "The Militia Movement." https://www.adl.org/education/resources/backgrounders/militia-movement (Accessed May 18, 2017).

Balleck, Barry J. 2015. *Allegiance to Liberty: The Changing Face of Patriots, Militias, and Political Violence in America.* Praeger.

CNN. April 8, 1997. "McVeigh Letter Bitterly Blames FBI for Waco Deaths." http://www.cnn.com/US/9704/08/mcveigh/ (Accessed May 18, 2017).

Danforth, John. C. Special Counsel. July 21, 2000. "Final Report to the Deputy Attorney General Concerning the 1993 Confrontation at the Mt. Carmel Complex, Waco Texas." Office of the Special Counsel. http://www.cesnur.org/testi/DanforthRpt.pdf (Accessed May 18, 2017).

Department of Justice. October 8, 1993. "Report to the Deputy Attorney General on the Events at Waco, Texas." https://www.justice.gov/publications/waco/report-deputy-attorney-general-events-waco-texas (Accessed May 18, 2017).

England, Mark and Darlene McCormick. February 27, 1993. "The Sinful Messiah, Part One." *Waco Tribune-Herald.* http://www.wacotrib.com/news/branch_davidians/sinful-messiah---part-feb---page-a/image_3ed4d566-a90a-11e2-b3ed-0019bb2963f4.html (Accessed May 18, 2017).

England, Mark and Darlene McCormick. February 28, 1993. "The Sinful Messiah, Part Two." *Waco Tribune-Herald.* http://www.wacotrib.com/news/branch_davidians/sinful-messiah---part-feb—page-a/image_44071c06-a90a-11e2-9550-0019bb2963f4.html (Accessed May 18, 2017).

Fantz, Ashley. April 14, 2011. "18 Years After Waco, Davidians Believe Koresh Was God." *CNN.* http://www.cnn.com/2011/US/04/14/waco.koresh.believers/ (Accessed May 18, 2017).

Federal Bureau of Investigation. "Project Megiddo." Center for Studies on New Religions. http://www.cesnur.org/testi/FBI_004.htm (Accessed May 18, 2017).

Klaidman, Daniel. September 19, 1999. "A Fire That Won't Die." *Newsweek.* http://www.newsweek.com/fire-wont-die-166178 (Accessed May 18, 2017).

Kopel, David B. September 8, 1999. "Fanning the Flames of Waco." CATO Institute. https://www.cato.org/publications/commentary/fanning-flames-waco (Accessed May 18, 2017).

Linedecker, Clifford L. 1993. *Massacre at Waco: The Shocking True Story of Cult Leader David Koresh and the Branch Davidians.* St. Martin's Paperbacks.

Sahagun, Louis. March 28, 1993. "Signs of Waco Drug Lab Led Guard Joining Raid: Standoff: Federal Agent Says There Were Indications that Koresh and Some Followers Were Making, Selling Methamphetamine as 'Fund-Raising Effort.'" *Los Angeles Times.* http://articles.latimes.com/1993-03-28/news/mn-16272_1_drug-lab (Accessed August 7, 2017).

Smith, J. B. April 13, 2013. "Scholar's Tackle 'Cult' Questions 20 Years After Branch Davidian Tragedy." *Waco Tribune-Herald.* http://www.wacotrib.com/news/religion/scholars-tackle-cult-questions-years-after-branch-davidian-tragedy/article_a3fa463e-d1b4-5eda-b49e-95327bc276d7.html (Accessed May 18, 2017).

Stange, Mary Zeiss. October 3, 2001. "U.S. Ignores Religion's Fringes." *USA Today*. https://usatoday30.usatoday.com/news/opinion/2001-10-04-ncguest2.htm (Accessed May 18, 2017).

United Press International. July 21, 2000. "Koresh's Lawyer Critical of Danforth Report." http://www.upi.com/Archives/2000/07/21/Koreshs-lawyer-critical-of-Danforth-report/7719964152000/ (Accessed May 18, 2017)

WEATHER UNDERGROUND

The Weather Underground was a left-wing revolutionary organization founded in 1969 with the aim of overthrowing the U.S. government (United States Senate 1975). More commonly referred to as the "Weathermen," the group was a far-left-wing organization with sympathies to the Black Power movement of the late 1960s and was distinguished by its violent actions in opposition to the Vietnam War. Members of the group were one-time members of the Students for a Democratic Society (SDS), whose primary intent was to form a clandestine revolutionary organization that would be capable of waging revolutionary war against the U.S. government (United States Senate 1975). The Weathermen grew out of a faction of the SDS, the Revolutionary Youth Movement (RYM), taking its name from a Bob Dylan song whose lyrics included, "You don't need to be a weatherman to know which way the wind blows." This phrase inspired what would become the founding document of the Weathermen. The document was distributed to SDS and RYM members at the SDS convention that was held in Chicago on June 18, 1969—the same city that only a year before had been the scene of the Democratic National Convention that saw four days of intense violence grip the city. The Weathermen "position paper" called for "a 'white fighting force' to be allied with the 'Black Liberation Movement' and other radical movements to achieve 'the destruction of US imperialism and achieve a classless world: world communism'" (Berger 2006).

The unifying force behind the Weathermen was their opposition to U.S. global policies, particularly the U.S. presence in Vietnam. Like other leftist movements of the late 1960s and early 1970s, the Weathermen grew out of the social and political turmoil elicited by the civil rights movement in the United States as well as the U.S. policy of global confrontation with communism. The RYM, which had inspired the formation of the Weathermen, believed that American youth "possessed the wherewithal to create a revolutionary force which would overthrow and destroy capitalism" (Encyclopedia of Anti-Revisionism). As author Ron Briley (2009) noted,

> With a growing protest movement in the United States and the global struggle in which anti-imperialist forces were on the march in Vietnam, Algeria, and Angola, the Weathermen believed they were on the winning side of history—creating new communities free from capitalist exploitation and embracing the Che Guevara prediction that numerous Vietnam-type conflicts would topple the American regime.

The Weathermen strongly identified with the Black Panther Party, and the killing of Black Panther member Fred Hampton in late 1969 galvanized the resolve of the organization, which "issued a 'Declaration of a State of War' against the United States Government in May 1970" (Balleck 2015). In a communique, Weathermen leader Bernardine Dohrn stated in part,

> All over the world, people fighting Amerikan [*sic*] imperialism look to Amerika's [*sic*] youth to use our strategic position behind enemy lines to join forces in the destruction of the empire.
>
> Black people have been fighting almost alone for years. We've known that our job is to lead white kids into armed revolution. We never intended to spend the next five or twenty-five years of our lives in jail. Ever since SDS became revolutionary, we've been trying to show how it is possible to overcome the frustration and impotence that comes from trying to reform this system. Kids know the lines are drawn revolution is touching all of our lives. Tens of thousands have learned that protest and marches don't do it. Revolutionary violence is the only way. (Dohrn 1970)

The Weathermen believed that the primary global struggle taking place in the 1960s and 1970s was the reality of "U.S. imperialism and the various national liberation struggles around the world which were confronting it" (Revolutionary Youth Movement). The Weathermen drew their inspiration from Vladimir Lenin's 1916 work, "Imperialism, the Highest Stage of Capitalism," in which Lenin argues that the forces of capitalism perpetuate generations of "oppressed people"

During what became known as the "Days of Rage" (October 8–11, 1969), members of the Weather Underground protest the Vietnam War in Chicago, Illinois. The Weather Underground was a radical, militant organization founded with the purpose of overthrowing the United States government. (Bettmann/Getty Images)

who are actually the creators of the wealth that capitalism enjoys, as the products bought and sold in the marketplace are the results of their labor. The goal of the revolutionary struggle against capitalism, then, had to be to seize wealth in the name of the oppressed peoples and "achieve a classless world, a world of communism" (Jacobs 1970). The Weathermen strived to make the point that their ideas were both anti-imperialist and antiracist, as they believed in a classless society where all the world's workers would share equally in the wealth that they created (Jacobs 1970).

The Weathermen engaged in their first act of public violence at a rally in Chicago on October 8, 1969. The "Days of Rage" were a series of direct actions from October 8 to 11 staged in opposition to the Vietnam War with "Bring the War Home" as its rallying cry (Wilkerson 2007). Members gathered in Grant Park in Chicago and listened to fiery speeches by SDS leaders about the world revolution and the activities of such revolutionaries as Che Guevara. When the rally spilled into the streets of Chicago, participants "vandalized businesses, smashed car windows and blew up a statue of a policeman known as the Haymarket statue" (Berger 2006). A mere nine months later, the Weathermen would declare war on the United States government, in part for Fred Hampton's shooting death at the hands of Cook County police officers.

Before issuing its Declaration of War against the United States, the Weathermen issued a communiqué in May 1970 in which it taunted the Federal Bureau of Investigation and challenged the organization to find its members. On June 9, 1970, "a bomb composed of ten sticks of dynamite exploded at the New York City Police headquarters. The explosion was preceded by a warning about the bombing as well as the claim of Weathermen responsibility" (Balleck 2015). After the Declaration of War in May 1970, the Weathermen conducted subsequent bombings on March 1, 1971, at the U.S. Capitol Building; on May 19, 1972, at the Pentagon; and on January 29, 1975, at the U.S. Department of State. In each of these cases, a communiqué issued prior to the bombings warned occupants of the buildings to evacuate so that no injuries or deaths occurred, though property damage was extensive (Berger 2006). The Weathermen claimed that all three bombings were in response to an escalation of events in Vietnam and U.S. involvement in these escalations. Of course, by 1975, the United States had largely withdrawn from Vietnam, but according to the Weathermen, its policies were still contributing to the deaths of tens of thousands of Vietnamese.

On February 21, 1970, "three gasoline-filled Molotov cocktails were thrown at the home of New York Supreme Court Justice John M. Mustagh who was presiding over the pretrial hearings of the 'Panther 21'—members of the Black Panther Party who had been accused of plots to bomb New York City landmarks and department stores" (Perlmutter 1970). Though the damage to the justice's home was relatively light, suspicion soon fell upon the Weathermen. Indeed, prior to the attack, an anonymous phone call to the police had reported prowlers in the area, prompting a strong police presence in the neighborhood. Earlier in the evening, "several Molotov cocktails had been thrown at the Columbia University Law Library and at a police car parked at a police station in the West Village in Manhattan." Similar devices were also thrown at the army and navy recruiting booths near Brooklyn College (Columbia Daily Spectator 1970). Bernardine Dohrn, who would within months issue the Weathermen's "Declaration of a State of War" against the United States, was quoted in a fellow Weather Underground member's 2007 memoir as saying that the fire bombings of the evening of February 21, 1970, were carried out by members of the cell that was decimated by the Greenwich Village townhouse explosion two weeks later, an incident in which three Weathermen were accidentally killed while constructing bombs (Dohrn 1974).

As the Vietnam War drew to a close for the United States, members of the Weathermen sought to more closely align their philosophies with Marxist-Leninist ideology. Bill Ayers, Bernardine Dohrn, Jeff Jones, and Celia Sojourn collaborated on a manifesto entitled *Prairie Fire: The Politics of Revolutionary Anti-Imperialism* (Dohrn et al. 1974). The name of the manifesto came from a quote by Mao Tse Tung, which stated that "a single spark can set a prairie fire." Among other things, "the manifesto urged the violent overthrow of the U.S. government and the establishment of a dictatorship of the proletariat—a Marxist term meant to denote control of political power by the proletariat, or working classes" (Balleck 2015). *Prairie Fire* was meant to outline the Weathermen's new way forward in light of the end of the Vietnam War and the spirit of détente that was then taking place between the United States and the Soviet Union. In light of these new realities,

> The only path to the final defeat of imperialism and the building of socialism is revolutionary war. . . . Socialism is the violent overthrow of the bourgeoisie, the establishment of the dictatorship of the proletariat, and the eradication of the social system based on profit. . . . Revolutionary war will be complicated and protracted. . . . It includes mass struggle and clandestine struggle, peaceful and violent, political and economic, cultural and military, where all forms are developed in harmony with the armed struggle. Without mass struggle there can be no revolution. Without armed struggle there can be no victory. (Asbley et al. 1969)

As the Weathermen struggled to find a new identity, they were accused by some groups of having abandoned their original ideologies in favor of a less racially inclusive message (Varon 2004). Several members of the organization turned themselves in under the terms of President Jimmy Carter's amnesty for Vietnam War draft dodgers, while others left their revolutionary rhetoric behind and tried to lead normal lives (Jacobs 1970). Bill Ayers and Bernardine Dohrn would turn themselves in in December 1980. Charges against Ayers were dropped, while Dohrn received three years' probation and was fined $15,000 (Jacobs 1970).

During its time and afterward, the Weathermen would be referred to as a terrorist organization (Ayers 2006). Yet Bill Ayers, undoubtedly the most recognized of the former members of the Weathermen because of his connections to President Barack Obama, wrote a book entitled *Fugitive Days* in which he stated that "terrorists terrorize, they kill innocent civilians, while we organized and agitated. Terrorists destroy randomly, while our actions bore, we hoped, the precise stamp of a cut diamond. Terrorists intimidate, while we aimed only to educate. No, we're not terrorists" (Ayers 2009). Ayers (2008) would later say,

> We did carry out symbolic acts of extreme vandalism directed at monuments to war and racism, and the attacks on property, never on people, were meant to respect human life and convey outrage and determination to end the Vietnam war. . . . The responsibility for the risks we posed to others in some of our most extreme actions in those underground years never leaves my thoughts for long. The antiwar movement in all its commitment, all its sacrifice and determination, could not stop the violence unleashed against Vietnam. And therein lies cause for real regret.

Other Weathermen have expressed similar ambivalence toward their violent actions. Brian Flanagan, for instance, has stated, "When you feel that you have right on your side, you can do some pretty horrific things" (The Guardian 2003). Mark Rudd has echoed similar sentiments of "mixed feelings" and "feelings of guilt and shame":

> These are things I am not proud of, and I find it hard to speak publicly about them and to tease out what was right from what was wrong. I think that part of the Weatherman phenomenon that was right was our understanding of what the position of the United States is in the world. It was this knowledge that we just couldn't handle; it was too big. We didn't know what to do. In a way I still don't know what to do with this knowledge. I don't know what needs to be done now, and it's still eating away at me just as it did 30 years ago. (Rudd 2009)

See also: Black Panther Party; Students for a Democratic Society

Further Reading

Asbley, Karin, Bill Ayers, Bernardine Dohrn, John Jacobs, Jeff Jones, Gerry Long, Home Machtinger, Jime Mellen, Terry Robbins, Mark Rudd, and Steve Tappis. June 18, 1969. "You Don't Need a Weatherman to Know Which Way the Wind Blows." *New Left Notes.* https://archive.org/stream/YouDontNeedAWeathermanToKnowWhichWayTheWind Blows_925/weather_djvu.txt (Accessed March 20, 2017).

Ayers, Bill. April 20, 2006. "Weather Underground Redux." *Bill Ayers Blog.* https://billayers .org/2006/04/20/weather-underground-redux/ (Accessed March 20, 2017).

Ayers, Bill. 2009. *Fugitive Days: Memoirs of an Antiwar Activist.* Beacon Press, p. 263.

Ayers, William. December 5, 2008. "The Real Bill Ayers." *The New York Times.* http://www .nytimes.com/2008/12/06/opinion/06ayers.html?_r=0 (Accessed March 20, 2017).

Balleck, Barry J. 2015. *Allegiance to Liberty: The Changing Face of Patriots, Militias, and Political Violence in America.* Praeger Press.

Berger, Dan. 2006. *Outlaws of America: The Weather Underground and the Politics of Solidarity.* AK Press.

Briley, Ron. July 20, 2009. "Bringing the War Home: The Weather Underground at Forty." *History News Network.* http://historynewsnetwork.org/article/93754 (Accessed March 20, 2017).

Columbia Daily Spectator. February 24, 1970. "Police Investigate Law Firebombing." http://spectatorarchive.library.columbia.edu/cgi-bin/columbia?a=d&d=cs19700224 -01.2.3&e=-------en-20--1--txt-txIN------ (Accessed March 20, 2017).

Dohrn, Bernardine. May 21, 1970. "Weathermen—First Communique: A Declaration of War." *The Berkeley Tribe* (July 31, 1970). http://www.lib.berkeley.edu/MRC/pacificaviet /scheertranscript.html (Accessed March 20, 2017).

Dohrn, Bernardine. 2006. "New Morning—Changing Weather." In Bill Ayers, Bernardine Dohrn, and Jeff Jones, editors. Sing a Battle Song: The Revolutionary Poetry, State- ments, and Communiqués of the Weather Underground, 1970–1974. Seven Stories Press, p. 163.

Dohrn, Bernardine, Jeff Jones, Celia Sojourn, and Bill Ayers. 1974. *Prairie Fire: The Politics of Revolutionary Anti-Imperialism*. Communications Co.

Encyclopedia of Anti-Revisionism. 1968. "Toward a Revolutionary Youth Movement." In "Debate Within SDS. RYM II vs. Weatherman." *Encyclopedia of Anti-Revisionism On-Line*. https://www.marxists.org/history/erol/ncm-1/debate-sds/rym.htm (Accessed March 20, 2017).

The Guardian. September 20, 2003. "The Americans Who Declared War on Their Country." https://www.theguardian.com/film/2003/sep/21/londonfilmfestival2003.londonfilm festival (Accessed March 20, 2017).

Jacobs, Harold. 1970. *Weathermen*. Ramparts.

Jacobs, Ron. 1997. *The Way the Wind Blew: A History of the Weather Underground*. Verso Press.

Kushner, Havey W. 2003. *Encyclopedia of Terrorism*. SAGE Publications.

Perlmutter, Emanuel. February 22, 1970. "Justice Murtagh's Home Target of 3 Fire Bombs." *The New York Times*. http://www.nytimes.com/1970/02/22/archives/justice -murtaghs-home-target-of-3-fire-bombs-judges-home-target-of.html?_r=0 (Accessed March 20, 2017).

Revolutionary Youth Movement. June 18, 1969. "You Don't Need to Be a Weatherman to Know Which Way the Wind Blows." https://archive.org/details/YouDontNeedAWeath ermanToKnowWhichWayTheWind Blows_925 (Accessed March 20, 2017).

Rudd, Mark. 2009. *Truth and Consequences: The Education of Mark Rudd*. Grove Press.

United States Senate. 1975. Committee on the Judiciary. "State Department Bombing by Weatherman Underground." U.S. Government Printing Office. https://archive.org /details/statedepartmentb00unit (Accessed March 20, 2017).

Varon, Jeremy. 2004. *Bringing the War Home: The Weather Underground, The Red Army Fac- tion and Revolutionary Violence in the Sixties and Seventies*. University of California Press, pp. 296–297.

Wilkerson, C. 2007. *Flying Close to the Sun: My Life and Times as a Weatherman*. Seven Stor- ies Press.

WEAVER, RANDY

Randy Weaver (b. 1948) is an antigovernment extremist whose arrest for the ille- gal modification of weapons in violation of federal gun laws prompted an 11-day standoff between federal agents and Weaver at his Ruby Ridge compound near Naples, Idaho, in August 1992. During the siege, one U.S. marshal was killed, after he had killed Weaver's 14-year-old son, and Weaver's wife was struck down by an FBI agent's sniper bullet as she stood in a doorway holding her 10-month- old baby. The incident, together with the action of the U.S. government against the Branch Davidian compound in Waco, Texas, several months later, galvanized antigovernment sentiment and prompted the formation of dozens of "patriot" and militia groups. Weaver and his family were later awarded $3.1 million in a wrongful death suit, though the U.S. government admitted no wrongdoing in the matter (Labaton 1995).

Weaver and his wife developed fundamentalist beliefs in the 1980s and wanted to move their family away from the "corrupted world." Weaver also believed that the Apocalypse was imminent (Walter 2002). As Weaver became more removed from the world, he began to associate with other extremists, particularly members of Aryan Nations. The neo-Nazi and anti-Semitic Aryan Nations was one of the most powerful and prominent hate groups in the United States in the 1980s and 1990s. Weaver began attending Aryan Nations meetings and found there kindred spirits who also expressed hatred of certain groups and shared their suspicions of the U.S. government.

Because of Aryan Nations' antigovernment sentiments, the Federal Bureau of Investigation (FBI) infiltrated it to monitor its activities. It was under these circumstances that an undercover FBI agent, posing as an illegal arms dealer, approached Randy Weaver and asked him to provide modified weapons that could be resold. Reportedly, Weaver modified two shotguns, in violation of federal law, after which he was arrested by a member of the Bureau of Alcohol, Tobacco, Firearms, and Explosives (ATF). After he failed to appear at a scheduled court hearing, a warrant for Weaver's arrest was issued. Weaver's failure to appear was actually prompted by a mix-up between the courts and Weaver's lawyer. Nevertheless, once the warrant was issued, Weaver was convinced of a conspiracy against him and his family and that he could not receive a fair trial in the courts of the federal government. As noted by one author, his "distrust grew when he was erroneously told by his magistrate that if he lost the trial he would lose the land that would essentially leave Vicki homeless and the government would take away his children" (Walter 2002).

With the failure-to-appear indictment, Weaver's case passed from the ATF to the United States Marshal's Service (USMS), the law enforcement arm of the federal court. Weaver had not fled the jurisdiction, however. He was simply holed up in his house on his land at Ruby Ridge, "threatening to resist any attempt to take him by force" (Balleck 2015). The USMS "made several attempts to have Weaver peacefully surrender, but he refused to leave his cabin or his property" (Balleck 2015).

On August 21, 1992, six U.S. marshals "were sent to Ruby Ridge to scout the area to determine a suitable place removed from Weaver's cabin where he could be apprehended and arrested" (Balleck 2015). At one point, one of the marshals threw rocks at the Weaver cabin to determine the reaction of the dogs that the Weavers maintained to alert them to intruders. As the dogs reacted, Weaver's friend, Kevin Harris, and Weaver's 14-year-old son Samuel ("Sammy") emerged from the cabin to investigate. Later, a confrontation between the marshals and Weaver and Harris left Deputy U.S. Marshal (DUSM) Bill Degan and Samuel Weaver dead. After the firefight, Harris, who had killed DUSM Degan, retreated to the Weaver cabin.

After the firefight, "the USMS was alerted by the FBI that a federal marshal had been killed. The FBI then mobilized the Hostage Rescue Team (HRT) from

Quantico, Virginia to Idaho" (Balleck 2015). The HRT commander at the scene briefed snipers who been deployed around the Weaver property. The rules of engagement (ROE) reportedly gave snipers the "green light" to "shoot on sight" (Department of Justice 1994). The ROE was drawn up on reports from the USMS and the FBI and was fueled by unconfirmed media reports that were accepted by the federal officers on the scene. The reports, most agree, exaggerated the threat posed by the Weavers (Balleck 2015).

Guided by the ROE, on August 22, 1992, the day after the deaths of Sammy Weaver and USMS Bill Degan, an FBI sniper, Lon Horiuchi, shot and wounded Randy Weaver from a position of more than 200 yards as Weaver "lifted the latch on a shed to visit the body of his dead son" (Balleck 2015). Agent Horiuchi then fired a second shot, which struck and killed Vicki Weaver, who was standing in the door through which those fleeing the shooting were attempting to enter the house. At the time of the shooting, Vicki Weaver "was holding her 10-month-old baby Elisheba in her arms" (Balleck 2015). A Department of Justice (DOJ) report (Office of Professional Responsibility Ruby Ridge Task Force Report) would state in 1994 that the second shot fired by Horiuchi, which killed Vicki Weaver, "did not satisfy constitutional standards for legal use of deadly force" (Department of Justice 1994). The DOJ report also found "that the lack of a request for surrender in the case of the shooting on August 22 was 'inexcusable' given that Harris and the Weavers were running for cover at the time of the second shot and that they did not pose an imminent threat as they were not returning fire" (Department of Justice 1994). On August 26, 1992, the Ruby Ridge rules of engagement were revoked.

The siege at Ruby Ridge was ultimately resolved when negotiators, including Bo Gritz, were told by federal authorities that if Weaver did not surrender the situation would be resolved through tactical assault (Walter 2002). Gritz, a decorated United States Army Special Forces officer, was sympathetic to Weaver. With Gritz's intervention, Randy Weaver and his daughters surrendered on August 31, 1992. Both "Kevin Harris and Weaver were arrested and his daughters were released to the custody of family members though there was some thought at the time of charging Weaver's oldest daughter—16-year-old Sara—as an adult" (Neiwert 1999).

At his trial, Weaver's defense attorney, Gerry Spence, would not call a single witness on behalf of the defense. Instead, he used as his defense strategy the "cross-examination and discrediting of government witnesses and the evidence which the government had presented" (Balleck 2015). Ultimately, Weaver was acquitted of all charges except failure to appear and violation of probation. He was "sentenced to 18 months and fined $10,000. Credited with time served, Randy Weaver served an additional four months in jail" (Balleck 2015). The defense of both Randy Weaver and Kevin Harris was that federal agents had themselves been guilty of serious wrongdoing in the siege that they perpetrated upon Weaver and his family and friends on Ruby Ridge. On June 10, 1994, the Department of Justice Ruby Ridge Task Force delivered a 542-page report to the DOJ Office of Professional Responsibility. Though the report was never officially released, a redacted version was later circulated.

In the aftermath of the siege at Ruby Ridge, a 1995 Senate subcommittee reported that the rules of engagement utilized at Ruby Ridge were unconstitutional (Judiciary Committee 1995). The "surviving members of the Weaver family filed a $200 million wrongful death lawsuit against the federal government. In an out-of-court settlement in 1995, the U.S. government awarded Randy Weaver $100,000 and his three daughters $1 million each, while never admitting any wrongdoing in the deaths of Weaver's son and wife" (Labaton 1995). On the condition of anonymity, "a DOJ official admitted in a *Washington Post* article that he believed that the Weavers would have been awarded the full amount of the lawsuit had it gone to trial" (Lowery 2015). FBI director Louis Freeh would admit before a U.S. Senate hearing investigation that the siege was "synonymous with the exaggerated application of federal law enforcement" and stated "law enforcement overreacted at Ruby Ridge" (Balleck 2015).

Randy Weaver and his daughters would eventually relocate to Montana. Weaver and his daughter Sara would write a book entitled *The Federal Siege at Ruby Ridge: In Our Own Words* (Weaver and Weaver 1998). The siege at Ruby Ridge was, for patriot and militia devotees, the epitome of "government gone wild." From the patriot/militia point of view, Randy Weaver and his family were falsely accused, harassed, and eventually targeted for death by a federal government that was accountable to no higher authority. The siege on Weaver's private property was for antigovernment extremists a prime example of a government that completely disregarded constitutional guarantees of freedom, liberty, and due process. In addition, the manner in which the siege was conducted (e.g., the Ruby Ridge rules of engagement) were testimony to a government apparatus that had degenerated into a lawless collection of agencies that answered to no authority and certainly not to the people. Although three individuals died in the case of Ruby Ridge, not one person spent even one day in jail as a result. The assault on liberties that Ruby Ridge represented to patriot/militia adherents was just one of the "last straws" that broke the proverbial camel's back, reinvigorating existing groups and creating new ones throughout the United States (Balleck 2015).

See also: Aryan Nations; Ruby Ridge

Further Reading

Balleck, Barry J. 2015. *Allegiance to Liberty: The Changing Face of Patriots, Militias, and Political Violence in America.* Praeger.

Department of Justice. June 10, 1994. "D.O.J. Office of Professional Responsibility Ruby Ridge Task Force Report." https://www.justice.gov/sites/default/files/opr/legacy/2006/11/09/rubyreportcover_39.pdf (Accessed May 18, 2017).

Judiciary Committee. September 6–October 19, 1995. "The Federal Raid on Ruby Ridge: Hearings Before the Subcommittee on Terrorism, Technology, and Government Information of the Committee on the Judiciary." United States Senate. http://www.famous-trials.com/rubyridge/1147-federalraid (Accessed May 18, 2017).

Labaton, Stephen. August 16, 1995. "Separatist Family Given $3.1 Million from Government." *The New York Times.* http://www.nytimes.com/1995/08/16/us/separatist-family-given-3.1-million-from-government.html (Accessed May 18, 2017).

Lowery, Wesley. November 4, 2015. "How Law Enforcement Officers Can Kill Someone and Avoid Prosecution." *The Washington Post*. https://www.washingtonpost.com/national /how-federal-agents-can-kill-someone-and-avoid-prosecution/2015/11/04/b25e927c -7f0b-11e5-b575-d8dcfedb4ea1_story.html?utm_term=.9303f0e29875 (Accessed May 18, 2017).

Neiwert, David A. 1999. *In God's Country: The Patriot Movement in the Pacific Northwest*. Washington State University Press.

Walter, Jess. 2002. *Ruby Ridge: The Truth and Tragedy of the Randy Weaver Family*. Harper Perennial.

Weaver, Randy and Sara Weaver. 1998. *The Federal Siege at Ruby Ridge*. Ruby Ridge, Inc.

WEBER, MARK

Mark Weber (b. 1952) directs the Institute for Historical Review (IHR), a group that promotes "revisionist" history in the form of Holocaust denial. Weber became involved in far-right causes when he joined William Pierce's neo-Nazi organization, the National Alliance, in 1978. During the 1980s, Weber became involved in the work of the IHR, and in 1992, he became the editor of the IHR's now-defunct *Journal of Historical Review*. In 1995, Weber wrested control of IHR from its founder, Willis Carto, and he has remained as the organization's director and leading spokesperson since then.

Weber attended Portland State University, where he received a BA degree in history. He later graduated with an MA in modern European history from Indiana University. In 1979, Weber served "as the editor of the *National Vanguard*, the premier publication of the National Alliance, which would later become the most influential neo-Nazi organization in the United States" (Southern Poverty Law Center, Weber). It was during this time that Weber "became interested in issues surrounding the Holocaust through his associations with the Committee for Open Debate on the Holocaust" (Gerstenfeld and Grant 2003). Weber was also writing articles for *The Spotlight*, "an anti-Semitic tabloid started by IHR founder Willis Carto" (Southern Poverty Law Center, Weber). Carto and the leader of the National Alliance, William Pierce, had been bitter enemies since 1970, when they both attempted to reconfigure the Youth for Wallace group, which was dedicated to the policies and plans of then Alabama governor George Wallace, into the National Youth Alliance. Pierce won and officially renamed the group the National Alliance. By 1984, Weber was editing Pierce's *National Vanguard* but also organizing annual conferences for Carto's Institute for Historical Review. In 1985, Weber joined the IHR's editorial board.

In 1992, Weber took over the editorial duties of the IHR's publication, *Journal of Historical Review*. At the time, the journal was the premier publication venue for the works of Holocaust denial, those who deny the genocide of the Jews and other groups by the Nazis during World War II. As started under Carter, the *Journal of Historical Review* attempted to gloss over its anti-Semitism by claiming that the articles found in the publication did not foster Holocaust denial but rather Holocaust "revisionism." As stated by several authors who published in the journal, history is something that is constantly revised through different decades, and attempts to reinterpret the Holocaust through a more modern lens simply follow from this path of inquiry.

In 1993, Weber, "with the support of the IHR board, ousted Carto as its leader, accusing him of interfering in editorial decisions" (Southern Poverty Law Center, Weber). Carto was later accused by Weber and the IHR board "of diverting some $10 million in funds that was left to IHR's parent company, the Legion for the Survival of Freedom, to his personal accounts" (Southern Poverty Law Center, Weber). In 1996, a California court handed down a $6.4 million judgment against Carto (Granberry 1996).

Weber and the IHR's fight with Carto took a toll. The publication of the *Journal of Historical Review* was interrupted for over a year, and by 2003, it ceased publication altogether. IHR was also unable to hold any annual conferences between 1994 and 2000, and after the conferences continued in 2000, they were much smaller events held over fewer days with fewer speakers.

In January 2009, Weber "shocked the world of Holocaust denial" by publishing an article entitled "How Relevant Is Holocaust Revisionism?" (Southern Poverty Law Center, Holocaust Denial). Weber's conclusion was "not very," which angered his former supporters, but his question did not signal a move toward the center. In fact, Weber "encouraged those on the radical right to struggle against the real enemy, Jewish-Zionist power" (Southern Poverty Law Center, Holocaust Denial). According to the Southern Poverty Law Center, "Weber had replaced his old suit-and-tie denialist friends with hard-core anti-Semites, including open neo-Nazis and heavily tattooed racist skinheads." Weber's ultimate conclusion was that the decades-long "Holocaust revision" effort had been "as much a hindrance as a help" (Beirich 2009).

Today, Weber continues to serve as the IHR's director and leading spokesperson.

See also: Carto, Willis; Holocaust Denial; Institute for Historical Review; National Alliance; Neo-Nazis; Pierce, William; White Supremacist Movement

Further Reading

Beirich, Heidi. November 30, 2009. "Holocaust Denial Movement Rocked by Infighting." *Southern Poverty Law Center—Intelligence Report.* https://www.splcenter.org /fighting-hate/intelligence-report/2009/holocaust-denial-movement-rocked-infighting (Accessed April 29, 2017).

Gerstenfeld, Phyllis B. and Diana R. Grant, editors. 2003. *Crimes of Hate: Selected Readings.* SAGE.

Granberry, Michael. November 16, 1996. "Judge Awards 6.4 Million to O.C. Revisionist Group." *Los Angeles Times.* http://articles.latimes.com/1996-11-16/local/me-65105_1 _judge-awards (Accessed April 29, 2017).

Institute for Historical Review. "Mark Weber: A Biographical Profile." http://www.ihr.org /other/weber_bio.html (Accessed April 29, 2017).

Southern Poverty Law Center. "Holocaust Denial." https://www.splcenter.org/fighting-hate /extremist-files/ideology/holocaust-denial (Accessed April 29, 2017).

Southern Poverty Law Center. "Mark Weber." https://www.splcenter.org/fighting-hate /extremist-files/individual/mark-weber (Accessed April 29, 2017).

WHITE ARYAN RESISTANCE

White Aryan Resistance (WAR) is a neo-Nazi and white supremacist organization founded by Tom Metzger, a former grand dragon of the Ku Klux Klan. WAR does not veil its racist propensities "but openly preaches racial discrimination and solidarity among the white, Anglo-Saxon segment of the American population, especially among white blue-collar workers" (Encyclopedia.com). WAR believes that the survival of the white race is under threat in the United States, and it promotes an anticapitalistic, antigovernment stance. WAR claims to fight against the Zionist Occupation Government, a worldwide conspiracy of Jews that purportedly controls countries around the world, including the United States. In its heyday, WAR openly courted racist skinheads and attracted such individuals to the organization through the use of hate rock festivals known as Aryan Fest. In 1988, three WAR skinhead members beat an Ethiopian graduate student to death in Portland, Oregon. A civil rights suit against Tom Metzger, WAR, and the three skinheads was brought by the Southern Poverty Law Center. A jury found Metzger "liable for intentionally inciting the skinheads to engage in violent confrontations with minorities and returned a $12.5 million judgment against Metzger and WAR" (Southern Poverty Law Center). The judgment bankrupted Metzger and WAR, though WAR continues to have an online presence, advocating for "the benefits of racial separation, [while] highlighting the dangers of multiculturalism and promoting racial identity and a territorial imperative" (White Aryan Resistance).

During the 1970s, Metzger was a member of David Duke's organization, the Knights of the Ku Klux Klan (KKKK). He rose to grand dragon of the KKKK in California but left the group to form his own organization. In the early 1980s, Metzger courted racist skinhead groups in California and formed the White Aryan Resistance. He also hosted *Race and Reason*, "a public-accessed cable television show, that aired WAR propaganda and featured neo-Nazis as guests" (Turner 1986). The show generated great controversy due to the topics that Metzger and his guests discussed, such as Holocaust denial, forced racial segregation, and antigovernment activism (Turner 1986).

In 1988, Metzger established the WAR hotline and encouraged people to call in and vent their frustrations. The recorded message on the hotline stated,

> You have reached WAR Hotline. White Aryan Resistance. You ask: What is WAR? We are an openly white-racist movement—Skinheads, we welcome you into our ranks. The federal government is the number one enemy of our race. When was the last time you heard a politician speaking out in favor of white people? . . . You say the government is too big; we can't organize. Well, by God, the SS did it in Germany, and if they did it in Germany in the thirties, we can do it right here in the streets of America. . . . We need to cleanse this nation of all nonwhite mud-races for the survival of our own people and the generations of our children. (Atkins 2011)

On November 13, 1988, three racist skinheads associated with WAR "beat to death Mulugeta Seraw, an Ethiopian man who had moved to the United States to attend graduate school. In October 1990, the Southern Poverty Law Center (SPLC) won a $12.5 million judgment against Metzger, WAR, and the skinheads" (Southern Poverty Law Center). Neither WAR nor Metzger had the assets to satisfy the judgment, so Seraw's family only received about $150,000 (AP 1990). Metzger declared bankruptcy, but WAR continued to operate (Southern Poverty Law Center) and today operates a Web site that continues to promote white nationalist, white supremacist, and neo-Nazi ideals (White Aryan Resistance). Metzger encourages white supremacists "to adopt a 'lone wolf' or 'leaderless resistance' strategy . . . that is, that they engage in criminal actions only individually or in small cells to avoid detection by law enforcement" (Southern Poverty Law Center).

Metzger continues to proclaim that WAR "serves the idea that what's good for the White European Race is the highest virtue. Whatever is bad for the White European Race is the ultimate Evil" (Southern Poverty Law Center).

See also: Duke, David; Holocaust Denial; Ku Klux Klan; Metzger, Tom; Neo-Nazis; Racist Skinheads; Southern Poverty Law Center; White Nationalism; White Supremacist Movement

Further Reading

Anti-Defamation League. "White Aryan Resistance." https://www.adl.org/education/references/hate-symbols/white-aryan-resistance (Accessed May 20, 2017).

AP. December 25, 1990. "Assets of White Supremacist Are Target of Legal Maneuver." *The New York Times.* http://www.nytimes.com/1990/12/25/us/assets-of-white-supremacist-are-target-of-legal-maneuver.html (Accessed May 20, 2017).

Atkins, Stephen E. 2011. *Encyclopedia of Right-Wing Extremism in Modern American History.* ABC-CLIO.

Encyclopedia.com. "White Aryan Resistance (WAR)." http://www.encyclopedia.com/politics/legal-and-political-magazines/white-aryan-resistance-war (Accessed May 20, 2017).

Southern Poverty Law Center. "Tom Metzger." https://www.splcenter.org/fighting-hate/extremist-files/individual/tom-metzger (Accessed May 20, 2017).

Turner, Wallace. October 7, 1986. "Extremist Finds Cable TV Is Forum for Right-Wing Views." *The New York Times.* http://www.nytimes.com/1986/10/07/us/extremist-finds-cable-tv-is-forum-for-right-wing-views.html (Accessed May 20, 2017).

White Aryan Resistance. "About." http://www.resist.com/About/index.html (Accessed May 20, 2017).

WHITE LIVES MATTER

White Lives Matter (WLM) is a racist movement formed in response to the Black Lives Matter (BLM) movement that came into being in 2014 "after George Zimmerman was acquitted in the shooting death of Trayvon Martin in Florida" (Mettler 2016). The Black Lives Matter movement surfaced "as a trending social media hashtag, and then grew into a nationwide political movement" as more and more incidents of police officers killing black people were picked up by the national media (Mettler 2016). WLM was meant to counter BLM's focus and emphasize that "all lives matter," putting across the point that blacks weren't the only victims of out-of-control law enforcement agencies. Republican presidential candidate and New Jersey governor Chris Christie stated that BLM was a movement that advocated "the murder of police officers" (Viets 2016). WLM "describes itself as dedicated to promotion of the white race and taking positive action as a united voice against issues facing our race." The group's Web site declares,

> The fiber and integrity our nation was founded on is being unraveled . . . [by] homosexuality and [racially] mix[ed] relationships. Illegal immigration, healthcare, housing, welfare, employment, education, social security, our children, our veterans and active military and their rights . . . are the issues we face as white Americans. The laws and immoral orders the current [Obama] administration are passing are drastically . . . targeting everything the white way of life holds dear. (White Lives Matter)

Since its founding in 2015, WLM appears to be populated by white supremacists and neo-Nazi adherents (Southern Poverty Law Center). Rebecca Barnette claims to be one of WLM's founders and has dedicated herself to spreading its message. Barnette has been involved in "several neo-Nazi groups and holds the post of the director of the Women's Division of the National Socialist Movement, the largest neo-Nazi organization in the United States" (Viets 2016). Barnette sounds the warning "that Jews and Muslims have formed an alliance to commit genocide of epic proportions" of the white race (Viets 2016). "Now is the time," Barnette has stated, for "the blood of our enemies [to] soak our soil to form new mortar to rebuild our landmasses" (Viets 2016). In reference to the Black Lives Matter movement, Barnette has stated that there is "a small army ready to blow their little party out of the water . . . in the proper way . . . the white way" (Viets 2016). In February 2016, a car containing six members of the Ku Klux Klan (KKK) with "White Lives Matter" signs arrived at a park in Anaheim, California, to protest "illegal immigration and Muslims. A confrontation with counter-protestors ensued and the KKK members stabbed three people, one critically" (Viets 2016). Five Klan members were arrested, though they were later released after claiming that the stabbings occurred in self-defense.

Several racist groups have joined the WLM movement, most likely in response to WLM fliers that have been posted in public places from Utah to Connecticut. Reading "It's Not Racist to Love Your People," the fliers urge supporters to find "like-minded people" and organize to confront issues affecting white communities, such as crime, illegal immigration, and health care (Southern Poverty Law Center).

The murder of eight Dallas and Baton Rouge police officers during the summer of 2016 prompted WLM members and conservative commentators to enjoin the Southern Poverty Law Center (SPLC), the civil rights organization that tracks hate groups in the United States, to designate the "Black Lives Matter movement a hate group" (Mettler 2016). In both the Dallas and Baton Rouge cases, police officers were killed by black men expressing sympathies for the Black Lives Matter movement. The killing of the Dallas police officers took place during a Black Lives Matter march.

Though the SPLC lists several black organizations, such as the New Black Panther Party, as hate groups, it has declined to affix this label to the Black Lives Matter movement. Richard Cohen, president of SPLC, has stated that "hate groups are, by our definition, those that vilify entire groups of people based on immutable characteristics such as race or ethnicity. Federal law takes a similar approach" (Cohen 2016) and notes,

> There's no doubt that some protesters who claim the mantle of Black Lives Matter have said offensive things, like the chant "pigs in a blanket, fry 'em like bacon" that was heard at one rally. But before we condemn the entire movement for the words of a few, we should ask ourselves whether we would also condemn the entire Republican Party for the racist words of its presumptive nominee—or for the racist rhetoric of many other politicians in the party over the course of years.
>
> Many of its harshest critics claim that Black Lives Matter's very name is anti-white, hence the oft-repeated rejoinder "all lives matter." This notion misses the point entirely. Black lives matter because they have been marginalized throughout our country's history and because white lives have always mattered more in our society. As BLM puts it, the movement stands for "the simple proposition that 'black lives also matter.'" (Cohen 2016)

Noting the rise of Donald Trump's intonation to "Make America Great Again," and that most of Trump's most ardent followers tend to be whites who feel themselves threatened in the changing social and political landscape of the United States, Cohen (2016) pointed out,

> The backlash to BLM, in some ways, reflects a broad sense of unease among white people who worry about the cultural changes in the country and feel they are falling behind in a country that is rapidly growing more diverse in a globalizing world. We consistently see this phenomenon in surveys showing that large numbers of white people believe racial discrimination against them is as pervasive, or more so, than it is against African Americans.

The WLM has stated that the movement is

> really about recognizing the contributions that people of European descent have made to civilization, and that we as a people and culture are worth preserving. We reject the notion that it is morally wrong for people of European descent to love and support their own race. We value Western civilization and believe that at the very least, immigrants should not make us dumber or poorer. (Mettler 2016)

After the Dallas murders, when law enforcement attempted to push forward a "Blue Lives Matter" movement, Kevin Harris, "one of WLM's co-founders, seemed less supportive, posting a photo of himself in front of a police car with his middle finger extended" (Southern Poverty Law Center). Rebecca Barnette echoed this sentiment, stating that "while White Lives Matter supports law and order and feels the terroristic attacks on law enforcement officers is a tragedy, we are not proponents for blue lives matter" (Southern Poverty Law Center).

See also: Neo-Nazis; New Black Panther Party; White Nationalism; White Supremacist Movement

402 **WHITE NATIONALISM**

Further Reading

Black Lives Matter. http://blacklivesmatter.com/ (Accessed May 13, 2017).

Cohen, Richard. July 19, 2016. "Black Lives Matter Is Not a Hate Group." *Southern Poverty Law Center—News*. https://www.splcenter.org/news/2016/07/19/black-lives-matter-not-hate-group (Accessed May 13, 2017).

Mettler, Katie. August 31, 2016. "Why SPLC Says White Lives Matter Is a Hate Group but Black Lives Matter Is Not." *The Washington Post*. https://www.washingtonpost.com/news/morning-mix/wp/2016/08/31/splc-the-much-cited-designator-of-hate-groups-explains-why-white-lives-matter-is-one/?utm_term=.e17453f98ed9 (Accessed May 13, 2017).

Southern Poverty Law Center. "White Lives Matter." https://www.splcenter.org/fighting-hate/extremist-files/group/white-lives-matter (Accessed May 13, 2017).

Viets, Sarah. August 3, 2016. "White Lives Matter." *Southern Poverty Law Center—Intelligence Report*. https://www.splcenter.org/fighting-hate/intelligence-report/2016/white-lives-matter (Accessed May 13, 2017).

White Lives Matter. http://www.whitelivesmatter.com/ (Accessed May 13, 2017).

WHITE NATIONALISM

White nationalism is a belief system that holds that the white race is distinct from other races, and, as such, should maintain a separate and distinct identity from other racial groups. The primary goal of white nationalism is to promote methods and means to ensure the survival of the white race and protect the cultural, political, and economic systems of historical white states. Most adherents of white nationalism abhor what they see as the devolution of American society as found in "miscegenation (mixed-race relations), multiculturalism, immigration of non-whites, and low birth rates among white populations are threatening the white race" (Federal Bureau of Investigation). Some argue that these factors are contributing to a systematic extermination of a purely white race (Federal Bureau of Investigation). In the United States, the overt expression of white nationalism first manifested itself in the presence and activities of the Ku Klux Klan (KKK) in the aftermath of the U.S. Civil War. Starting in the 1950s, white nationalism grew out of a conservative reaction to liberal politics and policies and became the organizing principle of many right-wing extremist groups in the post–World War II era. Harvard political scientist Samuel Huntington (2005) "argues that white nationalism developed as a reaction to a perceived decline in the essence of American identity as European, Anglo-Protestant and English-speaking." White nationalism may include tenets related to white supremacy and white separatism, though these are sometimes thought of as distinct and separate phenomenon (Anti-Defamation League; Taub 2016). Since World War II, several extremist groups in the United States have arisen that embrace the ideals of white nationalism, including Posse Comitatus, Aryan Nations, the National Alliance, The Order, and neo-Nazis. More recently, the alt-right movement, "a broad term covering many different far-right ideologies and groups in the United States, some of which endorse white nationalism, has gained traction as an alternative to mainstream conservatism in its national politics" (Welton 2015).

Following the defeat of the Confederate states in the U.S. Civil War, the KKK was founded by former Confederates as an insurgent group to maintain white supremacy in states that were subject to federal Reconstruction policies. Over time, the KKK has gone through several incarnations, but all the while the group has emphasized white nationalism and American nativism in the face of changing social conditions.

Starting in the 1950s, a new social and cultural milieu was being created in the United States that emphasized the inclusion of groups that had traditionally been left out of the power structure (e.g., blacks). The civil rights movement emphasized the displacement of social, cultural, economic, and political structures that had been in place for decades, most of which had greatly benefitted the white majority in all parts of the country. A new conservatism arose at the time in reaction to the perceived threat of communism, but the rising power of blacks in American society spawned the formation of groups that opposed the rapid changes taking place in society.

In the 1960s, Posse Comitatus was formed as an antigovernment organization that preached a message that white Christians were losing their social and political rights in the face of changing conditions in the United States. Though the 1960s and early 1970s tended to be dominated by extremist groups from the radical left, by the end of the 1970s worsening economic conditions gave rise to extremist right-wing groups that viewed government actions in support of greater social inclusion, support for minority groups, and support for heretofore cultural taboos (e.g., gay rights) as justification for antigovernment attitudes and actions.

In 1974, William Pierce founded the National Alliance, a white nationalist, anti-Semitic, and white supremacist political organization. In 1977, Richard Butler founded Aryan Nations as the political arm of his Church of Jesus Christ Christian. An adherent of Christian Identity, Butler taught his followers that the white race was God's chosen people and that Jews were the result of a sexual union between Eve and Satan. Both Butler's and Pierce's teachings would spawn spinoff groups even more virulent and disposed to hate than their parent organizations. The Order, for instance, preached that Aryans (whites) were the purest race. David Lane, a member of The Order, enunciated the slogan known as the "14 Words," which became the creed of the white supremacist and white nationalist cause: "We must secure the existence of our people and a future for white children" (Palmer 2008).

The farm crisis of the 1980s convinced many in the American heartland that the U.S. federal government no longer cared for white people as one family farm after another fell to worsening economic conditions and government indifference (Balleck 2015). Membership in groups that preached antigovernment extremism swelled during this time and exploded after the federal government killed antigovernment activists at Ruby Ridge in Idaho in 1992 and Waco in 1993. The formation of the present-day patriot and militia movements can trace their beginnings to this period, and though their numbers have waxed and waned over the years, they continue to be potent voices in the cause of white nationalism.

With the election of Barack Obama—the first African American president in U.S. history—in 2008, white nationalism was provided with "renewed clarity and focus" (Smithers 2016). Coupled with renewed antiblack, anti-immigrant, anti-Semitic, and the emerging anti-Islamic sentiments among white nationalists, Barack Obama's election in 2008, and his reelection in 2012, ignited a "counter-revolution" among whites that fanned the "flames of bigotry and intolerance" and reinvigorated old hate groups and gave rise to new ones (e.g., the alt-right). As noted by one commentator,

> This disparate collection of bigots, racists, and conspiracy theorists have found common cause in opposing Obama's presidency and leveling racist barbs at First Lady Michelle Obama—referred to by one West Virginia official as an "ape in heels."
>
> Racial prejudice is not a relic of American history; it's alive and thriving in twenty-first century America. Amid the smokescreens of anti-government, anti-tax, and pro-gun rights America, the racial animus that fuels the current white nationalist counterrevolution gains strength from the white supremacist traditions of the past as it is re-encoded in American political culture in new and subtle ways. (Smithers 2016)

Today, white nationalism "is the belief that national identity should be built around white ethnicity, and that white people should therefore maintain both a demographic majority and dominance of the nation's culture and public life" (Taub 2016). Like white supremacy, "white nationalism emphasizes placing the interests of whites over those of any other racial group or minority. White supremacists and white nationalists both believe that racial discrimination should be incorporated into law and policy" (Taub 2016). But while there may seem to be little difference between white nationalism and white supremacism, some believe that the terms are not synonymous. Eric Kaufmann, a professor of politics at Birkbeck University in London, says that "white supremacy is based on a racist belief that white people are innately superior to people of other races; white nationalism is about maintaining political and economic dominance, not just a numerical majority or cultural hegemony" (Taub 2016).

Thus, "for a long time white nationalism was less about an ideology as it was the presumptive belief about American life" (Taub 2016). Americans saw in their nation—in its laws, institutions, political system, culture, and social structures—"an extension of their own ethnic group. But the country's changing demographics, the civil rights movement and a push for multiculturalism in many quarters mean that white Americans are now confronting the prospect of a nation that is no longer built solely around their own identity" (Taub 2016).

Richard Spencer, founder of the alt-right movement, states that adherents to alt-right principles believe in protecting "the heritage, identity, and future of people of European descent in the United States, and around the world" (Taub 2016).

White nationalism can be epitomized in the remarks of a middle-aged white man from the U.S. state of Georgia who in 2016 proclaimed, "I believe our nation is ruined and has been for several decades and the election of Obama [was] merely the culmination of the change" (Smithers 2016). As noted by one commentator,

This sense of loss is galling to Americans who share this gentleman's perspective. What makes this sense of loss all the more difficult to stomach is the belief that a generation of intellectual and political elites have force-fed "political correctness" to unwilling citizens. Such Americans have had enough. Indeed, Obama's presidency did not usher in an era of post-racialism as millions hoped; it provided the hateful platform from which Donald Trump could rise to the presidency. (Smithers 2016)

See also: Alt-Right Movement; Aryan Nations; Butler, Richard; Christian Identity; Fourteen Words; Ku Klux Klan; Lane, David; Militia Movement; National Alliance; Neo-Nazis; Order, The; Patriot Movement; Pierce, William; Posse Comitatus; Ruby Ridge; Spencer, Richard Bertrand; Waco Standoff; White Supremacist Movement

Further Reading

Anti-Defamation League. "White Nationalism." https://www.adl.org/education/resources/glossary-terms/white-nationalism (Accessed May 20, 2017).

Balleck, Barry J. 2015. *Allegiance to Liberty: The Changing Face of Patriots, Militias, and Political Violence in America.* Praeger.

Federal Bureau of Investigation. "FOIA: FBI Monograph State of Domestic White Nationalist Extremist Movement in the U.S." https://archive.org/stream/foia_FBI_Monograph-State_of_Domestic_White_Nationalist_Extremist_Movement_in_the_U.S./FBI_Monograph-State_of_Domestic_White_Nationalist_Extremist_Movement_in_the_U.S._djvu.txt (Accessed May 20, 2017).

Huntington, Samuel P. 2005. *Who Are We?: The Challenges to America's National Identity.* Simon & Schuster.

Palmer, Brian. October 29, 2008. "White Supremacists by the Numbers." *Slate.* http://www.slate.com/articles/news_and_politics/explainer/2008/10/white_supremacists_by_the_numbers.html (Accessed May 20, 2017).

Smithers, Gregory D. December 23, 2016. "A White Nationalist Counterrevolution?" *Counter Punch.* http://www.counterpunch.org/2016/12/23/a-white-nationalist-counterrevolution/ (Accessed May 20, 2017).

Southern Poverty Law Center. "White Nationalist." https://www.splcenter.org/fighting-hate/extremist-files/ideology/white-nationalist (Accessed May 20, 2017).

Sterling, Joe. November 17, 2016. "White Nationalism, a Term Once on the Fringes, Now Front and Center." *CNN.* http://www.cnn.com/2016/11/16/politics/what-is-white-nationalism-trnd/ (Accessed May 20, 2017).

Taub, Amanda. November 21, 2016. "'White Nationalism' Explained." *The New York Times.* https://www.nytimes.com/2016/11/22/world/americas/white-nationalism-explained.html (Accessed May 20, 2017).

Welton, Benjamin. December 15, 2015. "What, Exactly, Is the 'Alternative Right?'" *Weekly Standard.* http://www.weeklystandard.com/what-exactly-is-the-alternative-right/article/2000310 (Accessed May 20, 2017).

WHITE PATRIOT PARTY

The White Patriot Party (WPP) "was a paramilitary, Christian Identity faction of the Ku Klux Klan founded by former Green Beret Frazier Glenn Miller in 1980" (Terrorist Research and Analysis Consortium). At its height, the group boasted some

3,000 members. Many believe that hard economic times in the 1980s attracted followers to the group, whose message blamed Jewish bankers and an alleged worldwide Jewish conspiracy for the poor economic conditions of white Americans. Frazier Glenn Miller, the group's founder, stated that the goal of WPP was "Southern independence—an all-white nation within the one million square miles of mother Dixie" (Terrorism Knowledge Base). Miller's focus on a white homeland in the South was based on his view of the rest of the country and its dominance by Jewish and other interests. As Miller stated, "We have no hope for Jew York City or San Fran-sissy-co and other areas that are dominated by Jews, perverts, and communists and non-white minorities and rectum-loving queers" (Ridgeway 1995).

During the height of its activities, the WPP was a paramilitary organization that stockpiled guns and ammunition, conducted paramilitary activities, and marched and demonstrated against what it considered the "mongrelization" of the white race in the United States. During the early to mid-1980s, it was one of dozens of militia groups that formed around the country in protest of the activities of the U.S. federal government. Like other groups of its ilk (e.g., white supremacist, white separatist, neo-Nazi, anti-Semitic), WPP believed in conspiracy theories of different kinds. Preeminent among these, however, was the notion of the Zionist Occupation Government (ZOG). For many in the militia movements of the 1980s, the worldwide Jewish conspiracy to control the world manifested itself in ZOG, a shadowy group of Jews who controlled economic systems, media outlets, popular culture, and even governments. Miller and the WPP believed that ZOG had taken control of the U.S. government. In 1987, while out on bond after being convicted of criminal contempt for his activities with WPP, "Miller disappeared and went underground" (Southern Poverty Law Center). From hiding, he issued a declaration of war and exhorted "Aryan warriors of The Order" to kill its enemies. In the declaration, Miller established a "point system" for each target that he encouraged his followers to attack: "N****** (1), White race traitors (10), Jews (10), Judges (50), Morris Seligman Dees (888)" (Southern Poverty Law Center). Morris Dees, founder of the Southern Poverty Law Center (SPLC), had brought suit against the WPP and forced Miller to publicly disband and disassociate himself from the WPP. The SPLC had found evidence that Miller and his confederates had planned to assassinate Dees, "after which a federal judge issued an injunction forbidding Miller and the WPP from engaging in any paramilitary activity" (Terrorism Knowledge Base).

When authorities caught up with Miller, they found him with "hand grenades, automatic weapons, thousands of rounds of ammunition, C-4 explosives, and $14,000 in cash" (Southern Poverty Law Center). The cash, it was later learned, had been given to Miller by Bob Mathews, the infamous leader of The Order, who had purloined the money from a series of robberies that The Order had perpetrated in order to fund white supremacist causes. When Miller cut a plea deal to lessen his sentence and testified against other white supremacists, his reputation within the community was effectively destroyed, and the WPP quietly faded away.

See also: Mathews, Bob; Militia Movement; Miller, Frazier Glenn; Neo-Nazis; Order, The; White Supremacist Movement

Further Reading

Ridgeway, James. 1995. *Blood in the Face: The Ku Klux Klan, Aryan Nations, Nazi Skinheads and the Rise of a New White Culture.* Thunder's Mouth Press.

Southern Poverty Law Center. "Frazier Glenn Miller." https://www.splcenter.org/fighting-hate/extremist-files/individual/frazier-glenn-miller (Accessed January 16, 2017).

Terrorism Knowledge Base. "White Patriot Party." http://web.archive.org/web/20070930013115/http://www.tkb.org/Group.jsp?groupID=127 (Accessed January 16, 2017).

Terrorist Research and Analysis Consortium. "White Patriot Party." https://www.trackingterrorism.org/group/white-patriot-party-wpp (Accessed January 16, 2017).

WHITE SUPREMACIST MOVEMENT

White supremacy has been the default reality in the United States since its founding. The millions of black African slaves kept by white slave owners made white supremacy both a de facto ("in fact") and de jure ("in law") reality, as evidenced by the social, cultural, economic, and political institutions that were created to perpetuate white dominance. White supremacy is at its core a racist ideology that "promotes the belief that the white race is superior to other races" in the basic characteristics, traits, and attributes that distinguish one race from another (Anti-Defamation League, White Hate in their Hearts). White supremacists believe that white people should dominate every society politically, economically, socially, and culturally inasmuch as the white race is the most morally evolved, socially just, and politically enlightened of all races. During the 1800s, Europeans spoke of the "white man's burden" as they colonized societies less "civilized" than themselves. In the United States, Americans believed in "Manifest Destiny," the idea that the superior attributes of white society must be spread from east to west and north to south in the Western Hemisphere. Thus, "white supremacists of any sort exhibit at least one of the following beliefs":

1. Whites should be dominant over people of other backgrounds.
2. Whites should live by themselves in a whites-only society.
3. White people have their own "culture" that is superior to other cultures.
4. White people are genetically superior to other people (Anti-Defamation League, White Hate in their Hearts).

"Anti-Semitism is also important for the majority of white supremacists, most of whom actually believe that Jews constitute a race of their own—a race with parasitic and evil roots" (Anti-Defamation League, White Hate in Their Hearts). The "white supremacist movement in the United States today is punctuated by a variety of extremist hate groups," but, as noted by the Anti-Defamation League, White Hate in Their Hearts, "most white supremacists do not belong to organized hate groups, but rather participate in the white supremacist movement as unaffiliated individuals. Thus the size of the white supremacist movement is considerably greater than just the members of hate groups." Because of the perception among right-wing individuals that American society is being threatened by a variety of forces beyond their control, the white supremacist movement is probably more active today than it has ever been in the past.

White supremacy in the United States is not confined to any one geographic region. Though many people believe that the American South, with its connections to the legacies of the Civil War, has a monopoly on white supremacist groups and individuals, white supremacists

> come from America's heartland—small towns, rural cities, swelling suburban sprawl outside larger Sunbelt cities. These aren't the prosperous towns, but the single-story working-class exurbs that stretch for what feels like forever in the corridor between Long Beach and San Diego (not the San Fernando Valley), or along the southern tier of Pennsylvania, or spread all through the Upper Peninsula of Michigan, across the vast high plains of eastern Washington and Oregon, through Idaho and Montana. There are plenty in the declining cities of the Rust Belt, in Dearborn and Flint, Buffalo and Milwaukee, in the bars that remain in the shadows of the hulking deserted factories that once were America's manufacturing centers. (Kimmel 2013)

Though a white supremacist may be somewhat indistinguishable from a white nationalist, this was not always the case. White supremacism was institutionalized by the Founding Fathers who, by and large, believed that the white race was unambiguously superior. The abolitionist movement of the 19th century galvanized white supremacist thought, which was reinforced by laws that perpetuated the dominance of the white majority. As blacks gained more political rights in the aftermath of the Civil War, white supremacist groups such as the Ku Klux Klan (KKK) attempted to prevent the rise of an equal class of political contenders. White supremacy was reinforced as different groups entered the United States, particularly those who did not come from predominantly white countries. Over time, however, white supremacism "evolved to reflect the new social and political realities that were found in the country" (Anti-Defamation League, White Hate in Their Hearts). Many white supremacists today have changed their rhetoric and tactics and moved away from a fight "to maintain white dominance to a fight to prevent white extinction" (Anti-Defamation League, White Hate in Their Hearts). This belief began to emerge in the 1970s and 1980s as white supremacists noted that miscegenation, immigration from nonwhite countries, and lower birth rates among whites threatened the majority status that whites had always enjoyed. This sentiment was captured in what became known as the "14 Words," enunciated by white supremacist and neo-Nazi David Lane: "We must secure the existence of our people and a future for white children" (Anti-Defamation League, White Hate in Their Hearts).

In the United States, though the white supremacist movement is characterized by hate groups that are well known on the American political landscape (e.g., Posse Comitatus, National Alliance, Aryan Nations, KKK, racist skinheads, neo-Nazis), the influence of these groups has been replaced by new, more virulent groups spewing hatred toward immigrants, Muslims, LGBT people, and conservative politicians ("cuckservatives") who have "sold out" and embraced key premises of the left and secretly sympathize with liberal values (Potok 2017). Among domestic extremist movements, "white supremacists are the most violent of all groups, committing about 83 percent of the extremist-related murders in the United States over the past 10 years and being involved in about 52 percent of the shootouts between extremists and police" (Anti-Defamation League, White Hate in Their Hearts). White supremacists also have a high degree of involvement in traditional forms of crime. Thus, a great deal of gang activity is associated with white supremacism, and the prisons are now one of the fastest-growing venues for the formulation and dissemination of white supremacist thought (Anti-Defamation League, White Hate in Their Hearts).

White supremacists in the United States tend to be Christian, but not just any Christian. White supremacists tend to be evangelical Protestants, Pentecostals, "and members of radical sects that preach the word of Christ from a perspective of racial purity" (Rikyrah 2013). Christian Identity, which was the founding belief of the white supremacist and anti-Semite group Aryan Nations, provided a theological justification for the superiority of whites over other racial groups, particularly Jews. It is from Christian Identity that white supremacists get the theological claim that

> Adam is the ancestor of the Caucasian race, whereas non-whites are pre-Adamic "mud people," without souls, and Jews are the children of Satan. According to this doctrine, Jesus was not Jewish and not from the Middle East; actually, he was northern European, his Second Coming is close at hand, and followers can hasten the apocalypse. It is the birthright of Anglo-Saxons to establish God's kingdom on earth; America's and Britain's "birthright is to be the wealthiest, most powerful nations on earth . . . able, by divine right, to dominate and colonize the world." (Kimmel 2013)

When President George H. W. Bush pronounced the arrival of the New World Order in 1991, he ignited among white supremacists a belief that a shadowy conspiracy was afoot to enslave the American people and destroy their freedoms. The unbridled actions of the federal government at Ruby Ridge, Idaho, and Waco, Texas, kick-started both the patriot and militia movements that rose in reaction to a post–Cold War environment in which the "enemy" was no longer a political ideology, such as communism, or its embodiment in the Soviet Union. Rather, for patriots and militia groups, the U.S. government became the enemy. Aside from its trampling of rights, the government was the catalyst for seismic cultural and social changes on the American landscape, from unchecked illegal immigration to tolerance for radical Muslims, to promotion of LGBT rights and gay marriage.

One of the most prominent purveyors of white supremacist thought today is the alt-right movement. The founder of alt-right, Richard Spencer, ran online journals that acted as forums for racists, anti-Semites, and others (Anti-Defamation League, Alt-Right, Alt-Right). White identity is at the core of the alt-right movement, and many "alt-righters" want the preservation of white identity—the cultural and genetic heritage that makes whites the dominant race. The alt-right movement wants to preserve what they claim are traditional Christian values, but from a uniquely white supremacist perspective (Anti-Defamation League, Alt-Right).

Alt-righters see threats to traditional American values in issues such as LGBT rights and gay marriage and view multiculturalism (evinced by unchecked immigration) and pluralism of any kind as diluting the dominance of whites in the political realm. After Donald Trump's surprise victory in the 2016 U.S. presidential election, Richard Spencer stood before the annual conference of the National Policy Institute and shouted, "Hail Trump, hail our people, hail victory!" (Lambroso and Appelbaum 2016). The gesture, a Nazi salute reminiscent of the kind offered to Adolf Hitler, was in exaltation of Trump's victory, which Spencer and others saw as a boon for the cause of whites in the United States. As Spencer stated, "America was until this past generation a white country designed for ourselves and our posterity. It is our creation, it is our inheritance, and it belongs to us" (Lambroso and Appelbaum 2016).

Though there is some debate as to whether white supremacism is waning or waxing in the United States (Shivani 2017; Kimmel 2013), there is no doubt that white supremacy movements and attitudes will continue inasmuch as "white supremacy as a type of group power is how individual white people in American society can still passively benefit from white racism and the psychological, material and political advantages it brings to their group" (DeVega 2014).

See also: Alt-Right Movement; Christian Identity; Fourteen Words; Ku Klux Klan; Lane, David; Militia Movement; National Alliance; National Policy Institute; Order, The; Patriot Movement; Posse Comitatus; Racist Skinheads; Ruby Ridge; Waco Standoff; White Nationalism

Further Reading

Anti-Defamation League. "Alt-Right: A Primer About the New White Supremacy." https://www.adl.org/education/resources/backgrounders/alt-right-a-primer-about-the-new-white-supremacy (Accessed May 20, 2017).

Anti-Defamation League. "White Hate in Their Hearts: The State of White Supremacy in the United States." https://www.adl.org/education/resources/reports/state-of-white-supremacy#white-supremacist-ideology (Accessed May 20, 2017).

DeVega, Chauncey. April 23, 2014. "10 Things Everyone Should Know About White Supremacy."*Alternet.* http://www.alternet.org/civil-liberties/10-things-everyone-should-know-about-white-supremacy (Accessed May 20, 2017).

Kimmel, Michael. November 17, 2013. "America's Angriest White Men: UP Close with Racism, Rage, and Southern Supremacy." *3ChicsPolitico.* Salon. https://www.salon.com/2013/11/17/americas_angriest_white_men_up_close_with_racism_rage_and_southern_supremacy/ (Accessed August 7, 2017).

Lambroso, Daniel and Yoni Appelbaum. November 21, 2016. "'Hail Trump!': White Nationalists Salute the President-Elect." *The Atlantic.* http://www.theatlantic.com/politics/archive/2016/11/richard-spencer-speech-npi/508379/ (Accessed May 19, 2017).

Potok, Mark. February 15, 2017. "The Year in Hate and Extremism." *Southern Poverty Law Center—Intelligence Report.* https://www.splcenter.org/fighting-hate/intelligence-report/2017/year-hate-and-extremism (Accessed May 20, 2017).

Shivani, Anis. April 23, 2017. "What Is 'White Supremacy?' A Brief History of a Term, and a Movement, That Continues to Haunt America." *Salon.* http://www.salon.com /2017/04/23/what-is-white-supremacy-a-brief-history-of-a-term-and-a-movement -that-continues-to-haunt-america/ (Accessed May 20, 2017).

WICKSTROM, JAMES

James Wickstrom (b. 1942) is a white supremacist and anti-Semite who spouts the ideology of Christian Ideology, which teaches "that Jews are the literal descendants of a union between Eve," the supposed mother of humankind, and Satan, or the devil (Southern Poverty Law Center). In the 1970s and 1980s, as farmers lost their livelihoods to foreclosures and auctions, Wickstrom became the national director of counterinsurgency for Posse Comitatus, the far-right, antigovernment movement that is virulently anti-Semitic and claims to speak on behalf of white Christians who have been marginalized in the contemporary United States (Southern Poverty Law Center). Wickstrom organized dispossessed farmers, conducted military training, spread conspiracy theories, and called for "Jews, non-whites and other enemies to be hanged from telephone poles" (Southern Poverty Law Center).

In 1982, Wickstrom illegally established a municipality known as the Constitutional Township of Tigerton Dells in Shawano County, Wisconsin. The township was meant to be a haven for antigovernment sentiment and a refuge against the increasing overreach of federal laws and regulations. In 1984, Wickstrom was convicted "of impersonating a public official in relation to the establishment of Tigerton Dells" (Southern Poverty Law Center). Having no legal authority, Wickstrom had established himself in the township as clerk, judge, and presiding officer. His actions were consistent with the ideology of Posse Comitatus, which holds that there is no higher authority above the county sheriff. Moreover, Wickstrom maintained that it was his right to establish the township as a "sovereign citizen," an individual who does not recognize the authority of the federal government to impose restrictions upon individual freedoms.

After serving 13 months in jail in the Tigerton Dells case, Wickstrom was later convicted on counterfeiting and weapons charges (Southern Poverty Law Center). After his release from prison a second time, he would find a renewed audience for his rantings at neo-Nazi gatherings. In the late 1990s, "Wickstrom became one of many individuals on the radical right" who predicted that Y2K would bring about the downfall of the United States as a race war would result from the ensuing economic, social, and political upheaval (Southern Poverty Law Center).

Today, Wickstrom's status within the white supremacist community is not what it was two decades ago, but he maintains his visibility by "preaching" white supremacy on his weekly Internet radio program called *Yahweh's Truth*.

See also: Christian Identity; Posse Comitatus; Sovereign Citizens Movement

Further Reading

Buchanan, Susy. December 21, 2004. "Return of the Pastor." *Southern Poverty Law Center—Intelligence Report*. https://www.splcenter.org/fighting-hate/intelligence-report/2004/james-wickstrom-faces-attacks-continues-preach-christian-identity-doctrine?page=0%2C2 (Accessed December 13, 2016).

Smith, Brent L. 1994. *Terrorism in America: Pipe Bombs and Pipe Dreams*. SUNY Press.

Southern Poverty Law Center. "James Wickstrom." *Extremist Files*. https://www.splcenter.org/fighting-hate/extremist-files/individual/james-wickstrom (Accessed December 13, 2016).

Y

YERUSHALMI, DAVID

David Yerushalmi (b. 1957) is one of the leading antisharia voices in the United States. Yerushalmi has been characterized by *The New York Times* as a "Hasidic Jew with a history of controversial statements about race, immigration and Islam" (Elliott 2011). Yerushalmi is senior counsel and cofounder of the American Freedom Law Center (AFLC), a self-described organization that touts itself as the "first truly authentic Judeo-Christian, public interest law firm" that seeks to "advance and defend [the United States'] Judeo-Christian heritage in courts" (Council on American-Islamic Relations). Yerushalmi is also a lawyer at the Center for Security Policy in Washington, D.C., an organization that focuses on claims that Muslims in the United States are engaging in a vast conspiracy to overthrow the U.S. government from within. Yerushalmi has been a major influence in shaping antisharia legislation in several U.S. states, "including Louisiana, Tennessee, Arizona, Kansas, South Dakota, North Carolina, and Oklahoma" (Sacirbey 2013). Yerushalmi has stated that, "the Mythical 'moderate' Muslim . . . the Muslim who embraces traditional Islam but wants a peaceful coexistence with the West, is effectively nonexistent" (Kedar and Yerushalmi 2011).

Yerushalmi founded the Society of Americans for National Existence in 2006. The virulently anti-Muslim organization promoted the idea that sharia, or Islamic religious law, was inherently violent and dedicated to overthrowing the U.S. government. According to Yerushalmi, sharia should be criminalized insomuch that any Muslim who espouses it should be deported. Yerushalmi holds the view that "only a Muslim who fully breaks with the customs of Shariah can be considered socially tolerable" (Southern Poverty Law Center).

Yerushalmi became involved with the anti-Islamic Center for Security Policy in 2007, and he has regularly defended anti-Muslim extremists, such as Pamela Geller. Yerushalmi engages in what he has called "lawfar"—"a multiplatform attack on Muslims' freedom, staged by pushing his model anti-Shariah bill in state legislatures and filing aggressive lawsuits against supposed enemies of free expression and America's 'Judeo-Christian' heritage" (Southern Poverty Law Center). Yerushalmi believes "that Shariah is inextricably linked with a global jihadist conspiracy that is intent on subjugating the West" (Kedar and Yerushalmi 2011).

Yerushalmi does not reserve his vitriol for only Muslims, however. As an Orthodox Jew, "he takes issue with liberal Jews and the 'progressive elites' that they influence." He has called blacks "the most murderous of peoples" and has called for "undocumented immigrants to be placed in 'special criminal camps,' where they would be detained for three years, and then deported" (Southern Poverty Law Center).

In 2012, Yerushalmi, together with Robert Muise, formed the American Freedom Law Center to advance and defend the United States' Judeo-Christian heritage. Within weeks of its founding, "the AFLC filed an amicus curiae brief in defense of S.B. 1070, Arizona's 'draconian' anti-immigration law" (Southern Poverty Law Center). Yerushalmi and the AFLC have been instrumental in helping to shape and pass antisharia laws in at least seven states (Sacirbey 2013). Legal experts have stated that the AFLC's activities are largely superfluous "because there is no mechanism by which any foreign criminal or civil code can trump U.S. laws" (Southern Poverty Law Center).

Yerushalmi has stated that the U.S. war on terror should ostensibly "be a war on Islam and all faithful Muslims." He has also proposed "outlawing Islam entirely in the United States and deporting Muslims and other non-Western, non-Christian people to protect the national character of the United States" (Southern Poverty Law Center).

In 2011, the Center for American Progress (CAP), a progressive Washington-based think tank, published a report entitled, "Fear, Inc.: The Roots of the Islamophobia Network in America." Yerushalmi and his activities figured prominently in the report (Center for American Progress). In 2015, the CAP updated the report by publishing "Fear, Inc. 2.0," which discussed several key elements of the "anti-Muslim fringe" by examining the narratives pushed by these groups, such as

> (1) the civilization jihad narrative and theories of Muslim Brotherhood infiltration of the U.S. government; (2) the Islamophobia network's influence among the religious right and faith groups combating anti-Muslim sentiment; (3) the impact of the Islamophobia network on law-enforcement training; (4) the response to the Boston Marathon bombing and the narrative of Islamic extremism; and, (5) the phenomenon of politically motivated Islamophobia and the pushback by mainstream conservatives. (Duss et al. 2015)

See also: Center for Security Policy; Gaffney, Frank, Jr.; Geller, Pamela

Further Reading

American Freedom Law Center. http://www.americanfreedomlawcenter.org/ (Accessed April 3, 2017).

Center for American Progress. 2011. "Fear Inc.: The Roots of the Islamophobia Network in America." *Islamophobianetwork*. https://islamophobianetwork.com/ (Accessed April 3, 2017).

Council on American-Islamic Relations. March 16, 2017. "American Freedom Law Center." http://www.islamophobia.org/islamophobic-orgs/american-freedom-law-center.html (Accessed April 3, 2017).

Duss, Matthew, Yasmine Taeb, Ken Gude, and Ken Sofer. February 11, 2015. "Fear, Inc. 2.0: The Islamophobia Network's Efforts to Manufacture Hate in America." Center for American Progress. https://www.americanprogress.org/issues/religion/reports/2015/02/11/106394/fear-inc-2-0/ (Accessed April 3, 2017).

Elliott, Andrea. July 30, 2011. "The Man Behind the Anti-Shariah Movement." *The New York Times*. http://www.nytimes.com/2011/07/31/us/31shariah.html (Accessed April 3, 2017).

Kedar, Mordechai and David Yerushalmi. Summer 2011. "Shari'a and Violence in American Mosques." *The Middle East Quarterly* 18: 597–592. http://www.meforum.org/2931/american-mosques (Accessed April 3, 2017).

Sacirbey, Omar. May 17, 2013. "Anti-Shariah Movement Gains Success." *Huffington Post.* http://www.huffingtonpost.com/2013/05/17/anti-shariah-movement-gains-success_n_3290110.html (Accessed April 3, 2017).

Southern Poverty Law Center. "David Yerushalmi." https://www.splcenter.org/fighting-hate/extremist-files/individual/david-yerushalmi (Accessed April 3, 2017).

YIANNOPOULOS, MILO

Milo Yiannopoulos (b. 1984), born Milo Hanrahan, is a British media personality associated with the alt-right movement and a former senior editor at the far-right-wing *Breitbart News*. Yiannopoulos has been criticized for his views on feminism and social justice and his anti-Islamic stances (Hankes 2017). Yiannopoulos "is openly gay, yet has stated that gay rights are detrimental to humanity, and that gay men should get back in the closet" (Milo 2015). Yiannopoulos has described his homosexuality as "aberrant" and a "lifestyle choice" that brings pain and unhappiness (Yiannopoulos 2011). In July 2016, Yiannopoulos was "permanently banned from Twitter for what the company cited as inciting or engaging in the targeted abuse or harassment of others" (Olheiser 2016). In February 2017, Yiannopoulos resigned his editorship at *Breitbart News* after a video clip surfaced in which he appeared to condone pedophilia (Peters, Alter, and Grynbaum 2017). As a result of the remarks, Yiannopoulos lost a lucrative book deal with Simon & Schuster and was uninvited from the American Conservative Union's Conservative Political Action Conference (Lynskey 2017).

Yiannopoulos has been called an advocate for the alt-right movement. Founded by Richard Spencer, the alt-right movement is a loose collection of individuals and ideas that promote far-right ideals while rejecting mainstream conservatism. The movement has been accused of being overtly racist, white supremacist, and anti-Semitic (Wallace-Wells 2016). As the "face" of the alt-right, Yiannopoulos advocates for its adherents and their views:

> They're angry about globalization—culturally even more than economically. They're angry about political correctness guilting them about insensitivity to women, minorities, gays, transgender people, the disabled, the sick—the everyone-but-them. They're angry about feminism. They don't like immigrants. They don't like military intervention. They aren't into free trade. They don't like international groups such as the European Union, United Nations, or NATO—even the International Olympic Committee. They admire the bravado of authoritarians, especially Vladimir Putin. Some are white supremacists. Most enjoy a good conspiracy theory. (Stein 2016)

In March 2016, Yiannopoulos coauthored a piece in *Breitbart News* that portended to explain the views of the alt-right (Bokhari and Yiannopoulos 2016). The piece was criticized from both the left and the far right for "whitewashing the nascent ideology's racist core tenets" (Hankes 2017). In July 2016, Yiannopoulos was "permanently banned from Twitter" after posting several racist tweets about *Ghost-busters* star Leslie Jones (Jones is black) (Olheiser 2016). Yiannopoulos's supporters blamed the banishment on his conservative views and stated that Yiannopoulos had done nothing wrong. But Twitter took decisive action after what it said was several warnings that had been issued to Yiannopoulos for his constant "trolling" (Olheiser 2016).

In February 2017, Yiannopoulos was scheduled to address the Conservative Political Action Conference. After the announcement, a 2016 video surfaced where Yiannopoulos "stated that sexual relationships between 13-year-old boys and adult men and women can be 'perfectly consensual,' because some 13-year-olds are, in his view, sexually and emotionally mature enough to consent to sex with adults; he spoke favorably both of gay 13-year-old boys having sex with adult men and straight 13-year-old boys having sex with adult women" (Suebsaeng and Kucinich 2017). Yiannopoulos went on to state that the current age of consent in most states (16 or above) is "about right" but "that there are people that are capable of consent at a younger age, himself included" (Peters, Alter, and Grynbaum 2017). Yiannopoulos's comments were generally interpreted as being supportive of pedophilia and were widely condemned (Peters, Alter, and Grynbaum 2017). Yiannopoulos later tried to explain himself, saying that "he had been a victim of child abuse and that his comments were a way to cope with the trauma he had experienced" (Helmore 2017). He stated,

> I will not apologize for dealing with my life experiences in the best way that I can, which is humour. No one can tell me or anyone else who has lived through sexual abuse how to deal with those emotions. But I am sorry to other abuse victims if my own personal way of dealing with what happened to me has hurt you. (Helmore 2017)

As a result of the controversy, Yiannopoulos resigned from *Breitbart News*, was disinvited from the Conservative Political Action Conference, and lost a book deal with Simon & Schuster.

Yiannopoulos is a supporter of Donald Trump, though he criticized Trump's missile strike on Syria in April 2017. He has been "compared to Ann Coulter and referred to as the 'face of a political movement,'" but he says his real concern is "pop culture and free speech. I don't care about politics, I only talk about politics because of Trump" (Stein 2016).

See also: Alt-Right Movement; Bannon, Steve; *Breitbart News*; Spencer, Richard Bertrand

Further Reading

Bokhari, Allum and Milo Yiannopoulos. March 29, 2016. "An Establishment Conservative's Guide to the Alt-Right." *Breitbart.com.* http://www.breitbart.com/tech/2016/03/29/an-establishment-conservatives-guide-to-the-alt-right/ (Accessed May 20, 2017).

Hankes, Keegan. February 23, 2017. "How Stephen Bannon Made Milo Dangerous." *Southern Poverty Law Center—Hatewatch.* https://www.splcenter.org/hatewatch/2017/02/23/how-stephen-bannon-made-milo-dangerous (Accessed May 20, 2017).

Helmore, Edward. February 22, 2017. "Milo Yiannopoulos Resigns from Breitbart News Over Pedophilia Remarks." *The Guardian.* https://www.theguardian.com/us-news /2017/feb/21/milo-yiannopoulos-resigns-breitbart-pedophilia-comments (Accessed May 20, 2017).

Lynskey, Dorian. February 21, 2017. "The Rise and Fall of Milo Yiannopoulos—How a Shallow Actor Played the Bad Guy for Money." *The Guardian.* https://www.theguardian .com/world/2017/feb/21/milo-yiannopoulos-rise-and-fall-shallow-actor-bad-guy -hate-speech (Accessed May 20, 2017).

Milo. June 17, 2015. "Gay Rights Have Made Us Dumber, It's Time to Get Back in the Closet." *Breitbart News.* http://www.breitbart.com/big-government/2015/06/17/gay-rights-have -made-us-dumber-its-time-to-get-back-in-the-closet/ (Accessed May 20, 2017).

Ohlheiser, Abby. July 21, 2016. "Just How Offensive Did Milo Yiannopoulos Have to Be to Get Banned from Twitter?" *The Washington Post.* https://www.washingtonpost.com /news/the-intersect/wp/2016/07/21/what-it-takes-to-get-banned-from-twitter/?utm _term=.722173965dfc (Accessed May 20, 2017).

Ohlheiser, Abby. February 21, 2017. "The 96 Hours That Brought Down Milo Yian-nopoulos." *The Washington Post.* https://www.washingtonpost.com/news/the-intersect /wp/2017/02/21/the-96-hours-that-brought-down-milo-yiannopoulos/?utm_term= .8a7c5ef8ac54 (Accessed May 20, 2017).

Peters, Jeremy W., Alexandra Alter, and Michael M. Grynbaum. February 20, 2017. "Milo Yiannopoulos's Pedophilia Comments Cost Him CPAC Role and Book Deal." *The New York Times.* https://www.nytimes.com/2017/02/20/us/politics/cpac-milo-yiannopoulos .html (Accessed May 20, 2017).

Stein, Joel. September 15, 2016. "Milo Yiannopoulos Is the Pretty, Monstrous Face of the Alt-Right." *Bloomberg.* https://www.bloomberg.com/features/2016-america-divided/milo -yiannopoulos/ (Accessed May 20, 2017).

Suebsaeng, Asawin and Jackie Kucinich. February 20, 2017. "CPAC Disinvites Milo Yian-nopoulos, Despite His Attempt at Contrition." *Daily Beast.* http://www.thedailybeast .com/articles/2017/02/20/cpac-disinvites-milo-yiannopoulos-despite-his-attempt-at -contrition (Accessed May 20, 2017).

Wallace-Wells, Benjamin. May 5, 2016. "Is the Alt-Right for Real?" *The New Yorker.* http:// www.newyorker.com/news/benjamin-wallace-wells/is-the-alt-right-for-real (Accessed May 20, 2017).

Yiannopoulos, Milo. July 11, 2011. "Why I'll Probably Never Be a Parent." Web Archive. https://web.archive.org/web/20110716015115/http://yiannopoulos.net:80/2011 /07/11/why-ill-probably-never-be-a-parent/ (Accessed May 20, 2017).

ZUNDEL, ERNST

Ernst Zundel (1939–2017) was a German-born publisher whose material focused mostly on Holocaust denial. Like many others who ascribe to this idea, Zundel contended that his publications focused on viewing the Holocaust through the lens of "historical revisionism" and not denial. Zundel was "jailed in Canada for publishing literature likely to incite hatred against an identifiable group; in the United States on being a threat to national security for overstaying his visa; and in Germany for charges of 'inciting racial hatred'" (Connolly 2007). On the Germany charge, Zundel spent five years in a German prison for violating that country's laws concerning hate speech. Zundel has described himself as being jailed for his "nonconformist views" and has called himself "the most prominent political prisoner in the western world today" (Zundelsite). Zundel was the author of such tracts as *The Hitler We Loved and Why*, *UFOs: Nazi Secret Weapon?*, and *Did Six Million Really Die?* (Sanchez 2008). After serving his five-year prison sentence in Germany, Zundel "retired to his home in the Black Forest (Germany) to regain his health" (Southern Poverty Law Center).

Zundel was born in Germany and immigrated to Canada in 1958. While in Canada, he began dabbling in fascist politics. During the late 1970s, Zundel gained some notoriety in Canada as the "spokesman for Concerned Parents of German Descent, a group that claimed that German-Canadian children were increasingly the target of discrimination due to anti-German stereotyping in Canadian media" (Zundel Explained). Zundel had complained about NBC's *Holocaust* miniseries that he contended portrayed Germans in a negative light. About the same time, a reporter unmasked Zundel as the author of neo-Nazi and anti-Semitic pamphlets, including *The Hitler We Loved and Why*. Zundel had been writing under the pseudonym Christof Friedrich (Bonokoski 2010).

In 1983, a Holocaust survivor living in Canada "filed a complaint against Zundel before the Canadian Human Rights Tribunal" (Zundel Explained). Zundel was charged for "knowingly publishing false news" in connection with his *Did Six Million Really Die? The Truth at Last* tract. Zundel was eventually convicted of "causing mischief to the public interest by promoting social and racial intolerance," a charge written into Canada's Criminal Code (Zundel Explained). Zundel's conviction was overturned, but a second trial in 1988 again found him guilty. He spent almost two years in prison before his conviction was finally overturned on appeal "when the Supreme Court of Canada ruled that the law against publishing false news was unconstitutional" (Southern Poverty Law Center).

Zundel left Canada in 2000, "while he was under investigation by the Canadian Human Rights Commission for promoting hatred against Jews" (Zundel

Explained). He settled in Tennessee, but in 2003, he was arrested for overstaying his visa and was deported back to Canada. Zundel had never gained Canadian citizenship, and upon his return to Canada he was deemed "a threat to national security for his alleged links to violent neo-Nazi groups" (Zundel Explained). He was therefore detained while his claim for refugee status was addressed by Canadian courts. Canadian neo-Nazi leader Paul Fromm held several rallies on behalf of Zundel, which observers noted did not help Zundel's case.

By this time, the German government had issued an arrest warrant for Zundel for "incitement of the masses." Though he had lived in Canada for 40 years, Zundel was still a German citizen. After exhausting his attempts to stay in Canada, Zundel was extradited to Germany in 2005 to face charges. In the indictment issued by the German court, Zundel was charged with 14 counts of inciting hatred, punishable by up to five years in prison. The indictment stated that Zundel "denied the fate of destruction for the Jews planned by National Socialist powerholders and justified this by saying that the mass destruction in Auschwitz and Treblinka, among others, were an invention of the Jews and served the repression and extortion of the German people" (Connolly 2007).

Zundel's trial began in November 2005, "but it was delayed after it was determined that a member of his defense team had been convicted of crimes against Jews himself" (Southern Poverty Law Center). In February 2007, Zundel was convicted in Germany "of 14 counts of inciting racial hatred and defaming the memory of the dead and sentenced to the maximum allowable sentence under the law—five years" (Southern Poverty Law Center). Zundel was "released from prison on March 1, 2010, five years after his deportation to Germany" (AP 2010). The Canadian minister of public safety announced that Zundel would not be permitted to return to Canada because he was seen as a danger to the security of the country. When Zundel was released, "a small group of fellow Holocaust deniers greeted him as he left a Mannheim prison" (Southern Poverty Law Center). He announced that he was "retiring to his home in the Black Forest to recuperate and regain his health" (Southern Poverty Law Center). Zundel died on August 5, 2017.

See also: Fromm, Paul; Holocaust Denial; Irving, David; Neo-Nazis; White Supremacist Movement

Further Reading

AP. March 1, 2010. "Convicted Holocaust Denier Zundel Freed." *The Jerusalem Post.* http://www.jpost.com/International/Convicted-Holocaust-denier-Zundel-freed (Accessed May 2, 2017).

Bonokoski, Mark. March 1, 2010. "Zundel Released from Germany Jail." *Toronto Sun.* http://www.torontosun.com/news/columnists/mark_bonokoski/2010/03/01/13074806.html (Accessed May 2, 2017).

Connolly, Kate. February 16, 2007. "Holocaust Denial Writer Jailed for Five Years." *The Guardian.* https://www.theguardian.com/world/2007/feb/16/historybooks.secondworldwar (Accessed May 2, 2017).

Sanchez, Casey. August 29, 2008. "Ernst Zundel Lauded by Other Holocaust Deniers." *Southern Poverty Law Center—Intelligence Report.* https://www.splcenter.org/fighting

-hate/intelligence-report/2008/ernst-zundel-lauded-other-holocaust-deniers (Accessed May 2, 2017).

Southern Poverty Law Center. "Ernst Zundel." https://www.splcenter.org/fighting-hate /extremist-files/individual/ernst-zundel (Accessed May 2, 2017).

Stern, Kenneth S. August 29, 2001. "Lying About the Holocaust: Inside the Denial Movement." *Southern Poverty Law Center—Intelligence Report.* https://www.splcenter.org /fighting-hate/intelligence-report/2001/lying-about-holocaust-inside-denial-movement (Accessed May 2, 2017).

Zundel Explained. "Ernst Zundel Explained." *Everything Explained Today.* http://everything .explained.today/Ernst_Z%C3%BCndel/ (Accessed August 7, 2017).

Zundelsite. "Who Is Ernst Zundel?" http://www.zundelsite.org/archive/zundel_persecuted /who_is_zundel.html (Accessed May 2, 2017).

Index

Boldfaced page numbers indicate main entries in the encyclopedia.

About the Author

Barry J. Balleck, PhD, is professor and chair of the Department of Political Science and International Studies at Georgia Southern University. He received a bachelor of arts degree in political science and a master's degree in international studies from Brigham Young University. Balleck received his doctorate in political science from the University of Colorado at Boulder with emphases in international relations, American politics, and political theory and then joined the faculty of Georgia Southern University, where he held a joint appointment in both the Department of Political Science and the Center for International Studies. For the past 22 years, he has also directed Georgia Southern University's Model United Nations program, one of the oldest and most continuous programs of its kind in the country. Balleck's primary research and teaching interests are in the fields of international and domestic terrorism, U.S. foreign policy, the rhetoric of politics, the United Nations, and international human rights. He has dozens of conference presentations to his credit and has published in journals such as *Presidential Studies Quarterly*, *Politics & Policy*, and *Peace Psychology Review*. His most recent publication is Praeger's *Allegiance to Liberty: The Changing Face of Patriots, Militias, and Political Violence in America*.